Android™ Application Development
ALL-IN-ONE

FOR

DUMMIES®

A Wiley Brand

Android™ Application Development
ALL-IN-ONE
FOR DUMMIES®
A Wiley Brand

by Barry Burd

Android™ Application Development All-in-One For Dummies®

Published by
John Wiley & Sons, Inc.
111 River Street
Hoboken, NJ 07030-5774

www.wiley.com

Copyright © 2012 by John Wiley & Sons, Inc., Hoboken, New Jersey

Published by John Wiley & Sons, Inc., Hoboken, New Jersey

Published simultaneously in Canada

About the Author

Barry Burd received an M.S. degree in Computer Science at Rutgers University and a Ph.D. in Mathematics at the University of Illinois. As a teaching assistant in Champaign-Urbana, Illinois, he was elected five times to the university-wide List of Teachers Ranked as Excellent by their Students.

Since 1980, Dr. Burd has been a professor in the Department of Mathematics and Computer Science at Drew University in Madison, New Jersey. When he's not lecturing at Drew University, Dr. Burd leads training courses for professional programmers in business and industry. He has lectured at conferences in the United States, Europe, Australia, and Asia. He is the author of several articles and books, including *Java For Dummies* and *Beginning Programming with Java For Dummies,* both from John Wiley & Sons, Inc.

Dr. Burd lives in Madison, New Jersey with his wife and two kids (both in their twenties, and mostly on their own). In his spare time, Dr. Burd enjoys being a workaholic.

Dedication

For

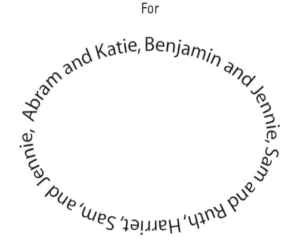

Abram and Katie, Benjamin and Jennie, Sam and Ruth, Harriet, Sam, and Jennie,

Acknowledgments

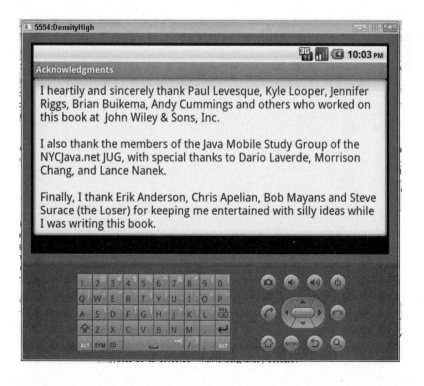

Publisher's Acknowledgments

We're proud of this book; please send us your comments at `http://dummies.custhelp.com`. For other comments, please contact our Customer Care Department within the U.S. at 877-762-2974, outside the U.S. at 317-572-3993, or fax 317-572-4002.

Some of the people who helped bring this book to market include the following:

Acquisitions and Editorial

Senior Project Editor: Paul Levesque

Acquisitions Editor: Kyle Looper

Copy Editor: Jennifer Riggs

Technical Editor: Brian Buikema

Editorial Manager: Leah Cameron

Editorial Assistant: Amanda Graham

Sr. Editorial Assistant: Cherie Case

Cover Photo: © iStockphoto.com / Cary Westfall

Cartoons: Rich Tennant (`www.the5thwave.com`)

Composition Services

Project Coordinator: Nikki Gee

Layout and Graphics: Joyce Haughey

Proofreaders: Melissa Cossell, Kathy Simpson

Indexer: BIM Indexing & Proofreading Services

Publishing and Editorial for Technology Dummies

Richard Swadley, Vice President and Executive Group Publisher

Andy Cummings, Vice President and Publisher

Mary Bednarek, Executive Acquisitions Director

Mary C. Corder, Editorial Director

Publishing for Consumer Dummies

Kathleen Nebenhaus, Vice President and Executive Publisher

Composition Services

Debbie Stailey, Director of Composition Services

Contents at a Glance

Table of Contents

Introduction

Android phones are everywhere. In January 2011, Android became the most popular operating system for mobile phones in the United States.[1] In that month, Android's market share managed to surpass those of the BlackBerry and the iPhone. And a month later, Android's presence grew to include one of every three smartphones in the United States.[2]

At the same time, Market Force Information, Inc., reported that "Android appears to be winning the smartphone popularity contest."[3] Among survey respondents in the United States, 34 percent said they would purchase an Android phone, compared with 21 percent for iPhone and 12 percent for BlackBerry. On the global scene, research firm Ovum predicts that by 2016, "We will see dramatic shifts in dominance for smartphone software platforms, with Android storming into the lead with 38 percent market share."[4]

So if you read this book in a public place (on a commuter train, at the beach, on the dance floor at the Coyote Ugly saloon), you can read proudly, with a chip on your shoulder and with your chest held high. Android is hot stuff, and you're cool because you're reading about it.

How to Use This Book

You can attack this book in either of two ways. You can go cover to cover, or you can poke around from one chapter to another. You can even do both (start at the beginning and then jump to a section that particularly interests you). I designed this book so that the basic topics come first and the more involved topics follow the basics. But you may already be comfortable with some basics, or you may have specific goals that don't require you to know about certain topics.

[1]*See* www.comscore.com/Press_Events/Press_Releases/2011/3/comScore_Reports_January_2011_U.S._Mobile_Subscriber_Market_Share.

[2]*See* www.comscore.com/Press_Events/Press_Releases/2011/4/comScore_Reports_February_2011_U.S._Mobile_Subscriber_Market_Share.

[3]*See* www.marketforce.com/2011/02/consumers-now-more-likely-to-buy-androids-than-iphones.

[4]*See* http://about.datamonitor.com/media/archives/5565.

In general, my advice is as follows:

✦ If you already know something, don't bother reading about it.

✦ If you're curious, don't be afraid to skip ahead. You can always sneak a peek at an earlier chapter if you really need to do so.

Conventions Used in This Book

Almost every technical book starts with a little typeface legend, and *Android Application Development All-in-One For Dummies* is no exception. What follows is a brief explanation of the typefaces used in this book:

✦ New terms are set in *italics*.

✦ If you need to type something that's mixed in with the regular text, the characters you type appear in bold. For example: "Type **MyNewProject** in the text field."

✦ You also see this `computerese` font. I use computerese for Java code, filenames, web page addresses (URLs), onscreen messages, and other such things. Also, if something you need to type is really long, it appears in computerese font on its own line (or lines).

✦ You need to change certain things when you type them on your own computer keyboard. For instance, I may ask you to type

```
public void Anyname
```

which means that you type **public void** and then some name that you make up on your own. Words that you need to replace with your own words are set in *`italicized computerese`*.

What You Don't Have to Read

Pick the first chapter or section that has material you don't already know and start reading there. Of course, you may hate making decisions as much as I do. If so, here are some guidelines that you can follow:

✦ If you've already created a simple Android application, and you have all the right software installed on your computer, skip Book I and go straight to Book II. Believe me, I won't mind.

✦ If you have a modest amount of experience developing Android apps, and you're looking for material that puts things together and fills in gaps, start with Book II.

✦ If you're thinking about writing a special kind of app (a text-messaging app, a location-based app, a game, or something like that), work your way quickly and impatiently through Books I, II, and III, and dive in seriously when you reach Book IV.

✦ If your goal is to publish (and maybe sell) your apps, set Book V as your ultimate goal. No one can tell you how to become the next Bill Gates, but Book V gets you thinking about the best ways to share your Android applications.

If you want to skip the sidebars and the Technical Stuff icons, please do. In fact, if you want to skip anything at all, feel free.

Foolish Assumptions

In this book, I make a few assumptions about you, the reader. If one of these assumptions is incorrect, you're probably okay. If all these assumptions are incorrect . . . well, buy the book anyway.

✦ **I assume that you can navigate through your computer's common menus and dialog boxes.** You don't have to be a Windows, Linux, or Macintosh power user, but you should be able to start a program, find a file, put a file into a certain directory . . . that sort of thing. Much of the time, when you practice the stuff in this book, you're typing code on your keyboard, not pointing and clicking your mouse.

On those occasions when you need to drag and drop, cut and paste, or plug and play, I guide you carefully through the steps. But your computer may be configured in any of several billion ways, and my instructions may not quite fit your special situation. So when you reach one of these platform-specific tasks, try following the steps in this book. If the steps don't quite fit, consult a book with instructions tailored to your system.

✦ **I assume that you can think logically.** That's all there is to application development — thinking logically. If you can think logically, you have it made. If you don't believe that you can think logically, read on. You may be pleasantly surprised.

✦ **I assume that you have some experience with Java.** In writing this book, I've tried to do the impossible. I've tried to make the book interesting for experienced programmers, yet accessible to people who don't write code for a living. If you're a Java guru, that's great. If you're a certified Linux geek, that's great, too. But I don't assume that you can recite the names of the Java's concurrency methods in your sleep, or that you can pipe together a chain of 14 Linux commands without reading the documentation or touching the Backspace key.

If you have a working knowledge of some Java-like language (C or C++, for example), all you need is a little Java overview. And if you have no experience with an object-oriented language, you can get some. Your favorite bookstore has a terrific book titled *Java For Dummies,* 5th Edition, by Barry Burd (John Wiley & Sons, Inc.). I recommend that book highly.

How This Book Is Organized

Android Application Development All-in-One For Dummies is divided into subsections, which are grouped into sections, which come together to make chapters, which are lumped finally into six books. (When you write a book, you get to know your book's structure pretty well. After months of writing, you find yourself dreaming in sections and chapters when you go to bed at night.) Each of the six books is listed here.

Book I: Android Jump Start

This part is your complete, executive briefing on Android. It includes some "What is Android?" material, instructions for setting up your system, and a chapter in which you create your first Android app. In this minibook, you visit Android's major technical ideas and dissect a simple Android application.

Book II: Android Background Material

When you create Android apps, you write Java programs and work with XML documents. Book II provides a quick look at the Java programming language and at the XML document standard. In addition, Book II has a chapter on Eclipse — a tool for creating Java programs that you will be using every minute of your Android-development day.

Book III: The Building Blocks

This minibook covers the big ideas in Android application programming. What is an activity? What is an intent? How do you handle button presses? How do you lay out the user's screen? The ideas in this minibook permeate all Android programming, from the simplest app on a cheapo phone to a killer app on an overpriced Android tablet.

Book IV: Programming Cool Phone Features

Some applications do very ordinary things, such as displaying lists or calculating sums. But other apps make use of a mobile device's unique capabilities. For example, apps can dial phone numbers, send text messages, surf the web, and track your travel direction. The Android platform has a rich set of built-in tools for programming each of these special capabilities. So in this minibook, you create apps that make the most of a device's vast feature set.

Book V: The Job Isn't Done Until . . .

Imagine earning a fortune selling the world's most popular Android app, being named *Time* magazine's Person of the Year, and having Tom Cruise or Julia Roberts buy the rights to star as you in a movie (giving you exclusive rights to the game for Android devices that's based on the movie, of course).

Okay, maybe your ambitions aren't quite that high, but when you develop a good Android app, you probably want to share that app with the rest of the world. Well, the good news is, sharing is fairly easy. And marketing your app isn't as difficult as you might imagine. This minibook provides the tips and pointers to help you spread the word about your fantastic application.

Book VI: Alternative Android Development Techniques

Deep in the bowels of a place called "computer nerd city," some programmers shun the easygoing life of the Android Java programmer and strive toward a simpler, more primitive existence. These "wonks" (as they're known by clinicians and other professionals) prefer the rugged, macho lifestyle that programming in C or C++ provides. Along with this lifestyle, they get the ability to reach the corners of a mobile device that are hidden by Android's layer of abstraction.

At the other end of the spectrum, some people prefer not to write code. These visual learners prefer dragging and dropping — designing a solution by imagining how it looks and feels. These people want a development technique that emphasizes intuition and big-picture planning.

If you're a wonk or an intuition-based learner, please include Book VI on your travel plans.

More on the Web!

You've read the *Android All-in-One* book, seen the *Android All-in-One* movie, worn the *Android All-in-One* t-shirt, and eaten the *Android All-in-One* candy. What more is there to do?

That's easy. Just visit this book's website — www.allmycode.com/Android. (You can also get there by visiting www.dummies.com/go/androidapplicationaio.) At the website, you can find updates, comments, additional information, and answers to commonly asked readers' questions. You can also find a small chat application for sending me quick questions when I'm online. When I'm not online (or if you have a complicated question), you can send me e-mail. I read messages sent to android@allmycode.com.

Icons Used in This Book

If you could watch me write this book, you'd see me sitting at my computer, talking to myself. I say each sentence in my head. Most of the sentences, I mutter several times. When I have an extra thought, a side comment, or something that doesn't belong in the regular stream, I twist my head a little bit. That way, whoever's listening to me (usually, nobody) knows that I'm off on a momentary tangent.

Of course, in print, you can't see me twisting my head. I need some other way of setting a side thought in a corner by itself. I do it with icons. When you see a Tip icon or a Remember icon, you know that I'm taking a quick detour.

Here's a list of icons that I use in this book.

A tip is an extra piece of information — something helpful that the other books may forget to tell you.

Everyone makes mistakes. Heaven knows that I've made a few in my time. Anyway, when I think people are especially prone to make a mistake, I mark it with a Warning icon.

Question: What's stronger than a Tip, but not as strong as a Warning?

Answer: A Remember icon.

"If you don't remember what *such-and-such* means, see *blah-blah-blah*," or "For more information, read *blahbity-blah-blah*."

This icon calls attention to useful material that you can find online. (You don't have to wait long to see one of these icons. I use one at the end of this introduction!)

Occasionally, I run across a technical tidbit. The tidbit may help you understand what the people behind the scenes (the people who developed Java) were thinking. You don't have to read it, but you may find it useful. You may also find the tidbit helpful if you plan to read other (more geeky) books about Android app development.

Where to Go from Here

If you've gotten this far, you're ready to start reading about Android application development. Think of me (the author) as your guide, your host, your personal assistant. I do everything I can to keep things interesting and, most important, help you understand.

If you like what you read, send me a note. My e-mail address, which I created just for comments and questions about this book, is `android@allmycode.com`. And don't forget — for the latest updates, visit this book's website. The site's address is `www.allmycode.com/android`.

Book I

Android Jump-Start

Contents at a Glance

Chapter 1: All about Android

In This Chapter

✔ Your take on Android (depending on who you are)

✔ A tour of Android technologies

*U*ntil the mid-2000s, the word "Android" stood for a mechanical humanlike creature — a root'n toot'n officer of the law with built-in machine guns, or a hyperlogical space traveler who can do everything except speak using contractions. But in 2005, Google purchased Android, Inc. — a 22-month-old company creating software for mobile phones. That move changed everything.

In 2007, a group of 34 companies formed the Open Handset Alliance. The Alliance's task is "to accelerate innovation in mobile and offer consumers a richer, less expensive, and better mobile experience." The Alliance's primary project is *Android* — an open, free operating system based on the Linux operating system kernel.

HTC released the first commercially available Android phone near the end of 2008. But in the United States, the public's awareness of Android and its potential didn't surface until early 2010. Where I'm sitting in August 2011, Canalys reports that nearly half all smartphones in the world run Android.* (I know. You're sitting sometime after August 2011. But that's okay.)

The Consumer Perspective

A consumer considers the alternatives.

✦ **Possibility #1: No mobile phone.**

Advantages: Inexpensive, no interruptions from callers.

Disadvantages: No instant contact with friends and family. No calls to services in case of an emergency. No handheld games, no tweeting, tooting, hooting, homing, roaming, or booping. And worst of all, to break up with your boyfriend or girlfriend, you can't simply send a text message.

---

* www.canalys.com/newsroom/google's-android-becomes-world's-leading-smart-phone-platform

✦ **Possibility #2: A feature phone.**

I love the way the world makes up fancy names for less-than-desirable things. A *feature phone* is a mobile phone that's not a smartphone. There's no official rule defining the boundary between feature phones and smartphones. But generally, a feature phone is one with an inflexible menu of home-screen options. A feature phone's menu items relate mostly to traditional mobile phone functions, such as dialing, texting, and maybe some web surfing and gaming. In contrast, a smartphone's home screen provides access to the underlying file system, has icons, customizable skins, and many other features that used to be available only to general-purpose computer operating systems.

Advantages: Cheaper than a smartphone.

Disadvantages: Not as versatile as a smartphone. Not nearly as cool as a smartphone. Nowhere near as much fun as a smartphone.

✦ **Possibility #3: An iPhone.**

Advantages: Great graphics. More apps than any other phone platform.

Disadvantages: Little or no flexibility with the single-vendor iOS operating system. Only a handful of different models to choose from. No sanctioned "rooting," "modding," or "jailbreaking" the phone. No hesitation permitted when becoming a member of the Mystic Cult of Apple Devotees.

✦ **Possibility #4: A Windows phone, a BlackBerry, a WebOS phone, or some other non-Android, non-Apple smartphone.**

Advantages: Having a smartphone without belonging to a crowd.

Disadvantages: The possibility of owning an orphan product when the smartphone wars come to a climax.

✦ **Possibility #5: An Android phone.**

Advantages: Using an open platform. Using a popular platform with lots of industry support and with powerful market momentum. Writing your own software and installing the software on your own phone (without having to post the software on a company's website). Publishing software without facing a challenging approval process.

Disadvantages: Security concerns when using an open platform. Worry over a number of lawsuits heaped upon Android manufacturers in 2011. Dismay when iPhone users make fun of your phone.

For me, Android's advantages far outweigh the possible disadvantages. And you're reading a paragraph from *Android Application Development All-in-One For Dummies,* so you're likely to agree with me.

Having decided to go with an Android phone, the consumer asks, "Which phone?" And the salesperson says, "This phone comes with Android 4.0" (which means "This phone comes with Android 2.3, which will eventually be upgraded to Android 4.0, or so claims the vendor"). So the consumer asks, "What are the differences among all the Android versions?"

Android comes with a few different notions of "version." Android has platform numbers, API levels, codenames, and probably some other versioning schemes. (The acronym *API* stands for *Application Programming Interface* — a library full of prewritten programs available for use by a bunch of programmers. In this case, the "bunch" consists of all Android developers.)

To complicate matters, the versioning schemes don't increase in lockstep. For example, from platform 1.5 to 1.6, the API level goes from 3 to 4. But platform 2.3 sports two API levels — level 9 for platform 2.3.1 and level 10 for platform 2.3.3. Versions that are skipped (such as API level 5 and platform 2.5) are lost in the annals of Android development history.

An Android version may have variations. For example, plain old Android 2.2 has an established set of features. To plain old Android 2.2, you can add the Google APIs (thus adding Google Maps functionality) and still use platform 2.2. You can also add a special set with features tailored for the Samsung Galaxy Tab.

Most consumers know Android's versions by their codenames. Unlike Apple (which names its operating systems after ferocious cats) or automakers (who name their SUVs after cowboys), Google names Android versions after desserts. (See Table 1-1.) I'm waiting impatiently for a version codenamed Chocolate. (Maybe one will be released by the time you read this book.)

Table 1-1	Android Codenames		
Version	*Codename*	*First Release Date*	*Some Noteworthy Improvements*
Android 1.5	Cupcake	April 2009	
Android 1.6	Donut	September 2009	Maturing Android market interface, better voice tools, support for an 800x480 screen
Android 2.1	Éclair	January 2010	Better user interface, more screen sizes, more camera functionality, Bluetooth 2.1 support, multitouch support

(continued)

Table 1-1 *(continued)*

Version	Codename	First Release Date	Some Noteworthy Improvements
Android 2.2	Froyo	May 2010	Better performance with a just-in-time (JIT) compiler, USB tethering, 720p screens, ability to install apps to the SD card
Android 2.3.1, 2.3.3	Gingerbread	December 2010	System-wide copy/paste, multi-touch soft keyboard, better native code development, concurrent garbage collection, native support for barometers (of all things!)
Android 3.0, 3.1, 3.2	Honeycomb	January 2011	Designed specifically for tablets, new soft keyboard, better Gmail interface, better web browser (with tabbed browsing), redesigned widgets, interface fragments
Android 4.0(?)	Ice Cream Sandwich	November 2011	Reintegration of phone and tablet platforms
	Jelly Bean	2012	

As a developer, your job is to balance portability with feature richness. When you create an app, you specify a target Android version and a minimum Android version. (You can read more about this in Chapter 3 of this minibook.) The higher the version, the more features your app can have. But the higher the version, the fewer devices that can run your app. Fortunately, this book has lots of tips and tricks for striking a happy medium between whiz-bang features and universal use.

The Developer Perspective

Android is a multi-faceted beast. When you develop for Android, you use many toolsets. This section has a brief rundown.

Java

James Gosling from Sun Microsystems created the Java programming language in the mid-1990s. (Sun Microsystems has since been bought out by Oracle.) Java's meteoric rise in use came from the elegance of the language and the well-conceived platform architecture. After a brief blaze of glory with applets and the web, Java settled into being a solid, general-purpose language with special strength in servers and middleware.

In the meantime, Java was quietly seeping into embedded processors. Sun Microsystems was developing Java ME (*M*obile *E*dition) for creating *midlets* to run on mobile phones. Java became a major technology in Blu-ray disc players. So the decision to make Java the primary development language for Android apps is no big surprise.

An *embedded processor* is a computer chip that's hidden from the user as part of some special-purpose device. The chips in today's cars are embedded processors, and the silicon that powers your photocopier at work is an embedded processor. Pretty soon, the flower pots on you windowsill will probably have embedded processors.

The trouble is, not everyone agrees about the fine points of Java's licensing terms. The Java language isn't quite the same animal as the Java software libraries, which in turn aren't the same as the *Java Virtual Machine* (the software that enables the running of Java programs). So in marrying Java to Android, the founders of Android added an extra puzzle piece — the Dalvik Virtual Machine. And instead of using the official Sun/Oracle Java libraries, Android uses *Harmony* — an open-source Java implementation from the Apache Software Foundation. Several years and many lawsuits later, companies are still at odds over the use of Java in Android phones.

For more information about Dalvik (the Virtual Machine, not the town in Iceland) see Book II, Chapter 2.

Fortunately for you, the soon-to-be Android developer, Java is deeply entrenched in the Android ecosystem. The time you invest in developing mobile Java-based apps will continue to pay off for a long, long time.

If you already have some Java programming experience, great! If not, you can find a fast-paced introduction to Java in Book II, Chapters 2, 3, and 4. For a more leisurely introduction to Java, buy *Java For Dummies,* 5th Edition.

XML

If you find View Source among your web browser's options, you see a bunch of Hypertext Markup Language (HTML) tags. A *tag* is some text enclosed in angle brackets. The tag describes something about its neighboring content.

For example, to create boldface type on a web page, a web designer writes

```
<b>Look at this!</b>
```

The angle-bracketed b tags turn boldface type on and off.

The *M* in HTML stands for *Markup* — a general term describing any extra text that annotates a document's content. When you annotate a document's content, you embed information about the document's content into the document itself. So, for example, in the line of code in the previous paragraph, the content is Look at this! The markup (information about the content) consists of the tags <b> and </b>.

The HTML standard is an outgrowth of SGML (*S*tandard *G*eneralized *M*arkup *L*anguage). SGML is an all-things-to-all-people technology for marking up documents for use by all kinds of computers running all kinds of software, and sold by all kinds of vendors.

In the mid-1990s, a working group of the World Wide Web Consortium (W3C) began developing XML — the e*X*tensible *M*arkup *L*anguage. The working group's goal was to create a subset of SGML for use in transmitting data over the Internet. They succeeded. Today, XML is a well-established standard for encoding information of all kinds.

For a technical overview of XML, see Book II, Chapter 5.

Java is good for describing step-by-step instructions, and XML is good for describing the way things are (or the way they should be). A Java program says, "Do this and then do that." In contrast, an XML document says, "It's this way, and it's that way." So Android uses XML for two purposes:

✦ **To describe an app's data.**

   An app's XML documents describe the look of the app's screens, the translations of the app into one or more languages, and other kinds of data.

✦ **To describe the app itself.**

   Each Android app comes with an AndroidManifest.xml file. This XML document describes features of the app. The operating system uses the AndroidManifest.xml document's contents to manage the running of the app.

For example, an app's `AndroidManifest.xml` file describes code that the app makes available for use by other apps. The same file describes the permissions that the app requests from the system. When you begin installing a new app, Android displays these permissions and asks for your permission to proceed with the installation. (I don't know about you, but I always read this list of permissions carefully. Yeah, right!)

For more information about the `AndroidManifest.xml` file and about the use of XML to describe an app's data, see almost any chapter in this book.

Concerning XML, there's bad news and good news. The bad news is, XML isn't always easy to compose. At best, writing XML code is boring. At worst, writing XML code is downright confusing.

The good news is, automated software tools compose most of the world's XML code. As an Android programmer, the software on your development computer composes much of your app's XML code. You often tweak the XML code, read part of the code for info from its source, make minor changes, and compose brief additions. But you hardly ever create XML documents from scratch.

Linux

An *operating system* is a big program that manages the overall running of a computer or a device. Most operating systems are built in layers. An operating system's outer layers are usually right up there in the user's face. For example, both Windows and Macintosh OS X have standard desktops. From the desktop, the user launches programs, manages windows, and so on.

An operating system's inner layers are (for the most part) invisible to the user. While the user plays Solitaire, the operating system juggles processes, manages files, keeps an eye on security, and generally does the kinds of things that the user shouldn't micromanage.

At the very deepest level of an operating system is the system's *kernel*. The kernel runs directly on the processor's hardware, and does the low-level work required to make the processor run. In a truly layered system, higher layers accomplish work by making calls to lower layers. So an app with a specific hardware request sends the request (directly or indirectly) through the kernel.

The best-known, best-loved general purpose operating systems are Windows, Macintosh OS X (which is really Unix), and Linux. Windows and Mac OS X are the properties of their respective companies. But Linux is open-source. That's one of the reasons why your TiVo runs Linux, and why the creators of Android based their platform on the Linux kernel.

Android's brand of Linux is an outlier among Linuxes (Linuces?). Based on the Linux 2.6.x kernel, Android uses stripped-down versions of many commonly -used Linux packages. The Android shell lacks many of the commands sported by desktop Linux shells. And instead of glibc, Android uses its own C-language library (named *Bionic*). There's also some tooth-gnashing among Linux geeks about the legitimacy of Android's drivers. So if you attend a Linux rally and you mention Android, be sure to do so with a wry look on your face. This protects you in case the person you're talking to doesn't think Android is "real" Linux.

Open-source software comes in many shapes and sizes. For example, there's the GNU General Public License (GPL), the Apache License, the GNU Lesser General Public License (LGPL), and others. When considering the use of other people's open-source software, be careful to check the software's licensing terms. "Open-source" doesn't necessarily mean "do anything at all for free with this software."

Figure 1-1 is a diagram of the Android operating system. At the bottom is the Linux kernel, managing various parts of a device's hardware. The kernel also includes a Binder, which handles all communication among running processes. (When your app asks, "Can any software on this phone tell me the current temperature in Cleveland, Ohio?", the request for information goes through the kernel's Binder.)

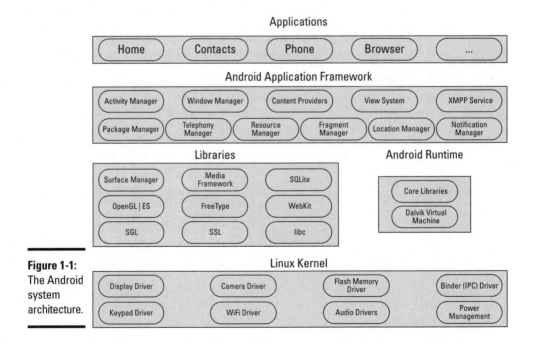

Figure 1-1:
The Android system architecture.

At the very top of Figure 1-1 are the applications — the web browser, the contacts list, the games, the dialer, your own soon-to-be-developed apps. Both developers and users interact mostly with this layer. Developers write code to run on this layer, and users see the outer surface of the apps created by developers.

As a developer, your most intimate contact with the Android operating system is through the command line, or the *Linux shell.* The shell uses commands, such as `cd` to change to a directory, `ls` to list a directory's files and subdirectories, `rm` to delete files, and many others.

Google's Android Market has plenty of free *terminal* apps. A terminal app's interface is a plain text screen in which you type Linux shell commands. And with one of Android's developer tools, the Android Debug Bridge, you can issue shell commands to an Android device through your development computer. If you like getting your virtual hands dirty, the Linux shell is for you.

For information about operating systems' command interfaces, see Book VI, Chapter 3. For a look at the Android Debug Bridge, see Chapter 2 of this minibook.

The Business Perspective

I admit it. I'm not an entrepreneur. I'm a risk-averse person with a preference for storing money in mattresses. My closest brush with a startup business was a cab ride in Kuala Lumpur. The driver wanted me to help finance his new restaurant idea. "Not Kentucky Fried Chicken!" he yelled. "Kentucky Fried Duck!"

Anyway, the creation and selling of mobile phone apps is an enormous cottage industry. Google's Android Market had 300,000 apps in mid-2011. By the time you read this book, the number 300,000 will seem pathetically obsolete. Add the marketing potential of Amazon's Appstore for Android, and you have some very natural distribution channels for your apps.

Anyone can post an app on Google's Android Market and on Amazon's Appstore. You can post free apps, paid apps, and programs with in-app billing. You can test an app with a select group of users before making your app available to everyone. You make a small one-time payment to register as an Android developer. Then you design apps, develop apps, and post apps for the general public.

Book V covers the business of posting apps on Google's Android Market and Amazon's Appstore for Android. I don't promise that you'll become a millionaire selling Android apps, but I promise that you'll have fun trying.

Chapter 2: Installing the Software Tools

In This Chapter

✔ Putting Android tools on your laptop or desktop

✔ Tweaking your installation settings

There are two kinds of people — people who love tools, and people who don't have strong feelings about tools. (As far as I know, no one dislikes tools.) I'm a tool lover because I enjoy the leverage that tools give me. With the right tool, I can easily do things that would otherwise require monumental effort. And I can do these things over and over again, getting better with practice using the tools so that the tasks I'm dealing with become easier as time goes on.

Of course, my tool-o-philia isn't always a good thing. I'm not handy with skills like carpentry, car repair, or plumbing, but I can't resist buying greasy old screwdrivers and other such tools at garage sales. Among other things, I have what I think is the world's biggest monkey wrench, which I bought several years ago for only seven dollars. But I'd be useless (if not dangerous) using the wrench, so it sits in my attic waiting for my kids to deal with it when, years from now, they inherit my house full of junk.

But software tools are great. They're not greasy; many good tools are free; and if you lose a tool, you can usually find it by searching your computer's hard drive.

Anyway, this chapter is about Android development tools. Enjoy!

Installing the Java Development Kit

Java is the *lingua franca* of Android application development. To write Android apps, you normally use Java.

In the preceding paragraph, I write that for Android apps, you *normally* use Java. I'm very careful not to imply that you always use Java. Android enjoys lots of different development modes. For example, with Android's *Native Development Kit* (NDK), you can write code that runs directly on a device's hardware in C or C++. You can develop in HTML and JavaScript to run code on the device's browser. You can even develop in Adobe AIR. And companies create other specialized development environments all the time. Even so, Java is the language of choice in the Android community. Google creates new versions of Android with Java in mind. And in general, you get a good power-to-ease-of-use ratio when you develop Android apps in Java.

For a closer look at Android's Native Development Kit, see Book VI.

To develop Android apps, you need the Java Development Kit. If you run Windows, Linux, or Solaris, you can get the kit at the Oracle.com website — more on that in the next section. Macintosh users have a few other possibilities, which I detail in just a bit.

Java for Windows, Linux, and Solaris

As I write this chapter, the exact URL for downloading the Java Development Kit for Windows, Linux, or Solaris is `http://www.oracle.com/tech network/java/javase/downloads`. I don't expect that URL to work forever and ever, but if you visit `http://www.oracle.com` and poke around for Java, you'll certainly reach the Java Development Kit download page. One way or another, keep a few things in mind:

✦ **Java comes in three separate editions.**

A bit of background here: A *programming language* is a bunch of rules describing the way you can write instructions for the computer to follow. An *application programming interface* (API) is a bunch of reusable code for performing common tasks in a particular language. (Another name for an API is a *library.*)

Now, there's only one Java language, but the Java language has three official APIs. When you download Java from `www.oracle.com` you download some Java language tools and one of the three Java APIs. Taken together, the big bundle containing the language tools and one of the three APIs is called an *edition* of the *Java Software Development Kit* (SDK). The three available Java SDK editions are as follows:

- *Java Platform, Standard Edition (Java SE)*

  The Standard Edition has code for anything you can imagine doing on a single desktop computer, and much more. This edition does text-handling, mathematical calculations, input/output, collections of objects, and much more.

  To develop Android apps, you want the Java Platform, Standard Edition.

- *Java Platform, Enterprise Edition (Java EE)*

  The Enterprise Edition has code for things you do on an industrial-strength server. This edition includes web server tools, sophisticated database tools, messaging between servers and clients, management of systems, and the entire kitchen sink.

- *Java Platform, Micro Edition (Java ME)*

  The Micro Edition has code for small devices, such as phones, TV set-top boxes, and Blu-ray players. This edition has limited capabilities that fit nicely into special-purpose devices that aren't as powerful as today's computers.

  At first glance, the Micro Edition seems perfect for Android app development. But the creators of Android decided to bypass Java ME and create their own micro edition of sorts. In a way, the Android SDK is an alternative to Java ME. To be more precise, the Android SDK is both an alternative to Java ME and a user of the Java SE. (That is, the Android SDK defers to Java SE to perform some important jobs.)

The stewards of Java flip-flop between the names *Java Software Development Kit* and *Java Development Kit* (JDK). The two names are synonymous.

To develop Android apps, you want the Java Platform, Standard Edition. If you already have Java's Enterprise Edition and you don't want more stuff on your hard drive, the Enterprise Edition is okay. But the Enterprise Edition has much more than you need for developing Android apps, and the extra Enterprise features might confuse you. (I know this because the extra Enterprise features confuse me!)

✦ **Java comes in several different versions, with several updates to each version.**

Java's version numbering demonstrates what can happen when the marketing department disrupts the timeline in the space-time continuum. Java's earliest releases were numbered "1.0." Next came version "1.1", and then the strangely named "Java 2, version 1.2." The extraneous digit 2 hung around through "Java 2, version 1.3", "Java 2, version 1.4", and finally "Java 2, version 5.0." (The spontaneous jump from 1.4 to 5.0 was lots of fun.)

Next up was "Java 6" (with no extra 2 and no ".0"). After that is Java 7. Each version is updated often, so a visit to www.oracle.com may offer Java SE 7 Update 13 for download.

Any version of Java starting with Java 2, version 5.0 and onward, is fine for Android development. Versions like 1.4 are not sufficient.

✦ **Java has two kinds of downloads.**

When you visit www.oracle.com, you see two acronyms floating around: *JRE* (Java Runtime Environment) and *JDK* (Java Development Kit). The JRE has everything you need in order to run existing Java programs. Whether you know it, your desktop computer probably has a version of the JRE.

The JDK has everything you need in order to run existing Java programs and everything you need in order to create new Java programs. The JDK has the entire JRE and more.

As an Android developer, you must create your own Java programs. So the download that you want is the JDK, which includes the JRE. You do *not* want the JRE alone.

Download and install the Java JDK, not the Java JRE.

✦ **Java might come with other tools.**

A glance at the Java download page shows several options — options to download Java with NetBeans, JavaFX, the Java source code, the Java SE documentation, and some other stuff. You might find the Java SE documentation helpful, especially if you don't want to repeatedly visit Oracle's online Java documentation. But the rest of the options (NetBeans, JavaFX, and the others) don't help with Android app development.

Those pesky filename extensions

On a Windows computer, the filenames displayed in My Computer or in Windows Explorer can be misleading. You may visit your `Downloads` directory and see the name `jdk-7u13-windows-x64`. Instead of just `jdk-7u13-windows-x64`, the file's full name is `jdk-7u13-windows-x64.exe`. In other directories you may see two `MyAndroidProgram` files. What you don't see is that one file's real name is `MyAndroidProgram.java` and the other file's real name is `MyAndroidProgram.class`.

The ugly truth is that My Computer and Windows Explorer can hide a file's extensions. This awful feature tends to confuse people. So if you don't want to be confused, modify the Windows Hide Extensions feature. To do this, you have to open the Folder Options dialog box. Here's how:

✔ **In Windows XP with the control panel's default (category) view:** Choose Start↔Control Panel↔Appearance and Themes↔Folder Options.

✔ **In Windows Vista or Windows 7 with the control panel's default (category) view:** Choose Start↔Control Panel↔Appearance and Personalization↔Folder Options.

✔ **In Windows XP, Windows Vista or Windows 7 with the control panel's classic view:** Choose Start↔Control Panel↔Folder Options.

In the Folder Options dialog box, click the View tab. Then look for the Hide Extensions for Known File Types option. Make sure that this check box is *not* selected.

After you've downloaded the Java SE JDK, follow the instructions at `www.oracle.com` for installing the software. On Windows, you normally double-click a file with the `.exe` extension. On Linux, you install an `.rpm` file or run a self-extracting `.bin` file. (I've never met a Linux geek who didn't know what to do with these files.)

Java for Macintosh

To develop Android programs on a Mac, you need OS X 10.5.8 or later, and your Mac must have an Intel processor. (The Android docs say that you can't develop Android apps on a PowerPC Mac or on a Mac with OS X 10.5.7. Of course, for every hardware or software requirement, someone tries to create a workaround, or *hack*. Anyway, apply hacks at your own risk.)

To find out which version of OS X you're running, do the following:

1. **Choose Apple⇨About This Mac.**

2. **In the About This Mac dialog that appears, look for the word *Version*.**

   You'll see Version 10.6.4 (or something like that) in very light gray text.

After deciding that you have OS X 10.5.8 or later, the next step is finding out whether your system already has the Java Development Kit. You have two choices:

✦ **You can trust me on the subject of OS X version numbers.**

   Macintosh OS X 10.5 (codenamed *Leopard)* and OS X 10.6 (codenamed *Snow Leopard*) have the Java Development Kit preinstalled. If you have either version of OS X (possibly with more dots in the version numbers, such as 10.6.4), from the Java point of view, you're good to go.

   Macintosh OS X 10.7 (codenamed *Lion)* comes without the Java Development Kit. So if you purchased OS X 10.7 thinking that you'd have the latest and the best, you may have gotten the latest, but (depending on your needs) you may not have gotten the best. But don't despair. Instead, keep reading.

   If you don't trust me about OS X version numbers (and frankly, you shouldn't trust everything you find in print), you have the following alternative:

✦ **You can perform tests on your development computer to discover the presence of a Java Development Kit and of a development kit's version number.**

   You have several choices for these tests. I explore two of the choices in this chapter — in fact, in the very next two sections.

Run Java Preferences to determine your JDK version

Here's how you run the utility:

1. **In the dock, select the Finder.**

A Finder window opens.

2. **In the Finder window's sidebar, select Applications.**

A list of applications appears in the Finder window's main panel.

3. **In the Finder window's main panel, double-click Utilities.**

A list of utilities appears in the Finder window's main panel.

4. **In the list of utilities, look for a Java Preferences entry.**

If you don't find a Java Preferences entry, don't fret (. . . not yet, anyway). You might still have a Java Development Kit. Skip to the test described in the next section.

5. **If you have a Java Preferences entry, double-click that entry.**

After an uncomfortable delay, your computer displays a window showing information about your computer's Java Development Kit. My Mac displays the name Java SE 6 (along with the more cryptic version number 1.6.0_22-b04-307). That's just fine.

To develop Android applications, you need Java SE 5 (also known as version number 1.5.0) or higher.

If the Java Preferences utility doesn't satisfy your needs, you can poke around in Macintosh's Unix command window. The next session tells you how.

Issue a Terminal command to determine your JDK version

To determine your Mac's JDK version, follow these steps:

1. **In the Spotlight search field, type the word** Terminal.

2. **When Terminal shows up as the Spotlight's top hit, press Enter.**

A Terminal window opens (usually with plain black text on a plain white background).

3. **In the Terminal window, type the following text and then press Enter:**

```
javac -version
```

On my computer, the Terminal window responds with the following text:

```
javac 1.6.0_22
```

If your computer responds with the number 1.5.0 or higher, you can pop open the champagne and look forward to some good times developing Android apps.

The Macintosh Terminal presents a strange (sometimes confusing) mix of case-sensitivity and "case-unsensitivity." For example, to see a list of users, you can type either **w** or **W** on the Terminal command line. To see a manual page describing that w command, you may type **man w**, **MAN w**, or even **mAn w**. But if you type **man W**, you get the unfriendly No manual entry for W response. In the same way, the javac -version command requires all the letters in version to be lower-case. Typing the incorrect javac -Version command gives you a dis-appointing invalid flag: -Version message.

If your computer responds with something like command not found, you may be running Mac OS X 10.7.0 or later. If your computer responds with a version number like 1.4.2 (or anything else that's less than 1.5.0), you may be running an older version of Mac OS X.

If your Mac doesn't have the Java JDK version 1.5.0 or greater . . .

As usual, here are a few things you can try:

✦ Visit www.oracle.com/technetwork/java/javase/downloads and look for a version of the Java JDK for the Mac. With the release of OS X 10.7, Apple agreed to let Oracle take charge of the JDK on the Macintosh. By the time you read this chapter, Oracle may have posted this software on its website. If you don't find the software on Oracle's site, you can also look for links at http://openjdk.org.

✦ Visit http://code.google.com/p/openjdk-osx-build/downloads/list?q=label:Featured and look for a prerelease version of Java for Mac OS X Lion.

✦ Choose Apple⇨Software Update. In the resulting window, look for any update having to do with Java.

✦ Search for *Java* at http://developer.apple.com. Poke around and look for a version of Java for your version of Mac OS X.

Installing the Android SDK Starter Package

The *Android Software Development Kit* (SDK) contains the libraries that you need for developing Android applications. The SDK has code for drawing forms on a device's screen, code for dialing phone numbers, code for taking pictures with the device's camera, and a lot more. The kit also contains bare-bones tools for creating, running, and testing your Android applications. By *barebones tools,* I mean tools that you can run by typing instructions in your development computer's command window (in the Command Prompt on Windows, or in the Terminal application on Linux and on a Mac). These tools perform all the logic required to do full-fledged Android development, but the SDK has no friendly user interface for invoking these tools. That friendly user interface comes in the next section, when you install Eclipse.

As you plow through various pieces of documentation, you'll see several uses of the acronym API. In the previous section, the Java API is a bunch of reusable code for performing common tasks with the Java programming language. In this section, the libraries in the Android SDK form the Android API — a bunch of reusable code for performing common tasks inside Android apps. To create Android apps, you need both APIs — the Java API and the Android API.

You normally drink down Android's SDK in two separate gulps. First, you get the Android SDK starter package — hence, the title for this section. Then you use the starter package to install the real Android SDK.

This separation between the SDK starter package and the actual SDK can be confusing because the Android website doesn't clearly highlight the distinction.

To install the Android SDK starter package, follow these steps:

1. **Visit** `http://developer.android.com`.

2. **On the main page that appears, click the link to download the Android SDK.**

3. **Find a link appropriate to your operating system (Windows, Mac OS X, or Linux).**

4. **Click the link to begin the download.**

For Windows, the web page provides two download options — a `.zip` file download and an `.exe` file download. If you're not sure which file you want, choose the `.exe` file download.

Today I stumbled on a little bug in the Android SDK starter package installation file for Windows. After installing the Java Development Kit and then launching the starter package installation program, I got a window telling me `Java SE Development Kit (JDK) not found`. Hey, what gives? I installed the JDK! Well, I searched online for a solution to the problem. If I click the window's Back button and then click the window's Next button again, the evil JDK Not Found message goes away. (Actually, if you encounter this bug, there's another way around it. Forget about the starter package's `.exe` file and instead download the alternative Android SDK starter package `.zip` file. Then extract the `.zip` file to a place on your computer's hard drive.)

For Mac OS X and for Linux, the web page provides a compressed archive file (a `.zip` file for Mac OS X and a `.tgz` file for Linux). Whichever file you download, double-click the file to view the file's contents and then drag the file's contents to a convenient place on your computer's hard drive.

If time has passed since I wrote this section and you find other formats for Android SDK downloads (.dmg files, .bin files, and so on), close your eyes and point to the screen. If you select any file that's appropriate for your operating system, you'll be okay.

Whatever operating system you run, whichever file format you download, make sure you know where (among the folders on your hard drive) the Android SDK starter package gets installed. (That's where the entire SDK will soon be installed.) I call this folder the *ANDROID_HOME directory.* You'll refer back to this location to find files that you need and to tell parts of your system where the Android libraries live.

You can find out a bit more by browsing your ANDROID_HOME directory's contents. The directory has folders named docs, platform-tools, platforms, samples, tools, and others.

Installing the Eclipse Development Environment

An *integrated development environment* (IDE) is a program that provides tools to help you create software easily and efficiently. You can develop software (including Android apps) without an IDE, but the time and effort you save using an IDE makes the IDE worthwhile. (Some hard-core developers disagree with me, but that's another matter.)

According to the Eclipse Foundation's website, *Eclipse* is "a universal tool platform — an open extensible IDE for anything and nothing in particular." Indeed, Eclipse is versatile. Most developers think of Eclipse as an IDE for developing Java programs, but Eclipse has tools for developing in C++, in PHP, and in many other languages. I've seen incarnations of Eclipse that have nothing to do with program development. (I've even seen *Lively Browser* — a web browser whose tabs are built from Eclipse components.)

Downloading Eclipse

Here's how you download Eclipse:

1. **Visit** www.eclipse.org.

2. **Look for a way to download Eclipse for your operating system.**

   Today, I visit www.eclipse.org and see a big button displaying the words *Get Started Now . . . Download Eclipse.* Tomorrow, who knows?

   After clicking the Download Eclipse button, I see a drop-down list with the names of three commonly used operating systems — Windows, Linux, and Mac OS X. In this drop-down list, I select the operating system that's installed on my development computer.

3. **Choose an Eclipse package from the available packages.**

   As I look at the Eclipse site today, I see Eclipse IDE for Java Developers, Eclipse IDE for Java EE Developers, Eclipse Classic, Eclipse IDE for C/C++ Developers, and others. To my great surprise, I also see MOTODEV Studio for Android.

   For developing Android apps, I recommend either Eclipse IDE for Java Developers or MOTODEV Studio for Android. As luck would have it, these are the two smallest downloads in the list. (Each is a mere 100MB.)

   In mid-2011 (where I live at the moment, probably ancient times for you, the reader), most of the Android developer documentation refers to plain old Eclipse (that is, Eclipse IDE for Java Developers). So I hesitate to recommend MOTODEV Studio exclusively. But from what I've heard, MOTODEV Studio has all the Android tools of Eclipse IDE for Java Developers, plus more. So if you don't mind seeing more options on your screen than the documentation normally describes, get MOTODEV Studio for Android. If you want a plainer environment, select Eclipse IDE for Java Developers.

   When winds blow to the northeast, and the moon is full, the Eclipse downloads page doesn't offer you the option of getting MOTODEV Studio. In that case, you can download MOTODEV Studio directly from `http://developer.motorola.com`.

   If you prefer, you can install the MOTODEV tools as a plug-in to your existing Eclipse installation. Visit `http://developer.motorola.com` for details.

4. **Select 32-bit or 64-bit.**

   For most Eclipse packages, you can choose between the 32-bit version and the 64-bit version. If you know that you're running a 64-bit operating system, choose the 64-bit package. If you're running a 32-bit operating system, or if you're not sure, choose the 32-bit package.

5. **Follow the appropriate links to get the download to begin.**

   The links you follow depend on which of the many mirror sites is offering up your download. Just wade through the possibilities and get the download going.

Installing Eclipse

Precisely how you install Eclipse depends on your operating system and on what kind of file you get when you download Eclipse. Here's a brief summary:

✦ **If you run Windows and the download is an `.exe` file:**

Double-click the `.exe` file's icon.

✦ **If you run Windows and the download is a `.zip` file:**

Extract the file's contents to the directory of your choice.

In other words, find the `.zip` file's icon in Windows Explorer. Then double-click the `.zip` file's icon. (As a result, Windows Explorer displays the contents of the `.zip` file, which consists of only one folder — a folder named `eclipse`.) Drag the `eclipse` folder to a convenient place in your development computer's file system.

My favorite place to drag the `eclipse` folder is directly onto the `C:` drive. So my `C:` drive has folders named `Program Files`, `Windows`, `eclipse`, and others. I avoid making the `eclipse` folder be a subfolder of `Program Files` because from time to time, I've had problems dealing with the blank space in the name `Program Files`.

After copying the `eclipse` folder to a place on your hard drive, you can run Eclipse by double-clicking the `eclipse.exe` file inside that folder.

✦ **If you run Mac OS X:**

If you download a `.tar.gz` file, find the file in your Downloads folder and double-click it. Double-clicking the file should extract the file's contents. After extraction, your Downloads folder contains a new Eclipse folder. Drag this new Eclipse folder to your Applications folder, and you're all set.

If you download a `.dmg` file, your web browser may open the file for you. If not, find the `.dmg` file in your Downloads folder and double-click the file. Follow any instructions that appear after this double-click. If you're expected to drag Eclipse or MOTODEV Studio into your Applications folder, do so.

✦ **If you run Linux:**

You might get a `.tar.gz` file, but there's a chance you'll get a self-extracting `.bin` file. Extract the `.tar.gz` file to your favorite directory, or execute the self-extracting `.bin` file.

Configuring Eclipse

Your Eclipse installation might need a bit of tuning. Here's what you do:

1. **Launch Eclipse.**

When you launch Eclipse, you see a Workspace Launcher dialog box. The dialog box asks where, on your computer's file system, you want to store the code that you will create using Eclipse.

2. **In the Workspace Launcher dialog box, click OK to accept the default.**

   Or don't accept the default! One way or another, it's no big deal.

   If this is your first time using a particular Eclipse workspace, Eclipse starts up with a Welcome screen. Through the ages, most of the Eclipse Welcome screens have displayed a few icons along with very little text.

3. **Hover over the icons on Eclipse's Welcome screen until you find an icon whose tooltip contains the word Workbench.**

4. **Click the Workbench icon to open Eclipse's main screen.**

   A view of the main screen, after opening Eclipse with a brand new work-space, is shown in Figure 2-1. If you downloaded MOTODEV Studio for Android (a particular version of Eclipse), you see the main screen in Figure 2-2.

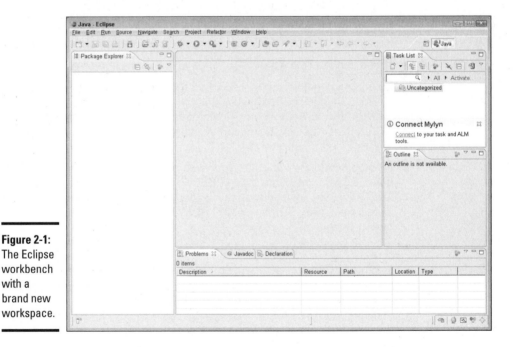

Figure 2-1:
The Eclipse workbench with a brand new workspace.

Eclipse is running. Now the fun begins.

Do I have the Eclipse Android Development Kit?

Eclipse is a generic platform. Eclipse doesn't owe its existence to Android. When you download Eclipse, you don't necessarily get any tools that are useful for developing Android apps.

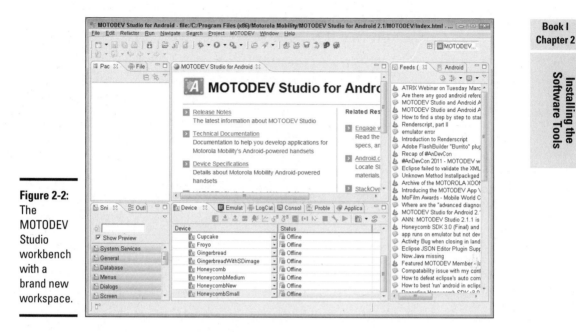

Figure 2-2:
The
MOTODEV
Studio
workbench
with a
brand new
workspace.

But Eclipse is well known for its plug-ins. Eclipse plug-ins add all kinds of tools to the barebones Eclipse platform. In fact, even Eclipse's signature tool, *Java Development Tools* (JDT), is a plug-in.

To develop Android apps, you need Eclipse's ADT — the *Android Development Tools* — plug-in. If you download Eclipse in the form of MOTODEV Studio for Android, you get the ADT along with the big download.

To find out if your Eclipse installation has the ADT plug-in, choose File↪New↪Project in Eclipse's main menu. If Eclipse displays anything about an Android project, you're home free.

If you already have Eclipse on your computer, or if you download a non-Android-specific version of Eclipse, your Eclipse installation probably doesn't have the ADT plug-in. You can add the ADT to Eclipse by following these instructions:

1. **In Eclipse's main menu, choose Help↪Install New Software.**

An Install dialog box opens.

2. **In the Install dialog box, click the Add button.**

An Add Repository dialog box opens.

3. **In the Add Repository dialog box, type a name (ideally, a name that reminds you of the Android ADT) and a location URL (see Figure 2-3).**

   The Add Repository dialog's Location field isn't like your Web browser's Address field. You can't surf to `https://dl-ssl.google.com/android/eclipse/` in a web browser. No ordinary web page has this address. Instead, you must use the URL in an Eclipse dialog box, as I describe in these steps. Also, when you type this URL, you can't abbreviate the URL by omitting the `https://` part. (The `s` in `https` stands for "secure.")

   The Add Repository dialog box's Location field isn't like your web browser's Address field. You can't abbreviate the URL by omitting the `https://` part. (And, by the way, the `s` in `https` stands for *secure.*)

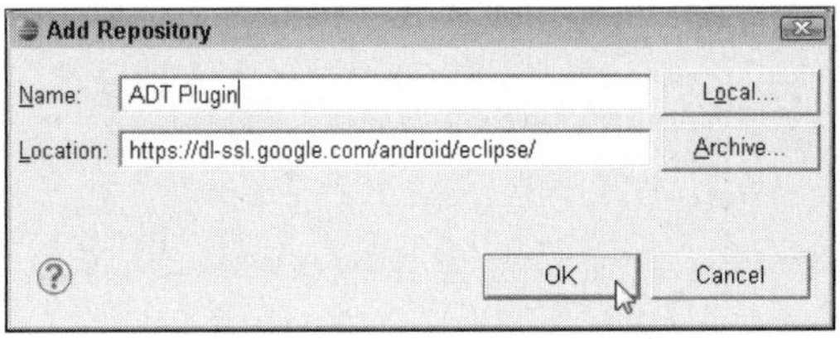

Figure 2-3: Eclipse's Add Repository dialog box.

Add Repository		
Name:	ADT Plugin	Local...
Location:	https://dl-ssl.google.com/android/eclipse/	Archive...
?		OK Cancel

4. **Click OK to close the Add Repository dialog box.**

   At this point in your journey, the Install dialog box displays a list of plug-ins that are available on your location URL's server. (See Figure 2-4.) If you're like me, you want everything.

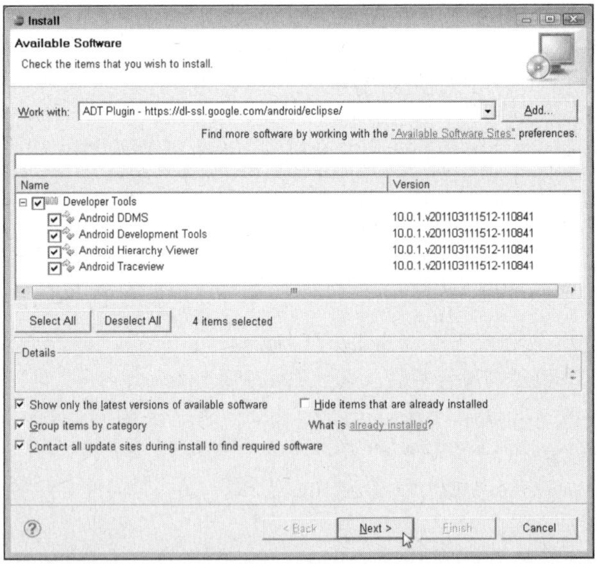

Figure 2-4: The Install dialog box.

Install

Available Software

Check the items that you wish to install.

Work with: ADT Plugin - https://dl-ssl.google.com/android/eclipse/   Add...

Find more software by working with the "Available Software Sites" preferences.

Name	Version
Developer Tools	
Android DDMS	10.0.1.v201103111512-110841
Android Development Tools	10.0.1.v201103111512-110841
Android Hierarchy Viewer	10.0.1.v201103111512-110841
Android Traceview	10.0.1.v201103111512-110841

Select All   Deselect All   4 items selected

Details

☑ Show only the latest versions of available software   ☐ Hide items that are already installed
☑ Group items by category   What is already installed?
☑ Contact all update sites during install to find required software

? | < Back | Next > | Finish | Cancel

5. **Click the Select All button and then click Next.**

   At this point, Eclipse asks for your acceptance of the license agreement's terms (which include no mention of your first-born child).

6. **Accept the agreement and follow any other instructions that Eclipse throws at you.**

   After some clicking and agreeing, your download begins. The plug-in installs itself automatically into Eclipse. When the download is finished, you have the Eclipse Android Development Tools plug-in.

Dude, where's my Android SDK?

After installing Eclipse's Android Development Tools, the next step is to make sure that Eclipse knows where to find the Android SDK (the stuff that you download a few sections back). To do this, follow these steps:

1. **In Eclipse's main menu, choose Window⇨Preferences.**

   Eclipse's Preferences dialog box opens.

2. **In the tree list on the left side of the Preferences dialog box, select Android.**

   Don't expand the Android branch of the tree. Simply click the word *Android.*

   An SDK Location field appears in the main body of the Preferences dialog box. (See Figure 2-5.)

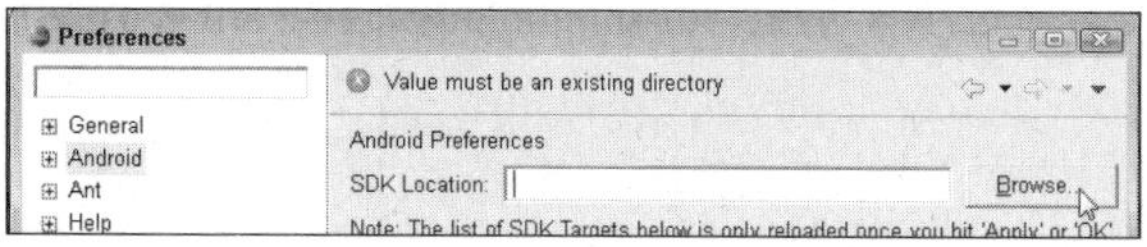

Figure 2-5:
Telling
Eclipse
about the
location
of your
Android
SDK.

At this point, the installing of Eclipse or MOTODEV Studio may have automatically filled in the SDK Location field (shown in Figure 2-5). If so, you're finished with this set of instructions. If so, skip Step 3.

3. **Click the Browse button and (of course) browse to the folder on your hard drive where you installed the Android SDK.**

   In a previous section, I called this folder your ANDROID_HOME directory.

4. **Click Apply, OK, and all those good things to return to the main Eclipse workbench.**

After selecting a location for the Android SDK, you may see a message saying `SDK Platform Tools component is missing! Please use the SDK Manager to install it.` As ferocious as this message looks, the message isn't disastrous. The message simply warns you that you must perform this chapter's next set of steps.

Look again at Figure 2-5 and notice the text field in the window's upper-left corner. That unlabeled text field is for filtering the names of Eclipse preference types. The tree of preference types (part of which is shown in Figure 2-5) expands to approximately 150 branches, and each branch refers to its own set of choices in the main body of the Preferences window. If you want to see a bunch of Eclipse preferences related to font (for example), type **font** in the little text field. When you type **font**, Eclipse displays only branches of the tree containing the word `font`.

Fattening Up the Android SDK

In the earlier "Installing the Android SDK Starter Package" section, you install the starter portion of the Android SDK. At this point in your travels, you install the rest of the SDK. The following section tells you how.

Installing platform tools

Like everything else in this world, Android changes. One month, developers work with Android 2.3, codenamed *Gingerbread.* Later that year, developers use Android 3.0, codenamed *Honeycomb.* Each version of Android represents a new *platform* or a new *API level,* depending on the way you refer to the version.

For more information about Android API levels, visit `http://developer.android.com/guide/appendix/api-levels.html#level.`

Terms like *platform* and *API level* have slightly different meanings in the Android world. But as a rule, platforms and API levels change in lockstep. For example, the Éclair Android release was platform 2.1, API level 7. The next release, Froyo ("frozen yogurt") was platform 2.2, API level 8.

Before you conclude that Éclair was once Android's "flavor of the month," I should point out that new Android releases tend to arrive every five or six months. Each Android release is installed on various devices, and those devices may keep these releases a long, long time.

Anyway, the Android SDK comes with several developer tools — tools for compiling, testing, and debugging Android code. Some of these tools don't change from one Android release to another. For example, to test your code, you usually start by running the code on an *emulator*. The emulator program runs on your development computer (your PC, your Mac, or your Linux computer). The emulator displays a picture of a mobile device (for example, a phone or a tablet device). The emulator shows you how your code will probably behave when you later run your code on a real phone or a real tablet device.

Now, an emulator doesn't change much from one Android platform to another. After all, an emulator represents the general capabilities of mobile devices in the marketplace. There are hundreds of makes and models of such devices, and the engineers who design all this hardware don't sit around waiting for the mythical Android 7.5, codenamed *Sugar High,* to be released in the year 2015. Emulators and Android platforms don't change in lockstep. So when you download the Android SDK starter package (as you do in an earlier section) you get the emulator tool as part of the package. This emulator tool lives in a `tools` folder inside your ANDROID_HOME directory.

As timeless as the emulator tool may be, some of the SDK's other tools are intimately tied to their respective Android versions. For example, the Android Debug Bridge (`adb`) is a tool to connect your development computer to a device that's executing your new code. (The `adb` also "connects" your development computer to a running emulator, even though the emulator is running on your development computer.) The `adb` is an invaluable tool for testing Android applications. The creators of Android revise the `adb` with every new Android platform, so the `adb` isn't in the `tools` folder, and the `adb` doesn't come with the Android SDK starter package. Instead, the `adb` is destined to reside in the `platform-tools` directory (a subdirectory of your ANDROID_HOME directory). To create the `platform-tools` directory and to populate the directory with things like `adb`, you run a program that comes with the starter package. Fortunately, you can do this by pointing and clicking within the Eclipse development environment.

1. **In Eclipse's main menu, choose Window⇨Android SDK and AVD Manager.**

    After selecting this option, Eclipse opens a new window. You'll never guess what the window's name is.

    After choosing Window⇨Android SDK and AVD Manager, you may see a troublesome message that tells you `Location of the Android SDK has not been setup in the preferences`. If you do, return to the section titled "Dude, where's my Android SDK?" earlier in this chapter.

2. **In the left panel of the Android SDK and AVD Manager window, select Available Packages.**

   In the main panel, you see a tree with a branch labeled Android Repository.

3. **Click the little plus sign to expand the Android Repository branch of the tree.**

   When the branch expands, you see a whole bunch of stuff, including Android SDK Platform-Tools, SDK Platform Android 2.2, Samples for SDK API 11, and many others.

4. **Place a check mark next to the Android Repository label.**

   When you do so, Eclipse automatically puts check marks in all the sub-branches of the Android Repository branch, as shown in Figure 2-6. Now you're ready to start downloading all the platform-specific stuff.

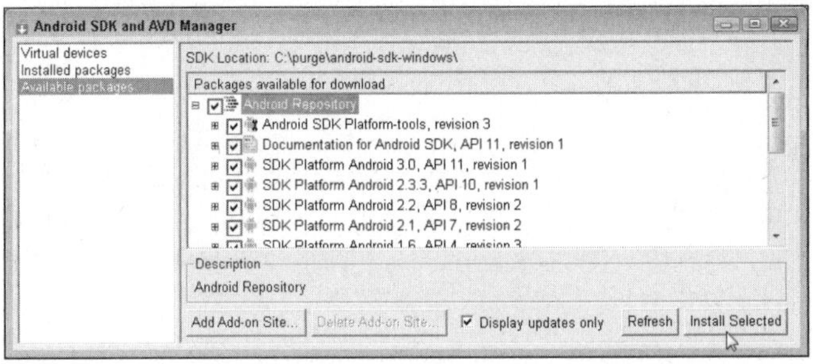

Figure 2-6:
Choosing
from the list
of available
packages.

5. **In the lower-right corner of the Android SDK and AVD Manager window, click Install Selected.**

6. **Do any remaining license accepting and clicking to make the download begin.**

Creating an Android Virtual Device

You might be itching to run some code, but first you must have something that can run an Android program. By "something," I mean either an Android device (a phone, a tablet, an Android enabled refrigerator, whatever) or a virtual device. An *Android Virtual Device* (AVD) is a test bed for Android code on your development computer (your PC, your Mac, or your Linux computer).

Steal this AVD!

You can copy an AVD from someone else's computer. That is, you don't really have to create an AVD. You can use an AVD that's already been created. On your development computer's hard drive, an AVD is an `.ini` file and a folder full of configuration information.

For example, my computer's `C:\Users\`*my-user-name*`\.android\avd\` folder has files named `Gingerbread.ini`, `Honeycomb.ini`, and so on. When I open `Honeycomb.ini` in a text editor, I see this:

```
target=android-11
path=C:\Users\my-user-name\.
    android\avd\Honeycomb.avd
```

Don't let the dot in the name `Honeycomb.avd` fool you. The name `Honeycomb.avd`

refers to a folder. This folder contains files like `config.ini`, which in turn describes the emulator's SD card size, RAM size, and so on. Here are a few lines from a `config.ini` file:

```
hw.lcd.density=160
sdcard.size=100M
hw.ramSize=256
```

To copy an AVD from someone else's computer, copy the `.avd` folder to your development computer's hard drive. Then create an `.ini` file like my `Honeycomb.ini` file. (Don't forget to replace my `target` and `path` values with values that are appropriate for your computer.) Put all this stuff in your user home's `.android\avd` folder (or wherever fine AVD files are stored).

Based on the stuff in the previous section, you may think that you download AVDs when you install the Android SDK starter package. After all, the starter package includes an emulator as part of its `tools` directory. The problem is, the SDK's emulator isn't the same as an AVD. The emulator is a generic program that translates Android code into code that your development computer can execute. But the emulator doesn't display a particular phone or tablet device on your screen. The emulator doesn't know what kind of device you want to display. Do you want a camera phone with 800-x-480-pixel resolution, or have you opted for a tablet device with its own built-in accelerometer and gyroscope? All these choices belong to a particular AVD. An AVD is actually a bunch of settings, telling the emulator all the details about the device to be emulated.

So before you can run Android apps on your computer, you must first create at least one AVD. In fact, you can create several AVDs and use one of them to run a particular Android app.

To create an AVD, follow these steps:

1. **In Eclipse's main menu, choose Window⇨Android SDK and AVD Manager.**

The Android SDK and AVD Manager window opens.

2. **In the Android SDK and AVD Manager window, click New, as shown in Figure 2-7.**

   The Create New Android Virtual Device (AVD) window opens. That's nice!

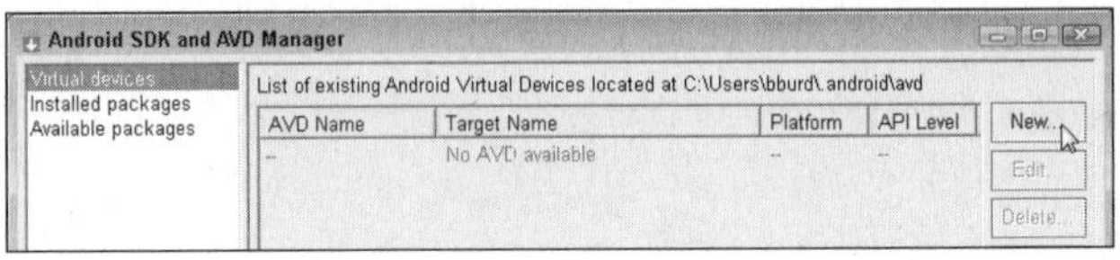

Figure 2-7:
An old
friend, the
Android
SDK and
AVD
Manager.

3. **Create a name for your virtual device.**

   You can name your device My Sweet Petunia, but in Figure 2-8, I name my device Gingerbread-800by480. The name serves to remind me of this device's capabilities.

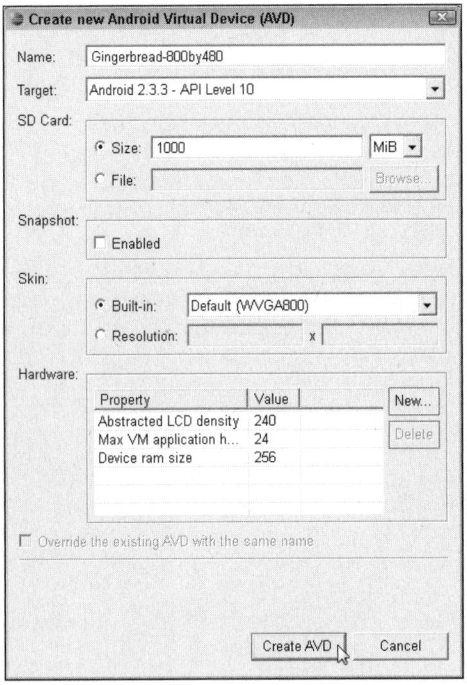

Figure 2-8:
Creating
a new
Android
virtual
device.

4. **Select a target platform for your virtual device.**

   In Figure 2-8, I select the Android 2.3.3 platform. My virtual device can run Android 2.3.3 programs.

5. **Decide what kind of secure digital (SD) card your device has.**

   In Figure 2-8, I decide on an SD card with a modest 1000 MiB, which is roughly 1GB. Alternatively, I could have selected the File radio button and specified the name of a file on my hard drive. That file would be storing information as if it were a real SD card on a real device.

   Recently, my department hired a new person. We offered a salary of $50K, which (we thought) meant $50,000 per year. Little did we know that the new person expected to be paid $51,200 each year. Computer scientists use the letter *K* (or the prefix "Kilo") to mean 1,024 because 1,024 is a power of 2 (and powers of 2 are very handy in computer science). The trouble is, the formal meaning of "Kilo" in the metric system is 1,000, not 1,024. To help clear things up (and to have fun creating new words) a commission of engineers created the *Kibibyte* (KiB) meaning 1,024 bytes, the *Mebibyte* (MiB) which is 1,048,576 bytes, and the *Gibibyte* (GiB) meaning 1,073,741,824 bytes. Most people (computer scientists included) don't know about KiBs or MiBs, and don't worry about the difference between MiBs and ordinary megabytes. I'm surprised that the developers of Android's SDK and AVD Manager thought about this issue.

6. **Select or specify a display resolution for your virtual device.**

   In Figure 2-8, I chose the default WVGA800 resolution, which is 800x480 pixels.

7. **Leave the other choices at their defaults (or don't, if you don't want to) and click the Create AVD button.**

   Your computer returns you to the Android SDK and AVD Manager window, where you see a brand-new AVD in the list. (See Figure 2-9.)

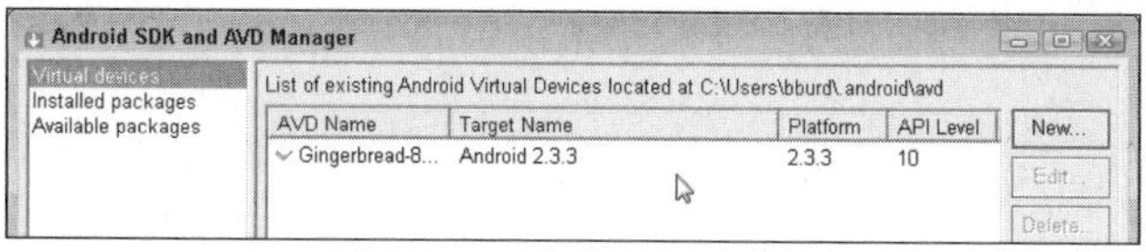

Figure 2-9:
You've created an Android virtual device.

Android SDK and AVD Manager

Virtual devices	List of existing Android Virtual Devices located at C:\Users\bburd\.android\avd				
Installed packages	AVD Name	Target Name	Platform	API Level	New...
Available packages	∨ Gingerbread-8...	Android 2.3.3	2.3.3	10	Edit...
					Delete...

This section's steps work with any copy of Eclipse that has the Android Development Tools plug-in. This includes MOTODEV Studio for Android, which is an enhanced copy of Eclipse. But MOTODEV Studio provides another way to create AVDs. The other way uses a wizard interface with an impressive number of options. To start the wizard, choose MOTODEV⇨New Android Virtual Device from the Studio's main menu. From then on, do what the nice wizard tells you to do.

And that does it! You're ready to run your first Android app. I don't know about you, but I'm excited. (Sure, I'm not watching you read this book, but I'm excited on your behalf.) Chapter 3 in this minibook guides you through the run of an Android application. Go for it!

Acting like a phone (when you're not a phone)

In computing, the words *emulator* and *simulator* have similar meanings. Some people use the words interchangeably, but if you're being picky, an *emulator* executes each program by doing what another kind of processor would do. In contrast, a *simulator* executes a program any way that's handy and ends up with the same result that an emulator would get. To be even pickier, an emulator mimics your processor's hardware, and a simulator mimics your application's software.

On your development computer's screen, a phone simulator would look like a picture of a phone and would carry out your mobile application's instructions for testing purposes. But on the inside, the simulator would be executing instructions the way your laptop or desktop executes instructions. The simulator would be translating instructions meant for a phone's processor into instructions meant for

your laptop's processor. This juggling act (of instructions and processors) works fine on the whole. But in some subtle situations, a simulator doesn't precisely mimic a real phone's behavior.

The goal of precise, reliable mimicry is one reason why the Android crew decided on an emulator instead of a simulator. Android's emulator (the emulator that you download with the SDK starter package) is based on a very popular open-source program named QEMU. On its own, QEMU takes code written for a certain kind of processor (an Intel chip, for example), translates this code, and then runs the code on another kind of processor (an ARM or a PowerPC, for example). The emulator that comes with Android's starter package has add-ons and tweaks to accommodate Android mobile devices. For more information about QEMU, visit `http://qemu.org`.

Chapter 3: Creating an Android App

In This Chapter

✔ Creating an elementary Android app

✔ Troubleshooting troublesome apps

✔ Testing an app on an emulator or a phone

✔ Dissecting an app

*I*n a quiet neighborhood in south Philadelphia, there's a maternity shop named Hello World. I stumbled on the store on my way to Pat's (to get a delicious Philly cheesesteak, of course), and I couldn't resist taking a picture of the store's sign.

Computer geek that I am, I'd never thought of Hello World as anything but an app. A *Hello World* app is the simplest program that can run in a particular programming language or on a particular platform.* Authors create Hello World apps to show people how to get started writing code for a particular system.

So I devote this chapter to an Android Hello World app. The app doesn't do much. (In fact, you might argue that the app doesn't do anything!) But the example shows you how to create and run new Android projects.

Creating Your First App

A typical gadget comes with a manual. The manual's first sentence is "Read all 37 safety warnings before attempting to install this product." Don't you love it? You can't get to the good stuff without wading through the preliminaries.

Well, nothing in this chapter can set your house on fire or even break your electronic device. But before you follow this chapter's instructions, you need a bunch of software on your development computer. To make sure that you have this software and that the software is properly configured, return to Chapter 2 of this minibook. (Do not pass Go; do not collect $200.)

---

* *For an interesting discussion of the phrase Hello World, visit* www.mzlabs.com/JMPubs/ HelloWorld.pdf .

When at last you have all the software you need, you're ready to start Eclipse and create a real, live Android app.

Starting Eclipse

In this book, almost everything starts with the Eclipse integrated development environment.

1. **Launch Eclipse.**

    For details, see Chapter 2 of this minibook. To read about hundreds of things you can do with Eclipse, see Book II, Chapter 1.

2. **If Eclipse shows you its Welcome screen, find that screen's Workbench icon and then click it to open Eclipse's main workbench.**

    For details, see Chapter 2 of this minibook.

3. **In the Eclipse workbench, make sure that the Java perspective is active.**

    Look for the word *Java* in the upper-right corner of the Eclipse workbench. If you see the word Java on an indented button (as in Figure 3-1), Eclipse's Java perspective is active.

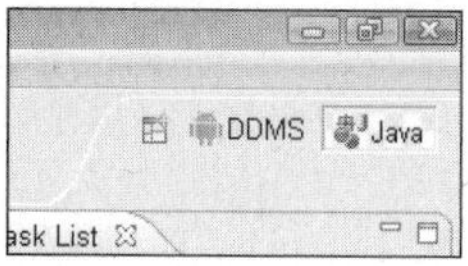

Figure 3-1:
Eclipse's
Java
perspective
is active.

For more information about Eclipse perspectives, see Book II, Chapter 1.

4. **If the Java perspective isn't active, choose Window⇨Open Perspective⇨Other⇨Java (Default).**

As a result, the Java perspective opens right before your eyes. You're ready to create an Android app.

Creating a project

To create your first Android application, do the following:

1. **In Eclipse's main menu, choose File⇨New⇨Project.**

The New Project dialog box opens.

2. **In the New Project dialog box, expand the Android branch. In that branch, select Android Project and then click Next. (See Figure 3-2.)**

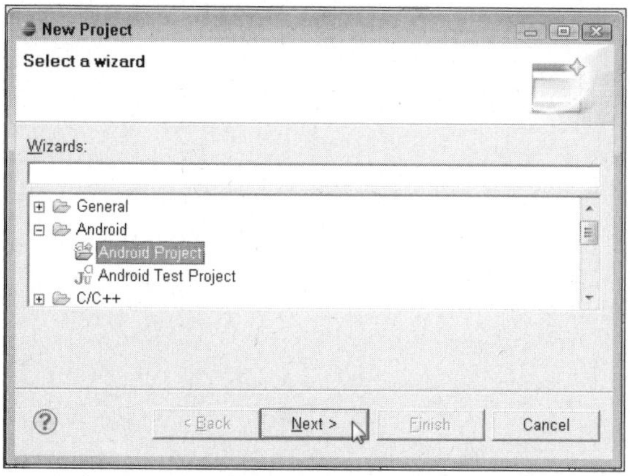

Figure 3-2:
The New
Project
dialog box.

As a result, Eclipse fires up its New Android Project dialog box. (The top half of the New Android Project dialog box is in Figure 3-3.)

3. **In the New Android Project dialog box, type a name for your project in the Project Name field.**

In Figure 3-3, I type **My First Android Project**.

4. **In the dialog box's Build Target panel, select a target.**

In Figure 3-3, I select Android 3.0. You can select any target that's listed, as long as you've created an Android Virtual Device (AVD, for short) that can run that target's projects. For example, an Android 2.3.3 AVD can run projects targeted to Android 2.3.1, Android 2.2, Android 1.6, and so on.

If you mistakenly select a target for which you have no AVD, Eclipse hollers at you when you try to run the project. (While it hollers, Eclipse offers to help you create the necessary AVD.)

For help creating an AVD, see Chapter 2 of this minibook.

5. **Find the Properties box of the New Android Project dialog box.**

On my computer, with its embarrassingly low screen resolution, the New Android Project dialog box comes with its own scroll bar. To find the Properties box, I have to scroll down to the lower half of the dialog box. (See Figure 3-4.)

New Android Project

New Android Project

Creates a new Android Project resource.

Project name: MyFirstAndroidProject

Contents

● Create new project in workspace
○ Create project from existing source
☑ Use default location

Location: C:/Users/bburd/workspaceJune2011/MyFirstAndr   Browse...

○ Create project from existing sample

Samples: ApiDemos

Build Target

Target Name	Vendor	Platform	AP...
☐ Android 1.5	Android Open Source Project	1.5	3
☐ Google APIs	Google Inc.	1.5	3
☐ Android 1.6	Android Open Source Project	1.6	4
☐ Google APIs	Google Inc.	1.6	4
☐ Android 2.1-upda...	Android Open Source Project	2.1-up...	7
☐ Google APIs	Google Inc.	2.1-up...	7
☐ Android 2.2	Android Open Source Project	2.2	8
☐ Google APIs	Google Inc.	2.2	8
☐ GALAXY Tab Ad...	Samsung Electronics Co., Ltd.	2.2	8
☐ Android 2.3.1	Android Open Source Project	2.3.1	9
☐ Google APIs	Google Inc.	2.3.1	9
☐ EDK	Sony Ericsson Mobile Comm...	2.3.1	9
☐ Android 2.3.3	Android Open Source Project	2.3.3	10
☐ Google APIs	Google Inc.	2.3.3	10
☑ Android 3.0	Android Open Source Project	3.0	11
☐ Google APIs	Google Inc.	3.0	11

Figure 3-3: The top half of the New Android Project dialog box.

6. **In the Application Name field, type a name for your app.**

In Figure 3-4, I type **My First Android App**. Whatever name you type appears below your app's icon in the device's Apps screen.

7. **In the Package Name field, type a name with a valid Java package name.**

   In Figure 3-4, I type **stuff.of.mine**. This isn't the world's best package name, but it'll do.

Using Android's versions

Android has a few different uses for version numbers. For example, in Figure 3-4, the *target* API is 11, and the *minimum SDK version* is also 11. What's the difference?

You design an Android app to run on a range of API versions. You can think informally of the minimum SDK version as the lowest version in the range, and the target version as the highest. So, if you select Android 2.2 as the target and select 4 as the minimum SDK, you design your app to run on Android 1.6 (API level 4), Android 2.1, and Android 2.2.

But the "lowest to highest version" idea needs some refining. Android's official documentation reports that " . . . new versions of the platform are fully backward-compatible." So an app that runs correctly on Android 1.6 should run correctly on all versions higher than Android 1.6. (I write "*should* run correctly" because in practice, full backward compatibility is difficult to achieve. Anyway, if the Android team is willing to promise full backward compatibility, I'm willing to take my chances.)

The *target version* (Android 3.0, API 11 near the top in Figure 3-4) is the version for which you test the app. When you run this chapter's example, Eclipse opens an emulator with Android 3.0 installed. To the extent that your app passes your testing, the app runs correctly on devices that run Android 3.0. What about devices that run other versions of Android?

✔ Maybe your app's target version is Android 3.0, but your app uses only features that are available in Android 2.2 and earlier versions. In that case, you can safely put the number 8 in Eclipse's Min SDK Version field.

✔ Maybe your app uses some features available only in Android 3.0 and later, but the app contains workarounds for devices that run Android 2.2. (Your app's code can detect a device's Android version and contains alternative code for different versions.) In that case, you can safely put the number 8 in Eclipse's Min SDK Version field.

✔ Maybe your app's target version is Android 3.0. In 2019, someone installs your app on a device running Android 16.0 (codenamed Artificial Sweetener). Because of backward compatibility, your app runs awkwardly but correctly on the Android 16.0 device. The target version isn't an upper limit.

When you select a target version and a min SDK version, Android stores these numbers in your project's files. The min SDK version lives in the project's `AndroidManifest.xml` file. The target version sits inside the project's `default.properties` file. The `AndroidManifest.xml` file guides the use of your app from start to finish. The `default.properties` file is used mainly to maintain the integrity of your app when you make modifications and store newer copies.

In addition to the min SDK version, the `AndroidManifest.xml` file may store a maximum SDK version. The maximum SDK version isn't an option in Figure 3-4 because hardly anyone specifies a maximum SDK version. In fact, the Android documentation discourages the use of a maximum SDK version. The docs warn that a maximum SDK version might cause an app to be uninstalled when the app is still usable.

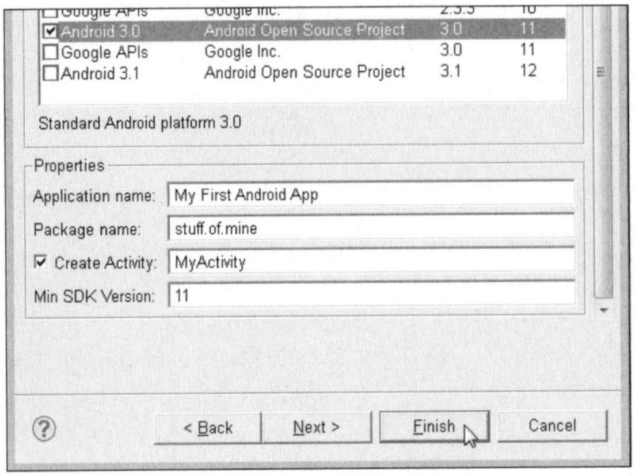

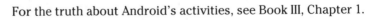

Figure 3-4:
The lower
half of
the New
Android
Project
dialog box.

For the lowdown on Java packages and package names, see Book II, Chapter 2.

Your project and application names may contain blank spaces, but your package name and (in the next step) your activity name must not contain blank spaces. In general, I'm not a fan of blank spaces. They can gum up the works when your software distinguishes the end of one name and the start of the next name. For example, in Windows, the folder name Program Files is a never-ending source of angst for me and other developers. Anyway, my advice is, use blank spaces only where an app's cosmetics demand blank spaces. If things go wrong, be suspicious of any names with blank spaces.

8. **With the Create Activity check box selected, type a name for your application's main activity.**

   In Figure 3-4, I type **MyActivity**. Lazy as I am, I use the name `MyActivity` quite often. For your project, you can type the name of any valid Java identifier. Make sure to start with a letter and then include only letters, digits, and underscores (_).

   Your activity is a Java class. So, to adhere to Java's stylistic conventions, start your activity's name with an uppercase letter. In the name, don't include any exotic characters (such as dots, blank spaces, dashes, dollar signs, or pictures of cows).

   For the truth about Android's activities, see Book III, Chapter 1.

9. **In the Min SDK Version field, type the number to the far right of whichever target you selected in Step 4.**

   In Figure 3-4, I type **11** because I find the number `11` at the end of the Android 3.0 target line in the Build Target panel. To find out what you're promising when you check Android 3.0 and minimum SDK 11, see the nearby "Using Android's versions" sidebar.

   For an overview of Android versions, see Chapter 1 of this minibook.

You can specify a min SDK version with a lower number than the number in the Build Target panel. For example, you can pick Build Target Android 2.3.1 with Min SDK Version 4. When you do this, Eclipse warns you that `The API level for the selected SDK target does not match the Min SDK Version`. You can safely ignore this warning.

10. **At the bottom of the New Android Project dialog box, click Finish.**

   As a result, the New Android Project dialog box closes, and the Eclipse workbench comes to the foreground. Eclipse's Package Explorer tree has a new branch. The branch's label is the name of your new project. (See Figure 3-5.)

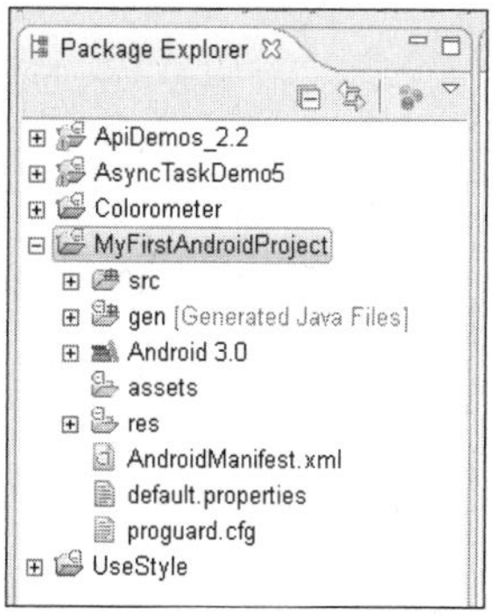

Figure 3-5:
The
Package
Explorer has
a MyFirst
Android
Project
branch.

Congratulations! You've created an Android application.

Running your project

To kick your new app's tires and take your app around the block, do the following:

1. **Select your app's branch in Eclipse's Package Explorer.**

   (See Figure 3-5.)

2. **In Eclipse's main menu, choose Run⇨Run As⇨Android Application.**

   As a result, Eclipse's Console view displays several lines of text. Among these lines, you might find the phrases `Launching a new emulator`; `Waiting for HOME`; and my personal favorite, `Success!` (See Figure 3-6.)

   If you don't see Eclipse's Console view, you have to coax this view out of hiding. For details, see Book II, Chapter 1.

   In general app development lingo, a *console* is a text-only window that displays the output of a running program. A console might also accept commands from the user (in this case, the app developer). A single Android run might create several consoles at once, so Eclipse's Console view can display several consoles at once. If the stuff you see in Eclipse's

Console view isn't anything like the text in Figure 3-6, the Console view may be displaying the wrong console. To fix this, look for a button with a picture of a computer terminal in the upper-right corner of the Console view. (See Figure 3-7.) Click the arrow to the right of the button. In the resulting drop-down list, choose Android.

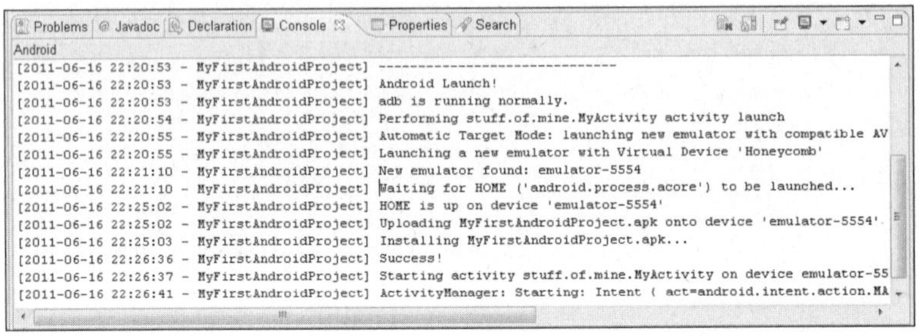

Figure 3-6:
The Console view during the successful launch of an app.

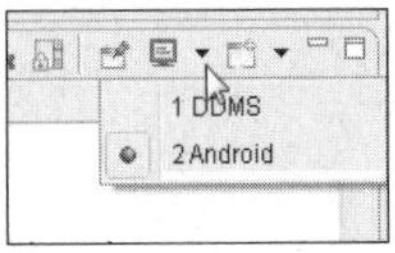

```
Problems  Javadoc  Declaration  Console  Properties  Search
Android
[2011-06-16 22:20:53 - MyFirstAndroidProject] ---------------------------------
[2011-06-16 22:20:53 - MyFirstAndroidProject] Android Launch!
[2011-06-16 22:20:53 - MyFirstAndroidProject] adb is running normally.
[2011-06-16 22:20:54 - MyFirstAndroidProject] Performing stuff.of.mine.MyActivity activity launch
[2011-06-16 22:20:55 - MyFirstAndroidProject] Automatic Target Mode: launching new emulator with compatible AV
[2011-06-16 22:20:55 - MyFirstAndroidProject] Launching a new emulator with Virtual Device 'Honeycomb'
[2011-06-16 22:21:10 - MyFirstAndroidProject] New emulator found: emulator-5554
[2011-06-16 22:21:10 - MyFirstAndroidProject] Waiting for HOME ('android.process.acore') to be launched...
[2011-06-16 22:25:02 - MyFirstAndroidProject] HOME is up on device 'emulator-5554'
[2011-06-16 22:25:02 - MyFirstAndroidProject] Uploading MyFirstAndroidProject.apk onto device 'emulator-5554'
[2011-06-16 22:25:03 - MyFirstAndroidProject] Installing MyFirstAndroidProject.apk...
[2011-06-16 22:26:36 - MyFirstAndroidProject] Success!
[2011-06-16 22:26:37 - MyFirstAndroidProject] Starting activity stuff.of.mine.MyActivity on device emulator-55
[2011-06-16 22:26:41 - MyFirstAndroidProject] ActivityManager: Starting: Intent ( act=android.intent.action.MA
```

Figure 3-7:
Choosing a console in Eclipse's Console view.

```
1 DDMS
● 2 Android
```

3. **Wait for the Android emulator to display a device locked screen, a home screen, or an app's screen.**

   First, you see the word ANDROID as if it's part of a scene from *The Matrix*. (See Figure 3-8.) Then you see the word ANDROID in shimmering, silvery letters. (See Figure 3-9.) Finally, you see Android's a device locked screen, a home screen, or an app's screen. (See Figure 3-10.)

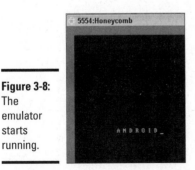

Figure 3-8:
The emulator starts running.

Figure 3-9:
Android
starts
running
on the
emulator.

4. **I can't overemphasize this point: Wait for the Android emulator to display a device locked screen, a home screen, or an app's screen.**

   Android's emulator takes a long time to start. For example, on my 2GHz processor with 4GB of RAM, the emulator takes a few minutes to mimic a fully booted Android device. Some people blame the fact that it's an emulator instead of a simulator. (See Chapter 2 of this minibook.) Others claim that translation of graphics hog the emulator's time. For whatever reason, you need lots of patience when you deal with Android's emulator.

5. **Keep waiting.**

Figure 3-10:
The device
locked
screen for
Android 3.0
appears.

While you're waiting, you might want to visit `http://youwave.com`. The people at YouWave have created an alternative to Android's emulator. The YouWave simulator runs on a Windows PC with a program named VirtualBox (a product from Oracle). YouWave can't run all Android apps, and I don't know how faithfully YouWave imitates Android. But one way or another, YouWave looks promising.

Oh! I see that your emulator is finally displaying the device locked screen. It's time to proceed . . .

6. **If the emulator displays the device locked screen, do whatever you normally do to unlock an Android device.**

 Normally, you slide something from one part of the screen to another. With Android Version 3.0 (pictured in Figure 3-10), you slide the lock from the center to the circumference of a circle.

7. **See your app on the emulator's screen.**

 Figure 3-11 shows the running of Android's Hello World app. (The screen even has `Hello World` on it.) Android's development tools create this tiny app when you create a new Android project.

Figure 3-11:
Your Hello
World app
in action.

For this chapter, you use Eclipse to create a project in the earlier "Creating a project" section. But you can create a Hello World project without Eclipse. For details, see Book VI, Chapter 3.

Android's Hello World app has no widgets for the user to push, and the app doesn't do anything interesting. But the appearance of an app on the Android screen is a very good start. Following this chapter's steps, you can start creating many exciting apps.

Don't close an Android emulator unless you know you won't be using it for a while. The emulator is fairly reliable after it gets going. (It's sluggish, but reliable.) While the emulator runs, you can modify your Android code and choose Run⇨Run As⇨Android Application yet again. When you do, Android reinstalls your app on the running emulator. The process isn't speedy, but you don't have to wait for the emulator to start. (Actually, if you run a different app — an app whose min SDK version is higher than the running emulator can handle — Android fires up a second emulator. But in many developer scenarios, jumping between emulators is the exception rather than the rule.)

What if . . .

You try to run your first Android app. If your effort stalls, don't despair. This section has some troubleshooting tips.

Error message: R cannot be resolved

Every Android app has an R.java file. Android's development tools generate this file automatically. So normally, you don't have to worry about R.java. Occasionally, the file takes longer than average to be generated. In that case, Eclipse finds references to the R class in the rest of your project's code and complains that your project has no R class. My advice is, wait!

If one minute of waiting doesn't bring good results, follow these steps to check your project settings:

1. **Highlight your project in Eclipse's Package Explorer.**

2. **In Eclipse's main menu, choose Project.**

   A list of sub-menu items appears.

3. **Look for a check mark next to the Build Automatically menu sub-item.**

4. **If you don't see a check mark, select the Build Automatically sub-item to add a one.**

   With any luck your R.java file appears almost immediately.

If your project is set to Build Automatically, and you still don't have an R.java file, try these steps:

1. **Highlight your project in Eclipse's Package Explorer.**

2. **In Eclipse's main menu, choose Project.**

   A list of sub-menu items appears.

3. **In Eclipse's Clean dialog box, select the project that's giving you trouble along with the Clean Projects Selected Below radio button.**

4. **Click OK.**

Cleaning the project should fix the problem. But if the problem persists, close Eclipse and then restart it. (Eclipse occasionally becomes "confused.")

Error message: No compatible targets were found

This message probably means that you haven't created an Android Virtual Device (AVD) capable of running your project. If Eclipse offers to help you create a new AVD, accept it. Otherwise, choose Window➪Android SDK and AVD Manager to create a new AVD.

For information about Android Virtual Devices, see Chapter 2 of this minibook.

The emulator stalls during startup

After five minutes or so, you don't see Android's device locked screen or Android's home screen. Here are several things you can try:

✦ **Lather, rinse, repeat.**

Close the emulator and launch your application again. Sometimes, the second or third time's a charm. On rare occasions, my first three attempts fail, but my fourth attempt succeeds.

✦ **Restart the Android Debug Bridge (adb) server.**

Here's what you do:

1. *Close Eclipse.*

2. *In a command window, go to your* ANDROID_HOME/platform-tools *directory.*

To read about your computer's command window, see Book VI, Chapter 3.

3. *In the* ANDROID_HOME/platform-tools *directory, type the following two commands:*

Windows:

```
adb kill-server
adb start-server
```

Macintosh and Linux:

```
./adb kill-server
./adb start-server
```

4. *Restart Eclipse.*

For help finding your ANDROID_HOME/platform-tools directory, see Chapter 2 of this minibook.

✦ **Switch to an older Android Virtual Device.**

In my experience, older AVDs consume fewer resources on your development computer. To change a project's target AVD, do the following:

1. *Close any running emulators.*

2. *With your project selected in Eclipse's Package Explorer, choose Project⟹Properties.*

A Properties dialog box opens. The Properties dialog box has a tree in its left panel. (See Figure 3-12.)

3. *In the Properties dialog box's tree, select Android.*

   A form full of options appears in the main body of the Properties dialog box. Among these options is a list of targets. (See Figure 3-12.)

4. *Select a new target AVD for your project.*

5. *Click OK to save the change and dismiss the Properties dialog box.*

   Wait! You're not finished yet . . .

6. *In your project's branch of Eclipse's Package Explorer, double-click the* `AndroidManifest.xml` *file.*

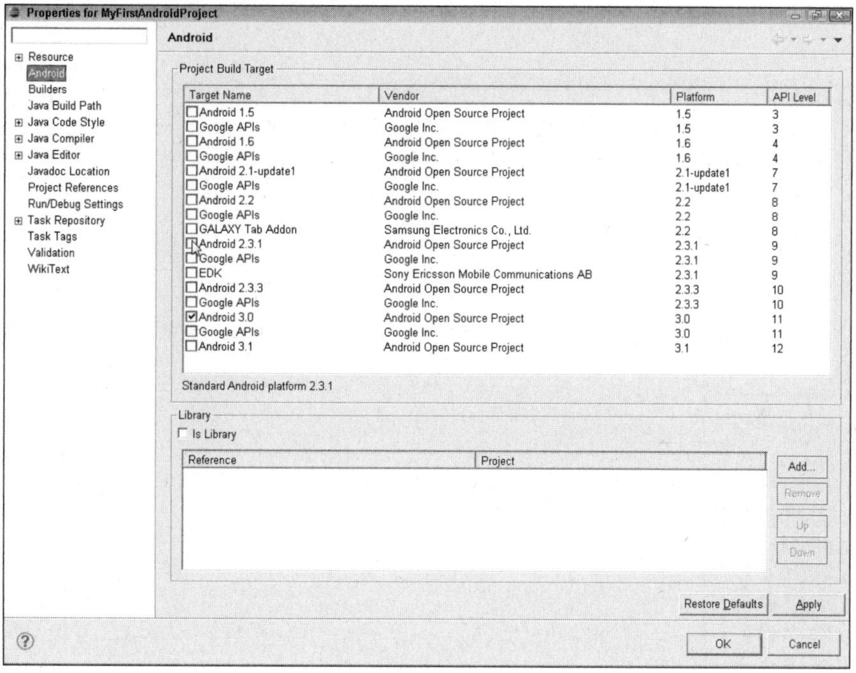

Figure 3-12:
A project's
Properties
dialog box.

Eclipse offers several ways to examine and edit this file.

7. *At the bottom of Eclipse's editor, select the Manifest tab.*

   Eclipse displays a form like the one shown in Figure 3-13.

8. *In the form, click Uses Sdk.*

   As a result, a set of options appears on the form. This set of options is labeled Attributes for Uses Sdk. (See Figure 3-13.)

9. *In the Min SDK Version field, type the number of your project's new API version.*

In Figure 3-13, I type **9**, but you can type any of Android's API version numbers. Just make sure that your min SDK version is no higher than the target you choose in Step 4.

10. *Choose File⇨Save to store the new* `AndroidManifest.xml` *file.*

You can use these instructions to lower an app's target and minimum SDK version. But if your app requires features that aren't available in the lower target or SDK version, you won't be happy with the results. In the best case, you see an error in Eclipse's Package Explorer as soon as you make the change. In the worst case, you see no error in the Package Explorer, but your app crashes when it runs.

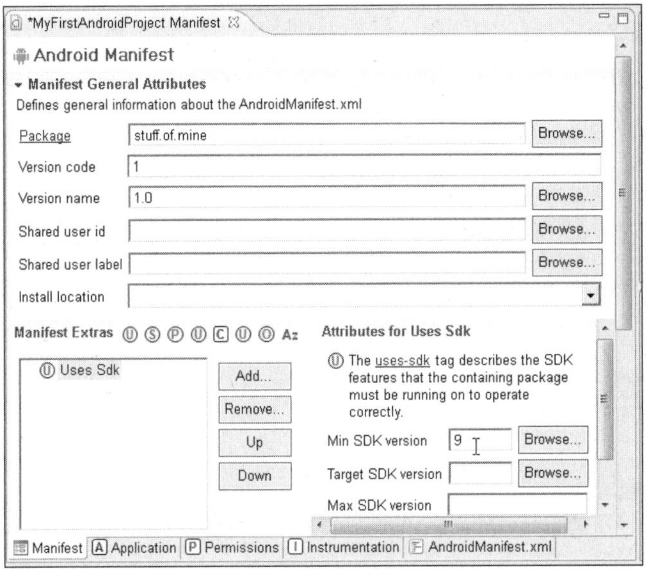

Figure 3-13:
The
Manifest
tab of a
project's
Android
Manifest.xml
file.

Continuing with my list of things to try if the emulator stalls during startup . . .

✦ **If you have a more powerful computer, try running your app on it.**

Horsepower matters.

✦ **Run your app on a phone, a tablet, or some other real Android device.**

Testing a brand-new app on a real device makes me queasy. But Android's sandbox is fairly safe for apps to play in. Besides, apps load quickly and easily on phones and tablets.

For instructions on installing apps to Android devices, see the section "Testing Apps on a Real Device," later in this chapter.

Error message: The user data image is used by another emulator

If you see this message, some tangle involving the emulator keeps Android from doing its job. First try closing and restarting the emulator.

If a simple restart doesn't work, try the following steps:

1. **Close the emulator.**

2. **In Eclipse's main menu, choose Window⇨Android SDK and AVD Manager.**

To read about the SDK and AVD Manager, see Chapter 2 in this minibook.

3. **In the list of virtual devices, select an AVD appropriate to your project and click Start.**

4. **In the resulting Launch Options dialog box, select the Wipe User Data check box and then click Launch.**

As a result, Android launches a new copy of the emulator, this time with a clean slate.

If the preceding set of steps doesn't work, take a firmer approach, as follows:

1. **Close the emulator.**

2. **Open whatever file explorer your computer uses to track down files.**

3. **In your home directory, look for a folder named .android (starting with a dot).**

The name of your home directory depends on your development computer's operating system.

- *On Windows 7 or Windows Vista,* your home directory is typically `c:\Users\`*your-user-name.*

- *On Windows XP,* your home directory is typically `c:\Documents and Settings\`*your-user-name.*

- *On a Mac,* your home directory is typically `/Users/`*your-user-name.*

For example, on my Windows 7 computer, I navigate to `c:\Users`. From there, I drill down into `c:\Users\bburd` (my home directory), and from there, I drill even further into `c:\Users\bburd\.android`.

4. **From the .android directory, drill down even further into the avd directory.**

The avd directory contains a folder for each AVD that you've created.

5. **Drill down one level more to the directory for the AVD that's giving you trouble.**

   For example, if you were running an AVD named *Froyo1* when you saw the `data image is used by another emulator` message, navigate to your `Froyo1.avd` directory.

6. **Inside your AVD's directory, delete the files named `cache.img.lock` and `userdata-qemu.img.lock`.**

7. **Return to the Eclipse workbench and run your app again.**

Error message: Unknown virtual device name

Android looks for AVDs in your home directory's `.android/avd` subdirectory, and occasionally Android's search goes awry. For example, one of my Windows 7 computers lists my home directory on an `i` drive. My AVDs are in `i:\Users\bburd\.android\avd`. But Android ignores the computer's home directory advice and instead looks in `c:\Users\bburd`. When Android doesn't find any AVDs, Android complains.

You can devise fancy solutions to this problem with *junctions* or *symbolic links.* But solutions of this kind require special handling of their own. So I prefer to keep things simple. I copy my `i:\Users\bburd\.android` directory's contents to `c:\Users\bburd\.android`. That fixes the problem.

Error message: INSTALL_PARSE_FAILED_ INCONSISTENT_CERTIFICATE

This error message indicates that an app that you previously installed conflicts with the app that you're trying to install. So, on the emulator screen, choose Settings⇨Applications⇨Manage Applications. In the list of applications to be managed, delete any apps that you installed previously.

If you have trouble finding your previously installed apps, you can uninstall using the `adb` tool in your development computer's command window. For example, the following exchange in the Windows command prompt deletes the app that I put in the `com.allmycode.menus` Java package. (The stuff that I type is in boldface type. Other stuff is the computer's response.)

```
C:\>adb shell
# cd data
cd data
# cd app
cd app
# rm com.allmycode.menus.apk
rm com.allmycode.menus.apk
# exit
```

Your app starts, but the emulator displays a Force Close or Wait dialog box

The formal name for this dialog box is the *Application Not Responding* (ANR) dialog box. Android displays the ANR dialog box when an app takes too long to do whatever it's supposed to do. When your app runs on a real device (a phone or a tablet device), the app shouldn't make Android display the ANR dialog box. (Other chapters in this book give you tips on how to avoid the dialog box.)

But on a slow emulator, a few Force Close or Wait messages are par for the course. When I see the ANR dialog box in an emulator, I usually select Wait. Within about ten seconds, the dialog box disappears and the app continues to run.

Changes to your app don't appear in the emulator

Your app runs and you want to make a few improvements. So, with the emulator still running, you modify your app's code. But after choosing Run➪Run As➪Android Application, the app's behavior in the emulator remains unchanged.

When this happens, something is clogged up. Close and restart the emulator. If necessary, use the Wipe User Data trick that I describe in the section "Error message: The user data image is used by another emulator," earlier in this chapter.

The emulator's screen is too big

This happens when your development computer's screen resolution isn't high enough. (Maybe your eyesight isn't what it used to be.) This symptom isn't a deal breaker, but if you can't see the emulator's lower buttons, you can't easily test your app. You can change the development computer's screen resolution, but adjusting the emulator window is less invasive.

To change the emulator window size, modify the instructions I gave in the "Running your project" section earlier in this chapter just a bit:

1. **Follow the steps in Book II, Chapter 1 for creating a run configuration.**

2. **In the Run Configurations dialog box, click the Target tab.**

3. **If necessary, scroll down to the bottom of the Target tab.**

4. **In the Additional Emulator Command Line Options text field, type** -scale 0.75.

    With the fraction 0.75, the emulator appears at three quarters of its normal size. If three quarters isn't optimal, change 0.75 to something more suitable.

For more troubleshooting advice, see my tidbits scattered throughout this book. Also visit `http://developer.android.com/resources/faq/troubleshooting.html`.

Testing Apps on a Real Device

You can bypass emulators and test your apps on a phone, a tablet device, or maybe an Android-enabled refrigerator. To do so, you have to prepare the device, prepare your development computer, and then hook together the two. This section describes the process.

1. **On an Android device, choose Settings⇨Applications⇨Development.**

2. **In the Development list, turn on USB debugging.**

   Here's what my Honeycomb device displays when I mess with this setting: `USB debugging is intended for development purposes. It can be used to copy data between your computer and your device, install applications on your device without notification, and read log data.`

   On my device, I keep USB Debugging on all the time. But if you're very nervous about security, turn off USB Debugging when you're not using the device to develop apps.

3. **In your project's branch of Eclipse's Package Explorer, double-click the `AndroidManifest.xml` file.**

   Eclipse offers several ways to examine and edit this file.

4. **At the bottom of Eclipse's editor, click the Application tab.**

   Eclipse displays a form like the one shown in Figure 3-14.

5. **In the Debuggable drop-down list, choose True. (Again, see Figure 3-14.)**

   With Debuggable set to True, your app allows Android's tools to examine and change things during a run of the app.

   The ability to debug is the ability to hack. Debugging also slows down an app. Never distribute an app to the public with Debuggable set to True.

6. **Choose File⇨Save to store the new `AndroidManifest.xml` file.**

7. **Set up your development computer to communicate with the device.**

   - *On Windows:* Visit `http://developer.android.com/sdk/oem-usb.html` to download your device's Windows USB driver. Install the driver on your development computer.

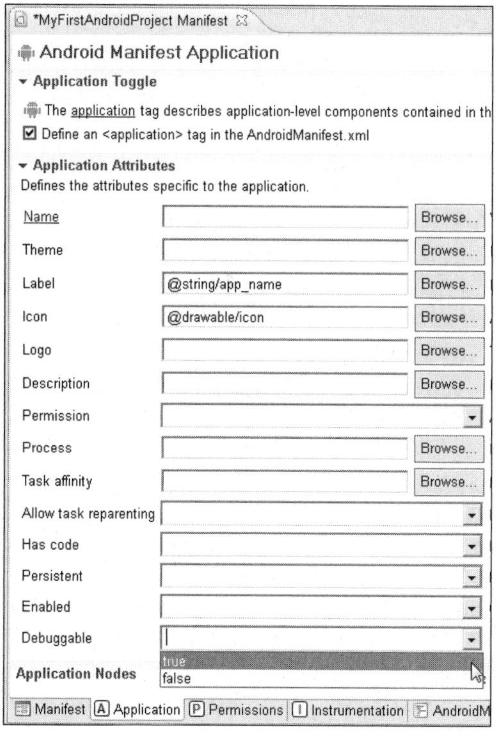

Figure 3-14:
The
Application
tab of a
project's
Android
Manifest.xml
file.

- *On a Mac:* /* Do nothing. It just works. */

- *On Linux:* Visit `http://developer.android.com/guide/developing/device.html` and follow the instructions that you find on that page. (Don't worry. To connect a device, you don't have to recompile the Linux kernel.)

8. **With a USB cable, connect the device to the development computer.**

   To find out whether your device is connected to the computer, open a command window on the computer. Navigate to the computer's ANDROID_HOME directory and then type **adb devices**. (On a Mac or a Linux computer, type **./adb devices**.) If your computer's response includes a very long hexadecimal number, that number represents your connected device. For example, with my Galaxy Tab connected, my computer's response is

   ```
   emulator-5554    device
   emulator-5556    device
   2885046445FF097  device
   ```

9. **In Eclipse, run your project.**

A connected device trumps a running emulator. So if your device's Android version can handle your project's minimum SDK version, choosing Run⇨Run As⇨Android Application installs your app on the connected device.

If you need more control over your app's destination, you can create a run configuration for your project. Book II, Chapter 1 describes run configurations. But if you don't want to jump to Book II, Chapter 1, choose Run As⇨Run Configurations. In the resulting Target tab, select one of the AVDs in the list.

The Target tab also has a radio button labeled Manual. When you choose Manual, Eclipse offers you a choice of devices. (See Figure 3-15.) To make Eclipse display its Android Device Chooser dialog box, deselect all the AVDs in the Run Configurations dialog box's Target tab.

Eventually, you want to disconnect your device from the development computer. If you're a Windows user, you dread reading `Windows can't stop your device because a program is still using it.` To disconnect your device, first issue the `adb kill-server` command as described in the "The emulator stalls during startup" section, earlier in this chapter. After that, you get the friendly `Safe to Remove Hardware` message.

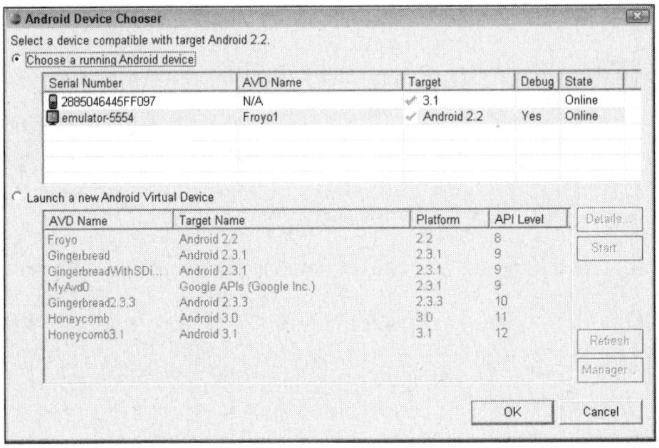

Figure 3-15: The Android Device Chooser dialog box.

Examining a Basic Android App

If you want to examine an app's basic building blocks, this chapter's Hello World app is a good place to start. So with your first project selected in Eclipse's Package Explorer, take this section's ten-cent tour.

A project's files

Figure 3-16 shows some of the directories and files in a simple Android project. When you use Eclipse to create a new project, Android generates all this stuff.

Figure 3-16:
The structure of a new Android project.

The project's directories are `src`, `gen`, `assets`, and `res` (and some other stuff that I cover near the end of this chapter).

The src directory

The `src` directory contains your project's Java source code. Files in this directory have names such as `MyActivity.java`, `MyService.java`, `DatabaseHelper.java`, `MoreStuff.java`, and so on.

You can cram hundreds of Java files in a project's `src` directory. But when you create a new project, Android typically creates just one file for you. In Figure 3-4 I type the name `MyActivity`, so Android creates a file named `MyActivity.java`. Listing 3-1 shows you the code in the `MyActivity.java` file.

Listing 3-1:   Android Creates This Skeletal Activity Class

```
package stuff.of.mine;

import android.app.Activity;
import android.os.Bundle;

public class MyActivity extends Activity {
```

(continued)

Listing 3-1 *(continued)*

```
/** Called when the activity is first created. */
@Override
public void onCreate(Bundle savedInstanceState) {
    super.onCreate(savedInstanceState);
    setContentView(R.layout.main);
}
}
```

An Android *activity* is one "screenful" of components. Think of an activity as a form — perhaps a form for entering information to make a purchase on a website. Unlike most online forms, Android activities don't necessarily have text boxes — places for the user to type credit card numbers and such. But Android activities have a lot in common with online forms. When you extend the `android.app.Activity` class, you create a new Android activity.

For more information about Java, see Book II, Chapters 2, 3, and 4.

An Android application can contain many activities. For example, an app's initial activity could list the films playing in your area. When you click a film's title, Android would then cover the entire list activity with another activity (perhaps an activity displaying a relevant film review).

Having one activity overlay another activity is typical of small phone screens. But on larger tablet screens, you can display a list of films and a particular film review side by side. Having side-by-side panels is a job for *fragments* rather than activities. To read about fragments, see Book IV, Chapter 4.

Here's another (possibly surprising) thing to keep in mind: An Android app can invoke an activity belonging to a different app. For example, your app might display a Help button, and pressing Help might open a web page. With the web page housed somewhere on the Internet, your app's button fires up an activity belonging to Android's built-in web browser application. In the Android world, applications don't Bogart their activities.

Every Android activity has a life cycle — a set of stages that the activity undergoes from birth to death to rebirth, and so on. I describe the activity lifecycle in Book III, Chapter 1. But in this chapter, you get a peek at the activity lifecycle with the method `onCreate` in Listing 3-1.

When Android creates an activity, Android calls the activity's `onCreate` method. This happens much more often than you'd think, because Android destroys and then re-creates activities while the user navigates from place to place. For example, if your phone runs low on memory, Android can kill some running activities. When you navigate back to a killed activity, Android re-creates the activity for you. The same thing happens when you turn the phone from portrait to landscape mode. If the developer doesn't override the default behavior, Android destroys an activity before displaying it in the other mode.

In Listing 3-1, the `onCreate` method executes two statements. The first statement, `super.onCreate(savedInstanceState)`, calls the parent class's `onCreate` method. The `savedInstanceState` variable stores information about the activity's values the last time the activity was destroyed. With `super.onCreate(savedInstanceState)`, the activity takes up where it last left off.

During what appears to the user to be a continuous run, Android might destroy and re-create an activity several times. An activity's `saved InstanceState` helps to maintain continuity between destructions and recreations. But if the user closes an activity (by pressing the Back button, for example), the next time the activity runs, its `savedInstanceState` is `null`.

The second method call in Listing 3-1 is `setContentView(R.layout. main)`. A call to `setContentView` plops a set of buttons, text fields, images, and other stuff on the activity screen. The method parameter, `R.layout. main`, is a roundabout way of coding the buttons, text fields, and the way they're all laid out. For more about this, read the next few sections.

The gen directory

The directory name `gen` stands for "generated." The `gen` directory contains `R.java`. Listing 3-2 shows the contents of `R.java` when you create a brand-new project.

Listing 3-2:   Don't Even Look at This File

```
/* AUTO-GENERATED FILE.   DO NOT MODIFY.
 *
 * This class was automatically generated by the
 * aapt tool from the resource data it found.  It
 * should not be modified by hand.
 */

package stuff.of.mine;

public final class R {
    public static final class attr {
    }
    public static final class drawable {
```

(continued)

Listing 3-2 *(continued)*

```
     public static final int icon=0x7f020000;
  }
  public static final class layout {
     public static final int main=0x7f030000;
  }
  public static final class string {
     public static final int app_name=0x7f040001;
     public static final int hello=0x7f040000;
  }
}
```

The hexadecimal values in R.java are the jumping-off points for Android's resource management mechanism. Android uses these numbers for quick and easy loading of the things you store in the res directory. For example, the code in Listing 3-1 sets the look of your activity to R.layout.main, and according to Listing 3-2, R.layout.main has the hex value 0x7f030000.

Android's documentation tells you to put R.java and its hex values out of your mind, and that's probably good advice (advice that I break in this section). Anyway, here are two things to remember about the role of R.java in an Android app:

✦ **You cannot edit R.java.**

Long after the creation of a project, Android continues to monitor (and if necessary, update) the contents of the R.java file. If you delete R.java, Android re-creates the file. If you edit R.java, Android undoes your edit. If you answer Yes in the Do You Really Want to Edit This File? dialog box, Eclipse accepts your change, but immediately after that, Android clobbers your change.

✦ **Many of Android's predeclared methods expect numbers in R.java as their parameters.**

This can lead to some confusion. Consider the following (very bad) chunk of code:

```
// THIS IS BAD CODE!
System.out.println("42");
System.out.println(42);

TextView textView =
   (TextView) findViewById(R.id.textView1);
textView.setText("42");
textView.setText(42);
```

Java's two System.out.println calls (rarely used in Android apps) add text to a log file. The first System.out.println sends the string "42" to the file, and the second System.out.println converts the integer value 42 to the string "42" and then sends the string "42" to the log file. (Java's System.out.println is prepared to print a string, an integer, and various other types of values.)

A call to findViewById fetches a text view (a place to display text) on your activity's screen. So in the bad code, textView refers to a label on the user's screen. A text view's setText method accepts a string parameter or an integer parameter. The call textView.setText("42") is okay. But the integer version of setText doesn't convert the integer to a string. Instead, textView.setText(42) looks for a resource with code number 42 (hex value 0x0000002A, that is). When Android finds nothing with code number 42 in the res directory, your app crashes.

The res directory

A project's res directory contains resources for use by the Android application. If you look at Figure 3-16, you see that res has five subdirectories — layout, values, and three drawable directories.

✦ The drawable directories contain images, shapes, and other such things.

✦ The layout directory contains descriptions of your activities' screens.

A minimal app's res/layout directory contains an XML file describing an activity's screen. (See the main.xml branch in Figure 3-16.) Listing 3-3 shows the code in the simple main.xml file.

Listing 3-3:   A Small Layout File

```
<?xml version="1.0" encoding="utf-8"?>
<LinearLayout xmlns:android=
        "http://schemas.android.com/apk/res/android"
    android:orientation="vertical"
    android:layout_width="fill_parent"
    android:layout_height="fill_parent"
    >
<TextView
    android:layout_width="fill_parent"
    android:layout_height="wrap_content"
    android:text="@string/hello"
    />
</LinearLayout>
```

An Android app consists of Java code, XML documents, and other stuff. The document in Listing 3-3 describes a *vertical linear layout* (a layout in which elements appear in a line, one beneath another). Because of its fill_parent attributes, the layout is large enough to fill its surroundings. Its "surroundings" are the entire screen minus a few doodads.

The only item inside the linear layout is an instance of `TextView` — a place to display text on the screen. The text view is wide enough to fill the screen. But because of the `wrap_content` attribute, the text view is only tall enough to enclose whatever characters it displays.

The `@string/hello` attribute in Listing 3-3 refers indirectly to the words *Hello World, MyActivity!* in Figure 3-11. Here's where Android's resource handling gets interesting. You don't hard-code character strings into your Java code. Instead, you put character strings in XML documents. To localize your app for French you point to a `res/values-fr/strings.xml` file. (*Bonjour tout le monde!*) To localize your app for Romanian, you point to a `res/values-ro/strings.xml` file. (*Salut lume!*)

A bare-bones app's `res/values` directory contains a `strings.xml` file. (See Figure 3-16.) Listing 3-4 shows the code in a simple `strings.xml` file.

Listing 3-4: A Small strings.xml File

```xml
<?xml version="1.0" encoding="utf-8" standalone="no"?>
<resources>
   <string name="hello">Hello World, MyActivity!</string>
   <string name="app_name">My First Android App</string>
</resources>
```

Listing 3-4 describes a `"hello"` string containing the characters `Hello World, MyActivity!`. To refer to the `"hello"` string in a `.java` file, you type **R.string.hello**. To refer to the `"hello"` string in another XML file (such as the file in Listing 3-3), you type **"@string/hello"**. Either way, you point to the words `Hello World, MyActivity!` in Listing 3-4.

To read all about XML documents, see Book II, Chapter 5.

The assets directory

When Android packages an app, a tool named aapt (short for *Android Asset Packaging Tool*) compiles the stuff in the app's `res` directory. In other words, aapt prepares the `res` directory's items for quick retrieval and use. So your application's access to items in the `res` directory is highly optimized.

But plain old Java has its own ways to fetch images and strings. Using Java's techniques, you generally read byte by byte from the Internet or from a device's file system. To grab an image or some other data using Java's standard tricks, put the image or data in the project's `assets` directory.

Other files in an Android project

In Figure 3-16, the tree's branches include the files `proguard.cfg`, `default.properties`, and `AndroidManifest.xml`.

The file `proguard.cfg` contains configuration information for *ProGuard,* a Java obfuscator program. *Obfuscation* is a way of making your Java code difficult to understand (which makes the code difficult to steal, difficult to modify, and difficult to infect). To read about ProGuard's role in Android app development, see Book V, Chapter 1.

The information in the `default.properties` file helps automated software keep track of a project's changes. Programs such as CVS (Concurrent *Versions System*), Subversion, and Git organize changes when one or more developers contribute updates to a project.

An app's `AndroidManifest.xml` file describes the things a device needs to run the app. (See Listing 3-5.)

Listing 3-5:   A Little AndroidManifest.xml File

```xml
<?xml version="1.0" encoding="utf-8"?>
<manifest xmlns:android=
  "http://schemas.android.com/apk/res/android"
    package="stuff.of.mine"
    android:versionCode="1"
    android:versionName="1.0">
  <uses-sdk android:minSdkVersion="11"/>

  <application android:icon="@drawable/icon"
               android:label="@string/app_name">
    <activity android:name=".MyActivity"
               android:label="@string/app_name">
      <intent-filter>
        <action android:name=
          "android.intent.action.MAIN" />
        <category android:name=
          "android.intent.category.LAUNCHER" />
      </intent-filter>
    </activity>

  </application>
</manifest>
```

I cover some `AndroidManifest.xml` elements in other chapters, and some of the elements in Listing 3-5 are self-explanatory. So in this chapter, I cover only a few of the listing's highlights.

In the document's root element, the `android:versionCode` and `android:versionName` attributes have similar (but slightly different) meanings. The `android:versionCode` attribute is an integer. For publication on the Android Market, the `android:versionCode` must increase from one version of your app to another. The numbers don't have to be consecutive. So your first published version can have `android:versionCode` 47, and the next published version can be number 63. The app's user doesn't see the `android:versionCode`.

The `android:versionName` can be any string of characters, so this attribute's value is largely cosmetic. The user sees the `android:versionName`.

The `application` element in Listing 3-5 has two attributes — `android:icon` and `android:label`. The user sees the application's icon and label on the device's Apps screen. The application's label (and sometimes the icon) appears when one of the app's activities is in the foreground. (See the words *My First Android App* and the Android icon in Figure 3-11.)

An app's activity can have its own icon and label, overriding the app's icon and label. But in an `AndroidManifest.xml` file, an activity element must have an `android:name` attribute. The `android:name` attribute has either of the following values:

✦ **The fully qualified name of the activity class.**

For example, the value of your activity's `android:name` attribute might be `com.`*`yourowndomainname`*`.MyActivity`. For Listing 3-1, the fully qualified name is `stuff.of.mine.MyActivity`.

✦ **The abbreviated activity class name, preceded by a dot.**

The name `.SomeClass` stands for "the class named `SomeClass` in this project's package." So in Listing 3-5, the name `.MyActivity` stands for `stuff.of.mine.MyActivity`.

The `manifest` element's `package` attribute isn't in the android namespace. In Listing 3-5, I type **package**, not **android:package**.

Within an `activity` element, an `intent-filter` element describes the kinds of duties that this activity can fulfill for apps on the same device. Intent filters consume an entire chapter (see Book III, Chapter 2). So in this section, I don't dare open the whole intent filter can of worms. But to give you an idea, action `android.intent.action.MAIN` indicates that this activity's code can be the starting point for an app's execution. And the category `android.intent.category.LAUNCHER` indicates that this activity's icon can appear in the device's Apps screen.

If you create a second activity for your app, you must declare the new activity in the app's `AndroidManifest.xml` file. If you don't, your app will crash with an `ActivityNotFoundException`.

The android.jar archive

The tree in Figure 3-16 has an `Android 3.0` branch, but that branch isn't a directory on your computer's file system. In the Package Explorer view, the `Android 3.0` branch reminds you that your project's CLASSPATH includes Android's predeclared Java code.

A `.jar` file is a compressed archive containing a useful bunch of Java classes. In fact, a `.jar` file is a Zip archive. You can open any `.jar` file with WinZip, StuffIt Expander, or your operating system's built-in unzipping utility. (You may or may not have to change the file's name from *whatever*`.jar` to *whatever*`.zip`.) Anyway, an `android.jar` file contains Android's Java classes for a particular version of Android. In Figure 3-16, a Package Explorer branch reminds you that your project contains a reference to someplace else on your hard drive (to a place containing the `.jar` file for Android 3.0).

The `android.jar` file contains code grouped into Java packages, and each package contains Java classes. (Figure 3-17 shows you the tip of the `android.jar` iceberg.) The `android.jar` file contains classes specific to Android and classes that simply help Java to do its job. Figure 3-17 shows a bunch of Android-specific packages, and Figure 3-18 displays some all-purpose Java packages.

Figure 3-17: Some of the packages and classes in android. jar.

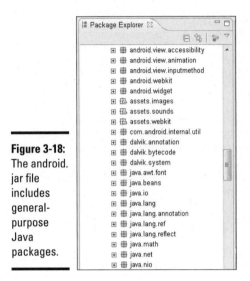

Figure 3-18:
The android.
jar file
includes
general-
purpose
Java
packages.

The bin directory

Each Android project has a `bin` directory, but Eclipse's Package Explorer doesn't display the `bin` directory. Android puts the output of its compiling, packaging and other "ing"s in the project's `bin` directory. In particular, the `bin` directory stores compiled Java `.class` files, doubly compiled Dalvik `.dex` files, packaged resource files, and complete `.apk` application files.

An *APK* file contains everything a user's device needs to know in order to run your app. To install a new app on your Android phone, you download and install a new APK file.

You can visit a project's `bin` directory with your operating system's file explorer. You can also see the `bin` directory in Eclipse's Navigator view. For information on opening a view in Eclipse, see Book II, Chapter 1.

Chapter 4: Conjuring and Embellishing an Android App

In This Chapter

✓ Creating an app with check boxes and other widgets

✓ Finding bugs in your app (not that there are any, of course)

✓ Adding interesting features to your app

*W*hen I set out to learn something, I follow a "ready, set, go" approach. I don't "go" right into the detailed technical manuals. Instead, I get ready by examining the simplest example I can find. I work with a Hello World scenario like the one in Chapter 3 of this minibook. Then (. . . and here's where this chapter fits in . . .) I do some probing and poking; I explore some possibilities; I peek around corners; I try some experiments. These are my initial "ready, set" steps.

When I'm firm on my feet, I do the kind of stuff you do in Books III through VI. I "go." If you feel confident, "go" directly to Book III. But if you want more "ready, set" material, march on into this chapter.

Dragging, Dropping, and Otherwise Tweaking an App

A general guideline in app development tells you to separate logic from presentation. In less technical terms, the guideline warns against confusing what an app does with how an app looks. The guideline applies to many things in life. For example, if you're designing a website, have artists do the layout and have geeks do the coding. If you're writing a report, get the ideas written first. Later, you can worry about fonts and paragraph styles. (Jen, this book's copy editor . . . do you agree?)

The literature on app development has specific techniques and frameworks to help you separate form from function. But in this chapter, I do the simplest thing — I chop an app's creation into two sets of instructions. The first set is about creating an app's look; the second set is about coding the app's behavior.

Creating the "look"

To add buttons, boxes, and other goodies to your app, do the following:

1. **Launch Eclipse, and create a new Android project.**

   For details, see Chapter 3 of this minibook.

2. **In the new project's `res/layout` directory (in Eclipse's Package Explorer), double-click `main.xml`.**

   As a result, Eclipse's editor displays the contents of `main.xml`. The bottom of the editor has two tabs — a Graphical Layout tab for visual editing and a `main.xml` tab for text-based editing.

3. **Click the editor's Graphical Layout tab.**

   The next several steps guide you through the creation of the stuff in Figure 4-1.

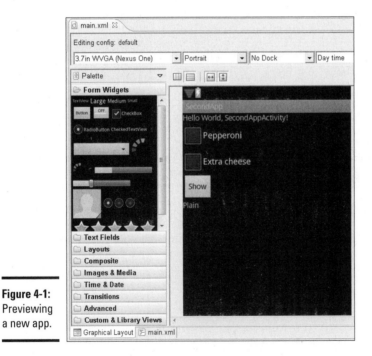

Figure 4-1:
Previewing
a new app.

If you can't see the Graphical Layout's palette, enlarge the layout. Drag the edges of Eclipse's editor. Better yet, double-click the `main.xml` tab at the top of Eclipse's editor. Doing so maximizes the editor within the Eclipse workbench.

4. **From the palette's Form Widgets group, drag two check boxes into the preview screen.**

5. **From the palette's Form Widgets group, drag a button and a TextView element into the preview screen.**

6. **In Eclipse's Outline view, select checkBox1. (See Figure 4-2.)**

   The Outline view appears on the right side of the Eclipse workbench. The Outline view's tree depicts the nesting of objects in `main.xml`. In Figure 4-2, all widgets are inside a `LinearLayout`.

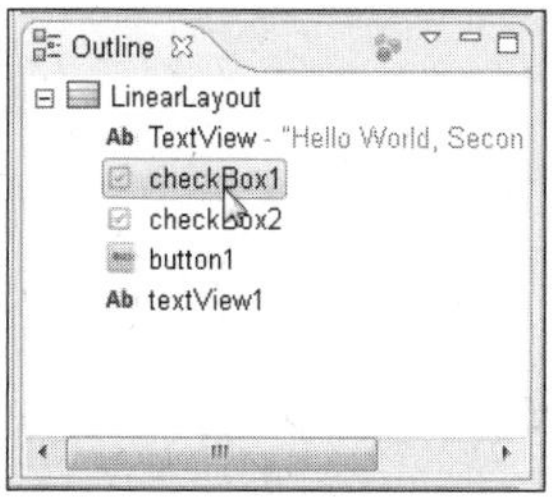

Figure 4-2:
The Outline
view.

Android's `LinearLayout` class arranges visible widgets in a line on the user's screen. (The line of widgets grows either vertically or horizontally, depending on the way you set things up.) For the full story on Android's `LinearLayout` class and on Android's other layout classes, see Book IV, Chapter 1. And, for more information on Eclipse's many views (like the Outline view in Figure 4-2), see Book II, Chapter 1.

7. **In Eclipse's Properties view, change the Text entry's value to Pepperoni. (See Figure 4-3.)**

   Eclipse's Properties view is normally in the bottom-right part of the Eclipse workbench.

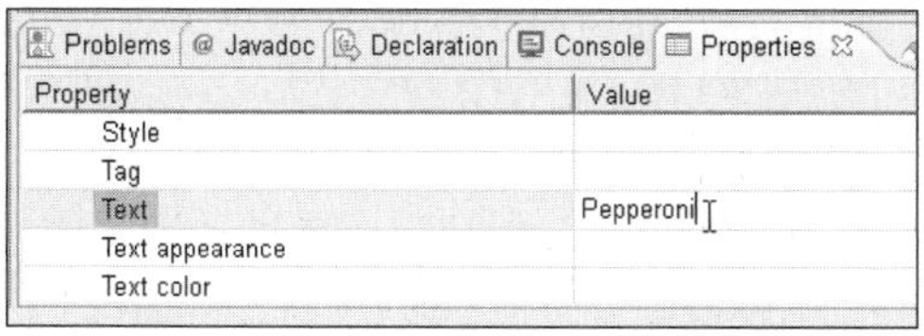

Figure 4-3:
The
Properties
view.

8. **Repeat Steps 6 and 7 a few times. Change the Text entry of each component in the Graphical Layout screen, so it looks like what you see in Figure 4-1.**

To see a component's attributes in the Properties view, you must select that component in the Outline view. Selecting the component's picture in the Graphical Layout isn't sufficient.

9. **Choose File⇨Save to save your work so far.**

With this section's steps, you edit your app visually. Behind the scenes, Eclipse is editing the text in your app's main.xml document. You can see what changes Eclipse has made to your app's main.xml document by selecting the main.xml tab at the bottom of Eclipse's editor. I've reproduced the main.xml document in Listing 4-1.

Listing 4-1: The main.xml Document

```xml
<?xml version="1.0" encoding="utf-8"?>
<LinearLayout
    xmlns:android=
        "http://schemas.android.com/apk/res/android"
    android:orientation="vertical"
    android:layout_width="fill_parent"
    android:layout_height="fill_parent">

    <TextView
        android:layout_width="fill_parent"
        android:layout_height="wrap_content"
        android:text="@string/hello" />
    <CheckBox android:id="@+id/checkBox1"
        android:layout_width="wrap_content"
        android:layout_height="wrap_content"
        android:text="Pepperoni"></CheckBox>
    <CheckBox android:id="@+id/checkBox2"
        android:layout_width="wrap_content"
        android:layout_height="wrap_content"
        android:text="Extra cheese"></CheckBox>
    <Button android:id="@+id/button1"
        android:layout_width="wrap_content"
        android:layout_height="wrap_content"
        android:text="Show"></Button>
    <TextView android:id="@+id/textView1"
        android:layout_width="wrap_content"
        android:layout_height="wrap_content"
        android:text="Plain"></TextView>

</LinearLayout>
```

Whenever you want, you can change the look of your app by directly editing the text in `main.xml`.

Disclaimer: In Listing 4-1, the file `main.xml` has been modified from its original version. It has been formatted to fit your page.

Coding the behavior

Assuming you've followed the instructions in this chapter's "Creating the 'look' " section, what's next? Well, what's next depends on your app's minimum SDK version.

For minimum SDK version 4 or higher (Android 1.6 and beyond)

Android 1.6 introduced a cool `android:onClick` attribute that streamlines the coding of an app's actions. Here's what you do:

1. **Follow the steps in this chapter's "Creating the 'look'" section.**

2. **In Eclipse's Outline view, select button1. (Refer to Figure 4-2.)**

3. **In Eclipse's Properties view, change the On Click entry's value to `onButton1Click`. (See Figure 4-4.)**

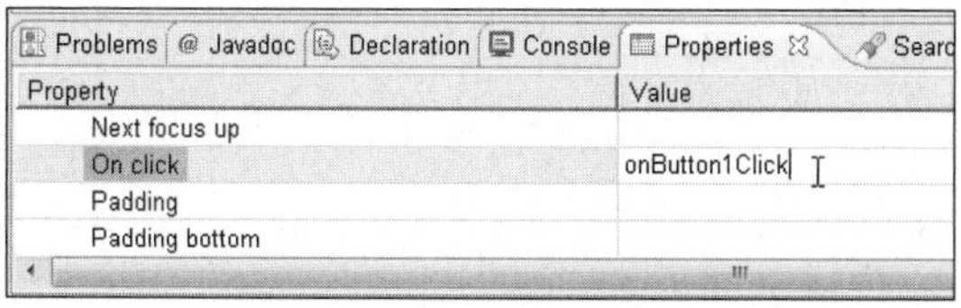

Figure 4-4:
Changing an object's On Click property.

Actually, you can change the entry's value to anything you want, as long as it forms a valid Java method name.

4. **In the Package Explorer, double-click the activity that Android created in your project's `src` directory.**

The activity's code appears in Eclipse's editor.

5. **Modify the activity's code, as shown in Listing 4-2.**

Listing 4-2: A Button Responds to a Click

```
package more.stuff.of.mine;

import android.app.Activity;
import android.os.Bundle;
import android.view.View;
import android.widget.CheckBox;
import android.widget.TextView;

public class SecondAppActivity extends Activity {
    TextView textView;
    CheckBox pepBox, cheeseBox;

    /** Called when the activity is first created. */
    @Override
    public void onCreate(Bundle savedInstanceState) {
        super.onCreate(savedInstanceState);
        setContentView(R.layout.main);

        pepBox =
            (CheckBox) findViewById(R.id.checkBox1);
        cheeseBox =
            (CheckBox) findViewById(R.id.checkBox2);
        textView =
            (TextView) findViewById(R.id.textView1);
    }

    public void onButton1Click(View view) {
        StringBuilder str = new StringBuilder("");
        if (pepBox.isChecked()) {
            str.append("Pepperoni" + " ");
        }
        if (cheeseBox.isChecked()) {
            str.append("Extra cheese");
        }
        if (str.length() == 0) {
            str.append("Plain");
        }
        textView.setText(str);
    }
}
```

6. **Run the app.**

When you click the app's button, you see one of the screens in Figure 4-5.

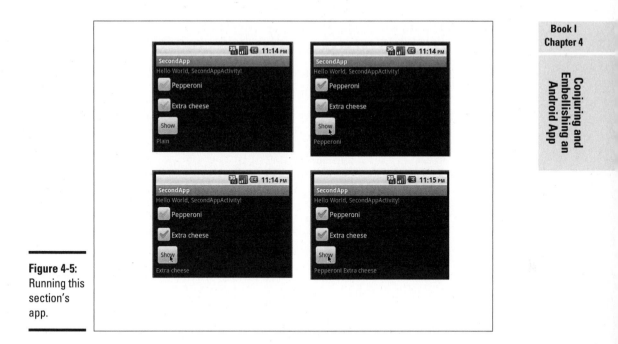

Figure 4-5:
Running this
section's
app.

In Listing 4-2, the statement

```
pepBox = (CheckBox) findViewById(R.id.checkBox1);
```

finds the first check box that you create in the "Creating the 'look' " section's
steps.

For info about the `findViewById` method, see Chapter 3 in this minibook.
To find out why I have `(CheckBox)` in parentheses before the call to `find`
`ViewById`, see the discussion of casting in Book II, Chapter 3.

The `onButton1Click` method in Listing 4-2 fulfills the promise that you
make in Step 3 of this section's instructions. Setting the button's On Click
property to `onButton1Click` gets Eclipse to add the attribute `android:`
`onClick="onButton1Click"` to the button's start tag in `main.xml`. As
a result, Android calls your `onButton1Click` method whenever the user
clicks the button. In the heading

```
public void onButton1Click(View view)
```

the method parameter `view` is whatever object the user clicked. In this example, you don't use the method's `view` parameter, but the parameter is available nonetheless. In fact, if you don't put a `View` parameter in your click-handling method, Android doesn't respond to the click.

Android also fails to respond if you don't declare `onButton1Click` to be `public`. The code that tries to call `onButton1Click` isn't a subclass of your activity and isn't in the same package. So if your event-handling method isn't public, your efforts are thwarted.

In Android, any widget on the device's screen, such as a button or a check box, is a subclass of `android.view.View`.

If your app's target version is 3, Eclipse's Properties view doesn't display an On Click entry. If your app's target version is 4 but the app's minimum SDK version is 3, Eclipse's Properties view displays an On Click entry, but the code doesn't work on devices running SDK version 3. The same kind of thing applies across the board in Android app development. What Eclipse allows you to do doesn't necessarily work on all versions of Android.

For any minimum SDK version

No matter what Android version you plan to use, this section's instructions get your app to respond to button clicks:

1. **Follow the steps in this chapter's "Creating the 'look' " section.**

2. **Modify the activity's code, as shown in Listing 4-3.**

Listing 4-3:   Event Handling (The Traditional Java Way)

```
package more.stuff.of.mine;

import android.app.Activity;
import android.os.Bundle;
import android.view.View;
import android.view.View.OnClickListener;
import android.widget.Button;
import android.widget.CheckBox;
import android.widget.TextView;

public class SecondAppActivity extends Activity
                           implements OnClickListener {
    TextView textView;
    CheckBox pepBox, cheeseBox;

    /** Called when the activity is first created. */
    @Override
```

```
public void onCreate(Bundle savedInstanceState) {
    super.onCreate(savedInstanceState);
    setContentView(R.layout.main);

    pepBox =
        (CheckBox) findViewById(R.id.checkBox1);
    cheeseBox =
        (CheckBox) findViewById(R.id.checkBox2);
    textView =
        (TextView) findViewById(R.id.textView1);

    ((Button) findViewById(R.id.button1))
                    .setOnClickListener(this);
}

public void onClick(View view) {
    StringBuilder str = new StringBuilder("");
    if (pepBox.isChecked()) {
        str.append("Pepperoni" + " ");
    }
    if (cheeseBox.isChecked()) {
        str.append("Extra cheese");
    }
    if (str.length() == 0) {
        str.append("Plain");
    }
    textView.setText(str);
}
}
```

3. **Run the app.**

Listing 4-3 uses Java's traditional event-handling pattern. The button registers your activity as its click-event listener. Your activity declares itself to be an `OnClickListener` and makes good on this click-listener promise by implementing the `onClick` method.

You can program any of Java's well-known variations on the event-handling pattern in Listing 4-3. For example, you can create a separate class to implement the `OnClickListener` interface, or you can implement the interface with an inner class.

A Bit of Debugging

In a perfect world, you wake up refreshed and energetic every morning. Every app you write runs correctly on the first test. Every word you write in *Android Application Development All-in-One For Dummies* is *le mot juste.*

But the world isn't perfect. And often, the first test of a new application forms a disappointing splat on your emulator's screen. So the next few sections contain some useful debugging techniques.

Try it!

To get a handle on Android debugging, follow these instructions:

***1.* In Eclipse, create a new Android project.**

Don't be shy. Almost any new Android project will do. To cook up this section's figures and listings, I named the project *DebugMe*.

***2.* Add a TextView element to your project's `main.xml` layout.**

For details, see the section "Creating the 'look'."

After adding a TextView element, the Graphical Layout screen looks like the one in Figure 4-6, and Eclipse's Outline view contains a `textView1` branch.

Figure 4-6: A layout containing a new TextView element.

***3.* Open the new project's activity for editing.**

The activity's `onCreate` method looks like this:

```
public void onCreate(Bundle savedInstanceState) {
    super.onCreate(savedInstanceState);
    setContentView(R.layout.main);
}
```

***4.* Add two statements to the `onCreate` method, as in Listing 4-4.**

Listing 4-4:   A Misguided Attempt to Add a TextView to an Activity

```
// THIS IS BAD CODE!

public void onCreate(Bundle savedInstanceState) {
    super.onCreate(savedInstanceState);
    TextView textView =
```

```
          (TextView) findViewById(R.id.textView1);
    setContentView(R.layout.main);
    textView.setText("Oops!");
}
```

5. **Run your app.**

   Your app comes crashing down with a big Has Stopped Unexpectedly
   message. You click the emulator's Force Close button and give up in
   despair. Or . . .

6. **Choose Window⮕Open Perspective⮕DDMS.**

   Eclipse's DDMS perspective opens. In the DDMS perspective, the LogCat
   view displays the running emulator's log. (See Figure 4-7.)

Devices view

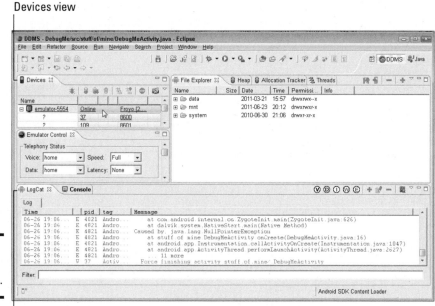

Figure 4-7:
The DDMS
perspective.

LogCat view

7. **If the LogCat view is empty, or if you're running more than one emulator or connected device, select your current app's emulator in the
   Devices view. (Again, see Figure 4-7.)**

8. **In the LogCat view, look for a Java stack trace.**

The Java stack trace, plus a few of the log's surrounding lines, looks like this:

```
AndroidRuntime( 4821): Shutting down VM
dalvikvm( 4821): threadid=1: thread exiting with uncaug
ht exception (group=0x4001d800)
AndroidRuntime( 4821): FATAL EXCEPTION: main
AndroidRuntime( 4821): java.lang.RuntimeException: Unab
le to start activity ComponentInfo{stuff.of.mine/stuff.
of.mine.DebugMeActivity}: java.lang.NullPointerExceptio
n
AndroidRuntime( 4821):          at android.app.ActivityTh
read.performLaunchActivity(ActivityThread.java:2663)
AndroidRuntime( 4821):          at android.app.ActivityTh
read.handleLaunchActivity(ActivityThread.java:2679)
AndroidRuntime( 4821):          at android.app.ActivityTh
read.access$2300(ActivityThread.java:125)
AndroidRuntime( 4821):          at android.app.ActivityTh
read$H.handleMessage(ActivityThread.java:2033)
AndroidRuntime( 4821):          at android.os.Handler.dis
patchMessage(Handler.java:99)
AndroidRuntime( 4821):          at android.os.Looper.loop
(Looper.java:123)
AndroidRuntime( 4821):          at android.app.ActivityTh
read.main(ActivityThread.java:4627)
AndroidRuntime( 4821):          at java.lang.reflect.Meth
od.invokeNative(NativeMethod)
AndroidRuntime( 4821):          at java.lang.reflect.Meth
od.invoke(Method.java:521)
AndroidRuntime( 4821):          at com.android.internal.o
s.ZygoteInit$MethodAndArgsCaller.run(ZygoteInit.java:86
8)
AndroidRuntime( 4821):          at com.android.internal.o
s.ZygoteInit.main(ZygoteInit.java:626)
AndroidRuntime( 4821):          at dalvik.system.NativeSt
art.main(Native Method)

AndroidRuntime( 4821): Caused by: java.lang.NullPointer
Exception
AndroidRuntime( 4821):          at stuff.of.mine.DebugMeA
ctivity.onCreate(DebugMeActivity.java:16)
AndroidRuntime( 4821):          at android.app.Instrument
ation.callActivityOnCreate(Instrumentation.java:1047)
AndroidRuntime( 4821):          at android.app.ActivityTh
read.performLaunchActivity(ActivityThread.java:2627)
AndroidRuntime( 4821):          ... 11 more
ActivityManager(   37):  Force finishing activity stuf
f.of.mine/.DebugMeActivity
```

A log file always contains more information than you need. But if you look for the most recent bunch of `at` words (each preceded by about eight blank spaces), you find the trace that you need.

9. **In the stack trace, look for lines relating directly to the code in your app.**

The *stack trace* shows which methods were calling which other methods when your app crashed. In this onslaught of details, you find a few lines containing names from your application — lines such as `stuff.of.mine.DebugMeActivity.onCreate(DebugMeActivity.java:16)`. Above that line, you see the words `java.lang.NullPointerException`.

So your app caused a `NullPointerException` at line 16 of the `DebugMeActivity.java` file.

10. **In Eclipse's editor, find the offending line in your app's code.**

In this section's example, the guilty line is `textView.setText("Oops!")` in your code's `Activity` class.

To make Eclipse's editor display line numbers, choose Window⇨ Preferences⇨General⇨Editors⇨Text Editors. Then, put a check mark in the Show Line Numbers check box.

11. **Figure out what part of the offending code might cause the error shown in the stack trace.**

Unfortunately, this step isn't always easy. You might need to make several guesses, try several possible solutions, or seek advice on some online forums.

Anyway, like a chef on a cooking show, I can quickly whip out a ready-made solution. When you call `textView.setText`, you get a `NullPointerException`. So `textView` is `null`. The problem in Listing 4-4 is the placement of the call to `findViewById`.

Until you set the activity's content view, the app knows nothing about `R.id.textView1`. So in Listing 4-4, calling `findViewById` before calling `setContentView` leads to disaster. To fix the problem, swap two statements as follows:

```
setContentView(R.layout.main);
TextView textView =
          (TextView) findViewById(R.id.textView1);
```

More than one way to skin a LogCat

With some clever use of Android's log, you can increase your chances of finding the source of an error.

See the long lines

Eclipse's LogCat view doesn't wrap long lines. So in the LogCat view, you might see a truncated line, such as

```
AndroidRuntime( 4821): Caused by: java.lang. ...
```

You can enlarge the LogCat view's Message column, but enlarging the column gets you only so far. If you need to see a very long line in the log file, open a command window and issue the `cd` command to change to your `ANDROID_HOME/platform-tools` directory. In the `platform-tools` directory, type **adb logcat**. Your emulator's log file appears in the command window.

For tips on using your development computer's command window, see Book VI, Chapter 3.

Read your device's log file

If you connect a device to your development computer, you can see the device's log file in Eclipse's LogCat view. But sometimes it's more convenient to view the log file right on the device. For example, you might want to debug an app when you're using it on the road.

The Android Market has apps to help you view your device's log file. I use an app called CatLog, but other apps might work well for you, too.

Filter the output

Android's logging has five levels. The *levels,* in decreasing order of seriousness, are ERROR, WARN, INFO, DEBUG, and VERBOSE. In general, only an ERROR entry is a show stopper. All other entries (WARN, INFO, and so on) are just idle chatter.

Eclipse's LogCat view has buttons: V, D, I, W, and E. You can click a button to filter entries of lesser severity. For example, if you click the W button, the view displays only entries with levels W or E.

You can also filter entries by their points of origin. In Step 8 of the "Try it!" section, the log output comes from two sources. Most of the output comes from `AndroidRuntime( 4821)`, but the last entry comes from `ActivityManager( 37)`. The name (such as `AndroidRuntime` or `ActivityManager`) is a *tag,* and the number (such as `4821` or `37`) is a *process identification number (PID).* As you see in the following section, the tag and PID don't always change in lockstep.

Anyway, to filter by tag or PID, click the plus-sign button next to the LogCat view's V, D, I, W, and E buttons. Doing so opens a Log Filter dialog box, where you can specify the tag or PID whose entries you want to see.

Write to the log file

What? You don't trust my diagnosis of the problem in Listing 4-4? "Is text View really null?", you ask. You can peek at your program's variables with Eclipse's Debug perspective, but for a quick answer to your question, you can write to Android's log file.

In Listing 4-4, add the following code before the textView. setText("Oops!") statement:

```
if (textView == null) {
    Log.i("READ ME!", "textView is null");
} else {
    Log.i("READ ME!",
            "-->" + textView.getText().toString());
}
```

The Log class's static i method creates an entry of level INFO in Android's log file. In this example, the entry's tag is READ ME!, and the entry's message is either textView is null or the characters displayed in the text View. When you run the app, you can check Eclipse's LogCat view to find out what this entry tells you.

By convention, a log entry's tag is the name of the class in which the log is created. For example, if your class's name is DebugMeActivity, the first parameter of Log.i is the string "DebugMeActivity". In this section, I don't follow that formula. But if other developers are involved in your project, coding conventions are very important.

Improving Your App

Face it — the app in this chapter's "Dragging, Dropping, and Otherwise Tweaking an App" section is boring! Who wants to click a button to see the words Pepperoni Extra Cheese on a device's screen?

I can't promise instant excitement in this section. But with modest efforts, you can add features to make the app more interesting. (I confess: In this chapter, the *real* reason for making the app interesting is to show you some additional Android developer tricks. Anyway, read on . . .)

Improving the layout

You can improve an app's look in two ways — the way it looks to a user and the way it looks to another developer. In this section, you do both. When you're done, you have a layout like the one in Figure 4-8.

Figure 4-8:
Your mission, should you decide to accept it.

Creating a reusable layout

1. **Launch Eclipse, and create a new Android project.**

   For details, see Chapter 3 of this minibook.

2. **Open Eclipse's dialog box for creating a new XML resource document.**

   On Windows, right-click (Control-click on a Mac) your project's branch in the Package Explorer.

   Then, in the resulting context menu, choose Android Tools⇨New Resource File. Eclipse's New Android XML File dialog box appears. (See Figure 4-9.)

3. **In the dialog box's File field, type the name of your new resource document.**

   In Figure 4-9, I type **reusable_layout.xml**.

   The names of Android's resource files must not contain capital letters. You can use lowercase letters and underscores. You cannot use Java's customary "camel-case" naming convention with names like `reUsable Layout.xml`. And, yes, a layout filename must end with the extension `.xml`.

4. **Select the Layout button among the dialog box's What Type of Resource . . . choices. (Again, see Figure 4-9.)**

5. **Click Finish to dismiss the dialog box.**

   As a result, the Graphical Layout editor appears.

6. **Select the new layout's `LinearLayout` in Eclipse's Outline view.**

   To read more about the `LinearLayout` class, see Book IV, Chapter 1.

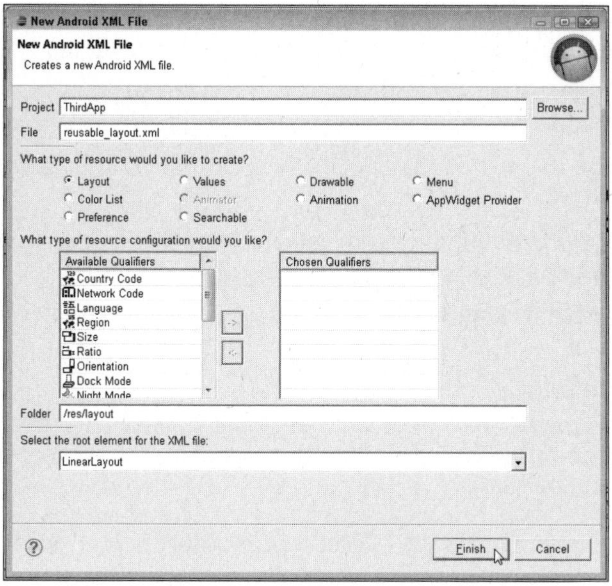

Figure 4-9:
The New
Android
XML File
dialog box.

7. **In Eclipse's Properties view, set the layout's Gravity property to `center_horizontal`.**

A layout's Gravity property helps determine the positions of objects inside the layout. The Gravity value `center_horizontal` makes objects center themselves across the layout screen.

8. **From the palette's Layouts group, drag a horizontal linear layout to the preview screen.**

The entire screen already contains a linear layout, so in this step, you're putting a linear layout inside of the existing linear layout.

In Android, any widget on the device's screen is a subclass of `android.view.View`. This includes the things on Eclipse's Graphical Layout palette. For example, the class `LinearLayout` is a subclass of `android.view.ViewGroup`, which is in turn a subclass of `android.view.View`.

9. **From the palette's Form Widgets group, drag two check boxes into your horizontal layout.**

Because of what you did in Step 8, your layout has a *horizontal* orientation; accordingly, your new check boxes line up beside one another.

10. **In Eclipse's Properties view, change your horizontal layout's `layout_width` property to `wrap_content`.**

As a result, your horizontal layout shrinks to a little over the size of its two check boxes (with their labels).

11. **From the palette's Form Widgets group, drag a button onto the pre-view screen and drop it below your horizontal layout.**

The outer layout's orientation is vertical, so the button falls below the two check boxes.

12. **Change the text on the check boxes and the button, as shown in Figure 4-8.**

Don't worry about the word *Plain* in Figure 4-8. You work on that in the "Reusing a layout" section.

For help changing the text, see the "Creating the 'look' " section.

Reusing a layout

In the "Creating a reusable layout" section, you create a layout with check boxes and a button. You can reuse this layout in many of this chapter's examples. Here's how:

1. **Follow the steps in the "Creating a reusable layout" section.**

If you're impatient, you can skip a few of that section's steps, but make sure to create a `reusable_layout.xml` file and to populate the file with a few widgets.

2. **Open your project's `res/layout/main.xml` file.**

3. **From the Layouts group in the Graphical Layout's palette, drag an Include Other Layout element onto your main layout.**

When you do this, a Resource Chooser dialog box appears. (See Figure 4-10.)

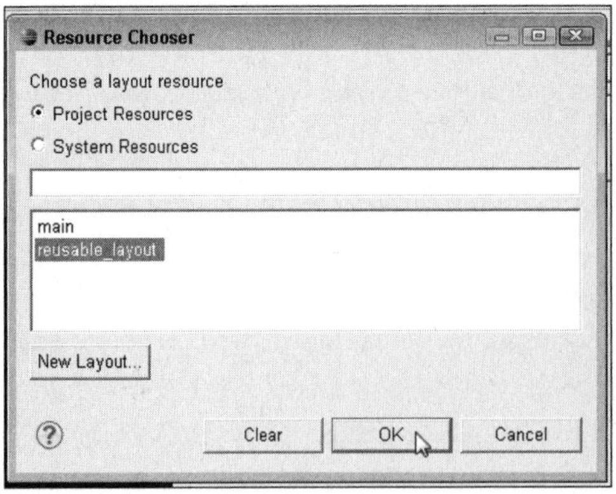

Figure 4-10:
The Resource Chooser dialog box.

4. **In the Resource Chooser dialog box, select your reusable layout — the one you named** `reusable_layout` **— and then click OK.**

    As if by magic, the stuff that you created in the "Creating a reusable layout" section appears on the main layout's preview screen. (Well, anyway, it looks like magic to me.)

5. **Change the main linear layout's Gravity property to** `center_` `horizontal`.

6. **From the Graphical Layout's palette, drag a TextView element onto the** `main.xml` **screen.**

7. **(Optional) If you're ambitious, change the TextView element's text to** `Plain`.

8. **(Optional) If you're very ambitious, follow the steps (starting with Step 2) in the section "Coding the behavior," and run your app.**

    Ambitious or not, you have a decent-looking layout with a reusable component. Nice work!

To copy your reusable layout from one Android project to another, do what you'd normally do to copy and paste a file. In Eclipse's Package Explorer, select this project's `reusable_layout.xml` file. In Eclipse's main menu, choose Edit⇨Copy. Then, select another project's `res/layout` directory. Finally, choose Edit⇨Paste. You can also use copying and pasting to apply your work from the "Coding the behavior" section to this section's project.

Starting another activity

An Android *activity* is one "screenful" of components. So juggling activities is a major endeavor for Android developers. This section's example does the simplest thing you can do with an activity —; namely, make an activity run.

1. **Launch Eclipse, and create a new Android project.**

    In this section's listings and screenshots, I call the project `FourthApp`; I call the main activity `FourthAppActivity`; and I use the package `more.stuff.of.mine`.

2. **Copy the** `reusable_layout.xml` **file from this chapter's "Creating a reusable layout" section to your new project's** `res/layout` **directory.**

3. **Follow Steps 2 to 5 in the "Reusing a layout" section to include** `reusable_layout` **in your project's** `main.xml` **file.**

4. **Open Eclipse's dialog box for creating a new XML resource document. Here's how:**

a. *On Windows, right-click (Control-click on a Mac) project's branch in the Package Explorer.*

b. *In the resulting context menu, choose Android Tools⇨New Resource File.*

Eclipse's New Android XML File dialog box appears. (See Figure 4-11.)

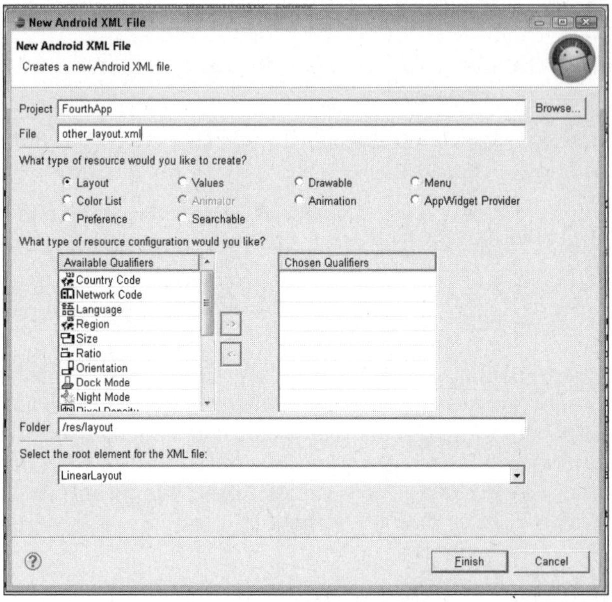

Figure 4-11:
The New Android XML File dialog box.

5. **In the dialog box's File field, type the name of your new resource document.**

In Figure 4-11, I type **other_layout.xml**.

WARNING!

The names of Android's resource files must not contain capital letters. You can use lowercase letters and underscores. And a layout filename must end with the extension `.xml`. You cannot use Java's customary camel-case naming convention with names like `otherLayout.xml` or `hasTwoHumps.xml`.

6. **Select the Layout button among the dialog box's What Type of Resource . . . choices. (Again, see Figure 4-11.)**

7. **Click Finish to dismiss the dialog box.**

As a result, the Graphical Layout editor appears. The editor displays your new layout's screen.

8. **Drag a TextView element from the palette to the Graphical Layout's screen.**

   Now, `other_layout` has a TextView element.

9. **Modify your main activity's code, as shown in Listing 4-5.**

Listing 4-5: Starting a New Activity

```
package more.stuff.of.mine;

import android.app.Activity;
import android.content.Intent;
import android.os.Bundle;
import android.view.View;
import android.view.View.OnClickListener;
import android.widget.Button;
import android.widget.CheckBox;

public class FourthAppActivity extends Activity
                    implements OnClickListener {
    CheckBox pepBox, cheeseBox;

    /** Called when the activity is first created. */
    @Override
    public void onCreate(Bundle savedInstanceState) {
        super.onCreate(savedInstanceState);
        setContentView(R.layout.main);

        pepBox =
            (CheckBox) findViewById(R.id.checkBox1);
        cheeseBox =
            (CheckBox) findViewById(R.id.checkBox2);

        ((Button) findViewById(R.id.button1))
                        .setOnClickListener(this);
    }

    /* If you use an onButton1Click method as in
       Listing 4-2, change this method's name from onClick
       to onButton1Click.
    */
    public void onClick(View view) {
        Intent intent =
            new Intent(this, OtherActivity.class);
        intent.putExtra
            ("Pepperoni", pepBox.isChecked());
        intent.putExtra
            ("Extra cheese", cheeseBox.isChecked());
        startActivity(intent);
    }
}
```

You don't start an activity by calling the activity's methods. Instead, you create an intent. An *intent* is like an open-ended method call. In Listing 4-5, you create an *explicit intent* — an intent that invokes a specific class's code.

- The intent in Listing 4-5 invokes the code in a class named `OtherActivity` (or whatever you name your app's second activity).

- The intent has two extra pieces of information. Each "extra piece" of information is a name/value pair. For example, if the user checks the Pepperoni box, `pepBox.isChecked()` is `true`, so the intent contains the extra pair `"Pepperoni", true`.

- The call `startActivity(intent)` invokes the `OtherActivity` class's code.

  If you follow these steps word for word, you see a little red error blip in the main activity's editor. That's because Listing 4-5 refers to `OtherActivity`, but you don't create the `OtherActivity` class until Step 12.

This section's explanation of Android's *intent* mechanism shows you the tiniest tip of the iceberg. To read all about activities and intents, see Book III, Chapter 1.

10. **In Eclipse's Package Explorer, select the `src/your.package` directory for your Android project.**

In Listing 4-5, the package name is `more.stuff.of.mine`. So I select my project's `src/more.stuff.of.mine` directory.

11. **In Eclipse's main menu, choose File⇨New⇨Class.**

Eclipse's New Java Class dialog box appears.

12. **In the New Java Class dialog box, type a name for your new class and then click Finish.**

In Listing 4-5, I refer to `OtherActivity`, so if you're following along letter for letter with these instructions, name your new class `OtherActivity`.

The New Java Class dialog box has all kinds of options for getting Eclipse to write your activity's code. But for my taste, the extra pointing and clicking in the New Java Class dialog box isn't worth the effort. I'd rather type a few lines myself after my `.java` file appears in Eclipse's editor.

13. **In your new `OtherActivity` class, type the code in Listing 4-6.**

Listing 4-6: Another Activity

```
package more.stuff.of.mine;

import android.app.Activity;
import android.content.Intent;
import android.os.Bundle;
import android.widget.TextView;

public class OtherActivity extends Activity {
  TextView textView;

  /** Called when the activity is first created. */
  @Override
  public void onCreate(Bundle savedInstanceState) {
    super.onCreate(savedInstanceState);
    setContentView(R.layout.other_layout);

    textView = (TextView) findViewById(R.id.textView1);

    Intent intent = getIntent();

    StringBuilder str = new StringBuilder("");
    if (intent.getBooleanExtra("Pepperoni", false)) {
        str.append("Pepperoni" + " ");
    }
    if (intent.getBooleanExtra("Extra cheese", false)) {
        str.append("Extra cheese");
    }
    if (str.length() == 0) {
        str.append("Plain");
    }
    textView.setText(str);
  }
}
```

In Listing 4-6, the call to `getIntent` gets the stuff that started this activity running. So by calling `getIntent` and `intent.getBooleanExtra`, the `OtherActivity` discovers the values of `pepBox.isChecked()` and `cheeseBox.isChecked()` from Listing 4-5. For example, the call

```
intent.getBooleanExtra("Pepperoni", false)
```

returns `true` if the value of `pepBox.isChecked()` in Listing 4-5 is `true`. The call returns `false` if the value of `pepBox.isChecked()` in Listing 4-5 is `false`. The call's second argument is a default value. So in Listing 4-6, the call to `intent.getBooleanExtra("Pepperoni", false)` returns `false` if the intent created in Listing 4-5 has no extra named `"Pepperoni"`.

14. **In your** project's `AndroidManifest.xml` document, **add the following element:**

    ```
    <activity android:name=".OtherActivity"></activity>
    ```

    Add this element after the document's existing `</activity>` end tag.

For each activity in your application, you must add an `<activity>` element to the `AndroidManifest.xml` file. Failure to do so results in runtime Cannot Find Activity messages, along with lots of pain and suffering.

In an `activity` element, the `android:name` attribute points to the name of the activity's Java class. In this step, the attribute's value is `".OtherActivity"`. The initial dot refers to the application's package name (the name `more.stuff.of.mine` from Step 1). The rest of the attribute refers to the class name in Listing 4-6.

15. **Run your app.**

    When you click the app's button, you see a new activity like the one pictured in Figure 4-12.

Figure 4-12:
A new activity appears on the device's screen.

FourthApp
Pepperoni Extra cheese

Localizing your app

The apps in this chapter's previous sections have too many strings. `"Pepperoni"` here; `"Extra cheese"` there! It's a wonder a developer can keep this stuff straight. It's too easy to type a string one way in one part of the code and misspell the string in a different part.

You can reduce the problem by creating string constants. For example, you can write

```
public final String pep = "Pepperoni";
```

at the top of your program. But then, to change from the English word *Pepperoni* to the Italian word *Merguez,* you have to mess with your Java code. In a world where only 6 percent of all mobile phones are in the United States*, you don't want to edit Java code for dozens of countries.

* *Source:* `http://en.wikipedia.org/wiki/List_of_countries_by_number_of_ mobile_phones_in_use`

The elegant answer is to use Android's *string externalization* feature. Here's what you do:

1. **Launch Eclipse, and create a new Android project.**

   In this section's listings and screenshots, I call the project `FifthApp`; I call the main activity `FifthAppActivity`; and I use the package `more.stuff.of.mine`.

2. **Copy the `reusable_layout.xml` file from this chapter's "Creating a reusable layout" section to your new project's `res/layout` directory.**

3. **Include `reusable_layout` in your project's `main.xml` file.**

   For details, see Steps 2 to 5 in the "Reusing a layout" section.

4. **Add a TextView element to your main layout.**

5. **Copy the text in Listing 4-3 to your project's activity file.**

   If necessary, change the class name from `SecondAppActivity` to `FifthAppActivity` (or to whatever your main activity's name is).

   Your main activity's code contains strings `"Pepperoni"`, `"Extra cheese"`, and `"Plain"`.

   If you want your code to run on Android 1.5 or earlier, you must copy the code in Listing 4-3. But if you don't care about Android 1.5, you can copy Listing 4-2 instead. If you copy Listing 4-2, you must remember to follow Steps 2 and 3 in this chapter's "For minimum SDK version 4 or higher (Android 1.6 and beyond)" section.

6. **In the editor, select the string `"Extra cheese"`.**

7. **In Eclipse's main menu, choose Refactor⇨Android⇨Extract Android String.**

   Well, wha' da' ya' know?! An Extract Android String dialog box appears!

   In Figure 4-13, Eclipse automatically creates a name for the externalized resource — the name `R.string.extra_cheese`. Notice how Eclipse replaces blank spaces in strings with underscores in resource names.

   If you want Eclipse to replace all occurrences of `Extra cheese` with references to the new string resource, select the dialog box's Replace in All Java files check box as well as the Replace in All XML files for Different Configuration check box. Doing so ensures uniform use of the `"Extra cheese"` string throughout your application.

8. **In the Extract Android String dialog box, click OK.**

   As a result, Eclipse replaces some code in your Java source file with the following code:

```
if (cheeseBox.isChecked()) {
    str.append(getString(R.string.extra_cheese));
}
```

Eclipse also adds the following element to your `res/values/strings.xml` file:

```
<string name="extra_cheese">Extra cheese</string>
```

Finally, Eclipse replaces one of your layout's `CheckBox` elements with the following element:

```
<CheckBox
    android:id="@+id/checkBox2"
    android:layout_width="wrap_content"
    android:layout_height="wrap_content"
    android:text="@string/extra_cheese"></CheckBox>
```

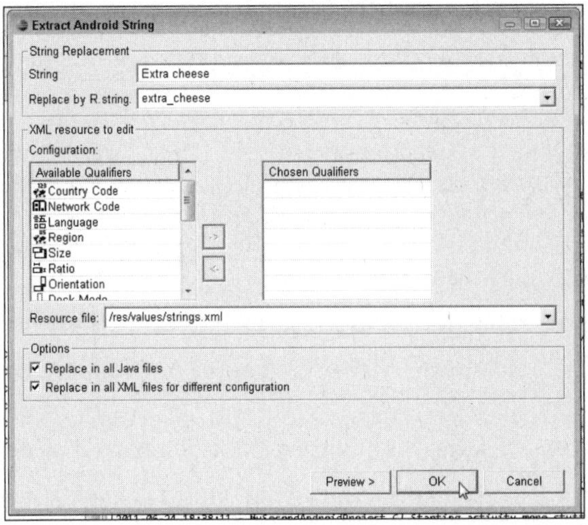

Figure 4-13:
The Extract
Android
String dialog
box.

Eclipse's Android string replacement tools can be buggy. After following this step, check your code to make sure that Eclipse's code changes are correct. The errors that I find are mostly in my XML documents. But in the Java code, Eclipse might forget to add the call to `getString` in `getString(R.string.extra_cheese)`. You need this call because the `append` method doesn't translate from numbers to resources on its own. So if Eclipse doesn't add the `getString` call, edit your activity's code yourself.

9. **Repeat Steps 3 through 5 for the strings "Pepperoni", "Plain", and (in the `reusable_layout.xml` file) "Show".**

With your app's strings externalized, you're ready to go international.

10. **Select your project's `res/values` folder in the Package Explorer.**

11. **In Eclipse's main menu, choose Edit⇨Copy.**

12. **Select your project's `res` folder in the Package Explorer.**

13. **In Eclipse's main menu, choose Edit⇨Paste.**

A Name Conflict dialog box appears.

14. **In the Name Conflict dialog box's Enter a New Name field, type** values-it **and then click OK.**

The two-letter it code stands for Italy. For the full scoop, visit www. iso.org/iso/country_names_and_code_elements.

15. **Open the `res/values-it/strings.xml` file in Eclipse's editor.**

16. **Modify the `res/values-it/strings.xml` file so it matches what is shown in Listing 4-7.**

Elenco 4-7:   Benvenuto in Italia!

```
<?xml version="1.0" encoding="utf-8"?>
<resources>
    <string name="hello">
        Ciao mondo, la mia attività!</string>
    <string name="app_name">
        Il mio secondo progetto Android</string>
    <string name="extra_cheese">Con più formaggio</
    string>
    <string name="pepperoni">Merguez</string>
    <string name="plain">Semplice</string>
    <string name="show">Mostra</string>
</resources>
```

17. **Test your app.**

As with most devices, the emulator has a setting for Language & Keyboard. Change this setting to Italiano (Italia), and suddenly, your app looks like the display in Figure 4-14.

Figure 4-14:
Buongiorno!

Responding to check box events

Why click twice when you can do the same thing by clicking only once? Think about the example in the "Dragging, Dropping, and Otherwise Tweaking an App" section. Your app responds to the contents of check boxes when the user clicks a button. In a streamlined scenario, your app might respond as soon as the user checks a box. Listing 4-8 shows you how to make this happen.

Listing 4-8:   Responding to Check Box Events

```
package more.stuff.of.mine;

import android.app.Activity;
import android.os.Bundle;
import android.widget.CheckBox;
import android.widget.CompoundButton;
import android.widget.CompoundButton.
                          OnCheckedChangeListener;
import android.widget.TextView;

public class MyActivity extends Activity
        implements OnCheckedChangeListener {

    TextView textView;

    @Override
    public void onCreate(Bundle savedInstanceState) {
        super.onCreate(savedInstanceState);
        setContentView(R.layout.main);

        ((CheckBox) findViewById(R.id.checkBox1))
                .setOnCheckedChangeListener(this);
        ((CheckBox) findViewById(R.id.checkBox2))
                .setOnCheckedChangeListener(this);
        textView =
```

```
                  (TextView) findViewById(R.id.textView1);
    }

    @Override
    public void onCheckedChanged(CompoundButton box,
                            boolean isChecked) {
        StringBuilder str =
                new StringBuilder(textView.getText());
        CharSequence boxText = box.getText();
        if (isChecked) {
            str.append(" " + boxText);
        } else {
            int start = str.indexOf(boxText.toString());
            int length = boxText.length();
            str.replace(start, start + length, "");
        }
        textView.setText(str.toString().trim());
    }
}
```

Like a button, each check box listens for `onClick` events. So you can write this section's code very much like the code in Listing 4-3. But in this section's listing, I avoid the use of `OnClickListener` and illustrate the use of a different event listener.

A check box listens for changes to its state (its "checked" versus "unchecked" state). So when the user touches a check box, Android fires an `onChecked Changed` event. By registering `this` (the entire `MyActivity` instance) as each check box's `OnCheckedChangeListener`, you make Android call the `onCheckedChanged` method in Listing 4-8.

The `onCheckedChanged` method has two parameters — the component that was touched and the state of the component as a result of the touch. I've contrived the code in Listing 4-8 to make use of these two method parameters.

A `CompoundButton` is a widget with checked and unchecked states. The `CheckBox` class is a subclass of `CompoundButton`. Other subclasses of `CompoundButton` are `RadioButton` and `ToggleButton`. A `ToggleButton` is that cute little thing that lights when it's checked.

In Listing 4-8, the `onCheckedChanged` method's `box` parameter refers to whichever check box the user touches. That check box has a `getText` method, so in Listing 4-8, I use the `getText` method to help fill the `text View` element. I use the `onCheckedChanged` method's `isChecked` parameter to decide whether to add text to the `textView` element or delete text from the `textView` element.

Displaying images

After designing an app and its variations in the previous sections, you might decide that your app needs some flair. When the user clicks the button, display a picture of the pizza being ordered.

Android has all kinds of features for drawing images and displaying bitmap files. I cover many of these features in Book IV, Chapter 3. In this section, I cover one possible approach:

1. **Launch Eclipse, and create a new Android project.**

In this section's listings and screenshots, I call the project `SixthApp`; I call the main activity `SixthAppActivity`; and I use the package `more.stuff.of.mine`.

2. **Copy the `reusable_layout.xml` file from this chapter's "Creating a reusable layout" section to your new project's `res/layout` directory.**

3. **Include `reusable_layout` in your project's `main.xml` file.**

For details, see Steps 2 to 5 in the "Reusing a layout" section.

4. **Find four images — one for plain, one for pepperoni, one for extra cheese, and one for pepperoni with extra cheese.**

Android's official documentation recommends the `.png` format for images. If you don't have `.png` images, Android's docs call the `.jpg` format "acceptable." If you don't have `.png` or `.jpg`, the docs tell you to hold your nose and use `.gif`. But remember, in this section, you're creating a practice application, not a work of art. Your images don't have to look good. They don't even have to look like pizzas. Besides, you can download my silly-looking drawings of pizzas from this book's website at `www.allmycode.com/Android`.

In creating my project, I use the names `plain.png`, `pepperoni.png`, `extracheese.png`, and `pep_extracheese.png`.

The names of Android's resource files must not contain capital letters. You can use only lowercase letters and underscores.

For working with image formats, the program IrfanView has always served me well. You can get this Windows program at `www.irfanview.com`. The program is free for noncommercial use.

5. **In Eclipse's Package Explorer, select your project's `res` folder.**

6. **In Eclipse's main menu, choose File⇨New⇨Folder.**

Eclipse prompts you for the name of the new folder.

7. **Name your folder** `drawable`.

   Now your project has a `res/drawable` folder. This new folder is the default for images and other image-worthy things.

   Your project already has folders named `drawable-hdpi`, `drawable-ldpi`, and `drawable-mdpi`. In a real-life app, you use these folders as alternatives for devices with high, low, and medium screen densities. But in this practice app, a default `drawable` folder is easier.

   The letters *dpi* stand for *dots per inch.* Android senses a device's screen density and uses the resources in the most appropriate `drawable-?dpi` folder. To find out what Android considers "most appropriate," visit http://developer.android.com/guide/practices/screens_support.html.

8. **Drag your four images from your development computer's file explorer to your project's `res/drawable` folder.**

9. **Open Eclipse's dialog box for creating a new XML resource document.**

   For details see the section "Starting another activity."

10. **Using the New Android XML File dialog box, add a new file (which I name `levels.xml`) to your `res/drawable` folder.**

11. **Use Eclipse's editor to populate your `levels.xml` file with the code in Listing 4-9.**

Listing 4-9: A Level-List Document

```xml
<?xml version="1.0" encoding="utf-8"?>
<level-list xmlns:android=
        "http://schemas.android.com/apk/res/android">
    <item android:drawable="@drawable/plain"
        android:maxLevel="0" />
    <item android:drawable="@drawable/pepperoni"
        android:maxLevel="1" />
    <item android:drawable="@drawable/extracheese"
        android:maxLevel="2" />
    <item android:drawable="@drawable/pep_extracheese"
        android:maxLevel="3" />
</level-list>
```

A *level-list* is a list of alternative drawables for a single image component to display. At any moment during an app's run, the image component has an integer level. You set the component's level using the `set ImageLevel` method.

When your app calls `setImageLevel`, Android starts at the top of the level-list and looks for the first item whose `android:maxLevel` is greater than or equal to the new image level. You can also assign an `android:minLevel` attribute to an item. But in most situations, `android:maxLevel` is all you need.

12. Add an ImageView element to your activity's layout.

You can drag an ImageView element from the Graphical Layout's palette, or you can add the following element to your app's `main.xml` file:

```
<ImageView android:id="@+id/imageView1"
           android:layout_height="wrap_content"
           android:layout_width="wrap_content"
           android:src="@drawable/levels"></ImageView>
```

13. Make sure that your ImageView element's `android:src` attribute refers to your new `levels.xml` document.

In Eclipse's Properties view, this attribute is called `Src`.

14. Code your project's activity file as in Listing 4-10.

Listing 4-10:   Changing Images

```
package more.stuff.of.mine;

import android.app.Activity;
import android.os.Bundle;
import android.view.View;
import android.view.View.OnClickListener;
import android.widget.Button;
import android.widget.CheckBox;
import android.widget.ImageView;

public class SixthAppActivity extends Activity
        implements OnClickListener {
    CheckBox pepBox, cheeseBox;
    ImageView imageView;

    @Override
    public void onCreate(Bundle savedInstanceState) {
        super.onCreate(savedInstanceState);
        setContentView(R.layout.main);
        ((Button) findViewById(R.id.button1))
            .setOnClickListener(this);

        pepBox =
            (CheckBox) findViewById(R.id.checkBox1);
        cheeseBox =
            (CheckBox) findViewById(R.id.checkBox2);
```

```
        imageView =
            (ImageView) findViewById(R.id.imageView1);
    }

    public void onClick(View view) {
        int level = 0;

        if (pepBox.isChecked()) {
            level += 1;
        }
        if (cheeseBox.isChecked()) {
            level += 2;
        }
        imageView.setImageLevel(level);
    }
}
```

In Listing 4-10, the `onClick` method calls the `setImageLevel` method. The method parameter's value depends on the states of the activity's check boxes.

15. **Run the app.**

The results, along with my beautiful drawings of pizza with toppings, are shown in Figure 4-15.

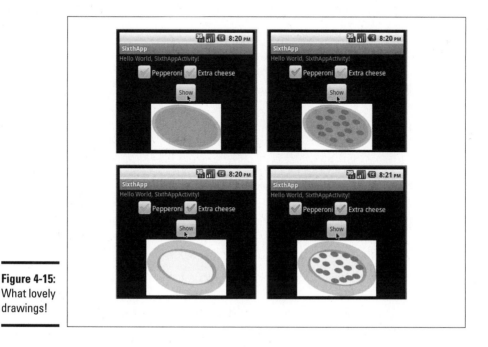

Figure 4-15:
What lovely
drawings!

Sending in your order

If you've read any of this chapter's previous sections, you're probably very hungry. An app with nothing but pictures and the names of pizza toppings is a real tease.

So you'd better add some purchasing power to this chapter's example. Real e-commerce functionality is the subject of several other books. But in this book, you can get a small taste of the online pizza-ordering process (pun intended). You can submit your choice of toppings to an existing web server — Google's search engine, to be precise. It's not as good as biting into a tasty pizza, but the example shows you one way to send information from a mobile device.

In a real application, you might program your own server to respond intelligently to users' requests. For passing money back and forth, you might use Android Market's in-app billing facilities.

Programming web servers isn't an Android-specific topic. To read all about servers, buy *Apache, MySQL, and PHP Web Development All-in-One Desk Reference For Dummies,* by Jeff Cogswell (John Wiley & Sons, Inc.).

1. **Launch Eclipse, and create a new Android project.**

In this section's listings and screenshots, I call the project `SeventhApp`; I call the main activity `SeventhAppActivity`; and I use the package `more.stuff.of.mine`.

2. **Copy the `reusable_layout.xml` file from this chapter's "Creating a reusable layout" section to your new project's `res/layout` directory.**

3. **Include `reusable_layout` in your project's `main.xml` file.**

For details, see Steps 2 to 5 in the "Reusing a layout" section.

4. **Add a WebView element to your main activity's layout.**

You can drag a WebView element from the Composite group of the Graphical Layout's palette. Alternatively, you can add the following element to your project's `main.xml` file:

```
<WebView android:id="@+id/webView1"
        android:layout_width="match_parent"
        android:layout_height="match_parent">
</WebView>
```

A WebView is a mini web browser that you can add to an existing activity.

5. **Code your project's activity file as in Listing 4-11.**

Listing 4-11:   Sending Info to a Server

```java
package more.stuff.of.mine;

import android.app.Activity;
import android.os.Bundle;
import android.view.View;
import android.view.View.OnClickListener;
import android.webkit.WebView;
import android.widget.Button;
import android.widget.CheckBox;

public class SeventhAppActivity extends Activity
                        implements OnClickListener {
  CheckBox pepBox, cheeseBox;
  WebView webView;

  @Override
  public void onCreate(Bundle savedInstanceState) {
    super.onCreate(savedInstanceState);
    setContentView(R.layout.main);
    ((Button) findViewById(R.id.button1))
      .setOnClickListener(this);

    pepBox = (CheckBox) findViewById(R.id.checkBox1);
    cheeseBox = (CheckBox) findViewById(R.id.checkBox2);
    webView = (WebView) findViewById(R.id.webView1);
  }

  public void onClick(View view) {
    StringBuilder str = new StringBuilder("");
    if (pepBox.isChecked()) {
      str.append("Pepperoni");
    }
    if (cheeseBox.isChecked()) {
      str.append("\"Extra cheese\"");
    }
    if (str.length() == 23) {
      str.insert(9, '+');
    }
    if (str.length() == 0) {
      str.append("Plain");
    }
    webView.loadUrl
      ("http://www.google.com/search?q="+str.toString());
  }
}
```

6. **Add the following element to your project's `AndroidManifest.xml` document:**

```
<uses-permission
    android:name="android.permission.INTERNET" />
```

Make this `uses-permission` element a direct sub-element of the document's `manifest` element.

This element grants your app permission to access the Internet. Access to the Internet will appear in the list the user sees before installing your app.

When you create an app, don't forget to add the appropriate permissions to the app's `AndroidManifest.xml` file. In a recent survey of *For Dummies* book authors, all respondents reported that they frequently forget to add permissions to their apps' manifest files. (Survey sample size: one.)

7. **Run your app.**

You might have to wait for the web page to load. When the page loads, your app looks something like the screen in Figure 4-16.

Figure 4-16: Your app sends stuff to a Web server.

Book II

Android Background Material

The 5th Wave   By Rich Tennant

Of course it doesn't make any sense, but it's the only chance we've got! Now hook the Droid into the override and see if you can bring this baby in!

Contents at a Glance

Chapter 1: Using the Eclipse Workbench

In This Chapter

✔ Finding your way around the Eclipse workbench

✔ Using views and perspectives

✔ Getting Eclipse's assistance to type your code

✔ Importing existing code

✔ Working with configurations and preferences

*W*hen you develop software, you have two options:

✦ **Be tough and use only command-line tools.**

Never touch your computer's mouse. Figure out all the commands with all their options. Edit programs in primitive text editors, such as Linux vi, GNU Emacs, Windows Notepad, or Macintosh TextEdit.

✦ **Be wimpy and use an integrated development environment (an IDE).**

Execute commands by clicking menu items. Edit programs with a full-featured editor — an editor customized for whatever programming language you use. Change object values with code-aware property sheets. Create forms by dragging widgets from a palette to a visual layout.

I admire toughness, but wimpiness is more efficient. Being wimpy makes you more productive and less prone to error. Also, being wimpy helps you to concentrate on the app that you're creating instead of having to focus on the commands to create the app.

Don't get me wrong. Tough command-line tools are great in a pinch. When your IDE covers up subtle (but important) details, you need command-line tools to show you what's going on behind the scenes. But for most developers, most of the time, IDEs are great time-savers. That's why the official Android developer docs say that "Developing in Eclipse . . . is highly recommended."

With or without Android, Eclipse is a mature platform, with tools for Java development, C/C++ development, PHP development, modeling, project management, testing, debugging, and much more.

So this chapter introduces Eclipse. I (naturally enough) focus on the aspects of Eclipse that help you build Android apps, but keep in mind that Eclipse has hundreds of (non-Androidish) features, as well as many ways to access each feature.

What's All That Stuff on the Eclipse Workbench?

The next few pages bathe you in vocabulary. Some of this vocabulary is probably familiar old stuff. Other vocabulary is new.

Before you jump into the next several paragraphs, please heed my advice: Don't take my descriptions of terms too literally. These are explanations, not definitions. Yes, they're fairly precise; but no, they're not airtight. Almost every description in this section has hidden exceptions, omissions, exemptions, and exclusions. Take the paragraphs in this section to be friendly reminders, not legal contracts.

✦ **Workbench:** The Eclipse desktop (see Figure 1-1).

The workbench is the environment in which you develop code.

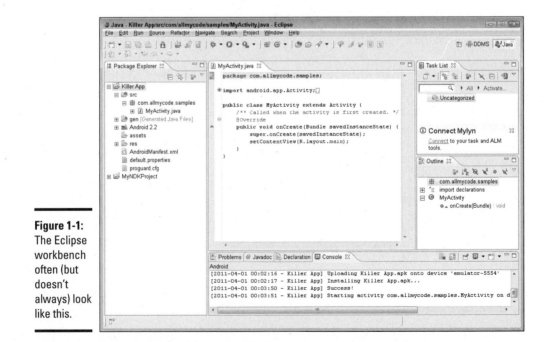

Figure 1-1:
The Eclipse workbench often (but doesn't always) look like this.

✦ **Area:** A section of the workbench.

The workbench in Figure 1-1 has five areas. In Figure 1-2 I draw a rectangle around each of the areas.

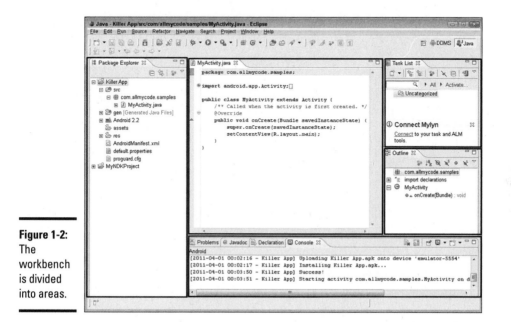

**Book II
Chapter 1**

**Using the Eclipse
Workbench**

Figure 1-2:
The
workbench
is divided
into areas.

✦ **Window:** A copy of the Eclipse workbench.

With Eclipse, you can have several copies of the workbench open at once. Each copy appears in its own window. (See Figure 1-3.)

To open a second window, go to the main Eclipse menu bar and choose Window⟶New Window.

✦ **Action:** A choice that's offered to you, typically when you click something.

For instance, when you choose File⟶New in Eclipse's main menu bar, you see a list of new things that you can create. The list usually includes Project, Folder, File, and Other, but it may also include things like Package, Class, and Interface. Each of these things (each item in the menu) is an *action*.

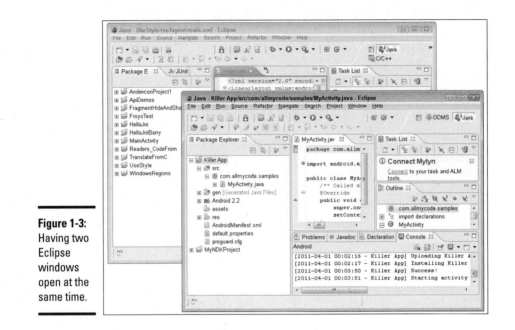

Figure 1-3:
Having two
Eclipse
windows
open at the
same time.

Views and editors

The next bunch of terms deals with things called views and editors. At first, you may have difficulty understanding the difference. (A view is like an editor, which is like a view, or something like that.) If views and editors seem the same to you, and you're not sure you can tell which is which, don't be upset. As an ordinary Eclipse user, the distinction between views and editors comes naturally as you gain experience using the workbench. You rarely have to decide whether the thing you're using is a view or an editor. But if you plan to develop Eclipse plug-ins, you eventually have to figure out what's a view and what's an editor.

✦ **View:** A part of the Eclipse workbench that displays information for you to browse.

In the simplest case, a view fills an area in the workbench. For instance, in Figure 1-1, the Package Explorer view fills up the leftmost area.

Many views display information as lists or trees. For example, in Figure 1-1, the Package Explorer and Outline views contain trees.

You can use a view to make changes to things. For example, to delete the `MyActivity.java` file in Figure 1-1, right-click the MyActivity.java branch in the Package Explorer view. Then, in the resulting context menu, choose Delete. (Macintosh users use Control-click in place of right-click.)

When you use a view to change something, the change takes place immediately. For example, when you choose Delete in the Package Explorer's context menu, whatever file you've selected is deleted immediately. In a way, this behavior is nothing new. The same kind of thing happens when you delete a file using My Computer or Windows Explorer.

✦ **Editor:** A part of the Eclipse workbench that displays information for you to modify.

A typical editor displays information in the form of text. This text can be the contents of a file. For example, an editor in the middle of Figure 1-1 displays the contents of the MyActivity.java source file.

Some editors display more than just text. For example, Figure 1-4 displays Android's *Graphical Layout editor*. Like many other editors, this Graphical Layout editor displays the contents of a file. But instead of showing you all the words in the file, the Graphical Layout editor displays the file's contents as they're rendered on a mobile device's screen.

**Book II
Chapter 1**

Using the Eclipse Workbench

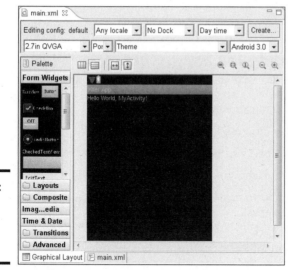

Figure 1-4:
The Graphical Layout editor.

To find out all about layouts and the Graphical Layout editor, see Book IV, Chapter 1.

When you use an editor to change something, the change doesn't take place immediately. For example, look at the editor in the middle of Figure 1-1. This editor displays the contents of the MyActivity.java source file. You can type all kinds of things in the Editor pane. Nothing permanent happens to MyActivity.java until you choose File⇨Save from Eclipse's menu bar. Of course, this behavior is nothing new.

The same kind of thing happens when you work in Microsoft Word or Macintosh TextEdit.

Like other authors, I occasionally become lazy and use the word "view" when I really mean "view or editor." When you catch me doing this, just shake your head and move onward. When I'm being very careful, I use the official Eclipse terminology. I refer to views and editors as *parts* of the Eclipse workbench. Unfortunately, this "parts" terminology doesn't stick in people's' minds very well.

That's all I'm going to say about the "view versus editor" distinction. For good measure, though, I explain a few related terms:

✦ **Tab group:** A bunch of views or editors stacked on top of one another.

For example, near the bottom of Figure 1-1, the Problems, Javadoc, Declaration, and Console views form a tab group.

✦ **Active view or active editor:** In a tab group, the view or editor that's in front.

In Figure 1-1, the Console view is the active view. The Problems, Javadoc, and Declaration views are inactive.

Understanding the big picture

The next two terms deal with Eclipse's overall look and feel.

✦ **Layout:** An arrangement of certain views.

The layout in Figure 1-1 has seven views:.

- At the far left, you see the Package Explorer view.

- On the far right, you have the Task List and Outline views.

- Near the bottom, you get the Problems, Javadoc, Declaration, and Console views.

Along with all these views, the layout contains a single *editor area.* Any and all open editors appear inside this editor area.

✦ **Perspective:** A very useful layout.

If a particular layout is really useful, someone gives that layout a name. And if a layout has a name, you can use the layout whenever you want.

For instance, the workbench of Figure 1-1 displays the Java perspective. By default, the Java perspective contains six views, in an arrangement very much like the one shown in Figure 1-1.

Along with all these views, the Java perspective contains an editor area. (Sure, the editor area has several tabs, but the number of tabs has nothing to do with the Java perspective.)

By default, the Console view isn't visible in the Java perspective. To find out how to add a view to an existing perspective, see the later section entitled "Where's my view?"

Eclipse's Java perspective is for writing Java code. In contrast, the DDMS perspective is for debugging a running Android application. (The acronym DDMS stands for Dalvik Debug Monitor Server. For more information, see Book I, Chapter 4; Book III, Chapter 1; and other sections in this chapter.)

The DDMS perspective, as shown in Figure 1-5, looks very different from the Java perspective. The two perspectives (Java and DDMS) sport different views and different area layouts. When you're in a Java mood, you can go with the Java perspective; when you're feeling DDMS, you can switch to the DDMS perspective. Eclipse comes with other ready-made perspectives, including the Debug perspective and the appealingly named Pixel Perfect perspective.

The point here is that you're not forced to stick with just one perspective. You can make the switch — the next section shows you how.

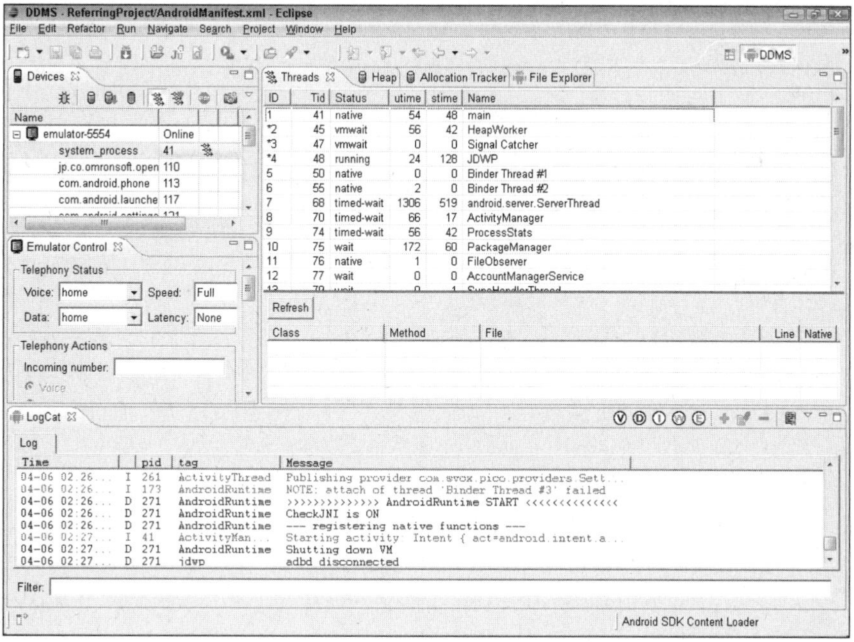

**Book II
Chapter 1**

**Using the Eclipse
Workbench**

Figure 1-5:
The DDMS
perspective.

Juggling among perspectives

Eclipse comes with several different perspectives. As an Android developer, your favorite perspectives are the Java perspective, the DDMS perspective, and the Debug perspective. You can easily switch from one perspective to another.

Look again at Figure 1-5, and notice the word *DDMS* in the upper-right corner. This DDMS button is part of the *Perspective bar*. Figure 1-6 shows what happens to the Perspective bar when you click the bar's Open Perspective icon (the picture of a very tiny perspective with a plus sign in the corner). You see a short list of the available perspectives and the ever-helpful word *Other*. (You see the same short list if you go Eclipse's main menu and choose Window⇨Open Perspective.)

Figure 1-6:
Using the
Perspective
bar's Open
Perspective
icon.

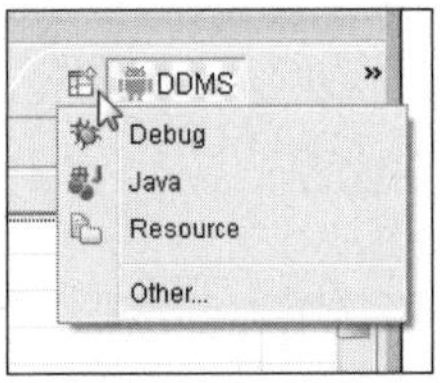

If you click anything except Other, Eclipse switches immediately to the selected perspective. If you click Other, Eclipse opens a new dialog box. (See Figure 1-7.) The dialog box lists the names of all the available perspectives. To switch to a perspective, double-click the perspective's name in the list.

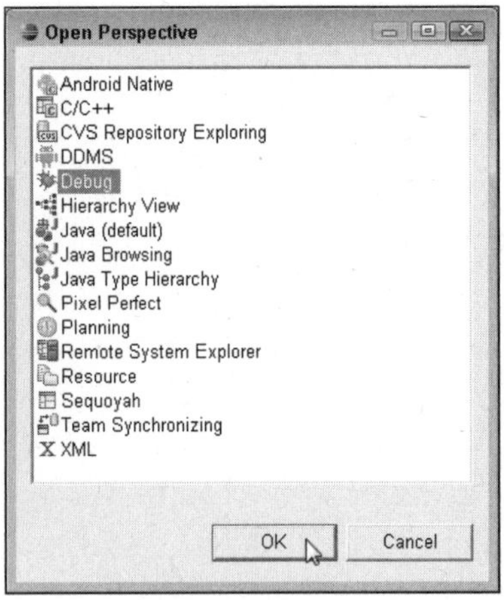

Figure 1-7:
A list of
perspec-
tives.

Changing the way a perspective looks

Believe me — I'm not big on cosmetic features. One look at the mess in my office will convince anyone of that. But if you work with Eclipse as much as I have, you become accustomed to having things exactly the way you want them.

In this section, you move things around within an Eclipse perspective. With the right amount of moving, you make Java coding much easier.

Where's my view?

You can add views to a perspective and remove views from a perspective. For example, in Figure 1-1, I've added the Console view to my existing Java perspective. To add the view, do the following:

1. **In the main Eclipse menu bar, choose Window⇨Show View.**

A list of views appears. Many of the available views are in this list. But some views aren't in the list.

2. **Choose the view that you want to show; if you don't see the view you want, choose Other. (See Figure 1-8.)**

Book II
Chapter 1

Using the Eclipse
Workbench

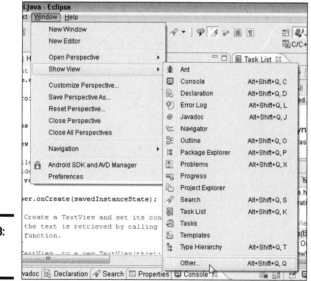

Figure 1-8:
Adding a
view.

If you choose a view, that view appears on your workbench. If you choose Other, a Show View dialog box appears. (See Figure 1-9.)

3. **Expand whatever branch you need to expand in the Show View dialog box's navigation tree to find the view that you want added to the workbench.**

   In Figure 1-9, I've expanded the General branch and hovered over the Properties view. (The views in the General branch apply to all kinds of application development, not to specific kinds such as Android, C++, or Java.)

4. **Double-click the view's name.**

   The view appears on your current Eclipse workbench.

If you know part of a view's name, you don't have to poke among tree branches in the Show View dialog box. Type the partial name in the text field at the top of the Show View dialog box. As a result, only views whose names contain your search text appear in the Show View dialog box.

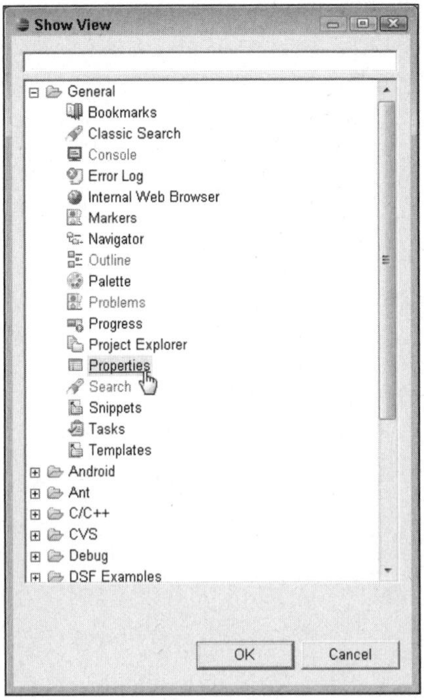

Figure 1-9:
The
Show View
dialog box.

> **Show View**
>
> ☐ 🗁 General
>   🕮 Bookmarks
>   ✐ Classic Search
>   🖳 Console
>   ⚑ Error Log
>   🌐 Internal Web Browser
>   🖾 Markers
>   🕮 Navigator
>   🝋 Outline
>   🎨 Palette
>   🖾 Problems
>   ☴ Progress
>   🗐 Project Explorer
>   🖿 Properties
>   ✐ Search
>   📄 Snippets
>   📄 Tasks
>   📄 Templates
> ⊞ 🗁 Android
> ⊞ 🗁 Ant
> ⊞ 🗁 C/C++
> ⊞ 🗁 CVS
> ⊞ 🗁 Debug
> ⊞ 🗁 DSF Examples
>
> [OK]   [Cancel]

If you lose a view (probably because you clicked the X on the view's tab and forgot that you did), you can follow this section's steps to add the view back to your perspective.

Some Useful Views

Eclipse comes stocked with a bunch of different views. For your convenience, I describe about ten of them in this chapter.

Views that normally live in the Java perspective

I start with the views that normally call the Java perspective home.

Package Explorer view

For me, the Package Explorer view is Eclipse's real workhorse. The *Package Explorer* displays things in an Android-specific way — meaning it displays things as you think of them inside an Android application. For example, in Figure 1-10 the com.allmycode.samples branch represents the com. allmycode.samples package — the Java package that houses the Killer App's code.

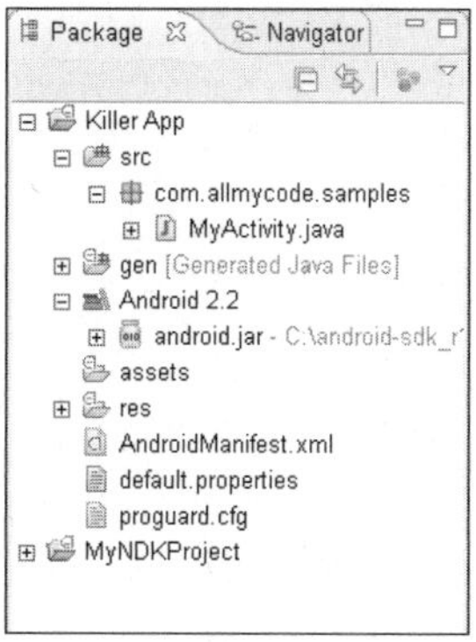

Figure 1-10:
The
Package
Explorer
view.

Navigator view

You can add the *Navigator* view to any existing perspective. The view part of the Navigator view is a lot like the Package Explorer view, but the Navigator's tree is less Android-centric and more Explorer-like. The Navigator view displays files and folders almost the way Windows Explorer and Macintosh Finder display files and folders.

Figure 1-11 shows a snapshot of a Navigator view. (This particular snapshot shows the files in my Killer App project.)

Contrast the trees in Figures 1-10 and 1-11. In Figure 1-11, you see things that you don't normally see in an Android-specific view. You see individual `com`, `allmycode`, and `samples` folders. You also see the `bin` directory, which contains the compiled Java class files, the compiled Android `.dex` files, and that Holy Grail — the application's installable `.apk` file.

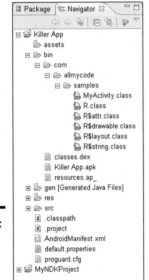

Figure 1-11:
The
Navigator
view.

Outline view

The *Outline view* displays a tree or list of whatever is in the active editor. In my mind, I typically use the Outline view to coax information out of another view — the Properties view. To find out what I do, read on.

Properties view

The Properties view lists the values of an object's attributes. For example, in Figure 1-12, the Graphical Layout editor displays the main layout of an app that I'm developing. In the editor, I selected TextView (the strip of text that's surrounded by dotted lines near the center of Figure 1-12).

To set the text I want this TextView to display, I look for the TextView's `text` attribute in the Properties view. I click the Value column of the `text` attribute's row, and then type **Are you listening?** After pressing Enter, the text shown in the Graphical Layout editor changes to `Are you listening?`

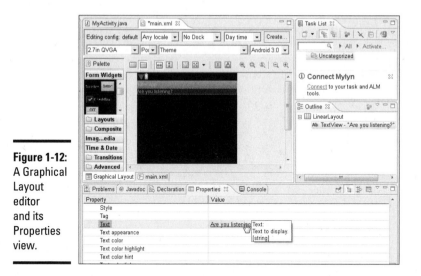

Figure 1-12:
A Graphical
Layout
editor
and its
Properties
view.

Sometimes, when I select an object in the Graphical Layout editor, the object's attributes appear immediately in the Properties view. But at other times, the Properties view doesn't respond. (I'm sure that this non-response is intentional, but I can't figure out why.) To remedy this situation, I go to the Outline view and select the object's branch in the Outline view's tree. (Refer to Figure 1-12.)

The Properties view doesn't appear on its own. To add the Properties view to your perspective, follow the earlier instructions in this chapter's "Where's my view?" section.

Console view

The Console view displays messages created by Android's development tools. For example, when I tell Eclipse to run my Android application, the Console view displays the progress of the application's launch. In Figure 1-13, the message `Success!` is particularly encouraging.

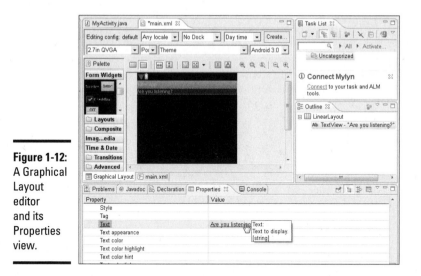

Figure 1-13:
The Console
view.

Javadoc view

The Javadoc view provides quick access to both the Java API documents and the corresponding Android API pages. When you select a name in Eclipse's source code editor, the Javadoc view displays the appropriate documentation page. (See Figure 1-14.)

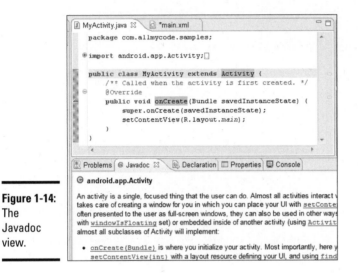

Figure 1-14:
The Javadoc view.

Views that normally live in the DDMS perspective

The previously mentioned views typically appear as part of the Java perspective. In this section, I describe views that you usually find in the DDMS perspective. The DDMS perspective displays information from Android's Dalvik Debug Monitor Server. The debug monitor watches your running emulator or your connected device and then reports useful information for the application developer.

LogCat view

Android's LogCat tool displays messages created by a running emulator or a connected device. The run reports all kinds of information — some relevant to your application and some having mostly to do with other running processes. Some of the messages may be a little scary, but in many cases, the errors and warnings are someone else's problem.

For example, in Figure 1-15, a log entry warns me that no available voice recognition services have been found. But that's okay because my application doesn't require voice recognition services. The LogCat view is simply reporting everything that happens in this run of the Android operating system, and Android is doing much more than just worrying about my little application.

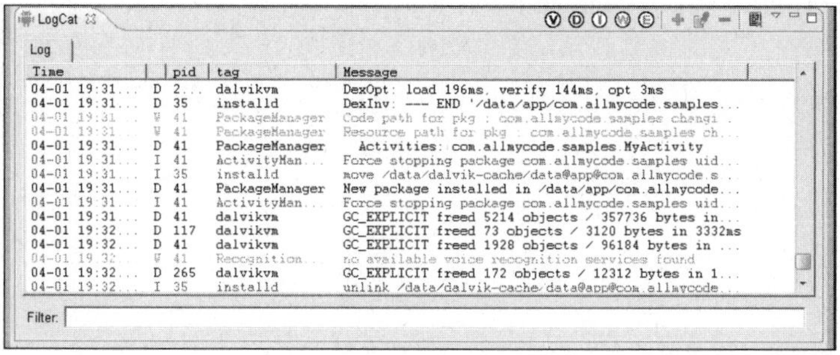

Figure 1-15: The LogCat view.

The LogCat view is great for helping you understand your application's behavior, especially because Java stack traces appear in the LogCat view. A Java *stack trace* is a kind of "snapshot" of your app at the moment when an error occurs. A stack trace tells you which methods are calling which other methods and which line of code triggers the error. To read more about stack traces and the LogCat view, see Book I, Chapter 4, and Book III, Chapter 1.

Devices view

The Devices view displays a navigation tree that includes running emulators and any attached phones or tablets. (See Figure 1-16.) You can expand each device's branch of the tree to show processes currently running on that device.

Eclipse links the Devices view to the other views in the DDMS perspective. So, if I want to see logging for a particular running emulator, I select that emulator in the Devices view. Then I can examine that emulator's LogCat output in the LogCat view. (In Figure 1-16, I select emulator-5554.)

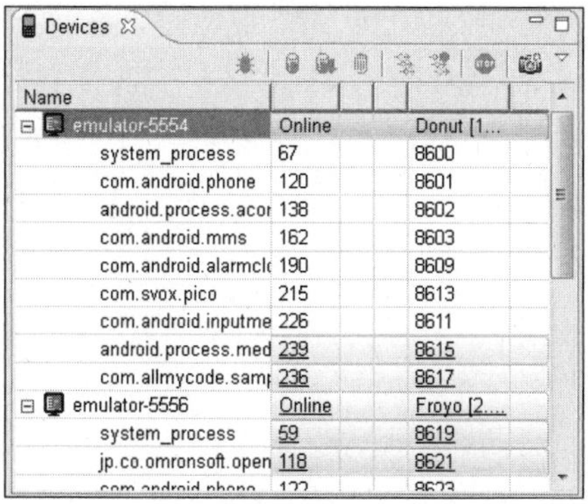

Figure 1-16: The Devices view.

File Explorer view

To explore the file system on a running emulator, I select that emulator in the Devices view and then examine the emulator's file system in the File Explorer view. (See Figure 1-17.)

Name	Size	Date	Time	Permissi...
⊟ 📂 data		2011-03-21	15:57	drwxrwx--x
⊞ 📂 anr		2011-04-02	02:07	drwxrwxr-x
⊞ 📂 app		2011-04-02	02:38	drwxrwx--x
⊞ 📂 app-private		2011-01-16	20:13	drwxrwx--x
⊞ 📂 backup		2011-01-16	20:14	drwx------
⊞ 📂 dalvik-cache		2011-04-02	02:38	drwxrwx--x
⊞ 📂 data		2011-03-31	19:57	drwxrwx--x
⊞ 📂 dontpanic		2011-01-16	20:13	drwxr-x--x
⊟ 📂 local		2011-01-16	20:13	drwxrwx--x
⊟ 📂 tmp		2011-04-02	02:37	drwxrwx--x
📄 Killer App.apk	13610	2011-04-02	02:37	-rw-rw-rw-
⊞ 📂 lost+found		2011-01-16	20:13	drwxrwx---
⊞ 📂 misc		2011-01-16	20:13	drwxrwx--t
⊞ 📂 property		2011-03-21	05:12	drwx------
⊞ 📂 system		2011-04-02	02:38	drwxrwxr-x
⊟ 📂 mnt		2011-04-02	02:37	drwxrwxr-x
⊞ 📂 asec		2011-04-02	02:37	drwxr-xr-x
⊟ 📂 sdcard		1970-01-01	00:00	d---rwxr-x
⊞ 📂 LOST.DIR		2011-01-16	15:15	d---rwxr-x

Tabs: Threads | Heap | Allocation Tracker | File Explorer ☒

Tooltip: Pull a file from the device

Figure 1-17:
The File
Explorer
view.

The File Explorer view lets you do more than simply examine a device's files. For example, in Figure 1-17, I'm getting ready to pull a copy of the `Killer App.apk` file from the emulator's file system to a location on my laptop's file system. (*Pulling* a file means copying the file from an emulator or phone to a development computer. *Pushing* a file means copying the file from a development computer to an emulator or a phone.)

Emulator Control view

The Emulator Control view gives you limited control over some features of a running emulator, and affords you the ability to trigger certain events on the emulator. For example, by clicking the view's buttons you can simulate an incoming call or make the emulator think that it's at Longitude –122.084095 and Latitude 37.422006. (See Figure 1-18.)

For even more control over an emulator, you can press certain keys on your development computer's keyboard. For a list of these keys, visit the official documentation at `http://developer.android.com/guide/ developing/tools/emulator.html`.

If you use MOTODEV Studio for Android, check out the cool Android Emulator view and the Database Explorer view.

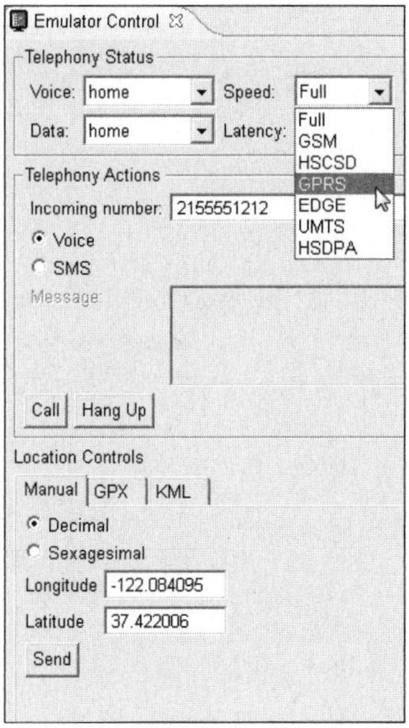

Book II
Chapter 1

Using the Eclipse
Workbench

Figure 1-18:
The
Emulator
Control
view.

Be Nice to Your Java Code

Eclipse has dozens of features to help you write better code. This section lists some of my favorites.

Making it pretty

Poorly formatted code is difficult to read. Well-formatted code is less expensive. You spend less time and money maintaining easy-to-read code.

When you choose Source➪Format in Eclipse's main menu, Eclipse formats an entire file or a whole bunch of files at once. As if by magic, your code becomes properly indented and consistently spaced.

Eclipse formats one or more files depending on which part of Eclipse's workbench has the focus. Does an editor have the focus? If so, choosing Source➪Format affects code in whatever file you're currently editing.

And what about the old Package Explorer? Does a branch of the Package Explorer have the focus? If so, Source➪Format affects all Java files in that branch. (For example, if you select a package's branch, Source➪Format affects all files in the package.)

Hocus-pocus! Who has the focus?

Imagine yourself working on a desktop or laptop computer. You're staring at a web page, thinking about submitting your entry in a random drawing. (If you win, you get a fully paid, one-week vacation to Kuala Lumpur in Malaysia.) When the web page first loaded, you saw a blinking cursor in a text field labeled Name. The blinking cursor indicates that this Name field has the focus. In other words, if the next thing you do is start typing on the computer keyboard, the characters that you type appear in the web page's Name field. The web page contains other widgets (in particular, an Email Address field and a Submit button), but the stuff that you type has no effect on those widgets. The stuff that you type goes directly into the Name field, because the Name field has the focus.

After typing your name, you can change the focus. To do this, you click your mouse in the Email Address field. Alternatively, you can press the Tab key after typing your name. Pressing Tab shifts the focus from the Name field to the Email Address field. So if you type `Barry Burd`*Tab*`android@allmycode. com`, then `Barry Burd` goes into the Name field and `android@allmycode.com` goes into the Email Address field. (As a pleasant side effect, typing these keystrokes increase Barry's chances of winning a trip to Kuala Lumpur!)

Pressing Tab once again shifts the focus to the Submit button. Sure, you can click the Submit button with your mouse. But to get practice with the notion of focus, you can also press your keyboard's spacebar. You see, any keystrokes go directly to whichever screen widget has the focus. When the Submit button has the focus, pressing the spacebar sends that spacebar keystroke to the button. And, by the way, a button's typical response to spacebar input is to "become clicked."

Getting back to the Eclipse workbench, try the following experiment:

1. Open a Java source file in Eclipse's editor. Click your mouse anywhere in the editor and begin typing. The editor has the focus, so whatever you type appears as text in the Java source file.

2. Now click the name of a project in the Package Explorer's tree. When you press Enter, the project branch expands to show its sub-branches. Press Enter again and the project branch collapses, hiding its sub-branches. The project in the Package Explorer has the focus, so that project branch responds to the Enter key.

3. Click again inside the editor. The editor has the focus, so when you press Enter, a line break appears in the Java source file. But looking back at the Package Explorer, the branch that you selected in Step 2 is still highlighted. The Package Explorer doesn't have the focus, so pressing Enter neither expands nor collapses the project branch.

So this experiment has a takeaway: At any moment, more than one item on the screen can be highlighted. But at any moment, only one item on the screen has the focus.

In fact, with the Package Explorer, you can quickly format a whole bunch of files. The files don't even have to live in the same project. Just do whatever you normally do to select more than one branch of the tree. In Windows and in many flavors of Linux, use Ctrl-click to add a branch to your selection. Use Shift-click to extend your selection from one branch to another (including all branches in between). After selecting a bunch of branches, choose Source➪Format.

Let Eclipse do the typing

Like so many modern development environments, Eclipse has a *Content Assist* feature. With Content Assist, you type enough code for Eclipse to make reasonable guesses about what you're trying to type. Then Eclipse's editor offers suggestions. Figure 1-19 shows what happens when I type **import android** and then a dot in the Java code editor. Eclipse suggests `import android.Manifest`, `import android.R`, `import android.accessibilityservice.*`, and others. Eclipse even displays a little documentation pop-up when it's feasible to do so.

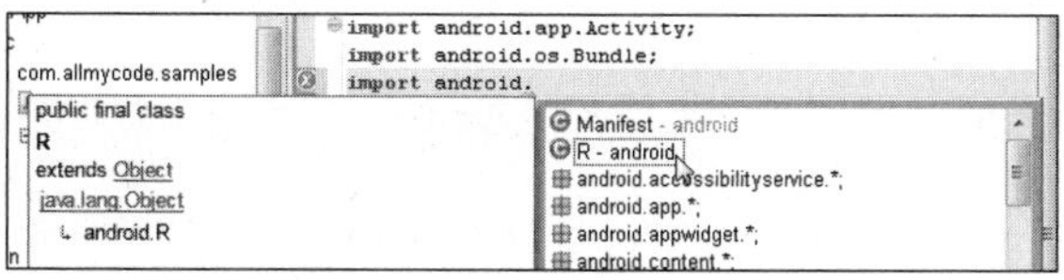

Figure 1-19:
The Eclipse editor offers to complete an import declaration for you.

In Figure 1-19, my mouse points to the *R* option. If I double click that *R* option, Eclipse types the code for me, changing my incomplete `import android.` to `import android.R;`.

Eclipse's Content Assist feature suggests names from Android's standard API, but it can also suggest other names — names that you define as part of your app. In Figure 1-20, Eclipse offers to complete my statement with the names `myCopyButton` and `myPasteButton` — names that I created as part of my activity's main layout.

```
@Override
public void onCreate(Bundle savedInstanceState) {
    super.onCreate(savedInstanceState);
    setContentView(R.layout.main);
    button = ((Button)findViewById(R.id.
}

                                            editText1 : int - R.id
                                            myCopyButton : int - R.id
                                            myPasteButton : int - R.id
                                            class : Class<com.allmycode.samp
                                            this
```

Sometimes Eclipse's Content Assist feature doesn't want to come out of its
shell. To coax this feature out of hiding, press Ctrl+spacebar.

Generating getter and setter methods

Take a look at the following code:

```
textView.setText("Boo!");

StringBuilder str = new StringBuilder(textView.getText());
```

Android's `TextView` class has its own private `text` variable. My examples
can't make direct references to a private variable such as the `text` variable.
(I get an error message if I write `textView.text = "Boo!"` or I write `new
StringBuilder(textView.text)`.) But my code can access the `text`
variable indirectly using the `TextView` class's *getter* and *setter* methods.

The folks who created Android coded getter and setter methods in the declaration of the `TextView` class:

```
public class TextView {

  private CharSequence text;

  public CharSequence getText() {
    return text;
  }

  public void setText(CharSequence text) {
    this.text = text;
  }

  // Much more code here ...
}
```

As an Android developer, you create many of your own getter and setter methods. Fortunately, you can create them without doing lots of typing. Eclipse can
type these methods for you. The following sections show you how.

Using Code Assist

Eclipse's Code Assist feature can be a great help when creating getter and setter methods. Start within a Java editor and place the cursor inside a class but outside of any method. Type the word **get** and then press Ctrl+spacebar. Code Assist offers to create a getter method for any of your class's fields. The method even includes an appropriate `return` statement.

In the getter method department, Code Assist is very smart. If a field already has a getter method, Code Assist doesn't suggest creating an additional getter.

Of course, everything I say about getters holds true of setters also. To create a setter method, place the cursor inside a class but outside of any method, type **set**, and then press Ctrl+spacebar. The new setter method has its own `this.field = field` statement.

Using menus

If you're partial to using menus rather than the Code Assist feature to create your getter and setter methods, start again in a Java editor and place the cursor anywhere inside a Java class. Then, in Eclipse's main menu, choose Source⇨Generate Getters and Setters. As a result, Eclipse displays a dialog box like the one in Figure 1-21. When you click OK, Eclipse creates the getters and setters whose boxes you've checked.

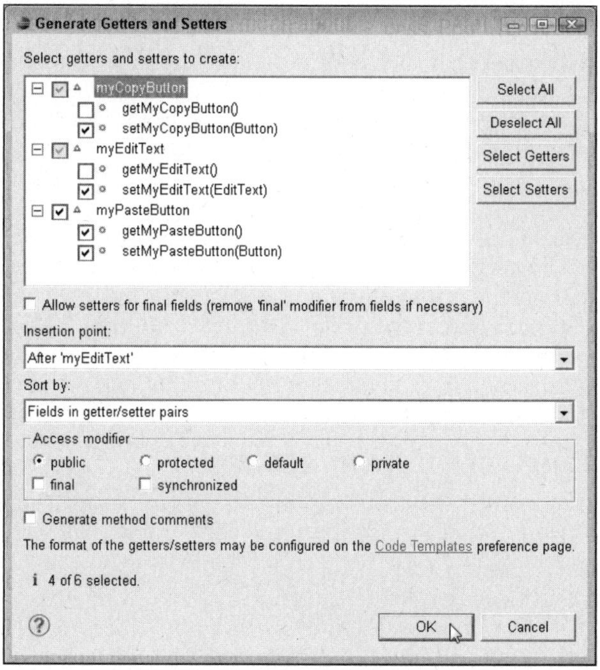

Figure 1-21:
Selecting
getters and
setters.

Renaming things

To change the name of a variable, a method, or something else in a Java program, click your mouse on that name in the editor and then choose Refactor➪Rename. Eclipse waits for you to edit the existing name. After you finish changing the name, press Enter. (To cancel the rename operation, press Esc.)

When you click a name in an editor, you don't have to click the name's defining occurrence. You can click anywhere in your code where the name occurs. After you edit the name, Eclipse changes all occurrences of that name in your project.

Eclipse is smart enough not to change identical names that have different meanings. For example, if a setter method contains the statement `this.myButton = myButton`, renaming `this.myButton` changes your class's field name. But renaming `myButton` on the right side of the assignment changes only the name of the method-local variable.

Creating Android strings

You're vigorously typing Java code (after having planned and designed the code carefully, of course), and you type a statement that includes a string literal:

```
button.setText("Click me!");
```

Then you remember that Java code shouldn't contain hard-coded strings. You should change `"Click me!"` to something like `R.string.click` and add a string tag to your `res/values/strings.xml` file. Then your French-speaking users grab data from a different `strings.xml` file — a file in which `R.string.click` refers to the text `"Cliquez-moi!"`

Eclipse's Android Development Tools plug-in provides a quick and easy way to turn a hard-coded string literal into an externalized Android string. Select any part of the string literal in the Java code editor. Then, in Eclipse's main menu, choose Refactor➪Android➪Extract Android String. After a brief encounter with the options in the Extract Android String dialog box, your string literal is turned into an element in `strings.xml`.

Using other refactoring actions

Eclipse comes with a host of refactoring actions for your Java code. For example, with a few menu selections, you can turn several lines of code into a separate method. You can create an interface from an existing class. You can even add generic type arguments to an old-fashioned raw collection type declaration. (Eclipse makes educated guesses about the generic argument types.)

To experiment with Eclipse's refactoring features, choose Refactor from Eclipse's main menu and start exploring.

The Organize Imports action

Eclipse has a cool Source⇨Organize Imports action. Many good things happen when you go to Eclipse's main menu and choose Source⇨Organize Imports:

✦ **Eclipse removes any import declarations that you don't use.**

If your code starts with

```
import android.widget.EditText;
```

but you never use an `EditText`, Eclipse deletes the `EditText` import declaration.

✦ **Eclipse adds any missing import declarations.**

If your code includes

```
((EditText) findViewById(R.id.editText1))
```

but you have no import declaration for `EditText`, Eclipse adds

```
import android.widget.EditText;
```

near the top of your code. I've even seen Eclipse uncomment a declaration that I'd commented out earlier.

✦ **Eclipse sorts your code's import declarations.**

By default, Eclipse sorts your declarations so that `java` packages come first, then the `javax` packages, then the `org` packages, then the `android` packages, and finally the `com` packages. Within each category, Eclipse sorts declarations alphabetically. (That way, the declarations are easy to find.)

Of course, you can change the sorting order. Visit the Java⇨Code Style⇨ Organize Imports page of the Window⇨Preferences dialog box. Move names up in the list, move names down in the list, add names, or remove names. It's all up to you.

✦ **Eclipse tries to eliminate import-on-demand declarations.**

Eclipse changes

```
import android.widget.*;
```

into something like

```
import android.widget.Button;
import android.widget.CheckBox;
import android.widget.ListView;
import android.widget.SimpleAdapter;
import android.widget.Toast;
```

using only the class names that you already use in your code.

Oops!

You notice some tiny icons on the left edge of the Java editor. (See Figure 1-22.) Each icon contains an X surrounded by a red shape and possibly a light bulb. These icons are *error markers,* and the whole left edge of the editor is a *marker bar.* Besides error markers, several other kinds of markers can appear in the editor's marker bar.

Figure 1-22:
Oh, no!
An error
marker!

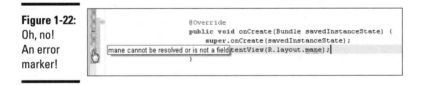

Each error marker represents a place in the code where Eclipse finds a compile-time error. The error in Figure 1-22 is the use of word `mane` (as opposed to `main`). If you find such an error, you can either retype **main**, or you can use Eclipse's Quick Fix feature. Here's how:

1. **Right-click the error marker, and in the resulting context menu, choose Quick Fix.**

A list with one or more alternatives appears. Each alternative represents a different way of fixing the compile-time error. When you highlight an alternative, another box shows what the revised code (after that alternative is applied) would look like, as shown in Figure 1-23.

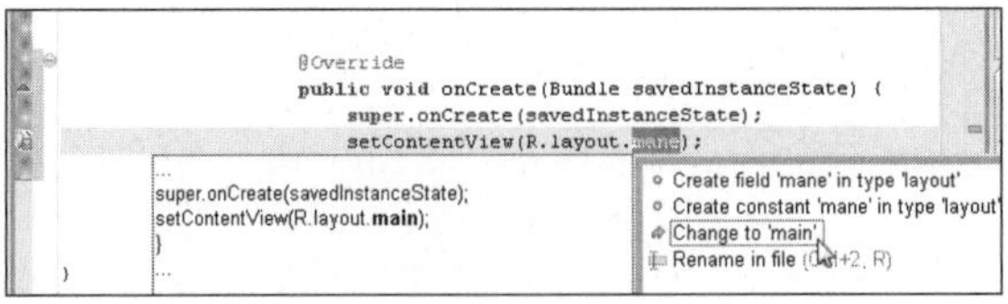

Figure 1-23:
Eclipse lets
you choose
among
several
quick fixes.

```
                    @Override
        public void onCreate(Bundle savedInstanceState) {
            super.onCreate(savedInstanceState);
            setContentView(R.layout.mane);

...                                          ○ Create field 'mane' in type 'layout'
super.onCreate(savedInstanceState);          ○ Create constant 'mane' in type 'layout'
setContentView(R.layout.main);               ✎ Change to 'main'
}                                            ↓≡ Rename in file (Ctrl+2, R)
...
```

2. **Double-click the alternative that you want to apply; or if you like using the keyboard, you can highlight the alternative and then press Enter.**

Eclipse rewrites your code, and the error marker goes away. What a cool feature!

In Figures 1-22 and 1-23, the error marker contains a tiny light bulb. The light bulb reminds you that Eclipse may have some Quick Fix ideas. If you don't see the bulb, Eclipse has no ideas. But occasionally, even though you see the little bulb, Eclipse doesn't have a clue. Okay, I can live with that.

Some Things You Can Do with Eclipse Projects

Eclipse has gazillions of features for managing Java and Android projects. So in this minibook, I'll do my best, but I can't cover every feature out there. I devote about five pages to the subject. Here goes!

Importing code

Importing code here means bringing somebody else's code into your own Eclipse project or bringing your own code (created with or without Eclipse) into an Eclipse project.

You have two import techniques to choose between. You can drag and drop, or you can use the Import Wizard.

Using drag and drop

As an importing technique, dragging and dropping works only with the Windows operating system. In addition, this technique is like a blunt instrument. The technique imports everything from a particular directory on your hard drive. If you want to import only a few files from a directory, this technique isn't your best bet.

Of course, if you use Windows and you like the intuitive feel of dragging and dropping, this technique is for you. Just drag the folders containing your code from your development computer's file explorer to the appropriate project folder in Eclipse's Package Explorer view.

In the preceding paragraph, I cleverly cover up my own clumsiness by instructing you to drag folders to "the appropriate project folder." I admit it. I forget which folder to drag where. I'm usually off by one level. (I drag either to the parent or to the child of the appropriate folder.) Then my project's directory structure isn't correct, and I see all kinds of red error markers in my code. So I have to drag items from one place to another in the Package Explorer, or delete the stuff that I imported and start dragging and dropping all over again. My brain doesn't process this particular concept of dragging and dropping folders very easily. Who knows? Maybe your brain does a better processing job.

Using the Import Wizard

If you don't use Microsoft Windows or if you want to carefully pick and choose what you import, you can't use drag and drop. Instead, you use the Import Wizard.

How you use the Import Wizard depends on the kind of thing that you want to import. To import an Eclipse project (perhaps from an old, currently unused Eclipse workspace), do the following:

1. **In Eclipse's main menu, choose File⇨Import.**

Eclipse's Import Wizard (magically) appears.

2. **In the General branch of the Import Wizard, click the Existing Projects into Workspace sub-branch. (See Figure 1-24.)**

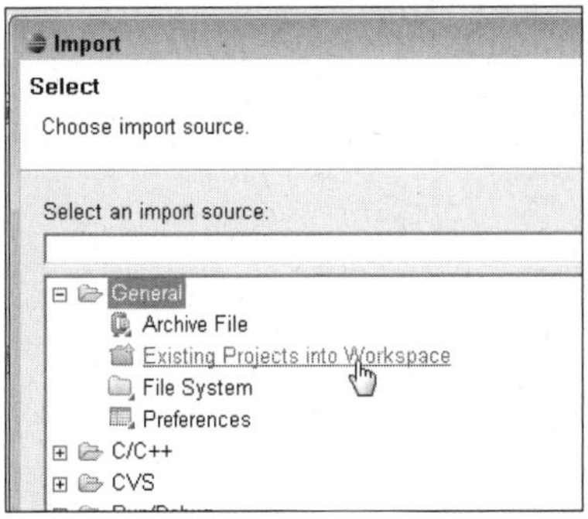

Figure 1-24: Telling Eclipse to import an existing project.

As a result of your clicking the Existing Projects into Workspace sub-branch, another Import dialog box (the Import Projects dialog box) appears.

3. **In the Import Projects dialog box, click the Select Root Directory radio button, and use the Browse button to locate a folder containing one or more Eclipse projects (projects that aren't in your current Eclipse workspace).**

An Eclipse *project* includes source code and other stuff. This "other stuff" includes the `.project` and `.classpath` files that you hardly ever notice inside an Eclipse project's folder.

To be considered an existing Eclipse project, a folder must contain a file named `.project`.

After you browse to a folder, Eclipse lists any and all projects that it finds in that folder. (See Figure 1-25.)

4. **Put check marks in the boxes next to each of the projects that you want Eclipse to import. (Again, see Figure 1-25.)**

5. **Put a check mark in the Copy Projects into Workspace box. (Or don't!)**

    If you check this box, Eclipse creates a new copy of your project inside your current workspace. Anything you do to that new copy has no effect on the original folder from which you imported projects. In other words, you have an easily accessible backup copy of the project.

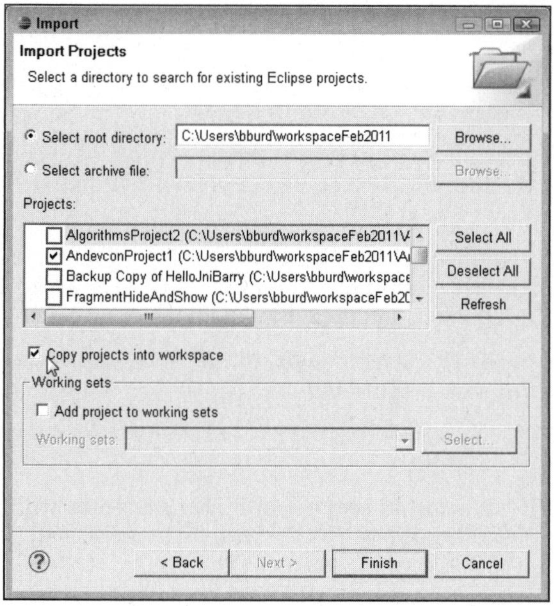

Figure 1-25:
Selecting one or more existing projects.

If you don't check this box, Eclipse doesn't make a new copy of the project. Instead, Eclipse works directly on whatever folder originally contained the projects. So whatever changes you make to the project's files affect the folder from which you imported projects. In other words, you have no easily accessible backup copy.

6. **In the Import Projects dialog box, click the Finish button.**

   That's it! Eclipse adds a new project to the Package Explorer's tree.

To import files or folders into your current Eclipse project, do this:

1. **In Eclipse's Package Explorer, select the *destination* folder (the folder that will contain the imported files).**

2. **In Eclipse's main menu, choose File⇨Import.**

   The Import Wizard appears (refer to Figure 1-24).

3. **In the Import Wizard, click either the Archive File option or the File System option.**

   An Import dialog box appears.

   Your choice of Archive File or File System depends on the location of the stuff that you want to import. Click Archive File if the stuff is inside a compressed file (a `.zip` file, a `.tar.gz` file, or something like that). Select File System if the stuff you want to import isn't inside a compressed file.

4. **In the Import dialog box, browse to the folder or to the archive file containing things that you want to import.**

   After browsing, two large panels in the Import dialog box display the subfolders and files inside your selected folder or archive file. (See Figure 1-26.)

   Sometimes you have to coax the Import dialog box's two large panels to display your folder's or archive file's contents. You "coax" the panels by clicking your mouse inside the leftmost panel.

5. **In the lists inside the large panels, put a check mark next to any folder or any file that you want to import.**

   In Figure 1-26, I put check marks next to the `com` folder and most of the files in the `res` folder.

6. **(Optional) If you want to import subfolder names as well as files, select the Create Complete Folder Structure check box.**

7. **Click Finish.**

   The Import dialog box disappears. The tree in Eclipse's Package Explorer view contains new entries.

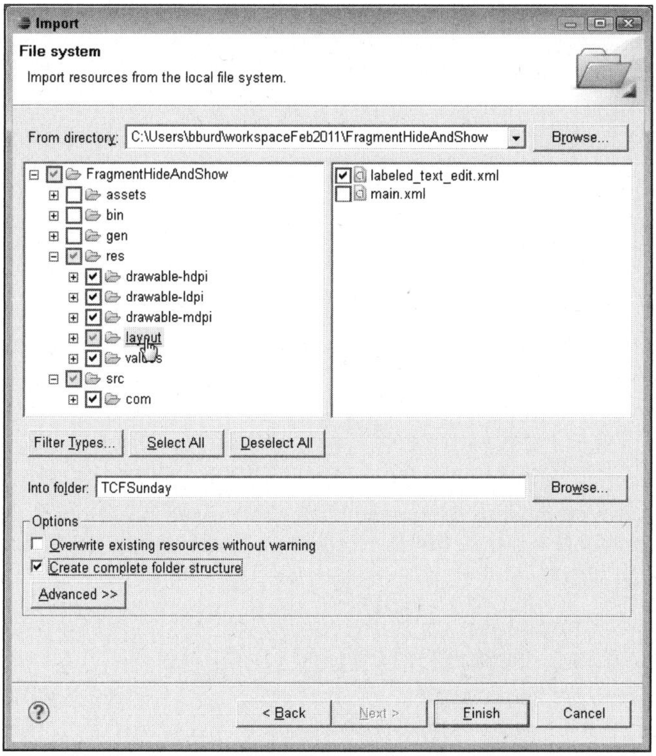

Figure 1-26:
The Import
dialog box.

Creating a run configuration

A *run configuration* is a set of guidelines that Eclipse uses for running an application. A particular run configuration stores the name of the project to be launched, the target Android platform (Gingerbread, Honeycomb, or whatever), and many other facts about an app's anticipated run.

Whenever you run an app, Eclipse uses one run configuration or another. If you don't create a custom run configuration, Eclipse uses a default configuration. Default is nice, but sometimes you want to micromanage the way your app runs on an emulator or on a device. So in this section, you get to create a customized run configuration. Here's how you do it:

1. **Right-click an Android project's branch in the Package Explorer view (or if you're a Mac user, Control-click).**

2. **In the resulting context menu, choose Run As⇨Run Configurations.**

The big Run Configurations dialog box appears.

3. **Click the New Launch Configuration button in the window's upper-left corner. (See Figure 1-27.)**

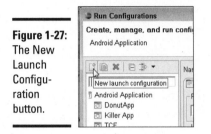

Figure 1-27:
The New Launch Configuration button.

A new branch (with a label like New_configuration) appears in the panel on the left side of the Run Configurations dialog box.

4. **In the main body of the Run Configurations dialog box, enter an informative name for your new configuration in the Name field. (See Figure 1-28.)**

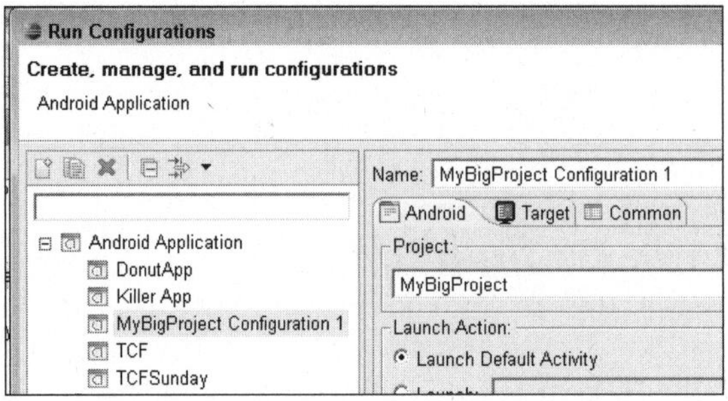

Figure 1-28:
Adding some information about your custom configuration.

5. **In the Project field of the Android tab (again, in the main body of the Run Configurations dialog box), type the name of the project this configuration applies to. (And again, see Figure 1-28.)**

6. **In the main body of the Run Configurations dialog box, click Apply.**

7. **Still in the main body of the Run Configurations dialog box, click the Target tab.**

The Run Configurations dialog box looks something like Figure 1-29.

8. **Change any (or none) of the default options in the Target tab.**

In Figure 1-29, I specify which of my emulators will run the application (the emulator named GingerbreadWithSDImage). I also supply the `-no-boot-anim` option for the startup of the emulator. (The `-no-boot-anim` option tells the emulator not to waste time displaying a glimmering rendition of the word *Android.*)

For more emulator options, visit `http://developer.android.com/guide/developing/tools/emulator.html`.

9. **In the main body of the Run Configurations dialog box, click Apply.**

10. **After doing all the tinkering you want to do with the Run Configurations dialog box, click Run or Close.**

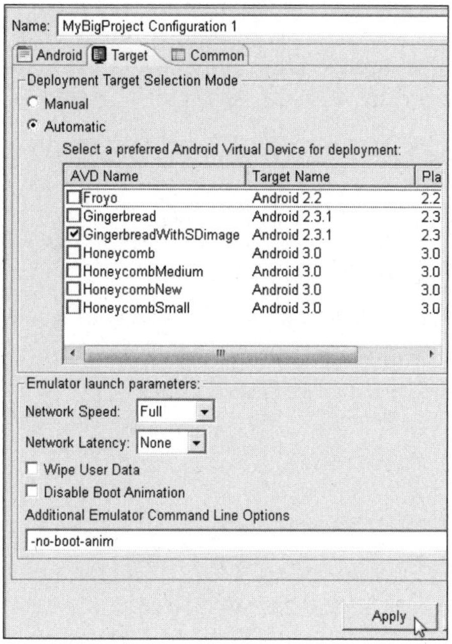

Name: | MyBigProject Configuration 1

☐ Android | 🖳 Target | ☐ Common

Deployment Target Selection Mode
○ Manual
◉ Automatic

Select a preferred Android Virtual Device for deployment:

AVD Name	Target Name	Pla
☐ Froyo	Android 2.2	2.2
☐ Gingerbread	Android 2.3.1	2.3
☑ GingerbreadWithSDimage	Android 2.3.1	2.3
☐ Honeycomb	Android 3.0	3.0
☐ HoneycombMedium	Android 3.0	3.0
☐ HoneycombNew	Android 3.0	3.0
☐ HoneycombSmall	Android 3.0	3.0

Emulator launch parameters:

Network Speed: | Full | ▼

Network Latency: | None | ▼

☐ Wipe User Data
☐ Disable Boot Animation

Additional Emulator Command Line Options

| -no-boot-anim |

Apply

Figure 1-29:
The Run Con-
figurations
dialog box's
Target tab.

The Run and Close buttons appear in the bottom-right corner of the Run Configurations dialog box. Clicking Run launches your project with the newly created configuration. Clicking Close saves the new configuration without launching the project.

Your custom run configuration becomes the default for whichever project you select in Step 5. So the next time you run this project, you can launch your project the easy way. To launch with your custom configuration, simply right-click the project's Package Explorer branch and choose Run As➪Android Application.

Adding extra stuff to a project's build path

In Java, a .jar file is a zipped collection of classes and other stuff. It's a bunch of goodies compressed into one file using the same compression method that .zip files use. A .jar file contains classes that you need in order to run one or more applications. For example, a file named junit.jar contains classes for running Java JUnit tests.

Depending on your mood, .jar stands for either *Java AR*chive or for a jar full of Java coffee beans.

JUnit is a cool software testing tool. For more information about JUnit, visit http://Junit.org/.

As you might have guessed already, you can add a .jar file to an Eclipse project. That way, you can use the .jar file's classes in your project's code. Here's how you do it:

1. **Select a project in Eclipse's Package Explorer.**

2. **In Eclipse's main menu, choose Project➪Properties.**

Eclipse displays the project's Properties dialog box. (Big surprise!) You can see a Properties dialog box in Figure 1-30.

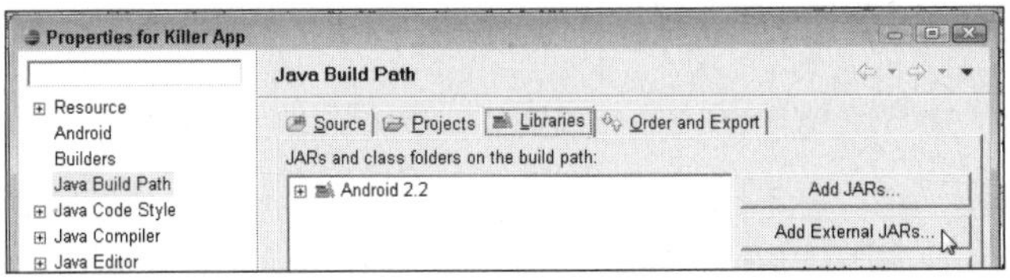

Figure 1-30: A project's Properties dialog box.

3. **In the tree on the left side of the Properties dialog box, click Java Build Path.**

This tree branch stores information about the places Eclipse checks when it compiles your project's code. The Java Build Path contains lots of options. In this section, I narrow down the example to one place Eclipse can check — a .jar file.

4. **In the main body of the Properties dialog box, click the Libraries tab.**

   Some buttons appear on the right side of the dialog box.

5. **Click the Add External JARs button.**

   When you click this button, Eclipse displays your operating system's "open a file" dialog box.

6. **In the "open a file" dialog box, navigate to the location of a .jar file on your development computer.**

   I can't tell you where to find all the .jar files you'll ever need. But if you're following these instructions just to practice adding .jar files, I have a suggestion Look for .jar files in your JAVA_HOME directory. In that directory's lib subdirectory, you'll find a bunch of nice .jar files.

   For help finding your development computer's JAVA_HOME directory, see Book VI, Chapter 3.

7. **Double-click the .jar file of your choice.**

   Lo and behold! The "open a file" dialog box closes, and now your chosen .jar file appears in your project's build path. (To get the result in Figure 1-31, I chose a file named tools.jar.)

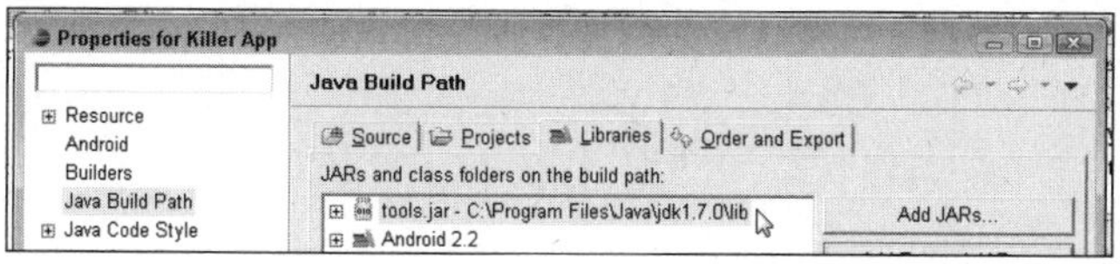

Book II
Chapter 1

Using the Eclipse
Workbench

Figure 1-31:
An
enhanced
Java build
path.

Chapter 2: It's Java!

In This Chapter

✔ How computers, phones and other devices run Java programs

✔ The parts of a typical Java program

*B*efore I became an Android guy, I was a Java guy. A *Java guy* is a person who revels in the workings of Java programs. I wrote Java programs, read about Java programs, went to Java user group meetings, and wore Java t-shirts. That's why I was thrilled to learn that Android's application programming language is Java.

In the early 1990s, James Gosling at Sun Microsystems created Java. He used ideas from many programming language traditions, including the object-oriented concepts in C++. He created an elegant platform with a wide range of uses. In mid-2011 (which is "now" as far as my chapter-writing goes), Java runs on more than 1.1 billion desktop computers,* and Java is the most popular programming language in the TIOBE Programming Community Index (www.tiobe.com/index.php/content/paperinfo/tpci). Do you have a Blu-ray player? Under the hood, your player runs Java.

In this minibook (Book II), this chapter and Chapters 3 and 4 introduce the ins and outs of the Java programming language. But these chapters don't offer a comprehensive guide to Java. (To badly paraphrase Geoffrey Chaucer, "This book never yet no complete not Java coverage.") Instead, these chapters hit the highlights of Java programming. For a more complete introduction to Java, read *Java For Dummies,* 5th Edition (John Wiley & Sons, Inc.). (Yes, I wrote that book, too.)

From Development to Execution with Java

Before Java became popular, most programs went almost directly from the developer's keyboard to the processor's circuits. But Java added an extra translation layer and then Android added yet another layer. This section describes the layers.

---

* *Source:* http://java.com/en/about

What is a compiler?

A Java program (such as an Android application program) goes through several translation steps between the time you write the program and the time a processor runs it. The reason for this is simple: What's convenient for processors to run is not convenient for people to write.

People can write and comprehend the code in Listing 2-1.

Listing 2-1:   Java Source Code

```
public void checkVacancy(View view) {
    if (room.numGuests == 0) {
        label.setText("Available");
    } else {
        label.setText("Taken :-(");
    }
}
```

The Java code in Listing 2-1 checks for a vacancy in a hotel. You can't run the code in Listing 2-1 without adding several lines. But at this stage of the game, those additional lines aren't important. What's important is that by staring at the code, squinting a bit, and looking past all the code's strange punctuation, you can see what the code is trying to do:

```
If the room has no guests in it,
    then set the label's text to "Available".
Otherwise,
    set the label's text to "Taken :-(".
```

The stuff in Listing 2-1 is *Java source code.*

The processors in computers, phones, and other devices don't normally follow instructions like the instructions in Listing 2-1. That is, processors don't follow Java source code instructions. Instead, processors follow cryptic instructions like the ones in Listing 2-2.

Listing 2-2:   Java Bytecode

```
 0 aload_0
 1 getfield #19 <com/allmycode/samples/MyActivity/room
Lcom/allmycode/samples/Room;>
 4 getfield #47 <com/allmycode/samples/Room/numGuests I>
 7 ifne 22 (+15)
10 aload_0
11 getfield #41 <com/allmycode/samples/MyActivity/label
```

```
 Landroid/widget/TextView;>
14 ldc #54 <Available>
16 invokevirtual #56
 <android/widget/TextView/setText(Ljava/lang/CharSequence;)V>
19 goto 31 (+12)
22 aload_0
23 getfield #41 <com/allmycode/samples/MyActivity/label
 Landroid/widget/TextView;>
26 ldc #60 <Taken :-(>
28 invokevirtual #56
 <android/widget/TextView/setText(Ljava/lang/CharSequence;)V>
31 return
```

The instructions in Listing 2-2 aren't Java source code instructions. They're *Java bytecode* instructions. When you write a Java program, you write source code instructions (like the instructions in Listing 2-1). After writing the source code, you run a program (that is, you apply a tool) to your source code. The program is a compiler. The *compiler* translates your source code instructions into Java bytecode instructions. In other words, the compiler takes code that you can write and understand (such as the code in Listing 2-1) and translates your code into code that a computer can execute (such as the code in Listing 2-2).

You might put your source code in a file named HotelActivity. java. If so, the compiler probably puts the Java bytecode in another file named HotelActivity.class. Normally, you don't bother looking at the bytecode in the HotelActivity.class file. In fact, the compiler doesn't encode the HotelActivity.class file as ordinary text, so you can't examine the bytecode with an ordinary editor. If you try to open HotelActivity.class with Notepad, TextEdit, KWrite, or even Microsoft Word, you see nothing but dots, squiggles, and other gobbledygook. To create Listing 2-2, I had to apply yet another tool to my HotelActivity. class file. That tool displays a text-like version of a Java bytecode file. I used Ando Saabas's Java Bytecode Editor (www.cs.ioc.ee/~ando/jbe).

No one (except for a few crazy developers in some isolated labs in faraway places) writes Java bytecode. You run software (a compiler) to create Java bytecode. The only reason to look at Listing 2-2 is to understand what a hard worker your computer is.

If compiling is a good thing, maybe compiling twice is even better. In 2007, Dan Bornstein at Google created *Dalvik bytecode* — another way of representing instructions for processors to follow. (To find out where some of Bornstein's ancestors come from, run your favorite Map application and look for Dalvik in Iceland.) Dalvik bytecode is optimized for the limited resources on a phone or a tablet device. Listing 2-3 contains some sample Dalvik instructions.*

---

* To see the code in Listing 2-3, I used the Dedexer program. See http://dedexer. sourceforge.net.

Listing 2-3:   Dalvik Bytecode

```
.method public checkVacancy(Landroid/view/View;)V
.limit registers 4
; this: v2 (Lcom/allmycode/samples/MyActivity;)
; parameter[0] : v3 (Landroid/view/View;)
.line 30
    iget-object
    v0,v2,com/allmycode/samples/MyActivity.room
    Lcom/allmycode/samples/Room;
; v0 : Lcom/allmycode/samples/Room; , v2 :
    Lcom/allmycode/samples/MyActivity;
    iget     v0,v0,com/allmycode/samples/Room.numGuests I
; v0 : single-length , v0 : single-length
    if-nez    v0,14b4
; v0 : single-length
.line 31
    iget-object
    v0,v2,com/allmycode/samples/MyActivity.label
    Landroid/widget/TextView;
; v0 : Landroid/widget/TextView; , v2 :
    Lcom/allmycode/samples/MyActivity;
    const-string    v1,"Available"
; v1 : Ljava/lang/String;
    invoke-virtual
    {v0,v1},android/widget/TextView/setText
    ; setText(Ljava/lang/CharSequence;)V
; v0 : Landroid/widget/TextView; , v1 : Ljava/lang/String;
14b2:
.line 36
    return-void
14b4:
.line 33
    iget-object
    v0,v2,com/allmycode/samples/MyActivity.label
    Landroid/widget/TextView;
; v0 : Landroid/widget/TextView; , v2 :
    Lcom/allmycode/samples/MyActivity;
    const-string    v1,"Taken :-("
; v1 : Ljava/lang/String;
    invoke-virtual
    {v0,v1},android/widget/TextView/setText ;
    setText(Ljava/lang/CharSequence;)V
; v0 : Landroid/widget/TextView; , v1 : Ljava/lang/String;
    goto     14b2
.end method
```

Java bytecode instructions use a *stack machine* format. In contrast, Dalvik bytecode instructions use a *register machine* format. The upshot of this (for those who don't know much about machine language formats) is that a typical Dalvik instruction is longer and more complicated than a Java bytecode instruction. Despite what you see in Listings 2-2 and 2-3, a big Dalvik instruction normally replaces several little Java bytecode instructions.

When you create an Android app, Eclipse performs at least two compilations. The first compilation creates Java bytecode from your Java source files. (Your source filenames have the `.java` extension; the Java bytecode filename have the `.class` extension.) The second compilation creates Dalvik bytecode from your Java bytecode files. (Dalvik bytecode filenames have the `.dex` extension.) To perform the first compilation, Eclipse uses a program named *javac,* or the *Java compiler.* To perform the second compilation, Eclipse uses a program named *dx* (known affectionately as *the dx tool).*

What is a virtual machine?

In the earlier "What is a compiler?" section, I make a big fuss about phones and other devices following instructions like the ones in Listing 2-3. As fusses go, it's a very nice fuss. But if you don't read every fussy word, you may be misguided. The exact wording is "... processors follow cryptic instructions *like* the ones in Listing *blah-blah-blah.*" The instructions in Listing 2-3 are a lot like instructions that a phone or tablet can execute, but in general, computers don't execute Java bytecode instructions, and phones don't execute Dalvik bytecode instructions. Instead, each kind of processor has its own set of executable instructions, and each operating system uses the processor's instructions in a slightly different way.

Imagine that you have two different devices — a smartphone and a tablet computer. The devices have two different kinds of processors. The phone has an ARM processor, and the tablet has an Intel Atom processor. (The acronym *ARM* once stood for *Advanced RISC Machine.* These days, *ARM* simply stands for ARM Holdings, a company whose employees design processors.) On the ARM processor, the *multiply* instruction is *000000.* On an Intel processor, the *multiply* instructions are D8, DC, F6, F7, and others. Many ARM instructions have no counterparts in the Atom architecture, and many Atom instructions have no equivalents on an ARM processor. An ARM processor's instructions make no sense to your tablet's Atom processor, and an Atom processor's instructions would give your phone's ARM processor a virtual headache.

So what's a developer to do? Does a developer provide translations of every app into every processor's instruction set? No.

Virtual machines create order from all this chaos. Dalvik bytecode is something like the code in Listing 2-3, but Dalvik bytecode isn't specific to one kind of processor or to one operating system. Instead, a set of Dalvik bytecode instructions runs on any processor. If you write a Java program and compile that Java program into Dalvik bytecode, your Android phone, your Android tablet, and even your grandmother's supercomputer can run the bytecode. (To do this, your grandmother must install *Android-x86,* a special port of the Android operating system, on her Intel-based machine.)

For a look at some Dalvik bytecode, look back at Listing 2-3. But remember, you never have to write or decipher Dalvik bytecode. Writing bytecode is the compiler's job. Deciphering bytecode is the virtual machine's job.

Both Java bytecode and Dalvik bytecode have virtual machines. With the Dalvik virtual machine, you can take a bytecode file that you created for one Android device, copy the bytecode to another Android device, and then run the bytecode with no trouble at all. That's one of the many reasons why Android has become popular so quickly. This outstanding feature, which gives you the ability to run code on many different kinds of computers, is called *portability.*

Imagine that you're the Intel representative to the United Nations Security Council. (See Figure 2-1.) The ARM representative is seated to your right, and the representative from Texas Instruments is on your left. (Naturally, you don't get along with either of these people. You're always cordial to one another, but you're never sincere. What do you expect? It's politics!) The distinguished representative from Dalvik is at the podium. The Dalvik representative speaks in Dalvik bytecode, and neither you nor your fellow ambassadors (ARM and Texas Instruments) understand a word of Dalvik bytecode.

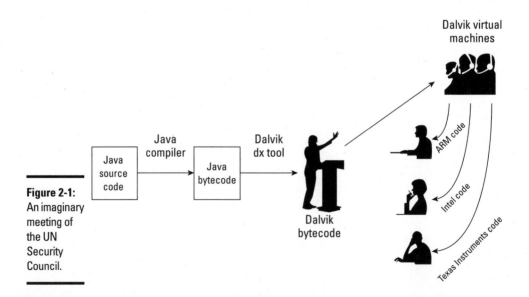

Figure 2-1: An imaginary meeting of the UN Security Council.

But each of you has an interpreter. Your interpreter translates from Dalvik bytecode to Intel instructions as the Dalvik representative speaks. Another interpreter translates from bytecode to ARM-ese. And a third interpreter translates bytecode into Texas Instruments speak.

Think of your interpreter as a virtual ambassador. The interpreter doesn't really represent your country, but the interpreter performs one of the important tasks that a real ambassador performs. The interpreter listens to Dalvik bytecode on your behalf. The interpreter does what you would do if your native language was Dalvik bytecode. The interpreter pretends to be the Intel ambassador and sits through the boring bytecode speech, taking in every word, and processing each word in some way or other.

You have an interpreter — a virtual ambassador. In the same way, an Intel processor runs its own bytecode interpreting software. That software is the Dalvik virtual machine.

A *Dalvik virtual machine* is a proxy, an errand boy, a go-between. The virtual machine serves as an interpreter between Dalvik's run-anywhere bytecode and your device's own system. As it runs, the virtual machine walks your device through the execution of bytecode instructions. The virtual machine examines your bytecode, bit by bit, and carries out the instructions described in the bytecode. The virtual machine interprets bytecode for your ARM processor, your Intel processor, your Texas Instruments chip, or whatever kind of processor you're using. That's a good thing. It's what makes Java code and Dalvik code more portable than code written in any other language.

**Book II
Chapter 2**

It's Java!

Grasping Java Code

When you create a new project, Android's tools create a small, no-nonsense Java class. I've copied the Java class in Listing 2-4.

Listing 2-4:   A Minimalistic Android Activity Class

```
package com.allmycode.samples;

import android.app.Activity;
import android.os.Bundle;

public class MyActivity extends Activity {
    /** Called when the activity is first created. */
    @Override
    public void onCreate(Bundle savedInstanceState) {
        super.onCreate(savedInstanceState);
        setContentView(R.layout.main);
    }
}
```

This chapter covers the Java language features used in Listing 2-4. So in this chapter, `android.app.Activity` (from the second line of Listing 2-4) is only the name of something to import — nothing more. To read all about the listing's implications for Android, see Book III, Chapter 1.

The Java class

Java is an object-oriented programming language. So, as a developer, your primary goal is to describe objects. Your closely related goal is to describe objects' close cousins —; namely, classes.

In Java, nothing happens unless it happens inside an object or a class. The code in Listing 2-4 is a class. I created the code, so I get to make up a name for my new class. I chose the name `MyActivity` because the code in Listing 2-4 describes one screen full of stuff on an Android device (and in Android, a screen full of stuff is an *activity*). So the code in Listing 2-4 contains the words `public class MyActivity`.

The words *public* and *class* are Java keywords. What that means is that no matter who writes a Java program, the word *class* always has the same meaning. The same holds true of the word *public* (although some classes aren't declared to be `public`).

On the other hand, the word *MyActivity* in Listing 2-4 is an identifier. I made up the word *MyActivity* while I was writing this chapter. The word *MyActivity* is the name of a particular class — the class that I'm creating by writing this program.

tHE jAVA PROGRAMMING LANGUAGE IS cASe-sEnsITiVE. iF YOU CHANGE A lowercase LETTER IN A WORD TO AN UPPERCASE LETTER, YOU CHANGE THE WORD'S MEANING.

If you define a public class named `DogAndPony`, the class's Java code must go in a file named `DogAndPony.java`, spelled and capitalized exactly the same way as the class name is spelled and capitalized. If you define a class named `MySecretStuff`, and if you write `class MySecretStuff` instead of `public class MySecretStuff`, you can put the `MySecretStuff` code in any file whose extension is `.java`. (Go ahead. Call your file `Urkshjk98t.java`. See if I care.)

Classes and objects

When you program in Java, you work constantly with classes and objects. Here's an analogy: A chair has a seat, a back, and legs. Each seat has a shape, a color, a degree of softness, and so on. These are the properties that a chair possesses. What I describe is *chairness* — the notion of something being a chair. In object-oriented terminology, I'm describing the `Chair` class.

In the preceding paragraph, I refer to the `Chair` class, not to the `chair` class. If you want to look like a very inexperienced developer, start the names of your Java classes with lowercase letters. With a class name such as `chair`, your code does what you want it to do, but you're committing a stylistic faux pas. Real Java developers start the names of their classes with uppercase letters.

Now peek over the edge of this book's margin and take a minute to look around your room. (If you're not sitting in a room right now, fake it.)

Several chairs are in the room, and each chair is an object. Each of these objects is an example of that ethereal thing called the `Chair` class. So that's how it works — the class is the idea of *chairness,* and each individual chair is an *object.*

A class isn't quite a collection of things. Instead, a class is the idea behind a certain kind of thing. When I talk about the class of chairs in your room, I'm talking about the fact that each chair has legs, a seat, a color, and so on. The colors may be different for different chairs in the room, but that doesn't matter. When you talk about a class of things, you're focusing on the properties that each of the things possesses.

It makes sense to think of an object as being a concrete instance of a class. In fact, the official terminology is consistent with this thinking. If you write a Java program in which you define a `Chair` class, each actual chair (the chair that you're sitting on, the empty chair right next to you, and so on) is called an *instance* of the `Chair` class.

Here's another way to think about a class. Imagine a table displaying three bank accounts. (See Table 2-1.)

Table 2-1	A Table of Accounts	
Name	*Address*	*Balance*
Barry Burd	222 Cyberspace Lane	24.02
John Q. Public	140 Any Way	−471.03
Jane Dough	800 Rich Street	247.38

Think of the table's column headings as a class, and think of each row of the table as an object. The table's column headings describe the `Account` class.

According to the table's column headings, each account has a name, an address, and a balance. Rephrased in the terminology of object-oriented programming, each object in the `Account` class (that is, each instance of the

`Account` class) has a name, an address, and a balance. So, the bottom row of the table is an object with the name `Jane Dough`. This same object has address *800 Rich Street* and a balance of *247.38*. If you opened a new account, you would have another object, and the table would grow an additional row. The new object would be an instance of the same `Account` class.

Java types

What does "six" mean? You can have six children, but you can also be six feet tall. With six children, you know exactly how many kids you have. (Unlike the average American family, you can't have 2.5 kids.) But if you're six feet tall, you could really be six feet and half an inch tall. Or you might be five feet eleven-and-three-quarter inches tall, and no one would argue about it.

A value's meaning depends on the value's *type*. If you write

```
int numberOfChildren = 6;
```

in a Java program, 6 means "exactly six." But if you write

```
double height = 6;
```

in a Java program, 6 means "as close to six as you care to measure." And if you write

```
char keystroke = '6';
```

in a Java program, `'6'` means "the digit that comes after the 5 digit."

In a Java program, every value has a *type*. Java has eight *primitive* types (types that are built into the language) and has as many *reference* types as you want to create.

Table 2-2 lists Java's eight primitive types.

Table 2-2	Java's Primitive Types	
Type Name	*What a Literal Looks Like*	*Range of Values*
Whole number types		
byte	(byte)42	−128 to 127
short	(short)42	−32768 to 32767
int	42	−2147483648 to 2147483647
long	42L	−9223372036854775808 to 9223372036854775807

Type Name	What a Literal Looks Like	Range of Values
Decimal number types		
float	42.0F	-3.4×10^{38} to 3.4×10^{38}
double	42.0	-1.8×10^{308} to 1.8×10^{308}
Character type		
char	'A'	Thousands of characters, glyphs, and symbols
Logical type		
boolean	true	true, false

A *literal* is an expression whose value doesn't change from one Java program to another. For example, the expression 42 means "the int value 42" in every Java program. Likewise, the expression 'B' means "the second upper-case letter in the Roman alphabet" in every Java program, and the word true means "the opposite of false" in every Java program.

In addition to its primitive types, Java has *reference types*. The code in Listing 2-4 contains the names of three reference types.

✦ **The reference type android.app.Activity is defined in the Android API (Android's enormous library of ready-made declarations).**

✦ **The reference type android.os.Bundle is also defined in the Android API.**

✦ **The reference type MyActivity is defined in Listing 2-4.**

How about that? Every class is a type!

When you write int numberOfChildren = 6, you declare the existence of a variable named numberOfChildren. The variable numberOfChildren has type int and has initial value 6.

But in Listing 2-4, android.os.Bundle is also a type (a reference type). In fact android.os.Bundle is the name of a class that's declared as part of Android's API. So just as you can write int numberOfChildren in a Java program, you can write Bundle savedInstanceState in Listing 2-4. (You can abbreviate android.os.Bundle to the simpler name Bundle because of the import declaration near the top of Listing 2-4.)

Because every class is a type, and because your newly declared MyActivity type is a class, you can add a line such as

```
MyActivity anActivity;
```

to the code in Listing 2-4. This new line declares that the name `anActivity` is a placeholder for a value (a value whose type is `MyActivity`). In case this idea muddies your mind, Listing 2-5 has another example.

Listing 2-5:   A Class Is a Type

```
public class Account {
    String name;
    String address;
    double balance;
}

Account myAccount = new Account();
Account yourAccount = new Account();

myAccount.name = "Burd";
yourAccount.name = "Dough";
myAccount.balance = 24.02;
```

Listing 2-5 doesn't contain a complete Java program. If you try to run the code in Listing 2-5 (without first adding some other stuff to the code), you get all kinds of error messages.

Listing 2-5 declares a class named `Account`. This blueprint for an account has three *fields*. The first field — the `name` field — refers to a Java `String` (a bunch of characters lined up in a row). The second field — the `address` field — refers to another Java `String`. The third field — the `balance` field — stores a `double` value. (See Table 2-2.)

A *class* is "the idea behind a certain kind of thing." (I quote myself frequently.) An *object* is "a concrete instance of a class." So in Listing 2-5, the variable `myAccount` refers to an actual `Account` object, and the variable `yourAccount` refers to another `Account` object. The last statement in Listing 2-5 assigns the value `24.02` to the `balance` field of the object referred to by `myAccount`.

The Java method

A *method* is a chunk of code that performs some actions and (possibly) produces a result. If you've written programs in other languages, you may know about functions, procedures, Sub procedures, or other such things. In Java, such things are called *methods*.

In Listing 2-4, the code

```
public void onCreate(Bundle savedInstanceState) {
    super.onCreate(savedInstanceState);
    setContentView(R.layout.main);
}
```

declares the existence of a method. The method's name is `onCreate`.

Real Java developers start the names of their methods with lowercase letters. You can ignore this convention. But if you ignore it, real Java developers will wince when they read your code.

Somewhere, buried deep inside the Dalvik virtual machine's caverns, lives a line of code that looks something like this:

```
onCreate(savedInstanceState);
```

That line of code *calls* the onCreate method of Listing 2-4. In other words, when the Dalvik virtual machine executes its onCreate(savedInstanceState) statement, the flow of execution jumps to the first instruction inside the Listing 2-4 onCreate method declaration.

A method declaration goes hand in hand with one or more calls. A method's declaration (such as the onCreate declaration in Listing 2-4) defines the actions that a method eventually performs. The method doesn't perform any of its actions until some other piece of code executes a call to that method.

The onCreate method's call hides inside some unseen Dalvik code. This situation isn't typical of methods and their calling statements. As an Android developer, you routinely declare a method in one part of your program and then call your own method in another part of the program.

The statements inside a method's declaration are collectively called the *method body*. The onCreate method's body contains two statements (two instructions). The second statement, setContentView(R.layout.main), is a call to a method named setContentView. (The setContentView method's declaration comes with every Android implementation, so you don't declare the setContentView method yourself.)

Like any method call, the call setContentView(R.layout.main) starts with a method name. The stuff in parentheses after the method's name is a *parameter list*. For insight into parameter lists, consider the code in Listing 2-6.

Listing 2-6:   A Method and Two Method Calls

```
double monthlyPayment(double principal,
                      double percentageRate,
                      int years) {

  int numPayments = 12 * years;
  double rate = percentageRate / 100.00;
  double effectiveRate = rate / 12;
  return principal * (effectiveRate /
    (1 - Math.pow(1 + effectiveRate, -numPayments)));
}

double myPayment = monthlyPayment(100000.00, 5.25, 30);

double yourPayment = monthlyPayment(100000.00, 5.00, 15);
```

The code in Listing 2-6 isn't a complete Java program. You can't run the code without adding a bunch of stuff to it. Even so, the code illustrates some important ideas about methods and their parameters.

✦ **The name of the method declared in Listing 2-6 is `monthlyPayment`.**

✦ **In the body of the `monthlyPayment` method declaration, the processor computes the monthly payments on a mortgage.**

You can follow this description of methods and method parameters without understanding anything about the calculations in Listing 2-6.

✦ **The body of the `monthlyPayment` method uses certain names as placeholders.**

For example, in the body of the `montlyPayment` method, the name `years` stands for the number of years in the mortgage's term. Likewise, the name `principal` stands for the total amount borrowed.

✦ **Some placeholders appear in parentheses at the beginning of the method's declaration.**

The names `principal`, `percentageRate` and `years` are the method's *parameters*. Each parameter is destined to stand for a particular value. But a parameter doesn't stand for a value until an app executes a method call.

In Listing 2-6, the call `monthlyPayment(100000.00, 5.25, 30)` gives the method's first parameter (namely, `principal`) the value `100000.00`. That same call gives the method's second parameter (`percentageRate`) the value `5.25`. Finally, that method call gives the method's third parameter (`years`) the value `30`.

The next method call in Listing 2-6 gives the `monthlyPayment` method's parameters different values (again `100000.00` for `principal`, but `5.00` for `percentageRate` and `15` for `years`). Each time you call a method, you supply values for the method's parameters.

✦ **The types of parameters in a method call must match the types of the parameters in a method declaration.**

The declaration of method `monthlyPayment` in Listing 2-6 has a `double` parameter (`principal`), another `double` parameter (`percentage Rate`), and an `int` parameter (`years`). Accordingly, the first method call in Listing 2-6 has two `double` parameters (`100000.00` and `5.25`) followed by an `int` parameter (`30`). The second method call in Listing 2-6 also has two `double` parameters followed by an `int` parameter.

You can declare the same method more than once, as long as each declaration has a different parameter list. For example, another method declaration in Listing 2-6 might have the same name `monthly Payment` but only two parameters: `double monthlyPayment(double principal, double percentageRate)`. To call this alternative `monthlyPayment` method, you write something like `monthlyPayment`

(100000.00, 5.25). In this situation, the body of the alternative monthlyPayment method probably contains a statement like years = 30. You don't call this two-parameter method unless you know that the mortgage's term is 30 years.

✦ **A method call might stand for a value.**

The first method call in Listing 2-6 (in the listing's next-to-last line) stands for the double value 552.20 (or a value very close to the number 552.20). The value 552.20 comes from all the calculations in the body of the monthlyPayment method when the principal is 100000.00, the percentageRate is 5.25, and the number of years is 30. Near the end of the monthlyPayment method's body, the formula

```
principal * (effectiveRate /
    (1 - Math.pow(1 + effectiveRate, -numPayments)))
```

**Book II
Chapter 2**

It's Java!

has the value 552.20, and the word return says "send 552.20 back to the statement that called this method." So, in Listing 2-6, the end of the monthlyPayment method body effectively says

```
return 552.20;
```

and the next-to-last line in the listing effectively says

```
double myPayment = 552.20;
```

Similarly, the second method call in Listing 2-6 (the listing's last line) stands for the value 790.79. Because of the second method call's parameter values, the end of the monthlyPayment method body effectively says

```
return 790.79;
```

and the next-to-last line in the listing effectively says

```
double yourPayment = 790.79;
```

✦ **A method's declaration begins (much of the time) with the name of the return type.**

In Listing 2-6, the monthlyPayment method declaration begins with the type name double. That's good because the value returned at the end of the method's body (either 552.20 or 790.79) is of type double. Also, the names myPayment and yourPayment store double values, so it's okay to assign the value of the call monthlyPayment(100000.00, 5.25, 30) to myPayment, and to assign the value of the call monthly Payment(100000.00, 5.00, 15) to yourPayment.

✦ **A method call doesn't necessarily stand for a value.**

In Listing 2-1, the word void in the first line of the checkVacancy method indicates that a call to checkVacancy doesn't stand for a value. That is, a call to checkVacancy performs some actions, but the call doesn't calculate an answer of any kind.

Similarly, the method onCreate in Listing 2-4 doesn't return a value.

Objects and their constructors

Earlier, I introduce you to the Chair class example, and how it's the idea of *chairness,* and each individual chair is an object . . . If you write a Java program in which you define a Chair class, each actual chair (the chair that you're sitting on, the empty chair right next to you, and so on) is called an *instance* of the Chair class. I also encourage you to think of the table's column headings as a class, and think of each row of the table as an object.

To drive this point home, consider the code in Listing 2-7.

Listing 2-7:   What Is an Account?

```
package com.allmycode.samples;

public class Account {
    public String name;
    public String address;
    public double balance;

    public Account(String name,
                   String address,
                   double balance) {
        this.name = name;
        this.address = address;
        this.balance = balance;
    }

    public String infoString() {
        return name + " (" + address +
            ") has $" + balance;
    }
}
```

Listing 2-7 is a souped-up version of the code in Listing 2-5. In Listing 2-7, an Account has a name, an address, a balance, and an infoString method. The infoString method describes a way of composing a readable description of the account.

The variables name, address, and balance are *fields* of the Account class. In addition, the variables name, address, balance, and the method infoString are *members* of the Account class.

The Account class also has something that looks like a method, but isn't really a method. In Listing 2-7, the text beginning with public Account(String name is the start of a constructor. A *constructor* describes a way of creating a new instance of a class.

According to the code in Listing 2-7, each object created from the `Account` class has its own `name`, its own `address`, and its own `balance`. So, in Listing 2-7, the `Account` constructor's instructions say:

✦ **this.name = name;**

When creating a new object (a new instance of the `Account` class), make `this` new object's `name` be whatever `name` has been passed to the constructor's parameter list. (See Figure 2-2.)

Elsewhere in your app:

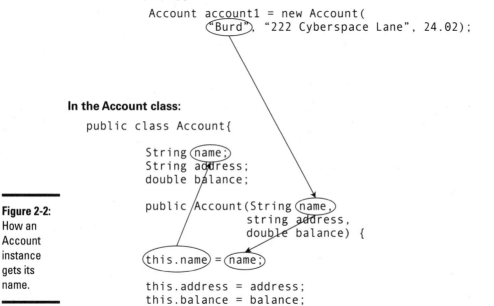

```
Account account1 = new Account(
                "Burd", "222 Cyberspace Lane", 24.02);
```

In the Account class:

```
public class Account{

        String name;
        String address;
        double balance;

        public Account(String name,
                       string address,
                       double balance) {

        this.name = name;

        this.address = address;
        this.balance = balance;
```

Book II
Chapter 2

It's Java!

Figure 2-2:
How an
Account
instance
gets its
name.

✦ **this.address = address;**

When creating a new object (a new instance of the `Account` class), make `this` new object's `address` be whatever `address` has been passed to the constructor's parameter list.

✦ **this.balance = balance;**

When creating a new object (a new instance of the `Account` class), make `this` new object's `balance` be whatever `balance` has been passed to the constructor's parameter list.

You can tell a constructor from a method by checking two things. First, the constructor's name is the same as the class's name. In Listing 2-7, both the class and the constructor have the name Account. Second, a constructor has no return type, not even void. In Listing 2-7, the infoString method has return type String. But the Account constructor has no return type.

Listing 2-8 shows you how to use the code in Listing 2-7. In Listing 2-8, the statement Account account1 = new Account("Burd", "222 Cyberspace Lane", 24.02) calls the constructor from Listing 2-7. As a result, the app has a brand-new instance of the Account class. The variable account1 refers to that new object.

Listing 2-8: Using the Account Class

```
package com.allmycode.samples;

import android.app.Activity;
import android.os.Bundle;
import android.widget.TextView;

public class MyActivity extends Activity {
    TextView textView1;

    @Override
    public void onCreate(Bundle savedInstanceState) {
        super.onCreate(savedInstanceState);
        setContentView(R.layout.main);
        Account account1 = new Account(
                "Burd", "222 Cyberspace Lane", 24.02);

        textView1 =
            ((TextView) findViewById(R.id.textView1));
        textView1.setText(account1.infoString());
    }
}
```

Later in Listing 2-8, the text account1.infoString() calls the new account1 object's infoString method. The method returns a handsome-looking string of characters, which the activity displays on its screen.

To refer to a member belonging to an object, use the dot notation. For example, to call the account1 object's infoString method, write account1. infoString(). To refer to the account1 object's balance, write account1.balance. Method calls require parentheses, and field names don't use parentheses.

When you run the code in Listing 2-8, you get the screen shown in Figure 2-3.

Figure 2-3:
A run of
the app in
Listings 2-7
and 2-8.

Classes grow on trees

Listing 2-4 contains the words `extends Activity`. Apparently, the new `MyActivity` class, declared in Listing 2-4, is some kind of extension of something called `Activity`. So what's this all about?

You can download the Android source code (the Java code that comprises Android's many predeclared classes). When you do, you can open the `Activity.java` file with your favorite editor. Listing 2-9 contains an (admittedly unrepresentative) portion of the code in that file.

For more information about downloading Android's source code, visit `http://source.android.com/source/downloading.html`.

Book II
Chapter 2

It's Java!

Listing 2-9: **A Seriously Abridged Version of Android's Activity Class**

```java
package android.app;

public class Activity extends ContextThemeWrapper {

  protected void onCreate(Bundle savedInstanceState) {
    mVisibleFromClient =
      !mWindow.getWindowStyle().getBoolean(
        com.android.internal.R.styleable.
        Window_windowNoDisplay, false);
    mCalled = true;
  }

  protected void onDestroy() {
    mCalled = true;

    // dismiss any dialogs we are managing.
    if (mManagedDialogs != null) {
      final int numDialogs = mManagedDialogs.size();
      for (int i = 0; i < numDialogs; i++) {
        final ManagedDialog md =
          mManagedDialogs.valueAt(i);
        if (md.mDialog.isShowing()) {
          md.mDialog.dismiss();
        }
      }
```

(continued)

Listing 2-9 *(continued)*

```
      mManagedDialogs = null;
    }

    // Close any open search dialog
    if (mSearchManager != null) {
      mSearchManager.stopSearch();
    }
  }
}
```

The Android SDK comes with an `Activity` class, and the `Activity` class contains methods named `onCreate` and `onDestroy`. (Actually, the Android's `Activity` class contains at least 140 methods. But who's counting?) In Listing 2-4, the words `MyActivity extends Activity` establish a relationship between the `MyActivity` class and Android's `Activity` class. Among other things, the `MyActivity` class *inherits* fields and methods belonging to the `Activity` class. So without adding any code to Listing 2-4, you can rest assured that `MyActivity` has an `onDestroy` method. It's as if you copied the `onDestroy` method declaration from Listing 2-9 and pasted that declaration into Listing 2-4.

Aside from the `extends` terminology, Java has several names for the relationship between the `MyActivity` class and the `Activity` class:

✦ The `MyActivity` class is a **subclass** of the `Activity` class.

✦ The `MyActivity` class is a **child** of the `Activity` class.

✦ The `Activity` class is the **superclass** of the `MyActivity` class.

✦ The `Activity` class is the **parent** of the `MyActivity` class.

If all this parent/child business reminds you of a family tree, you're not alone. Java developers draw upside-down trees all the time. For example, a small part of the tree for the class in Listing 2-4 is pictured in Figure 2-4.

At the top of Figure 2-4, the tree's root is Java's ancestor of all classes — the `Object` class. Android's `Context` class is a subclass of the `Object` class. The `Context` class has many subclasses, two of which (`Application` and `ContextWrapper`) are pictured in Figure 2-4. From there on, `ContextWrapper` begets `ContextThemeWrapper`, which begets `Activity`, which begets the main activity class in a typical Android app.

A class can have many subclasses, but a class has only one superclass. The only class with no superclass is Java's `Object` class.

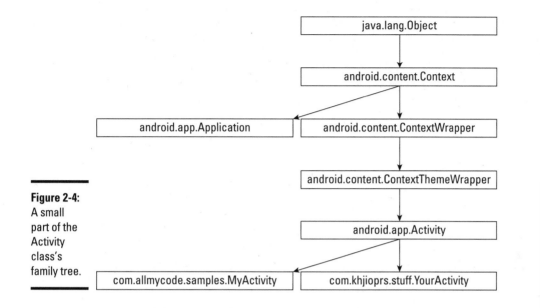

Figure 2-4:
A small
part of the
Activity
class's
family tree.

The Java package

Java has a feature that lets you lump classes into groups of classes. Each
lump of classes is a *package*. The class in Listing 2-4 belongs to the `com.`
`allmycode.samples` package because of the listing's first line of code.

In the Java world, developers customarily give packages long, dot-filled
names. For instance, because I've registered the domain name `allmycode.`
`com`, I name a package `com.allmycode.samples` or `com.allmycode.`
whateverIwant. The Java API is actually a big collection of packages. The
API has packages with names like `java.lang`, `java.util`, `java.awt`,
`javax.swing`, and so on. The Android SDK is also a bunch of packages,
with package names such as `android.app`, `android.view`, and `android.`
`telephony.gsm`.

An `import` declaration starts with the name of a package and ends with
either of the following:

✦ The name of a class within that package

✦ An asterisk (indicating all classes within that package)

For example, in the declaration

```
import android.app.Activity;
```

`android.app` is the name of a package in the Android SDK, and `Activity` is the name of a class in the `android.app` package. The dotted name `android.app.Activity` is the *fully qualified name* of the `Activity` class. A class's fully qualified name includes the name of the package in which the class is defined.

With an `import` declaration, you don't have to repeatedly use a class's fully qualified name. For example, in Listing 2-4, you *could* write

```
public class MyActivity extends android.app.Activity
```

but because of the Listing's `import` declaration, you can get away with plain old

```
public class MyActivity extends Activity
```

In a declaration such as

```
import android.app.*;
```

the asterisk refers to all classes in the `android.app` package. With this `import` declaration at the top of your Java code, you can use abbreviated names for all classes in the `android.app` package — names like `Activity`, `AlertDialog`, `Fragment`, `ListActivity`, and many others.

A public class

A class can be either public or non-public. If you see something like

```
public class SomeClass
```

you're looking at the declaration of a public class. But, if you see plain old

```
class SomeClass
```

the class that's being declared isn't public.

If a class is public, you can refer to the class from anywhere in your code. The following example illustrates the point.

In one file, you have

```
package com.allmycode.somepackage;

public class SomeClass {

}
```

And in another file, you have

```
package com.allmycode.someotherpackage;

import com.allmycode.somepackage.*;

//You CAN extend SomeClass:
class SomeOtherClass extends SomeClass {

    public String infoString() {

        //This works too:
        SomeClass someObject = new SomeClass();
    }
}
```

Book II
Chapter 2

It's Java!

If a class *isn't* public, you can refer to the class only from code within the class's package. The following code makes that crystal clear.

In one file, you have

```
package com.burdbrain.somepackage;

class SomeClass {

}
```

And in another file, you have

```
package com.burdbrain.someotherpackage;

import com.burdbrain.somepackage.*;

//You can't extend SomeClass:
class SomeOtherClass extends SomeClass {

    public String infoString() {

        //This doesn't work either:
        SomeClass someObject = new SomeClass();
    }
}
```

Other public things

The *scope* of a name is the range of code in which you (the developer) can use the name. So, to sum up the preceding section's long-winded explanation:

✦ The scope of a **public** class's name includes all Java code.

✦ The scope of a **non-public** class's name is limited to the package in which the class is declared.

A public class's name doesn't really include *all* Java code. If I'm running a Java program on a computer at my moon base, and you're running a program on your phone while vacationing in orbit around Mars, your phone can't access my code's public classes. For code to access my public classes, that code must be running on the same Java virtual machine.

A class's members (the class's methods and fields) can also be public. For example, the class in Listing 2-7 has the public fields name, address, and balance, and has the public method infoString. In fact, the story for class members is a bit more involved. The word public is an *access modifier,* and a member of a class can be public, private, or protected, or have no access modifier. (For example, the textView1 field in Listing 2-8 has no access modifier. The onCreate and onDestroy methods in Listing 2-9 have protected access.)

Your access modifier choices break down as follows:

✦ A public member's scope includes all Java code.

✦ A private member's scope includes the class in which the member is declared.

✦ A protected member's scope includes the class in which the member is declared. The scope also includes any subclasses of the class in which the member is declared and all classes belonging to the package in which the member is declared.

✦ The scope of a member with no access modifier includes the class in which the member is declared. The scope also includes all classes belonging to the package in which the member is declared.

I don't know about you, but I have trouble wrapping my head around the idea of protected access. One of the difficulties is that, contrary to my intuitions, sporting the word protected is less restrictive than sporting no access modifier at all. Anyway, when I encounter a member with protected access, I stop and think about it long enough for my queasiness to go away.

Defying your parent

In families, children often rebel against their parents' values. The same is true in Java. The MyActivity class (in Listing 2-4) is a child of the Activity class (in Listing 2-9). So at first glance, MyActivity should inherit the onCreate method declared in the Activity class's code.

But both the Activity and MyActivity classes have onCreate method declarations. And the two onCreate declarations have the same parameter list. In this way the `MyActivity` class rebels against its parent. The `MyActivity` class says to the `Activity` class, "I don't want your stinking `onCreate` method. I'm declaring my own `onCreate` method."

So when you fire up an app, and your phone creates a `MyActivity` object, the phone executes the `MyActivity` version of `onCreate`, not the parent `Activity` version of `onCreate`.

Like all rebellious children, `MyActivity` can't break completely from its parent class's code. The first statement in the `MyActivity` class's `onCreate` method is a call to `super.onCreate`. (My kids don't usually refer to me as `super`, but a class refers to its parent that way.) Anyway, the statement `super.onCreate` calls the parent class's `onCreate` method. So, before the `onCreate` method in Listing 2-4 does anything else, the processor runs the `onCreate` method in Listing 2-9. (The creators of Android rigged things so that your `onCreate` method must call `super.onCreate`. If you forget to call `super.onCreate`, Android displays a blunt, annoying error message.)

Book II
Chapter 2

It's Java!

Java annotations

The word `@Override` in Listing 2-4 is an example of an annotation. An *annotation* tells Java something about your code. In particular, the `@Override` annotation in Listing 2-4 tells the Java compiler to be on the lookout for a common coding error. The annotation says, "Make sure that the method immediately following this annotation has the same stuff (the same name, the same parameters, and so on) as one of the methods in the `Activity` class. If not, display an error message."

So if I accidentally misspell a method's name, as in

```
@Override
public void nCreate(Bundle savedInstanceState)
```

the compiler reminds me that my new `nCreate` method doesn't really override anything that's in Android's pre-declared `Activity` class. Oops!

Java comments

A *comment* is part of a program's text. But unlike declarations, method calls, and other such things, a comment's purpose is to help people understand your code. A comment is part of a good program's documentation.

The Java programming language has three kinds of comments:

✦ **Block comments**

A *block* comment begins with `/*` and ends with `*/`. Everything between the opening `/*` and the closing `*/` is for human eyes only. No information between `/*` and `*/` is translated by the compiler.

A block comment can span across several lines. For example, the following code is a block comment:

```
/* This is my best
   Android app ever! */
```

✦ **End-of-line comments**

An *end-of-line* comment starts with two slashes and goes to the end of a line of type. So in the following code snippet, the text `// A required call` is an end-of-line comment:

```
super.onCreate(savedInstanceState); // A required call
```

Once again, no text inside the end-of-line comment gets translated by the compiler.

✦ **Javadoc comments**

A *Javadoc* comment begins with a slash and two asterisks (`/**`). In Listing 2-4, the text `/** Called when the activity is first created. */` is a Javadoc comment.

A Javadoc comment is meant to be read by people who never even look at the Java code. But that doesn't make sense. How can you see the Javadoc comment in Listing 2-4 if you never look at Listing 2-4?

Well, a certain program called `javadoc` (what else?) can find the Javadoc comment in Listing 2-4 and turn this comment into a nice-looking web page. The page is shown in Figure 2-5.

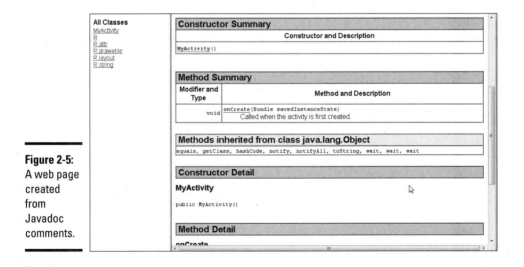

Figure 2-5:
A web page created from Javadoc comments.

To generate a web page like the one in Figure 2-5, do the following:

1. **In Eclipse's main menu, choose Project⇨Generate Javadoc.**

A Generate Javadoc dialog box opens. (See Figure 2-6.)

2. **In the dialog box's Javadoc Command field, type the path to your development computer's `javadoc` (or `javadoc.exe`) file.**

Alternatively, you can navigate to the `javadoc` or `javadoc.exe` file by using the dialog box's Configure button.

3. **In the Select Types pane, check the projects whose code you want to document.**

The Select Types pane is actually two side-by-side panes. (See Figure 2-6.) The left pane is for selecting entire projects or entire packages; the right pane is for selecting or deselecting `.java` files within the packages.

4. **In the Destination field, type the name of the folder that will contain your Javadoc pages (or click the Browse button and let your mouse do the work).**

5. **Click Finish.**

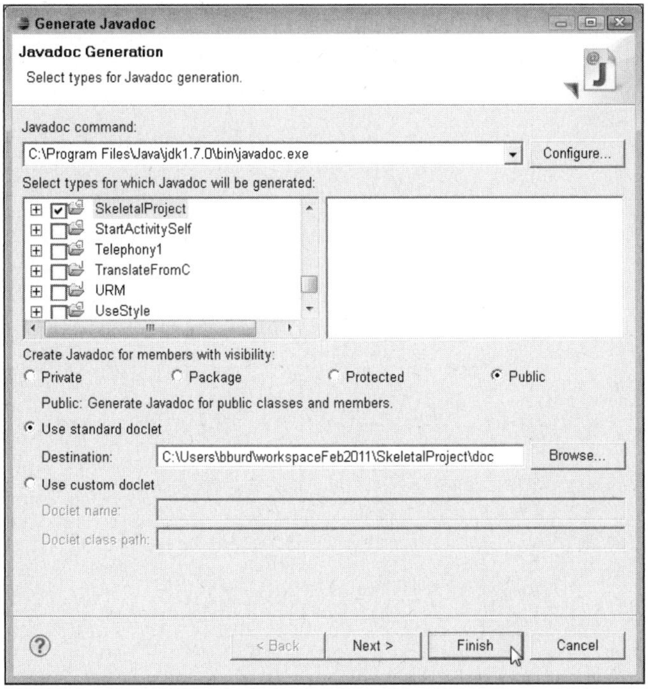

Figure 2-6:
Eclipse's
Generate
Javadoc
dialog box.

In the Generate Javadoc dialog box, you can select Use Custom Doclet instead of Use Standard Doclet. A *doclet* determines the look of a Java documentation page. So selecting Use Custom Doclet lets you change the appearance of your documentation pages. For example, with a doclet named `DroidDoc`, you get pages similar to the docs at `http://developer.` `android.com/reference/packages.html` (Android's official documentation website).

Chapter 3: What Java Does (and When)

In This Chapter

✔ Making decisions with Java statements

✔ Repeating actions with Java statements

✔ Adding exception handling

Human thought centers on nouns and verbs. Nouns are the "stuff," and verbs are the stuff's actions. Nouns are the pieces, and verbs are the glue. Nouns are, and verbs do. When you use nouns, you say, "book," "room," or "stuff." When you use verbs, you say "Do this," "Do that," "Hoist that barge," or "Lift that bale."

Java also has nouns and verbs. Java's nouns include `String`, `ArrayList`, and `JFrame`, along with Android-specific things such as `Activity`, `Application`, and `Bundle`. Java's verbs involve assigning values, choosing among alternatives, repeating actions, and other courses of action.

This chapter covers some of Java's verbs. In Chapter 4 of this minibook, you bring in the nouns.

Making Decisions (Java if Statements)

When you're writing computer programs, you're constantly hitting forks in roads. Did the user correctly type his or her password? If yes, let the user work; if no, kick the bum out. So the Java programming language needs a way of making a program branch in one of two directions. Fortunately, the language has a way: It's called an `if` statement. The use of an `if` statement is illustrated in Listing 3-1.

Listing 3-1:   A Method with an if Statement

```
public void onClick(View v) {
    if (((CheckBox) v).isChecked()) {
        textview.setTextColor(Color.GREEN);
        textview.setText("Thank you!");
```

(continued)

Listing 3-1 *(continued)*

```
    } else {
        textview.setTextColor(Color.RED);
        textview.setText("No harm done.");
    }
}
```

Android calls the onClick method in Listing 3-1 when the user clicks a particular check box. (Android uses the parameter v to pass this check box to the onClick method. That's how the onClick method finds out which object the user clicked.) If clicking puts a check mark in the check box, the text view displays Thank you! in green letters. Otherwise, the text view displays No harm done. in red letters. (See the colorless Figure 3-1.)

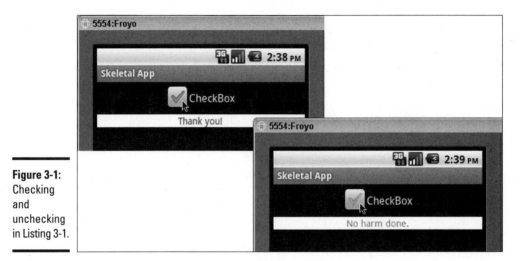

Figure 3-1: Checking and unchecking in Listing 3-1.

Central casting

In Listing 3-1, the variable v represents a View of some kind (or so says the onClick method's parameter list). Like all Java classes, the View class is part of a class family tree. The figure below shows some of the View class's nearest and dearest relatives. The lower you go in the tree, the more specific the class's characteristics are. For example, at the top of the tree you have the very nebulous thing called Object. Below Object you have the View class. A View is something that that you put on the user's screen (something the user sees). Not all View instances display text, so below View on the hierarchy are the more specific ImageView and TextView classes.

The CheckBox class is at the very bottom of the figure. A CheckBox is a specific kind of TextView — a TextView that's always in one of two states — checked or unchecked.

Meanwhile, back in Listing 3-1, the onClick method's v parameter is any kind of View.

This non-specific "any kind of `View`" business comes because you never know what kind of `View` the user will click. Android's predeclared `onClick` method (which you override in Listing 3-1) works with `TextView` instances, `ImageView` instances, `Button` instances, `CheckBox` instances, and all kinds of other instances.

Many kinds of `View` instances have no checked state and no unchecked state. For example, an ordinary `TextView` (displaying a line of text) is neither checked no unchecked. So in Android's grand hierarchy of `Object` instances, `View` instances, and `CheckBox` instances, the humble `View` class has no `isChecked` method. If you replace the condition in Listing 3-1 with the simpler `v.isChecked()` condition, the modified code doesn't compile. Java realizes that `v`, being declared as a parameter of type `View`, might not have an `isChecked` method.

The issue in this example is the balance between generality and specificity. Android's `onClick` method must be prepared to work with any `View` instance, but for this particular app, you (the developer) know that the thing being clicked is a `CheckBox` instance. And in the Android API, every `CheckBox` instance has an `isChecked` method.

So what do you do? In Listing 3-1, you do *casting.* When you *cast* a value, you precede the value with a class's name in parentheses. The code `(CheckBox) v` represents "v, when we think of v as a `CheckBox`." In other words, by writing `(CheckBox) v`, the developer assures Java that when the time comes to execute this code, v will not only be a `View` of some kind or other. The v object will be a `CheckBox` and will have an `isChecked` method. So the condition `((CheckBox) v).isChecked()` is received warmly and graciously by the Java compiler.

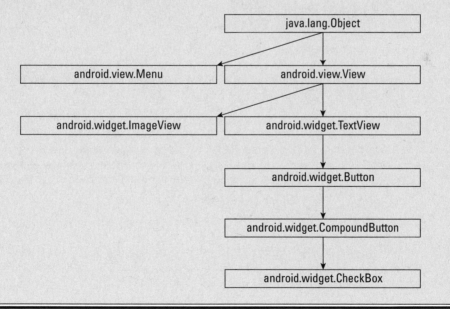

An `if` statement has the following form:

```
if (condition) {
    statements to be executed when the condition is true
} else {
    statements to be executed when the condition is false
}
```

In Listing 3-1, the condition being tested is

```
((CheckBox) v).isChecked()
```

In this condition, variable `v` is the `onClick` method's parameter — the thing that Android passes to the `onClick` method. Listing 3-1 is far from being a complete Android app. But presumably, `v` is a check box. (See the nearby sidebar, "Central casting.")

Android's `isChecked` method returns either `true` or `false` — `true` when the `v` check box is checked,; `false` when the `v` check box isn't checked.

The condition in an `if` statement must be enclosed in parentheses. The condition must be a `boolean` expression — an expression whose value is either `true` or `false`. (See Chapter 2 of this minibook for information about Java's primitive types, including the `boolean` type.) So, for example, the following condition is okay:

```
if (numberOfTries < 17) {
```

But the strange kind of condition that you can use in languages, such as C++, is not okay:

```
if (17) { //This is incorrect.
```

You can omit curly braces when only one statement comes between the condition and the word `else`. You can also omit braces when only one statement comes after the word `else`. For example, the following code is right and proper:

```
if (((CheckBox) v).isChecked())
    textview.setText("Thank you!");
else {
    textview.setTextColor(Color.RED);
    textview.setText("No harm done.");
}
```

An `if` statement can also enjoy a full and happy life without an `else` part. So the following code forms a complete `if` statement:

```
if (((CheckBox) v).isChecked()) {
    textview.setTextColor(Color.GREEN);
    textview.setText("Thank you!");
}
```

Primitive and reference types

The int type is a primitive type. When you declare a variable to have type int, you can visualize what that declaration means in a fairly straightforward way. It means that, somewhere inside the computer's memory, a storage location is reserved for that variable's value. In that storage location is a bunch of bits. The arrangement of the bits ensures that a certain whole number is represented.

That explanation is fine for primitive types like int or double, but every Java class is a *reference* type. If you declare a variable to have some type that's not a primitive type, the variable's type is (most of the time) the name of a Java class.

What does it mean when you declare a variable to have a reference type? What does it mean to declare response to be of type String or to declare v to be of type View?

Because String is a class, you can create objects from that class. Each such object (each instance of the String class) is a sequence of characters. By declaring the variable response to be of type String, you're reserving the use of the name response. This reservation tells Java that response can refer to an actual String-type object. In other words, response can become a nickname for a sequence of characters. The situation is illustrated in the figure below, where the storage story for primitive types and reference types is told.

If you're familiar with other programming languages and you like talking about pointers, you can safely think of String response as a declaration whose meaning is "response stores a pointer to a sequence of characters."

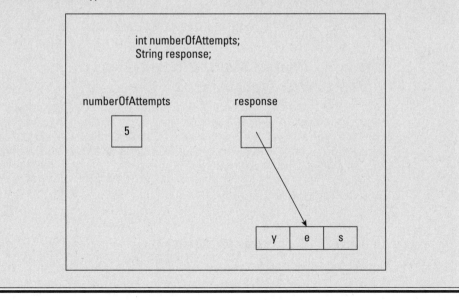

```
int numberOfAttempts;
String response;
```

numberOfAttempts

| 5 |

response

| y | e | s |

Testing for equality

Java has several ways to test for equality ("Is this value the same as that value?"). None of these ways is the first thing you'd think of doing. In particular, to find out whether the parameter v is the thing you call checkbox1,

you *don't* write if (v = checkbox1). Instead, you use a double equal sign
(==). You write if (v == checkbox1). In Java, the single equal sign (=) is
reserved for *assignment*. So n = 5 means "Let n stand for the value 5," and
v = checkbox1 means "Let v stand for the checkbox1 object."

Comparing two strings is yet another story. When you compare two strings
with one another, you don't want to use the double equal sign. Using the
double equal sign would ask, "Is this string stored in exactly the same place
in memory as that other string?" That's usually not what you want to ask.
Instead, you usually want to ask, "Does this string have the same characters
in it as that other string?" To ask the second question (the more appropriate
question), Java's String type has a method named equals:.

```
if (response.equals("yes")) {
```

The equals method compares two strings to see whether they have the
same characters in them. In this paragraph's tiny example, the variable
response refers to a string, and the text "yes" refers to a string. The condition response.equals("yes") is true if response refers to a string
whose letters are 'y', then 'e', and then 's'.

Like most programming languages, Java has the usual complement of comparison operators (such as < for "less than") and logical operators (such as && for
"and"). For a list of such operators, visit http://download.oracle.com/
javase/tutorial/java/nutsandbolts/opsummary.html.

Choosing among many alternatives (Java switch statements)

I'm the first to admit that I hate making decisions. If things go wrong, I would
rather have the problem be someone else's fault. Writing the previous sections (on making decisions with Java's if statement) knocked the stuff-
ing right out of me. That's why my mind boggles as I begin this section on
choosing among many alternatives.

Consider the code in Listing 3-2.

Listing 3-2:   A Java switch Statement

```
public void onClick(View v) {

    String message;
    Editable edit = textfield.getText();
    if (edit.length() != 0) {
        int number =
            Integer.valueOf(edit.toString());

        switch (number) {
```

```
case 0:
    message = "none";
    break;
case 1:
    message = "one";
    break;
case 2:
    message = "two";
    break;
case 3:
    message = "three";
    break;
default:
    message = "many";
}

label.setText(message);
    }
}
```

The code in Listing 3-2 is part of an app, and the app's screen is pictured in Figure 3-2.

Figure 3-2:
A TextView
object
reports on
an EditText
object's
content.

The user clicks something or other (something not specified in Listing 3-2 or in Figure 3-2). As a result of the user's click, Android does the stuff in Listing 3-2. Some of that stuff involves a Java `switch` statement. The `switch` statement examines the characters in a text field. (In Figure 3-2, the text field contains `011`.) To make sure that the text field characters are all digits, I included the following element in the app's layout document:

```
<EditText android:layout_height="wrap_content"
    android:id="@+id/editText1"
    android:layout_width="match_parent"
    android:inputType="number"></EditText>
```

In the first line of the `switch` statement, `number` is a whole number. If `number` is 0, the code makes `message` be `"none"`. If `number` is 1, the code makes `message` be `"one"`. If `number` is not 0, 1, 2, or 3, the `default` part of the `switch` statement takes over, and the code makes `message` be `"many"`.

Each break statement in Listing 3-2 says, "Jump past any remaining cases." You can omit a break statement, but do so at your own peril! For example, if you write

```
case 2:
    message = "two";
case 3:
    message = "three";
default:
    message = "many";
}
```

and number is 2, Java executes three cases, one after another — namely, message = "two" followed by message = "three" followed immediately by message = "many". The lack of break statements tells Java to *fall-through* from one case to the next. The end result is that the message is "many", and that's probably not what you want.

A switch statement has the following form:

```
switch (expression) {
case constant1:
    statements to be executed when the
    expression has value contstant1
case constant2:
    statements to be executed when the
    expression has value contstant2
case ...

default:
    statements to be executed when the
    expression has a value different from
    any of the constants
}
```

You can't put any old expression in a switch statement. The expression that's tested at the start of a switch statement must have

✦ One of the primitive types char, byte, short, or int, or

✦ One of the reference types Character, Byte, Short, or Integer, or

✦ An enum type

An enum type is a type whose values are limited to the few that you declare. For example, the code

```
enum TrafficSignal {GREEN, YELLOW, RED};
```

defines a type whose only values are GREEN, YELLOW, and RED. Elsewhere in your code, you can write

```
TrafficSignal signal;
signal = TrafficSignal.GREEN;
```

to make use of the `TrafficSignal` type.

Starting with Java 7, you can put a `String` type expression at the start of a `switch` statement. But until Java 7 settles in a bit, you may want to avoid using this feature in Android code.

Repeating Instructions Over and Over Again

In 1966, the company that brings you Head & Shoulders shampoo made history. On the back of the bottle, the directions for using the shampoo read, "Lather, rinse, repeat." Never before had a complete set of directions (for doing anything, let alone shampooing your hair) been summarized so succinctly. People in the direction-writing business hailed this as a monumental achievement. Directions like these stood in stark contrast to others of the time. (For instance, the first sentence on a can of bug spray read, "Turn this can so that it points away from your face." Duh!)

Aside from their brevity, the thing that made the Head & Shoulders directions so cool was that, with three simple words, they managed to capture a notion that's at the heart of all instruction-giving — the notion of repetition. That last word, *repeat,* took an otherwise bland instructional drone and turned it into a sophisticated recipe for action.

The fundamental idea is that when you're following directions, you don't just follow one instruction after another. Instead, you take turns in the road. You make decisions ("If HAIR IS DRY, then USE CONDITIONER"), and you go into loops ("LATHER-RINSE and then LATHER-RINSE again"). In application development, you use decision-making and looping all the time.

Java while statements

In an Android app, a content provider feeds a *cursor* to your code. You can think of the cursor as a pointer to a row in a table. In Listing 3-3, each table row has three entries — an _id, a name, and an amount. Supposedly, the _id uniquely identifies a row, the name is a person's name, and the amount is a huge number of dollars owed to you by that person.

For the rundown on content providers, see Book III, Chapter 5.

Listing 3-3: A while Loop

```
cursor.moveToFirst();

while (!cursor.isAfterLast()) {
    String _id = cursor.getString(0);
    String name = cursor.getString(1);
    String amount = cursor.getString(2);
    textViewDisplay.append(_id + " " +
                          name + " " + amount + "\n");
    cursor.moveToNext();
}
```

A cursor's `moveToFirst` method makes the cursor point to the first row of the table. Regardless of the row a cursor points to, the cursor's `moveToNext` method makes the cursor point to the next row of the table. The cursor's `isAfterLast` method returns `true` when, having tried to move to the next row, there's no next row.

In Java, an exclamation point (`!`) means "not,", so `while (!cursor.isAfterLast())` means "while it's not true that the cursor has reached past the table's last row . . ." So the code in Listing 3-3 repeatedly does the following:

```
As long as the cursor has not reached past the last row,
    get the string in the row's initial column and
        make _id refer to that string,
    get the string in the row's middle column and
        make name refer to that string,
    get the string in the row's last column and
        make amount refer to that string, and
    append these strings to the textViewDisplay, and then
    move the cursor to the next row in preparation
        for returning to the top of the while statement.
```

Imagine that a particular cursor's table has 100 rows. Then a processor executes the statements inside Listing 3-3's `while` loop 100 times. Using the official developer lingo, the processor performs 100 loop *iterations*.

A `while` statement has the following form:

```
while (condition) {
    statements to be executed
}
```

You can omit the curly braces when the loop has only one *statement to be executed*.

In Listing 3-3, the characters \n form an *escape sequence*. When you put \n inside a string, you're escaping from the normal course of things by displaying neither a backslash nor a letter n. Instead, \n in a Java string always means "Go to the next line." So in Listing 3-3, \n puts a line break between one _id, name, amount group and the next.

Java for statements

Life is filled with examples of counting loops. And app development mirrors life — or is it the other way around? When you tell a device what to do, you're often telling the device to display three lines, process ten accounts, dial a million phone numbers, or whatever.

Listing 3-3 displays all the rows in a table full of data. Sometimes, all the data is too much data. To get the idea of what the table has to offer, you might want to display only the first ten rows of data. The code in Listing 3-4 does the job.

Listing 3-4:   A for Loop

```
cursor.moveToFirst();

for (int i = 0; i < 10; i++) {
    String _id = cursor.getString(0);
    String name = cursor.getString(1);
    String amount = cursor.getString(2);
    textViewDisplay.append(i + ": " + _id + " " +
                              name + " " + amount + "\n");
    cursor.moveToNext();
}
```

Listing 3-4 declares an int variable named i. The starting value of i is 0. As long as the condition i < 10 is true, the processor executes the instructions inside the for statement. In this example, the for statement's instructions include getting an _id, getting a name, getting an amount, and appending all that stuff to the textViewDisplay. In addition to that stuff, the textViewDisplay gets the value of i (be it 0, 1, 2, or any number less than 10).

To keep the ball rolling, the last instruction in the for statement moves the cursor to the next line. But wait! What happens when the processor goes to the beginning of the loop again? Before starting the loop anew, the processor does i++, which is Java-speak for "Add 1 to i." So after ten loop iterations, the value of i finally reaches 10 and the execution of the for loop's instructions comes to an end.

A `for` statement has the following form:

```
for (initialization ; condition ; update) {
    statements to be executed
}
```

✦ An *initialization* (such as `int i = 0` in Listing 3-4) defines the action to be taken before the first loop iteration.

✦ A *condition* (such as `i < 10` in Listing 3-4) defines the thing to be checked before an iteration. If the condition is `true`, the processor executes the iteration. If the condition is `false`, the processor doesn't execute the iteration and moves on to execute whatever code comes after the `for` statement.

✦ An *update* (such as `i++` in Listing 3-4) defines an action to be taken at the end of each loop iteration.

As always, you can omit the curly braces when the loop has only one *statement to be executed.*

Like the protagonist in an ancient Greek tragedy, the loop in Listing 3-4 has a fatal flaw. The loop comes crashing down if the cursor's table has fewer than ten rows. To remedy this (and to save the protagonist), you can add a check for "rowlessness" inside the loop:

```
for (int i = 0; i < 10; i++) {
    if (cursor.isAfterLast())
        break;
    String _id = cursor.getString(0);
    String name = cursor.getString(1);
    String amount = cursor.getString(2);
    textViewDisplay.append(i + ": " + _id + " " +
                           name + " " + amount + "\n");
    cursor.moveToNext();
}
```

Inside a loop (a `while` loop, a `for` loop, or some other kind of loop), a `break` statement says, "This looping is done" and "We're outta here." The processor moves on to execute whatever statement comes immediately after the loop's code.

Java do statements

To find a particular row of a cursor's table, you normally do a *query*. (For straight talk about queries, see Book IV.) You almost never perform a do-it-yourself search through a table's data. But just this once, look at a loop that iterates through row after row — the loop is in Listing 3-5.

Listing 3-5: Leap before You Look

```
cursor.moveToFirst();
String name;

do {
    String _id = cursor.getString(0);
    name = cursor.getString(1);
    String amount = cursor.getString(2);
    textViewDisplay.append(_id + " " +
                        name + " " + amount + "\n");
    cursor.moveToNext();
} while (!name.equals("Burd") && !cursor.isAfterLast());
```

With a do loop, the processor jumps right in, takes action, and then checks a condition to see whether the result of the action is what you want. If the result is what you want, execution of the loop is done. If not, the processor goes back to the top of the loop for another go-around.

In Listing 3-5, you're looking for a row with the name *Burd*. (After all, the bum owes you lots of money.) When you enter the loop, the cursor points to the table's first row. Before checking a row for the name *Burd,* you fetch that first row's data and add the data to the textViewDisplay where the user can see what's going on.

Before you march on to the next row (the next loop iteration), you check a condition to make sure that another row is worth visiting. (Check to make sure that you haven't yet found that Burd guy, and that you haven't moved past the last row of the table.)

To get the code in Listing 3-5 working, you have to move the declaration of name outside the do statement. A declaration that's inside a pair of curly braces (such as the _id, name, and amount declarations in Listing 3-4) cannot be used outside curly braces. So, in Listing 3-5, if you don't move the name declaration outside the loop, Java complains that !name. equals("Burd") is incorrect.

Arrays in Java

An *array* is a bunch of values of the same type. Each value in the array is associated with an *index*. For example, the following code puts 15.020999999999999 in an app's textView1:

```
double[] measurements = new double[3];
measurements[0] = 5.7;
measurements[1] = 9.32;
measurements[2] = 0.001;
textView1.setText(Double.toString(measurements[0]
        + measurements[1] + measurements[2]));
```

Arithmetic with `float` values and `double` values suffers from the woes of numeric errors. The sum 5.7 + 9.32 + 0.001 is 15.021, not 15.020999999999999. But computers use the bits 0 and 1 (instead of the digits 0 through 9) to store numbers internally. The use of zeros and ones, along with the fact that computers can't store infinitely long decimal expansions, leads inevitably to arithmetic errors. Sorry about that!

The following code puts *Barry Burd and Jane Dough* in an app's `textView1`:

```
String[] names = new String[3];
names[0] = new String("Barry Burd");
names[1] = new String("John Public");
names[2] = new String("Jane Dough");

textView1.setText(names[0] + " and " + names[2]);
```

You can step from value to value in an array using a `for` loop. For example, the following code puts *Barry Burd John Public Jane Dough* in an app's `textView1`:

```
String[] names = new String[3];
names[0] = new String("Barry Burd ");
names[1] = new String("John Public ");
names[2] = new String("Jane Dough ");
textView1.setText("");

for (int i = 0; i < 3; i++) {
  textView1.append(names[i]);
}
```

Java's enhanced for statements

In the mid-1960s, a company advertised its product by announcing, "Our product used to be perfect. But now, our product is even better!"

In the mid-2000s, the newly created Java 5 specification had a brand- new kind of loop. This feature has been part of Java for several years, but it's still called the enhanced `for` loop. The following code uses an enhanced `for` loop to put *Barry Burd John Public Jane Dough* in an app's `textView1`:.

```
String[] names = new String[3];
names[0] = new String("Barry Burd ");
names[1] = new String("John Public ");
names[2] = new String("Jane Dough ");
textView1.setText("");

for (String s : names) {
  textView1.append(s);
}
```

Here's another example. Suppose you have a cursor, and the cursor points to a table's row. (To keep this example simple, I assume that each column contains `String` data.) You don't know the table's column names, and you don't know how many columns the table has. Java's enhanced `for` statement provides an elegant way to deal with this kind of situation. Listing 3-6 shows you the story.

Listing 3-6:   An Enhanced for Loop

```
cursor.moveToFirst();

while (!cursor.isAfterLast()) {

    String[] columnNames = cursor.getColumnNames();

    for (String colName : columnNames) {
        int index = cursor.getColumnIndex(colName);
        textViewDisplay.append(colName + ":" +
                cursor.getString(index) + ", ");
    }

    textViewDisplay.append("\n");
    cursor.moveToNext();
}
```

In Listing 3-6, a cursor's `getColumnNames` method returns an array of `String` values. The code assigns this array to the `columnNames` variable. Then the enhanced `for` loop creates a variable (`colName`) that steps through the `String` values in the array. The line

```
for (String colName : columnNames)
```

says, "Repeat the instructions in the `for` statement once for each of the `String` values stored in the `columnNames` array. During each value in the array, let the variable `colName` stand for that value during one of the loop's iterations." So, for example, if the `columnNames` array contains the strings `_id`, `name`, and `amount`, the processor performs three iterations of the enhanced loop in Listing 3-6. During the first iteration, `colName` stands for `"_id"`. During the second iteration, `colName` stands for `"name"`. During the third iteration, `colName` stands for `"amount"`.

With or without enhanced loops, a cursor's `getString` method needs a column number. In Listing 3-5 (and in previous listings), I hand column numbers 0, 1, and 2 to the `getString` method. In Listing 3-6, I fetch these column numbers from the column names, using the cursor's `getColumn Index` method.

An enhanced `for` statement has the following form:

```
for (TypeName variable : ArrayOrCollection) {
    statements to be executed
}
```

The *TypeName* is the type of each element in the *ArrayOrCollection*. The loop performs an iteration for each element of the *ArrayOrCollection*. During each iteration, the variable refers to one of the elements in the *ArrayOrCollection*.

Jumping Away from Trouble

The Java programming language has a mechanism called *exception handling*. With exception handling, a program can detect that things are about to go wrong and respond by creating a brand-new object. In the official terminology, the program is said to be *throwing* an exception. That new object, an instance of the `Exception` class, is passed like a hot potato from one piece of code to another until some piece of code decides to *catch* the exception. When the exception is caught, the program executes some recovery code, buries the exception, and moves on to the next normal statement as if nothing had ever happened.

The whole thing is done with the aid of several Java keywords. These keywords are as follows:

+ **throw:** Creates a new exception object.

+ **throws:** Passes the buck from a method up to whatever code called the method.

+ **try:** Encloses code that has the potential to create a new exception object. In the usual scenario, the code inside a `try` clause contains calls to methods whose code can create one or more exceptions.

+ **catch:** Deals with the exception, buries it, and then moves on.

For example, Java's `Integer.parseInt` method turns a `String` value into an `int` value. The value of `"279" + 1` is `"2791"`, but the value of `Integer.parseInt("279") + 1` is 280. A call to `Integer.parseInt` throws a `NumberFormatException` if the call's parameter isn't a whole number. So if your code calls `Integer.parseInt("3.5")`, your code has to deal with a `NumberFormatException`. (The String value `"3.5"` doesn't stand for a whole number.)

Here's a simple method to add one to a number that's represented as a
`String` value:

```
int increment(String str) {
  return Integer.parseInt(str) + 1;
}
```

If you call `increment("985")`, you get `986`. That's good.

But if you call `increment("2.71828")`, your code crashes and your app
stops running. Java leaves clues about the crash in Eclipse's LogCat view.
The clues (which form a Java *stack trace*) look something like this:

```
Exception in thread "main" java.lang.NumberFormatException:
For input string: "2.71828"
    at java.lang.NumberFormatException.forInputString
    at java.lang.Integer.parseInt
```

If you add some exception handling code to the increment method, your
code keeps running with or without the `increment("2.71828")` call.

```
int increment(String str) {
  try {
    return Integer.parseInt(str) + 1;
  } catch (NumberFormatException e) {
    return 0;
  }
}
```

With the `try` and `catch` in the revised method, Java attempts to evaluate
`Integer.parseInt(str)`. If evaluation is successful, the method returns
`Integer.parseInt(str) + 1`. But if `str` has a weird value, the call
to `Integer.parseInt` throws a `NumberFormatException`. Fortunately,
the revised `increment` method catches the `NumberFormatException`,
returns the value `0`, and continues running without bothering the user.

Chapter 4: Object-Oriented Programming in Java

In This Chapter

✔ **Using classes with finesse**

✔ **Working with Java's classes and interfaces**

✔ **Being part of Java's inner circle**

If you remember nothing else about Java, remember these ideas from Chapter 2 of this minibook:

> *Java is an object-oriented programming language. So, as a developer, your primary goal is to describe objects. Your closely related goal is to describe objects' close cousins —; namely, classes. A class is the idea behind a certain kind of thing. An object is a concrete instance of a class.*

And if you remember nothing else about those ideas, remember the following two-word summary:

> *Classes; objects.*

Chapter 2 in this minibook covers the highlights of object-oriented programming in Java. This chapter covers some of object-oriented programming's finer points.

Static Fields and Methods

In Listing 4-1, I reproduce a small portion of the source code of Android's Toast class.

Listing 4-1: An Unrepresentative Sample of Android's Toast Class Code

```
public class Toast {

  public static final int LENGTH_LONG = 1;

  public static Toast makeText(Context context,
```

(continued)

Listing 4-1 *(continued)*

```
                                   CharSequence text,
                                   int duration) {
    Toast result = new Toast(context);

    LayoutInflater inflate = (LayoutInflater) context.
       getSystemService(Context.LAYOUT_INFLATER_SERVICE);
    View v = inflate.inflate
       (com.android.internal.
       R.layout.transient_notification, null);
    TextView tv = (TextView)v.findViewById
       (com.android.internal.R.id.message);
    tv.setText(text);

    result.mNextView = v;
    result.mDuration = duration;

    return result;
  }

  public void show() {
    if (mNextView == null) {
      throw new RuntimeException
        ("setView must have been called");
    }

    INotificationManager service = getService();

    String pkg = mContext.getPackageName();

    TN tn = mTN;

    try {
      service.enqueueToast(pkg, tn, mDuration);
    } catch (RemoteException e) {
      // Empty
    }
  }
}
```

According to the code in Listing 4-1, the `Toast` class has a static field named `LENGTH_LONG` and a static method named `makeText`. Anything that's declared to be static belongs to the whole class, not to any particular instance of the class. When you create the static field, `LENGTH_LONG`, you create only one copy of the field. This copy stays with the entire `Toast` class. No matter how many instances of the `Toast` class you create — one, nine, or none — you have just one `LENGTH_LONG` field.

Contrast this with the situation in Chapter 2 of this minibook. In that chapter, the `Account` class has fields `name`, `address`, and `balance`. The fields aren't static, so every instance of the `Account` class has its own `name`, its own `address`, and its own `balance`. One instance has name `Barry Burd` and balance `24.02`, and another instance has name `John Q. Public` with balance `-471.03`. To refer to Burd's balance, you may write something like `myAccount.balance`, as in the following code

```
Account myAccount = new Account();

myAccount.name = "Burd";
myAccount.address = "222 Cyberspace Lane";
myAccount.balance = 24.02;
```

To refer to a non-static member of a class, you write the name of an object (such as `myAccount`), followed by a dot, and then the name of the member (such as `balance`).

Book II Chapter 4

Object-Oriented Programming in Java

But the `Toast` class's `LENGTH_LONG` field is static. When you create a `Toast` instance, you don't create a new `LENGTH_LONG` field. Your Dalvik virtual machine's `Toast` class has one `LENGTH_LONG` field, and that's that. Accordingly, you refer to `LENGTH_LONG` by prefacing the field name with the `Toast` class name, followed by a dot:

```
Toast.LENGTH_LONG
```

In fact, a typical use of `Toast` in an Android app refers to the static field `LENGTH_LONG` and the static method `makeText`:

```
Toast.makeText
   (getApplication(), "Whoa!", Toast.LENGTH_LONG).show();
```

A call to the `Toast` class's `makeText` method returns an actual object — an instance of the `Toast` class. (You can verify this by looking at the first line of the `makeText` method in Listing 4-1.) So in an Android app, an expression such as

```
Toast.makeText
   (getApplication(), "Whoa!", Toast.LENGTH_LONG)
```

stands for an object. And (again according to Listing 4-1) each object created from the `Toast` class has its own non-static `show` method. That's why you normally follow a `Toast.makeText` call with `.show()`.

Here's one final word about Listing 4-1: In addition to being `static`, the `LENGTH_LONG` field is also `final`. A `final` field is one whose value cannot be changed. In other words, when you declare `LENGTH_LONG`, you can initialize its value to `1` (as in Listing 4-1). But elsewhere in the code, you can't write `LENGTH_LONG = 2`. (For that matter, you can't even write `LENGTH_LONG = 1` elsewhere in the code.)

Many programming languages use the word *constant* (or the abbreviation `const`) to refer to a variable whose value cannot be changed.

Interfaces and Callbacks

Listing 4-2 contains a snippet from Android's predeclared Java code. The listing contains a Java *interface.*

Listing 4-2:   Android's OnClickListener Interface

```
public interface OnClickListener {
    void onClick(View v);
}
```

An interface is like a class, but it's different. (So, what else is new? A cow is like a planet, but it's quite a bit different. Cows moo; planets hang in space.) Anyway, when you hear the word *interface,* you can start by thinking of a class. Then, in your head, note the following things:

✦ **A class doesn't extend an interface. Instead, a class *implements* an interface.**

Later in this chapter, you can see the following line of code:

```
class MyListener implements OnClickListener
```

✦ **A class can extend only one parent class, but a class can implement more than one interface.**

For example, if you want `MyListener` objects to listen for long clicks as well as regular clicks, you can write

```
class MyListener implements OnClickListener,
                            OnLongClickListener {
```

A long click is what non-developers would probably call a touch-and-hold motion.

✦ **An interface can extend another interface.**

For example, in the following line of code, a homegrown interface named `SomeListener` extends Android's built-in `OnClickListener` interface:

```
public interface SomeListener extends OnClickListener {
```

✦ **An interface can extend more than one interface.**

✦ **An interface's methods have no bodies of their own.**

In Listing 4-2, the `onClick` method has no body — no curly braces and no statements to execute. In place of a body, there's just a semicolon.

A method with no body, like the method defined in Listing 4-2, is an *abstract method*.

✦ **When you implement an interface, you provide bodies for all the interface's methods.**

That's why the MyListener class in Listing 4-3 has an onClick method. By announcing that it will implement the OnClickListener interface, the MyListener class agrees that it will give meaning to the interface's onClick method. In this situation, *giving meaning* means declaring an onClick method with curly braces, a body, and maybe some statements to execute.

Book II
Chapter 4

Object-Oriented
Programming
in Java

Listing 4-3: Implementing Android's OnClickListener Interface

```java
package com.allmycode.samples;

import android.app.Activity;
import android.os.Bundle;
import android.view.View;
import android.view.View.OnClickListener;
import android.widget.Button;

public class MyActivity extends Activity {

    Button button;

    @Override
    public void onCreate(Bundle savedInstanceState) {
        super.onCreate(savedInstanceState);
        setContentView(R.layout.main);

        button = ((Button) findViewById(R.id.button1));

        button.setOnClickListener(new MyListener(this));
    }
}

class MyListener implements OnClickListener {
    Activity activity;

    MyListener (Activity activity) {
        this.activity = activity;
    }

    @Override
    public void onClick(View arg0) {
        ((MyActivity) activity).button.setBackgroundColor
                            (android.graphics.Color.GRAY);
    }
}
```

Listing 4-3 doesn't illustrate the most popular way to implement the `OnClickListener` interface, but the listing presents a straightforward use of interfaces and their implementations.

When you announce that you're going to implement an interface (as in `class MyListener implements OnClickListener`), the Java compiler takes this announcement seriously. In the body of the class, if you fail to give meaning to any of the interface's methods, the compiler yells at you.

If you're really lazy, you can quickly find out what methods need to be declared in your interface-implementing code. Try to compile the code, and the compiler lists all the methods that you should have declared but didn't.

Chapter 2 in this minibook introduces the use of `@Override` — a Java annotation. Normally, you use `@Override` to signal the replacement of a method that's already been declared in a superclass. But from Java 6 onward, you can also use `@Override` to signal an interface method's implementation. That's what I do in Listing 4-3.

You can think of an interface as a kind of contract. When you write

```
class MyListener implements OnClickListener
```

you're binding `MyListener` to the contract described in Listing 4-2. That contract states, "You, the implementing class, hereby agree to provide a body for each of the abstract methods declared in the interface and to indemnify and hold harmless this interface for any damages, mishaps, or embarrassments from wearing pocket protectors."

As a member of society, you have exactly two biological parents, but you can enter into agreements with several companies. In the same way, a Java class has only one parent class, but a class can implement many interfaces.

The interface-implementing hierarchy (if you can call it a "hierarchy") cuts across the class-extension hierarchy. This idea is illustrated in Figure 4-1, where I display class extensions vertically and display interface implementations horizontally. (Android's `KeyboardView` class lives in the `android.inputmethod service` package. Both `KeyboardView` and the homegrown `MyListener` class in Listing 4-3 implement Android's `OnClickListener` interface.)

Figure 4-1:
The interface hierarchy cuts across the class hierarchy.

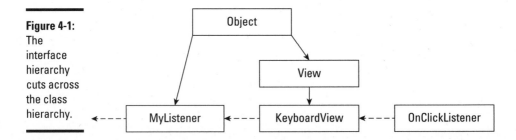

Event handling and callbacks

The big news in Listing 4-3, shown in the preceding section, is the handling of the user's button click. Anything the user does (such as pressing a key, touching the screen, or whatever) is an *event*. The code that responds to the user's press or touch is the *event-handling* code.

Some things that the user doesn't do are also events. For example, when you turn on a device's GPS sensor and the sensor gets its first fix, Android calls the onGpsStatusChanged event handler.

Listing 4-3 deals with the click event with three parts of its code:

✦ The MyListener class declaration says that this class implements OnClickListener.

✦ The activity's onCreate method sets the button's click handler to a new MyListener object.

✦ The code for the MyListener class has an onClick method.

Taken together, all three of these tricks make the MyListener class handle button clicks. Figure 4-2 illustrates the process.

Book II
Chapter 4

Object-Oriented
Programming
in Java

```
Your application                              Android

                                   ┌──────────────────────────────┐
                                   │ Android's list of classes that│
                                   │ implement OnClickListener     │
                                   │ and should have their onClick │
                                   │ methods called whenever the   │
                                   │ button is clicked:            │
button.setOnClickListener          │                              │
        (new MyListener(this));────┼──▶1. The new MyListener object│
                                   └──────────────────────────────┘

                       (Time passes...
               and then the user clicks the button...)


class MyListener implements
OnClickListener {
                                       Call the MyListener
public void onClick (View arg0)◀────── object's mono method
{                                      and pass the button to the
        setBackgroundColor...         method's View parameter.

}
```

Figure 4-2:
Handling
an event.

When the user clicks the button, Android says, "Okay, the button was clicked. So, what should I do about that?" And the answer is, "Call an `onClick` method." It's as if Android has code that looks like this:

```
OnClickListener object1;
if (buttonJustGotClicked()) {
    object1.onClick(infoAboutTheClick);
}
```

Of course, behind every answer is yet another question. In this situation, the follow-up question is, "Where does Android find `onClick` methods to call?" And there's another question: "What if you don't want Android to call certain `onClick` methods that are lurking in your code?"

Well, that's why you call the `setOnClickListener` method. In Listing 4-3, the call

```
button.setOnClickListener(new MyListener(this));
```

creates a new `MyListener` object. You tell Android to "put the new object's `onClick` method on your list of methods to be called. Call this object's `onClick` method whenever the button is clicked."

And in response to this request, Android asks, "Oh, yeah? How do I know that your `MyListener` object has an `onClick` method that I can call?" And before you can answer the question, Android notices that your `MyListener` class implements the `OnClickListener` interface. So (because of the code in Listing 4-2) your `MyListener` object has an `onClick` method.

Of course, Android doesn't really ask, "How do I know that your `MyListener` object has an `onClick` method?" For one thing, Android doesn't say anything because Android doesn't have a mouth. And for another thing, Android's code to call `onClick` declares the object containing the `onClick` method to be of type `OnClickListener`. So if your `MyListener` method doesn't implement `OnClickListener`, Java notices a type inconsistency (and Java complains vigorously).

So here's the sequence of events (follow along in Figure 4-2): Your app registers a listener with Android. Then your app goes about its business. When a relevant event takes place (such as the clicking of a button) Android calls back to your app's code. Android calls the `onClick` method inside whatever object you registered.

Android calls back to your app's code, so the term *callback* describes the mechanism that Android uses to handle events.

An object remembers who created it

In the preceding section, I raise several questions about the interaction between your app and Android's callback. But in that section, I miss one of the questions. The question is this: In the `onClick` method of Listing 4-3, how does the code know what `button` means? Listing 4-3 contains two classes — `MyActivity` and `MyListener`. Without jumping through some hoops, one class doesn't know anything about another class's fields.

In Listing 4-3, the keyword `this` sits inside the code that defines the `MyActivity` class:

```
button.setOnClickListener(new MyListener(this));
```

Book II
Chapter 4

In Java, `this` refers to "the object that contains the current line of code." So, in Listing 4-3, the word `this` refers to an instance of `MyActivity` — the activity that's being displayed on the device's screen. The current `MyActivity` instance has a button. So far, so good.

Later in Listing 4-3, the `MyListener` constructor tucks a reference to the current activity into one of its fields. (See Figure 4-3.)

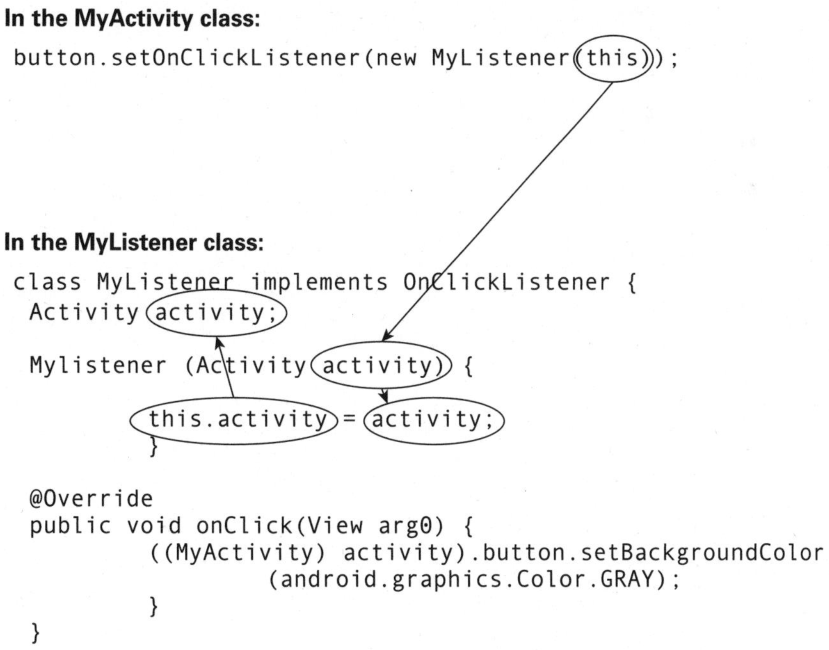

In the MyActivity class:

```
button.setOnClickListener(new MyListener(this));
```

In the MyListener class:

```
class MyListener implements OnClickListener {
  Activity activity;

  Mylistener (Activity activity) {
    this.activity = activity;
  }

  @Override
  public void onClick(View arg0) {
      ((MyActivity) activity).button.setBackgroundColor
              (android.graphics.Color.GRAY);
      }
  }
```

Figure 4-3:
How a listener remembers its creator.

For more information about constructors and about the use of the word `this` inside a constructor, see Chapter 2 in this minibook.

Looking again at Figure 4-3, `MyListener` refers to an `activity`, and that activity contains a button. When Android calls the `onClick` method, the method executes an instruction that's very much like this one:

```
activity.button.setBackgroundColor
                        (android.graphics.Color.GRAY);
```

The instruction takes the referenced activity's button and sets the button's background color to gray. (To make things work properly, you have to do some casting in the `onClick` method of Listing 4-3, but you can worry about the casting when you glance at Chapter 3 of this minibook.)

An easier way to handle an event

If you read the preceding section and then you read this section, you'll probably want to send me a nasty e-mail message. The preceding section describes an admittedly convoluted way to make a listener remember which activity's button to tweak. It's important to know how Listing 4-3 works, but if you modify Listing 4-3 so that the activity is its own listener, things become much simpler. Listing 4-4 shows you how to do it.

Listing 4-4:   An Activity Eats Its Own Dog Food

```
package com.allmycode.samples;

import android.app.Activity;
import android.os.Bundle;
import android.view.View;
import android.view.View.OnClickListener;
import android.widget.Button;

public class MyActivity extends Activity
                        implements OnClickListener {

    Button button;

    @Override
    public void onCreate(Bundle savedInstanceState) {
        super.onCreate(savedInstanceState);
        setContentView(R.layout.main);

        button = ((Button) findViewById(R.id.button1));

        button.setOnClickListener(this);
    }

    @Override
    public void onClick(View arg0) {
        button.setBackgroundColor
```

```
                                 (android.graphics.Color.GRAY);
    }
}
```

The earlier section starts with a question: "In the `onClick` method, how does the code know what `button` means?" In this section, that question goes away just as my lap goes away when I stand up.

In Listing 4-4, both the button and the `onClick` method are members inside the activity. So the `onClick` method has free and easy access to the button. You don't need an `Activity` field as in Listing 4-4, and you don't need any fancy casting from `Activity` to `MyActivity`.

You have to remind Android that `MyActivity` contains an `onClick` method; you do that by adding `implements OnClickListener` to the declaration of `MyActivity`. You must also remind Android to notify the current `MyActivity` object whenever the button gets clicked. You do this reminding by writing

```
button.setOnClickListener(this);
```

which, roughly speaking, translates to "Hey, Android! When someone clicks the button, call the `onClick` method that's inside `this` object (a `MyActivity` object, which fortunately implements `OnClickListener`)."

The pattern in Listing 4-4 (having an `Activity` implement whatever interface it requires) is a very common Java programming idiom.

Classes That Must (And Must Not) Be Extended

If a Java class isn't broken, don't fix it.

Suppose you want to add functionality to an existing Java class. You like Android's `Activity` class, but the predeclared `Activity` class displays nothing on the screen. Do you rewrite Android's `Activity` class? No.

Instead of rewriting an existing class, you extend the class. Even in a do-nothing Android "Hello" application, you write

```
public class MyActivity extends Activity
```

Then, in the `MyActivity` class's declaration, you write

```
@Override
public void onCreate(Bundle savedInstanceState) {
    super.onCreate(savedInstanceState);
    setContentView(R.layout.main);
}
```

Your `MyActivity` class creates new functionality by extending most of Android's `Activity` functionality while overriding the `Activity` class's brain-dead `onCreate` method.

Java's final classes

In object-oriented programming, extending a class is the noblest thing you can do.

But some classes aren't meant to be extended. Take, for example, Java's `String` class. A `String` is a `String` is a `String`. You don't want somebody's `MyString.length` method to return the length of time it takes to scramble a string's characters. To prevent someone from doing something unexpected, unconventional, or unusual with a string's methods, the creators of Java made the `String` class final:

```
public final class String
```

Some of Android's predeclared classes are also final, including the `Calendar` class, the `Telephony` class, and (one of my favorites) the `MathUtils` class.

Java's abstract classes

Just as a final class hates to be extended, an *abstract class* insists on being extended. Android's `ViewGroup` is an example of an abstract class. (See Listing 4-5.)

Listing 4-5:   A Small Part of Android's ViewGroup Class

```
public abstract class ViewGroup {

    public void bringChildToFront(View child) {
        int index = indexOfChild(child);
        if (index >= 0) {
            removeFromArray(index);
            addInArray(child, mChildrenCount);
            child.mParent = this;
        }
    }

    protected abstract void onLayout(boolean changed,
                int l, int t, int r, int b);
}
```

Android's `ViewGroup.java` file is more than 3,700 lines long. So Listing 4-5 has only a tiny fraction of the file's code. But you can see from Listing 4-5 how a class becomes abstract. To no one's surprise, the word `abstract` precedes the word `class`. But the word `abstract` also starts the declaration of some methods belonging to the class.

The founders of Android decided that the idea of a `ViewGroup` is useful. They were correct because your favorite Android layouts (`LinearLayout`, `RelativeLayout`, and so on) are subclasses of `ViewGroup`. They also understood that from one kind of `ViewGroup` to another, some functionality doesn't change. For example, Listing 4-5 defines a `bringChildToFront` method, and subclasses of `ViewGroup` inherit this method.

But the founders also realized that some aspects of a `ViewGroup` make no sense unless you work with a particular kind of group. For example, a `LinearLayout` positions things one after another, and an `AbsoluteLayout` positions things according to specified coordinates. So Listing 4-5 doesn't have a full-blown `onLayout` method. The `onLayout` declaration in Listing 4-5 has no method body. But Android requires each subclass of the `ViewGroup` class to declare its own `onLayout` method. Java enforces this requirement when (as in Listing 4-5) you declare method `onLayout` to be `abstract`.

Book II
Chapter 4

Object-Oriented
Programming
in Java

As a developer, you can't create an object from an abstract class. If you write

```
ViewGroup group = new ViewGroup();
```

Java tells you that you're behaving badly. To do something useful with the `ViewGroup` class, you need a subclass of the `ViewGroup` class. The subclass has a concrete version of each abstract method in the `ViewGroup` class:

```
package com.allmycode.samples;

import android.content.Context;
import android.view.ViewGroup;

public class MyLayout extends ViewGroup {

    public MyLayout(Context context) {
        super(context);
    }

    @Override
    protected void onLayout(boolean changed,
            int l, int t, int r, int b);
    }
}
```

Inner Classes

Here's big news! You can define a class inside another class! Most classes don't live inside another class, and most classes don't contain other classes. But when the idea behind one class screams out to be part of another class, feel free to create a class within a class.

Named inner classes

For the user, Listing 4-6 behaves the same way as Listings 4-3 and 4-4. But in Listing 4-6, the `MyActivity` class contains its own `MyListener` class.

Listing 4-6:   A Class within a Class

```
package com.allmycode.samples;

import android.app.Activity;
import android.os.Bundle;
import android.view.View;
import android.view.View.OnClickListener;
import android.widget.Button;

public class MyActivity extends Activity {

    Button button;

    @Override
    public void onCreate(Bundle savedInstanceState) {
        super.onCreate(savedInstanceState);
        setContentView(R.layout.main);

        button = ((Button) findViewById(R.id.button1));

        button.setOnClickListener(new MyListener());
    }

    class MyListener implements OnClickListener {

        @Override
        public void onClick(View arg0) {
            button.setBackgroundColor
                        (android.graphics.Color.GRAY);
        }
    }
}
```

The `MyListener` class in Listing 4-6 is an *inner class.* An inner class is a lot like any other class. But within an inner class's code, you can refer to the enclosing class's fields. For example, the `onClick` method inside

MyListener uses the name button, and button is defined in the enclosing MyActivity class.

Listings 4-4 and 4-6 are very similar. In both listings, you circumvent the complexities described in the section "An object remembers who created it," earlier in this chapter. For this chapter's example, the choice of Listing 4-4 or Listing 4-6 is largely a matter of taste.

Anonymous inner classes

Notice that the code in Listing 4-6 uses the MyListener class only once. (The only use is in a call to button.setOnClickListener.) So I ask, do you really need a name for something that's used only once? No, you don't. You can substitute the entire definition of the inner class inside the call to button.setOnClickListener. When you do this, you have an *anonymous inner class*. Listing 4-7 shows you how it works.

Listing 4-7:   A Class with No Name (Inside a Class with a Name)

```java
package com.allmycode.samples;

import android.app.Activity;
import android.os.Bundle;
import android.view.View;
import android.view.View.OnClickListener;
import android.widget.Button;

public class MyActivity extends Activity {

    Button button;

    @Override
    public void onCreate(Bundle savedInstanceState) {
        super.onCreate(savedInstanceState);
        setContentView(R.layout.main);

        button = ((Button) findViewById(R.id.button1));

        button.setOnClickListener(new OnClickListener() {

            @Override
            public void onClick(View arg0) {
                button.setBackgroundColor
                        (android.graphics.Color.GRAY);
            }
        });
    }

}
```

Inner classes are good for things like event handlers, such as the `onClick` method in this chapter's examples. The most difficult thing about an anonymous inner class is keeping track of the parentheses, the curly braces, and the indentation. So my humble advice is, start by writing code without any inner classes, such as the code in Listing 4-3 or Listing 4-4. Later, when you become bored with ordinary Java classes, experiment by changing some of your ordinary classes into inner classes.

Chapter 5: A <brief> Look at XML

In This Chapter

✔ **What XML can do for you**

✔ **What goes into an XML document**

✔ **How XML handles the names of things**

*M*odern software takes on several forms:

✦ **Some software is *procedural*.**

The software tells the computer to "Do this, then do that."

✦ **Some software is *declarative*.**

The software says, "Here's what I want the form to look like" or "Here's a list of things my application should be allowed to do."

✦ **Some software is neither procedural nor declarative.**

The software lists functions to be executed in the order in which they apply or lists logical rules to be checked for validity.

One way or another, a development platform should use the best software for the job. That's why the Android platform uses both procedural and declarative software.

✦ Android's **procedural** Java code tells a device what to do.

✦ Android's **declarative** XML code describes a layout, an application, a set of strings, a set of preferences, or some other information that's useful to a mobile device.

A typical Android application is a mix of Java code, XML code, and a few other things. So when you develop for Android, you write lots of Java code and you mess with XML code.

What? You "mess with" XML code? What does that mean?

The truth is, XML code is painful to type. A typical XML file involves many elements, each requiring very precise wording and all looking very much alike at first glance. So in the Android world, most XML files are generated automatically. You don't type all the file's angle brackets. Instead, you fill in a form and let Eclipse's tools create the XML code on your behalf.

So in many situations, you don't have to compose XML code. But I often encounter situations in which I want to bypass Eclipse's forms and tweak the XML code myself. Maybe the form doesn't readily provide an option that I want to use in my XML code. Or maybe my app isn't behaving the way I want it to behave, and I read over the XML code to check for subtle errors.

For these reasons and others, you're best off understanding the fundamentals of XML. So this chapter covers XML basics.

If you're new to Java, you may wonder why this book doesn't have a chapter on Java fundamentals. Well, Java is an intricate beast. Years ago I tried to summarize Java fundamentals in a few side chapters of a book, and the whole endeavor didn't feel right to me. If you want to figure out Java, you're better off with a complete book on the subject. Fortunately, I have just the book! It's *Java For Dummies,* 5th Edition, by Barry Burd (John Wiley & Sons, Inc.). It's available in fine bookstores around the world. And when you buy a copy, please pay double the asking price.

XML Isn't Ordinary Text

You may already be familiar with *Hypertext Markup Language* (HTML) because HTML is the universal language of the World Wide Web. Choose View⇨Source in your favorite web browser, and you'll see a bunch of HTML tags — tags like `<head>`, `<title>`, `<meta>`, and so on. An HTML document describes the look and layout of a web page.

An XML document is something like an HTML document. But an XML document differs from an HTML document in many ways. The two most striking ways are as follows:

✦ An XML file doesn't describe only look and layout. In fact, very few XML files describe anything visual at all. Instead, most XML files describe data — a list of stock trades; a hierarchical list of automobile makes and models; or a nested list of movements, measures, and notes in a Beethoven symphony.

✦ Certain rules describe what you can and cannot write in an HTML or an XML document. The rules for HTML are very permissive. The rules for XML are very strict.

In HTML, a missing character or word often goes unnoticed. In XML, a missing character or word can ruin your whole day.

The formal definitions of an XML document's parts can be daunting. But you can think of an XML document as a bunch of elements, with each element having one or two tags.

Of tags and elements

Tags and elements are the workhorses of XML. Here's the scoop:

✦ **A *tag* is some text surrounded by angle brackets.**

For example, Listing 5-1 contains a basic `AndroidManifest.xml` file. In this file, `<intent-filter>` is a tag, `</intent-filter>` (which comes a bit later in the file is another tag. Text such as `<application android:icon="@drawable/icon" android:label="@string/app_name">` is also a tag.

Listing 5-1: An AndroidManifest.xml File

```
<?xml version="1.0" encoding="utf-8"?>
<manifest xmlns:android=
  "http://schemas.android.com/apk/res/android"
     package="com.allmycode.andevcon"
     android:versionCode="1"
     android:versionName="1.0">
   <uses-sdk android:minSdkVersion="8" />

   <application android:icon="@drawable/icon"
     android:label="@string/app_name">
        <activity android:name=".MyActivity"
                android:label="@string/app_name">
           <intent-filter>
              <action android:name=
                "android.intent.action.MAIN" />
              <category android:name=
                "android.intent.category.LAUNCHER" />
           </intent-filter>
        </activity>

   </application>
</manifest>
```

Not everything with angle brackets qualifies as an XML tag. For example, the text `<This is my application.>` violates many of the rules of grammatically correct XML. For more about what an XML tag can and cannot contain, read on.

An XML document is *well formed* when its text obeys all the rules of grammatically correct XML.

✦ **An XML document may have three different kinds of tags:**

• A *start tag* begins with an open angle bracket and a name. The start tag's last character is a closing angle bracket.

In Listing 5-1, `<intent-filter>` is a start tag. The start tag's name is `intent-filter`.

What element names can you use?

In HTML, the tags `<b>` and `</b>` surround text that appears in bold type. That's the way web pages are encoded.

But in XML, tags like `<cat>` and `</cat>` might represent a Windows security catalog, catenary-shaped wire hanging down from telephone poles, or a pet who's climbing on your computer keyboard (while you write *Android Application Development All-in-One For Dummies*, I might add).

How do you know whether the names in your XML document are meaningful?

The short answer is, "Meaning is as meaning does." (Whatever that means!) An element's name is meaningful as long as a computer program can do the things that you intend programs to do with that element. For example, a program that checks security catalogues to distinguish trustworthy from malicious downloads probably does nothing useful with an element like

```
<cat name="Felix" age="7"
    breed="calico" />
```

On the other hand, a security catalog program may include instructions to deal with the following element:

```
<cat name="Firefox"
    verified="true"
    publisher="mozilla.org"
    version="7.0.1" />
```

Even so, the XML specs provide two ways to describe the names in a document. The older way is with a *DTD* (*Document Type Definition*). A DTD looks something like this:

```
<!ELEMENT CatThoughts
(Image, Thought+)>
<!ATTLIST CatThoughts
```

```
frequency CDATA #REQUIRED>

<!NOTATION JPEG SYSTEM
"image/jpeg">
<!ENTITY CuteCat SYSTEM
"weelie.jpg" NDATA JPEG>
<!ELEMENT Image EMPTY>
<!ATTLIST Image source
ENTITY #REQUIRED>

<!ELEMENT Thought
(#PCDATA)>
<!ENTITY meow "Feed me">
```

A DTD describes the names that you can use in a particular XML document (or in a bunch of XML documents) and describes the order in which you can use those names. But a DTD doesn't describe all the fine points of element-naming (like the fact that a name must refer to an integer value, or to a date). So the newer way to describe the names in a document is with a *schema.* A schema looks something like this:

```
<?xml version="1.0"?>
<!-- Children.xsd -->

<xsd:schema xmlns:xsd="http://
    www.w3.org/2001/XMLSchema">
<xsd:element name="Children"
    type="xsd:integer"/>
</xsd:schema>
```

This schema says that a certain XML document (or a bunch of XML documents) uses the element name `Children`, and that the value stored in the `Children` element must be an integer. (A family can't have 2.5 children.) Even better, a schema is itself an XML document (with start tags, end tags, and everything else), so all the tools that you apply to ordinary XML documents can be applied to schema documents as well. (A DTD may look something like an XML document, but in a DTD, the exclamation points and the lack of end tags break the grammar rules of an XML document.)

Not every XML document is connected to a DTD or to a schema — and even if an XML document has a DTD or a schema, that document may or may not be valid. A *valid* XML document is a document whose names obey the rules described in the document's DTD or schema.

To test the validity of an XML document use the online test application at `www.w3schools.com/XML/xml_validator.asp`.

- An *end tag* begins with an open angle bracket followed by a forward slash and a name. The end tag's last character is a closing angle bracket.

  In Listing 5-1, `</intent-filter>` is an end tag. The end tag's name is `intent-filter`.

- An *empty element tag* begins with an open angle bracket followed by a name. The empty element tag's last two characters are a forward slash, followed by a closing angle bracket.

  In Listing 5-1, the text `<uses-sdk android:minSdkVersion="8" />` is an empty element tag.

I rattle on about tags a bit more in the next several paragraphs. But in the meantime, I want to describe an XML element.

✦ **An XML *element* either has both a start tag and an end tag, or it has an empty element tag.**

The document in Listing 5-1 contains several elements. For example, the document's `intent-filter` element has both a start tag and an end tag. (Both the start and end tags have the same name, `intent-filter`, so the name of the entire element is `intent-filter`.)

In Listing 5-1, the document's `action` element has only one tag — an empty element tag.

✦ **The names of XML elements are not cast in stone.**

In an HTML document, a b element creates boldface text. For example, the text `<b>Buy this!</b>` in an HTML document looks like **Buy this!** in your web browser's window.

In an HTML document, the element name b is cast in stone. But in XML documents, names like `manifest`, `application`, `activity`, and `intent-filter` are not cast in stone. An XML document has its own set of element names, and these names are likely to be different from the names in most other XML documents. You can create your own well-formed XML document as follows:

```
<pets>
    <cat>
        Felix
    </cat>
    <cat>
        Sylvester
    </cat>
</pets>
```

If your goal is to store information about kitty cats, your XML document is just fine.

The text in an XML document is case-sensitive. An element named APPLICATION doesn't have the same name as another element named application.

✦ **A non-empty XML element may contain *content*.**

The content is stuff between the start tag and the end tag. For example, in Listing 5-1, the intent-filter element's content is

```
<action android:name=
    "android.intent.action.MAIN" />
<category android:name=
    "android.intent.category.LAUNCHER" />
```

An element's content may include other elements. (In this example, the intent-filter element contains an action element and a category element.)

An element's content may also include ordinary text. For example, in Listing 5-2, the resources element contains two string elements, and each string element contains ordinary text.

Listing 5-2:   An Android strings.xml File

```
<?xml version="1.0" encoding="utf-8" standalone="no"?>
<resources>
    <string name="hello">Hello World!</string>
    <string name="app_name">AnDevCon App</string>
</resources>
```

You can even have mixed content. For example, between an element's start and end tags, you may have some ordinary text, followed by an element or two, followed by more ordinary text.

✦ **In some cases, two or more elements may have the same name.**

In Listing 5-2, two distinct elements have the name string. To find out more about the names used in an XML file, see the nearby sidebar "What element names can you use?"

✦ **Elements are either nested inside one another, or they don't overlap at all.**

In Listing 5-1, the `manifest` element contains a `uses-sdk` element and an `application` element. The `application` element contains an `activity` element, which in turn contains an `intent-filter` element, and so on.

```
<manifest>

    This code demonstrates element nesting.
    This code is NOT a real AndroidManifest.xml file


    <uses-sdk />

    <application>

        <activity>
            <intent-filter>
                <action />
                <category />
            </intent-filter>
        </activity>

    </application>

</manifest>
```

In Listing 5-1 (and in the fake listing inside this bullet) the `uses-sdk` and `application` elements don't overlap at all. The `action` and `category` elements don't overlap at all. But whenever one element overlaps another, one of the elements is nested completely inside the other.

For example, in Listing 5-1, the `intent-filter` element is nested completely inside the `activity` element. The following sequence of tags, with overlapping and not nesting, would be illegal:

```
<activity>
    <intent-filter>
    This is NOT well-formed XML code.
</activity>
    </intent-filter>
```

Near the start of this chapter, I announce that the rules governing HTML aren't as strict as the rules governing XML. In HTML, you can create non-nested, overlapping tags. For example, the code `<b>Use <i>irregular</b> fonts</i> sparingly` appears in your web browser as

Use *irregular* fonts sparingly

with "Use irregular" in bold and "irregular fonts" italicized.

Microsoft Internet Explorer is a decent XML viewer. When you visit an XML document with Internet Explorer, you see a colorful, well-indented display of your XML code. The code's elements expand and collapse on your command. And if you visit an XML document that's not well-formed (for example, a document with overlapping, non-nested tags), Internet Explorer displays a blank page. (That's good. Internet Explorer reminds you that you've goofed.)

✦ **Each XML document contains one element in which all other elements are nested.**

In Listing 5-1, the `manifest` element contains all other elements. That's good. The following outline would not make a legal XML document:

```
<manifest>
    <uses-sdk />
    <application>
    </application>

    This is NOT a well-formed XML document
    because another element comes after the
    following manifest end tag:
</manifest>


<manifest>
    <uses-sdk />
    <application>
    </application>
</manifest>
```

In an XML document, the single element that encloses all other elements is the *root* element.

✦ **Start tags and empty element tags may contain *attributes*.**

An *attribute* is a name-value pair. Each attribute has the form

```
name="value"
```

The quotation marks around the value are required.

In Listing 5-1, the start tags and empty element tags contain many attributes. For example, in the `manifest` start tag, the text

```
xmlns:android=
    "http://schemas.android.com/apk/res/android"
```

is an attribute. In the same tag, the text

```
package="com.allmycode.andevcon"
```

is an attribute. All in all, the `manifest` start tag has four attributes. Later in Listing 5-1, the empty element `uses-sdk` tag has one attribute.

Other things you find in an XML document

There's more to life than tags and elements. This section describes all the things you can look forward to.

✦ **An XML document begins with an XML declaration.**

The declaration in Listing 5-1 is

```
<?xml version="1.0" encoding="utf-8"?>
```

The question marks distinguish the declaration from an ordinary XML tag.

This declaration announces that Listing 5-1 contains an XML document (big surprise!), that the document uses version 1.0 of the XML specifications, and that bit strings used to store the document's characters are to be interpreted with their meanings as UTF-8 codes.

In practice, you seldom have reason to mess with a document's XML declaration. For a new XML document, simply copy and paste the declaration in Listing 5-1.

The version="1.0" part of an XML declaration may look antiquated, but XML hasn't changed much since the initial specs appeared in 1998. In fact, the only newer version is XML 1.1, which developers seldom use. This reluctance to change is part of the XML philosophy — to have a universal, time-tested format for representing information about almost any subject.

✦ **An XML document may contain comments.**

A comment begins with the characters <!-- and ends with the characters -->. For example, the lines

```
<!-- This application must be tested
     very, very carefully. -->
```

form an XML comment. A document's comments can appear between tags (and in a few other places that aren't worth fussing about right now).

Comments are normally intended to be read by humans. But programs that input XML documents are free to read comments and to act on the text within comments. Android doesn't normally do anything with the comments it finds in its XML files, but you never know.

✦ **An XML document may contain processing instructions.**

A processing instruction looks a lot like the document's XML declaration. Here's an example of a processing instruction:

```
<?chapter number="x" Put chapter number here ?>
```

A document may have many processing instructions, and these processing instructions can appear between tags (and in a few other places).

But in practice, most XML documents have no processing instructions. (For reasons too obscure even for a Technical Stuff icon, the document's XML declaration isn't a processing instruction.)

Like a document's XML declaration, each processing instruction begins with the characters <? and ends with the characters ?>. Each processing instruction has a name. But after the processing instruction's name, anything goes. The processing instruction near the start of this bullet has the name chapter followed by some free-form text. Part of that text looks like a start tag's attribute, but the remaining text looks like a comment of some sort.

You can put almost anything inside a processing instruction. Most of the software that inputs your XML document will simply ignore the processing instruction. (As an experiment, I added my chapter processing instruction to the file in Listing 5-1. This change made absolutely no difference in the running of my Android app.)

So what good are processing instructions anyway? Well, if you stumble into one, I don't want you to mistake it for a kind of XML declaration. Also, certain programs may read specific processing instructions and get particular information from these instructions.

For example, a *style sheet* is a file that describes the look and the layout of the information in an XML document. Typically, an XML document and the corresponding style sheet are in two different files. To indicate that the information in your pets.xml document should be displayed using the rules in the animals.css style sheet, you add the following processing instruction to the pets.xml document:

```
<?xml-stylesheet href="animals.css" type="text/css"?>
```

✦ **An XML document may contain entity references.**

I poked around among Android's official sample applications and found the following elements (spread out among different programs):

```
<Key android:codes="60" android:keyLabel="&lt;"/>
<Key android:codes="62" android:keyLabel="&gt;"/>
<Key android:codes="34" android:keyLabel="&quot;"/>
<string name="activity_save_restore">
    App/Activity/Save &amp; Restore State
</string>
```

The first element contains a reference to the < entity. You can't use a real angle bracket just anywhere in an XML document. An angle bracket signals the beginning of an XML tag. So if you want to express that the name three-brackets stands for the string "<<<", you can't write

```
<string name="three-brackets"><<<</string>
```

The extra brackets will confuse any program that expects to encounter ordinary XML tags.

So to get around XML's special use of angle brackets, the XML specs include the *entities* `&lt;` and `&gt;`. The first, `&lt;`, stands for an opening angle bracket. The second, `&gt;`, stands for the closing angle bracket. So to express that the name `three-brackets` stands for the string `"<<<"`, you write

```
<string name="three-brackets">&lt;&lt;&lt;</string>
```

In the entity `&lt;`, the letters `lt` stand for "less than." And after all, an opening angle bracket looks like the "less than" sign in mathematics. Similarly, in the entity `&gt;`, the letters `gt` stand for "greater than."

What's in a Namespace?

The first official definition of XML was published in 1998 by the World Wide Web Consortium (W3C). This first standard ignored a sticky problem. If two XML documents have some elements or attributes with identical names, and if those names have different meanings in the two documents, how can you possibly combine the two documents?

Here's a simple XML document:

```
<?xml version="1.0" encoding="utf-8"?>
<banks>
    <bank>First National Bank</bank>
    <bank>Second Regional Bank</bank>
    <bank>United Trustworthy Trusty Trust</bank>
    <bank>Federal Bank of Fredonia (Groucho Branch)</bank>
</banks>
```

And here's another XML document:

```
<?xml version="1.0" encoding="utf-8"?>
<banks>
    <bank>Banks of the Mississippi River</bank>
    <bank>La Rive Gauche</bank>
    <bank>La Rive Droite</bank>
    <bank>The Banks of Plum Creek</bank>
</banks>
```

An organization with seemingly limitless resources aims to collect and combine knowledge from all over the Internet. The organization's software finds XML documents and combines them into one super all-knowing document. (Think of an automated version of Wikipedia.)

But when you combine documents about financial institutions with documents about rivers, you get some confusing results. If both First National and the Banks of Plum Creek are in the same document's `bank` elements, analyzing the document may require prior knowledge. In other words, if you don't already know that some banks lend money and that other banks flood during storms, you might draw some strange conclusions. And unfortunately, computer programs don't already know anything. (Life becomes really complicated when you reach an XML element describing the Red River Bank in Shreveport, Louisiana. This river bank has teller machines in Shreveport, Alexandria, and other towns.)

To remedy this situation, members of the XML standards committee created XML namespaces. A *namespace* is a prefix that you attach to a name. You separate the namespace from the name with a colon (`:`) character. For example in Listing 5-1, almost every attribute name begins with the `android` prefix. The listing's attributes include `android:versionCode`, `android:versionName`, `android:minSdkVersion`, `android:icon`, and more.

So to combine documents about lending banks and river banks, you create the XML document in Listing 5-3.

Listing 5-3:   A Document with Two Namespaces

```
<?xml version="1.0" encoding="utf-8"?>

<banks xmlns:money=
            "http://schemas.allmycode.com/money"
       xmlns:river=
            "http://schemas.allmycode.com/river">

    <money:bank>First National Bank</money:bank>
    <money:bank>Second Regional Bank</money:bank>
    <money:bank>
        United Trustworthy Trusty Trust
    </money:bank>
    <money:bank>
        Federal Bank of Fredonia (Groucho Branch)
    </money:bank>

    <river:bank>
        Banks of the Mississippi River
    </river:bank>
    <river:bank>La Rive Gauche</river:bank>
    <river:bank>La Rive Droite</river:bank>
    <river:bank>The Banks of Plum Creek</river:bank>

</banks>
```

In a name such as `android:icon`, the word `android` is a `prefix`, and the word `icon` is a `local name`.

At this point, the whole namespace business branches into two possibilities:

✦ **Some very old XML software is not namespace-aware.**

The original XML standard had no mention of namespaces. So the oldest XML-handling programs do nothing special with prefixes. To an old program, the names `money:bank` and `river:bank` in Listing 5-3 are simply two different names with no relationship to each other. The colons in the names are no different from the letters.

✦ **Newer XML software is namespace-aware.**

In some situations, you want the software to recognize relationships between names with the same prefixes and between identical names with different prefixes. For example, in a document containing elements named `consumer:bank`, `investment:bank`, and `consumer:confidence`, you may want your software to recognize two kinds of banks. You may also want your software to deal with two kinds of consumer elements.

Most modern software is namespace-aware. That is, the software recognizes that a name like `river:bank` consists of a prefix and a local name.

To make it easier for software to sort out an XML document's namespaces, every namespace must be defined. In Listing 5-3, the attributes

```
xmlns:money=
        "http://schemas.allmycode.com/money"
xmlns:river=
        "http://schemas.allmycode.com/river"
```

define the document's two namespaces. The attributes associate one URL with the `money` namespace and another URL with the `river` namespace. The special `xmlns` namespace doesn't get defined because the `xmlns` namespace has the same meaning in every XML document. The `xmlns` prefix always means, "This is the start of an XML namespace definition."

In Listing 5-3, each namespace is associated with a URL. So if you're creating a new XML document, you may ask, "What if I don't have my own domain name?" You may also ask, "What information must I post at a namespace's URL?" And the surprising answers are "Make up one" and "Nothing."

The string of symbols doesn't really have to be a URL. Instead, it can be a URI — a *Universal Resource Identifier*. A URI looks like a URL, but a URI doesn't have to point to an actual network location. A URI is simply a name, a string of characters "full of sound and fury" and possibly "signifying nothing." Some XML developers create web pages to accompany each of their URIs. The web pages contain useful descriptions of the names used in the XML documents.

But most URIs used for XML namespaces point nowhere. For example, the URI `http://schemas.android.com/apk/res/android` in Listing 5-1 appears in almost every Android XML document. If you type that URI into the address field of your favorite web browser, you get the familiar `cannot display the webpage` or `Server not found` message.

An *unbound prefix* message indicates that you haven't correctly associated a namespace found in your XML document with a URI. Some very old software (software that's not namespace-aware) doesn't catch errors of this kind, but most modern software does.

The package attribute

In Listing 5-1, the attribute name `package` has no prefix. So you might say, "What the heck! I'll change the attribute's name to `android:package` just for good measure." But this change produces some error messages. One message reads `<manifest> does not have a package attribute.` What's going on here?

In an `AndroidManifest.xml` file, the `package` attribute has more to do with Java than with Android. (The `package` attribute points to the Java package containing the application's Java code.) So the creators of Android decided not to make this `package` attribute be part of the `android` namespace. The creators coded the `android` namespace words (such as `android:versionCode` and `android:versionName`) in some of the Android SDK files.

When you create an `AndroidManifest.xml` file, Eclipse starts building parts of your project immediately. The Android software compares the names in your `AndroidManifest.xml` file with the words in the `android` namespace. As soon as the Android software encounters the evil `android:package` (the `android` prefix followed by a non-android name), the software sounds the alarms.

Each Android platform, from Cupcake onward, has a file named `public.xml` among the files you get when you download the Android SDK. If you open a `public.xml` file in a text editor, you see a list of names in the `android` namespace.

The style attribute

The same business about not being an `android` name holds for `style` and `package`. A *style* is a collection of items (or *properties)* describing the look of something on the mobile device screen. A style's XML document might contain Android-specific names, but the style itself is simply a bunch of items, not an Android property in its own right.

To see how this works, imagine creating a very simple app. The XML file describing the app's basic layout may look like the code in Listing 5-4.

Listing 5-4: Using the style Attribute

```xml
<?xml version="1.0" encoding="utf-8"?>
<LinearLayout xmlns:android=
  "http://schemas.android.com/apk/res/android"
    android:orientation="vertical"
    android:layout_width="fill_parent"
    android:layout_height="fill_parent"
    >
<TextView
    android:layout_width="fill_parent"
    android:layout_height="wrap_content"
    android:text="@string/callmom"
    style="@style/bigmono"
    />
</LinearLayout>
```

In Listing 5-4, all attribute names except `style` (and the name `android` itself) are in the `android` namespace. The value `"@style/bigmono"` points Android to an XML file in your app's `res/values` folder. Listing 5-5 contains a very simple file named `styles.xml`.

Listing 5-5: A File with Style

```xml
<?xml version="1.0" encoding="utf-8"?>
<resources>
    <style name="bigmono">
        <item name="android:textSize">50dip</item>
        <item name="android:typeface">monospace</item>
    </style>
</resources>
```

Again, notice the mix of words that are inside and outside of the `android` namespace. The words `android:textSize` and `android:typeface` are in the `android` namespace, and the other words in Listing 5-5 are not.

The style in Listing 5-5 specifies a whopping 50 device-independent pixels for the size of the text and monospace (traditional typewriter) font for the type-face. When Android applies the style in Listing 5-5 to the layout in Listing 5-4, you see the prominent message in Figure 5-1.

Figure 5-1:
Be a good
son or
daughter.

For more information about styles, layouts, device-independent pixels, and the use of XML to describe these things, see Book IV, Chapter 1.

Book III

The Building Blocks

The 5th Wave   By Rich Tennant

"This model comes with a particularly useful app — a simulated static button for breaking out of long-winded conversations."

Contents at a Glance

Chapter 1: Android Activities

In This Chapter

✔ **Launching an activity**

✔ **Going through an activity's lifecycle**

✔ **Getting information from an activity**

On a desktop computer, everything starts with a window. Open a window, and run a word processor. Open another window, and read your e-mail. Move a window, minimize a window, resize a window. It's a very familiar story.

But mobile devices aren't desktop computers. A smartphone has a relatively small screen, and if by chance you *could* open several windows at once, the phone's processor would fall over from exhaustion. On a mobile phone, the "window" metaphor would lead to nothing but trouble.

Tablet devices have larger screens and better processors than their telephone cousins. You can probably squeeze a few windows on a tablet screen, but the power that you would allocate to window-handling could be put to better use.

So where does that leave you? The earliest computers had no windows and no multi-tasking. You can't have that. Without some kind of multi-tasking, "smartphones" wouldn't be smart.

Along comes Android's solution — namely, the *activity.* In other chapters, I refer to an activity as "one 'screenful' of components." I liken activities to online forms, such as "a form for entering information to make a purchase on a website." I write, "Unlike most online forms, Android activities don't necessarily have text boxes — places for the user to type credit card numbers and such. But Android activities have a lot in common with online forms." I love quoting myself.

All about Activities

Here's what the official Android docs say about an activity:

"An activity is a single, focused thing that the user can do. Almost all activities interact with the user, so the `Activity` *class takes care of creating a window for you in which you can place your UI with* `setContentView(View)`.... *Activities are often presented to the user as full-screen windows . . ."*

The `android.app.Activity` class's code is a complete, official definition describing what an activity is and what an activity isn't. But from an app designer's point of view, no formal definition of *activity* paints the complete picture. So maybe the way to describe an activity is behaviorally. Here's my informal description:

At some point during the run of an app, an app designer fills up the screen with stuff. At that point, the designer thinks, "I have to move all this stuff out of the way so the user can deal sensibly with whatever has become most important." So the designer creates a new screen layout, codes the layout's behavior, and refers to the whole business (the layout and its behavior) as a new activity.

At that (newer) point, the designer has two different activities — the original activity that filled up the screen with stuff and the new activity that deals with whatever has become most important. On a smaller device (or on a device running anything earlier than Honeycomb), each activity fills the entire screen. The original activity invokes the new activity and then the new activity covers the original activity.

Under normal circumstances, the two activities form part of a *stack* — a *first in, last out* structure. Imagine that Activity A invokes Activity B, which in turn invokes Activity C. Then the activities A, B, and C form a stack, with Activity C being on top of the stack (and visible to the user). When the user presses the Back button, Activity C pops off the stack to reveal Activity B. When the user presses the Back button again, Activity B pops off the stack to reveal Activity A.

A stack of Android activities is called a *task*. So now you have apps, activities, and tasks. Unfortunately, these words have different meanings for Android developers than they have for the rest of the world.

An *application* is a collection of things meant to accomplish a particular user goal. Some of the things belonging to an app are activities.

The other things belonging to an app are services, broadcast receivers, and content providers. I cover these things in Chapters 3, 4 and 5 of this minibook.

Applications and processes

A typical operating system (Android included) has users, processes, and threads.

- **Each person who logs onto the system is a** *user.* **But the system may also create virtual users — things that the operating system treats as separate users, but that don't correspond to people using keyboards.**

 With users who aren't real people, a system can create specialized pathways for access to resources. For example, a database might be the only "user" with permission to access certain data. A real, human user gets the data indirectly. The human user logs in to the database and asks the database to fetch the data on his or her behalf.

 Each user on a system (a session conducted by a real person or a virtual user) has a *user identification number (UID).*

 Throughout most of this book, I refer to the person who touches the device's screen as "the user." I don't worry too much about virtual users.

- **The operating system divides its work into** *processes.*

 Each process has its own memory space, separate from the space belonging to other processes. Processes interact with one another only through narrow, well-policed pathways.

 The system schedules the running of processes. To do this, the system executes a sequence of statements in one process, then a sequence of statements in another process, then a sequence in a third, eventually returning to the place where the first process left off.

 Each process has a *process identification number (PID).*

- **A process may divide its work into** *threads.*

 The operating system schedules threads in an interleaved fashion. In this respect, a

thread is a lot like a process. But a single process's threads share the process's memory space. So a single process's threads can communicate freely with one another.

With Android, each app runs in its own process as well as bearing its own PID and its own UID. (Apps don't hold onto their PIDs or UIDs from one run to another. The operating system assigns these numbers at the start of a run and then dumps them at the end of the run. The system assigns new numbers for the app's next run.)

Android assigns PIDs incrementally as new processes are created. So when your app starts running, it may have PID 1900. Later, your device may be running low on memory. Android might notice that none of your app's components are needed in the short term. (For example, the device is displaying a different app's activity, and your app contains no long-running services.) To save space, Android might kill your app's process. Poof! The process is gone.

Of course, the user knows nothing of this process assassination. (I'm referring to the human user, not some virtual figment of the system's imagination.) The user simply wanders away from your app's activities by invoking another activity, by pressing Home, by answering a phone call, or some other way. So at some point, the user says, "Hey, wait! I want to get back to what I was doing a few minutes ago." The user navigates back to one of your process's activities. So Android (clever operating system that it is) starts a new process to run your application, re-creates your app's activity as it was before the murder, and displays the activity as if nothing unusual happened. Now your application has a new PID (maybe 1921) because Android created several other processes between the time of your app's murder and the time of your app's rebirth.

Each application runs in its own Android Linux process, with its own user ID. This is one of Android's security strengths. Separate processes don't share any memory. So in effect, each application is sandboxed from the rest of the system, with very narrowly defined (tightly guarded) paths of communication between one application and another. If an application does something wrong (either maliciously or unintentionally), the chance of that wrongdoing affecting the rest of the system is limited. As a developer, you create an application using the XML <application> element in the app's AndroidManifest.xml file.

An activity can (and frequently does) invoke activities belonging to other apps. (For example, an e-mail message might contain a link. So an e-mail app's activity might invoke a web browser app's activity.) That means that a particular task might contain activities from several applications. (See Figure 1-1.)

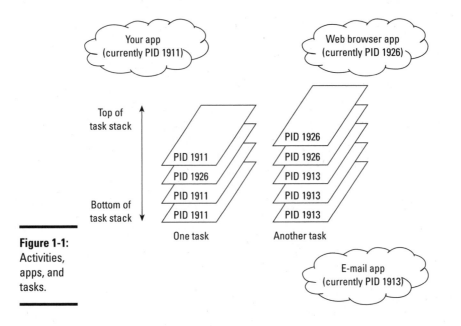

Figure 1-1: Activities, apps, and tasks.

The scenario often works this way:

1. The user starts an app. (Call it Application 1.)

Android creates a new process for the app, creates an instance of the app's main activity, and puts the main activity onto a brand-new task stack. (Call it Task 1.)

2. From the app's main activity, the user invokes another activity (say, a secondary activity belonging to the same app).

Android creates a new instance of the secondary activity. Android pushes the secondary activity onto the task stack. (See Figure 1-2.) The device's screen displays only the secondary activity. (Think of the app's main activity as being hidden underneath the secondary activity. Call the main activity Activity 1; call the secondary activity Activity 2.)

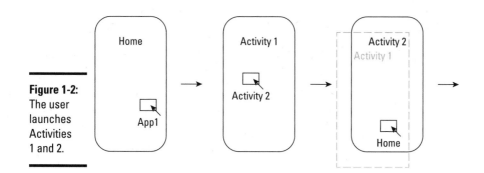

Figure 1-2:
The user launches Activities 1 and 2.

3. The user presses Home.

   Android moves Task 1 off the screen and displays the Home screen, as shown in Figure 1-3.

4. The user starts a second app. (How about calling it Application 2?)

   With the Task 1 still waiting in the wings, Android creates a second task (Task 2) with the second app's main activity.

5. The user presses Home again and presses the icon for Application 1.

   See Figure 1-4. Android displays the top of the Task 1 stack. Activity 2 is still at the top of Task 1. So the user sees Activity 2. Happily, Activity 2 is in the same state as it was when the user first pressed Home. Any text fields still have whatever text the user previously entered, and so on.

6. The user presses the Back button.

   Android pops Activity 2 off the Task 1 stack and destroys this instance of Activity 2. The user sees Activity 1, which is in the same state as it was immediately before Android covered up Activity 1 with Activity 2.

7. From Activity 1, the user again invokes the secondary activity belonging to Application 1.

   Android creates a brand-new instance of the secondary activity. Android pushes the secondary activity onto the task stack. The device's screen displays only the secondary activity. This new instance is *not* in the same state that Activity 2 was in when Activity 2 was destroyed. This new instance is initialized with new values (which is normal for brand-new objects).

**Book III
Chapter 1**

Android Activities

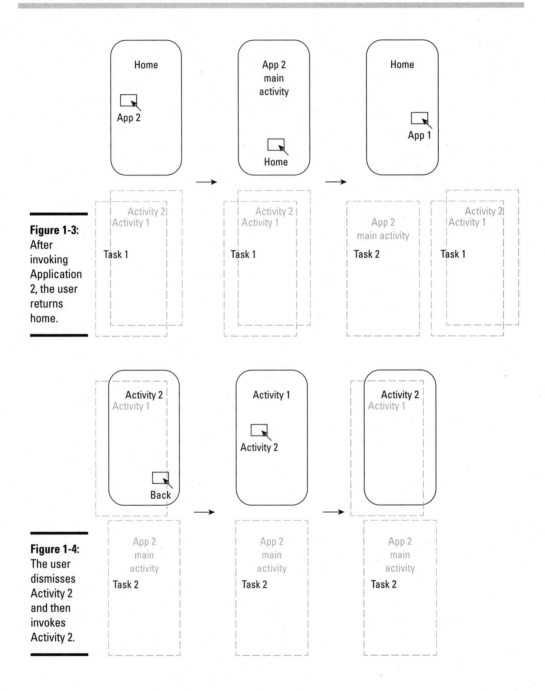

Figure 1-3:
After invoking Application 2, the user returns home.

Figure 1-4:
The user dismisses Activity 2 and then invokes Activity 2.

The scenario in these steps can have many variations. For starters, the user doesn't necessarily press buttons and icons in the order described in the steps. For another thing, a developer can change the way in which activities pile onto tasks. (See Chapter 2 in this minibook.) And from Honeycomb onward, Android has *fragments,* which are like activities but take up only part of a tablet device's screen. (See Chapter 4 in minibook IV.)

State your intention

The Android programming model is based on the use of scarce resources. Compared to a desktop or laptop computer, a smartphone has a small screen, limited memory, and a wimpy processor. With that in mind, the original creators of Android focused on reuse.

Imagine that my app includes a link to my website. When the user clicks the link, Android opens a web browser. But which browser does Android open? Android comes with its own browser (based on Apple's WebKit engine). But the user might have also installed Firefox for Android, Opera Mini, or any number of other web browsers.

In Microsoft Windows, the choice of browser depends on filename extensions and protocol associations. But in Android, the developer invokes a browser by issuing an intent.

In Android development, an *intent* is like an open-ended method call. Instead of coding something like

```
firefox("http://www.google.com");
```

or

```
android_built_in_browser("http://android.allmycode.com");
```

you code the following:

```
String url = "http://android.allmycode.com";
Intent intent = new Intent(Intent.ACTION_VIEW);
intent.setData(Uri.parse(url));
startActivity(intent);
```

In this example, calling `startActivity(intent)` is like throwing an I-want-to-browse ball into the air and expecting another app's activity to catch it. Another app announces its intentions to catch the I-want-to-browse ball by putting an element of the following kind in the app's `AndroidManifest.xml` file:

Book III
Chapter 1

Android Activities

```
<activity android:name=".Catcher"
          android:label="Catcher">
  <intent-filter>
    <action
      android:name="android.intent.action.VIEW" />
    <category
      android:name="android.intent.category.DEFAULT" />
    <category
      android:name="android.intent.category.BROWSABLE" />
    <data android:scheme="http" />
  </intent-filter>
</activity>
```

Again, I quote Android's official documentation:

> *"An intent is an abstract description of an operation to be performed. It can be used with startActivity to launch an Activity, ... An Intent provides a facility for performing late runtime binding between the code in different applications. Its most significant use is in the launching of activities, where it can be thought of as the glue between activities. It is basically a passive data structure holding an abstract description of an action to be performed."*

In truth, Android has two kinds of intents — *implicit* and *explicit* intents.

✦ The kind of intent that I describe in the previous paragraphs (to start any activity claiming to be a web browser) is an *implicit* intent. An implicit intent doesn't call for a particular activity to be launched. Instead, an implicit intent names an action to be taken, along with other information required to fulfill the intent.

The intent

```
Intent intent = new Intent(Intent.ACTION_VIEW);
intent.setData(Uri.parse(url));
```

is an implicit intent.

I cover implicit intents in Chapter 2 of this minibook.

✦ An *explicit* intent actually names an activity class whose instance is to be launched.

In this chapter's examples, I use explicit intents to launch activities. So the next section covers explicit intents.

The explicit intent

To use an explicit intent, you can write something like code in Listing 1-1.

Listing 1-1:   Calling Your Own App's Activity Using an Explicit Intent

```
package my.pack;

import android.app.Activity;
import android.os.Bundle;

public class SomeActivity extends Activity {
  // ... code of some sort belongs here

  Intent intent = new Intent();
  intent.setClassName("my.pack", "my.pack.OtherActivity");
  startActivity(intent);
}
```

In Listing 1-1, the intent's `setClassName` method takes two `String` parameters. The first parameter is the name of the package containing the target activity, and the second parameter is the activity's *fully qualified* class name. So in Listing 1-1, the call to `setClassName` has two strings containing `"my.pack"`. (There may be a reasonable way to avoid repetition, where you'd write something like `setClassName("my.pack", "OtherActivity")`. But if there is one, no one's told *me* about it.)

To invoke another app's activity, you can write something like the code in Listing 1-2.

Book III
Chapter 1

Android Activities

Listing 1-2:   Calling another App's Activity Using an Explicit Intent

```
package my.pack;

import android.app.Activity;
import android.os.Bundle;

public class SomeActivity extends Activity {
  // ... code of some sort belongs here

  intent = new Intent();
  intent.setClassName("other.pack",
                      "other.pack.OtherAppActivity");
  startActivity(intent);
}
```

Listing 1-2 is almost exactly like Listing 1-1. The only difference is that in Listing 1-2, the two activities (the invoking and the invoked activities) belong to two different applications. *Different applications* means different packages. So Listing 1-1 has `"my.pack"`, and Listing 1-2 has `"other.pack"`.

For each activity in your application, you must add an `<activity>` element to the `AndroidManifest.xml` file. If one project's activity invokes another project's activity, you must make Eclipse aware of the connection between the two projects. In the Package Explorer, select the project that contains the `startActivity` call. Then choose Project➪Properties. In the resulting Properties dialog box, choose Java Build Path➪Projects. Add the target activity's project and then click OK. Failure to do any of this stuff results in a runtime `Cannot Find Activity` message. And when you see such a message, screaming "Whadaya mean, Cannot Find Activity?" won't solve the problem.

Using a context

Another way to start a specific activity is with a context. In Listing 1-3, an activity calls another activity within the same application.

Listing 1-3: Calling Your Own App's Activity Using an Explicit Intent with a Context

```
package my.pack;

import android.app.Activity;
import android.os.Bundle;

public class SomeActivity extends Activity {
  // ... code of some sort belongs here

  Intent intent =
    new Intent(this, OtherActivity.class);
  startActivity(intent);
}
```

In Listing 1-3, the last two statements are really saying, "With `this` activity's own context, start running an instance of `OtherActivity`." (If all goes well, the class `OtherActivity` extends Android's `Activity` class, and you're good to go.)

In Listing 1-3, the `Intent` class's constructor takes two parameters — a context and a Java class. The word `this` represents the enclosing `SomeActivity` instance. That's good, because the constructor's first parameter is of type `Context`, and Android's `Activity` class is a subclass of the abstract `Context` class.

A `Context` object is an "interface to global information about an application environment." (Again, I'm quoting the Android docs.) An activity is a context because (aside from being a subclass of `Context`) an activity has a bunch of files, a package name, a bunch of resources, a theme, wallpaper, and other things. All this stuff is available programmatically by way of the activity's context. In Listing 1-3, the `Intent` constructor gets the `OtherActivity`'s package name from `this` — the `SomeActivity` object's context.

Each activity is part of an application, and an `Application` instance is also a context. So in many programs, you can use any of the following method calls (instead of `this`) to obtain a `Context` instance:

```
getContext()
getApplicationContext()
getBaseContext()
```

The `getApplicationContext` and `getBaseContext` methods have limited, specialized uses in Android programs. In this book's examples, you'll never need to call `getApplicationContext` or `getBaseContext`.

In Listing 1-4, an activity from one app uses a context to call another app's activity.

Listing 1-4: Calling another App's Activity Using an Explicit Intent with a Context

```
package my.pack;

import android.app.Activity;
import android.os.Bundle;

public class SomeActivity extends Activity {
  // ... code of some sort belongs here

  try {
    otherContext =
      createPackageContext("other.pack",
      Context.CONTEXT_IGNORE_SECURITY |
      Context.CONTEXT_INCLUDE_CODE);
  } catch (NameNotFoundException e) {
    e.printStackTrace();
  }
  Class<?> otherClass = null;
  try {
    otherClass = otherContext.getClassLoader().
      loadClass("other.pack.OtherAppActivity");
  } catch (ClassNotFoundException e) {
    e.printStackTrace();
  }
  Intent intent = new Intent(otherContext, otherClass);
  startActivity(intent);
}
```

Listing 1-4 is more complicated than Listing 1-3. But most of the complexity comes from the way Java loads classes. One way or another, Listing 1-4 creates an intent from a context and a class name, and then starts the intent's activity.

The Activity Lifecycle

"... And one man in his time plays many parts, His acts being seven ages."

— from *As You Like It,* by William Shakespeare

The human lifecycle is infancy, childhood, adolescence, young adulthood, middle age, old age, and finally, the end.

Android activities have a lifecycle, too. Here are the stages:

+ **Active (or Running):** The activity is in the foreground on the device's screen at the top of a task stack. The user can interact with the activity.

+ **Stopped:** The activity is on a task stack, but the activity isn't visible. Maybe the activity isn't at the top of its stack and other activities on the stack are covering up that activity. Alternatively, the activity isn't visible because the device's screen displays something that's not part of this activity's stack.

+ **Paused:** The Paused state is a kind of limbo between Active and Stopped. Officially, an activity is paused if it's on the currently active stack but it's partially obscured by another activity (such as a transparent activity or a non-full-screen activity that's at the top of the stack).

  In practice, an activity that's transitioning from Active to Stopped goes through a brief period of being Paused, even if the user doesn't see a "partially obscured" phase.

+ **Destroyed:** How sad! But wait! *Destroyed* doesn't mean "dead and gone forever." Android might destroy an activity in order to revive it with a different configuration. Or Android might temporarily clobber an activity while the user isn't actively using that activity.

Lifecycle methods

Most cultures have rites of passage. A *rite of passage* is something that you do when you transition from one life stage to another. For example, where I come from, a child does the following when transitioning to adolescence: "Ye shall stand at the highest point in all of thy land (which is normally the Dauphin Street station of the Frankford El train) and swing a raw fish thrice over thy head. All the while, thou shalt exclaim, 'I shall be a troublesome, raving lunatic for the next few years.' "

Android activities have their own rites of passage, dubbed *lifecycle methods*. Figure 1-5 illustrates the methods.

Unlike people, activities don't step predictably from one stage to the next. For example, a typical activity goes back and forth from being Active to Stopped and back to Active again, with several interludes of being Paused. And when Destroyed, an activity can unceremoniously be revived. For an activity, destruction and reconstruction are parts of the normal course of events.

An Android activity has seven lifecycle methods — namely, onCreate, onRestart, onStart, onResume, onPause, onStop, and onDestroy. In addition, an activity has a few on*Something* methods (such as onSave InstanceState) that aren't formally part of the lifecycle and aren't guaranteed to be called. Anyway, Listing 1-5 contains a bunch of these methods.

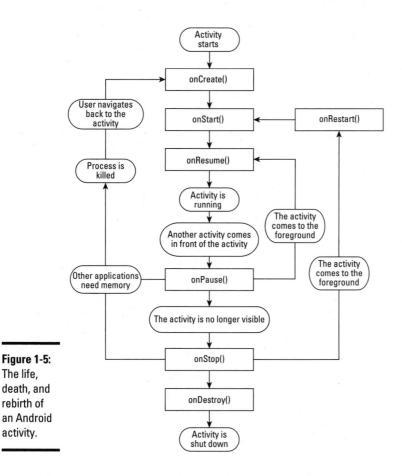

Figure 1-5:
The life, death, and rebirth of an Android activity.

Listing 1-5:   Add Some Logging to Your Activity

```
package com.allmycode.demo1;

import android.app.Activity;
import android.content.res.Configuration;
import android.os.Bundle;
import android.view.View;

public abstract class MyActivity extends Activity {

    abstract void logStuff(String message);

    public void addBreak(View view) {
        logStuff("------");
    }

    /** Called when the activity is created (either
     *  for the first time or after having been
     *  Destroyed. */
    @Override
    public void onCreate(Bundle savedInstanceState) {
        super.onCreate(savedInstanceState);
        logStuff("onCreate");
    }

    /** Called when the activity transitions to
     *  Paused (on its way to Active) after having
     *  been Stopped.
     */
    @Override
    public void onRestart() {
        super.onRestart();
        logStuff("onRestart");
    }

    /** Called when the activity transitions to
     *  Paused (on its way to Active), either for
     *  the first time or after the activity has
     *  been Stopped.
     */
    @Override
    public void onStart() {
        super.onStart();
        logStuff("onStart");
    }

    /** Called when the activity transitions
     *  from Paused to Active.
     */
    @Override
    public void onResume() {
        super.onResume();
```

```
        logStuff("onResume");
    }

    /** Never called unless you set
     * android:configChanges in the
     * AndroidManifest.xml file.
     */
    @Override
    public void onConfigurationChanged
                          (Configuration config) {
        super.onConfigurationChanged(config);
        logStuff("onConfigurationChanged");
    }

    /** Usually (but not always) called during the
     * transition from Active to Paused, or during
     * the transition from Paused to Stopped.
     */
    @Override
    public void onSaveInstanceState(Bundle state) {
        super.onSaveInstanceState(state);
        logStuff("onSaveInstanceState");
    }

    /** Called when the activity transitions from
     * Active to Paused.
     */
    @Override
    public void onPause() {
        super.onPause();
        logStuff("onPause");
    }

    /** Called when the activity transitions from
     * Paused to Stopped.
     */
    @Override
    public void onStop() {
        super.onStop();
        logStuff("onStop");
    }

    /** Called when the activity transitions from
     * Stopped to Destroyed.
     */
    @Override
    public void onDestroy() {
        super.onDestroy();
        logStuff("onDestroy");
    }
}
```

My goal in creating Listing 1-5 is to provide logging that helps you see the lifecycle methods in action. You can drop Listing 1-5 into almost any app to get a Burd's-eye view of your activities and their transitions. To this end, I've created an app that lets you bounce back and forth among different kinds of activities. Listings 1-6, 1-7, and 1-8 describe the app's main activity, and Figure 1-6 shows the main activity's screen.

Listing 1-6:   The com.allmycode.demo1.Demo1Activity Class

```
package com.allmycode.demo1;

import android.content.Intent;
import android.os.Bundle;
import android.util.Log;
import android.view.View;

public class Demo1Activity extends MyActivity {

    @Override
    public void onCreate(Bundle savedInstanceState) {
        super.onCreate(savedInstanceState);
        setContentView(R.layout.main);
    }

    @Override
    void logStuff(String message) {
        Log.i("Demo1Activity", message);
    }

    public void startOtherActivity(View view) {
        Intent intent = new Intent();
        intent.setClassName("com.allmycode.demo1",
            "com.allmycode.demo1.OtherActivity");
        startActivity(intent);
    }

    public void startOtherAppActivity(View view) {
        Intent intent = new Intent();
        intent.setClassName("com.allmycode.demo1A",
            "com.allmycode.demo1A.OtherAppActivity");
        startActivity(intent);
    }

    public void startTransparentActivity(View view) {
        Intent intent = new Intent();
        intent.setClassName("com.allmycode.demo1",
            "com.allmycode.demo1.TranslucentActivity");
        startActivity(intent);
    }
}
```

Listing 1-7:   The main.xml File

```xml
<?xml version="1.0" encoding="utf-8"?>
<LinearLayout xmlns:android=
        "http://schemas.android.com/apk/res/android"
    android:orientation="vertical"
    android:layout_width="fill_parent"
    android:layout_height="fill_parent">

    <TextView android:layout_width="fill_parent"
            android:layout_height="wrap_content"
            android:text="@string/hello" />

    <Button android:layout_width="wrap_content"
            android:id="@+id/button1"
            android:onClick="startOtherActivity"
            android:layout_height="wrap_content"
            android:text="@string/start_this_app_other">
    </Button>

    <EditText android:layout_height="wrap_content"
            android:id="@+id/editText1"
            android:layout_width="match_parent"
            android:hint="Type anything here">
        <requestFocus></requestFocus>
    </EditText>

    <include android:id="@+id/include1"
            android:layout_width="wrap_content"
            layout="@layout/add_break"
            android:layout_height="wrap_content">
    </include>

    <Button android:id="@+id/button2"
            android:layout_width="wrap_content"
            android:layout_height="wrap_content"
            android:onClick="startOtherAppActivity"
            android:text="@string/start_other_app">
    </Button>

    <Button android:id="@+id/button3"
            android:layout_width="wrap_content"
            android:layout_height="wrap_content"
            android:onClick="startTransparentActivity"
            android:text="@string/start_translucent">
    </Button>

</LinearLayout>
```

Listing 1-8: The add_break.xml File

```xml
<?xml version="1.0" encoding="utf-8"?>
<LinearLayout xmlns:android=
        "http://schemas.android.com/apk/res/android"
    android:orientation="vertical"
    android:layout_width="match_parent"
    android:layout_height="match_parent"
    android:gravity="center">

    <Button android:id="@+id/button1"
            android:layout_width="wrap_content"
            android:layout_height="wrap_content"
            android:onClick="addBreak"
            android:text="@string/add_break">
    </Button>

</LinearLayout>
```

Figure 1-6:
The main
activity's
screen.

I cover most of the Android coding tricks in Listings 1-6, 1-7, and 1-8 in Book I, Chapters 3 and 4. But these listings form the basis for an app that lets you experiment with the activity lifecycle. The next section describes what the widgets in Figure 1-6 (and a few other buttons) do.

The next section describes a number of experiments involving the code in Listings 1-6, 1-7, 1-8, and 1-9, and some other Android code. To try the experiments yourself, download all the code from this book's website.

Taking an activity lifecycle through its paces

No two lives are the same, so it would make sense that there is an infinite variety as well to the lifecycles of individual activities. If you dutifully followed my advice about downloading the code from Listings 1-6, 1-7, 1-8, and 1-9 from this book's website, you can follow along as I demonstrate the kinds of curveballs I can throw at an activity lifecycle.

Starting another activity in the same app

In Figure 1-6, you can click the Start This App's Other Activity button to cover up the main activity with another activity from the same application. When you click the button, Eclipse's LogCat view displays the following entries:

```
INFO/Demo1Activity(4526): onSaveInstanceState
INFO/Demo1Activity(4526): onPause
WARN/OtherActivity(4526): onCreate
WARN/OtherActivity(4526): onStart
WARN/OtherActivity(4526): onResume
INFO/Demo1Activity(4526): onStop
```

An `OtherActivity` instance goes from not existing to being Active, and the `Demo1Activity` instance goes from being Active to being Stopped.

In Listing 1-6, I code `Demo1Activity`'s `logStuff` method with an `i` for *INFO*. And in the `OtherActivity` (which can download from this book's website), I code `logStuff` with a `w` for *WARN*. I don't mean to imply that `OtherActivity`'s methods are more important than `Demo1Activity`'s methods. I use INFO and WARN because Eclipse's LogCat view displays different levels (such as INFO and WARN) with different colors. So on your computer screen, you can distinguish one activity's entries from another with a casual glance. In this book, instead of asking for four-color printing, I set some of the entries in boldface type.

You can filter the LogCat view to see only your own app's entries. Your app and all its activities run in one process. So with the filtering trick from Book I, Chapter 4, create a filter with your app's PID. In the LogCat output shown a few paragraphs above, both activities run in the process with PID 4526.

Taking a break

In Figure 1-6, you can click the Add Break in Log File button to add an entry whose message is a dashed line. Press this button to help you keep track of the parts in a long log file.

The Back button

Your device's Back button pops an activity off the task stack.

Imagine that with `Demo1Activity` and `OtherActivity` on the stack, you press the Back button. As a result, Eclipse's LogCat view displays the following entries:

```
WARN/OtherActivity(4526):  onPause
INFO/Demo1Activity(4526):  onRestart
INFO/Demo1Activity(4526):  onStart
INFO/Demo1Activity(4526):  onResume
WARN/OtherActivity(4526):  onStop
WARN/OtherActivity(4526):  onDestroy
```

Notice that pressing the Back button destroys the `OtherActivity` instance.

Saving (and not saving) an activity's state

In Figure 1-6, the Type Anything Here text field helps you understand when an activity's state is preserved (and when it's not).

Try this experiment:

1. **Type something in the text field and then click the Start This App's Other Activity button.**

   `OtherActivity` obscures `Demo1Activity`, and `Demo1Activity` is Stopped.

2. **Dismiss `OtherActivity` with the Back button.**

   The `Demo1Activity` reappears with your typed characters still in the text field. In spite of `Demo1Activity`'s being stopped, Android has preserved the state of `Demo1Activity`.

Try another experiment:

1. **Type something in the text field and then click the Home button.**

   The Home screen appears, and `Demo1Activity` is Stopped.

2. **Find the Demo1 icon and touch the icon to invoke `Demo1Activity`.**

   The `Demo1Activity` reappears with your typed characters still in the text field. Android has preserved the state of the `Demo1Activity`.

Here's another experiment:

1. **Type something in the text field and then click the Back button.**

   The `Demo1Activity`'s screen goes away. In the LogCat view, you see `Demo1Activity` execute its `onPause`, `onStop`, and `onDestroy` methods.

2. **Find the Demo1 icon and touch the icon to invoke `Demo1Activity`.**

   The `Demo1Activity` reappears, but the Type Anything Here text field has been re-initialized. Android hasn't preserved the `Demo1Activity`'s state.

3. **(Optional) To preserve a state between Back-button clicking and an activity's next invocation, add the following code to your activity's `onPause` method:**

   ```
   SharedPreferences prefs =
                      getPreferences(MODE_PRIVATE);
   SharedPreferences.Editor editor = prefs.edit();
   editor.putString("EditTextString",
                      editText.getText().toString());
   editor.commit();
   ```

4. **Add the following code to your activity's `onResume` method:**

   ```
   SharedPreferences prefs =
                      getPreferences(MODE_PRIVATE);
   String str = prefs.getString("EditTextString", "");
   editText.setText(str);
   ```

5. **Save an activity's relevant information in your override of the `onPause` method.**

   Don't wait to save the information in the `onStop` or `onDestroy` method.

   The code in Step 4 uses `SharedPreferences`. For more about `SharedPreferences`, see Chapter 3 in this minibook.

Here's your next experiment:

1. **Type something in the text field.**

2. **Turn your device sideways.**

   If you're running an emulator, you can do a virtual turn by pressing Ctrl+F11. Your activity's screen adjusts (from portrait to landscape or vice versa) and your typed characters are still in the text field.

   But when you look at Eclipse's LogCat view, you see the following entries:

```
INFO/Demo1Activity(4526): onSaveInstanceState
INFO/Demo1Activity(4526): onPause
INFO/Demo1Activity(4526): onStop
INFO/Demo1Activity(4526): onDestroy
INFO/Demo1Activity(4526): onCreate
INFO/Demo1Activity(4526): onStart
INFO/Demo1Activity(4526): onResume
```

Surprise! In order to rotate your activity's screen, Android destroys and then re-creates the activity. And between destruction and subsequent creation, Android preserves your activity instance's state. The text field's content is restored.

This leads you to one more experiment:

1. **Add the following attribute to the `Demo1Activity`'s `<activity>` element in the `AndroidManifest.xml` file:**

```
android:configChanges="orientation"
```

2. **Turn the app and change the orientation of the emulator or the device.**

You see the following entries in Eclipse's LogCat view:

```
INFO/Demo1Activity(4588): onSaveInstanceState
INFO/Demo1Activity(4588): onPause
INFO/Demo1Activity(4588): onStop
INFO/Demo1Activity(4588): onDestroy
INFO/Demo1Activity(4588): onCreate
INFO/Demo1Activity(4588): onStart
INFO/Demo1Activity(4588): onResume
INFO/Demo1Activity(4588): onConfigurationChanged
```

The `android:configChanges="orientation"` attribute tells Android to notify the activity about orientation changes. So Android calls the activity's `onConfigurationChanged` method which, in Listing 1-5, logs the event. Under normal circumstances, you'd use the attribute to intercept the default actions when the user tilts the device so you could then handle the event with your own code.

Starting another app's activity

In Figure 1-6, you can click the Start Other App's Activity button to cover up the main activity — you essentially cover the main activity with an activity from a different application. When you click the button, Eclipse's LogCat view displays the following entries:

```
INFO/Demo1Activity(4688): onSaveInstanceState
INFO/Demo1Activity(4688): onPause
VERBOSE/OtherAppActivity(4697): onCreate
VERBOSE/OtherAppActivity(4697): onStart
VERBOSE/OtherAppActivity(4697): onResume
INFO/Demo1Activity(4688): onStop
```

The only difference between these entries and the entries in previous examples is that these entries use two PID numbers. In this example, the Demo1Activity has PID 4688, and the OtherAppActivity has PID 4697. As promised, two different apps run in two different operating system processes, and each process has its own PID. You can get independent verification of this fact by examining Eclipse's Devices view (in the DDMS perspective). Figure 1-7 shows you the Devices view.

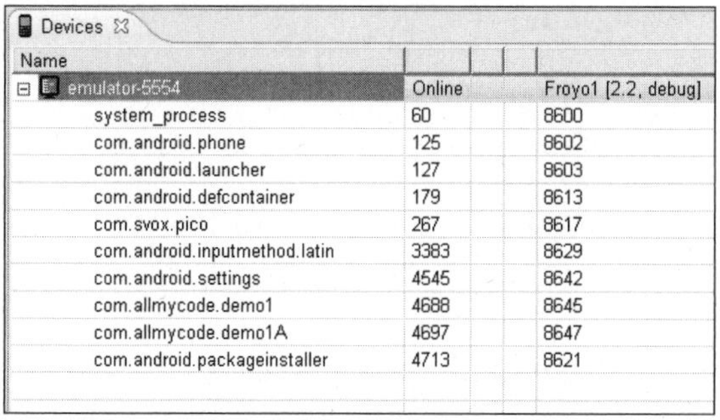

Figure 1-7:
The Devices view.

Name	Online	Froyo1 [2.2, debug]
⊟ 📱 emulator-5554	Online	Froyo1 [2.2, debug]
system_process	60	8600
com.android.phone	125	8602
com.android.launcher	127	8603
com.android.defcontainer	179	8613
com.svox.pico	267	8617
com.android.inputmethod.latin	3383	8629
com.android.settings	4545	8642
com.allmycode.demo1	4688	8645
com.allmycode.demo1A	4697	8647
com.android.packageinstaller	4713	8621

In Figure 1-7, the process running Demo1Activity (in package com.allmy code.demo1) has PID 4688. And the process running OtherAppActivity (in package com.allmycode.demo1A) has PID 4697.

Book III
Chapter 1

Android Activities

Overloading the system

As the sun sets on the "Starting another app's activity" section, you're running two com.allmycode processes. (Refer to Figure 1-7.) On your emulator's screen, the com.allmycode.demo1.Demo1Activity is obscured by the com.allmycode.demo1A.OtherAppActivity.

So you can conduct another experiment:

1. **Get your emulator (or device) in the state described at the end of the "Starting another app's activity" section.**

   To do so, start the app whose main activity is in Listing 1-6. Then click the Start Other App's Activity button.

2. **Press the emulator's Home button.**

   See Figure 1-8. You're not pressing the Back button, so you're not backing out of the OtherAppActivity or the Demo1Activity. Those two activities are Stopped, not Destroyed. (You can verify this by looking at the Eclipse's LogCat view.)

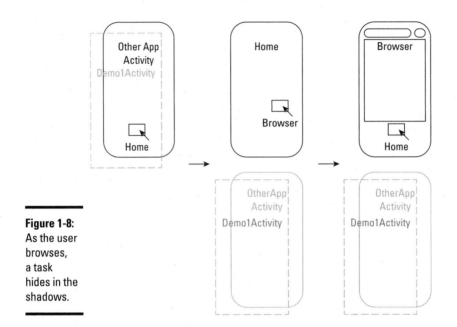

Figure 1-8:
As the user
browses,
a task
hides in the
shadows.

3. **With your eye on Eclipse's Devices and LogCat views, start several of the emulator's built-in apps.**

   Start apps such as the browser, e-mail, contacts, and maybe more. In each case, keep the current activity alive by pressing Home instead of Back.

   At some point, you see the `com.allmycode.demo1` process disappear from Eclipse's Devices view. (See Figure 1-9.) Android has reclaimed memory by killing off a process. After all, the `com.allmycode.demo1.Demo1Activity` instance is Stopped, so Android figures it can destroy that activity. The `com.allmycode.demo1A.OtherAppActivity` is also Stopped. But the last time you saw `OtherAppActivity`, that activity was at the top of a task stack.

Figure 1-9:
The package
`com.allmycode.demo1` has
disappeared.

Devices ✕		
Name		
⊟ 🖳 emulator-5554	Online	Froyo1 [2.2, debug]
system_process	60	8600
com.android.phone	125	8602
com.android.launcher	127	8603
com.android.inputmethod.latin	3383	8629
com.android.settings	4545	8642
com.allmycode.demo1A	4697	8647
com.android.browser	4743	8633
com.android.email	4770	8613

Android kills a process in order to reclaim space, and the user has no clue that the process has been killed. This is business as usual for the Android operating system.

At this point in the experiment, the Demo1Activity is Stopped, the activity's process has been killed, and the activity isn't on top of its current task.

4. **Return to the emulator's Apps screen and click the Demo1 icon (the icon for the `com.allmycode.demo1.Demo1Activity` instance).**

   The `OtherAppActivity` reappears on the screen. (See Figure 1-10.) Android interprets your click as a wish to return to the *top of the task stack* containing Demo1Activity, and not to Demo1Activity itself. In the LogCat view, OtherAppActivity has restarted, started, and resumed. In Eclipse's Devices view, you still don't see `com.allmycode.demo1`.

5. **Press the emulator's Back button.**

   Android remembers that `com.allmycode.demo1.Demo1Activity` was hidden (conceptually) underneath `OtherAppActivity` on the task stack. Because the `com.allmycode.demo1` process no longer exists, Android creates a new process with a new PID to run the `com.allmycode.demo1.Demo1Activity` code.

   As a result, Demo1Activity appears on your emulator's screen, `com.allmycode.demo1` reappears in Eclipse's devices view with a new PID, and the following entries appear in Eclipse's LogCat view:

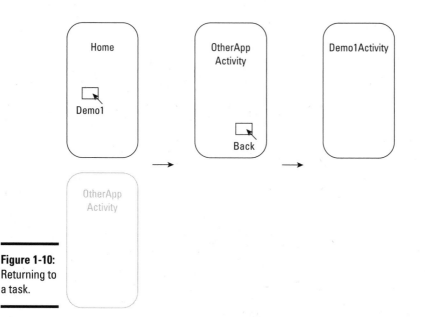

Figure 1-10: Returning to a task.

```
VERBOSE/OtherAppActivity(4697): onPause
INFO/Demo1Activity(4783): onCreate
INFO/Demo1Activity(4783): onStart
INFO/Demo1Activity(4783): onResume
VERBOSE/OtherAppActivity(4697): onStop
VERBOSE/OtherAppActivity(4697): onDestroy
```

Unbeknownst to the user, Android has restored the Demo1Activity in a new process.

Partially covering an activity

In Figure 1-6, clicking the Start Translucent Activity button does what you think it should do. The button makes Android invoke a see-through activity. (App development terminology tends to blur the difference between "translucent" and "transparent." Get it? "Blur" the difference?) Of course, you can't invoke a translucent activity unless you have a translucent activity to invoke. So Listing 1-9 shows you how to create a translucent activity.

Listing 1-9: The AndroidManifest.xml File for One of This Chapter's Big Projects

```xml
<?xml version="1.0" encoding="utf-8"?>
<manifest xmlns:android=
        "http://schemas.android.com/apk/res/android"
    package="com.allmycode.demo1"
    android:versionCode="1"
    android:versionName="1.0">
    <uses-sdk android:minSdkVersion="8" />

    <application android:icon="@drawable/icon"
                 android:label="@string/app_name"
                 android:name=".Demo1App">

        <activity android:name=".Demo1Activity"
                  android:label="@string/app_name" >
            <intent-filter>
                <action android:name=
                    "android.intent.action.MAIN" />
                <category android:name=
                    "android.intent.category.LAUNCHER" />
            </intent-filter>
        </activity>

        <activity android:name=".OtherActivity" />
        <activity android:name=".TranslucentActivity"
                  android:theme=
                    "@android:style/Theme.Translucent" />
    </application>

</manifest>
```

To create a translucent activity, create a Java class that extends Android's `Activity` class. Then, in your `AndroidManifest.xml` file, declare the activity's `theme` to be Android's predefined `Theme.Translucent` style.

My `TranslucentActivity` class has only one button — an Add Break in Log File button in the center of the activity. So after pressing the Start Translucent Activity button in Figure 1-6, I see the stuff in Figure 1-11. True to its word, Android superimposes the Translucent Activity's button on top of the next activity on the stack.

Referring to the list of activity states in the "The Activity Lifecycle" section, one of the Paused state's duties is to house activities that are partially obscured. So if you look at Eclipse's LogCat view after clicking the Start Translucent Activity button, you see the following entries:

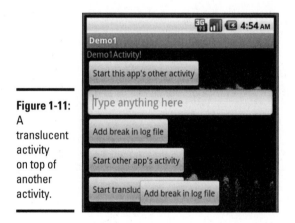

Figure 1-11: A translucent activity on top of another activity.

```
INFO/Demo1Activity(4783): onSaveInstanceState
INFO/Demo1Activity(4783): onPause
WARN/TranslucentActivity(4783): onCreate
WARN/TranslucentActivity(4783): onStart
WARN/TranslucentActivity(4783): onResume
```

`Demo1Activity` pauses but doesn't stop.

Getting Results Back from an Activity

Earlier in this book, I compare an intent to a method call. To start an activity, you don't call a method. Instead, you fire up an intent.

So far, so good. But what feature of an intent takes the place of a method call's return value? Listings 1-10 and 1-11 have the answer.

Listing 1-10:   An Activity Asks for a Result

```java
package com.allmycode.results;

import android.app.Activity;
import android.content.Intent;
import android.os.Bundle;
import android.view.View;
import android.view.View.OnClickListener;
import android.widget.Button;
import android.widget.TextView;

public class GetResultActivity extends Activity
                               implements OnClickListener {
  final int MY_REQUEST_CODE = 42;
  TextView textView;
  Button button;

  @Override
  public void onCreate(Bundle savedInstanceState) {
    super.onCreate(savedInstanceState);
    setContentView(R.layout.main);
    textView = (TextView) findViewById(R.id.textView1);
    button = (Button) findViewById(R.id.button1);
    button.setOnClickListener(this);
  }

  @Override
  public void onClick(View v) {
    Intent intent = new Intent();
    intent.setClassName("com.allmycode.results",
      "com.allmycode.results.GiveResultActivity");
    startActivityForResult(intent, MY_REQUEST_CODE);
  }

  @Override
  protected void onActivityResult(int requestCode,
                                  int resultCode,
                                  Intent intent) {

    if (requestCode == MY_REQUEST_CODE &&
                       resultCode == RESULT_OK) {
      textView.setText(intent.getStringExtra("text"));
    }
  }
}
```

Listing 1-11: An Activity Provides a Result

```java
package com.allmycode.results;

import android.app.Activity;
import android.content.Intent;
import android.os.Bundle;
import android.view.KeyEvent;
import android.view.View;
import android.view.View.OnClickListener;
import android.view.View.OnKeyListener;
import android.widget.Button;
import android.widget.EditText;

public class GiveResultActivity extends Activity
        implements OnKeyListener, OnClickListener {

  Button button;
  EditText editText;
  StringBuffer buffer = new StringBuffer();

  @Override
  public void onCreate(Bundle state) {
    super.onCreate(state);

    setContentView(R.layout.giver);
    editText = (EditText) findViewById(R.id.editText1);
    editText.setOnKeyListener(this);

    button = (Button) findViewById(R.id.button2);
    button.setOnClickListener(this);
  }

  @Override
  public boolean onKey(View v, int keyCode,
                                 KeyEvent event) {
    buffer.append(keyCode);
    return false;
  }

  @Override
  public void onClick(View arg0) {
    Intent intent = new Intent();
    intent.putExtra
      ("text", editText.getText().toString());
    setResult(RESULT_OK, intent);
    finish();
  }
}
```

The action of Listings 1-10 and 1-11 takes place in three stages. First, the user sees the `GetResultActivity` in Listing 1-10. (See Figure 1-12.)

Figure 1-12:
The
activity in
Listing 1-10.

When the user clicks the Get a Result button, Android calls `startActivity ForResult(intent, MY_REQUEST_CODE)`.

The `startActivityForResult` method takes an intent and a request code. In Listing 1-10, the intent points explicitly to the activity being started. The request code is any `int` value. The request code identifies the return result when the result arrives. (You can call `startActivityForResult` more than once before you get any results. When results arrive, you use the request code to distinguish one result from another.)

After clicking the button in Figure 1-12, the user sees the `GiveResult Activity` in Listing 1-11. (See Figure 1-13.)

Figure 1-13:
The
activity in
Listing 1-11.

The user types text into the text field in Figure 1-13 and then clicks the Go Back button. The button click causes the code in Listing 1-11 to create an intent. The intent has extra information — namely, the user's text input.

The call to `setResult` sends a result code (`RESULT_OK`, `RESULT_ CANCELED`, or any positive `int` value that's meaningful to the receiver) along with the intent full of useful information.

At the end of Listing 1-11, the `finish` method call ends the run of the activity shown in Figure 1-13. The screen returns to the `GetResultActivity`. (See Figure 1-14.)

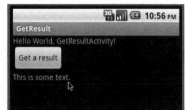

Figure 1-14:
The activity in Listing 1-10 after getting a result.

At this point, Android calls the `onActivityResult` method in Listing 1-10. The method uses the result in some way or other. (In this example, the `onActivityResult` method simply displays the result in a `TextView` element.)

Applications Don't Feel Left Out

In any operating system, things come and things go. Users log on and log off, and activities are created and destroyed. But what about applications? Applications are created and terminated.

If you check Listing 1-9, you see an `application` element with an `android: name=".Demo1App"` attribute. An app doesn't need an `android:name` attribute, but if it has one, you must create a class with the name that you specify. You can keep track of an app's global values (values that transcend the app's individual activities) with this class.

Calls to an `Application` class's methods aren't predictable. Listing 1-12 sheds light on the situation.

Book III Chapter 1

Android Activities

Listing 1-12: An Android Application

```
package com.allmycode.demo1;

import android.app.Application;
import android.content.res.Configuration;
import android.util.Log;

public class Demo1App extends Application {
    private static final String CLASSNAME = "Demo1App";

    @Override
    public void onCreate() {
```

(continued)

Listing 1-12 *(continued)*

```
        Log.v(CLASSNAME, "onCreate");
    }

    @Override
    public void onConfigurationChanged
                            (Configuration config) {
        Log.v(CLASSNAME, "onConfigurationChanged");
    }

    @Override
    public void onLowMemory() {
        Log.v(CLASSNAME, "onLowMemory");
    }

    @Override
    public void onTerminate() {
        Log.v(CLASSNAME, "onTerminate");
    }
}
```

Android's `Application` class has only four of its own methods — the methods declared in Listing 1-12. In previous sections, I didn't show you the log entries from Listing 1-12. So if you rerun the experiment in the "Overloading the system" section and you don't hide the app's log entries, you see slightly enhanced results.

When you first launch the `Demo1` app, you see the following log entries:

```
VERBOSE/Demo1App(638): onCreate
INFO/Demo1Activity(638): onCreate
INFO/Demo1Activity(638): onStart
INFO/Demo1Activity(638): onResume
VERBOSE/Demo1App(638): onConfigurationChanged
```

Android creates the app and notifies the app that its configuration has changed (from not existing to existing).

When you click the Start Other App's Activity button, you see these entries:

```
INFO/Demo1Activity(638): onSaveInstanceState
INFO/Demo1Activity(638): onPause
VERBOSE/OtherApp(645): onCreate
VERBOSE/OtherAppActivity(645): onCreate
VERBOSE/OtherAppActivity(645): onStart
VERBOSE/OtherAppActivity(645): onResume
VERBOSE/OtherApp(645): onConfigurationChanged
INFO/Demo1Activity(638): onStop
```

Android has created your other app and has notified the other app to get its configuration act together.

Next, you launch some of Android's built-in apps (the browser, e-mail, and so on). You see none of the log messages from Listing 1-12 (not even when Android kills your apps' processes). If you read the fine print in Android's docs, you see the following:

> *"While the exact point at which this [*onLowMemory *method] will be called is not defined, generally it will happen around the time all background process have [sic] been killed . . . [The* onTerminate *method] will never be called on a production Android device, where processes are removed by simply killing them; no user code (including this callback) is executed when doing so."*

During my run of this chapter's apps, Android never calls either onLow Memory or onTerminate.

Some of Android's doc entries are concisely worded. This makes the docs easy to misinterpret. Your confidence in a doc entry's interpretation should be proportional to your experience using and testing that entry's claims.

When you return to your original app's task (as in Step 4 of the "Overloading the system" section), you see the OtherApp startup entries:

```
VERBOSE/OtherApp(698): onCreate
VERBOSE/OtherAppActivity(698): onCreate
VERBOSE/OtherAppActivity(698): onStart
VERBOSE/OtherAppActivity(698): onResume
VERBOSE/OtherApp(698): onConfigurationChanged
```

One of your "other" app's activities is on top of the stack. So Android creates a new process (with a new PID) for your other app.

Chapter 2: Intents and Intent Filters

In This Chapter

↙ **Making a match**

↙ **Getting the lowdown on intents and intent filters**

↙ **Practicing with intents on an emulator or device**

↙ **Stacking up your activities and tasks**

You can judge people's mental ages by the kinds of foods they eat. For example, one of my friends seeks out new tastes from strange and exotic lands. Mentally, he's a mature adult. As for me, I like cheeseburgers and chocolate. Mentally, I'm 12 years old.

So here's an experiment: Put a meal on a table and then put a bunch of people in the room. Each person has a list of foods that he is willing to eat. Now use the people's lists to figure out who is (and who isn't) willing to eat the meal.

Things can become complicated. I love cheeseburgers . . . but no toppings, please! . . . unless the topping is mayonnaise. Yes, I want fries with that, but not if they're sweet potato fries. And above all, if the food's slimy, or if you have to explain where it comes from, I'm not eating it.

How to Make a Match

Android has two kinds of intents — explicit and implicit:

✦ An *explicit* intent names an activity class whose instance is to be launched.

✦ An *implicit* intent doesn't call for a particular activity to be launched. Instead, an implicit intent describes some work to be done. An implicit intent names an action to be taken, along with other information required to perform the action.

I cover explicit intents in Chapter 1 of this minibook.

Android's use of implicit intents is like the meal-in-a-room experiment in this chapter's introduction. An intent is like a meal. An *intent filter* is like a person's list of acceptable foods.

First, an activity sends an intent. Then the system compares that intent with other activities' intent filters to find out which activities have filters that match the intent (which activities can perform the desired action). See Figure 2-1.

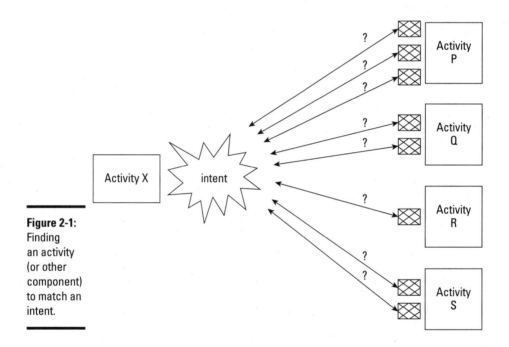

Figure 2-1:
Finding
an activity
(or other
component)
to match an
intent.

In Figure 2-1, Android checks for a match between the intent and the first of Activity P's filters. If the intent doesn't match Activity P's first filter, Android checks for a match between the intent and the second Activity P filter. If Android finds a match in one of Activity P's filters, Android marks Activity P as one possible way to fulfill the intent (one possible component that may perform the work described by the intent).

Still in Figure 2-1, Android proceeds to test Activity Q's, Activity R's, and Activity S's filters. Android keeps a list of all the activities that have at least one matching filter.

✦ If exactly one activity has a matching intent filter, that activity starts running.

✦ If no activities have any matching intent filters, the system throws an exception.

✦ If more than one activity has a matching intent filter, the system chooses among the matching activities, or the system displays a menu asking the user to choose among the matching activities.

Android's `startActivity`, `bindService`, and `sendBroadcast` methods all take arguments of type `Intent`. So a component that matches an intent can be an activity, a service, or a broadcast receiver. For most of this chapter's examples, you can safely think *activity* when you read the word *component*. Sometimes I blur the terminology and use *activity* as an example, even though a more complete explanation would use the word *component*.

In this minibook, I cover services in Chapter 3 and broadcast receivers in Chapter 4.

The parts of an intent

Figure 2-2 shows you the parts of an implicit intent. An intent has an action, data, categories, extras, and flags. Some of these things might be omitted, but Android sets stiff restrictions about what may or may not be omitted, and when.

Each item in Figure 2-2 consists of one or more Java strings. Some typical sample values are in italics. So the string `"android.intent.action.MAIN"` is a sample action value, and the predeclared `android.content.Intent.FLAG_ACTIVITY_NO_HISTORY` constant is a sample flag value.

The conventions surrounding Android intents make it difficult to distinguish between strings and predeclared constants. In Figure 2-2, `"android.intent.action.MAIN"` is a string and `android.content.Intent.FLAG_ACTIVITY_NO_HISTORY` is a predeclared constant (a static final field named `FLAG_ACTIVITY_NO_HISTORY` in the `android.content.Intent` class). Oddly, the dots in the string `"android.content.intent.MAIN"` don't mean very much. There's no member named `MAIN` in any `android.content.intent` class.

You can use strings, constants, or references to string resources in Java source files, but you can use only strings in XML documents.

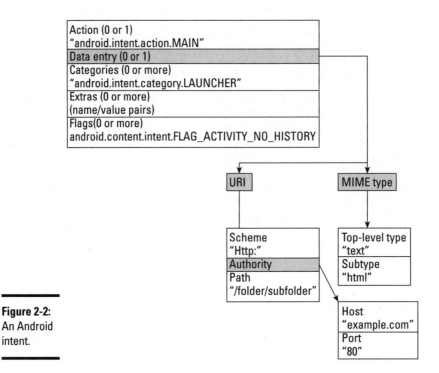

Figure 2-2:
An Android
intent.

Figure 2-2 indicates that an intent's data parts come in two flavors — URI and MIME type. An intent may have neither of these, one of the two, or both.

Still looking at Figure 2-2, the *MIME* in MIME type stands for *Multipurpose Internet Mail Extensions.* The original MIME standard describes the kinds of data that can be encoded and sent in e-mail messages. For example, when your e-mail program receives a message with `Content-Type: text/ html`, your program interprets the message as an HTML document and displays the content the way web browsers display web pages. When a program receives bits declared with MIME type `audio/mp3`, `image/jpeg`, or `application/zip`, the program interprets the bits as sounds, images, or ZIP files. In each case, the word before the slash is a *top-level type,* and the word after the slash is a *subtype.* Familiar top-level-type/subtype pairs include `text/plain`, `text/html`, `text/xml`, `image/png`, `image/jpeg`, and `image/gif`.

Many of the names in Android's SDK use the shortened term *type* instead of the full name *MIME type.*

Unlike the use of MIME types in ordinary e-mail handling, the matching of Android's MIME types is case-sensitive. So, for example, `TEXT/PLAIN` in an intent doesn't match `text/plain` in a filter. Android's developer guidelines recommend using only lowercase letters in the names of MIME types.

A *Uniform Resource Locator (URL)* is any familiar web address that you dictate when someone asks, "Where can I find that on the web?" A *Uniform Resource Identifier (URI)* looks like a URL, but URIs describe more than just web pages. Every URL is a URI, but a URI isn't necessarily a URL.

In Android, a URI has from one to four parts, depending on how you count and on what you choose to omit. Figure 2-3 has some examples.

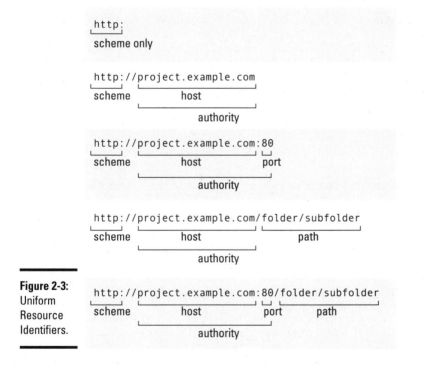

**Book III
Chapter 2**

**Intents and Intent
Filters**

Figure 2-3:
Uniform
Resource
Identifiers.

The kind of URI that I illustrate in Figure 2-3 is a *hierarchical* URI. The alternative to a hierarchical URI is an *opaque* URI. An opaque URI, such as `tel:6502530000` or `mailto:android@allmycode.com`, has a single colon instead of `://`. Also, in an opaque URI, what comes after the colon varies widely depending on the scheme. In fact, what comes after the colon in an opaque URI is the URI's *scheme-specific part*. So, for example, in the URI `mailto:android@allmycode.com`, the scheme is `mailto` and the scheme-specific part is `android@allmycode.com`. An opaque URI has neither an authority nor a path.

What r u?

If you don't live under a rock, you've used hundreds of URLs (*Uniform Resource Locators*). As the name suggests, a URL locates something. For example, the URL `www.panynj.gov:80/path` locates the main page of the website for the Port Authority Trans-Hudson Corporation — the organization in charge of trains that run between New Jersey and New York City. This URL's scheme is `http`. Its host is `www.panynj.gov`. Its port is `80`. Its authority is `www.panynj.gov:80`. Its path happens to be `/path`.

Every URL is a URI (*Uniform Resource Identifier*), but a URI isn't necessarily a URL. Some URIs don't locate anything. For example, every `AndroidManifest.xml` document contains the attribute `xmlns:android="http://schemas.android.com/apk/res/android"`. The URI's scheme is `http`. Both the host and authority are `schemas.android.com`. (This URI has no port.) The URI's path is `/apk/res/android`.

If you type **http://schemas.android.com/apk/res/android** into your web browser's address field, your browser goes nowhere. The URI `http://schemas.android.com/apk/res/android` doesn't locate anything. Like the URIs that start many XML documents, this URI is nothing but a name.

This URI is a URN (*Uniform Resource Name*). According to the Internet Engineering Task Force document RFC 3986, URNs "are required to remain globally unique and persistent even when the resource ceases to exist or becomes unavailable . . ." In other words, a URN names something — something whose name always applies — something that might never need to be found.

Here's another example. The Android SDK comes with a folder full of sample apps. One of the apps (the SearchableDictionary example) uses the URI `content://com.example.android.searchable dict.DictionaryProvider/dictionary`. The URI's scheme is `content`, and so on. This URI doesn't work in a web browser's address field. But within Android's SearchableDictionary example, the URI locates a particular content provider (in this case, a provider of dictionary words and definitions). The things that a URI locates don't have to be web pages.

The World Wide Web Consortium is currently working on IRIs (*Internationalized Resource Identifiers*). An IRI is like a URI except that an IRI's characters aren't restricted to characters in the Roman alphabet. The following figure has an example of an IRI.

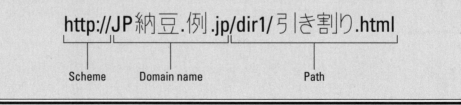

Scheme   Domain name   Path

The parts of an intent filter

Your app creates an intent and then calls `startActivity(intent)`. Then what happens? Android has a list of activities installed on the device, and each activity has its intent filters. Android tries to match the intent with each intent filter. If an activity has any matching intent filters, that activity goes on the list of possible responders to the `startActivity` method call.

An activity's non-matching filters don't harm the activity's chances of going on the list. Even if only one of an activity's filters matches, the activity still goes on the list of possible responders.

So what constitutes a match between an intent and an intent filter? Funny you should ask! The answer is far from simple.

An intent filter can have actions, data entries, and categories. (Unlike an intent, an intent filter can have more than one action and more than one data entry. Like an intent, an intent filter can have more than one category.) Intent filters don't have extras or flags. (See Figure 2-4.)

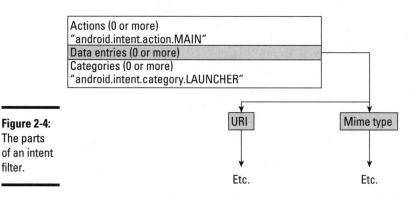

Book III Chapter 2

Intents and Intent Filters

Figure 2-4:
The parts
of an intent
filter.

To find a match between an implicit intent and an intent filter, Android performs three tests:

+ Android tests the intent's action for a match with the filter's actions.
+ Android tests the intent's categories for a match with the filter's categories.
+ Android tests the intent's data for a match with the filter's data.

Android's rules for matching an intent's action with a filter's action are fairly straightforward. And the rules for matching the intent's categories with the filter's categories are okay. But neither of these rules is a memorable, one-sentence slogan. And the rules for matching the intent's data with the filter's data are quite complicated. Unfortunately, the official documentation about filter matching (`http://developer.android.com/guide/topics/intents/intents-filters.html`) is ambiguous and contains some errors.

So to help you understand how intents match intent filters, I take a multi-faceted approach. (That's a fancy way to say that I explain matching a few times in a few different ways.)

Matching: The general idea using a (silly) analogy

Two kinds of people sign up to participate in a speed-dating event. On one side of the room, each participant represents a part of an Android intent. (So one person is an action, the next two people are categories, and so on. I warned you that this analogy would be silly!) On the other side of the room, each participant represents a part of a filter. (See Figure 2-5.)

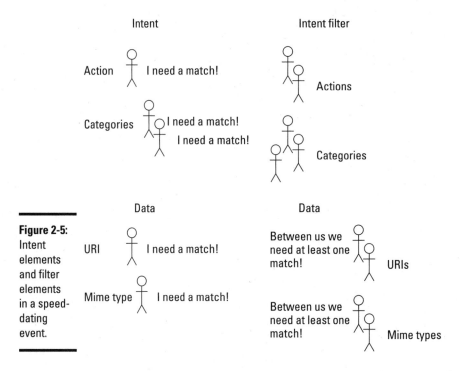

Figure 2-5: Intent elements and filter elements in a speed-dating event.

Like all dating situations, the room might be imbalanced. The filter might have more actions or more categories. The intent might have more data. It's almost never a fairy tale, one-to-one mix of people.

In this arena, some people are needier than others. For example, on the intent side, you have an action that absolutely insists on finding a match among the filters. On the filter side, you have a category that's speed dating only to keep a friend company. This nonchalant category doesn't need to find a match among the intent's categories.

As a quick (and not entirely accurate) rule, the entire intent matches the entire filter if and only if each needy person finds a match. Anyone who isn't needy doesn't have to be matched. That is, the whole speed-dating event is successful even if no one who's along only for the ride finds a match. Non-needy parts don't derail the overall match between the intent and the filter.

So who's needy and who isn't? Figure 2-5 gives you a rough idea.

The matching rules in Figures 2-5, 2-6, and 2-7 are general guidelines. The official rules include some important exceptions. For more info, see the next few sections.

The real story

An intent filter has three parts — actions, categories, and data. Android tests each part to determine whether a particular intent matches a particular filter. Each part consists of one or more Java strings. So, roughly speaking, an intent's part matches a filter's part if and only if `intent_part.equals(filter_part)`. In this situation, `equals` is Java's `String` comparison method.

In the preceding paragraph I write "roughly speaking" because Android's rules for matching actions aren't quite the same as the rules for matching categories, which in turn are different from the rules for matching data entries. How do you decide whether the one action in an intent matches the many actions in a filter? And what do you do with each part of a URI? Stay tuned, because the next several sections answer these questions.

In the next few sections, be aware of the many kinds of matching — an intent with a filter, an intent with an activity, an intent action with a filter action, a scheme with an entire URI, and several other kinds of matching.

Java methods and XML elements

An intent's Java methods include the following:

+ **setAction:** Sets the intent's action.

+ **addCategory:** Adds a category to the intent.

+ **setData:** Sets the intent's URI and removes the intent's MIME type (if the intent has a MIME type).

✦ **setType:** Sets the intent's MIME type and removes the intent's URI (if the intent has a URI).

✦ **setDataAndType:** Sets both the intent's URI and the intent's MIME type. According to the docs, "This method should very rarely be used."

You can describe an intent filter in an `AndroidManifest.xml` document or in Java code. In an `AndroidManifest.xml` document, the `<intent-filter>` element has `<action>`, `<category>`, and `<data>` subelements.

```
<action android:name="string" />

<category android:name="string" />

<data android:scheme="string"
      android:host="string"
      android:port="string"
      android:path="string"
      android:pathPattern="string"
      android:pathPrefix="string"
      android:mimeType="string" />
```

The intent methods and the data element's attributes aren't parallel. For example, with an intent's `setAction` method, you set an intent's action (if you want the intent to have an action). But with a filter's `<action>` element, you add one of possibly many actions to the filter. With an intent's `setData` method, you set an intent's URI (if you want the intent to have a URI). But with a filter's `<data>` elements, you add individual pieces of a URI.

You typically set a filter's values in the `AndroidManifest.xml` file. But in Java code, the `android.content.IntentFilter` class has lots of useful methods. I list a few here:

✦ **addAction:** Adds an action to the filter.

✦ **addCategory:** Adds a category to the filter.

✦ **addDataScheme:** Adds a scheme to the filter.

✦ **addDataAuthority:** Adds an authority to the filter.

✦ **addDataPath:** Adds a path to the filter.

✦ **addDataType:** Adds a MIME type to the filter.

As was the case with the intent methods and the data element's attributes, the intent methods and the filter methods aren't parallel. An intent's `setAction` method does the obvious — it sets an intent's action (if you want the intent to have an action). A filter's `addAction` method, however, lets you add one of possibly many actions to the filter. An intent's `setData` method sets an intent's URI (if you want the intent to have a URI). A filter's `addDataScheme`, `addDataAuthority`, and `addDataPath` methods, on the other hand, let you separately add pieces of a URI.

Matching actions

According to Figure 2-5, an intent's action must be matched with one of the filter's actions. That makes sense because an intent's action says, "I want a component that can do *such-and-such*." And the filter's action says, "I can do *such-and-such*." The filter might have other actions (be able to do other things), but having additional filter actions doesn't prevent an intent from matching with a filter.

Exactly what is an action? The simplest answer is that an *action* is a string. You can create your own action string `"thisismyaction"` or `"allmy code.intent.action.DO_THIS"` — Android's docs recommend the latter form. But Android also has a bunch of standard actions — actions reserved for certain kinds of work. For example, when a developer creates an activity that can display something (a document, a web page, an image, or whatever) the developer includes `"android.intent.action.VIEW"` in the activity's filter. Then, when you want someone else's activity to display something, you put `"android.intent.action.VIEW"` (or the constant `android.content.Intent.ACTION_VIEW` whose value is `"android.intent.action.VIEW"`) in your intent.

Table 2-1 lists some of my favorite standard actions.

Book III
Chapter 2

Intents and Intent
Filters

Table 2-1	Some Standard Actions for Activities	
String Value	*Constant Name*	*An Activity with This Action in One of Its Filters Can . . .*
`"android. intent. action.MAIN"`	`Intent.ACTION_ MAIN`	Be the first activity in a brand-new task stack (the task's *root* activity).
`"android. intent. action.VIEW"`	`Intent.ACTION_ VIEW`	Display something.
`"android. intent. action.GET_ CONTENT"`	`Intent.ACTION_ GET_CONTENT`	Show the user a certain kind of data and then let the user choose an item from the displayed data. With this action, you don't specify the source (URI) of the data.

(continued)

Table 2-1 *(continued)*

String Value	Constant Name	An Activity with This Action in One of Its Filters Can . . .
`"android. intent. action.PICK"`	`Intent.ACTION_ PICK`	Show the user a certain kind of data and then let the user choose an item from the displayed data. With this action, you specify the source (URI) of the data.
`"android. intent. action. INSERT_OR_ EDIT"`	`Intent.ACTION_ INSERT_OR_EDIT`	Same as `Intent. ACTION_PICK` except that the user can create a new item.
`"android. intent. action.EDIT"`	`Intent.ACTION_ EDIT`	Edit something.
`"android. intent. action. INSERT"`	`Intent.ACTION_ INSERT`	Add a new empty item to something. (You fill the item later.)
`"android. intent. action. DELETE"`	`Intent.ACTION_ DELETE`	Delete something.
`"android. intent. action.PASTE"`	`Intent.ACTION_ PASTE`	Paste something from the Clipboard.
`"android. intent. action. SEARCH"`	`Intent.ACTION_ SEARCH`	Search for something.
`"android. intent. action. ANSWER"`	`Intent.ACTION_ ANSWER`	Handle an incoming call.
`"android. intent. action.CALL"`	`Intent.ACTION_ CALL`	Make a phone call.
`"android. intent. action.DIAL"`	`Intent.ACTION_ DIAL`	Launch a dialer with a particular phone number in place, but let the user press the Dial button.

For a complete list of Android's standard actions, visit `http://developer.` `android.com/reference/android/content/Intent.html`.

Here's a useful experiment:

1. **Create a new Android project with two activities — the main activity created by Eclipse and a second `OtherActivity.java` activity.**

2. **Add the following `activity` element to the project's `AndroidManifest.xml` file:**

   ```
   <activity android:name=".OtherActivity">
     <intent-filter>
       <action
         android:name="com.allmycode.action.MY_ACTION" />
       <category
         android:name="android.intent.category.DEFAULT" />
     </intent-filter>
   </activity>
   ```

3. **In the main activity, add the following code:**

   ```
   final String THE_ACTION =
       "com.allmycode.action.MY_ACTION";
   Intent intent = new Intent();
   intent.setAction(THE_ACTION);
   startActivity(intent);
   ```

4. **Using Eclipse's Graphical Layout editor, change the layout of the other activity.**

   Any change is okay. The only reason for changing the other activity's layout is to help you recognize which of the two activities (the main activity or the other activity) is on the emulator's screen.

5. **Run the project.**

   As soon as your emulator executes the code in Step 3, Android launches the other activity. The intent's `"com.allmycode.action.MY_ACTION"` matches the filter's `"com.allmycode.action.MY_ACTION"`, so the other activity starts running.

Real Android developers use a standard action (such as the actions in Table 2-1), or they make up dotted action names, such as `"com.allmy` `code.action.MY_ACTION"`. Real developers type that `"com.allmy` `code.action.MY_ACTION"` string in the `AndroidManifest.xml` file (because they must). But in the Java code, real developers create a constant value to represent the string (because it's good programming practice).

The `category` element in Step 2 of this section's instructions is an anomaly that I cover in the later section "The fine print." If you don't want to skip to that section, simply add the category `"android.` `intent.category.DEFAULT"` to each filter in your `Android}` `Manifest.xml` file.

Continuing the experiment . . .

6. Comment out (or delete) the following element from your project's AndroidManifest.xml file:

```
<action
   android:name="com.allmycode.action.MY_ACTION" />
```

7. Run your project again.

When your emulator executes the Java code in Step 3, your app crashes. The filter has no action matching your intent's "com.allmycode.action.MY_ACTION", and (in all likelihood) no other activity on your emulator has a filter containing "com.allmycode.action.MY_ACTION".

In Step 7, your app intentionally crashes. Crashes make good learning experiences, but users don't appreciate such learning experiences. To avoid the kind of disaster you see in Step 7, call the PackageManager class's queryIntentActivities method before attempting to call startActivity. Alternatively, you can put your startActivity call in a *try/catch block* with the ActivityNotFoundException:

```
try {
   startActivity(intent);
} catch (ActivityNotFoundException e) {
   e.printStackTrace();
}
```

This code tells Java to call startActivity. If Android can't start an activity (that is, if Android can't find an activity to match the intent), Java jumps to the statement e.printStackTrace(), which displays error information in Eclipse's LogCat view. After displaying the information, Java marches on to execute whatever code comes after the attempt to call startActivity. Therefore, the app doesn't crash.

For more on try/catch blocks, see Book II, Chapter 3.

8. Uncomment the element that you commented out in Step 6.

9. Modify the other activity's element in the AndroidManifest.xml file as follows:

```
<activity android:name=".OtherActivity">
  <intent-filter>
    <action
      android:name="com.allmycode.action.MY_ACTION" />
    <action
      android:name="com.allmycode.action.X_ACTION" />
    <category
      android:name="android.intent.category.DEFAULT" />
  </intent-filter>
</activity>
```

***10.* Run the project again.**

> When your emulator executes the Java code in Step 3, Android launches the other activity. The intent's `"com.allmycode.action.MY_ACTION"` matches the filter's `"com.allmycode.action.MY_ACTION"`, and the filter's additional `"com.allmycode.action.X_ACTION"` doesn't require a match.

TIP

Following this example's steps for each intent and filter that you want to test can become very tedious. So to help you test matches, I've created a special Android app. For details, see the "Practice, Practice, Practice" section, later in this chapter.

Matching categories

According to Figure 2-5, each of an intent's categories must be matched with one of the filter's categories. That makes sense because an intent's category says, "I want a component of *such-and-such* kind." And the filter's category says, "I'm a *such-and-such* kind of component." The filter might have other categories, but having additional filter categories doesn't prevent an intent from matching with a filter.

Exactly what is a category? Like an action, a *category* is a string. You can create your own category string `"thisismycategory"` or `"allmycode.intent.category.THIS_KIND"`, and Android's docs recommend the latter form. But Android also has a bunch of standard categories — categories reserved for certain kinds of components. Table 2-2 lists some of my favorites.

Table 2-2	Some Standard Categories	
String Value	*Constant Name*	*An Activity with This Category in One of Its Filters Is . . .*
`"android.intent.category.DEFAULT"`	`Intent.CATEGORY_DEFAULT`	Able to respond to user actions and to be launched by calls to the `start Activity` and `start ActivityForResult` methods.
`"android.intent.category.BROWSABLE"`	`Intent.CATEGORY_BROWSABLE`	Able to work in a web browser.
`"android.intent.category.LAUNCHER"`	`Intent.CATEGORY_LAUNCHER`	Displayed as an icon on the device's app launcher screen.

(continued)

Table 2-2 *(continued)*

String Value	Constant Name	An Activity with This Category in One of Its Filters Is . . .
`"android.intent.category.ALTERNATIVE"`	`Intent.CATEGORY_ALTERNATIVE`	When the system offers the user a choice of activities to do a job, the system lists activities with filters possessing this category.

Consider the kitty-cat intent created with the following Java code:

```
final String THE_ACTION =
      "com.allmycode.action.MY_ACTION";
final String THE_CATEGORY =
      "com.allmycode.category.KITTY";
Intent intent = new Intent();
intent.setAction(THE_ACTION);
intent.addCategory(THE_CATEGORY);
startActivity(intent);
```

This kitty-cat intent matches a filter with the following XML code:

```
<activity android:name=".OtherActivity">
  <intent-filter>
    <action
      android:name="com.allmycode.action.MY_ACTION" />
    <category
      android:name="com.allmycode.category.KITTY" />
    <category
      android:name="android.intent.category.DEFAULT" />
  </intent-filter>
</activity>
```

The kitty-cat intent also matches the following intent because (in the language of speed dating) *filter* categories aren't needy.

```
<activity android:name=".OtherActivity">
  <intent-filter>
    <action
      android:name="com.allmycode.action.MY_ACTION" />
    <category
      android:name="com.allmycode.category.KITTY" />
    <category
      android:name="Otto.Schmidlap" />
    <category
```

```
      android:name="android.intent.category.DEFAULT" />
  </intent-filter>
</activity>
```

The kitty-cat intent does not match the following intent because *an intent's* categories are needy:

```
<activity android:name=".OtherActivity">
  <intent-filter>
    <action
      android:name="com.allmycode.action.MY_ACTION" />
    <category
      android:name="Otto.Schmidlap" />
    <category
      android:name="android.intent.category.DEFAULT" />
  </intent-filter>
</activity>
```

Matching data

Figure 2-5 illustrates an interesting relationship between an intent's data and a filter's data:

✦ If an intent has a URI or if a filter has a URI, one of the filter's URIs must match the intent's URI.

✦ If an intent has a MIME type or if a filter has a MIME type, one of the filter's MIME types must match the intent's MIME type.

These rules have some corollaries:

✦ An intent without a URI cannot match a filter without a URI. A filter without a URI cannot match an intent without a URI.

✦ An intent without a MIME type cannot match a filter without a MIME type. A filter without a MIME type cannot match an intent without a MIME type.

How does all this stuff about URIs and MIME types make sense? The deal is, data doesn't perform the same role as an action or a category in matching a filter with an intent. Imagine that an intent announces, "I want a component to perform `android.intent.action.VIEW`," and a certain activity's filter announces, "I can perform `android.intent.action.VIEW`." The intent doesn't care if the filter announces that it can perform other actions.

But what if an intent announces, "I want a component to handle the URI `tel:6502530000`"? (The URI `tel:6502530000` places a call to Google's corporate headquarters in Mountain View, California.) An appropriate filter contains the `tel` scheme. (See Figure 2-6.) Now imagine another intent with no `tel:` URI and a filter whose only scheme is the `tel` scheme. (Again, see Figure 2-6.) In this case, the filter says, "I can do something useful with a telephone number, and when I'm invoked, I expect to receive a telephone number." If the intent has no `tel:` URI, a match isn't appropriate.

So the coupling between an intent's and a filter's data is stronger than the coupling between actions or the coupling between categories. With the URI part of the data, both the intent and the filter are needy. The same is true of the data's MIME types.

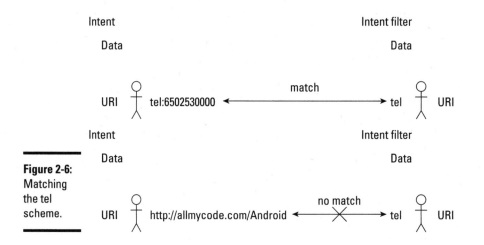

Figure 2-6: Matching the tel scheme.

The following intent and filter form a match:

```
final String THE_ACTION =
        "com.allmycode.action.MY_ACTION";
Intent intent = new Intent();
intent.setAction(THE_ACTION);
intent.setData(Uri.parse("http:"));
startActivity(intent);

<intent-filter>
  <action
    android:name="com.allmycode.action.MY_ACTION" />
  <category
    android:name="android.intent.category.DEFAULT" />
  <data android:scheme="http" />
  <data android:scheme="mymadeupscheme" />
</intent-filter>
```

The same intent with a slightly modified filter does *not* form a match because the set of MIME types in a filter is needy:

```
<intent-filter>
  <action
    android:name="com.allmycode.action.MY_ACTION" />
  <category
    android:name="android.intent.category.DEFAULT" />
  <data android:scheme="http" />
  <data android:scheme="mymadeupscheme" />
  <data android:mimeType="text/html" />
</intent-filter>
```

To match this modified filter, you need either of the following intents:

```
final String THE_ACTION =
        "com.allmycode.action.MY_ACTION";
Intent intent = new Intent();
intent.setAction(THE_ACTION);
intent.setDataAndType(Uri.parse("http:"), "text/html");
startActivity(intent);

final String THE_ACTION =
        "com.allmycode.action.MY_ACTION";
Intent intent = new Intent();
intent.setAction(THE_ACTION);
intent.setDataAndType
    (Uri.parse("mymadeupscheme:"), "text/html");
startActivity(intent);
```

Finally, the following intent and filter form a match because the MIME type in the intent matches one of the MIME types in the filter:

```
final String THE_ACTION =
        "com.allmycode.action.MY_ACTION";
Intent intent = new Intent();
intent.setAction(THE_ACTION);
intent.setType("text/html");
startActivity(intent);

<intent-filter>
  <action
    android:name="com.allmycode.action.MY_ACTION" />
  <category
    android:name="android.intent.category.DEFAULT" />
  <data android:mimeType="abc/xyz" />
  <data android:mimeType="text/html" />
</intent-filter>
```

Matching parts of the data

The "Java methods and XML elements" section, earlier in this chapter, lists methods and XML elements. With an intent's setData method, you set an intent's URI (if you want the intent to have a URI). With a filter's `<data>` elements, you add individual pieces of a URI. The filter's pieces don't have to fit together. For example, the following intent and filter form a match:

```
final String THE_ACTION =
        "com.allmycode.action.MY_ACTION";
Intent intent = new Intent();
intent.setAction(THE_ACTION);
intent.setData(Uri.parse("abc://example.com:2222"));
startActivity(intent);
```

```xml
<intent-filter>
  <data android:scheme="xyz" android:host="example.com" />
  <data android:port="2222" />
  <action
    android:name="com.allmycode.action.MY_ACTION" />
  <category
    android:name="android.intent.category.DEFAULT" />
  <data android:scheme="abc" />
</intent-filter>
```

A filter can have schemes `"abc"` and `"xyz"`, and authority `"example.com"`. Then the filter's data matches both intent data `"abc://example.com"` and intent data `"xyz://example.com"`. This works even if you lump `"xyz"` and `"example.com"` in the same `<data>` element.

With a filter's `addDataScheme`, `addDataAuthority`, and `addDataPath` methods, you separately add pieces of a URI. For example, the following intent and filter form a match:

```
final String THE_ACTION =
        "com.allmycode.action.MY_ACTION";
Intent intent = new Intent();
intent.setAction(THE_ACTION);
intent.setData(Uri.parse("abc://example.com:2222"));
```

```
final IntentFilter filter = new IntentFilter();
filter.addAction(THE_ACTION);
// Constant com.content.Intent.CATEGORY_DEFAULT has
//   value "android.intent.category.DEFAULT"
filter.addCategory(Intent.CATEGORY_DEFAULT);
filter.addDataScheme("abc");
filter.addDataScheme("xyz");
filter.addDataAuthority("example.com", "2222");
```

At this point, a few observations are in order.

✦ An intent has three similar methods — setData, setDataAndType, and setType. You call setData for an intent with a URI but no MIME type. You call setType for an intent with a MIME type but no URI. You call setDataAndType only for an intent with both a URI and a MIME type.

✦ You don't pass a string to the setData method or to the first parameter of the setDataAndType method. Instead, you pass an instance of the android.net.Uri class. You do this by applying the method Uri. parse to a string of characters.

✦ Here's a silly but important detail: A call to intent.setData(Uri. parse("http:")) with a colon after http matches the filter element <data android:scheme="http" /> *without* a colon after the http. Other combinations of colon/no-colon for a URI scheme fail to make a match.

Matching URIs

Figure 2-5 illustrates an imaginary speed-dating event for the parts of an intent and an intent filter. The figure doesn't address the matching of one URI with another. So imagine that the URIs in Figure 2-5 bring their darling little children (their schemes, authorities, and paths) to the speed-dating event. As the evening begins, the kids go off to a separate room for a speed-dating event of their own. (Sure, they're too young to date. But it's good practice for adolescence.) Figure 2-7 illustrates the neediness situation in the kids' event.

The situation with the URI's kids is similar to the situation with all data. Everybody's happy as long as each thing on the intent side matches something on the filter side. For example, the following intent and filter form a match:

```
final String THE_ACTION =
        "com.allmycode.action.MY_ACTION";
Intent intent = new Intent();
intent.setAction(THE_ACTION);
intent.setData(Uri.parse("abc://example.com:2222"));
startActivity(intent);
<intent-filter>
  <action
    android:name="com.allmycode.action.MY_ACTION" />
  <category
    android:name="android.intent.category.DEFAULT" />
  <data android:scheme="abc" />
</intent-filter>
```

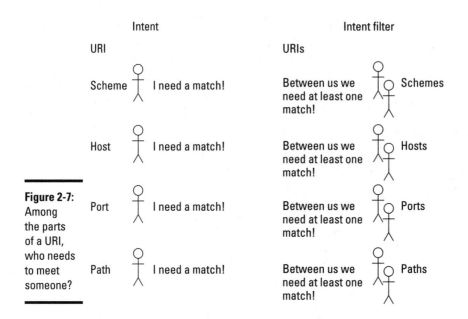

Intent   Intent filter

URI   URIs

Scheme — I need a match! Between us we need at least one match! — Schemes

Host — I need a match! Between us we need at least one match! — Hosts

Port — I need a match! Between us we need at least one match! — Ports

Path — I need a match! Between us we need at least one match! — Paths

Figure 2-7:
Among
the parts
of a URI,
who needs
to meet
someone?

But with the same intent, the following filter isn't a match:

```
<intent-filter>
  <action
    android:name="com.allmycode.action.MY_ACTION" />
  <category
    android:name="android.intent.category.DEFAULT" />
  <data android:scheme="abc" />
  <data android:host="example.com" />
  <data android:port="2222" />
  <data android:path="/some/stuff" />
</intent-filter>
```

The fine print

With all the fuss about filter matching in the previous sections, you'd think the issue was covered and done with. But the work is never done. Here's a list of filter matching's most important gotchas and exceptions:

✦ Android treats activities differently from other components (such as services and broadcast receivers).

You can create an implicit intent with no actions. If you do, a call to `startActivity(intent)` doesn't find a match among any activity filters. However, calls to `sendBroadcast(intent)` or to `bindService(intent, ...)` may find matches.

According to the Android docs, "… an Intent object that doesn't specify an action automatically passes the test — as long as the filter contains at least one action." As far as I can tell, this statement in the docs is incorrect.

✦ With respect to categories, Android treats activities differently from other components.

When you try to start an activity, Android behaves as if the intent contains the `"android.intent.category.DEFAULT"` category. (Android does this even if you don't execute code to add that category to the intent.) Because of this, an activity filter without the `"android.intent.category.DEFAULT"` category never matches an intent. Broadcast receivers and services don't suffer from this anomaly.

The activity that starts when the user first presses an app's icon is the app's *main activity*. A main activity's filter normally contains the action `"android.intent.action.MAIN"` and the category `"android.intent.category.LAUNCHER"`. If you want an activity to function only as a main activity (and never be started by an app's call to `startActivity`), you can safely omit `"android.intent.category.DEFAULT"` from the activity's filter.

✦ Flip back to Figure 2-3 to see the kinds of URIs you can create. A URI with an authority must have a scheme, and a URI with a path must have an authority and a scheme. Also, a port without a host is ignored. So the following strings are not valid URIs:

- `example.com` — has an authority but no scheme.

- `http:///folder/subfolder` — has a path but no authority.

The official Android docs provide the following loophole: " . . . if a host is not specified, the port is ignored." So a URI like `http://:2000/folder` is strange but valid. I've created such URIs in captivity, but I've never encountered one in the wild.

✦ A filter URI with nothing but a scheme matches any intent URI with the same scheme. Take, for example, the intent URI to call Google's corporate headquarters, `tel:6502530000`. An appropriate filter probably contains the `tel` scheme but not the number `6502530000`. (A filter whose sole URI is `tel:6502530000` can call *only* Google's corporate headquarters. The filter would be useful only for an Unsatisfied Google Customer app.)

In the same way, a filter URI with a scheme, an authority, and no path matches any intent filter with the same scheme and the same authority.

✦ The schemes `content` and `file` get special treatment. If the intent's URI has scheme `content` or scheme `file`, and the intent has a MIME type, you can omit the scheme from the filter. (You must still have a match between the intent's MIME type and one of the filter's MIME types.) Someday this rule will make sense to me.

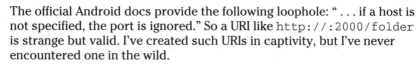

✦ Certain parts of the data may contain wildcards or simplified regular expressions. Here are a few examples:

- The type `text/*` matches `text/plain`. The type `text/*` also matches `text/html` and `text/whatever`. The type `text/*` matches `text/` (with a slash and no subtype) but does not match `text` (with no slash and no subtype).

- The type `*/*` matches `text/plain`. The type `*/*` also matches `image/jpeg`, and so on.

- The type `*` (one wildcard with no slash) and `*/html` don't seem to match anything.

- The type `text/ht*` doesn't match `text/html`. (With a top-level type or a subtype, the wildcard must be "all or nothing.")

- Paths use a simplified regular expression form. (In other words, paths can include wildcards and other funky symbols.) For example, the intent URI `http://example.com/folder` matches the filter URI with scheme `http`, authority `example.com`, and path pattern `/fol.*`. In the `AndroidManifest.xml` file, the data element's `android:path`, `android:pathPrefix`, and `android:pathPattern` attributes distinguish among the various possibilities.

  For more information about path expressions, visit `http://developer.android.com/guide/topics/manifest/data-element.html`.

- With the exception of the host name, the strings in an intent and its filter are case-sensitive. So `text/html` doesn't match `TEXT/HTML`, and `HTTP` doesn't match `http`. But `http://example.com` matches `http://EXAMPLE.com`. Android's docs recommend using mostly lowercase letters.

Practice, Practice, Practice

If I had a nickel for every time I misinterpreted something in Android's Intent Filters documentation, I'd have enough to fill my tank with gas. (That's pretty impressive, isn't it?) I want to believe that this chapter's sections on intent and filter matching are clear and unambiguous. But in my heart, I know that almost all spoken-language sentences are moving targets. Take, for example, the following sentences:

Put Mommy in the car behind us.

I want David Copperfield to read.

I'll put the bandage on myself.

Everything shouldn't be blue.

Chew one tablet three times a day until finished.

I saved everyone five dollars.

Cars towed at owner's expense.

Our cream is so gentle that it never stings most people, even after shaving.

I hope someday that you love me as much as Amy.

If he were to learn that wild bears are related to dogs, and never hurt people, then he'd be happier.

The best test of your understanding is not the way you nod while you read this book's paragraphs. Instead, the best test is when you try your own examples on an emulator or a device. If you can accurately predict the results much of the time, you understand the subject.

Unfortunately, testing intent and filter matching can be tedious. For every change, you have to edit Java code, then edit the `AndroidManifest.xml` file, and then reinstall your app. Some time ago, after many hours of such testing, I was "mad as hell and I wasn't going to take it anymore." I wrote an app to test filter matches one after another without modifying files or reinstalling anything. I named it the Intentsity app (because, as an author, I'm tired of worrying about things being spelled correctly). Needless to say, the app is available for your use through this book's website — `www.allmy code.com/android`. (You can thank me later.)

The upper half of the app's main screen is shown in Figure 2-8.

Figure 2-8:
A screen for entering intent and intent filter strings.

The Intentsity app's screen has an Intent part and a Filter part. Both parts have EditText fields for filling in `String` values. Each EditText field represents an `Intent` instance method or an `IntentFilter` instance method. (For a list of such methods, see the "Java methods and XML elements" section, earlier in this chapter.)

Android has no features for setting an activity's intent filter using Java code. But you can create another component — a broadcast receiver — and set the broadcast receiver's filter using Java code. (You use the `IntentFilter` method calls described in the "Java methods and XML elements" section.) Accordingly, my Intentsity app tests the values you type in the EditText fields by attempting to communicate with a broadcast receiver. The fields in the lower part of the app (the Filter fields) match with the Java methods for creating an `IntentFilter` object, not with the attributes in the `AndroidManifest.xml` document. To keep things as faithful as possible to Android's real behavior, my app respects the fact that a broadcast receiver's filter can do without the category `"android.intent.category.DEFAULT"`. So when you move from the Intentsity app to your own project, remember to add `"android.intent.category.DEFAULT"` to your activities' filters.

The "Java methods and XML elements" section, earlier in this chapter, lists methods like `setAction` and `addCategory`. Methods beginning with the `set` are for things like an intent's action because an intent can't have more than one action. Methods beginning with the `add` are for things like an intent's category because an intent can have more than one category.

Figure 2-8 shows a New Intent Category button. When you click this button, the app creates an additional `addCategory` row.

Figure 2-9 shows the bottom of the Intentsity app's scrolling screen.

Figure 2-9:
Press Test
to check for
a match.

After filling in some EditText fields, click the Test button, and the app does what it does best:

✦ The app calls the `Intent` class's methods to compose an intent from your Intent fields' entries.

✦ The app calls the `IntentFilter` class's methods to compose a filter from your Filter fields' entries.

✦ The app calls `registerReceiver(myReceiver, filter)` to create a broadcast receiver with the new filter.

✦ The app calls `sendBroadcast(intent)` to shout out to all the system's broadcast receivers.

If the receiver's filter matches your intent, the receiver displays a screen like the one in Figure 2-10.

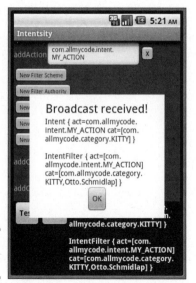

Figure 2-10:
It's a match!

**Book III
Chapter 2**

**Intents and Intent
Filters**

With or without a match, the app displays `toString` versions of your intent and intent filter. Figure 2-11 shows the display for a failed attempt to match.

Figure 2-11:
The app
displays the
values in an
intent and a
filter.

The Intentsity app doesn't want you to type variables in the EditText fields. In your own Java code, the call `setAction(Intent.ACTION_VIEW)` sets the intent's action to the string `"android.intent.action.VIEW"`. But in the Intentsity app, typing `Intent.ACTION_VIEW` in the topmost field sets the intent's action to the string `"Intent.ACTION_VIEW"`, which is not equal to (and therefore doesn't match) a filter string `"android.intent.action.VIEW"`.

With the Intentsity app, you can test your understanding of intents and intent filters. But you can also examine the app's source code for some tips and tricks. The following sections have a few highlights.

No magic

I keep things as simple as possible in order to turn your EditText entries into an intent and a filter. The simplicity guards against discrepancies between the Intentsity app's behavior and the behavior you get when you code your own app. In the following code snippet, I grab text from EditText fields and plug that text into Android's `set` and `add` methods. To grab text from the `addCategory` fields, I loop through the fields that the user has created.

```
private Intent createIntentFromEditTextFields() {
  String theAction =
          actionText.getText().toString().trim();

  Intent intent = new Intent();
  if (theAction.length() != 0) {
    intent.setAction(theAction);
  }

  if (intentCategoriesLayout != null) {
    int count =
            intentCategoriesLayout.getChildCount();
    for (int i = 0; i < count; i++) {
      String cat =
        ((EditText) ((ViewGroup) intentCategoriesLayout
          .getChildAt(i))... // More code goes here
          .getText().toString().trim();
      if (cat.length() != 0) {
        intent.addCategory(cat);
      }
    }
  }

  // Et cetera, et cetera, ...

  return intent;
}
```

Using a ScrollView

The app's main screen takes up more space than is typically available on a mobile phone. So I enclose the whole screen in a ScrollView. As its name suggests, a ScrollView lets the user slide things onto the screen as other things slide off. The big restriction on a ScrollView is that a ScrollView may contain only one direct child. So in the following code, you can't put another View element between the end tags `</LinearLayout>` and `</ScrollView>`:

```
<?xml version="1.0" encoding="utf-8"?>
<ScrollView xmlns:android=
   "http://schemas.android.com/apk/res/android"
   android:id="@+id/scrollView1"
   android:layout_width="match_parent"
   android:layout_height="wrap_content">

   <LinearLayout android:orientation="vertical"
     android:layout_width="match_parent">

       <!-- More layout stuff within
            the LinearLayout goes here.
            This stuff may include
            additional view elements. -->

   </LinearLayout>
     <!-- No additional view elements may appear here. -->
</ScrollView>
```

Defining a layout in Java code

With my Intentsity app, a user can add new elements to an existing layout. Android has a `ListView` class that handles runtime additions to a layout. With the Intentsity app, though, I found Android's `addView` and `removeView` methods easier to wield. The `addView` and `removeView` methods allow you to manipulate layouts dynamically in Java code rather than statically in XML resource files. The following excerpt gives you a taste of this technique:

```
void addRow(final LinearLayout layout,
        String label, String hintStr,
        boolean addRadioGroup) {
   LinearLayout.LayoutParams rowLayoutParams =
           new LinearLayout.LayoutParams(
           LinearLayout.LayoutParams.FILL_PARENT,
           ViewGroup.LayoutParams.WRAP_CONTENT);
   LinearLayout.LayoutParams editTextLayoutParams =
           new LinearLayout.LayoutParams(
           180, LinearLayout.LayoutParams.WRAP_CONTENT);

   LinearLayout row = new LinearLayout(this);
   row.setOrientation(LinearLayout.HORIZONTAL);
   row.setGravity(Gravity.CENTER_VERTICAL);
```

```
TextView textView = new TextView(this);
textView.setText(label);
row.addView(textView);
EditText editText = new EditText(this);
editText.setTextSize(TypedValue.COMPLEX_UNIT_SP, 12);
editText.setHint(hintStr);
editText.setLayoutParams(editTextLayoutParams);
if (!isFirstTime) {
    editText.requestFocus();
}
row.addView(editText);

// Blah, blah, blah,...

Button button = new Button(this);
button.setTextSize(10);
button.setTypeface(null, Typeface.BOLD);
button.setText("X");
button.setTypeface(
        Typeface.SANS_SERIF, Typeface.BOLD);
button.setOnClickListener(new OnClickListener() {
    public void onClick(View view) {
        layout.removeView(
                (LinearLayout) view.getParent());
    }
});
row.addView(button);
row.setLayoutParams(rowLayoutParams);
layout.addView(row);
}
```

Activities and Stacks

The activity that starts when the user first presses an app's icon is the app's *main activity*. When the user first presses the app's icon, this main activity becomes the *root activity* in a new task stack. (At first, the root activity is the only activity on the task stack. As the stack grows, the root activity normally remains at the bottom of the stack.)

To learn more about tasks, see Chapter 1 of this minibook.

A call to startActivity in Activity A's code can launch an activity (Activity B) belonging to a different app. When this happens, Android launches Activity B by pushing Activity B onto Activity A's task stack. So one task may contain activities belonging to more than one application.

But each task is associated with a single application — namely, the app containing the task's root activity. And typically, that single application has an icon on the device's Home screen or Apps screen. (See Figure 2-12.)

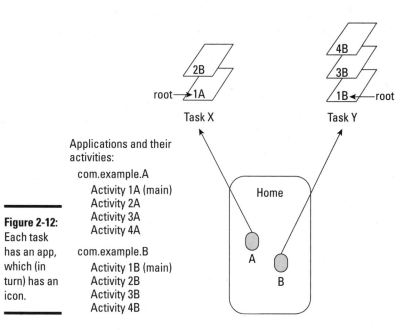

Figure 2-12:
Each task
has an app,
which (in
turn) has an
icon.

Task X

Task Y

Applications and their
activities:

com.example.A

Activity 1A (main)
Activity 2A
Activity 3A
Activity 4A

com.example.B

Activity 1B (main)
Activity 2B
Activity 3B
Activity 4B

Home

A

B

The user can switch between tasks by pressing the Home button and then pressing the icon whose app is associated with the desired task. In this sense, the user has task-level control over the device's behavior. The user doesn't have activity-level control. (For example, the user can't routinely return to an activity that's in the middle [rather than the top] of a task stack.)

The activity stack

In most of Android's documentation, *stack* doesn't refer to a task stack. Instead, the docs refer to the *activity stack* (or the *back stack*). The activity stack is the system's ever-changing, last-in/first-out history list.

You can think of the activity stack as a list of activities. But more precisely, the items in the activity stack are tasks, and the tasks themselves contain the activities.

When the user presses the Back button, Android pops an activity off the activity stack. (That is, Android pops an activity off whatever task is at the top of the activity stack.)

When the user presses Home and then presses an icon to return to an older task, Android reorders the activity stack so that the task being revisited is on top of the activity stack. (Because of this reordering, the activity stack isn't strictly a last-in/first-out list. For that matter, an individual task doesn't always behave like a last-in/first-out list either.)

Imagine starting an emulator by running an application in Eclipse. (Call this application *App A.*) With App A showing in the emulator, pressing Home brings you to Android's own *launcher* task (the Home screen). Then, when you press a second application's icon (the icon representing *App B*), the activity stack contains three tasks, as shown at the start of Figure 2-13.

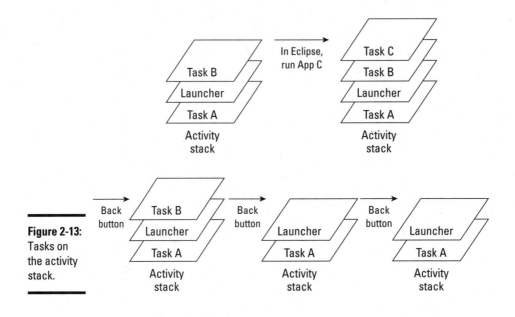

Figure 2-13: Tasks on the activity stack.

Because the activity stack is normally a last-in/first-out list, Android's own launcher task is sandwiched between the two application tasks.

With three tasks on the emulator's activity stack, run another app *(App C)* in Eclipse. Starting an app from Eclipse doesn't involve Android's launcher, so the emulator's activity stack now contains four tasks, as shown in Figure 2-13.

Pressing the Back button pops App C off the stack and returns you to App B. Pressing the Back button a second time pops App B off the stack and returns you to the launcher. (Again, see Figure 2-13.)

Pressing the Back button a third time keeps you at the launcher because you can't back up beyond the Home screen.

Fly the flag

An intent can contain six kinds of information:

✦ The name of a component to be invoked (making the intent an *explicit* intent rather than an *implicit* intent)

✦ A set of extras

✦ One action

✦ A set of categories

✦ Some data (one URI and/or one MIME type)

✦ A set of flags

I cover the first two kinds of information in Chapter 1 of this minibook, and I beat the third, fourth, and fifth kinds of information to death in this chapter's previous sections. So this section deals with the sixth kind of information — namely, flags.

A *flag* tells Android how to deal with a component. In most cases, the *component* is an activity that you're launching by calling `startActivity` or `startActivityForResult`. A typical programming pattern is as follows:

```
Intent intent = new Intent();
intent.setAction(someActionString);
intent.addCategory(someCategoryString);
intent.addFlags(int_value_representing_one_or_more_flags);
startActivity(intent);
```

Examples of Android's standard flags include the following:

✦ **Intent.FLAG_ACTIVITY_NO_ANIMATION:** When starting the new activity, don't animate the activity's entrance. That is, if the norm is to slide the new activity over the existing activity, don't slide it. Just make the new activity "poof" onto the screen.

✦ **Intent.FLAG_ACTIVITY_NO_HISTORY:** Start the new activity, but destroy this new activity as soon as the user navigates away from it. For example, if the user presses Home and then returns to this task, restore the task as if this new activity had never been added. (See Figure 2-14.)

✦ **Intent.FLAG_ACTIVITY_SINGLE_TOP:** If an instance of the activity is already on top of the activity stack, don't start another instance of that activity. Instead, use the instance that's already on top of the stack. (See Figure 2-15.)

✦ **Intent.FLAG_ACTIVITY_CLEAR_TOP:** If the activity being started already has an instance somewhere on the task stack, don't add a new instance at the top of the task stack. Instead, grab all activities above the existing instance, and pop them off the stack. (Yes, destroy them.) See Figure 2-16.

✦ **Intent.FLAG_ACTIVITY_NEW_TASK:** Each task is associated with an application. Imagine that you have two applications — App A and App B — and that the currently active task is associated with App A. Inside this task, you call `startActivity` to launch an activity in the other app — App B. What happens?

Without the FLAG_ACTIVITY_NEW_TASK flag, Android pushes the newly starting activity on top of the current stack. (See Figure 2-17.) But with the FLAG_ACTIVITY_NEW_TASK flag, Android looks for a task associated with App B.

Without FLAG_ACTIVITY_NO_HISTORY:

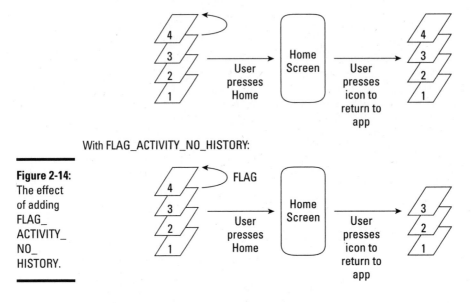

With FLAG_ACTIVITY_NO_HISTORY:

Figure 2-14:
The effect
of adding
FLAG_
ACTIVITY_
NO_
HISTORY.

Without FLAG_ACTIVITY_SINGLE_TOP:

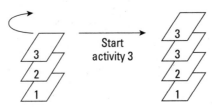

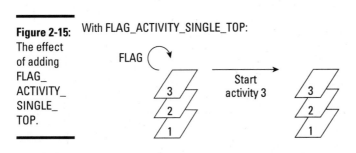

Figure 2-15:
The effect
of adding
FLAG_
ACTIVITY_
SINGLE_
TOP.

With FLAG_ACTIVITY_SINGLE_TOP:

Without FLAG_ACTIVITY_CLEAR_TOP:

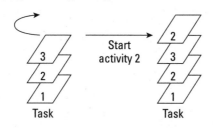

With FLAG_ACTIVITY_CLEAR_TOP:

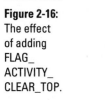

Figure 2-16:
The effect
of adding
FLAG_
ACTIVITY_
CLEAR_TOP.

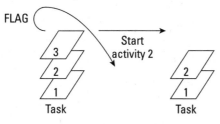

- *If Android finds such a task,* Android pushes the newly starting activity onto that task.

- *If Android doesn't find such a task,* Android creates a task associated with App B. (See Figure 2-17.)

With or without a previously existing App B task, Android displays the newly started activity on the user's screen.

Without FLAG_ACTIVITY_NEW_TASK:

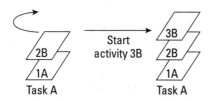

Installed applications:
com.example.A
com.example.B

Figure 2-17:
The effect
of adding
FLAG_
ACTIVITY_
NEW_TASK.

With FLAG_ACTIVITY_NEW_TASK:

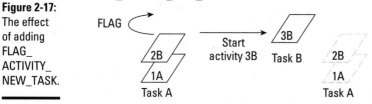

✦ **Intent.FLAG_ACTIVITY_EXCLUDE_FROM_RECENTS:** Don't display this activity's app when the user holds down the Home button.

Android creates a "Recents" item when you create a new task. Combining FLAG_ACTIVITY_EXCLUDE_FROM_RECENTS with FLAG_ACTIVITY_NEW_TASK suppresses the creation of a new "Recents" item.

✦ **Intent.FLAG_ACTIVITY_CLEAR_TASK:** When used with FLAG_ACTIVITY_NEW_TASK and the new activity is already part of a task, make the task containing the activity be the active task *and* obliterate all other activities currently on that task. (See Figure 2-18.)

The FLAG_ACTIVITY_CLEAR_TASK feature joined Android's SDK with the release of Honeycomb. If your target is older than Honeycomb, don't try to use FLAG_ACTIVITY_CLEAR_TASK.

✦ **Intent.FLAG_ACTIVITY_REORDER_TO_FRONT:** If an instance of the activity being started is already part of the current task, reorder the task's activities so that the instance is on top. (See Figure 2-19.)

✦ **Intent.FLAG_EXCLUDE_STOPPED_PACKAGES:** When searching for an activity to start, consider only activities that are currently active or paused.

Each of these flags has a Java int value, and you can combine two or more flags with Java's bitwise OR operator (|). For example, you can write

```
intent.addFlags(FLAG_ACTIVITY_NEW_TASK |
                FLAG_ACTIVITY_CLEAR_TASK);
```

The result is 0x10000000 | 0x00008000, which is 0x10008000.

The FLAG_ACTIVITY_CLEAR_TASK feature joined Android's SDK with the release of Honeycomb. If you try to use this flag's numeric value (0x00008000) on a pre-Honeycomb system, you don't get a compile-time error. After all, the compiler thinks 0x00008000 is a perfectly good hexadecimal number, even when you pass the number to the addFlags method. But at runtime, a pre-Honeycomb system says, "I can't do addFlags(0x00008000), so I think I'll display a rude application has stopped unexpectedly message." So to catch such errors before runtime, always use the constant name FLAG_ACTIVITY_CLEAR_TASK as well as other SDK constants.

Needless to say, I've created an app to help you experiment with intent flags. My flag-testing app is very much like the Intentsity app that I describe previously in this chapter. I haven't given my flag-testing app a fancy name, but you can download the app and its source code from this book's website — `www.allmycode.com/android`.

To test your intent flags, you must keep track of the apps, tasks, and activities as they run on your emulator or device. This isn't always straightforward. Fortunately, Android's `dumpsys` command can show you a snapshot of the current state of affairs. To see an up-to-date list of your emulator's activity stack and its tasks, type **adb shell dumpsys activity** in your development computer's command window. Alternatively, you can log on to the emulator's shell (by typing **adb shell**) and then issue the `dumpsys activity` command within the emulator's own command window.

Without flags:

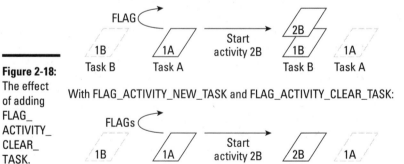

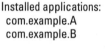

With FLAG_ACTIVITY_NEW_TASK:

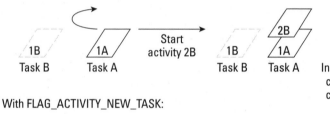

Figure 2-18: The effect of adding FLAG_ ACTIVITY_ CLEAR_ TASK.

With FLAG_ACTIVITY_NEW_TASK and FLAG_ACTIVITY_CLEAR_TASK:

Without FLAG_ACTIVITY_REORDER_TO_FRONT:

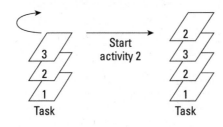

With FLAG_ACTIVITY_REORDER_TO_FRONT:

Figure 2-19:
The effect
of adding
FLAG_
ACTIVITY_
REORDER_
TO_FRONT.

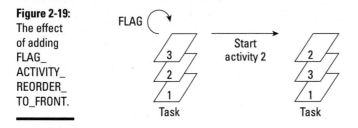

Chapter 3: Services

In This Chapter

✔ **Running code without bothering the user**

✔ **Running code when a device starts**

✔ **Starting, binding, and querying**

✔ **Sending messages from one process to another**

Some things are of no concern to the user of an Android device. "A process on your phone is checking for e-mail right now . . . Nope, no new e-mail. Sorry about the interruption. Get back to what you were doing. You'll hear from me again in exactly one minute." Such notices are intrusive and unnecessary, especially on a device with limited screen real estate.

To do something behind the scenes, you don't want an Android activity. An activity normally has a layout file, and the user deals with the layout's gizmos on the screen. Instead, you want the kind of component that runs quietly in the background. In other words, you want an Android service.

A Very Simple Service

I start this chapter with an embarrassingly simple example — a service that doesn't do anything. This lazy service simply illustrates the minimum service source code requirements.

The service

Listing 3-1 contains the good-for-nothing service.

Listing 3-1: An Un-Weather Service

```
package com.allmycode.services;

import android.app.Service;
import android.content.Intent;
import android.os.IBinder;
import android.widget.Toast;

public class MyWeatherService extends Service {

    @Override
```

(continued)

Listing 3-1 *(continued)*

```java
public IBinder onBind(Intent intent) {
    Toast.makeText(this, R.string.service_bound,
                   Toast.LENGTH_SHORT).show();
    return null;
}

@Override
public int onStartCommand(Intent intent,
                          int flags, int startId) {
    Toast.makeText(this, R.string.service_started,
                   Toast.LENGTH_SHORT).show();
    return START_STICKY;
}

@Override
public void onDestroy() {
    Toast.makeText(this, R.string.service_destroyed,
                   Toast.LENGTH_SHORT).show();
}
}
```

In truth, the service in Listing 3-1 has more code than is absolutely necessary. As a subclass of the abstract `android.app.Service` class, the only required method in Listing 3-1 is `onBind`. Still, the listing's `onStart Command` and `onDestroy` methods are a bit more useful than the methods that would be inherited from the `android.app.Service` class.

The required `onBind` method in Listing 3-1 returns `null`. Normally, the object returned by an `onBind` method implements the `android. os.IBinder` interface, and an object that implements `IBinder` allows one process to exchange information with another process. That's nice, but in this simple example, the service doesn't exchange information.

I put the service from Listing 3-1 in its own Eclipse project, with its own package name. So this service runs as its own application in its own process on an emulator or a device. The service has no user interface (and, therefore, no layout file). The application's `AndroidManifest.xml` file has no `<activity>` element but instead has the `<service>` element shown in Listing 3-2.

Listing 3-2:   An Element in the Un-Weather Service's AndroidManifest.xml File

```xml
<service android:name=".MyWeatherService">
    <intent-filter>
        <action android:name="com.allmycode.WEATHER" />
    </intent-filter>
</service>
```

A client activity

To start the service in Listing 3-1, other components refer to the action named in Listing 3-2. Listing 3-3 shows you how.

Listing 3-3:   A Client for the Un-Weather Service

```
package com.allmycode.demos;

import android.app.Activity;
import android.content.Intent;
import android.os.Bundle;
import android.view.View;

public class ServiceConsumerActivity extends Activity {
    Intent intent = new Intent();

    @Override
    public void onCreate(Bundle savedInstanceState) {
        super.onCreate(savedInstanceState);
        setContentView(R.layout.main);
        intent.setAction("com.allmycode.WEATHER");
    }

    public void onStartClick(View view) {
        startService(intent);
    }

    public void onStopClick(View view) {
        stopService(intent);
    }
}
```

**Book III
Chapter 3**

Services

The activity in Listing 3-3 has two buttons — a Start button and a Stop button. (See Figure 3-1.)

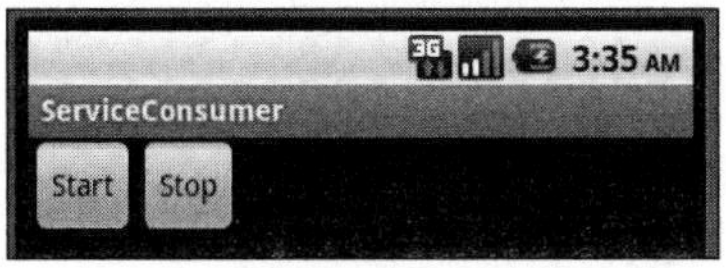

Figure 3-1:
Start and
stop a
service.
How simple
is that?

In creating the layout, I took the liberty of assigning listener method names to the two buttons:

```
<Button android:text="Start"
        android:onClick="onStartClick"
        android:id="@+id/button1"
        android:layout_height="wrap_content"
        android:layout_width="wrap_content">
</Button>
<Button android:text="Stop"
        android:onClick="onStopClick"
        android:id="@+id/button4"
        android:layout_height="wrap_content"
        android:layout_width="wrap_content">
</Button>
```

So clicking the Start button calls `startService(intent)`, and clicking the Stop button calls `stopService(intent)`. In addition to starting and stopping the service, each click displays a `Toast` view.

For a brief treatise on Android's `Toast` class, see the "Informing the user" section, later in this chapter.

A service's primary purposes are to run in the background (independent of any obvious user interaction) and to offer help to other apps. So if the code in Listing 3-1 represented a useful service, this code would be doing something about the weather. (For code that does something useful, see this chapter's "Talking about the Weather" section.)

Here's what happens when you play with the buttons in Figure 3-1:

✦ **Press Start and then press Stop.**

After pressing Start, you see the Service Started toast. Then, after pressing Stop, you see the Service Destroyed toast. No surprises here!

✦ **Press Stop twice in a row.**

If the service is running, the first call to `stopService` (in Listing 3-3) destroys the service. The second call to `stopService` doesn't display a Service Destroyed toast because a component that's not running can't be destroyed.

✦ **Press Start twice in a row and then press Stop twice in a row.**

As a result, you see two Service Started toasts followed by only one Service Destroyed toast. Each `startService` call (from Listing 3-3) triggers a call to `onStartCommand` in Listing 3-1. But the first `stopService` call (again, from Listing 3-3) destroys the service. Subsequence `stopService` calls have no effect.

✦ **Press Start and then press the emulator's Back button.**

When you press the Back button, you *don't* see a Service Destroyed toast. And that's the essence of an Android service. A service can live on after the activity that started the service has been destroyed.

Services start, stop, and start again

A service has no user interface, and it may continue to run after you destroy the service's starting activity. That can be a dangerous combination of traits. Services without interfaces can hang around indefinitely like Rasputin — the mad monk of czarist Russia that no one could kill. If developers don't include code to manage their services, the services clog up the system. No one's happy.

Of course, Android can kill services in order to reclaim needed memory. The http://developer.android.com/reference/android/app/ Service.html page lists all the situations in which Android kills or doesn't kill a service, and it doesn't make light reading.

One insight about the lifetime of a service comes from the onStartCommand method in Listing 3-1. The onStartCommand method takes an Intent parameter. The parameter's value points to whatever Intent object the startService method sends. (See Listing 3-3.) The onStartCommand method returns an int value. In Listing 3-1, the int value is Service. START_STICKY. This constant value tells Android how to restart the service at some time interval after killing it. The alternative int values are as follows:

✦ **START_STICKY:** If Android kills the service, Android waits for a certain time interval and then restarts the service. Upon restart, Android feeds the service the intent from whatever startService call is next in the queue of such commands. If no startService calls are waiting to start this particular service, Android feeds null to the onStartCommand method's Intent parameter.

✦ **START_REDELIVER_INTENT:** If Android kills the service, Android waits for a certain time interval and then restarts the service. Upon restart, Android feeds the service the intent that came as a parameter in the current call to onStartCommand.

✦ **START_NOT_STICKY:** If Android kills the service, Android doesn't automatically restart the service. Android restarts the service if and when the next startService call queues up to start this particular service.

✦ **START_STICKY_COMPATIBILITY:** If Android kills the service, Android tries to restart the service the way START_STICKY restarts services. But Android doesn't promise to restart the service.

Services, threads, and processes

When you were a child, resting happily on your mother's knee, she told you that an Android service runs in its own separate thread. Unfortunately, your mother was wrong. A service runs in its app's main thread. You can verify this fact by displaying the value of `Thread.currentThread().get-Name()` from the service's code. When you do, you see the name `main`. A service runs in its app's main thread, also known (somewhat misleadingly) as the app's *UI thread.*

An app's activities also run in the app's main thread. So another way to verify a service's behavior is to do something nasty — time-consuming work in a service's code. *Time-consuming work* includes such things as retrieving data from a network connection or computing several elements' positions in a graphic scene. Doing heavy lifting in the main thread makes you vulnerable to ANR (application not responding) conditions. An ANR dialog box appears after five seconds of inactivity and offers the user a Force Close option.

An app has its own package name and runs in its own process. A process has several threads, but a thread belongs to one and only one process. So the components in Listings 3-1 and 3-3 belong to separate processes and don't clash with one another's runs. But you can combine activities and services in the same app. When you do, the activities and services run in the same thread — meaning that the run of a service isn't as independent as Mom once claimed.

You can force an activity or a service to run in its own process. To do so, add the attribute `android:process="other.process.name"` to a `<service>` element or an `<activity>` element in an app's `AndroidManifest.xml` file. The `other.process.name` can be anything you want as long as it includes at least one dot. (Normally, the `other.process.name` is a package name, such as `com.example.mystuff`, but the name doesn't have to be part of an existing package name.) As a bonus, you can start the process name with a colon (as in `android:process=":other.process.name"`). In true Unix/Linux geek fashion, the keystroke-efficient colon symbol indicates that this additional process is private to the component's own application. Other apps can't communicate with this coveted process.

The bottom line is, you should be proactive in starting and stopping your own service. Don't be a memory hog by relying on the system to clean up after you. Be aware of your service's lifespan, and destroy your service when it's no longer needed. Add a `stopService` call to your activity's `onPause` or `onDestroy` method if it makes sense to do so. And if a service knows that it's no longer useful, have the service call its own `stopSelf` method.

Android calls an activity's `onDestroy` method whenever the user turns the device (from portrait to landscape, for example). If you put a `stopService` call in an activity's `onDestroy` method, you must deal with all possible situations in which the service halts. For details, see this chapter's "Talking about the Weather" section.

Running a Service at Boot Time

How important is your service? Does your service start on rare occasions when the user presses a certain button? Or does your service start when the device powers up?

If Android users can't survive without running your service, you can start the service at boot time. To do so, you create another kind of component — a broadcast receiver.

A *broadcast receiver* responds to intents that you fling into the air using the `sendBroadcast` or `sendOrderedBroadcast` method. Android provides special treatment for an intent sent with either of these methods.

✦ **When you call `startActivity` or `startService`, Android looks for** *one* **component to satisfy the intent.**

   If the system finds more than one suitable activity (two installed web browsers, for example), Android displays a dialog box prompting the user to choose among the alternatives.

✦ **When you call `sendBroadcast` or `sendOrderedBroadcast`, Android fires up** *all* **the receivers whose filters satisfy the intent.**

   With `sendOrderedBroadcast`, Android runs receivers one after the other. Each receiver can pass the intent on to the next receiver in line or can break the chain by calling its `abortBroadcast` method.

   With `sendBroadcast`, Android may interleave the running of several receivers. In this scenario, having a receiver abort a broadcast doesn't make sense.

Consider the Weather service in Listing 3-1. In the same application, create a Java class with the code from Listing 3-4.

Book III
Chapter 3

Services

Listing 3-4: A Simple Broadcast Receiver

```
package com.allmycode.services;

import android.content.BroadcastReceiver;
import android.content.Context;
import android.content.Intent;

public class MyBootReceiver extends BroadcastReceiver {
  @Override
  public void onReceive(Context context, Intent intent) {
    Intent serviceIntent = new Intent();
    serviceIntent.setClass(context,
                           MyWeatherService.class);
    context.startService(serviceIntent);
  }
}
```

When `MyBootReceiver` runs, it starts an instance of the `MyWeather` `Service` class. The not-too-difficult trick is to make `MyBootReceiver` run when the emulator or device starts.

Listing 3-5 shows you the mechanics of launching the receiver in Listing 3-4.

Listing 3-5: Manifest Elements for the Receiver in Listing 3-4

```
<uses-permission android:name=
  "android.permission.RECEIVE_BOOT_COMPLETED"/>

<application android:icon="@drawable/icon"
             android:label="@string/app_name">

  <service android:name=".MyWeatherService">
    <intent-filter>
      <action android:name="com.allmycode.WEATHER" />
    </intent-filter>
  </service>


  <receiver android:name=".MyBootReceiver">
    <intent-filter>
      <action android:name=
        "android.intent.action.BOOT_COMPLETED" />
      <category android:name=
        "android.intent.category.HOME" />
    </intent-filter>
  </receiver>

</application>
```

The `<uses-permission>` element in Listing 3-5 grants this app permission to receive `BOOT_COMPLETED` broadcasts. In the receiver's `<action>` element, the `android:name` attribute says, "Wake me up if anyone hollers `android.intent.action.BOOT_COMPLETED`." When you launch your emulator or you turn on your device, Android runs through its normal boot sequence and then sends an intent containing the `BOOT_COMPLETED` action. At that point, Android finds the receiver in Listing 3-4 and calls the receiver's `onReceive` method. In turn, the `onReceive` method in Listing 3-4 gooses the Weather service in Listing 3-1.

A broadcast receiver lives long enough to run its `onReceive` method and then the receiver stops running. A receiver doesn't have any `onCreate` or `onDestroy` methods, or any of the lifecycle methods belonging to other kinds of components. A broadcast receiver does its work and then hides in the shadows until the next relevant broadcast comes along.

You can download this section's example from the book's website. To test the code, install the code, shut down the emulator, and then restart the emulator. Ay, there's the rub! Starting an emulator once is annoying enough. Starting it several times (because you got some detail wrong the first few times) is a pain in the class.

Your code can't test Listing 3-4 by creating an ACTION_BOOT_COMPLETED intent. Android reserves ACTION_BOOT_COMPLETED for system-level code only. By using the Android Debug Bridge, though, you can launch an intent as a Linux shell superuser. Here's how:

1. **Install this section's code onto an emulator.**

2. **On your development computer, launch a command window.**

   For details, see Book VI, Chapter 3.

3. **In the command window, issue the cd command to make the ANDROID_HOME/platform-tools directory your working directory.**

   Again, see Book VI, Chapter 3 for details.

4. **Type the following command, all on one line:**

```
adb shell am broadcast
        -a android.intent.action.BOOT_COMPLETED
```

   Using Android's am command, you can call startActivity, startService, and sendBroadcast as if you were Android itself (or himself, or herself, or whoever). When you issue the command in Step 4, Android behaves as if the system has just finished booting.

You can see all the am command's options by typing **adb shell am** in your development computer's command window.

For more information about the Android Debug Bridge, see Book I, Chapter 2. For more information about broadcast receivers, see Chapter 4 in this minibook.

Starting and Binding

You can do two kinds of things with a service:

+ **You can start and stop a service.**

   You do this by calling the Context class's startService and stop Service methods. Also, a service can take the bull by the horns and call its own stopSelf or stopSelfResult method.

When you call `startService`, you create only a momentary relationship with the service. Android creates an instance of the service if no instances are already running. In addition, Android calls the service's `onStartCommand` method. (See Listing 3-1.)

Calls to `startService` don't pile up. To illustrate the point, consider this sequence of method calls, along with their resulting Android responses:

```
Activity A calls startService to start MyService.
    Android instantiates MyService and
        calls the instance's onStartCommand method.

Activity B calls startService to start MyService.
    Android calls the existing instance's
        onStartCommand method.

Activity A calls stopService to stop MyService.
    Android destroys the MyService instance.

Activity B calls stopService to stop MyService.
    Android says "The joke's on you." There's no
        instance of MyService to stop.
```

✦ **You can bind to, and unbind from, a service.**

You do this by calling the `Context` class's `bindService` and `unbindService` methods. Between binding and unbinding, you have an ongoing connection with the service. Through this connection, you can send messages to the service and receive messages from the service. That's useful!

When you call `bindService`, Android creates an instance of the service if no instances are running already. In addition, Android calls the service's `onBind` method. (For an example, skip ahead to Listings 3-6 and 3-7.)

When you call `bindService`, Android doesn't call the service's `onStartCommand` method.

Calls to `bindService` pile up. A service can have many bindings at once, each to a different activity. Your service's code can keep track of all this hubbub by maintaining a collection of binding objects (an `ArrayList`, or whatever). When you call `unbindService`, you don't destroy the service instance. Android keeps the service alive as long as any activities are bound to the service.

Services can receive Start requests and Bind requests all at the same time. When all bound activities unbind themselves from a particular service, the system checks whether anybody started the service this time around. If so, the system waits for somebody to call `stopService` before destroying the service.

Android can terminate activities to reclaim memory. If I were a service and Android terminated the activities that were bound to me, I'd be afraid for my own survival. Test your apps for unwanted results from the untimely termination of activities and their services. If, in testing, you experience any unexpected behavior due to the early termination of a service, please fix the code.

The previous sections' examples started and stopped a service. The rest of this chapter binds and unbinds with a service.

Talking about the Weather

Every Android book needs a Weather Service example, and this book is no exception. In this section, your activity binds to a service, which in turn reaches out for weather information over the Internet.

A service

I build the example in stages. The first stage is *essence de service*. An activity binds to the service, gets back some fake responses to nonsense queries, and then unbinds. Listing 3-6 contains the service.

Listing 3-6:   A Weather Service with a Fear of Commitment

```
package com.allmycode.services;

import android.app.Service;
import android.content.Intent;
import android.os.Bundle;
import android.os.Handler;
import android.os.IBinder;
import android.os.Message;
import android.os.Messenger;
import android.os.RemoteException;
import android.widget.Toast;

public class MyWeatherService extends Service {

  Messenger messengerToClient = null;

  MyIncomingHandler myIncomingHandler =
      new MyIncomingHandler();
  Messenger messengerToService =
      new Messenger(myIncomingHandler);
```

(continued)

Listing 3-6 *(continued)*

```
@Override
public IBinder onBind(Intent intent) {
  doToast(R.string.service_bound);
  return messengerToService.getBinder();
}

class MyIncomingHandler extends Handler {
  @Override
  public void handleMessage(Message incomingMessage) {
    messengerToClient = incomingMessage.replyTo;

    Bundle reply = new Bundle();
    reply.putString("weather", "It's dark at night.");
    Message replyMessage = Message.obtain();
    replyMessage.setData(reply);
    try {
      messengerToClient.send(replyMessage);
    } catch (RemoteException e) {
      e.printStackTrace();
    }
    doToast(R.string.message_handled);
  }
}

@Override
public boolean onUnbind(Intent intent) {
  doToast(R.string.service_stopped_itself);
  stopSelf();
  return false;
}

@Override
public void onDestroy() {
  myIncomingHandler = null;
  doToast(R.string.service_destroyed);
}

void doToast(int resource) {
  Toast.makeText(this, resource,
      Toast.LENGTH_SHORT).show();
}
}
```

The flow of control in Listing 3-6 isn't simple, so I've created Figure 3-2 to
help you understand what's going on. The first thing to notice in Figure 3-2
is that the service doesn't interact directly with a client application. Instead,
the service gets calls indirectly through the Android operating system.

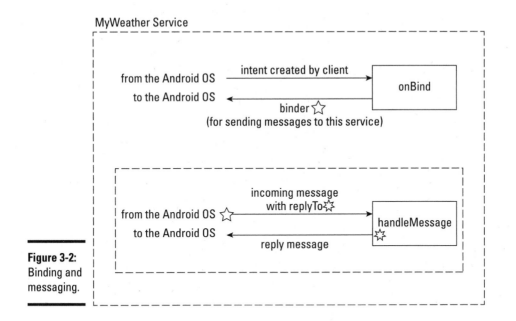

MyWeather Service

Figure 3-2:
Binding and
messaging.

Like many other communication regimens, the talk between a client and a service has two phases:

✦ The first phase (the binding phase) establishes a line of communication.

✦ In the second phase, the client and the service exchange useful information via messages. In general, the client sends a request for information and the service sends a reply.

To bind to a service, a client sends an intent. Android hands this intent to the service's onBind method. In response, the onBind method returns a *binder* — an object that implements the IBinder interface. (See Listing 3-6 and Figure 3-2.) The binder is like a business card. By returning a binder, the service says, "Android, tell the client application that it can reach me at this address." That's why, in Listing 3-6, the service creates the binder from an instance of MyIncomingHandler. (It's the same as printing a business card from an instance of "my answering machine's phone number.")

Android delivers the binder to the client app. Eventually, the client app queries the service. The query contains a request for specific information. But the query also contains a replyTo field. The service's inner class (in this example, MyIncomingHandler) uses the replyTo information to send an answer back to the client app. In Listing 3-6, I keep things simple by replying It's dark at night no matter what query the client sends. (A weather report like this is always correct.)

A client

Listing 3-7 contains a client for the service in Listing 3-6.

Listing 3-7: A Client for the Service in Listing 3-6

```
package com.allmycode.demos;

import android.app.Activity;
import android.content.ComponentName;
import android.content.Context;
import android.content.Intent;
import android.content.ServiceConnection;
import android.content.SharedPreferences;
import android.os.Bundle;
import android.os.Handler;
import android.os.IBinder;
import android.os.Message;
import android.os.Messenger;
import android.os.RemoteException;
import android.view.View;
import android.view.View.OnClickListener;
import android.widget.Button;
import android.widget.EditText;
import android.widget.TextView;
import android.widget.Toast;

public class ServiceConsumerActivity extends Activity
    implements OnClickListener {

  Messenger messengerToService = null;

  MyIncomingHandler myIncomingHandler =
      new MyIncomingHandler();
  Messenger messengerFromService =
      new Messenger(myIncomingHandler);

  ServiceConnection connection =
      new MyServiceConnection();
  SharedPreferences prefs;
  boolean isBound = false;

  void bind() {
    Intent intent = new Intent();
    intent.setAction("com.allmycode.WEATHER");
    isBound =
        bindService(intent, connection,
            Context.BIND_AUTO_CREATE);
  }
```

```
public void queryService() {
  if (isBound) {
    Bundle bundle = new Bundle();
    bundle.putString("location", "Philadelphia");

    Message message = Message.obtain();
    message.replyTo = messengerFromService;
    message.setData(bundle);
    try {
      messengerToService.send(message);
    } catch (RemoteException e) {
      e.printStackTrace();
    }
  } else {
    textView1.setText(R.string.service_not_bound);
  }
}

class MyIncomingHandler extends Handler {
  @Override
  public void handleMessage(Message msg) {
    Bundle bundle = msg.getData();
    textView1.setText(bundle.getString("weather"));
  }
}

void unbind() {
  if (isBound) {
    unbindService(connection);
    isBound = false;
  }
}

class MyServiceConnection implements ServiceConnection {
  public void onServiceConnected(
      ComponentName className, IBinder binder) {
    messengerToService = new Messenger(binder);
    doToast(R.string.service_connected);
  }

  public void onServiceDisconnected(ComponentName n) {
    messengerToService = null;
    doToast(R.string.service_crashed);
  }
}

void doToast(int resource) {
  Toast.makeText(this, resource,
      Toast.LENGTH_SHORT).show();
}
```

(continued)

Listing 3-7 *(continued)*

```
@Override
public void onDestroy() {
  super.onDestroy();
  prefs = getSharedPreferences("PREFS", MODE_PRIVATE);
  SharedPreferences.Editor editor = prefs.edit();
  editor.putBoolean("isBound", isBound);
  editor.putString("report", textView1.getText()
      .toString());
  editor.commit();

  unbind();
}

@Override
public void onCreate(Bundle savedInstanceState) {
  super.onCreate(savedInstanceState);
  setContentView(R.layout.main);
  prefs = getSharedPreferences("PREFS", MODE_PRIVATE);
  if (prefs != null) {
    textView1 = (TextView) findViewById(R.id.textView1);

    textView1.setText(prefs.getString("report",
      getString(R.string.report_appears_here)));
    if (prefs.getBoolean("isBound", false)) {
      bind();
    }
  }

  // The rest of the code is boilerplate stuff
  // such as onCreate.
}
```

The first several lines of Listing 3-7 are parallel to the code in Listing 3-6. Like the service in Listing 3-6, the client in Listing 3-7 has messengers and an incoming handler class.

Figure 3-3 shows a layout that I created for the activity in Listing 3-7. The bind, queryService, and unbind methods in Listing 3-7 handle the button clicks in Figure 3-3. (This section's service doesn't care what city you're in, so the EditText view set up for a city name or zip code in Figure 3-3 doesn't serve any purpose. It's a placeholder for user input in subsequent examples.)

Informing the user

Near the bottom of Figure 3-3, there's a rounded rectangle containing the words *Message handled.* The rectangle illustrates the use of Android's Toast class. A *toast* is an unobtrusive little view that displays some useful information for a brief period of time. A toast view pops up on the screen, the way a hot piece of bread pops up from a toaster. (Rumor has it that the Android class name Toast comes from this goofy analogy.)

Figure 3-3:
A user
interface for
the activity
in Listing
3-7.

A toast view typically displays a message for the user to read. So Android developers often talk about *toast messages*. In principle, there's nothing wrong with the term *toast message*. But much of this chapter deals with instances of the `android.os.Message` class — messages sent between a service and its client. And near the bottom of Figure 3-3, the words *Message handled* refer to a message between a service and its client, not to a toast message. So in Figure 3-3, a toast message informs the user about a completely different kind of message. What's an author to do? In this chapter, I use the word *message* to refer to communication between a service and its client. In other chapters, I throw around the words *toast message* without worrying about the problem.

The `Toast` class has two extremely useful methods: `makeText` and `show`.

✦ **The static `Toast.makeText` method creates an instance of the `Toast` class.**

The `makeText` method has three parameters.

- The first parameter is a context (the word `this` in Listing 3-7).

- The second parameter is either a resource or a sequence of characters (a `String`, for example).

  If you call `makeText` with a `String`, the user sees the `String` when Android displays the toast. If you call `makeText` with a resource, Android looks for the resource in your app's `res` directory. In Listing 3-7, the code calls `makeText` twice — once with resource `R.string.service_connected` and once with `R.string.service_crashed`.

Book III
Chapter 3

Services

If you use an `int` value (42, for example) for the second parameter of the `makeText` method, Android doesn't display the characters *42* in the toast view. Instead, Android looks for a resource whose value in `R.java` is 42. Your `R.java` file probably doesn't contain the number 42. So instead of a toast view, you get a `ResourceNotFound` exception. Your app crashes, and you groan in dismay.

- The `makeText` method's third parameter is either `Toast.LENGTH_LONG` or `Toast.LENGTH_SHORT`. With `LENGTH_LONG`, the toast view appears for about four seconds. With `LENGTH_SHORT`, the toast view appears for approximately two seconds.

✦ **The `show` method tells Android to display the toast view.**

In Listing 3-7, notice that I call both `makeText` and `show` in one Java statement. If you forget to call the `show` method, the toast view doesn't appear. You stare in disbelief wondering why you don't see the toast view. ("Who stole my toast?" you ask.) When you finally figure out that you forgot to call the `show` method, you feel foolish. (At least that's the way I felt when I forgot earlier today.)

Binding to the service

In Listing 3-7, the call to `bindService` takes three parameters — an intent, a service connection, and an `int` value representing flags.

✦ **The intent helps determine which service to invoke.**

In Listing 3-7, the intent has action `"com.allmycode.WEATHER"`. That's good because my service's `AndroidManifest.xml` file contains the following elements:

```
<application android:icon="@drawable/icon"
   android:label="@string/app_name">

  <service android:name=".MyWeatherService">
    <intent-filter>
      <action android:name="com.allmycode.WEATHER" />
    </intent-filter>
  </service>

</application>
```

(Only a snippet from the `AndroidManifest.xml` file appears in this chapter.)

✦ **The connection is the virtual rope between the client and the service.**

The `connection` parameter in Listing 3-7 implements the `android.content.ServiceConnection` interface. I define the `MyServiceConnection` class later in Listing 3-7.

Notice that in one of the `MyServiceConnection` class's methods, Android hands the service's business card (the binder) to the client. This is a bit different from the code in Listing 3-6, where the service gets `replyTo` information from each incoming message. The difference stems from the way the client and the service talk to each other. The client initiates communications, and the service twiddles its virtual thumbs waiting for communications.

Another thing to notice about `MyServiceConnection` is the peculiar role of the `onServiceDisconnected` method. As the toast implies, Android doesn't call `onServiceDisconnected` unless the service takes a dive prematurely.

✦ **The flags provide additional information about the run of the service.**

When Android needs more memory, Android terminates processes. In Listing 3-7, the flag `BIND_AUTO_CREATE` tells Android to avoid terminating the service's process while your activity runs. An alternative, `BIND_NOT_FOREGROUND`, tells Android not to consider your activity's needs when deciding whether to terminate the service's process.

Querying the service

In Listing 3-7, the `queryService` method asks the service for the answer to a question. Here's what the `queryService` method does:

1. The `queryService` method obtains a blank *message* from the `android.os.Message` class.

2. The `queryService` method adds a question (the *bundle*) to the message.

3. The `queryService` method tells a *messenger* to send the message to the service.

A *bundle* (an instance of `android.os.Bundle`) is something that a process can write to and that another process can read from. You see a bundle in every activity's `onCreate` method. In the world of data communications, sending a message is likened to writing data. So in Listing 3-7, the code juggles bundles.

✦ The `queryService` method puts a bundle on a message and then "writes" the message to an Android message queue.

✦ The `handleMessage` method in the `MyIncomingHandler` class "reads" a message from an Android message queue and then gets the message's bundle for display on the device's screen.

Using shared preferences to restart a connection

Listing 3-7 contains an important lesson about the life of a service. A service that's bound to another component (an activity, for example) tends to stay alive. If developers don't explicitly unbind from services, the services build up and start clogging Android's pipes. So a good citizen does the housekeeping to unbind services.

So in Listing 3-7, the `onDestroy` method unbinds the service. So far, so good. But what happens when the user turns the device sideways? Chapter 1 of this minibook reminds you what happens when the user reorients the device — Android destroys the current activity and re-creates the activity in the new orientation. So if you're not careful, the user loses the service just by moving the device. That's probably not what you want.

To defend against this problem, use *shared preferences*. With shared preferences, you can store information. Later, your app (or, if you want, someone else's app) can retrieve the information.

Here's how you wield a set of shared preferences:

✦ **To create shared preferences, call the `android.content.Context` class's `getSharedPreferences` method.**

For parameters, feed a name and a mode to the method call. In Listing 3-7, the name is the string `"PREFS"` and the mode is the `int` value `android.content.Context.MODE_PRIVATE`. The alternatives are

- *MODE_PRIVATE:* No other process can read from or write to these preferences.

- *MODE_WORLD_READABLE:* Other processes can read from these preferences.

- *MODE_WORLD_WRITEABLE:* Other processes can write to these preferences.

- *MODE_MULTI_PROCESS:* Other processes can write to these preferences even while a process is in the middle of a read operation. Weird things can happen with this much concurrency. So watch out!

You can combine modes with Java's bitwise `or` operator. So a call such as

```
getSharedPreferences("PREFS",
    MODE_WORLD_READABLE | MODE_WORLD_WRITEABLE);
```

makes your preferences both readable and writable for all other processes.

✦ **To add values to a set of shared preferences, use an instance of the `android.content.SharedPreferences.Editor` class.**

In Listing 3-7, the `onDestroy` method creates a new editor object. Then the code uses the editor to add a name/value pair (`"isBound"`,

isBound) to the shared preferences. The `Editor` class has methods such as `putInt`, `putString`, `putStringSet`, and so on.

✦ **To finish the job, call the editor's `commit` method.**

Again, see Listing 3-7.

✦ **To retrieve an existing set of shared preferences, call `getShared-Preferences`, using the same name as the name you used to create the preferences.**

Can you guess which listing contains an example of this code? Yes! Listing 3-7. Look at the listing's `onCreate` method.

✦ **To read values from an existing set of shared preferences, call `get-Boolean`, `getInt`, `getFloat`, or one of the other get methods belonging to the `SharedPreferences` class.**

In Listing 3-7, the call to `getBoolean` takes two parameters. The first parameter is the name in whatever name/value pair you're trying to get. The second parameter is a default value. So when you call `prefs.getBoolean("isBound", false)`, if `prefs` has no pair with name `"isBound"`, the method call returns `false`.

In Listing 3-7, the `onDestroy` method saves the value of `isBound`. Then, when Android revives the activity, the `onCreate` method retrieves the `isBound` value. In effect, the `onCreate` method "finds out" whether the service was bound before the activity was destroyed. If the service was bound, the code renews its connection, making another call to the `bind-Service` method.

Using attributes in an app's `AndroidManifest.xml` document, you can keep Android from destroying an activity when the user reorients the device. For information, see Chapter 1 of this minibook.

Getting Real Weather Data

After this book printed, Google's weather service became defunct. As a result, Listings 3-9 and 3-10 are out of date. Visit `allymcode.com/android` for updated examples. In this section, you supplement the code in Listings 3-6 and 3-7 so that your app retrieves real weather data. The code changes don't require major surgery. Here's what you do:

✦ **In the client app, get the user's input from the EditText widget and send this input to the service.**

That is, change the statement

```
bundle.putString("location", "Philadelphia");
```

in Listing 3-7 to a statement such as

```
bundle.putString("location", locationText.getText()
    .toString().trim());
```

✦ **In the service, send the incoming message's text to the Google's weather server.**

That is, change the statement

```
reply.putString("weather", "It's dark at night.");
```

in Listing 3-6 to a statement such as

```
reply.putString("weather",
    getWeatherString(incomingMessage));
```

Google's weather server takes a city name or a zip code and returns an XML document describing the weather at that location. Here's an abridged version of a response from Google's weather API:

```
<xml_api_reply version="1">
  <weather module_id="0" tab_id="0" mobile_row="0"
      mobile_zipped="1" row="0" section="0">
    <forecast_information>
      <city data="San Francisco, CA" />
      <postal_code data="San Francisco" />
      <latitude_e6 data="" />
      <longitude_e6 data="" />
      <forecast_date data="2011-08-07" />
      <current_date_time
        data="2011-08-07 18:56:00 +0000" />
      <unit_system data="US" />
    </forecast_information>
    <current_conditions>
      <condition data="Overcast" />
      <temp_f data="59" />
      <temp_c data="15" />
      <humidity data="Humidity: 77%" />
      <icon data="/ig/images/weather/cloudy.gif" />
      <wind_condition data="Wind: W at 10 mph" />
    </current_conditions>
    <forecast_conditions>
      <day_of_week data="Sun" />
      <low data="54" />
      <high data="63" />
      <icon
        data="/ig/images/weather/mostly_sunny.gif" />
      <condition data="Mostly Sunny" />
    </forecast_conditions>
  </weather>
</xml_api_reply>
```

You can get a similar XML response by typing **http://www.google.com/ig/api?weather=San%20Francisco** in your web browser's address field. In this address, the characters %20 are the web's way of encoding a blank space.

✦ **In the service, submit Google's response to an XML parser.**

An *XML parser* is a program that sifts information from XML files. This section's code contains a parser that ferrets out the Fahrenheit temperature and the weather condition from Google's response. (I apologize in advance to non-U.S., non-Belize readers for the use of the Fahrenheit scale. Bad habits are difficult to break.)

In the old days, before XML was commonly used, your app would be screen scraping. *Screen scraping* refers to the practice of fishing for data in an ordinary web page. In the pre-XML era, your code had to eliminate the page's colors, font tags, advertisements, and any other irrelevant material. Then your code had to search the page for the current Fahrenheit temperature, making every effort to avoid grabbing next week's forecast or the cost of a subscription to *Weather and Wine Weekly*. Then you hoped that any future changes in the website's layout didn't spoil the correctness of your code. Undoubtedly, parsing XML is more reliable.

✦ **As a final step, your service gets the result returned from the XML parser and forwards that result to the client app.**

Dealing with XML

Listing 3-8 contains a harmless-looking `Weather` class, and Listing 3-9 contains an XML parser.

Listing 3-8:   A Weather Class

```
package com.allmycode.services;

public class Weather {

  private int temperature = 0;
  private String condition = "";

  public Weather() {
  }

  public Integer getTemperature() {
    return temperature;
  }

  public void setTemperature(Integer temperature) {
    this.temperature = temperature;
  }

  public String getCondition() {
    return condition;
  }

  public void setCondition(String condition) {
    this.condition = condition;
  }

}
```

Listing 3-9:   What to Do When You Find XML Elements

```java
package com.allmycode.services;

import org.xml.sax.Attributes;
import org.xml.sax.SAXException;
import org.xml.sax.helpers.DefaultHandler;

public class MySaxHandler extends DefaultHandler {

  private static final String CURRENT_CONDITIONS =
      "current_conditions";
  private static final String DATA = "data";
  private static final String CONDITION = "condition";
  private static final String TEMP_F = "temp_f";

  private Weather weather = new Weather();

  private boolean current_conditions = false;

  public Weather getWeather() {
    return weather;
  }

  @Override
  public void startElement(String namespaceURI,
      String localName, String qName,
      Attributes attributes) throws SAXException {

    if (localName.equals(CURRENT_CONDITIONS)) {
      current_conditions = true;
    } else {
      if (current_conditions) {
        if (localName.equals(TEMP_F)) {
          String dataAttribute =
              attributes.getValue(DATA);
          weather.setTemperature(Integer
              .parseInt(dataAttribute));
        } else if (localName.equals(CONDITION)) {
          String condAttribute =
              attributes.getValue(DATA);
          weather.setCondition(condAttribute);
        }
      }
    }
  }

  @Override
  public void endElement(String namespaceURI,
      String localName, String qName) throws SAXException {
    if (localName.equals(CURRENT_CONDITIONS)) {
      current_conditions = false;
    }
  }
}
```

The code in Listing 3-9 has more to do with XML than with Android, so I don't go into detail about the code in Listing 3-9. Briefly, XML parsers come in two popular flavors: SAX parsers and DOM parsers. The acronym *SAX* stands for *S*imple *A*PI for *X*ML, and the acronym *DOM* stands for *D*ocument *O*bject *M*odel. Listing 3-9 uses SAX because SAX parsers have a smaller memory footprint than DOM parsers.

A DOM parser picks apart an entire XML document, loads all this information into memory, and then lets you query the parser for values anywhere in the document. "What's the value of the data attribute inside the `<temp_f>` element in the `<current_conditions>` element?", you ask. The DOM parser answers, but only after analyzing the entire document.

A SAX parser scans an XML document one piece at a time, keeping only the current piece in memory. At every step, the parser offers to report its findings. "I found a start tag" or "I found an attribute," says the parser. The code in Listing 3-9 monitors parser findings for relevant data and adds any useful data to an instance of the `Weather` class.

For some tips on deciphering the contents of XML documents, see Book II, Chapter 5.

Getting info from an online server

Listing 3-10 contains the code to submit a location to Google's weather API, to call an XML parser, and to turn the parser's result into a usable string. Simply add Listing 3-10's code to the code in Listing 3-6.

**Book III
Chapter 3**

Services

Listing 3-10: Getting Weather Information from Google

```
String getWeatherString(Message message) {
  Bundle query = message.getData();
  String location = query.getString("location");
  String weatherString;
  if (location != null && !location.equals("")) {
    Weather weather = getWeather(location);
    weatherString =
        Integer.toString(weather.getTemperature())
            + (char) 0x00B0 + "F "
            + weather.getCondition();
  } else {
    weatherString = "It's dark at night.";
  }
  return weatherString;
}

private static final String GOOGLE_WEATHER_URL =
    "http://www.google.com/ig/api?weather=";
```

(continued)

Listing 3-10 *(continued)*

```
public Weather getWeather(String location) {
  URL url;
  Weather weather = null;
  try {
    url =
        new URL(GOOGLE_WEATHER_URL
            + location.replace(" ", "%20"));
    SAXParser parser =
        SAXParserFactory.newInstance().newSAXParser();
    XMLReader reader = parser.getXMLReader();
    MySaxHandler saxHandler = new MySaxHandler();
    reader.setContentHandler(saxHandler);
    reader.parse(new InputSource(url.openStream()));

    weather = saxHandler.getWeather();

  } catch (Exception e) {
    e.printStackTrace();
  }
  return weather;
}
```

In Listing 3-10, the `getWeatherString` method extracts the user's input from the message sent to the service. The method then submits the user's input to the `getWeather` method (also in Listing 3-10). In Listing 3-10, the only other excitement comes from the `(char) 0x00B0` value. The hex value `B0` (decimal value 176) is the Unicode representation for the degree symbol. (See the text view in Figure 3-4.)

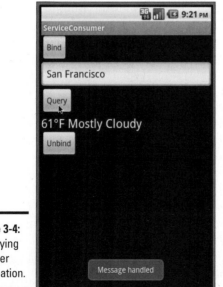

Figure 3-4:
Displaying
weather
information.

The `getWeather` method in Listing 3-10 does what Java programs do when they get a response from a web server and submit the response to a SAX parser. I review the steps briefly because the code is mostly boilerplate. You can paste it into your own app with barely any changes.

1. **Create a URL pointing to Google's weather server.**

2. **Create a `SAXParser` instance and then use the parser to get an `XMLReader` instance (whatever an `XMLReader` instance is).**

3. **Create a `MySaxHandler` instance (see Listing 3-9) and feed the `MySaxHandler` instance to the `XMLReader` instance.**

4. **Connect to Google by creating new `InputSource(url.open Stream())`.**

5. **Call the reader's `parse` method, feeding Google's response to the reader.**

6. **Get a `Weather` instance from the SAX handler.**

Whew!

Talking to a Service as if You're Right Next Door

Where I come from, you're thought to be sophisticated if you're multilingual. Do you speak a foreign language? If so, you're cool.

Learning a second language is easy. Just find something whose acronym ends with the letter *L,* and learn how to use it. In this section, you read about *AIDL* — the *Android Interface Definition Language.*

Aside from being a language, AIDL is a programming idiom. AIDL is a way of rewriting some of your Java code to make it more natural and more straightforward.

In Listings 3-6 and 3-7, a service and its client pass messages back and forth. The message-passing paradigm is nice, but wouldn't life be simpler if the client could simply call one of the service's methods? That's exactly what AIDL does for your code.

Using AIDL

Here's how AIDL works:

1. **Start with a service and a client, such as the code in Listings 3-6 and 3-7, and create an `.aidl` file.**

   The `.aidl` file describes the kind of information to be passed between the service and the client.

2. **Put copies of the `.aidl` file in both the service's and the client's projects.**

   The `.aidl` file belongs to the service's package. So to place a copy of the `.aidl` file in the client's project, you create a version of the service's package in the client project. See Figure 3-5, in which, with the help of some fancy photo-editing software, the source folders for both projects are visible.

   When you add `.aidl` files to the two projects, Eclipse automatically generates new Java code. You see evidence of this in Figure 3-5 in the projects' `gen` folders.

3. **In the client, remove the message-sending code and add code that (at least in appearance) calls the service's methods directly.**

4. **In the service, remove references to the `Messenger` class and the incoming handler class.**

   With AIDL, neither the client nor the service needs an explicit messenger. In addition, a method inside the service is being called directly (at least in appearance), so the service no longer needs an incoming handler class. (Well, that's almost true.)

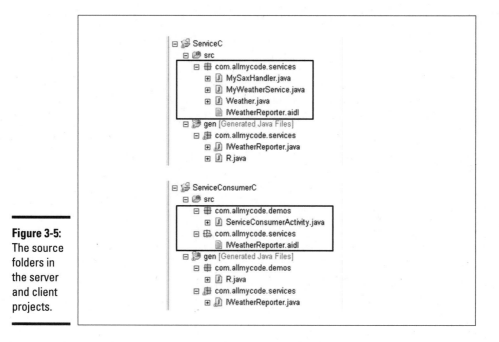

Figure 3-5:
The source folders in the server and client projects.

AIDL and Java code

Listing 3-11 shows my `WeatherInterface.aidl` file. The file is almost a plain old Java source file. The big difference is the use of the non-Java keyword `in`. This `in` keyword tells the world that the service's code *receives* a `String` value (rather than sends a `String` value).

Listing 3-11:   The WeatherInterface.aidl File

```
package com.allmycode.services;

interface WeatherInterface
{
    String fetchWeather(in String location);
}
```

Eclipse automatically generates a `WeatherInterface.java` file based on the information you supply in the `WeatherInterface.aidl` file. The `WeatherInterface.java` code defines a Java interface that extends Android's own `android.os.IInterface`. (You see? You don't write `WeatherInterface.java` because `WeatherInterface.java` belongs to one of Android's packages — not to your package.) You can peek at the `gen` folder's `WeatherInterface.java file`, but you'll be just as happy if you don't.

Listing 3-12 contains the AIDL version of the service in Listing 3-6. For your reading pleasure, I've set the AIDL-specific code in bold.

Listing 3-12:   A Service That Uses AIDL

```
package com.allmycode.services;

import java.net.URL;

import javax.xml.parsers.SAXParser;
import javax.xml.parsers.SAXParserFactory;

import org.xml.sax.InputSource;
import org.xml.sax.XMLReader;

import android.app.Service;
import android.content.Intent;
import android.os.Bundle;
import android.os.IBinder;
import android.os.Message;
import android.widget.Toast;
```

(continued)

Listing 3-12 *(continued)*

```java
public class MyWeatherService extends Service {

  @Override
  public IBinder onBind(Intent intent) {
    doToast(R.string.service_bound);
    return new WeatherFetcher();
  }

  class WeatherFetcher extends WeatherInterface.Stub {
    public String fetchWeather(String city) {
      String weatherString = null;
      if (city != null) {
        Weather weather = getWeather(city);
        weatherString =
            Integer.toString(weather.getTemperature())
                + (char) 0x00B0 + "F "
                + weather.getCondition();
      }
      return weatherString;
    }
  }

  String getWeatherString(Message message) {
    Bundle query = message.getData();
    String location = query.getString("location");
    String weatherString;
    if (location != null && !location.equals("")) {
      Weather weather = getWeather(location);
      weatherString =
          Integer.toString(weather.getTemperature())
              + (char) 0x00B0 + "F "
              + weather.getCondition();
    } else {
      weatherString = "It's dark at night.";
    }
    return weatherString;
  }

  private static final String GOOGLE_WEATHER_URL =
      "http://www.google.com/ig/api?weather=";

  public Weather getWeather(String location) {
    URL url;
    Weather weather = null;
    try {
      url =
          new URL(GOOGLE_WEATHER_URL
              + location.replace(" ", "%20"));
      SAXParser parser =
          SAXParserFactory.newInstance().newSAXParser();
```

```
    XMLReader reader = parser.getXMLReader();
    MySaxHandler saxHandler = new MySaxHandler();
    reader.setContentHandler(saxHandler);
    reader.parse(new InputSource(url.openStream()));

    weather = saxHandler.getWeather();

  } catch (Exception e) {
    e.printStackTrace();
  }
  return weather;
}

@Override
public boolean onUnbind(Intent intent) {
  doToast(R.string.service_stopped_itself);
  stopSelf();
  return false;
}

@Override
public void onDestroy() {
  doToast(R.string.service_destroyed);
}

void doToast(int resource) {
  Toast.makeText(this, resource, Toast.LENGTH_SHORT)
      .show();
}
}
```

**Book III
Chapter 3**

Services

The code in Listing 3-6 has a messenger and an incoming message handler. The message handler sends a message to be delivered to the client. In contrast, the code in Listing 3-12 has a `fetchWeather` method, which simply returns a `String` value. The class in Listing 3-12 can't shoot the messenger because the class doesn't even see the messenger.

Listing 3-13 contains the AIDL version of the stuff in Listing 3-7. Once again, I've set the AIDL-specific code in bold.

Listing 3-13:   A Client That Uses AIDL

```
package com.allmycode.demos;

import android.app.Activity;
import android.content.ComponentName;
import android.content.Context;
import android.content.Intent;
import android.content.ServiceConnection;
import android.content.SharedPreferences;
```

(continued)

Listing 13-13 *(continued)*

```java
import android.os.Bundle;
import android.os.IBinder;
import android.os.RemoteException;
import android.view.View;
import android.view.View.OnClickListener;
import android.widget.Button;
import android.widget.EditText;
import android.widget.TextView;
import android.widget.Toast;

import com.allmycode.services.WeatherInterface;

public class ServiceConsumerActivity extends Activity
    implements OnClickListener {

  WeatherInterface reporter;

  ServiceConnection connection =
      new MyServiceConnection();
  SharedPreferences prefs;
  boolean isBound = false;

  void bind() {
    Intent intent = new Intent();
    intent.setAction("com.allmycode.WEATHER");
    isBound =
        bindService(intent, connection,
            Context.BIND_AUTO_CREATE);
  }

  public void queryService() {
    if (isBound) {
      try {
        String report =
            reporter.fetchWeather(locationText.getText()
                .toString());
        textView1.setText(report);
      } catch (RemoteException e) {
        e.printStackTrace();
      }
    } else {
      textView1.setText(R.string.service_not_bound);
    }
  }

  void unbind() {
    if (isBound) {
      unbindService(connection);
      isBound = false;
    }
  }
```

```
class MyServiceConnection implements ServiceConnection {
   public void onServiceConnected(
      ComponentName className, IBinder binder) {

      reporter =
         WeatherInterface.Stub.asInterface(binder);

      doToast(R.string.service_connected);
   }

   public void onServiceDisconnected(ComponentName n) {
      doToast(R.string.service_crashed);
   }
}

void doToast(int resource) {
   Toast.makeText(this, resource, Toast.LENGTH_SHORT)
      .show();
}

@Override
public void onDestroy() {
   super.onDestroy();
   prefs = getSharedPreferences("PREFS", MODE_PRIVATE);
   SharedPreferences.Editor editor = prefs.edit();
   editor.putBoolean("isBound", isBound);
   editor.putString("report", textView1.getText()
      .toString());
   editor.commit();
   unbind();
}

@Override
public void onCreate(Bundle savedInstanceState) {
   super.onCreate(savedInstanceState);
   setContentView(R.layout.main);
   prefs = getSharedPreferences("PREFS", MODE_PRIVATE);
   if (prefs != null) {
      textView1 = (TextView) findViewById(R.id.textView1);

      textView1.setText(prefs.getString("report",
         getString(R.string.report_appears_here)));
      if (prefs.getBoolean("isBound", false)) {
         bind();
      }
   }

   // The rest of the code is boilerplate stuff
   // such as onCreate.
}
```

Upon connecting to the service, the client in Listing 3-13 creates an instance of the AIDL-generated code. The client does this by executing `reporter = WeatherInterface.Stub.asInterface(binder)`. Then, with this new `reporter` object, the client makes what appears to be an ordinary call to the `reporter` object's `fetchWeather` method.

In Listings 3-12 and 3-13, the developer is free of the messy messaging business when one process communicates with another. So the developer — that's you! — can concentrate instead on the underlying application logic. Nice stuff!

Chapter 4: Broadcast Receivers

In This Chapter

✔ **Creating broadcast receivers**

✔ **Organizing data from broadcast receivers**

✔ **Restricting a receiver's access**

Chapter 3 of this minibook introduces a broadcast receiver for the purpose of running code at boot time. Here's a summary of that chapter's broadcast receiver news:

✦ When you send a broadcast, Android fires up all the receivers whose filters satisfy the intent.

✦ A broadcast receiver runs long enough to execute the code in the receiver's onReceive method. A receiver has no onCreate, on Destroy, or on*AnythingElse* methods — only onReceive. After Android finishes executing the onReceive method's code, the broadcast receiver becomes dormant, doing nothing until an app sends another matching broadcast.

This chapter describes broadcast receivers in more detail.

Receivers 101

This chapter's first example contains the world's simplest broadcast receiver. To be precise, Listing 4-1 contains the receiver class (MyReceiver, which extends BroadcastReceiver), Listing 4-2 contains code to broadcast to the receiver, and Listing 4-3 contains the example's AndroidManifest.xml file.

Listing 4-1: A Simple Broadcast Receiver

```
package com.allmycode.rec1;

import android.content.BroadcastReceiver;
import android.content.Context;
import android.content.Intent;
import android.util.Log;

public class MyReceiver extends BroadcastReceiver {

  @Override
  public void onReceive(Context arg0, Intent arg1) {
    Log.i("MyReceiver", "Received a broadcast");
  }
}
```

A class that extends `android.content.BroadcastReceiver` must implement the `onReceive` method. The class in Listing 4-1 says, "When I receive a broadcast, I'll write an entry in Android's log file."

Listing 4-2: A Simple Broadcaster

```
package com.allmycode.rec1;

import android.app.Activity;
import android.content.Intent;
import android.os.Bundle;
import android.view.View;

public class MyActivity extends Activity {
  @Override
  public void onCreate(Bundle savedInstanceState) {
    super.onCreate(savedInstanceState);
    setContentView(R.layout.main);
  }

  public void onButtonClick(View view) {
    Intent intent = new Intent();
    intent.setAction("com.allmycode.ACTION");
    sendBroadcast(intent);
  }
}
```

In Listing 4-2, the `onButtonClick` method sends a broadcast. The method creates an intent and then feeds the intent to the `sendBroadcast` broadcast method.

Listing 4-3:   Declaring a Broadcast Receiver

```
<?xml version="1.0" encoding="utf-8"?>
<manifest xmlns:android=
    "http://schemas.android.com/apk/res/android"
  package="com.allmycode.rec1"
  android:versionCode="1"
  android:versionName="1.0">
  <uses-sdk android:minSdkVersion="8" />

  <application android:icon="@drawable/icon"
               android:label="@string/app_name">

    <activity android:name=".MyActivity"
              android:label="@string/app_name">
      <intent-filter>
        <action android:name=
          „android.intent.action.MAIN" />
        <category android:name=
          „android.intent.category.LAUNCHER" />
      </intent-filter>
    </activity>

    <receiver android:name=".MyReceiver">
      <intent-filter>
        <action android:name="com.allmycode.ACTION" />
      </intent-filter>
    </receiver>

  </application>
</manifest>
```

In Listing 4-3, the receiver's action is `"com.allmycode.ACTION"`. And, sure enough, in Listing 4-2, the broadcast intent's action is also `"com.allmy-code.ACTION"`. With no other constraints in either listing, the broadcast matches the receiver. So when you run the code in Listings 4-1, 4-2, and 4-3, Android calls the receiver's `onReceive` method. The method writes an entry to Android's log file.

Creating a receiver on the fly

Of Android's four components (`Activity`, `Service`, `BroadcastReceiver`, and `ContentProvider`), the `BroadcastReceiver` is the only component that doesn't require its own `AndroidManifest.xml` element. Instead of creating a `<receiver>` element the way I do in Listing 4-3, you can register a broadcast receiver on the fly in your code. Listing 4-4 shows you how.

Book III
Chapter 4

Broadcast
Receivers

Listing 4-4:   Registering a New Broadcast Receiver

```
public void onButtonClick(View view) {
    IntentFilter filter = new IntentFilter();
    filter.addAction("com.allmycode.ACTION");
    registerReceiver(new MyReceiver(), filter);

    Intent intent = new Intent();
    intent.setAction("com.allmycode.ACTION");
    sendBroadcast(intent);
}
```

With the bold code in Listing 4-4, you eliminate the need for the
<receiver> element in Listing 4-3.

Juggling receivers and broadcasts

You can create several instances of a broadcast receiver and send several
broadcasts. Listings 4-5 and 4-6 illustrate the situation.

Listing 4-5:   Registering Several Receivers

```
public void onButtonClick(View view) {
    IntentFilter filter = new IntentFilter();
    filter.addAction("com.allmycode.ACTION");
    MyReceiver receiver = new MyReceiver();

    registerReceiver(receiver, filter);
    registerReceiver(receiver, filter);
    registerReceiver(new MyReceiver(), filter);

    Intent intent = new Intent();
    intent.setAction("com.allmycode.ACTION");
    sendBroadcast(intent);

    Log.i("MyActivity",
        "Sent a broadcast; about to send another...");

    sendBroadcast(intent);
}
```

Listing 4-6:   Entries in the Log

```
MyActivity(280): Sent a broadcast; about to send another...
MyRecevier(280): Received a broadcast
MyRecevier(280): Received a broadcast
MyRecevier(280): Received a broadcast
MyRecevier(280): Received a broadcast
```

Listing 4-5 contains an alternative to the `onButtonClick` method in Listing 4-2, and Listing 4-6 shows the output (using the `MyReceiver` class from Listing 4-1). Here's how it all works:

✦ **Listing 4-5 registers two instances of `MyReceiver`.**

Sure, the code in Listing 4-5 calls `registerReceiver` three times. But the second call is redundant because it contains the same `MyReceiver` instance as the first `registerReceiver` call.

✦ **Listing 4-5 sends two broadcasts.**

No argument about that.

✦ **After sending the first of the two broadcasts, the activity logs the words `Sent a broadcast; about to send another....`**

But in Listing 4-6, you see log entries in a different order. In Listing 4-6, you see the activity bragging about having sent one broadcast. Then you see two broadcasts landing on two receivers (for a total of four log entries).

Remember that a broadcast isn't a method call. *Sending a broadcast* means flinging a message to the Android operating system. The system then calls `onReceive` methods in its own good time. So calls to `on Receive` (and their corresponding log entries) arrive out of sync with the sender's code. That asynchronous affect happens even if the sender and receiver classes belong to the same app.

How to unregister a receiver

You can unregister, reregister, and re-unregister broadcast receivers. You can even un-re-un-re-unregister broadcast receivers. Listings 4-7 and 4-8 illustrate all this with some code.

Listing 4-7: Registering and Unregistering

```
public void onButtonClick(View view) {
  IntentFilter filter = new IntentFilter();
  filter.addAction("com.allmycode.ACTION");
  filter.addDataScheme("letter");
  MyReceiver receiver1 = new MyReceiver(1);
  MyReceiver receiver2 = new MyReceiver(2);

  registerReceiver(receiver1, filter);
  registerReceiver(receiver2, filter);

  Intent intent = new Intent();
  intent.setAction("com.allmycode.ACTION");
  intent.setData(Uri.parse("letter:A"));
  sendBroadcast(intent);
```

(continued)

Listing 4-7 *(continued)*

```
    unregisterReceiver(receiver1);

    sendBroadcast(intent);

    intent.setData(Uri.parse("letter:B"));
    sendBroadcast(intent);

    registerReceiver(receiver1, filter);
}
```

In Listing 4-7, I give each receiver its own `int` value in the receiver's constructor call. This helps the receiver identify itself in a log entry. I also add identifying letters to the code's intents. But I break my bad habit of pasting extras onto intents. Instead, I create my own URI scheme (the Letter scheme) and send an opaque URI along with each intent.

An *opaque URI* is a URI that has no particular structure to the right of the first colon. I describe opaque URIs in Chapter 2 of this minibook.

Listing 4-8 contains the receiver's code. The receiver writes its number and the broadcast's letter to each log entry.

Listing 4-8: A More Verbose Broadcast Receiver

```
package com.allmycode.rec1;

import android.content.BroadcastReceiver;
import android.content.Context;
import android.content.Intent;
import android.util.Log;

public class MyReceiver extends BroadcastReceiver {
  private int number;

  public MyReceiver(int number) {
    this.number = number;
  }

  @Override
  public void onReceive(Context context, Intent intent) {
    String letter =
        intent.getData().getSchemeSpecificPart();
    Log.i("MyRecevier", number + " Received a broadcast "
        + letter);
  }
}
```

What's the log output of the code in Listings 4-7 and 4-8? Listing 4-9 has the answer.

Listing 4-9: Entries in the Log

```
MyRecevier(278): 1 Received a broadcast A
MyRecevier(278): 2 Received a broadcast A
MyRecevier(278): 2 Received a broadcast A
MyRecevier(278): 2 Received a broadcast B
```

Here's what happens when you run the code in Listing 4-7:

✦ **The code registers two instances of `MyReceiver`, numbered 1 and 2.**

✦ **The code sends a broadcast with letter `A`.**

Both receivers get the broadcast. (See the first two lines in Listing 4-9.)

✦ **The code unregisters `receiver1`.**

At this point, only `receiver2` is registered.

✦ **The code sends another broadcast with letter `A`.**

Only `receiver2` gets the broadcast. (See the third line in Listing 4-9.)

✦ **The code sends another broadcast with letter `B`.**

Again, `receiver2` gets the broadcast. (See the last line in Listing 4-9.)

✦ **The code re-registers `receiver1`.**

Too late. All the broadcasts have propagated through the system, and each broadcast has died its own quiet death. So `receiver1` doesn't get a broadcast, and nothing new appears in Listing 4-9.

A receiver can continue to receive until you unregister the receiver. (Notice how `receiver2` gets all three broadcasts in this section's example.)

In contrast, Android wipes away a broadcast after the broadcast reaches all currently registered receivers. (At the end of this section's example, re-registering `receiver1` has no visible affect because all the code's broadcasts have run their course.)

The preceding paragraph says, "Android wipes away a broadcast after the broadcast reaches all currently registered receivers." That's a half-truth. You can send a broadcast that sticks around on the system long after the broadcast has finished reaching all currently registered receivers. In other words, you can create a *sticky* broadcast. To find out more about it, skip ahead to the "How to be a stickler" section.

When I write "registered receivers," I include any receivers declared in the `AndroidManifest.xml` file. You don't call `registerReceiver` to start these manifest file broadcast receivers. Android registers an instance of each manifest file receiver when you install the file's app. If you happen to call `registerReceiver` for a receiver that you've declared in the `AndroidManifest.xml` file, Android responds by registering an additional instance of your broadcast receiver class.

Broadcast receivers and contexts

Like the `startActivity` and `start Service` methods, the `sendBroadcast` method belongs to the class `android. content.Context`. The familiar `Activity` class is a subclass of the `Context` class, so an activity's code can call `start Activity`, `startService`, and `send Broadcast`. Android's `Service` class is also a subclass of the `Context` class. But the `BroadcastReceiver` class isn't a subclass of the `Context` class. So a broadcast receiver's code can't directly call `start Activity` or any of the other methods that require a context. For a workaround, have the broadcast receiver use the `context` parameter in its `onReceive` method:

```
@Override
public void onReceive(Context
    context, Intent intent) {
  Intent newIntent = new
  Intent();
  newIntent.setClassName("com.
  allmycode.rec3",
      "com.allmycode.rec3.
  OtherActivity");
  newIntent.addFlags(Intent.
  FLAG_ACTIVITY_NEW_TASK);
  context.
  startActivity(newIntent);
}
```

Another way to hack the code is to code the receiver as an inner class of a component with a context:

```
package com.allmycode.rec3;

import android.app.Activity;
import android.content.
  BroadcastReceiver;
import android.content.
  Context;
import android.content.Intent;
import android.content.
  IntentFilter;
import android.os.Bundle;
```

```
public class
  ReceiverContextActivity
  extends Activity {

@Override
public void onCreate(Bundle
  savedInstanceState) {
  super.onCreate(saved
  InstanceState);
  setContentView(R.layout.
main);

  IntentFilter filter = new
  IntentFilter();
  filter.addAction("MY_
ACTION");
  registerReceiver(new
MyReceiver(), filter);

  Intent intent = new
  Intent();
  intent.setAction("MY_
ACTION");
  sendBroadcast(intent);
}

class MyReceiver extends
  BroadcastReceiver {

  @Override
  public void
onReceive(Context context,
Intent intent) {
    Intent newIntent = new
Intent();
    newIntent.
setClassName("com.
allmycode.rec3",
        "com.allmycode.rec3.
OtherActivity");
    ReceiverContextActivity.
this
        .startActivity
(newIntent);
  }
}
}
```

Beyond the Fundamentals

The earlier section deals with some minimalist, no-nonsense broadcast receiver examples. This section covers some additional broadcast receiver features.

Managing receivers

The previous section's code is nice and simple. At least I think it's nice because I'm a teacher, both by profession and in spirit. I like the little examples, even if they're not sturdy enough to survive real-world use.

But some hard-core developers don't agree with me. They'd call Listings 4-4, 4-5, and 4-7 "bad and simple" because (and I'm being painfully honest) the code in these listings can't take a beating in the real world. In fact, the code in these listings probably wouldn't survive gentle petting. To find out why, try this experiment:

1. **Create a brand-new Android project with target API 8 or greater.**

   Actually, APIs earlier than API 8 are okay. But with earlier APIs, views don't have the nice `android:onClick` attribute. So with an earlier API you extend `OnClickListener` and do some other boring stuff.

2. **Start with the activity code in Listing 4-2.**

3. **Change the activity's `onButtonClick` method to match the code in Listing 4-4.**

4. **In the `main.xml` layout, add a button whose click-handler is the activity's `onButtonClick` method.**

5. **Use the `AndroidManifest.xml` document in Listing 4-3.**

6. **Run the app.**

7. **While you wait for the app to load, switch to Eclipse's DDMS perspective.**

   For details on switching between Eclipse perspectives, see Book II, Chapter 1.

   When the app finishes loading, you see a button on the emulator's screen. It's the button that you created in Step 4.

8. **Click the button, and look at the resulting entries in Eclipse's LogCat view.**

   You see two `MyReceiver Received a broadcast` entries because Android is running two `MyReceiver` instances. One instance comes from the `<receiver>` element in the `AndroidManifest.xml` document. The other receiver comes from the `registerReceiver` method call in Listing 4-4.

   Having two `MyReceiver` instances isn't bad. But in most cases, it's probably not what you want. Observing these two instances is a side benefit that comes from performing this experiment.

9. While the app is still running, press the emulator's Back button, and look again at Eclipse's LogCat view.

In Eclipse's LogCat view, you see a big, ugly `activity has leaked IntentReceiver` error message. The message tells you that Android has destroyed your activity and (because you forgot to do it . . .) Android has also unregistered one of your `MyReceiver` instances.

If you call `registerReceiver`, Android wants you to unregister the receiver before terminating your activity. When you press the Back button, Android calls your activity's `onPause`, `onStop`, and `onDestroy` methods. In this experiment's code, you don't override the inherited `onPause`, `onStop`, and `onDestroy` methods, so Android calls these inherited methods.

In this experiment, Android finds the inherited `onDestroy` method particularly painful. You're getting rid of your activity and leaving your registered receiver in limbo. If lots of developers do the same thing, the user's Android device experiences the *Night of the Living Broadcast Receivers.*

So Android says, "If you refuse to clean up after yourself, I'll clean up for you. I'll terminate your broadcast receiver. And just like your mother, I'll show my disapproval by writing an entry to the log file." (If only Mom had been so even-tempered!)

Android doesn't like the `MyReceiver` instance that I register and don't unregister in Listing 4-4. But Android isn't upset about the `MyReceiver` instance from the `AndroidManifest.xml` file (see Listing 4-3). Android expects receivers declared this way to have a life of their own, surviving past the lifetime of any activities in the application.

The error message `activity has leaked IntentReceiver` hints that the SDK has an `IntentReceiver` class. But that's misleading. The name `IntentReceiver` is an artifact from Android's early history. What used to be called an `IntentReceiver` is now a `BroadcastReceiver`.

You might not be impressed by Step 9's `activity has leaked IntentReceiver` message. After all, Android doesn't alert the user, so your app doesn't look bad. And when the user clicks the Back button, you probably don't mind that Android terminates your broadcast receiver. So what's the big deal? Well, try the next few steps . . .

10. Restart this section's app.

11. Again, press the button on the activity's screen to invoke the code in Listing 4-4.

12. While the app is still running, turn the emulator sideways by pressing Ctrl+F11.

Of course, if you're testing on a real device, simply turn the device sideways.

In Eclipse's LogCat view, look again for the insulting `activity has leaked IntentReceiver` error message. Unless you override the default behavior, Android destroys and re-creates your activity when the device's orientation changes. As far as the user is concerned, the activity is still alive and well. But unbeknownst to the user, Android killed the broadcast receiver and hasn't revived it.

This anomaly makes little difference in Listing 4-4, where you register the receiver and send a broadcast using the same button. But the state of your process has changed considerably. In a real-life app, you've lost a broadcast receiver just by tilting the device. It's difficult to imagine a scenario in which you want that to happen.

In most of this chapter's simple examples, I register and unregister receivers in an `onButtonClick` method. That's okay if I include logic to deal with the nastiness in this section's example. Of course, the logic can become complicated, and it's easy to make mistakes.

In general, the easiest way to deal with runtime receiver registrations is to register and unregister in the activity's complementary lifecycle methods. Listing 4-10 shows you what to do.

Listing 4-10: Dealing with the Component Lifecycle

```
package com.allmycode.rec1;

import android.app.Activity;
import android.content.Intent;
import android.content.IntentFilter;
import android.os.Bundle;
import android.view.View;

public class MyActivity extends Activity {
  MyReceiver receiver = new MyReceiver();

  @Override
  public void onCreate(Bundle savedInstanceState) {
    super.onCreate(savedInstanceState);
    setContentView(R.layout.main);
  }

  @Override
  public void onResume() {
    super.onResume();
    IntentFilter filter = new IntentFilter();
    filter.addAction("com.allmycode.ACTION");
    registerReceiver(receiver, filter);
  }

  @Override
```

(continued)

Listing 4-10: *(continued)*

```
public void onPause() {
  super.onPause();
  unregisterReceiver(receiver);
}

public void onButtonClick(View view) {
  Intent intent = new Intent();
  intent.setAction("com.allmycode.ACTION");
  sendBroadcast(intent);
  }
}
```

I can state the big message in Listing 4-10 very simply: Make things in an activity's onResume method and then get rid of these things in the activity's onPause method. If you want things to live longer, make things in the activity's onCreate method and get rid of these things in the activity's on Destroy method. That's it. (And yes, I'm aware that I wrote this three-page section to pontificate about something that I can summarize at the end in only two sentences. Thanks for noticing!)

How to be a stickler

An ordinary broadcast disintegrates after it's sent to all the matching, currently running receivers. But another kind of broadcast — a *sticky* broadcast — hangs on until someone or something explicitly removes the broadcast. To remove a sticky broadcast, you can call removeStickyBroadcast. Alternatively, you can turn off your device, hit your device with a hammer, or do other unpleasant things. Listing 4-11 contains some informative code.

Listing 4-11:   Sending a Sticky Broadcast

```
public void onButtonClick(View view) {
  IntentFilter filter = new IntentFilter();
  filter.addAction("com.allmycode.ACTION");
  filter.addDataScheme("letter");
  MyReceiver receiver1 = new MyReceiver(1);
  MyReceiver receiver2 = new MyReceiver(2);
  MyReceiver receiver3 = new MyReceiver(3);

  Intent intent = new Intent();
  intent.setAction("com.allmycode.ACTION");
  intent.setData(Uri.parse("letter:A"));

  registerReceiver(receiver1, filter);

  sendStickyBroadcast(intent);

  registerReceiver(receiver2, filter);
```

```
removeStickyBroadcast(intent);

registerReceiver(receiver3, filter);
}
```

With the sending and registering business in Listing 4-11 and the receiver I set up back in Listing 4-8, Android logs the entries shown in Listing 4-12.

Listing 4-12:   Log File Entries

```
MyRecevier(282): 1 Received a broadcast A
MyRecevier(282): 2 Received a broadcast A
```

In Listing 4-11, I register `receiver1` before sending the broadcast. So `receiver1` receives the broadcast. No big deal here.

At this point in the run of Listing 4-11, `receiver1` is the only currently registered receiver, and `receiver1` has received the broadcast. But the broadcast is sticky, so the broadcast lives on. On the next line of code, when I register `receiver2` in Listing 4-11, `receiver2` receives the broadcast. That's what stickiness does.

In the last two statements of Listing 4-11, I remove the sticky broadcast (with a method call, not with turpentine), and I register `receiver3`. Because I've removed the only matching broadcast, `receiver3` receives nothing.

A component that calls `sendStickyBroadcast` (or calls the closely related `sendStickyOrderedBroadcast` method) must have the `<uses-permission android:name="android.permission.BROADCAST_STICKY" />` element in its app's `AndroidManifest.xml` document. A component that calls `sendBroadcast` (or its friend, the `sendOrderedBroadcast` method) doesn't need permission to do so.

Book III
Chapter 4

**Broadcast
Receivers**

Using receiver intents

At some point, you might have several receivers and several sticky broadcasts vying for attention in a multiprocess, nondeterministic fashion. Sounds like fun, doesn't it? You may also be dealing with broadcasts from other apps and from the system itself. To help you keep track of the comings and goings, the `registerReceiver` method returns an intent. This intent comes from one of the (possibly many) broadcasts that the newly registered receiver catches.

In Listing 4-13, I register two receivers and fling two sticky broadcasts (`"letter:A"` and `"letter:O"`) into the air. For each receiver registration, Listing 4-13 logs an intent caught by the receiver.

Listing 4-13: Getting an Intent from a Receiver's Registration

```
MyReceiver receiver1 = new MyReceiver(1);
MyReceiver receiver2 = new MyReceiver(2);
Intent intentAct = new Intent();
Intent intentOth = new Intent();

public void onButtonClick(View view) {
  IntentFilter filter = new IntentFilter();
  filter.addAction("com.allmycode.ACTION");
  filter.addAction("com.allmycode.OTHER_ACTION");
  filter.addDataScheme("letter");

  Intent returnedIntent =
    registerReceiver(receiver1, filter);
  Log.i("MyActivity", getStatus(returnedIntent));

  intentAct.setAction("com.allmycode.ACTION");
  intentAct.setData(Uri.parse("letter:A"));
  sendStickyBroadcast(intentAct);

  intentOth.setAction("com.allmycode.OTHER_ACTION");
  intentOth.setData(Uri.parse("letter:O"));
  sendStickyBroadcast(intentOth);

  returnedIntent = registerReceiver(receiver2, filter);
  Log.i("MyActivity", getStatus(returnedIntent));
}

private String getStatus(Intent returnedIntent) {
  if (returnedIntent == null) {
    return "null";
  } else {
    return returnedIntent.toString();
  }
}
```

Listing 4-14 shows the results of a run of Listing 4-13's code (using the receiver in Listing 4-8). The first registration returns `null` rather than an actual intent. This happens because no broadcast is alive when the code executes this first registration.

Listing 4-14: Log This!

```
MyActivity(313): null
MyActivity(313):
  Intent { act=com.allmycode.ACTION dat=letter:A }
MyRecevier(313): 1 Received a broadcast A
MyRecevier(313): 1 Received a broadcast O
MyRecevier(313): 2 Received a broadcast A
MyRecevier(313): 2 Received a broadcast O
```

The second receiver registration returns the `"com.allmycode.ACTION"` intent. The receiver's filter has both `"com.allmycode.ACTION"` and `"com.allmycode.OTHER_ACTION"`, and both of these actions belong to active sticky broadcasts. But the call to `registerReceiver` returns only one of the broadcasts' intents.

One way or another, two receivers catch two broadcasts. The final four entries in Listing 4-14 contain reports from the receivers themselves. Notice how, in its typical asynchronous flurry, Android logs all the receivers' steps after returning from the second `registerReceiver` call. Without concurrent processing, Android would complete a receiver's `onReceive` method before returning from the second `registerReceiver` call. You'd see lines in Listing 4-14 in a different order.

Ordered broadcasts

Android takes a regular broadcast and throws it into the air. Then the receivers with matching filters jump like basketball players, catching the broadcast in no particular order. This "no particular order" behavior can be nice because it frees up the system to make the most of any available processing time.

But occasionally you want a predictable sequence of `onReceive` calls. To achieve such behavior, you assign priorities to the receivers' intent filters and then send an ordered broadcast.

In this chapter's log listings, receivers seem to form a first-come/first-served waiting line to catch broadcasts. That's fine. But in general, Android makes no promises about this polite behavior. In fact, Android might run two receivers at once. You never know.

Listing 4-15 prioritizes receivers and sends an ordered broadcast.

Listing 4-15: Set Your Priorities

```
public void onButtonClick(View view) {
  IntentFilter filter = new IntentFilter();
  filter.addAction("com.allmycode.ACTION");
  filter.addDataScheme("letter");

  IntentFilter filter1 = new IntentFilter(filter);
  IntentFilter filter2 = new IntentFilter(filter);
  IntentFilter filter3 = new IntentFilter(filter);

  filter1.setPriority(17);
  filter2
      .setPriority(IntentFilter.SYSTEM_HIGH_PRIORITY - 1);
  filter3.setPriority(-853);
```

(continued)

Listing 4-15 *(continued)*

```
MyReceiver receiver1 = new MyReceiver(1);
MyReceiver receiver2 = new MyReceiver(2);
MyReceiver receiver3 = new MyReceiver(3);

registerReceiver(receiver1, filter1);
registerReceiver(receiver2, filter2);
registerReceiver(receiver3, filter3);

Intent intent = new Intent();
intent.setAction("com.allmycode.ACTION");
intent.setData(Uri.parse("letter:A"));

sendOrderedBroadcast(intent, null);
Log.i("MyActivity",
    "Now watch the log entries pour in...");
}
```

From a single intent filter, Listing 4-15 stamps out three copies. Then the code assigns a priority to each copy. Priorities are `int` values, ranging from @nd999 to 999. Android reserves the values –1000 (`IntentFilter.SYSTEM_LOW_PRIORITY`) and 1000 (`IntentFilter.SYSTEM_HIGH_PRIORITY`) for its own private use.

You can set an intent filter's priority in an app's `AndroidManifest.xml` document. Do so with an attribute, such as `android:priority="17"`.

After registering three receivers (one for each of the three filters), Listing 4-15 sends an ordered broadcast and lets the chips fall where they may. The chips fall in Listing 4-16.

Listing 4-16:   Yet Another Log

```
MyActivity(284): Now watch the log entries pour in...
MyRecevier(284): 2 Received a broadcast A
MyRecevier(284): 1 Received a broadcast A
MyRecevier(284): 3 Received a broadcast A
```

Listing 4-16 confirms that `receiver2` — the receiver with highest priority — receives the broadcast first. Poor `receiver3` — the receiver with the lowest priority — receives the broadcast last.

Stopping a broadcast in its tracks

In the preceding section, an ordered broadcast travels from one receiver to another. The sequence of receivers depends on their relative priorities.

In this section, you play a nasty trick on all but one of the receiver instances. Change the `MyReceiver` class's code, as in Listing 4-17.

Listing 4-17:   Aborting a Broadcast

```
package com.allmycode.rec1;

import android.content.BroadcastReceiver;
import android.content.Context;
import android.content.Intent;
import android.util.Log;

public class MyReceiver extends BroadcastReceiver {
  private int number;

  public MyReceiver(int number) {
    this.number = number;
  }

  @Override
  public void onReceive(Context context, Intent intent) {
    String letter =
        intent.getData().getSchemeSpecificPart();
    Log.i("MyRecevier", number + " Received a broadcast "
        + letter);
    abortBroadcast();
  }
}
```

With the call to `abortBroadcast` in Listing 4-17, a run of the code in Listing 4-15 creates only two log entries:

```
MyActivity(281): Now watch the log entries pour in...
MyRecevier(281): 2 Received a broadcast A
```

The second log entry comes from an instance of the receiver in Listing 4-17. The listing's call to `abortBroadcast` stops the ordered broadcast in its tracks. Other instances of `MyReceiver` never see the broadcast.

The `abortBroadcast` method works only with ordered broadcasts. Normally, you have a `MyReceiver` instance abort a broadcast so that some other receiver (maybe a `YourReceiver` instance) doesn't get the broadcast. But in this chapter's examples, I keep things simple by creating only one `MyReceiver` class and several instances of the class.

Getting results from receivers

What will they think of next? You have sticky broadcasts and ordered broadcasts. Why not have a broadcast that's both sticky and ordered? Developers typically use sticky, ordered broadcasts to collect results from several broadcast receivers.

Listing 4-18 contains a receiver on steroids.

Listing 4-18:   A Receiver Manages Data

```java
package com.allmycode.rec1;

import java.util.ArrayList;

import android.app.Activity;
import android.content.BroadcastReceiver;
import android.content.Context;
import android.content.Intent;
import android.os.Bundle;
import android.util.Log;

public class MyReceiver extends BroadcastReceiver {
  private int number;
  private boolean INTENTIONALLY_FAIL = false;

  public MyReceiver(int number) {
    this.number = number;
  }

  @Override
  public void onReceive(Context context, Intent intent) {
    String letter =
        intent.getData().getSchemeSpecificPart();
    Log.i("MyRecevier", number + " Received a broadcast "
        + letter);

    if (INTENTIONALLY_FAIL) {
      setResultCode(Activity.RESULT_CANCELED);
      return;
    }

    if (getResultCode() == Activity.RESULT_OK) {
      Bundle bundle = getResultExtras(true);
      ArrayList<Integer> receiverNums =
          bundle.getIntegerArrayList("receiverNums");
      if (receiverNums != null) {
        receiverNums.add(new Integer(number));
      }
      setResultExtras(bundle);
    }
  }
}
```

An ordered broadcast goes to an ordered chain of receiver instances. Along with the broadcast, each receiver instance gets *result extras* from the previous receiver in the chain. These result extras take the form of a bundle.

For the lowdown on bundles, see Chapter 3 of this minibook.

An instance of the receiver in Listing 4-18 gets a bundle containing an ArrayList of integers. This ArrayList happens to contain the numbers of all the previous receiver instances in the ordered broadcast's chain. The instance in Listing 4-18 adds its own number to the ArrayList and then sets its own result to be the newly enhanced ArrayList. The next receiver instance in the chain gets this newly enhanced ArrayList.

An ordered broadcast also comes with an int valued code. In Listing 4-18, the call to getResultCode checks for the android.app.Activity. RESULT_OK code. Any receiver instance in the chain can mess up the works with a result code that's not OK.

In Listing 4-18, I add an extra INTENTIONALLY_FAIL constant to test undesirable situations. Changing the constant's value to true forces Listing 4-18 to set the result code to android.app.Activity.RESULT_CANCELED. After that, any result from the ordered broadcast can't be trusted.

Always remove testing and debugging code (such as the INTENTIONALLY_ FAIL code in Listing 4-18) before you publish your app.

Listing 4-19 puts the receiver in Listing 4-18 through its paces.

Listing 4-19: Dealing with the Result from a Chain of Receivers

```
package com.allmycode.rec1;

import java.util.ArrayList;

import android.app.Activity;
import android.content.BroadcastReceiver;
import android.content.Context;
import android.content.Intent;
import android.content.IntentFilter;
import android.net.Uri;
import android.os.Bundle;
import android.util.Log;
import android.view.View;

public class MyActivity extends Activity {

  @Override
  public void onCreate(Bundle savedInstanceState) {
    super.onCreate(savedInstanceState);
    setContentView(R.layout.main);
  }

  public void onButtonClick(View view) {
    IntentFilter filter = new IntentFilter();
    filter.addAction("com.allmycode.ACTION");
    filter.addDataScheme("letter");
```

(continued)

Listing 4-19 *(continued)*

```
IntentFilter filter1 = new IntentFilter(filter);
IntentFilter filter2 = new IntentFilter(filter);
IntentFilter filter3 = new IntentFilter(filter);

MyReceiver receiver1 = new MyReceiver(1);
MyReceiver receiver2 = new MyReceiver(2);
MyReceiver receiver3 = new MyReceiver(3);

registerReceiver(receiver1, filter1);
registerReceiver(receiver2, filter2);
registerReceiver(receiver3, filter3);

Intent intent = new Intent();
intent.setAction("com.allmycode.ACTION");
intent.setData(Uri.parse("letter:A"));

MyEndResultReceiver resultReceiver =
    new MyEndResultReceiver();
ArrayList<Integer> receiverNums =
    new ArrayList<Integer>();
Bundle bundle = new Bundle();
bundle.putIntegerArrayList("receiverNums",
    receiverNums);

sendStickyOrderedBroadcast(intent, resultReceiver,
    null, Activity.RESULT_OK, null, bundle);
  }
}

class MyEndResultReceiver extends BroadcastReceiver {

  final static String CLASSNAME = "MyEndResultReceiver";

  @Override
  public void onReceive(Context context, Intent intent) {
    if (getResultCode() == Activity.RESULT_OK) {
      Bundle bundle = getResultExtras(true);
      ArrayList<Integer> receiverNums =
          bundle.getIntegerArrayList("receiverNums");
      Log.i(CLASSNAME, receiverNums.toString());
    } else {
      Log.i(
          CLASSNAME,
          "Result code: "
              + Integer.toString(getResultCode()));
    }
  }
}
```

In Listing 4-19, the call to sendStickyOrderedBroadcast takes a boatload of parameters. The official signature of method sendStickyOrdered-Broadcast is as follows:

```
public void
sendStickyOrderedBroadcast(Intent intent,
                          BroadcastReceiver resultReceiver,
                          Handler scheduler,
                          int initialCode,
                          String initialData,
                          Bundle initialExtras)
```

✦ **The `intent` parameter plays the same role as any other broadcast's intent.**

The `intent` presents a list of criteria to test against receivers' filters.

✦ **The `resultReceiver` is the last instance in the ordered broadcast's calling chain.**

By specifying the result receiver, you know where to look for the accumulated results.

✦ **The `scheduler` (if it's not `null`) handles messages coming from the `resultReceiver`.**

✦ **The `initialCode` is the starting value for the sequence of result codes passed from one receiver to the next.**

In most apps, the `initialCode`'s value is `Activity.RESULT_OK`. You give the `initialCode` a different value only when you're making up your own custom result code values. When you do such a thing, you program your app to respond sensibly to each of the made-up values.

✦ **The `initialData` (if it's not `null`) is a starting value for a string that's passed from receiver to receiver in the chain.**

An ordered broadcast carries a bundle (the result extras) and a code (an `int` value, such as `Activity.RESULT_OK`). In addition, an order broadcast carries *result data* — a `String` value that can be examined and modified by each receiver instance in the chain.

✦ **The `initialExtras` is a starting value for the broadcast's bundle of extra stuff.**

In Listing 4-19, the `initialExtras` bundle is an empty `ArrayList`. Each receiver instance that gets the broadcast adds its number to this `ArrayList`.

Listing 4-20 shows the output of the code in Listings 4-18 and 4-19.

Listing 4-20:   More Log Entries

```
MyRecevier(3602): 1 Received a broadcast A
MyRecevier(3602): 2 Received a broadcast A
MyRecevier(3602): 3 Received a broadcast A
MyEndResultReceiver(3602): [1, 2, 3]
```

The broadcast ends its run at an instance of MyEndResultReceiver — the instance named *last in the chain* by the sendStickyOrderedBroadcast call in Listing 4-19. When this last receiver does it stuff, the receiver logs [1, 2, 3] — the accumulated ArrayList of receiver numbers.

Using permissions and other tricks

To send a broadcast, you toss an intent into the ether. A broadcast receiver gets the intent if the receiver's filter matches the intent. And that's the whole story. Or is it?

When you send a broadcast, you can also specify a permission. Permissions come from those <uses-permission> elements that you put in your AndroidManifest.xml document (after first forgetting to do it and getting an error message). In Listing 4-21, the sendBroadcast call's second parameter is a permission.

Listing 4-21: Requiring a Permission

```
public void onButtonClick(View view) {
  Intent intent = new Intent();
  intent.setAction("THIS_ACTION");

  sendBroadcast(intent,
      android.Manifest.permission.INTERNET);
}
```

The receiver declared in Listing 4-22 catches the broadcast in Listing 4-21.

Listing 4-22: Declaring That an App Has a Permission

```
<?xml version="1.0" encoding="utf-8"?>
<manifest xmlns:android=
    "http://schemas.android.com/apk/res/android"
        package="com.allmycode.receiver2"
        android:versionCode="1"
        android:versionName="1.0">

  <uses-sdk android:minSdkVersion="8" />

  <uses-permission
    android:name="android.permission.INTERNET" />
```

```
<application android:icon="@drawable/icon"
              android:label="@string/app_name">

  <receiver android:name=
    "com.allmycode.receiver2.MyReceiverWithPermission">

    <intent-filter>
      <action android:name="THIS_ACTION" />
    </intent-filter>
  </receiver>

</application>
</manifest>
```

Another receiver, in an app whose manifest doesn't have the <uses-permission> element, can't receive the broadcast from Listing 4-21.

Android's built-in android.Manifest.permission.INTERNET constant (used in Listing 4-21) has String value "android.permission.INTERNET". At the risk of being gauche, you can use the quoted string "android.permission.INTERNET" in the Java code of Listing 4-21. But you can't use the android.Manifest.permission.INTERNET constant in Listing 4-13 or in any other AndroidManifest.xml document.

Android has all kinds of mechanisms for shielding components from other components. For example, you can add an attribute to the <receiver> start tag in Listing 4-22:

```
<receiver android:name=
  "com.allmycode.receiver2.MyReceiverWithPermission"
  android:exported="false">
```

If you do, no component outside the receiver's app can send a broadcast to this receiver.

Standard Broadcasts

Chapter 2 of this minibook contains a list of some standard actions for starting activities. Android's SDK also contains standard actions for sending broadcasts. Table 4-1 has a list of some actions that your app can broadcast.

**Book III
Chapter 4**

**Broadcast
Receivers**

Table 4-1	Some Standard Broadcast Actions	
String Value	*Constant Name*	*A Broadcast Receiver with This Action in One of Its Filters Can . . .*
`"android.intent.action.CAMERA_BUTTON"`	`Intent.ACTION_CAMERA_BUTTON`	Respond to the user pressing the camera button.
`"android.intent.action.HEADSET_PLUG"`	`Intent.ACTION_HEADSET_PLUG`	Respond to a wired headset being plugged or unplugged.
`"android.intent.action.DATE_CHANGED"`	`Intent.ACTION_DATE_CHANGED`	Respond to the system's date being changed.
`"android.intent.action.TIME_SET"`	`Intent.ACTION_TIME_CHANGED`	Respond to the system's time being changed.

The actions in Table 4-1 are both *libre* and *gratis*. Or, to paraphrase Richard Stallman, the actions are free as in "free speech" and free as in "free beer."* Whatever metaphor you prefer, you can broadcast or receive intents with the actions in Table 4-1.

The actions in Table 4-2 resemble beer more than they resemble speech. In your app's code, a broadcast receiver's filter can include these actions. But your app can't broadcast an intent having any of these actions. Only the operating system can broadcast intents that include the actions in Table 4-2.

* *From "The Free Software Definition,"* `www.gnu.org/philosophy/free-sw.html`.

Table 4-2   **Some Standard System Broadcast Actions**

String Value	Constant Name	A Broadcast Receiver with This Action in One of Its Filters Can . . .
`"android. intent.action. SCREEN_OFF"`	`Intent.ACTION_ SCREEN_OFF`	Respond to the device's screen turning off.
`"android. intent.action. SCREEN_ON"`	`Intent.ACTION_ SCREEN_ON`	Respond to the device's screen turning on.
`"android. intent.action. BOOT_COMPLETED"`	`Intent.ACTION_ BOOT_COMPLETED`	Respond to the end of system startup.
`"android. intent.action. BATTERY_LOW"`	`Intent.ACTION_ BATTERY_LOW`	Respond to a low-battery condition.
`"android. intent.action. BATTERY_OKAY"`	`Intent.ACTION_ BATTERY_OK`	Respond to the battery's condition no longer being low.
`"android. intent.action. DEVICE_STORAGE_ LOW"`	`Intent.DEVICE_ STORAGE_LOW`	Respond to memory becoming low.
`"android. intent.action. DEVICE_STORAGE_ OK"`	`Intent.DEVICE_ STORAGE_OK`	Respond to memory no longer being low.
`"android. intent.action. ACTION_POWER_ CONNECTED"`	`Intent.ACTION_ POWER_CONNECTED`	Respond to a power cord being connected.
`"android. intent.action. ACTION_POWER_ DISCONNECTED"`	`Intent. ACTION_POWER_ DISCONNECTED`	Respond to a power cord being removed.
`"android. intent.action. LOCALE_CHANGED"`	`Intent.LOCALE_ CHANGED`	Respond to a change in locale (from the United States to the United Kingdom, for example).

(continued)

**Book III
Chapter 4**

**Broadcast
Receivers**

Table 4-2 *(continued)*

String Value	Constant Name	A Broadcast Receiver with This Action in One of Its Filters Can . . .

`"android.`
`intent.action.`
`TIMEZONE_`
`CHANGED"`
	`Intent.ACTION_`
	`TIMEZONE_`
	`CHANGED`
		Respond to the system's time zone being changed.

`"android.`
`intent.action.`
`TIME_TICK"`
	`Intent.ACTION_`
	`TIME_TICK`
		Respond when the system broadcasts this `TIME_`
		`TICK` action once each minute.

`"android.`
`intent.action.`
`NEW_OUTGOING_`
`CALL"`
	`Intent.NEW_`
	`OUTGOING_CALL`
		Respond to the start of an outgoing call.

As an Android developer, you can test the effect of broadcasting any of the actions in Table 4-2. To do so, you become superuser on the Android shell and issue an am command. (In Linux, a *superuser* has administrative privileges. A consumer becomes superuser when he or she *roots* a device.) For an example of the use of the am command, see Chapter 3 of this minibook.

For a complete list of Android's standard actions, visit `http://developer.`
`android.com/reference/android/content/Intent.html`.

Chapter 5: Content Providers

In This Chapter

 ✔ **A primer on databases**

 ✔ **Database processing in Android**

 ✔ **Sharing data using a content provider**

*I*n his introduction to *Napalm & Silly Putty* (Hyperion Books), George Carlin wrote, "For the next few hundred pages, I will be your content provider." Carlin was poking fun at business-speak phrases and other phrases that seem artificially lofty or commercially sanitized. Little did he know that a few years later, the introduction to his book would compare him to an Android SDK component.

Databases: From the Stone Age to the Present Day

A *database* is a place to store lots of data. Nobody's surprised about that. A *database management system* is a bunch of software for creating the data, finding the data, and doing other useful things with the data.

Until the mid-1970s, people didn't agree on the best structure for storing data in a database. Some argued for hierarchical structures, whereas others swore that networked structures were the only way to go. But in the 1970s, Edgar Codd (working at IBM) published papers on relational structures for storing data. Since the mid-1980s, the relational database has been the all-around favorite.

A relational database is of a bunch of *tables*. Like a table in this book, a database table has *rows* and *columns*. Each row represents an instance (a customer, an employee, an appointment, or whatever), and each column represents a property of some kind (such as the customer's name, the employee's salary, or the appointment's time). Table 5-1 is a table in this book, but it might as well be a table in a relational database.

Table 5-1		Customers	
Account Number	*Name*	*Outstanding Balance*	*Comment*
001	Boris Bleeper	25.00	Valued, long-time customer
002	Barry Burd	454.21	Deadbeat
003	Jane Q. Customer	0.00	Valued, long-time customer

A Java programmer might compare a database table to a Java class. Each instance is a row, and each public field is column. In fact, this similarity between tables and classes has been apparent to people for quite a while. Many software frameworks specialize in *object-relational mapping (ORM)*, in which the software automatically manages the correspondence between Java objects and relational database tables.

A *database management system (DBMS)* stores database data and provides access to the data for administrators and users. A *database administrator (DBA)* is a person who keeps the DBMS software running. A *user* is a person who gets information from the database and (with the right privileges) modifies values stored in the database. A user might directly or indirectly add rows to a table, but a user doesn't add columns to a table or change a table's structure in any way.

A database management system uses sophisticated data structures and algorithms to efficiently store and retrieve data. So the data in a database seldom lives in a flat file.

A *flat file* is an ordinary bunch of data on a hard drive, with no special pointers or indices to important places inside the file. Database management systems offer the option to store data in flat files, but only as a necessary evil for quick-and-dirty data storage. With database tables in a flat file, the DBMS has to chug slowly and inefficiently through the file for any data that you need.

Database management systems come from many different vendors, with many different price ranges and many different feature sets. The big commercial players are IBM (with its DB2 software), Microsoft (with its Access and SQL Server products), and Oracle (with its aptly named Oracle Database). Some popular noncommercial products include MySQL (owned by Oracle), PostgreSQL, and SQLite. Each Android device comes with SQLite software.

In general, you communicate with a database in the following way:

✦ You connect to the database (whatever that means).

✦ You query the database, asking for rows and columns matching criteria that you specify.

In response, the database management system hands you a cursor. A *cursor* is a minitable; it's a table of the rows and columns that match your query. The database management system distills the information in the database in order to deliver the cursor to you.

Like a regular database table, a cursor consists of rows and columns. At any point in time, the cursor points to one of the rows in the table (or to the never-never land after the table's last row).

✦ You step from row to row with the cursor, doing whatever you need to do with each row of data.

✦ Finally (and not unimportantly), you close the connection to the database.

Depending on your permissions, you can also create a table, modify the values in rows of the table, insert rows into the table, and do other things. The four major table operations go by the name *CRUD,* which stands for *C*reate, *R*ead, *U*pdate, and *D*elete.

The most common way of issuing commands to a DBMS is with SQL — the *S*tructured *Q*uery *L*anguage. (Depending on your mood, you can pronounce the SQL acronym *ess-kyoo-el* or *sequel.*) An SQL statement looks something like this:

```
SELECT * FROM CUSTOMER_TABLE WHERE COMMENT='Deadbeat';
```

Each database management system has its own dialect of SQL, so the only way to study SQL in detail is to work exclusively with one DBMS. With Android's SDK, you can add strings containing SQL commands to your code. But you can also call methods that compose SQL commands on your behalf.

For the rules governing SQLite's use of SQL, visit `http://sqlite.org/lang.html`.

Working with a Database

With Android's SDK, an app has two ways to access a database:

✦ An app can access its own database directly with commands to SQLite. (See Figure 5-1.)

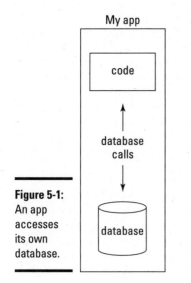

Figure 5-1:
An app
accesses
its own
database.

✦ An app can access another app's database indirectly with commands to the other app's content provider. (See Figure 5-2.)

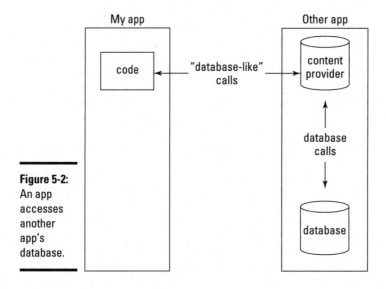

Figure 5-2:
An app
accesses
another
app's
database.

A *content provider* is one of Android's four big component types. (The four types are activities, services, broadcast receivers, and content providers.)

In the interest of full disclosure, I must write that content providers don't work exclusively with databases. A content provider is a bridge between an app's code and another app's data. The other app's data doesn't have to be part of a database. But the content provider's publicly exposed methods look like database calls. So to anyone living outside the provider's app, the provider's data looks like database data. (See Figure 5-3.) The provider creates an abstract database-like view of whatever data lives underneath it.

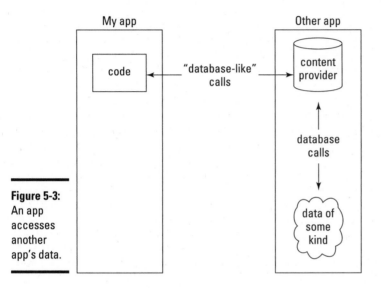

Figure 5-3:
An app accesses another app's data.

Book III
Chapter 5

Content Providers

The rest of this chapter consists of three examples. The first example demonstrates an app creating its own SQLite database and making calls directly to that database. In the second example, an app exposes data using a content provider, and another app accesses the first app's data through the provider. (The third example illustrates some newer Android API features.)

As you compare the first and second examples, you'll notice some striking similarities. The second example is very much like the first. To get the second example, I (figuratively) tear the first example in half, giving half of the first example's code to the new content provider and giving the other half of the first example's code to a brand-new app.

Coding for SQLite using Android's SDK

Listing 5-1 contains code to access an SQLite database. When the activity begins running, the code inserts data, then modifies the data, and then deletes the data. To keep things simple, I intentionally omit much of the fail-safe checking that database code normally has. I also have a dirt-simple user interface. The activity's screen has only one widget — a text view for displaying data at various stages of processing.

Headaches involving concurrency

Any computing device worth its salt runs several processes simultaneously. In other words, the processes are *concurrent*.

Concurrency is great for taking full advantage of device's resources, but if two or more processes write to a database at the same time, nasty things can happen. For example, I might discover that Table 5-1 has three rows and decide to add a fourth row. In the meantime, you might discover the same thing and issue your own command to add a fourth row. In the end, the table has only one additional row, and the row contains a mix of your data and my data. Ouch!

To combat the two-process-writing problem, database management systems have locks. A *lock* enforces read-only status for all but one process at a time. So two processes can't perform write operations at the same time. The trick for the database management system (and sometimes for the developer) is to choose options that maintain the data's integrity while locking the smallest chunk of data for the smallest amount of time. Long-lived, widely applied locks tend to slow down the system.

Another possible pitfall with database handling is the danger of incomplete write operations. Imagine that my rich uncle calls the company to pay my bill in Table 5-1. A representative keys in the new information for account number 002 — my rich uncle's name; the new 0.00 balance; and the Valued, long-time customer comment. The DBMS changes the name and the new balance, but the network connection fails before the DBMS receives the request to change the comment. Then account number 002 has values `Rich Burd`, `0.00`, `Deadbeat`. You may not think much of my uncle, but he's certainly not a deadbeat!

To fight against incomplete write operations, database management systems perform transactions. A *transaction* is a collection of operations to be performed in all-or-nothing fashion. "Either do them all, or do none of them," says the DBMS. The collection of operations in a transaction is *atomic;* the collection of operations cannot be subdivided.

As you might guess, enforcing atomicity isn't easy. How does a DBMS ensure all-or-nothing writing when some heinous network error gums up the whole system?

Fortunately, the mechanisms used to enforce atomicity aren't your problem if you are a database user. If your app requires atomicity (and if the database management system doesn't automatically enforce atomicity), you simply write a sequence of regular database commands. At the end of an all-or-nothing sequence, you issue a special `commit` command or a special `rollback` command. A `commit` command says, "Cast all the changes in this sequence of operations stone," and a `rollback` command says, "Discard all the changes in this sequence." The database management system implements the special `commit` and `rollback` commands cleanly and reliably.

(In case you're wondering, these `commit` and `rollback` commands normally belong in alternative branches within your code. You don't just issue a bunch of commands and then roll them back for the fun of it.)

Listing 5-1:   Sending Commands to a Database

```
package com.allmycode.db1;

import android.app.Activity;
import android.content.ContentValues;
import android.database.Cursor;
import android.database.sqlite.SQLiteDatabase;
import android.os.Bundle;
import android.widget.TextView;

public class MyActivity extends Activity {

  TextView textView;
  Cursor cursor = null;
  DBHelper helper = null;
  SQLiteDatabase db = null;
  ContentValues values = null;

  @Override
  public void onCreate(Bundle savedInstanceState) {
    super.onCreate(savedInstanceState);
    setContentView(R.layout.main);

    textView = (TextView) findViewById(R.id.textView1);

    helper = new DBHelper(this, "simple_db", null, 1);
    db = helper.getWritableDatabase();
    values = new ContentValues();

    values.put("name", "Barry");
    values.put("amount", "100");
    db.insert("simpletable", "", values);
    values.clear();
    values.put("name", "Harriet");
    values.put("amount", "300");
    db.insert("simpletable", "", values);

    addToTextView();

    values.clear();
    values.put("amount", "500");
    db.update("simpletable", values, "name='Barry'", null);

    addToTextView();

    db.delete("simpletable", "1", null);

    addToTextView();
  }
```

(continued)

Listing 5-1 *(continued)*

```
@Override
public void onDestroy() {
  super.onDestroy();
  helper.close();
}

void addToTextView() {
  cursor =
      db.rawQuery("SELECT * FROM simpletable;", null);

  if (cursor != null && cursor.moveToFirst()) {

    String name;
    do {
      String _id = cursor.getString(0);
      name = cursor.getString(1);
      int amount = cursor.getInt(2);
      textView.append(_id + " " + name + " " + amount
          + "\n");
    } while (cursor.moveToNext());
    }
    textView.append("-----------\n");
  }
}
```

The first new and exciting statement in Listing 5-1 is the call to a `DBHelper` constructor. My `DBHelper` class (to be unveiled in Listing 5-2) extends the abstract `android.database.sqlite.SQLiteOpenHelper` class. The purpose of such a class is to manage the creation and modification of an SQLite database. In particular, the code in Listing 5-1 uses the helper to grab hold of an actual database.

Details about the friendly helper class

Listing 5-2 contains my `DBHelper` code.

Listing 5-2:   A Subclass of the SQLiteOpenHelper Class

```
package com.allmycode.db1;

import android.content.Context;
import android.database.sqlite.SQLiteDatabase;
import android.database.sqlite.SQLiteOpenHelper;

public class DBHelper extends SQLiteOpenHelper {

  public DBHelper(Context context, String dbName,
      SQLiteDatabase.CursorFactory factory, int version) {
```

```
      super(context, dbName, factory, version);
    }

    @Override
    public void onCreate(SQLiteDatabase db) {
      String createString =
          "CREATE TABLE IF NOT EXISTS simpletable "
            + "( _id INTEGER PRIMARY KEY AUTOINCREMENT, "
            + "name TEXT NOT NULL, "
            + "amount INTEGER NOT NULL);";
      db.execSQL(createString);
    }

    @Override
    public void onUpgrade(SQLiteDatabase db,
        int oldVersion, int newVersion) {
      String dropString =
          "DROP TABLE IF EXISTS simpletable;";
      db.execSQL(dropString);
      onCreate(db);
    }
}
```

In Listing 5-2, I implement the parent class's abstract methods (as I must). I also create a constructor that takes the lazy way out, passing all its parameters to the parent constructor.

The most important part of Listing 5-2 is the onCreate method. You never call this method directly. Instead, Android calls the method on your behalf when you set up a helper the way I do in Listing 5-1.

Android delays the call to the helper's onCreate method until your code actually uses the database. That bodes well for your app's performance.

Android hands the onCreate method an *SQLite database* (a database belonging to the app in which the helper is located). That SQLite database (called db in the onCreate method's parameter list) has an execSQL method. Listing 5-2 calls the database's execSQL method, feeding the method an ordinary Java string. Luckily for me, this ordinary Java string happens to be an SQL command.

In Listing 5-2's onCreate method, lots of good things happen without much fanfare. If the database doesn't already exist, Android creates one. If the database doesn't already have a table named simpletable, SQLite creates one. If the database already exists and has a simpletable, the onCreate method doesn't rock the boat.

Databases normally live on after the hosting process terminates. If you run this example's code in March and then turn off your device for three months, the database still exists (along with any data that you added in March) when you turn on the device again in June.

**Book III
Chapter 5**

Content Providers

I don't cover SQL commands in this book. I'd go crazy trying to cover them all. But fortunately, other authors have covered SQL without going crazy. So to read all about SQL commands, buy either the standard *SQL For Dummies* or the supersize version *SQL All-in-One For Dummies*, both by Allen G. Taylor (John Wiley & Sons, Inc.).

SQL is more readable than some other languages, so with or without a thorough introduction, you can probably make sense of most of the SQL commands in this book. The SQL command midway through Listing 5-2, for example, says the following:

```
If the database doesn't have a table named simpletable,
  create simpletable with three columns, called
  _id, name, and amount.
    The _id column stores an integer value,
        which serves to identify its row,
        and is incremented by 1 for each newly added row,
    The name column stores a string value
        which cannot be null, and
    The amount column stores an integer value
        which cannot be null.
```

Android's SDK wants you to use the name _id for a table's auto-incremented primary key. I haven't experimented with other column names, but from what I've read, something will break if I try it.

An SQLiteOpenHelper's onUpgrade method deals with new versions of the database. For example, when I modify the database in Listing 5-2 so that each row has an additional column (a *comment* column, perhaps), I'm changing the table's structure. A change of this kind requires me to obliterate the existing table (that is, to *drop* the table) and to create another table as if from scratch. In a helper's onUpgrade method, you manage this (admittedly delicate) procedure.

Details about the mainstream SQLite code

In Listing 5-1, after the call to getWritableDatabase, the code performs some fairly commonplace operations — namely, inserting, updating, deleting, and querying.

Inserting

Each call to db.insert adds a row of values to the simpletable. Each *value* is actually a name/value pair, the name being a database column name and the value being something to stuff into that column.

The put method belonging to the ContentValues class takes two String parameters. In the call values.put("amount", "100"), the first parameter is a column name. The second parameter is the value to be placed into that column in the current row. Notice that the second parameter "100" is a Java String even though the database's *amount* column stores an integer. That's just the way it works. Oh, and while you're remembering things, don't forget to call values.clear() between using one set of values and assembling another.

In Listing 5-1, the insert method takes three parameters — a table name, a null column hack, and a set of values constituting the newly created row. The *null column hack* is a value that you add to deal with the possibility of a completely empty insert. SQLite behaves badly if you try to insert a row containing no data.

As a result of the calls to insert in Listing 5-1, the activity's screen contains the first two lines in the text view of Figure 5-4.

Figure 5-4:
Running
the code in
Listing 5-1.

```
1 Barry 100
2 Harriet 300
----------
1 Barry 500
2 Harriet 300
----------
```

Updating

In Listing 5-1, the call to db.update takes four parameters. The first two parameters — a table name and a set of values — are old hat. The update method's third parameter is part of an SQL WHERE clause. A *WHERE clause* tells SQLite which rows should be chosen for processing. For example, the WHERE clause in the "Databases: From the Stone Age to the Present Day" section tells SQLite to select only those rows whose Comment column contains the value Deadbeat.

For the third parameter in an update method call, you supply a string containing the entire WHERE clause, but you omit the word *WHERE*. So in Listing 5-1, the update method call generates an SQL statement containing WHERE name = 'Barry'. At this point in the game, it's easy to become confused with nested single quotes and double quotes. The SQL command rules require a value such as 'Barry' to be quoted, and a Java string must be double-quoted. If things become more complicated, you have to use escape sequences and other tricks.

In Listing 5-1, the update method's last parameter is a set of *WHERE arguments* — values to plug into the holes in your WHERE clause. For example, you can gain some flexibility (and in some cases, slightly better performance) by substituting the following two statements for the update call in Listing 5-1:

```
String[] whereArgs = {"Barry"};
db.update("simpletable", values, "name=?", whereArgs);
```

Deleting

The delete method call in Listing 5-1 takes three parameters — a table name, a WHERE clause, and a set of WHERE arguments. The WHERE clause is normally something like "name='Barry'". (Get rid of that deadbeat!) But in Listing 5-1, the WHERE clause is "1" — the SQL code for *everything*. In Listing 5-1, the delete method removes every row in the database table.

Querying

After each change to the database, the code in Listing 5-1 adds text to the activity's text view. To do this, the code executes a *query*. The database's rawQuery method takes two parameters — an SQL command string and a (possibly null) set of WHERE arguments.

In Listing 5-1, the call to rawQuery returns a cursor. The cursor.moveTo First call returns true as long as the attempt to reach the cursor table's first row is successful. (Failure typically means that the table has no rows.)

For an introduction to database cursors, see the "Databases: From the Stone Age to the Present Day" section, earlier in this chapter.

From that point on, the code in Listing 5-1 loops from row to row, moving the cursor to the next table row each time through the loop. The cursor. moveToNext call returns false when there's no next row to move to.

Every time through the loop, the code uses the cursor to get the values in each of the table's three columns. The columns' indices start at 0 and increase in the order in which I declare the columns in Listing 5-2. Notice how I call get methods particular to the types of data in the database. Nothing good can happen if, for one column or another, I use a get method with the wrong type.

As the code in Listing 5-1 takes its last breath, the activity's onDestroy method closes the helper instance. Doing so shuts down the entire database connection and frees up resources for use by other apps. As is the case with all onDestroy methods, you should eschew my overly simple code. Before calling the helper's `close` method, make sure that the helper isn't `null`. Also include code to handle the possibility that the Android is temporarily destroying (and later re-creating) the activity. For some help with that, see Chapter 3 of this minibook.

How to find out what's really going on

SQLite expects each SQL command to end with a semicolon. So, for example, near the end of the `onCreate` method in Listing 5-2, a line contains two semicolons — one to end the SQL command and another to end the Java statement. Android's methods let you omit an SQL command's ending semicolon. So the line in Listing 5-2 works just as well if you write `"amount INTEGER NOT NULL")`; with only one semicolon. But I like to include the extra semicolon. That way, I remember SQLite's punctuation rules when I'm not composing Java code.

And when do I write SQL commands without Java code? I'm glad you asked! Imagine that I'm testing some of this section's code. I'm using an emulator or a real, Android-powered device attached to my development computer. Before installing this section's code, I comment out the `delete` method call in Listing 5-1. (That way, the database has two rows when the code finishes its run.)

The figure nearby shows a session in my development computer's command window.

✔ **I invoke Android's `adb` command with the `shell` option.**

This deposits me into the emulator's Linux command interface. On the emulator, the prompt is the pound sign (#).

✔ **I issue the Linux `cd` command four times.**

As a result, my working directory is `/data/data/com.allmycode.db1/`

`databases`. Notice that my humble little app has a directory for its own databases.

✔ **The Linux `ls` command lists files in my working directory.**

The directory contains a file that stores the `simple_db` database (the database created by the code in Listing 5-1).

✔ **I invoke the `sqlite3` executable a program to help me explore and modify an SQLite database.**

The sqlite3 program displays the `sqlite>` prompt. My next several commands are specific to the `simple_db` database. Commands that start with a dot are instructions to the sqlite3 program. (These may include instructions such as `.help`, `.log` and `.exit`.)

Commands that don't start with a dot are actual SQL commands. These SQL commands read and update the `simple_db` database.

✔ **Two times during the session, I type the `SELECT * FROM simpletable;` SQL command.**

When I issue this command, I see exactly what's in the `simple_db` database. I can use this information to help me debug my Java code. (Not that my Java code ever needs debugging . . .)

(continued)

**Book III
Chapter 5**

Content Providers

(continued)

✔ **In the nearby figure, when I type an SQL INSERT command, I forget to end the command with a semicolon.**

As a result, the sqlite3 program prompts me with `...>`. To complete the command, I type the required semicolon and press Enter. (Is it time for me to say, "I told you so?")

✔ **I type `.exit` to terminate the sqlite3 program and then type `exit` to end the emulator's shell session.**

All things considered, it's a very enlightening session. Communicating directly with the database management system can be extremely helpful.

```
C:\>\android-sdk\platform-tools\adb shell
# cd data
cd data
# cd data
cd data
# pwd
pwd
/data/data
# cd com.allmycode.db1
cd com.allmycode.db1
# cd databases
cd databases
# ls
ls
simple_db
# sqlite3 simple_db
sqlite3 simple_db
SQLite version 3.6.22
Enter ".help" for instructions
Enter SQL statements terminated with a ";"
sqlite> .tables
.tables
android_metadata  simpletable
sqlite> .schema
.schema
CREATE TABLE android_metadata (locale TEXT);
CREATE TABLE simpletable ( _id INTEGER PRIMARY KEY AUTOINCREMENT, name TEXT NOT
NULL, amount INTEGER NOT NULL);
sqlite> SELECT * FROM simpletable;
SELECT * FROM simpletable;
1|Barry|500
2|Harriet|300
sqlite> INSERT INTO simpletable ("name", "amount") VALUES ("Alex", "29")
INSERT INTO simpletable ("name", "amount") VALUES ("Alex", "29")
...> ;
;
sqlite> SELECT * FROM simpletable;
SELECT * FROM simpletable;
1|Barry|500
2|Harriet|300
3|Alex|29
sqlite> .exit
.exit
# exit
exit

C:\>_
```

Creating and Using a Content Provider

A *content provider* is a gateway to an app's data. Other apps approach the gateway as if it's a database. But under the hood, the data can take many different forms.

This section's example involves two apps — an app with a content provider and a separate client app. (Refer to Figures 5-2 and 5-3.) The client app's code looks very much like the code in Listing 5-1.

This section's client code is in Listing 5-3. (The result of executing the code is in Figure 5-5.)

Listing 5-3: Getting Data from a Content Provider

```
package a.b.c;

import android.app.Activity;
import android.content.ContentResolver;
import android.content.ContentValues;
import android.database.Cursor;
import android.net.Uri;
import android.os.Bundle;
import android.widget.TextView;

public class ClientActivity extends Activity {
  TextView textView;
  Cursor cursor = null;
  ContentValues values = null;
  ContentResolver resolver = null;

  public static final Uri CONTENT_URI = Uri
      .parse("content://com.allmycode.db/names_amounts");

  public static final Uri SILLY_URI = Uri
      .parse("content://com.allmycode.db/silly_stuff");

  @Override
  public void onCreate(Bundle b) {
    super.onCreate(b);
    setContentView(R.layout.main);

    textView = (TextView) findViewById(R.id.textView1);

    values = new ContentValues();
    resolver = getContentResolver();

    values.put("name", "Sam");
    values.put("amount", "100");
    resolver.insert(CONTENT_URI, values);
    values.clear();
    values.put("name", "Jennie");
    values.put("amount", "300");
    resolver.insert(CONTENT_URI, values);

    addToTextView(CONTENT_URI);

    values.clear();
    values.put("amount", "500");
    resolver.update(CONTENT_URI, values,
        "name='Sam'", null);
```

(continued)

**Book III
Chapter 5**

Content Providers

Listing 5-3 *(continued)*

```
      addToTextView(CONTENT_URI);

      resolver.delete(CONTENT_URI, "1", null);

      addToTextView(CONTENT_URI);

      addToTextView(SILLY_URI);
  }

  void addToTextView(Uri uri) {
    cursor = resolver.query(uri, null, "1", null, null);
    startManagingCursor(cursor);

    if (cursor != null && cursor.moveToFirst()) {

      String name;
      do {
        String _id = cursor.getString(0);
        name = cursor.getString(1);
        int amount = cursor.getInt(2);
        textView.append(_id + " " + name + " " + amount
            + "\n");
      } while (cursor.moveToNext());
    }
    textView.append("-----------\n");
  }
}
```

Figure 5-5:
A run of
the code in
Listing 5-3.

```
1 Sam 100
2 Jennie 300
-----------
1 Sam 500
2 Jennie 300
-----------

-----------
Table 4 2
-----------
```

Many of the differences between Listings 5-1 and 5-3 are cosmetic. The big noncosmetic difference is the use of a content resolver instead of a helper and a database. In Listing 5-3, the client app has no direct communication with the provider's database. Instead, the client app talks to the database through a *content resolver*.

Each content resolver method takes a URI — a reference to some data offered by a content provider. Here's what happens when your code calls a content resolver method:

✦ **Android examines the URI's scheme and finds the `content: scheme`.**

The `content: scheme` tells Android to look for a matching content provider.

✦ **Android compares the URI's authority with the authorities in the intent filters of available content providers. (See Figure 5-6.)**

A content provider must declare one or more authorities in its app's `AndroidManifest.xml` document. Listing 5-4 has the `AndroidManifest.xml` document for this section's example. Notice that in this example, the app containing the content provider has no activity. The app has no direct interface to the user.

Listing 5-4:   A Content Provider's XML Element

```
<?xml version="1.0" encoding="utf-8"?>
<manifest xmlns:android=
        "http://schemas.android.com/apk/res/android"
    package="com.allmycode.db" android:versionCode="1"
    android:versionName="1.0">
<uses-sdk android:minSdkVersion="10" />

    <application android:icon="@drawable/icon"
        android:label="@string/app_name">

        <provider android:name=".MyContentProvider"
            android:authorities="com.allmycode.db">
        </provider>

    </application>
</manifest>
```

If an `android:authorities` attribute contains more than one authority, you separate authorities from one another using semicolons:

```
android:authorities="this.is.one;this.is.another"
```

So far, so good. Here's what happens when Android finds a matching content provider:

✦ **Android hands the client's database-like call (URI and all) to the matching content provider.**

After Android hands the call to a content provider, the ball is in the content provider's court.

✦ **The content provider parses the URI's path to further refine the client app's request.**

✦ **The content provider uses its own app's data to fulfill the client app's request.**

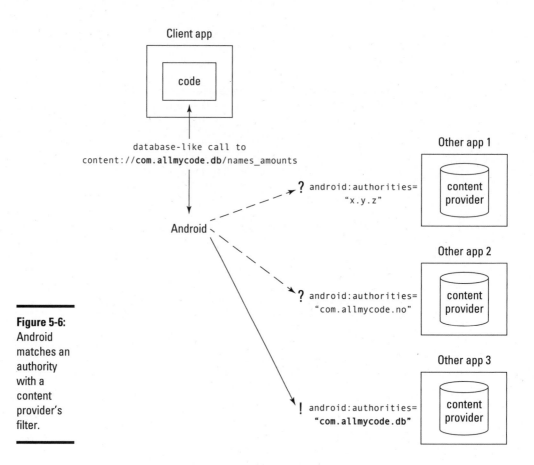

Client app

code

database-like call to
content://**com.allmycode.db**/names_amounts

Android

? android:authorities=
"x.y.z"

Other app 1

content provider

? android:authorities=
"com.allmycode.no"

Other app 2

content provider

! android:authorities=
"com.allmycode.db"

Other app 3

content provider

Figure 5-6:
Android matches an authority with a content provider's filter.

Listing 5-3 has another special feature. The startManagingCursor(cursor) call tells the activity to automatically deactivate the cursor when the activity stops and to automatically query the cursor when the activity starts again. This handy method call eliminates the need for elaborate housekeeping in the activity's lifecycle methods.

In Listing 5-1, I make a meager attempt to be tidy by closing the helper in the activity's onDestroy method. But in practice, manually closing and reopening database resources can be much more complicated. That's why methods like startManagingCursor are so handy.

At last! A content provider!

Listing 5-5 contains a content provider for this section's ongoing example.

Listing 5-5:   Look; It's a Content Provider

```
package com.allmycode.db;

import android.content.ContentProvider;
import android.content.ContentUris;
import android.content.ContentValues;
import android.content.UriMatcher;
import android.database.Cursor;
import android.database.MatrixCursor;
import android.database.sqlite.SQLiteDatabase;
import android.net.Uri;

public class MyContentProvider extends ContentProvider {
  public static final Uri CONTENT_URI = Uri
      .parse("content://com.allmycode.db/names_amounts");
  public static final Uri SILLY_URI = Uri
      .parse("content://com.allmycode.db/silly_stuff");

  private static final String SIMPLE_DB = "simple_db";
  private static final String SIMPLETABLE = "simpletable";

  Cursor cursor = null;
  DBHelper helper = null;
  SQLiteDatabase db = null;
  ContentValues values = null;
  UriMatcher uriMatcher = null;
  {
    uriMatcher = new UriMatcher(UriMatcher.NO_MATCH);
    uriMatcher.addURI("com.allmycode.db",
                             "names_amounts", 1);
    uriMatcher.addURI("com.allmycode.db",
                             "silly_stuff", 2);
  }

  @Override
  public boolean onCreate() {
    try {
      helper =
          new DBHelper(getContext(), SIMPLE_DB, null, 1);
      db = helper.getWritableDatabase();
      values = new ContentValues();
      return true;
    } catch (Exception e) {
      return false;
    }
  }

  @Override
  public Uri insert(Uri ure, ContentValues values) {
    long id = db.insert(SIMPLETABLE, "", values);
    return ContentUris.withAppendedId(CONTENT_URI, id);
  }
```

(continued)

Listing 5-5 *(continued)*

```java
@Override
public int update(Uri uri, ContentValues values,
    String whereClause, String[] whereArgs) {

  int numOfChangedRows =
      db.update(SIMPLETABLE, values, whereClause,
          whereArgs);

  return numOfChangedRows;
}

@Override
public int delete(Uri uri, String whereClause,
    String[] whereArgs) {
  int numOfChangedRows =
      db.delete(SIMPLETABLE, whereClause, whereArgs);
  return numOfChangedRows;
}

@Override
public Cursor query(Uri uri, String[] columns,
    String whereClause, String[] whereArgs,
    String sortOrder) {
  Cursor cursor = null;
  int code = uriMatcher.match(uri);
  if (code == 1) {

    cursor =
        db.query(SIMPLETABLE, columns, whereClause,
            whereArgs, null, null, sortOrder);

  } else if (code == 2) {
    String[] columnNames = { "_id", "name", "amount" };
    String[] rowValues = { "Table ", "4 ", "2" };
    MatrixCursor matrixCursor =
        new MatrixCursor(columnNames);
    matrixCursor.addRow(rowValues);
    cursor = matrixCursor;
  }
  return cursor;
}

@Override
public String getType(Uri uri) {
  return null;
}
}
```

Listing 5-5 implements the six abstract methods declared in the `android.content.ContentProvider` class. The implementation code bears a striking resemblance to some of the code in Listing 5-1.

✦ Both `onCreate` methods use `DBHelper` (which extends Android's `SQLiteOpenHelper` class) to get a writable database.

✦ Both listings call the database's `insert`, `update`, and `delete` methods.

✦ Both listings issue a query to the database.

> Actually, Listing 5-1 uses the `rawQuery` method and an SQL command string. In contrast, Listing 5-5 uses the `query` method with a bunch of parameters. The difference has nothing to do with content providers. It's just my whim in using different methods to illustrate different ways of issuing a query.

The bottom line is this: A content provider does with its app's data what an ordinary activity does with its own app's data.

Listing 5-5 has some features that I choose not to use in Listing 5-1. For example, Android's `update` and `delete` methods return `int` values. In Listing 5-1, I simply ignore the return values. But in Listing 5-5, I pass each method's return value back to the client code. (Don't congratulate me on my diligence. I pass on each value because the content provider's abstract `update` and `delete` methods must have `int` return values.)

Listing 5-5 also has some features that are unique to content providers. For example, to effectively dish out data, a content provider must manage URIs. Normally, a content provider examines each method's incoming URI and uses the information to decide on its next move. In Listing 5-5, I keep things simple with only a minor bit of URI handling in the `query` method.

Outside the Android world, the use of URIs to connect to databases is commonplace. For example, in a Java JDBC program, you may connect to a database with a statement, such as `DriverManager.getConnection("jdbc:derby:AccountDatabase")`. In this statement's opaque URI, the scheme `jdbc:` forwards a request to another scheme — namely, the `derby:` scheme.

In Listing 5-5, the `query` method calls on a `UriMatcher` instance to distinguish one path from another. As it's defined near the start of Listing 5-5, the `UriMatcher` instance returns 1 for the `names_amounts` path and returns 2 for the `silly_stuff` path.

A return value of 1 makes the `query` method do its regular old database query. But a return value of 2 does something entirely different. To show that I can do it, I respond to a URI's `silly_stuff` path without consulting a real database. Instead, I use arrays to concoct something that looks like a `simpletable` row. I squish the arrays into a `MatrixCursor` (a cursor built from an array rather than a database), and I send the cursor back to the client.

The `insert` method in Listing 5-5 returns a URI. What's that all about? Each row associated with the `content:` scheme has its own individual URI. For example, in a run of this section's code, the first two row insertions have URIs `content://com.allmycode.db/names_amounts/1` and `content://com.allmycode.db/names_amounts/2`. The `android.content.ContentUris` class's `withAppendedId` method fetches the URI for a particular database row. The client can use this row-specific URI to refer to one database row at a time.

The latest and greatest cursor code

With the arrival of Honeycomb (Android 3.0), managing cursors is a whole new ballgame. In particular, the `startManagingCursor` method from Listing 5-3 is deprecated. As horrible as it sounds for something to be "deprecated," you can still run the code from Listing 5-3 on devices running Honeycomb. *Deprecated* simply means "the creators of Android recommend that you don't continue to use this method because they might not continue to support it in future Android releases." Fair enough.

To replace things like managed cursors, Honeycomb has a `CursorLoader` class. Like a teenager off to college, a `CursorLoader` instance manages itself by leaving its parent thread, going out on its own, and eventually returning with the desired result. And like any real teenager, a `CursorLoader` instance, with all its asynchronous behavior, can behave in strange and surprising ways.

Anyway, you can get a head start with the `CursorLoader` class by looking at a simple example of its use. Listing 5-6 has just such an example.

Listing 5-6:   A Simple CursorLoader Example

```
package a.b.c;

import android.app.Activity;
import android.content.ContentResolver;
import android.content.ContentValues;
import android.content.CursorLoader;
import android.content.Loader;
import android.content.Loader.OnLoadCompleteListener;
import android.database.Cursor;
import android.net.Uri;
```

```
import android.os.Bundle;
import android.widget.TextView;

public class ClientActivity extends Activity {
  TextView textView;
  Cursor cursor = null;
  ContentValues values = null;
  ContentResolver resolver = null;

  public static final Uri CONTENT_URI = Uri
      .parse("content://com.allmycode.db/names_amounts");

  @Override
  public void onCreate(Bundle b) {
    super.onCreate(b);
    setContentView(R.layout.main);

    textView = (TextView) findViewById(R.id.textView1);

    values = new ContentValues();
    resolver = getContentResolver();

    values.put("name", "Sam");
    values.put("amount", "100");
    resolver.insert(CONTENT_URI, values);
    values.clear();
    values.put("name", "Jennie");
    values.put("amount", "300");
    resolver.insert(CONTENT_URI, values);

    addToTextView(CONTENT_URI);
  }

  CursorLoader loader = null;

  void addToTextView(Uri uri) {
    loader =
        new CursorLoader(this, uri, null, "1", null, null);
    loader.registerListener(42,
        new MyOnLoadCompleteListener());
    loader.startLoading();
    textView.append("Here it comes...");
  }

  class MyOnLoadCompleteListener implements
      OnLoadCompleteListener<Cursor> {

    @Override
    public void onLoadComplete(Loader<Cursor> loader,
        Cursor cursor) {
      if (cursor != null && cursor.moveToFirst()) {
```

(continued)

Listing 5-6 *(continued)*

```
        String name;
        do {
          String _id = cursor.getString(0);
          name = cursor.getString(1);
          int amount = cursor.getInt(2);
          textView.append(_id + " " + name + " " + amount
              + "\n");
        } while (cursor.moveToNext());
      }
      textView.append("-----------\n");
    }
  }
}
```

The result of running the code in Listing 5-6 is shown in Figure 5-7.

Figure 5-7:
A run of
the code in
Listing 5-6.

ClientProject

Here it comes...
1 Sam 100
2 Jennie 300

Listing 5-6 simply adds two rows to a database table and displays the results in the activity's text view. The call to the `CursorLoader` constructor looks very much like the call to `resolver.query` in Listing 5-3. (In fact, I copied and pasted code to create the `CursorLoader` constructor's parameter list.) The big difference between the `CursorLoader` constructor and a `resolver.query` call is that the `CursorLoader` constructor requires a context parameter. In Listing 5-6, the context is this activity itself.

From the constructor call onward, the activity's thread registers a callback listener and calls the loader's `startLoading` method. As in most of Java's listener scenarios, the loader's callback listener (the `MyOnLoadCompleteListener`) is a class whose methods sit and wait for a holler from another thread.

In Listing 5-6, the listener's `onLoadComplete` method does nothing while it waits for a result from the loader. In the meantime, the rest of the activity's code (namely, the appending of `Here it comes` to the text view) continues on its merry way.

When at last the loading of the data is complete, the `onLoadComplete` method does what you want it to do with the data from the cursor. In Listing 5-6, the method follows the lead from this chapter's previous examples and displays the data in the activity's text view.

Book IV

Programming Cool Phone Features

The 5th Wave — By Rich Tennant

HORNER BROS.
MAKERS OF PREMIUM
BELLS & WHISTLES

"As an application developer, I never thought I'd say this, but your app needs more bells and whistles."

Contents at a Glance

Chapter 1: Lay Out Your Stuff

In This Chapter

↳ **Organizing the widgets on the device's screen**

↳ **Dealing with colors, sizes, and positions**

↳ **Working with various layouts**

*W*hich description do you prefer?

✦ *In my entire line of sight, I see a polygon with convex vertices at the points (1.5, 0), (0, 1.2), (3, 1.2), (0.6, 3), (2.4, 3), and with concave vertices at the points (1.15, 1.2), (1.85, 1.2), (0.95, 1.8), (2.05, 1.8), (1.5, 2.2). The units are in inches.*

✦ *In my entire line of sight, I see a five-pointed star.*

The first description is more precise, but the first is also more brittle. As I type this introduction, I anticipate the e-mail messages from readers: "You got one of the numbers wrong in the first description."

The second description is also more versatile. The second description makes sense whether you describe an image on a laptop screen or on a highway billboard. In a world with all kinds of mobile devices, all kinds of screen sizes, screen resolutions, display qualities, refresh rates, and who-knows-what-other variations, the big picture is often more useful than the picky details. When you describe your app's screen, you should avoid measurements in favor of concepts.

Android supports four basic layout concepts — linear layout, relative layout, table layout, and frame layout. In many cases, choosing one kind of layout over another is a matter of taste. A table layout with only one row looks like a horizontal linear layout. A set of nested linear layouts may look exactly like a complicated relative layout. The possibilities are endless.

Android Layouts

The game with Android's layouts is to place visible things into a container in an orderly way. In a typical scenario, one of these "visible things" is a *view*, and one of these "containers" is a *view group*.

The formal terminology is a bit hazy. But fortunately, the fine distinctions between the terms aren't terribly important. Here's some formal terminology:

✦ A *view* appears on the user's screen and (either directly or indirectly) involves user interaction. The word *view* often refers to an instance of the `android.view.View` class. A broader use of the word *view* includes any class or interface in the `android.view` package.

✦ A *widget* appears on the user's screen and (either directly or indirectly) involves user interaction. (Sounds a lot like a view, doesn't it?) The word *widget* commonly refers to a class or interface in the `android.widget` package.

Views can be widgets, and widgets can be views. As long as your `import` declarations work and your method parameter types match, the distinction between widgets and views is unimportant.

Commonly used widgets and views include buttons, check boxes, text views, toasts, and more exotic things such as digital clocks, sliding drawers, progress bars, and other good junk.

(Android or no Android, I think *widget* is a wonderful word. The playwrights George S. Kaufman and Marc Connelly made up the word "widget" for dialogue in their 1924 comedy *Beggar on Horseback*. I learned about widgets from the fictitious Universal Widgets company — an enterprise featured in *The Wheeler Dealers* from 1963.)

✦ A *view group* (an instance of `android.view.ViewGroup`) is a view that contains other views (including other view groups). The views contained in a view group are the view group's *children*.

Examples of view groups are the linear layouts, relative layouts, table layouts, and frame layouts mentioned at the beginning of this chapter, as well as some more special-purpose things such as the list view and the scroll view.

One way or another, I usually write about putting a "view" on a "layout."

Linear Layout

Linear layouts have either vertical or horizontal orientation. When you create a new Android project, Eclipse fills your `main.xml` file with a vertically orientated linear layout.

Views in a vertical linear layout line up one beneath the other. Views in a horizontal linear layout line up one beside the other. (See Figure 1-1.)

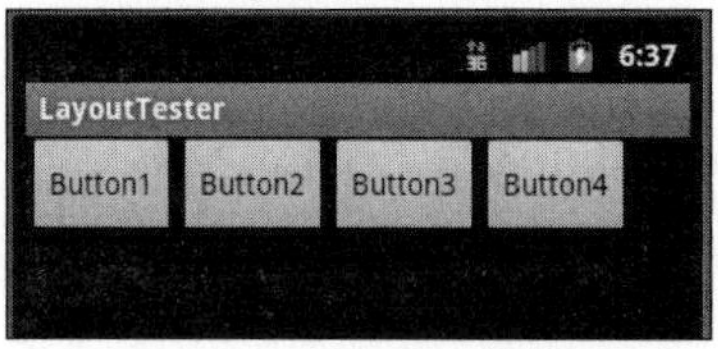

Figure 1-1:
Four
buttons in a
horizontal
linear
layout.

You can create the layout in Figure 1-1 with the XML code in Listing 1-1.

Listing 1-1: A Horizontal Linear Layout

```xml
<?xml version="1.0" encoding="utf-8"?>
<LinearLayout xmlns:android=
    "http://schemas.android.com/apk/res/android"
  android:layout_width="match_parent"
  android:layout_height="match_parent"
  android:orientation="horizontal">

  <Button android:text="Button1"
    android:layout_height="wrap_content"
    android:layout_width="wrap_content"
    android:id="@+id/button1">
  </Button>

  <Button android:text="Button2"
    android:layout_height="wrap_content"
    android:layout_width="wrap_content"
    android:id="@+id/button2">
  </Button>

  <Button android:text="Button3"
    android:layout_height="wrap_content"
    android:layout_width="wrap_content"
    android:id="@+id/button3">
  </Button>

  <Button android:text="Button4"
    android:layout_height="wrap_content"
    android:layout_width="wrap_content"
    android:id="@+id/button4">
  </Button>

</LinearLayout>
```

**Book IV
Chapter 1**

**Lay Out Your
Stuff**

You can also create the layout in Figure 1-1 by dragging and dropping views in Eclipse's Graphical Layout editor.

Linear layouts don't wrap, and they don't scroll. So if you add six buttons to a horizontal layout, and the user's screen is wide enough for only five of the buttons, the user sees only five buttons. (See Figure 1-2.)

Figure 1-2:
Six (yes, six) buttons in a horizontal linear layout.

Attributes (A Detour)

Using XML attributes, you can change a layout's default behavior. This section has several examples.

android:layout_width and android:layout_height

You can tweak the size of a view using the android:layout_width and android:layout_height attributes. Listing 1-2 has some code, and Figure 1-3 shows the resulting layout.

Listing 1-2: Setting a View's Width and Height

```
<?xml version="1.0" encoding="utf-8"?>
<LinearLayout xmlns:android=
    "http://schemas.android.com/apk/res/android"
  android:orientation="vertical"
  android:layout_width="match_parent"
  android:layout_height="match_parent">

  <Button
    android:layout_width="match_parent"
    android:layout_height="wrap_content"
    android:text='1. android:layout_height="wrap_content"
      android:layout_width="match_parent"'>
    android:id="@+id/button1"
  </Button>
```

```
<Button
  android:layout_width="wrap_content"
  android:layout_height="wrap_content"
  android:text="2. wrap/wrap">
  android:id="@+id/button2"
</Button>

<Button
  android:layout_width="60dp"
  android:layout_height="wrap_content"
  android:text="3. width 60dp">
  android:id="@+id/button3"
</Button>

<Button
  android:layout_width="160dp"
  android:layout_height="wrap_content"
  android:text='4. android:layout_width="160dp"'>
  android:id="@+id/button4"
</Button>

<Button
  android:layout_width="wrap_content"
  android:layout_height="match_parent"
  android:text="5. width wrap_content,
    height match_parent"
  android:id="@+id/button5">
</Button>

</LinearLayout>
```

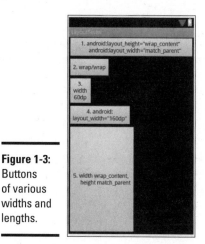

Figure 1-3:
Buttons
of various
widths and
lengths.

You can describe a view's size using general guidelines or numbers of units, as spelled out in the next two sections.

Using general size guidelines

To create general guidelines, use the `"wrap_content"`, `"match_parent"`, or `"fill_parent"` value. (See Listing 1-2.) With `"wrap_content"`, Android shrinks a view's width or length so that the view tightly encloses whatever it contains. With `"match_parent"` and `"fill_parent"`, Android expands a view's width or length so that the view fits tightly inside its container.

 What it means to "tightly enclose" something or "fit tightly inside" something depends on the amount of breathing room you specify for the boundaries around things. This breathing room comes in two forms — padding and margins. (If you want, you can look ahead to this chapter's section on padding and margins.)

 The strings `"match_parent"` and `"fill_parent"` have the same meaning. Before API Level 8, only `"fill_parent"` works. Starting with API Level 8, the string `"fill_parent"` is deprecated in favor of `"match_parent"`. According to Java's official documents, deprecated features are obsolete and "are supported only for backwards compatibility." In the Java world, a feature that's deprecated might be unavailable in future software versions. But Java's deprecated features tend to linger on for years. Both `"fill_parent"` and `"match_parent"` work up to (and possibly beyond) API Level 13 (Honeycomb).

In Listing 1-2, the first button has attributes `android:layout_width="match_parent"` and `android:layout_height="wrap_content"`. So in Figure 1-3, the top button is as wide as it can be and only tall enough to contain the words displayed on the button's face.

 In Listing 1-2, the first button's `android:text` attribute illustrates two out-of-the-way features. First, I enclose the attribute's value in single quotation marks. I do this because the value itself contains double quotation marks. Next, the attribute's value straddles two lines. As a result, Android breaks the content on the top button into two lines of text. (See Figure 1-3.)

Using numbers of units

In Listing 1-2, I describe the third button's width in units. The value *60dp* stands for 60 *density-independent pixels.* A density-independent pixel is a measurement based on a 160 pixels-per-inch benchmark.

"And what," you ask, "is a 160 pixels-per-inch benchmark?" A *pixel* is a single dot on a device's screen. A pixel can be invisible, glow brightly, or anything in between.

Different devices have different pixel densities. For example, a low-density screen might have 120 pixels per inch, and a high-density screen might have 260 pixels per inch. To adjust for these differences, each Android screen has several metrics. Each *metric* is a numeric value describing some characteristic of the display:

✦ **widthPixels (an int value)**: The number of pixels from the left edge to the right edge of the screen.

✦ **heightPixels (an int value)**: The number of pixels from the top to the bottom of the screen.

✦ **xdpi (an int value)**: The number of pixels from left to right along one inch of the screen.

✦ **ydpi (an int value)**: The number of pixels from top to bottom along one inch of the screen. (In a square inch, some screens stuff more pixels across than up and down, so xdpi isn't necessarily the same as ydpi.)

✦ **densityDpi (an int value)**: A general measure of the number of pixels per inch. For screens with equal xdpi and ydpi values, densityDpi is the same as xdpi and ydpi. For screens with unequal xdpi and ydpi values, somebody figures out what the screen's densityDpi is (but they don't tell me how they figure it out).

✦ **density (a float value)**: The number of pixels per inch, divided by 160.

✦ **scaledDensity (a float value)**: The density measure, but with some extra stretching or squeezing to account for any default font size chosen by the user. (Some versions of Android don't let the user adjust the default font size. Other versions have font size options in the Spare Parts application. If all else fails, it never hurts to look at the Settings app.)

When you specify 160dp (as in Listing 1-2), you're telling Android to display density × 160 pixels. So on my tiny screen, a width of 160dp is one inch, and on the Android home theater that you transport through time from the year 2055, a width of 160dp is one inch. Everybody gets the inch that they want.

The letters *dpi* stand for *dots per inch.* Your Android project has folders named res/drawable-hdpi, res/drawable-ldpi, and res/drawable-mdpi. At runtime, Android senses a device's or emulator's screen density and uses the resources in the most appropriate res/drawable-dpi folder. To find out what Android considers "most appropriate" for various screen densities, visit http://developer.android.com/guide/practices/screens_support.html.

Another handy unit of measurement is *sp — scale-independent pixels.* Like the dp unit, the size of an sp unit adjusts nicely for different screens. But the size of an sp unit changes in two ways. In addition to changing based on the screen's pixel density, the sp unit changes based on the user's font size preference settings.

TIP

The abbreviations *dp* and *dip* are interchangeable. Both stand for *device-independent pixels*. But *sp* is always *sp*. Android has no unit named *sip*.

If you want to be ornery, you can use physical units. For example, value *1 in* stands for one inch. Other unsavory physical units include *mm* (for millimeters), *pt* (for points, with 1 point being 1/72 of an inch), and *px* (for pixels — actual dots on the device's screen). In almost all situations, you should avoid physical units. Use dp to specify a view's size, and use sp to specify a text font size.

Figures 1-4 and 1-5 illustrate the relationship between pixels and density-independent pixels. The screen in Figure 1-4 has density 0.75. So an inch-wide button consumes $0.75 \times 160 = 120$ pixels. You can confirm this by comparing the sizes of the 160dp and 160px buttons. The 160dp button is roughly three quarters the width of the 160px button.

Figure 1-4:
A low-density display.

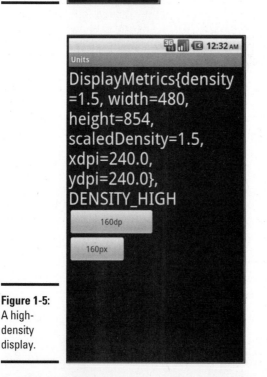

Figure 1-5:
A high-density display.

This book's figures might have stretched or shrunk in printing. Objects may be larger than they appear. What measures an inch across in this book's pages or on your e-reader's screen isn't necessarily an inch on an Android device's screen.

The screen in Figure 1-5 has a density 1.5, so in Figure 1-5, a 160dp button is 1.5 times as wide as a 160px button.

The XML document describing the layout in Figures 1-4 and 1-5 is shown in Listing 1-3.

Listing 1-3: Using Size Units

```xml
<?xml version="1.0" encoding="utf-8"?>
<LinearLayout xmlns:android=
      "http://schemas.android.com/apk/res/android"
    android:orientation="vertical"
    android:layout_width="fill_parent"
    android:layout_height="fill_parent">

  <TextView android:textSize="30sp"
      android:layout_width="wrap_content"
      android:layout_height="wrap_content"
      android:textColor="#FFFF"
      android:id="@+id/textView1"></TextView>

  <Button android:layout_width="160dp"
      android:text="160dp"
      android:layout_height="wrap_content"
      android:id="@+id/button1"></Button>

  <Button android:layout_width="160px"
      android:text="160px"
      android:layout_height="wrap_content"
      android:id="@+id/button2"></Button>

</LinearLayout>
```

Notice the metric information in the text view in Figures 1-4 and 1-5. To display this information, I use the `android.util.DisplayMetrics` class in my app's main activity:

```
package com.allmycode.screen;

import android.app.Activity;
import android.os.Bundle;
import android.util.DisplayMetrics;
import android.widget.TextView;
```

```java
public class ScreenActivity extends Activity {
  TextView textView;
  DisplayMetrics metrics;
  String densityDpiConstant;

  @Override
  public void onCreate(Bundle savedInstanceState) {
    super.onCreate(savedInstanceState);
    setContentView(R.layout.main);

    textView = (TextView) findViewById(R.id.textView1);

    metrics = new DisplayMetrics();
    getWindowManager().getDefaultDisplay().
      getMetrics(metrics);

    switch (metrics.densityDpi) {
    case DisplayMetrics.DENSITY_LOW:
      densityDpiConstant = "DENSITY_LOW";
      break;
    case DisplayMetrics.DENSITY_MEDIUM:
      densityDpiConstant = "DENSITY_MEDIUM";
      break;
    case DisplayMetrics.DENSITY_HIGH:
      densityDpiConstant = "DENSITY_HIGH";
      break;
    default:
      densityDpiConstant = "Huh?";
      break;
    }

    textView.setText(metrics.toString()
        + ", " + densityDpiConstant);
  }
}
```

android:padding and android:margin

Objects on a screen need room to breathe. You can't butt one text field right up against another. If you do, the screen looks horribly cluttered. So Android has things called *padding* and *margin:*

✦ A view's *padding* is space between the view's border and whatever is contained inside the view.

✦ A view's *margin* is space between the view's border and whatever is outside the view.

In Figure 1-6, I superimpose labels onto a screen shot from Eclipse's Graphical Layout editor. The rectangle with eight little squares along its perimeter is the text view's border. Think of the border as the text view's clothing. The padding keeps the clothing from being too tight, and the margins determine how much "personal space" the text view wants.

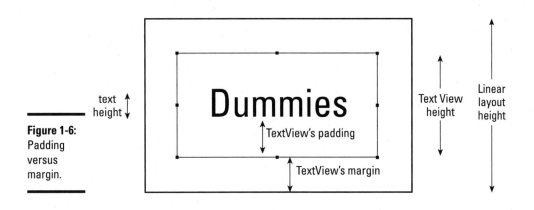

Figure 1-6:
Padding
versus
margin.

Listing 1-4 contains the code that generates the layout in Figure 1-6.

Listing 1-4:   Using Margin and Padding

```xml
<?xml version="1.0" encoding="utf-8"?>
<LinearLayout xmlns:android=
     "http://schemas.android.com/apk/res/android"
    android:orientation="vertical"
    android:layout_width="match_parent"
    android:layout_height="match_parent"
    android:gravity="center">

    <LinearLayout android:id="@+id/LinearLayout1"
        android:layout_height="wrap_content"
        android:layout_width="wrap_content"
        android:background="@color/opaque_white">

        <TextView android:text="Dummies"
            android:layout_margin="30dip"
            android:padding="30dip"
            android:textSize="30sp"

            android:layout_height="wrap_content"
            android:layout_width="wrap_content"

            android:id="@+id/textView1"
            android:textColor="@color/opaque_black">
        </TextView>

    </LinearLayout>

</LinearLayout>
```

**Book IV
Chapter 1**

**Lay Out Your
Stuff**

android:gravity and android:layout_gravity

I once asked a button what it wanted to be when it grows up. The button replied, "I want to be an astronaut." So I placed the button inside a layout with attribute `android:layout_gravity="center"`. A layout with this attribute is like the International Space Station. Things float in the middle of it. (Well, they don't actually bob to and fro the way things do in the space-station videos, but that's beside the point.)

Android has two similarly named attributes, and it's very easy to confuse them with one another. The `android:gravity` attribute tells a layout how to position the views within it. The `android:layout_gravity` attribute tells a view how to position itself within its layout. Figure 1-7 illustrates the idea.

The screen in Figure 1-7 contains a shortened linear layout and a button. The linear layout is only 220dip tall, and its `android:layout_gravity` is `center_vertical`. (See Listing 1-5.) So the gray linear layout floats downward to the center of the screen. But the layout's `android:gravity` attribute is `center_horizontal`. So the button within the layout shimmies horizontally to the layout's center. The button hangs along the top edge of the layout because, by default, things rise to the top and hug the left.

Figure 1-7:
The gray layout gravitates to the center of the screen; the button gravitates to the top of the gray layout.

Listing 1-5: Using layout_gravity and gravity

```
<?xml version="1.0" encoding="utf-8"?>
<LinearLayout xmlns:android=
     "http://schemas.android.com/apk/res/android"

   android:layout_gravity="center_vertical"
   android:gravity="center_horizontal"

   android:background="#F999"
   android:orientation="vertical"
   android:layout_width="match_parent"
   android:layout_height="220dip">

   <Button android:text="Button"
      android:id="@+id/button1"
      android:layout_width="wrap_content"
      android:layout_height="wrap_content">
   </Button>

</LinearLayout>
```

Figures 1-8 through 1-11 illustrate some other android:gravity attribute values.

Figure 1-8:
<Linear
Layout
android:
gravity=
"center_
vertical"...

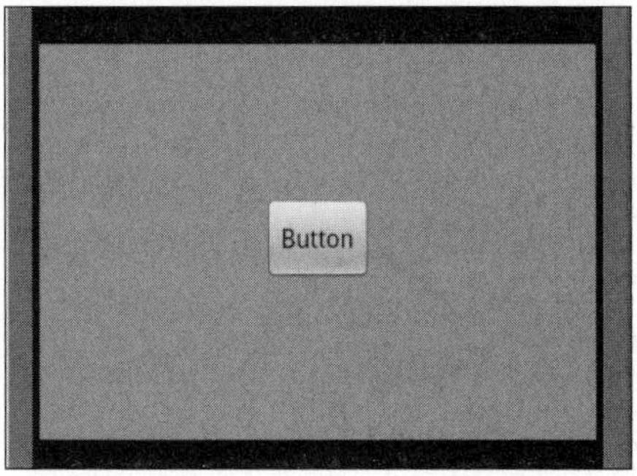

Figure 1-9:
<Linear
Layout
android:
gravity=
"center"...

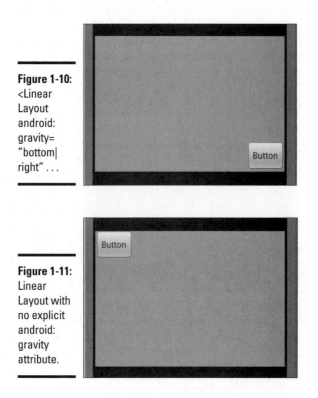

Figure 1-10:
<Linear
Layout
android:
gravity=
"bottom|
right"...

Figure 1-11:
Linear
Layout with
no explicit
android:
gravity
attribute.

Figure 1-10 shows what you can do by combining gravity values using Java's `bitwise or` operator (|).

android:color

You can apply colors to all kinds of things — things such as text, backgrounds, shadows, links, and other stuff. In Listing 1-5, I use the attribute `android:background="#F999"`, making a layout's background a quiet, dignified shade of gray.

As an Android developer, the most grown-up way to create a color is to declare it in a `res/values/colors.xml` file. The file looks something like the stuff in Listing 1-6.

Listing 1-6:   A colors.xml File

```
<?xml version="1.0" encoding="utf-8"?>
<resources xmlns:android=
    "http://schemas.android.com/apk/res/android">
```

```
<color name="bright_red">#F00</color>
<color name="bright_red2">#FF00</color>
<color name="bright_red3">#FF0000</color>
<color name="translucent_red">#7F00</color>
<color name="invisible_good_for_nothing_red">
   #00FF0000
</color>
<color name="white">#FFF</color>
<color name="black">#000</color>
<color name="puce">#CC8898</color>
</resources>
```

A color value begins with a pound sign (#) and then has three, four, six, or eight hexadecimal digits. With three digits, the leftmost digit is an amount of redness, the middle digit is an amount of greenness, and the rightmost digit is an amount of blueness. (The colors always come in that order — red, then green, and then blue. It's called *RGB* color.) So, for example, the color value #F92 stands for a decent-looking orange color — 15 units of red, 9 units green, and 2 units of blue, each out of a possible 16 units.

With only three hexadecimal digits you can't express fine color differences. So Android permits you to express a color as a sequence of six hex digits. For example, the value #FEF200 is a good approximation to the yellow on this book's cover. It's 254 units of red, 242 units of green, and no blue, each out of a possible 255 units.

With three RGB digits, you can add a fourth *alpha* digit immediately after the pound sign. And with six RGB digits, you can add two additional alpha digits immediately after the pound sign. The alpha value is the amount of opaqueness, with 15 being fully opaque and 0 being completely transparent. So the value #7F00 in Listing 1-6 is partially transparent red ("translucent red," if you will). Against a black background, the value #7F00 is a dull, depressing reddishness.

```
<?xml version="1.0" encoding="utf-8"?>
<LinearLayout xmlns:android=
    "http://schemas.android.com/apk/res/android"
  android:background="@color/black"
  android:id="@+id/linearLayout1"
  android:layout_height="wrap_content"
  android:layout_width="match_parent"
  android:orientation="vertical">

  <Button android:background="@color/translucent_red"
    android:layout_width="match_parent"
    android:layout_height="wrap_content"
    android:text="Button"
    android:id="@+id/button8"></Button>
</LinearLayout>
```

Against a white background, the value #7F00 looks like elementary-school pink.

A hexadecimal digit is an ordinary decimal digit or one of the letters *A, B, C, D, E,* or *F.* (Either uppercase or lowercase letters are okay.) The letter *A* stands for 10, *B* stands for 11, and so on up to *F,* which stands for 15. A two-digit hex number stands for "the right digit, plus 16 times the left digit." For example, A5 stands for 5 + (16 × 10), which is 165. With only one hex digit, you can represent the `int` values from 0 to 15, inclusive. With two hex digits, you can represent the `int` values from 0 to 255, inclusive.

android:visibility

An Android view has one of three visibility values — `android.view.View.VISIBLE`, `android.view.View.INVISIBLE`, or `android.view.View.GONE`. The first value — `VISIBLE` — is self-explanatory. The difference between `INVISIBLE` and `GONE` is as follows: An `INVISIBLE` view takes up space; a view that's `GONE` takes up no space. For example, in Figure 1-12, an `INVISIBLE` view (Button2) separates Button1 from Button3. If I change Button2's visibility to `GONE`, Button1 butts up against Button3. (See Figure 1-13.)

Figure 1-12: Button2 is INVISIBLE.

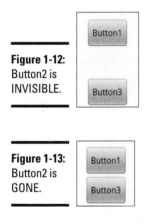

Figure 1-13: Button2 is GONE.

In Figure 1-13, Button2 is gone but not forgotten. See this chapter's "Frame Layout" section for more details.

Relative Layout

A relative layout describes the placement of each view compared with other views. For example, in a relative layout, you might place Button2 beneath Button1 and place Button3 to the right of Button1. Listing 1-7 has some code, and Figure 1-14 shows the resulting screen.

Listing 1-7: Using a Relative Layout

```xml
<?xml version="1.0" encoding="utf-8"?>
<RelativeLayout xmlns:android=
        "http://schemas.android.com/apk/res/android"
    android:orientation="vertical"
    android:layout_height="match_parent"
    android:layout_width="match_parent">

    <Button android:layout_alignParentTop="true"
            android:layout_alignParentLeft="true"

        android:text="Button1" android:id="@+id/button1"
        android:layout_height="wrap_content"
        android:layout_width="wrap_content"></Button>

    <Button android:layout_alignParentLeft="true"
            android:layout_below="@+id/button1"

        android:text="Button2" android:id="@+id/button2"
        android:layout_height="wrap_content"
        android:layout_width="wrap_content"></Button>

    <Button android:layout_alignParentTop="true"
            android:layout_toRightOf="@+id/button1"

        android:text="Button3" android:id="@+id/button3"
        android:layout_height="wrap_content"
        android:layout_width="wrap_content"></Button>

    <Button android:layout_below="@+id/button2"
            android:layout_alignLeft="@+id/button3"

        android:text="Button4" android:id="@+id/button4"
        android:layout_height="wrap_content"
        android:layout_width="wrap_content"></Button>

</RelativeLayout>
```

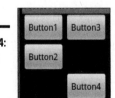

Figure 1-14:
Buttons in
a relative
layout.

Coding Android's relative layouts can be complicated. I have trouble remembering which `android:id` goes with which view's `android:layout_toRightOf`. I can easily goof up by creating a circular reference.

But don't give up on relative layouts! For complicated designs, people try creating vast nests of linear layouts within other linear layouts. Things go well until someone runs the code. Excessive nesting of linear layouts slows down a processor.

Android has two tools to help wean you away from nested linear layouts. One is the hierarchy viewer. The *hierarchy viewer* is an executable file in your SDK's tools directory. The hierarchy viewer's tree displays the nesting of your layout's objects.

Figure 1-15 contains an embarrassing hierarchy viewer analysis of one of my recent projects. Each rounded rectangle represents a view, and the length of the tree (from left to right) shows how deep the nesting goes for this particular project. Some of the tree's branches are seven levels deep, and the processor can't draw a view without first calculating the views to its left along the tree's branches. So the processor chugs slowly as it tries to render the whole scene.

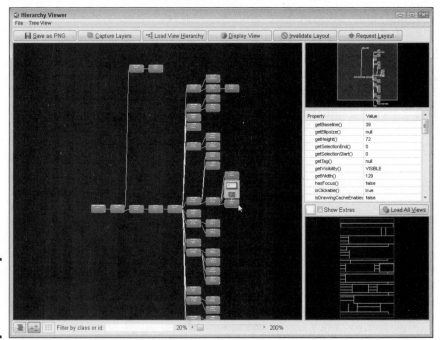

Figure 1-15: The hierarchy viewer.

A run of the hierarchy viewer tells you how deeply nested your layouts are. With the viewer's tree in mind, you can look for ways to eliminate some of the nesting.

Another tool that's useful in the fight against nested layouts is a refactoring tool in Eclipse. Here's how you use it:

1. **Use Eclipse's Graphical Layout editor to create a horrible collection of linear layouts within linear layouts.**

2. **In the Graphical Layout editor, select the outermost linear layout.**

3. **In Eclipse's main menu, choose Refactor⇨Android⇨Change Layout.**

   The Change Layout dialog box appears.

4. **In the Change Layout dialog box's drop-down list, choose Relative Layout.**

5. **Just for fun, click Preview.**

   Eclipse shows you all the ways it plans to change your XML code. (See Figure 1-16.)

6. **Click OK.**

   Voilá! You have an efficient relative layout. The new relative layout looks exactly like your old network of linear layouts. But unlike a bunch of nested linear layouts, the relative layout is computationally efficient.

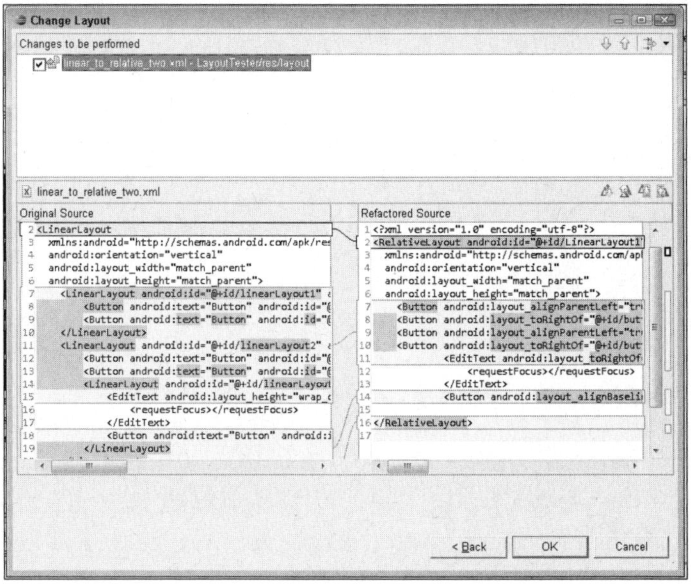

Figure 1-16: Eclipse compares your old code to your new code.

Book IV
Chapter 1

Lay Out Your Stuff

Table Layout

A table layout has rows, and each row contains some views. If you do nothing to override the defaults, the views line up to form columns.

For example, the table layout in Figure 1-17 has three table rows. Each table row contains buttons.

```
<TableLayout ... >
    <TableRow ...>
        <Button ... android:layout_width="wrap content"
                ... android:text="Button">
        <Button ... android:layout_width="wrap content"
                ... android:text="Button">
        <Button ... android:layout_width="wrap content"
                ... android:text="Button">
    </TableRow>

    <TableRow ...>
        <Button ... android:layout_width="wrap content"
                ... android:text="Button">
        <Button ... android:layout_width="wrap content"
                ... android:text="Wide button">
    </TableRow>

    <TableRow ...>
        <Button ... android:layout_width="wrap content"
                ... android:text="Button">
        <Button ... android:layout_width="wrap content"
                ... android:text="Btn.">
        <Button ... android:layout_width="wrap content"
                ... android:text="Button">
    </TableRow>

</TableLayout>
```

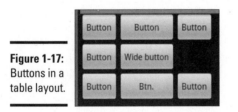

Figure 1-17: Buttons in a table layout.

Frame Layout

A frame layout displays one view. What good is that?

Well, to be more precise (and less sensational), a frame layout displays views one in front of another. (Put on your 3D glasses and think of a frame layout as an outward-pointing linear layout.) Because views tend to cover the stuff behind them, a frame layout normally displays only one view — namely, whatever's in front.

Frame layouts usually serve one of two purposes:

+ A frame layout might display a small view superimposed on a larger view (such as text on an image).

+ A frame layout might store several views, only one of which is visible at any point in time. Using the frame layout, you change what appears in a certain place on the screen.

This section's example illustrates both ideas. You start with a word superimposed on an image, which is in turn superimposed on top of another image. (See Figure 1-18.)

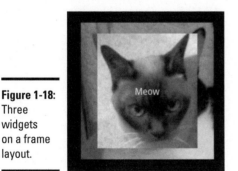

Figure 1-18:
Three
widgets
on a frame
layout.

When the user touches the screen, two of the three items disappear. (See Figure 1-19.) The screen cycles through the three images, changing the image whenever the user touches the screen. (See Figures 1-20 and 1-21.)

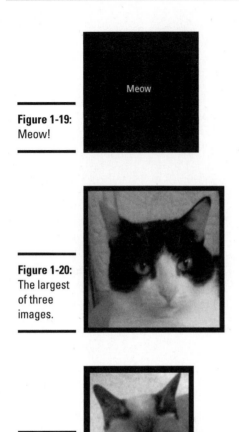

Figure 1-19:
Meow!

Figure 1-20:
The largest
of three
images.

Figure 1-21:
The midsize
image.

(I know what you're thinking: "The author looks for excuses to show pictures of his cats." That's only partly true. I include lots of illustrations to help you visualize the code's behavior. Anyway, pictures of cats make perfect clip art. Cats don't complain when you use their least favorite profiles. Pictures of cats are better than pictures of your family members because readers seldom stalk cats. Best of all, no one's figured out how to patent the domestic cat. I can't be sued for putting cat pictures in my book. Not yet, anyway.)

Listing 1-8 shows you the XML code for the app in Figures 1-18 to 1-21.

Listing 1-8:   Creating a Frame Layout

```xml
<?xml version="1.0" encoding="utf-8"?>

<FrameLayout xmlns:android=
        "http://schemas.android.com/apk/res/android"
    android:id="@+id/mainlayout"
    android:layout_height="fill_parent"
    android:layout_width="fill_parent"
    android:orientation="vertical"
    android:onClick="rotate">

    <ImageView android:src="@drawable/calico"

        android:layout_height="wrap_content"
        android:layout_width="wrap_content"
        android:padding="5px"
        android:layout_gravity="center"
        android:id="@+id/imageViewCalico"/>

    <ImageView android:src="@drawable/burmese"

        android:layout_height="wrap_content"
        android:layout_width="wrap_content"
        android:padding="5px"
        android:layout_gravity="center"
        android:id="@+id/imageViewBurmese"/>

    <TextView android:text="@string/meow"

        android:textColor="#FFF"
        android:textSize="15sp"
        android:layout_width="wrap_content"
        android:layout_height="wrap_content"
        android:layout_gravity="center"
        android:id="@+id/textView"/>

</FrameLayout>
```

The only important business in Listing 1-8 is the order in which I declare the views. The largest image (the Calico) is the `FrameLayout` element's first child. So in Figure 1-18, the Calico appears behind the other images. If the Burmese's image was as large as the Calico's image, you wouldn't see the edges of the Calico's image in Figure 1-18. The last element in Listing 1-8 is the text view, so in Figure 1-18, the text is superimposed on top of the other elements.

Listing 1-9 has the code that rotates from image to image.

**Book IV
Chapter 1**

**Lay Out Your
Stuff**

Listing 1-9:   Coding Java with a Frame Layout

```java
package com.allmycode.layouts;

import android.app.Activity;
import android.os.Bundle;
import android.view.View;
import android.widget.ImageView;
import android.widget.TextView;

public class LayoutTesterActivity extends Activity {
  ImageView imageCalico, imageBurmese;
  TextView textView;

  @Override
  public void onCreate(Bundle savedInstanceState) {
    super.onCreate(savedInstanceState);
    setContentView(R.layout.frame);
    imageCalico =
        (ImageView) findViewById(R.id.imageViewCalico);
    imageBurmese =
        (ImageView) findViewById(R.id.imageViewBurmese);
    textView = (TextView) findViewById(R.id.textView);
  }

  int count = 0;

  public void rotate(View view) {
    switch (count++ % 3) {
    case 0:
      textView.setVisibility(View.VISIBLE);
      imageCalico.setVisibility(View.INVISIBLE);
      imageBurmese.setVisibility(View.INVISIBLE);
      break;
    case 1:
      textView.setVisibility(View.INVISIBLE);
      imageCalico.setVisibility(View.VISIBLE);
      imageBurmese.setVisibility(View.INVISIBLE);
      break;
    case 2:
      textView.setVisibility(View.INVISIBLE);
      imageCalico.setVisibility(View.INVISIBLE);
      imageBurmese.setVisibility(View.VISIBLE);
      break;
    }
  }
}
```

When the app starts running, all three views (the two images and the text view) are visible. But then Listing 1-9 cycles from one view to another. Each call to the `rotate` method makes one view visible and makes the other two views invisible.

Chapter 2: Menus, Lists, and Notifications

In This Chapter

✔ **Building options menus and context menus**

✔ **Using lists in activities as well as stand-alone activities**

✔ **Adding notifications to the status bar**

Sure, I wish I were down at my favorite cheap restaurant, ordering something that a gourmet would never eat. Alas, I am not. As much as I would prefer to talk about menus dealing with food, I'm actually going to talk about menus inside an Android application!

All about Menus

Android provides a simple mechanism for you to add menus to your applications. With Android's help, you can add the following types of menus:

✦ **Options menu:** An options menu is the menu that appears when a user presses the Menu key on a pre-Honeycomb device. (See Figure 2-1.) On a device running Android 3.0 or greater, an options menu appears when a user presses a little menu icon. (Figure 2-2 illustrates this with my development computer's emulator. Instead of a finger touching the icon, you see my mouse cursor.)

In addition, Honeycomb has an *action bar*. The action bar appears in the upper-right corner of the screen. (See Figure 2-3.)

✦ **Context menu:** A context menu is floating list of menu items that is presented when a user long-presses a view. (See Figure 2-4.)

✦ **Submenu:** A submenu is a floating list of menu items that the user opens by clicking a menu item on an options menu or on a context menu. A submenu item cannot support nested submenus.

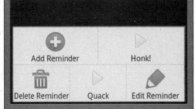

Figure 2-1:
An options menu on Gingerbread (or earlier).

Figure 2-2:
An options menu on Honeycomb (or later).

Figure 2-3:
An options menu in the action bar (Honeycomb or later).

Figure 2-4:
A context menu.

Within an options menu, you find two groups:

✦ **Icon:** These are the menu items that are available at the bottom of the screen on a pre-Honeycomb device. The device supports up to six icon-type menu items. (Again, see Figure 2-1.)

✦ **Expanded:** The expanded menu is a list of menu items that goes beyond the original six icon-type menu items.

On pre-Honeycomb devices, Android automatically adds a More item when you put more than six items on an options menu. (See Figure 2-5.) When the user clicks the More item, an expanded menu appears. (See Figure 2-6.)

In a post-Honeycomb world, items can stack up in the action bar and in the action bar's overflow bin. (See Figure 2-7.) You control this behavior with an `android:showAsAction="ifRoom|withText"` attribute.

In this chapter, you create an options menu and a context menu.

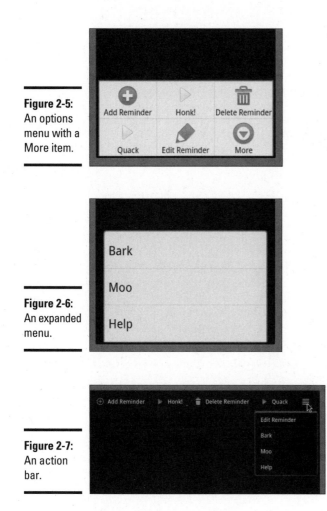

Figure 2-5:
An options menu with a More item.

Figure 2-6:
An expanded menu.

Figure 2-7:
An action bar.

Book IV Chapter 2

Menus, Lists, and Notifications

Creating an Options Menu

You can use Java code or an XML document to create a menu. If you use XML, your document lives in a `res/menu` directory. The preferred method of creating menus is to define menus through XML. This helps separate the menu definition from the actual application code.

Defining the XML file

To define an XML menu, follow these steps:

1. **Create a menu folder in the res directory.**

2. **Add a list_menu.xml file to the menu directory.**

3. **Type the code here into the list_menu.xml file:**

```
<?xml version="1.0" encoding="utf-8"?>
<menu xmlns:android=
    "http://schemas.android.com/apk/res/android">
  <item android:id="@+id/menu_insert"
        android:icon="@android:drawable/ic_menu_add"
        android:title="@string/menu_insert" />
  <item android:id="@+id/make_noise"
        android:icon="@android:drawable/ic_media_play"
        android:title="@string/honk" />
</menu>
```

The values @android:drawable/ic_menu_add and @android:drawable/ic_media_play are built-in Android icons. You don't have to provide these bitmaps in your res/drawable folders. The ldpi, mdpi, and hdpi versions of this icon are all built into the Android platform.

All resources in the android.R class are available for you to use in your application and are recommended because they give your application a common and consistent user interface and user experience with the Android platform. To view other resources available to you, view the android.R.drawable documentation here: http://developer.android.com/reference/android/R.drawable.html.

4. **Create new string resources with the names menu_insert and honk.**

5. **Add the code shown in bold here to your project's main activity class:**

```
@Override
public boolean onCreateOptionsMenu(Menu menu) {
    super.onCreateOptionsMenu(menu);
    MenuInflater inflater = getMenuInflater();
    inflater.inflate(R.menu.list_menu, menu);
    return true;
}
```

When you *inflate* an XML document, Android turns the XML code into something resembling Java code (a Java object, perhaps).

In the preceding code, I get a MenuInflater that's capable of inflating menus from XML resources. Then I inflate the XML code to get a real live Java object.

When you implement the onCreateOptionsMenu method, you must return either true or false. If you return false, Android doesn't display your menu! How rude!

6. **Run the application.**

Depending on the current wind direction, you see the stuff in Figure 2-2 or Figure 2-8 when you click the Menu button or menu icon. You might even see the action bar items in Figure 2-3 (without having to click anything).

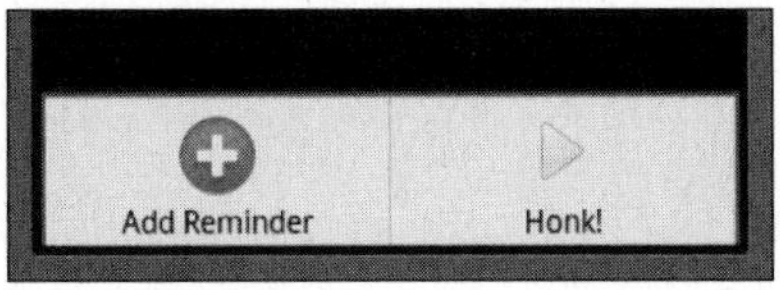

Figure 2-8:
Menu items
in the action
bar.

Handling user actions

The menu has been created, and now you want to perform some type of action when it's clicked. To do this, add the method in Listing 2-1 to your app's main activity.

Listing 2-1:   Responding to a Menu Item Click

```
@Override
public boolean onOptionsItemSelected(MenuItem item) {

  switch (item.getItemId()) {

  case R.id.menu_insert:
    createReminder();
    return true;

  case R.id.make_noise:
    MediaPlayer mediaPlayer =
        MediaPlayer.create(this, R.raw.honk);
    mediaPlayer.start();
    return true;

  }
  return super.onOptionsItemSelected(item);
}
```

In your `onOptionsItemSelected` method, you do the old switcheroo to find out exactly which item the user clicks. You match the clicked item's ID with the ID of the items in your `list_menu.xml` document. In this example, your menu has two items. One item creates a reminder, and the other plays a sound.

You still have to define the `createReminder` method, but in the meantime, you can add a sound to your project. To add a sound, first create a `res/raw` folder and then copy an MP3 file into that `res/raw` folder. After renaming the file `honk.mp3`, you're ready to make some noise.

**Book IV
Chapter 2**

**Menus, Lists, and
Notifications**

The method in Listing 2-1 returns `true`. This `true` value tells Android that you've finished handling the user's selection. If you return `false`, Android passes the selection event to whatever other code might be waiting for it.

Creating a reminder

The method in Listing 2-2 responds to a call in Listing 2-1. Add Listing 2-2's code to your project's main activity.

Listing 2-2:   Calling an Activity to Create a New Reminder

```
private static final int ACTIVITY_CREATE = 0;

private void createReminder() {
  Intent intent =
      new Intent(this, ReminderEditActivity.class);
  startActivityForResult(intent, ACTIVITY_CREATE);
}
```

The `createReminder` method starts an instance of `ReminderEditActivity`. The `startActivityForResult` call allows you to get a result back from the `ReminderEditActivity`. In this app, you use the result to repopulate a list with the newly added reminder.

For straight talk about the `startActivityForResult` method, see Book III, Chapter 1.

Listing 2-3 contains an embarrassingly simple `ReminderEditActivity` class.

Listing 2-3:   Creating a Reminder

```
package com.allmycode.menus;

import android.app.Activity;
import android.content.Intent;
import android.os.Bundle;
import android.view.View;
import android.widget.EditText;

public class ReminderEditActivity extends Activity {
  EditText editText;

  @Override
  public void onCreate(Bundle b) {
    super.onCreate(b);
    setContentView(R.layout.reminder_edit);
    editText = (EditText) findViewById(R.id.editText1);
  }
```

```
public void onPostButtonClick(View view) {
  Intent intent = new Intent();
  intent
    .putExtra("text", editText.getText().toString());
  setResult(Activity.RESULT_OK, intent);
  finish();
  }
}
```

When the user clicks a button, the ReminderEditActivity sets its result and finishes its run. The result comes from the activity's EditText widget.

When you create a new Android project, Eclipse automatically adds an <activity> element to the project's AndroidManifest.xml document. But when you add an additional activity to an *existing* project, you must manually add an <activity> element. And yes, I made this mistake for the thousandth time when I first created this section's example.

My no-nonsense layout for the activity in Listing 2-3 is shown in Listing 2-4. The activity's screen is shown in Figure 2-9.

Listing 2-4:   A Layout for the Activity in Listing 2-3

```xml
<?xml version="1.0" encoding="utf-8"?>
<LinearLayout xmlns:android=
      "http://schemas.android.com/apk/res/android"
    android:orientation="vertical"
    android:layout_width="match_parent"
    android:layout_height="match_parent"
    android:gravity="center_horizontal">

    <EditText android:layout_height="wrap_content"
            android:id="@+id/editText1"
            android:layout_width="match_parent"
            android:hint="Type a reminder here.">
        <requestFocus></requestFocus>
    </EditText>

    <Button android:layout_height="wrap_content"
            android:id="@+id/button1"
            android:layout_width="wrap_content"
            android:text="@string/post"
            android:onClick="onPostButtonClick"></Button>

</LinearLayout>
```

Figure 2-9:
Adding a
reminder.

Finish writing Chapter 2.

Post

Putting the new reminder in a list

To do what is spelled out in this section's title — putting the new reminder in a list — add the code in Listing 2-5 to your project's main activity.

Listing 2-5: Using another Activity's Result

```
ListView listView;
ArrayList<String> listItems = new ArrayList<String>();
ArrayAdapter<String> adapter;

@Override
public void onCreate(Bundle savedInstanceState) {
  super.onCreate(savedInstanceState);
  setContentView(R.layout.main);
  listView = (ListView) findViewById(R.id.listView1);
  adapter =
      new ArrayAdapter<String>(this,
          R.layout.my_list_layout, listItems);
  listView.setAdapter(adapter);
}

@Override
protected void onActivityResult(int requestCode,
    int resultCode, Intent intent) {
  if (resultCode == RESULT_OK) {
    listItems.add(intent
        .getStringExtra("reminder_text"));
    adapter.notifyDataSetChanged();
  }
}
```

The code in Listing 2-5 refers to two new resources — namely, R.id.listView1 and R.layout.my_list_layout. The first is a ListView widget. You create it by adding a <ListView> element to your main.xml layout file. The following element works just fine:

```
<ListView android:id="@+id/listView1"
          android:layout_height="wrap_content"
          android:layout_width="match_parent">
</ListView>
```

The `R.layout.my_list_layout` resource in Listing 2-5 is new and different. This layout describes an item in the list view. Android uses this layout many times (as many times as there are items in the list view). So create a `res/layout/my_list_layout.xml` file, and put the code from Listing 2-6 into the file.

Listing 2-6: The res/layout/my_list_layout.xml Document

```xml
<?xml version="1.0" encoding="utf-8"?>
<TextView xmlns:android=
        "http://schemas.android.com/apk/res/android"
    android:id="@+id/identView"
    android:layout_width="wrap_content"
    android:layout_height="wrap_content">
</TextView>
```

According to the code in Listing 2-6, each list view item has its own text view. That's all!

With the Android SDK, you don't add an item directly to an onscreen list. Instead, you add items to a Java list (an `ArrayList`, for example). Then you tie the Java list to the onscreen list using an adapter. An *adapter* separates your code's business logic from the app's visible presentation. The adapter also smooths the look of changes in the onscreen list.

In Listing 2-5, I create a new adapter using three parts:

✦ The ever-present context — namely, `this`

✦ The list view's layout — namely, `R.layout.my_list_layout`

✦ An `ArrayList` of items

The `ArrayList` of items contains Java `String` objects, each of which is a reminder for me to do something (such as `Pay your taxes`, `Take out the trash`, or `Come up for air`). The new adapter contains enough information to connect the `ArrayList` with the visible `listView` object. Then, still in Listing 2-5, I marry the `ArrayList` to the `listView` by calling `listView.setAdapter(adapter)`.

When the code in Listing 2-3 finishes running, Android calls the `onActivity Result` method in Listing 2-5. The `onActivityResult` method grabs the newly created result and adds that result to the code's `ArrayList` (the `listItems` object). Finally, to make sure that the screen knows about this addition, the code calls `adapter.notifyDataSetChanged()`.

Calling `setAdapter` (as in Listing 2-5) binds a Java list to an onscreen list. The call does *not* bind one variable name to another. So, for example, in Listing 2-5, if you follow the `listView.setAdapter(adapter)` call with a second `adapter = new ArrayAdapter` statement, the second assignment has no effect.

The code in Listing 2-5 overrides an `onActivityResult` method. For several nice paragraphs about Android's `onActivityResult` method, see Book III, Chapter 1.

After all is said and done (or after all is written and read; or all is developed, published, and then downloaded) the user sees a screen like the one in Figure 2-10.

Figure 2-10:
A list of
items
created
by this
section's
example.

Figure 2-10 illustrates the result of a few of the Add Reminder menu item selections. (Refer to Figure 2-8.) I thought for a while about illustrating a Honk item selection. My only idea was to ask Wiley to add a little speaker to this page, like one of those greeting cards that plays "Somewhere My Love" when you open it. But in the end, I didn't have the nerve to make that request. What do you think? It's a very practical idea, isn't it?

Creating a Context Menu

When the user long-presses a view, Android displays a context menu. The context menu hovers above the current activity and allows users to choose various options. (Refer to Figure 2-4.)

Making the context menu appear

Listing 2-7 contains the XML document describing this section's context menu.

Listing 2-7:   The res/menu/list_menu_item_longpress.xml Document

```
<?xml version="1.0" encoding="utf-8"?>
<menu xmlns:android=
        "http://schemas.android.com/apk/res/android">
    <item android:id="@+id/menu_delete"
          android:title="@string/menu_delete" />
    <item android:id="@+id/make_noise2"
          android:title="Make a quacking sound" />
</menu>
```

Notice that I don't put any `icon` attributes in this menu. Context menus don't have icons. They're simply lists of menu options that float above the current activity.

You want Android to inflate Listing 2-7's menu when the user long-presses a list view item. To achieve this, you make two connections:

✦ Connect the `listView` object (declared in Listing 2-5) with context menus in general. You do this by adding one statement to Listing 2-5's `onCreate` method.

```
registerForContextMenu(listView);
```

✦ Connect context menus in general with the menu in Listing 2-7. Listing 2-8 shows you how.

Listing 2-8:   Handling a Long Click

```
@Override
public void onCreateContextMenu(ContextMenu menu,
    View view, ContextMenuInfo menuInfo) {
  super.onCreateContextMenu(menu, view, menuInfo);
  MenuInflater inflater = getMenuInflater();
  inflater.inflate(R.menu.list_menu_item_longpress,
      menu);
}
```

Listing 2-8 is very much like the code used in Step 5 earlier in the "Defining the XML file" section. The method name is different, and the method in Listing 2-8 doesn't return a `boolean` value. Other than that, it's the same old stuff.

Handling context menu item selections

To handle the selection of a context menu item, add the code from Listing 2-9 to your main activity.

Listing 2-9: Responding to a Context Menu Click

```
@Override
public boolean onContextItemSelected(MenuItem item) {

  switch (item.getItemId()) {

  case R.id.menu_delete:
    deleteReminder(item);
    return true;

  case R.id.make_noise2:
    MediaPlayer mediaPlayer =
        MediaPlayer.create(this, R.raw.quack);
    mediaPlayer.start();
    return true;

  }
  return super.onContextItemSelected(item);
}

void deleteReminder(MenuItem item) {
  AdapterContextMenuInfo info =
      (AdapterContextMenuInfo) item.getMenuInfo();
  listItems.remove(info.position);
  adapter.notifyDataSetChanged();
}
```

Listing 2-9 looks a lot like Listings 2-1 and 2-2. The most significant difference is in the code to delete a list view item. Listing 2-9 doesn't start a secondary activity, so you don't need an intent, and you don't need an `onActivityResult` method like the one in Listing 2-5.

Grabbing information about the selected list view item is one step more complicated that you might expect. The reason for this is that you're dealing with two different items — the list view item that the user long-pressed and the context menu item that the user clicked.

In Listing 2-9, I call `getMenuInfo` to create an `AdapterContextMenuInfo` instance. Then I use the instance's public `position` field to tell me which list view item the user long-pressed. I remove the list view item corresponding to the `info.position` value.

More Stuff about Lists

The previous sections describe list views, but there are tons more to lists than list views. This section covers Android's `ListActivity` class and shows more tricks you can do with lists.

Creating a list activity

On a typical phone screen, you might not have room to add a list view to an existing activity's layout. An alternative is to create a separate activity containing nothing but the list. This strategy is so commonly used that the makers of Android created a special class for it. A `ListActivity` instance is an activity whose sole purpose is to display a list.

And speaking of lists, Listing 2-10 lists a `ListActivity`'s code.

Listing 2-10:   An Activity That's Also a List

```
package com.allmycode.lists;

import java.util.ArrayList;

import android.app.ListActivity;
import android.content.Intent;
import android.os.Bundle;
import android.widget.ArrayAdapter;

public class MyListActivity extends ListActivity {

  public void onCreate(Bundle savedInstanceState) {
    super.onCreate(savedInstanceState);
    Intent intent = getIntent();
    String isChecked =
        intent.getData().getSchemeSpecificPart();

    ArrayList<Integer> listItems =
        new ArrayList<Integer>();
    for (int i = 0; i < 5; i++) {
      if (isChecked.charAt(i) == '1') {
        listItems.add(i);
      }
    }

    setListAdapter(new ArrayAdapter<Integer>(this,
        R.layout.my_list_layout, listItems));
  }
}
```

The code in Listing 2-10 extends `android.app.ListActivity`, which is a subclass of `Activity`. So the listing's `MyListActivity` class is an Android activity. But notice that Listing 2-10 has no `setContentView` call. Instead, a `ListActivity` instance gets its layout from the call to `setListAdapter`. This `setListAdapter` call is strikingly similar to some code in Listing 2-5, and that's no accident. After all, a list is a list is a list (whatever that means).

Anyway, Listings 2-5 and 2-10 even use the same `R.layout.my_list_layout` resource — the layout described in Listing 2-6. Like a `ListView` instance's layout, a `ListActivity` instance's layout describes only one list item.

This section's example works best if you start a brand-new project for Listing 2-10. That being the case, copy the `res/layout/my_list_layout.xml` file from Listing 2-6 to this section's project.

The code in Listing 2-10 isn't the project's main activity. So to get information about the list's contents, the main activity passes an intent containing a URI of the following kind:

```
checked:01011
```

I made up this opaque URI format in order to pass five yes-or-no values from the main activity to the list activity. With the `01011` URI, the list activity's screen looks like the stuff in Figure 2-11.

Figure 2-11: The result of sending checked: 01011 to this section's list activity.

The sequence `01011` is my way of representing "no" 0, "yes" 1, "no" 2, "yes" 3, and "yes" 4. So the numbers 1, 3, and 4 appear as items in the list. The loop in Listing 2-10 picks the 0s and 1s out of the incoming intent's URI.

Here's one more thing to remember about this section's list activity. The activity's incoming intent has my made-up `checked` data scheme. So in the project's `AndroidManifest.xml` document, I specify the `checked` scheme in the list activity's intent filter:

```
<activity android:name=".MyListActivity">
    <intent-filter>
        <data android:scheme="checked" />
    </intent-filter>
</activity>
```

A client for the list activity

Listing 2-11 contains the code for a main activity. This main activity gives the user a way to fire up the app's list activity.

Listing 2-11:   Code to Trigger the List Activity

```
package com.allmycode.lists;

import android.app.Activity;
import android.content.Intent;
import android.net.Uri;
import android.os.Bundle;
import android.view.View;
import android.widget.CheckBox;

public class MainActivity extends Activity {
    CheckBox[] checkBoxes = new CheckBox[5];

    @Override
    public void onCreate(Bundle savedInstanceState) {
        super.onCreate(savedInstanceState);
        setContentView(R.layout.main);
        checkBoxes[0] = (CheckBox) findViewById(R.id.a);
        checkBoxes[1] = (CheckBox) findViewById(R.id.b);
        checkBoxes[2] = (CheckBox) findViewById(R.id.c);
        checkBoxes[3] = (CheckBox) findViewById(R.id.d);
        checkBoxes[4] = (CheckBox) findViewById(R.id.e);
    }

    public void onShowListClick(View view) {
      Intent intent =
          new Intent(this, MyListActivity.class);

      StringBuffer isChecked = new StringBuffer("");

      for (CheckBox box : checkBoxes) {
        isChecked.append(box.isChecked() ? "1" : "0");
      }
      intent.setData(Uri.parse("checked:"
          + isChecked.toString()));

      startActivity(intent);
    }
}
```

Listing 2-11 maintains an array of CheckBox instances. A loop composes a string of 0s and 1s from the states of the five boxes. Then Listing 2-11 wraps these 0s and 1s in an intent's URI, and passes the intent to the list activity.

Listing 2-12 describes the main activity's layout, and Figure 2-12 shows the layout as it appears on the user's screen.

Listing 2-12:   The res/layout/main.xml Document

```xml
<?xml version="1.0" encoding="utf-8"?>
<LinearLayout xmlns:android=
      "http://schemas.android.com/apk/res/android"
    android:orientation="vertical"
    android:layout_width="fill_parent"
    android:layout_height="fill_parent"
    android:gravity="center_horizontal">

    <CheckBox android:id="@+id/a"
              android:text="@string/box0"
              android:layout_height="wrap_content"
              android:layout_width="wrap_content">
    </CheckBox>
    <CheckBox android:id="@+id/b"
              android:text="@string/box1"
              android:layout_height="wrap_content"
              android:layout_width="wrap_content">
    </CheckBox>
    <CheckBox android:id="@+id/c"
              android:text="@string/box2"
              android:layout_height="wrap_content"
              android:layout_width="wrap_content">
    </CheckBox>
    <CheckBox android:id="@+id/d"
              android:text="@string/box3"
              android:layout_height="wrap_content"
              android:layout_width="wrap_content">
    </CheckBox>
    <CheckBox android:id="@+id/e"
              android:text="@string/box4"
              android:layout_height="wrap_content"
              android:layout_width="wrap_content">
    </CheckBox>

    <Button android:text="@string/show_list"
            android:onClick="onShowListClick"
            android:layout_height="wrap_content"
            android:id="@+id/button1"
            android:layout_width="wrap_content">
    </Button>

</LinearLayout>
```

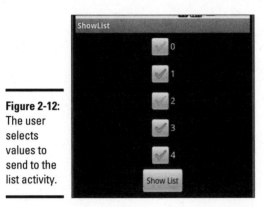

Figure 2-12: The user selects values to send to the list activity.

Displaying Two (or More) Values in a List

When you display a list on the user's screen, you often display more than one value per entry. Maybe each entry has a title and a subtitle, or a keyword and an icon. Anyway, the preceding section's list has only one value in each list entry. Displaying more than one value is both easy and difficult. (Huh?)

It's easy because switching from single-value entries to multi-value entries doesn't involve any large strategy changes in your code. You still have a Java list, an onscreen list, and an adapter. Whatever tricks you use to pass data to a list activity work equally well with both single- and multi-value entries.

Displaying more than one value is difficult because you have to wield a complicated data structure in which the Java list meshes with the onscreen list. Figure 2-13 describes the situation.

A Java *map* is a list of key/value pairs. To create an adapter, you create a Java list of maps. Each map in the Java list represents one entry in the onscreen list.

So now the trick is to tell Android how one map turns into one onscreen entry. To do this, you create two arrays — an array containing the map key names and an array containing an entry's views. Android associates the key names with the views as if they're partners in a contra dance. Listing 2-13 contains the code.

The Java data structure
Adapter:

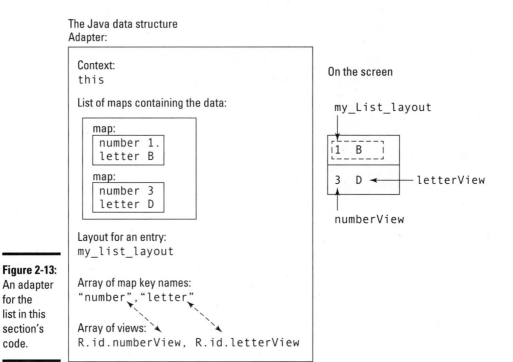

Figure 2-13:
An adapter
for the
list in this
section's
code.

Listing 2-13:   Putting Two Values in Each List Entry

```
package com.allmycode.lists;

import java.util.ArrayList;
import java.util.HashMap;

import android.app.ListActivity;
import android.content.Intent;
import android.os.Bundle;
import android.widget.SimpleAdapter;

public class MyListActivity extends ListActivity {

  public void onCreate(Bundle savedInstanceState) {
    super.onCreate(savedInstanceState);
    Intent intent = getIntent();
    String isChecked =
        intent.getData().getSchemeSpecificPart();

    ArrayList<HashMap<String, String>> data =
        new ArrayList<HashMap<String, String>>();
```

```
    for (int i = 0; i < 5; i++) {
      if (isChecked.charAt(i) == '1') {
        HashMap<String, String> map =
            new HashMap<String, String>();
        map.put("number", Integer.toString(i));
        map.put("letter",
            (new Character((char) (i + 65))).toString());
        data.add(map);
      }
    }

    String[] columnNames = { "number", "letter" };
    int[] textViews = new int[2];
    textViews[0] = R.id.numberView;
    textViews[1] = R.id.letterView;

    setListAdapter(new SimpleAdapter(this, data,
        R.layout.my_list_layout, columnNames, textViews));
  }

  static final String
      letterToIntegerString(String letter) {
    return Integer
        .toString((int) (letter.charAt(0) - 65));
  }
}
```

This section's example uses the main activity from Listing 2-11. Other than the enhanced list activity in Listing 2-13, the only other change from single-valued to double-valued entries is the use of a new layout. The new layout for a list entry (see Listing 2-14) has two text views instead of one.

Listing 2-14:   A res/layout/my_list_layout.xml Document with Two Text Views

```
<?xml version="1.0" encoding="utf-8"?>
<LinearLayout xmlns:android=
    "http://schemas.android.com/apk/res/android"
    android:layout_width="match_parent"
    android:layout_height="match_parent"
    android:orientation="horizontal">

    <TextView android:id="@+id/numberView"
        android:layout_width="wrap_content"
        android:layout_height="wrap_content"></TextView>
    <TextView android:id="@+id/letterView"
        android:layout_width="wrap_content"
        android:layout_height="wrap_content"
        android:padding="20dp"></TextView>

</LinearLayout>
```

Listing 2-13 puts into code what Figure 2-13 illustrates with a drawing. The most noteworthy feature in Listing 2-13 is the use of a `SimpleAdapter`. Unlike the `ArrayAdapter` of Listing 2-10, a `SimpleAdapter` can handle multi-value list entries.

To connect an onscreen list with the rows in a database table, use the `android.widget.SimpleCursorAdapter`.

Figure 2-14 shows the result of sending the numbers 1, 3, and 4 to this section's list activity. To keep the example tidy, I don't do anything fancy to associate a second value with each number. Instead, I call my `letterTo IntegerString` method. The method converts from `int` values 0, 1, 2, 3, and 4 to `char` values `'A'`, `'B'`, `'C'`, `'D'`, and `'E'`.

Figure 2-14:
A list with two values in each entry.

Notifying the User

One of Android's cool features is its status bar. On a small-screen phone, the status bar appears at the top of the screen. The user drags the bar downward to see all the current notifications. (See Figure 2-15.) On a big-screen tablet, the status bar appears near the lower-right corner. The user taps the lower-right corner to make notifications appear. (See Figure 2-16.)

In this section, you add notifications to the device's status bar. In addition to its visual elements, a notification can have its own intent. The intent triggers an activity when the user clicks the notification.

Figure 2-15:
Notifications on a small-screen phone.

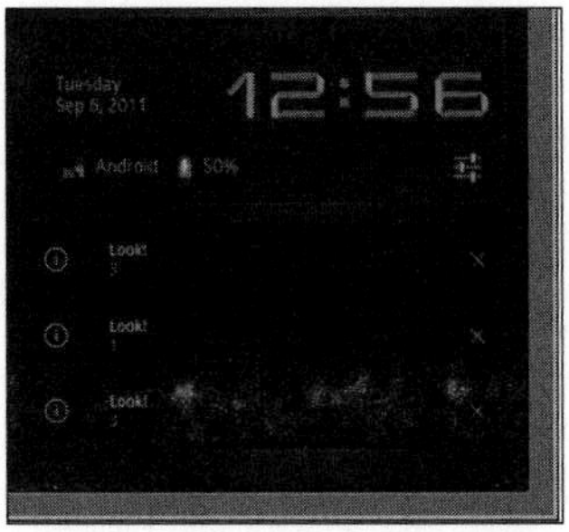

Figure 2-16:
Notifications
on a tablet
device.

Notify the user on any device

In the previous sections, you create a list activity from a bunch of check boxes. But in those sections, the list items are passive. If the user clicks an item, nothing happens. (Well, the user smudges the screen at bit, but that doesn't count.)

This section adds code to the activity in Listing 2-10. The new code, which responds to the clicking of a list item, is in Listing 2-15.

Listing 2-15:   Using the onListItemClick Method

```
package com.allmycode.lists;

import java.util.ArrayList;

import android.app.ListActivity;
import android.app.Notification;
import android.app.NotificationManager;
import android.app.PendingIntent;
import android.content.Context;
import android.content.Intent;
import android.net.Uri;
import android.os.Bundle;
import android.view.View;
import android.widget.ArrayAdapter;
import android.widget.ListView;

public class MyListActivity extends ListActivity {
  int notificationNumber = 0;
  NotificationManager notificationMgr;

  /* Code copied from Listing 2-10... */

  public void onCreate(Bundle savedInstanceState) {
    super.onCreate(savedInstanceState);
    Intent intent = getIntent();
    String isChecked =
        intent.getData().getSchemeSpecificPart();
```

(continued)

Listing 2-15 *(continued)*

```java
    ArrayList<Integer> listItems =
        new ArrayList<Integer>();
    for (int i = 0; i < 5; i++) {
      if (isChecked.charAt(i) == '1') {
        listItems.add(i);
      }
    }

    setListAdapter(new ArrayAdapter<Integer>(this,
        R.layout.my_list_layout, listItems));
  }

  /* Code to respond to a list item click... */

  @Override
  public void onListItemClick(ListView listView,
      View view, int position, long id) {

    makeNewNotification(listView, position);
  }

  /* Code to create a status bar notification... */

  private void makeNewNotification(ListView listView,
      int position) {

    String numberValue =
        ((Integer) listView.getItemAtPosition(position))
            .toString();

    Notification notification = new Notification();
    notification.icon =
        android.R.drawable.ic_menu_info_details;
    notification.flags = Notification.FLAG_AUTO_CANCEL;

    Intent intent =
        new Intent(this, YetAnotherActivity.class);
    intent.setData(Uri.parse("number:" + numberValue));
    intent.addFlags(Intent.FLAG_ACTIVITY_NEW_TASK);
    PendingIntent pendingIntent =
        PendingIntent.getActivity(this, 0, intent, 0);

    notification.setLatestEventInfo(this, "Look!",
        numberValue, pendingIntent);

    notificationMgr = (NotificationManager)
        getSystemService(Context.NOTIFICATION_SERVICE);

    notificationMgr.notify(notificationNumber++,
        notification);
  }
```

```
@Override
public void onDestroy() {
  super.onDestroy();
  for (int i = 0; i <= notificationNumber; i++) {
    notificationMgr.cancel(i);
  }
 }
}
```

To respond to a list item click, simply add an `onListItemClick` method to your code. This section's example uses two of the method's four parameters — namely, the list view that the user clicked and the position number of the clicked entry. In Listing 2-15, I pass those parameters' values to my homegrown `makeNewNotification` method.

All the excitement surrounding the status bar is inside my `makeNew Notification` method. Here's what happens inside the method:

✦ Using the list view's `getItemAtPostion` method, I find the number value of the list item that the user clicked. I store this value for safekeeping in my `numberValue` string.

✦ I create a new `android.app.Notification` instance, and assign values to the instance's `icon` and `flags` fields:

   • The `icon` field's `int` value refers to one of Android's standard icons.

   • The `flags` field's `FLAG_AUTO_CANCEL` value tells Android to remove the notification after the user clicks the notification.

This example has several kinds of things for the user to click. The user clicks a list item to create a notification in the status bar. The user can also click one of the notifications. That is, the user can click one of the *Look!* entries in Figure 2-15 or Figure 2-16.

In the Android SDK, you don't often assign values directly to an object's fields. That's why, in Listing 2-15, the direct assignments to `notification. icon` and to `notification.flags` might look strange. In fact, they *are* strange! Object-oriented programmers don't like messing with public fields from other people's classes. Public fields that aren't final don't shield the object's data. Anyway, if these assignments in Listing 2-15 give you the willies, just be patient. Everything's better in this chapter's final section.

✦ Continuing on the tour of Listing 2-15, the next step in displaying a notification is to create an intent:

   • The intent's purpose is to invoke `YetAnotherActivity`.

   • The intent has a URI, such as `number:3`, indicating that the user clicked either the topmost or bottommost notification in Figure 2-15.

The code in Listing 2-15 does not start an instance of `YetAnotherActivity`.

Book IV Chapter 2

Menus, Lists, and Notifications

✦ The code in Listing 2-15 turns the `YetAnotherActivity` intent into a pending intent. A *pending intent* is an intent that one component asks another component to execute.

✦ With the call to `notification.setLatestEventInfo`, the code attaches the pending intent to a new status bar notification.

The `setLatestEventInfo` method has four parameters:

- The first parameter (`this`) is a context. (So what else is new?)

- The second parameter (`"Look!"`) is the title to be displayed on the new notification. (See Figures 2-15 and 2-16.)

- The third parameter (`numberValue`) is the text to be displayed on the new notification (for example, the number 1 or the number 3 shown in Figure 2-15).

- The fourth parameter is the pending intent — the intent that Android executes if and when the user clicks the notification.

✦ Finally, the code grabs hold of a notification manager and calls the manager's `notify` method. Calling the `notify` method places the notification in the device's status bar.

The `notify` method has two parameters:

- After all the fuss in this section about creating a `notification` object, the method's second parameter (the notification itself) is old news.

- The `notify` method's first parameter is an `int` value. This `int` value — a notification's ID number — identifies the notification for future reference. For example, the `onDestroy` method in Listing 2-15 uses ID numbers to cancel all the notifications.

Notifications' ID numbers don't cross application boundaries. If two different applications create notifications with ID number 1, there's no conflict. But within an application, ID numbers shouldn't conflict. If you call `notificationMgr.notify` twice with the same ID number, Android replaces the first notification with the second. Only one of the two notifications appears in the status bar.

By the time Android calls the `onDestroy` method in Listing 2-15, some of the original notifications may have already been canceled. (The notification's `FLAG_AUTO_CANCEL` value does some of that housekeeping.) Fortunately, nothing bad happens when you try to cancel a nonexistent notification.

In case you're wondering, Listing 2-16 contains my `YetAnotherActivity` code. In the `YetAnotherActivity` class, I grab the notification's number and display it on the screen.

Listing 2-16:   Using the Result of the Pending Intent

```
package com.allmycode.lists;

import android.app.Activity;
import android.content.Intent;
import android.os.Bundle;
import android.widget.TextView;

public class YetAnotherActivity extends Activity {
  TextView textView;

  @Override
  public void onCreate(Bundle b) {
    super.onCreate(b);
    setContentView(R.layout.yet_another_layout);
    textView = (TextView) findViewById(R.id.textView1);

    Intent intent = getIntent();

    String numberValue =
        intent.getData().getSchemeSpecificPart();

    textView.setText("You selected " + numberValue + ".");
  }
}
```

Notify the user on Honeycomb and beyond

The preceding section's code works on almost any version of Android. But the code is a bit clunky. So Android's overseers recommend that you chuck some of the clunky code in favor of Honeycomb's `Notification.Builder` class.

The `Builder` class is an inner class of the `Notification` class.

So if your target device runs Honeycomb or better, don't create notifications the way your grandparents did. Instead, use the code in Listing 2-17.

Listing 2-17:   The Modern Way to Create a Status Bar Notification

```
private void makeNewNotification(ListView listView,
    int position) {

  String numberValue =
      ((Integer) listView.getItemAtPosition(position))
          .toString();
```

(continued)

Listing 2-17 *(continued)*

```
Notification.Builder builder =
    new Notification.Builder(this);
builder.setSmallIcon
    (android.R.drawable.ic_menu_info_details);
builder.setAutoCancel(true);

Intent intent =
    new Intent(this, YetAnotherActivity.class);
intent.setData(Uri.parse("number:" + numberValue));
intent.addFlags(Intent.FLAG_ACTIVITY_NEW_TASK);
PendingIntent pendingIntent =
    PendingIntent.getActivity(this, 0, intent, 0);

builder.setContentIntent(pendingIntent);
builder.setContentTitle("Look!");
builder.setContentText(numberValue);

notificationMgr = (NotificationManager)
    getSystemService(Context.NOTIFICATION_SERVICE);

notificationMgr.notify(notificationNumber++,
    builder.getNotification());
}
```

In Listing 2-17, I set the new `Notification.Builder` statements in bold-face type. The new statements are cleaner and safer because they don't rely on a notification instance's public fields. What a relief!

Chapter 3: An Android Potpourri

In This Chapter

✔ **Programming Android to make phone calls**

✔ **Working with text messages and device sensors**

✔ **Responding to multi-touch events**

✔ **Drawing things**

✔ **Distracting the user with a progress bar**

✔ **Putting Java threads to good use**

A *potpourri* is an assortment — a little of this and a little of that. It's a mixture of pleasant things related in one way or another, but not dependent on one another. It's a medley of songs or a bunch of nice-smelling dried plants. It's a salmagundi with meats, eggs, vegetables, fruits, and nuts. It's a pastiche such as Queen's "Bohemian Rhapsody." It's a plate of gefilte fish with a mix of carp, pike, perch, salmon, mullet, whitefish, and other things whose odors form an orange haze that spreads throughout the house. But in this book, a potpourri is a collection of useful programming goodies.

Making Phone Calls

Before smartphones came along, the most techno-savvy people around carried personal digital assistants (PDAs). A PDA (a PalmPilot or an iPAQ with Windows CE) did many of the things that today's smartphones do. But the early PDAs didn't make phone calls. So they didn't catch on with the general public.

An explosion in mobile device usage came when companies merged computing with telephony. In retrospect, it's not surprising. After all, communication is a "killer app." People need to share. People talk to friends, arrange meetings, send photos, and post recommendations. Exchanging ideas is one of humanity's greatest strengths.

This section puts the *phone* in *smartphone*.

Two ways to initiate a call

Making a phone call requires two steps:

1. *Dial* a phone number.

2. Press the *Call* button.

Accordingly, Android has two intent actions — one for dialing and another for calling. This section's code in Listing 3-1 illustrates both situations.

Listing 3-1:   Dialing and Calling

```
package com.allmycode.samples;

import android.app.Activity;
import android.app.AlertDialog;
import android.content.Context;
import android.content.DialogInterface;
import android.content.Intent;
import android.net.Uri;
import android.os.Bundle;
import android.telephony.TelephonyManager;
import android.view.View;
import android.view.View.OnClickListener;
import android.widget.Button;

public class MyActivity extends Activity implements
    OnClickListener {

  @Override
  public void onCreate(Bundle savedInstanceState) {
    super.onCreate(savedInstanceState);
    setContentView(R.layout.main);

    ((Button) findViewById(R.id.dialButton))
        .setOnClickListener(this);
    ((Button) findViewById(R.id.callButton))
        .setOnClickListener(this);
  }

  @Override
  public void onClick(View view) {
    boolean isOk = true;
    Intent intent = new Intent();

    if (!deviceIsAPhone()) {
      displayAlert();
      isOk = false;
    }
```

```
      if (isOk) {
        switch (view.getId()) {
        case R.id.dialButton:
          intent.setAction(Intent.ACTION_DIAL);
          break;
        case R.id.callButton:
          intent.setAction(Intent.ACTION_CALL);
          break;
        default:
          isOk = false;
        }
        intent.setData(Uri.parse("tel:234-555-6789"));
      }

      if (isOk) {
        startActivity(intent);
      }
    }

    boolean deviceIsAPhone() {
      TelephonyManager manager = (TelephonyManager)
          getSystemService(Context.TELEPHONY_SERVICE);
      return manager.getPhoneType() !=
                    TelephonyManager.PHONE_TYPE_NONE;
    }

    void displayAlert() {
      AlertDialog.Builder alertBuilder =
          new AlertDialog.Builder(this);
      alertBuilder
        .setTitle("Not a telephone!")
        .setMessage("This device can't phone make calls!")
        .setPositiveButton("OK", new MyDialogListener())
        .show();
    }

    class MyDialogListener implements
        DialogInterface.OnClickListener {
      public void onClick(DialogInterface dialog,
          int whichButton) {
      }
    }
  }
```

Before testing the code in Listing 3-1, I lay out the main activity's screen as shown in Figure 3-1.

When I run the code and press the activity's Dial button, I see my phone's familiar dialer. The dialer has my fake phone number 234-555-6789 at the top of the screen, just waiting for me to press the little phone icon. (See Figure 3-2.)

Figure 3-1:
The main
layout for
the code in
Listing 3-1.

Figure 3-2:
The result of
clicking the
Dial button.

(If your ego needs a lift, dialing a phone number with the fake 555 exchange makes you feel like an actor in a Hollywood movie.)

Pressing the activity's Call button is another story. Pressing the Call button in Figure 3-1 takes me immediately to the calling screen in Figure 3-3.

To start an activity with `Intent.ACTION_CALL`, your app must have `"android.permission.CALL_PHONE"`. (You need no special permission for `Intent.ACTION_DIAL`.)

The basic strategy in Listing 3-1 isn't complicated. You create an intent with action `Intent.ACTION_DIAL` (or `Intent.ACTION_CALL`). You add a `tel` URI to the intent and then call `startActivity`.

In Listing 3-1, you can modify the `tel` URI so that the URI has no scheme-specific part:

```
intent.setData(Uri.parse("tel:"));
```

Figure 3-3:
The result of clicking the Call button.

To read more than you ever wanted to know about URIs and scheme-specific parts, see Book III, Chapter 2.

```
intent.setData(Uri.parse("tel:"));
```

Modifying the `tel` URI in this fashion changes the way `Intent.ACTION_DIAL` works. Now the phone launches the dial screen with no phone number. (See Figure 3-4.) The user enters a phone number and then presses the Call button.

Figure 3-4:
A blank dialer.

If you combine `"tel:"` with `Intent.ACTION_CALL`, Android tries to place a call with no phone number. (It's a call to "nowhere" — the stuff science-fiction plots are made of.) The result on my phone is a dialog box warning me that something's very wrong. (See Figure 3-5.)

Figure 3-5:
Trying to
dial no one
in particular.

Oops! No phone

Some Android devices aren't phones. Running the preceding section's
example on a ten-inch tablet is like trying to call Paris using a can opener.
You might expect users to know this, but life is complicated, and users have
other things to think about. (Doesn't everyone?)

It's best to anticipate the worst and to remind users when they press the wrong
buttons. So in Listing 3-1, I add code to check for "phone-ness." I display an alert
if the user tries to make a call from an Android-based dishwasher.

What kind of phone is this?

In Listing 3-1, the deviceIsAPhone method gets a TelephonyManager. Then
the method uses the TelephonyManager to check the device's phone type.

The phone type options are PHONE_TYPE_GSM, PHONE_TYPE_CDMA, PHONE_
TYPE_SIP, and PHONE_TYPE_NONE.

+ **Global System for Mobile Communications (GSM):** It's used by most of
  the world's carriers, including AT&T and T-Mobile in the United States.

+ **Code Division Multiple Access (CDMA):** It's used in the United States by
  carriers Sprint and Verizon.

+ **Session Initiation Protocol (SIP):** It's a telephone standard based on
  Internet packets. SIP isn't commonly used on commercial mobile phones.

+ The value PHONE_TYPE_NONE applies to devices with no telephony
  capabilities. It's the telephone standard used by tablet devices, rocks,
  table lamps, ham sandwiches, and other things that neither place nor
  receive phone calls.

I need your attention

In Listing 3-1, the displayAlert method creates the dialog box shown in
Figure 3-6.

Figure 3-6:
An alert
dialog box.

An alert dialog box can have one, two, or three buttons. If you use the `AlertDialog.Builder` class to construct an alert dialog box, the buttons' names are `positive`, `negative`, and `neutral`. (So, for example, to create a `NO` button, you call `alertBuilder.setNegativeButton`.)

If you skip the `AlertDialog.Builder` class and instead call the `Alert Dialog` class's methods, the corresponding method calls are `setButton`, `setButton2`, and `setButton3`.

The `displayAlert` method in Listing 3-1 illustrates an interesting feature of Android's builder classes. A builder has setter methods, and each setter method returns a newly modified builder. For example, you start with a vanilla new `AlertDialog.Builder(this)`. You assign the new builder to your `alertBuilder` variable. Then you call `alertBuilder.setTitle`, which returns a builder whose title is `"Not a telephone!"` To this enhanced builder you apply `setMessage`, returning a builder with title `"Not a telephone!"` and message `"This device can't make phone calls!"`

The chain continues until you feed a builder to the `show` method. The `show` method displays the dialog box created by the builder.

An example in Chapter 2 of this minibook uses the `Notification. Builder` class. In that example, I don't use the result returned by each of the builder's setter methods. The choice to use (or not use) a builder's return results is simply a matter of taste.

In Listing 3-1, I check for the presence of telephony hardware using Android's `TelephonyManager`. In the first draft of this section's code, I relied on the `PackageManager` class as follows:

```
PackageManager manager = getPackageManager();
ComponentName name = intent.resolveActivity(manager);
return name != null;
```

As strategies go, this first draft wasn't a bad one. An intent's `resolveActivity` method tells you which activity, if any, has an intent filter matching the intent. But the plan stumbled when I learned that my device's Contacts app matches the phone intents. When I ran the code on a tablet device, I expected to see the `"Not a telephone!"` dialog box. Instead, the device offered to add the new phone number to my Contacts list. Okay. No harm done.

On being a dialer

In Listing 3-1, you call `startActivity` to invoke the default Android dialer. You can also *become* a dialer by adding stuff to your activity's intent filter. (See Listing 3-2.) A quick search on the Android shows that many developers create alternatives to the standard system dialer. I see dialers integrated with enhanced contacts lists, dialers customized for particular businesses, old-style rotary dialers, dialers designed for sliding your fingers across the keys, dialers that play music, and many more.

Listing 3-2: Responding to a Dial Intent

```
<activity android:name=".DialerActivity">
  <intent-filter>
    <action android:name="android.intent.action.DIAL" />
    <category
      android:name="android.intent.category.DEFAULT" />
    <data android:scheme="tel" />
  </intent-filter>
</activity>
```

The value of the constant `Intent.ACTION_DIAL` (used in Listing 3-1) is the string `"android.intent.action.DIAL"`.

In Java code, you can use either the constant `Intent.ACTION_DIAL` or the string `"android.intent.action.DIAL"`. But in the `AndroidManifest.xml` document, you must use the string.

Listing 3-2 also contains a `<data>` element, and without this `<data>` element, the code is worthless. Any app that invokes a dialer sends dialing information (empty or not) as part of the intent. The dialing information is a URI with the `tel` scheme. If an intent's data has a scheme, a matching intent filter must have the same scheme.

To read all about the matching of intents and intent filters, see Book III, Chapter 2.

Keep an eye on the phone

The `android.telephony` package has a useful `PhoneStateListener` class. With this class, you can "listen in" on a phone's state transitions. Here's a code snippet:

```
PhoneStateListener listener = new PhoneStateListener() {
  private static final String CLASSNAME =
      "PhoneStateListener";

  @Override
  public void onCallStateChanged(int state,
      String incomingNumber) {
    String stateString = "N/A";
    switch (state) {
    case TelephonyManager.CALL_STATE_IDLE:
      stateString = "Idle";
      break;
    case TelephonyManager.CALL_STATE_OFFHOOK:
      stateString = "Off Hook";
      break;
    case TelephonyManager.CALL_STATE_RINGING:
      stateString = "Ringing";
      break;
    }
    Log.i(CLASSNAME, stateString);
  }
};
```

Android calls the listener's `onCallStateChanged` method when an incoming call arrives.

With an emulator, you can simulate an incoming call using Eclipse's Emulator Control view. The view is visible by default in the DDMS perspective.

The listener's other useful methods include `onCellLocationChanged`, `onDataActivity`, `onDataConnectionStateChanged`, and `onSignal StrengthsChanged`. To use any of these methods, you must add the following element to your `AndroidManifest.xml` document:

```
<uses-permission
    android:name="android.permission.READ_PHONE_STATE">
</uses-permission>
```

Book IV Chapter 3

An Android Potpourri

Sending a Text Message

Where I come from, people send "text messages" to one another. Apparently, the rest of the world calls this SMS (*S*hort *M*essaging *S*ervice). Whatever you call it, the business of sending brief, phone-to-phone messages is an important feature of today's communications.

Listing 3-3 shows you how an Android program sends a text message.

What's an SMS service center?

When you send a text message, the message goes first to a service center. The service center stores the message before forwarding it to the desired recipient.

This *store and forward* mechanism might sound cumbersome. But the reality is, text messages aren't synchronous. When you talk on the phone, you interact in real time with another voice. But when you send a text

message, the other person might not read the message immediately. Indeed, the recipient's phone might be turned off.

Because of this gap in timing, text messaging requires a buffer — a service center. If it weren't for this buffer, messages that weren't processed immediately would never be delivered. Text messaging would require careful coordination between the sender and the receiver.

Listing 3-3: Sending Text

```
SmsManager smsMgm = SmsManager.getDefault();

smsMgm.sendTextMessage("2345556789", null,
    "Hello world", null, null);
```

The `sendTextMessage` method has five parameters:

+ **The first parameter, a Java string, is the destination's phone number.**

+ **The second parameter, a Java string, is a *service center* address (see the nearby sidebar).**

   The value `null` in Listing 3-3 says, "I don't care how the message gets to its destination. Just send it!"

+ **The third parameter, also a Java string, is the message content.**

+ **The fourth and fifth parameters are pending intents.**

   Android uses both intents to send broadcasts. The fourth parameter's broadcast notifies the system when the message is sent. The fifth parameter's broadcast notifies the system when the message is received.

For an introduction to pending intents, see Chapter 2 in this minibook.

To run the code in Listing 3-3, your app must have `android.permission.SEND_SMS "`.

Working with Device Sensors

A full-featured Android device is more than just a telephone. To emphasize this point, I include a list of constants from the `android.content.PackageManager` class:

```
FEATURE_BLUETOOTH
FEATURE_CAMERA
FEATURE_CAMERA_AUTOFOCUS
FEATURE_CAMERA_FLASH
FEATURE_CAMERA_FRONT
FEATURE_FAKETOUCH
FEATURE_FAKETOUCH_MULTITOUCH_DISTINCT
FEATURE_FAKETOUCH_MULTITOUCH_JAZZHAND
FEATURE_LIVE_WALLPAPER
FEATURE_LOCATION
FEATURE_LOCATION_GPS
FEATURE_LOCATION_NETWORK
FEATURE_MICROPHONE
FEATURE_NFC
FEATURE_SCREEN_LANDSCAPE
FEATURE_SCREEN_PORTRAIT
FEATURE_SENSOR_ACCELEROMETER
FEATURE_SENSOR_BAROMETER
FEATURE_SENSOR_COMPASS
FEATURE_SENSOR_GYROSCOPE
FEATURE_SENSOR_LIGHT
FEATURE_SENSOR_PROXIMITY
FEATURE_SIP
FEATURE_SIP_VOIP
FEATURE_TELEPHONY
FEATURE_TELEPHONY_CDMA
FEATURE_TELEPHONY_GSM
FEATURE_TOUCHSCREEN
FEATURE_TOUCHSCREEN_MULTITOUCH
FEATURE_TOUCHSCREEN_MULTITOUCH_DISTINCT
FEATURE_TOUCHSCREEN_MULTITOUCH_JAZZHAND
FEATURE_USB_ACCESSORY
FEATURE_USB_HOST
FEATURE_WIFI
```

Some of these constants are self-explanatory, but others need some clarification. For example, with FAKETOUCH, a device without a real touchscreen has some support for touch events. (For the FAKETOUCH_MULTITOUCH constants, DISTINCT stands for simulation of two-finger touches, and JAZZHAND stands for simulation of five-finger touches.)

**Book IV
Chapter 3**

**An Android
Potpourri**

A device can sense LOCATION in several ways. A crude method is to guess location using the known locations of nearby cellphone towers. Using GPS (*Global Positioning System*) is much more accurate.

Among all the PackageManager's FEATURE constants, my favorite is FEATURE_ SENSOR_BAROMETER. I can't imagine shopping for a phone and thinking, "That model isn't good enough. I can't use it to measure barometric pressure."

Anyway, when you start programming a device's sensors, you grapple with new kinds of problems. What's the underlying physics of the sensor measurement? How do you handle the necessary mathematics? How do you deal with tiny adjustments in an inherently analog world? The GPS sensor notices a location change. Should my code do processing in its onLocationChanged method, or is the change so small that I should call it background noise and ignore it?

Quantifying location and orientation

You're probably familiar with the terms *latitude* and *longitude,* but just in case:

✦ **Latitude** is 0 on the Earth's equator, 90 degrees at the North Pole, and –90 degrees at the South Pole.

✦ **Longitude** is 0 at the Royal Observatory in Greenwich, UK. Longitude is negative to the west of Greenwich and positive to the east of Greenwich. Longitude is 180 degrees at the International Date Line in the Pacific Ocean.

In the Android world, the term *orientation* has two different (but closely related) meanings:

✦ The **screen's orientation** can be either *portrait* or *landscape.*

✦ The **device's orientation** is a measurement consisting of three numbers — yaw, pitch, and roll.

Usually, when people talk about orientation (or write about orientation), they don't say "screen orientation" or "device orientation." They simply say, "orientation." Fortunately, you can distinguish the two kinds of orientation from the surrounding terminology:

✦ If you hold the device so that the screen's height is greater than the screen's width, the screen's orientation is *portrait.*

If you hold the device so that the screen's width is greater than the screen's height, the screen's orientation is *landscape.*

You can use most Android devices in either portrait or landscape mode. So as a developer, you must design your app's interface with both modes in mind. True, users tend to hold phones in portrait mode and hold tablets in landscape mode. But when you define an activity's layouts, you must consider all possibilities. Does your app look good when a user lies flat on a couch and looks up at the device?

✦ If you lay the device flat on the ground so that the top of the device points to the Earth's magnetic North Pole, the device's yaw, pitch, and roll values are all 0. (This assumes that the ground is perfectly horizontal.)

Android doesn't use degrees to measure yaw, pitch, and roll. Instead, Android's methods return *radian* measure. A half turn of the device is Π radians. A full 360-degree turn is 2Π radians. The easiest way to convert between degrees and radians is as follows:

✦ To change degrees into radians, multiply the number of degrees by 0.01745327777777777778.

✦ To change radians into degrees, multiply the number of radians by 57.2958279087977743754.

Don't fret at the number of digits in each of the conversion factors. Use fewer digits if you want. No matter how many digits you use, the numbers aren't completely accurate.

For a more detailed description of yaw, pitch, and roll, see Book VI, Chapter 2.

Sending location and orientation

The program in Listing 3-4 displays a device's location and orientation. The program's run is shown in Figure 3-7.

Listing 3-4: Sensing Device Orientation

```
package com.allmycode.sensor;

import static android.hardware.Sensor.TYPE_ACCELEROMETER;
import static android.hardware.Sensor.TYPE_MAGNETIC_FIELD;
import android.app.Activity;
import android.content.Context;
import android.hardware.Sensor;
import android.hardware.SensorEvent;
import android.hardware.SensorEventListener;
import android.hardware.SensorManager;
import android.location.Location;
import android.location.LocationListener;
import android.location.LocationManager;
import android.os.Bundle;
import android.widget.TextView;
import android.widget.Toast;
```

(continued)

Book IV
Chapter 3

An Android
Potpourri

Listing 3-4 *(continued)*

```java
public class MyActivity extends Activity {
  SensorManager sensorManager;
  Sensor magFieldSensor, accelerometer;
  SensorEventListener sensorListener;
  LocationListener locationListener;
  LocationManager locationManager;
  TextView orientationView, locationView;

  private float[] gravityValues = new float[3];
  private float[] geoMagnetValues = new float[3];
  private float[] orientation = new float[3];
  private float[] rotationMatrix = new float[9];

  @Override
  protected void onCreate(Bundle savedInstanceState) {
    super.onCreate(savedInstanceState);

    setContentView(R.layout.main);
    sensorManager = (SensorManager)
        getSystemService(Context.SENSOR_SERVICE);
    magFieldSensor = sensorManager
            .getDefaultSensor(TYPE_MAGNETIC_FIELD);
    accelerometer = sensorManager
            .getDefaultSensor(TYPE_ACCELEROMETER);

    sensorListener = new MySensorEventListener();

    locationListener = new MyLocationListener();
    locationManager = (LocationManager)
        getSystemService(Context.LOCATION_SERVICE);

    orientationView =
        (TextView) findViewById(R.id.orientationView);
    locationView =
        (TextView) findViewById(R.id.locationView);
  }

  @Override
  protected void onResume() {
    super.onResume();
    sensorManager.registerListener(sensorListener,
        magFieldSensor, SensorManager.SENSOR_DELAY_UI);
    sensorManager.registerListener(sensorListener,
        accelerometer, SensorManager.SENSOR_DELAY_UI);

    locationManager.requestLocationUpdates
    (LocationManager.GPS_PROVIDER,
        0, 0, locationListener);
  }
```

```
@Override
protected void onPause() {
  super.onPause();
  sensorManager.unregisterListener(sensorListener);
  locationManager.removeUpdates(locationListener);
}

class MySensorEventListener implements SensorEventListener {

  @Override
  public void onSensorChanged(SensorEvent event) {

    int sensorEventType = event.sensor.getType();

    if (sensorEventType == Sensor.TYPE_ACCELEROMETER) {
      System.arraycopy
        (event.values, 0, gravityValues, 0, 3);

    } else if (sensorEventType ==
                          Sensor.TYPE_MAGNETIC_FIELD) {
      System.arraycopy
        (event.values, 0, geoMagnetValues, 0, 3);

    } else {
    return;
    }

    if (SensorManager.getRotationMatrix(rotationMatrix,
        null, gravityValues, geoMagnetValues)) {

      SensorManager.getOrientation(rotationMatrix,
          orientation);

      orientationView.setText
          ("Yaw:   " + orientation[0] + "\n"
        + "Pitch: " + orientation[1] + "\n"
        + "Roll:  " + orientation[2]);
    }
  }

  @Override
  public void onAccuracyChanged(Sensor sensor,
      int accuracy) {
    if (accuracy <= 1) {
      Toast.makeText(MyActivity.this, "Please shake the " +
        "device in a figure eight pattern to " +
        "improve sensor accuracy!", Toast.LENGTH_LONG)
        .show();
    }
  }
}
```

(continued)

Listing 3-4 *(continued)*

```
class MyLocationListener implements LocationListener {

    @Override
    public void onLocationChanged(Location location) {
      locationView.setText
          ("Latitude:  " + location.getLatitude() + "\n"
          + "Longitude: " + location.getLongitude());
    }

    @Override
    public void onProviderDisabled(String provider) {
    }

    @Override
    public void onProviderEnabled(String provider) {
    }

    @Override
    public void onStatusChanged(String provider,
        int status, Bundle extras) {
    }
  }
}
```

Figure 3-7:
Displaying
orientation
and
location.

```
SensorDemo
Yaw:    0.9403192
Pitch: -0.010684388
Roll:  -0.04408906
Latitude:  37.802109
Longitude: -122.432691
```

Listing 3-4 illustrates a bunch of sensor features — some that are specific to location and orientation, and others that apply to sensors in general. One way or another, most sensors use the same programming constructs:

✦ Instances of the Manager classes connect your code to the device's hardware sensors.

In Listing 3-4, calling getSystemService provides access to sensor managers. The managers belong to android.hardware. SensorManager and android.location.LocationManager.

The LocationManager isn't in the android.hardware package because sensing location is abstracted for various sensing techniques. The LocationManager class represents GPS readings, cell tower usage, and other things. The `LocationManager` deals generically with places on Earth, not specifically with GPS hardware.

✦ Instances of `android.hardware.Sensor` represent the sensors themselves.

In Listing 3-4, calls to the `getDefaultSensor` method return values for `magFieldSensor` and for `accelerometer`.

✦ Objects that implement `Listener` interfaces receive notice of changes to sensor values.

In Listing 3-4, instances of `MySensorEventListener` and `MyLocation Listener` fill these rolls. I register the listeners in the activity's `onResume` method and unregister the listeners in the activity's `onPause` method.

Your app should stop listening when the activity pauses. If you forget to unregister, the user's battery might die of exhaustion.

The code to get useful values from sensor events depends on the kind of event. In Listing 3-4, getting location information means simply calling `location.getLatitude()` and `location.getLongitude()`. For orientation, the story is more complicated. One way or another, you feed values from the device's level gravity sensor or the device's magnetometer into the `SensorManager.getRotationMatrix` method.

A few miscellaneous tidbits in Listing 3-4 are worth noting:

✦ To sense the device's location, your app must have `"android.permission.ACCESS_FINE_LOCATION"`. Sensing orientation requires no particular permission. (Hackers rarely benefit from knowing the tilt of the user's device.)

✦ When you test this section's app, you probably tilt your device in several directions. By default, this tilting can change the display from portrait to landscape and back. Oddly enough, these display changes can be very annoying. (With most apps, your mind zones out while you're turning the device. But with this app, the turning motion is the app's *raison d'être*.)

To keep changes in screen orientation from driving you crazy, add either `android:screenOrientation="landscape"` or `android:screenOrientation="portrait"` to the `<activity>` element in the `AndroidManifest.xml` document.

✦ Calls to `registerListener` in Listing 3-4 have delay parameters. The delay parameter's value tells the device how often to check the sensor's value. The choices are `SENSOR_DELAY_FASTEST`, `SENSOR_DELAY_GAME`, `SENSOR_DELAY_NORMAL`, and `SENSOR_DELAY_UI`. The `SENSOR_DELAY_GAME` value is appropriate for game playing, and the `SENSOR_DELAY_UI` value is best for displaying the information. Of course, to figure out what's best for your app, ignore the guidelines and do lots of testing.

Book IV Chapter 3

An Android Potpourri

✦ When you implement the `SensorEventListener` interface, you must create an `onAccuracyChanged` method. The predefined accuracy values are `SENSOR_STATUS_UNRELIABLE` with `int` value 0, `SENSOR_STATUS_ACCURACY_LOW` with `int` value 1, `SENSOR_STATUS_ACCURACY_MEDIUM` with `int` value 2, and `SENSOR_STATUS_ACCURACY_HIGH` with `int` value 3. For some reason, shaking the device in a figure-eight pattern tends to improve orientation sensitivity.

Finally, notice the austere-looking typeface in Figure 3-7. I added `android:typeface="monospace"` to each of the `TextView` start tags in the app's `AndroidManifest.xml` document. A font that's *monospace* reserves the same width for each character. So, for example, with a monospace font, the letter *i* consumes as much width as the letter *m,* and each blank space is as wide as the letter *m.*

In this section's example, I use monospace to help align the numeric values. So in Figure 3-7, the three orientation numbers form a column, and the two location numbers form a column. Without a monospace font, the display would have the jagged look in Figure 3-8.

Figure 3-8:
The display from this section's app without a monospace font.

SensorDemo
Yaw: -1.8083397
Pitch: -0.05866862
Roll: -0.20562357
Latitude: 37.802109
Longitude: -122.432691

I could have aligned the numbers by creating separate text views and specifying the width of each text view. Alternatively, I could try adding tabs to my single text view:

```
locationView.setText
          ("Latitude:\t\t" + location.getLatitude() + "\n"
    + "Longitude:\t" + location.getLongitude());
```

The escape sequence `\t` tells Java to space to the next tab stop. If you use tabs, the display looks like the stuff in Figure 3-9.

When I'm tempted to use tabs, I stop and remember how flakey tabs can be. For example, in Figure 3-9 the word *Latitude* is narrower than the word *Longitude.* So my code snippet compensates by having two tabs after the word *Latitude* and only one tab after the word *Longitude.* The extra tab works fine on my test device, but with different font settings on another user's device, the same tabs might throw the numbers out of alignment.

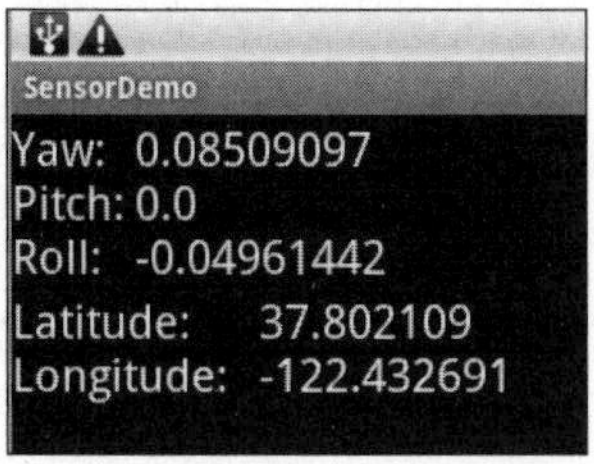

Figure 3-9:
The display
from this
section's
app using
tabs.

SensorDemo

Yaw: 0.08509097
Pitch: 0.0
Roll: -0.04961442
Latitude: 37.802109
Longitude: -122.432691

Drawing, Dragging, and Zooming

No doubt about it — touchscreens are cool. You press plain old glass, and the device responds! (Okay. It's not plain old glass. But it's still mysterious.) When you slide your finger, a drawing of some kind moves! And with multi-touch screens, you can zoom things, rotate things, and reshape things.

Android's software supports events involving up to 256 fingers. That's about two-and-a-half centipedes walking on the screen at the same time. Of course, humans seldom apply more than two fingers to a device's screen.

The big picture

Listing 3-5 demonstrates the handling of touch events. A *touch event* is a lot like a click. The most important difference is that touch events may involve motion — the sliding of your finger (or stylus) along the screen's surface.

Listing 3-5: Handling Touch Events

```
package com.allmycode.draw;

import android.app.Activity;
import android.content.Context;
import android.graphics.Canvas;
import android.graphics.Color;
import android.graphics.Paint;
import android.graphics.Rect;
import android.os.Bundle;
import android.util.DisplayMetrics;
import android.view.MotionEvent;
import android.view.View;
import android.view.View.OnTouchListener;

public class DrawStuffActivity extends Activity implements
    OnTouchListener {
```

**Book IV
Chapter 3**

**An Android
Potpourri**

(continued)

Listing 3-5 *(continued)*

```java
MyView myView;
int numberOfFingers = 0;
float oldX[] = new float[2], oldY[] = new float[2];
Rect rectangle = new Rect(0, 0, 100, 100);
DisplayMetrics metrics = new DisplayMetrics();

@Override
public void onCreate(Bundle savedInstanceState) {
  super.onCreate(savedInstanceState);

  myView = new MyView(this);
  setContentView(myView);
  myView.setOnTouchListener(this);

  getWindowManager().getDefaultDisplay().
    getMetrics(metrics);
}

@Override
public boolean onTouch(View view, MotionEvent event) {
    switch (event.getActionMasked()) {
    case MotionEvent.ACTION_DOWN:
      numberOfFingers = 1;
      oldX[0] = event.getX(0);
      oldY[0] = event.getY(0);
      break;
    case MotionEvent.ACTION_POINTER_DOWN:
      numberOfFingers = 2;
      oldX[1] = event.getX(1);
      oldY[1] = event.getY(1);
      break;
    case MotionEvent.ACTION_MOVE:
      handleMove(event);
      break;
    case MotionEvent.ACTION_POINTER_UP:
    case MotionEvent.ACTION_UP:
      numberOfFingers--;
      break;
    }

    view.invalidate();
    return true;
}

// The handleMove method is in Listing 3-6.

class MyView extends View {
  Paint whitePaint = new Paint();
```

```
MyView(Context context) {
    super(context);
    whitePaint.setColor(Color.WHITE);
}

@Override
public void onDraw(Canvas canvas) {
    canvas.drawRect(rectangle, whitePaint);
}
    }
}
```

Figure 3-10 has an unexciting screen shot from a run of this section's example.

Figure 3-10:
Believe
me! You
can move
and resize
the white
rectangle.

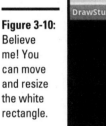

Listing 3-5 has the basic outline of most other Android activity classes. The `onCreate` method sets the activity's content view and registers a listener. But unlike most of the examples scattered through this book's various mini-books, the content view in Listing 3-5 isn't a resource. Instead, Listing 3-5 gets its content view from an object constructed in the code.

The content view is an instance of the `MyView` class, which I define at the end of Listing 3-5. The `MyView` class isn't fancy. The class's primary purpose is to override the `View` class's `onDraw` method. When Android draw's a `MyView` instance, Android places a white rectangle on a canvas. The rectangle itself (an instance of Android's `Rect` class) has four properties: `left`, `top`, `right`, and `bottom`. (See Figure 3-11.) Each property is a number of pixels.

In Listing 3-5, the `onTouch` method responds to motion events. The motion event's `getActionMasked` method returns the type of motion:

✦ Android fires `MotionEvent.ACTION_DOWN` when the user places one finger on the screen.

✦ Android fires `MotionEvent.ACTION_POINTER_DOWN` when the user places a second finger on the screen.

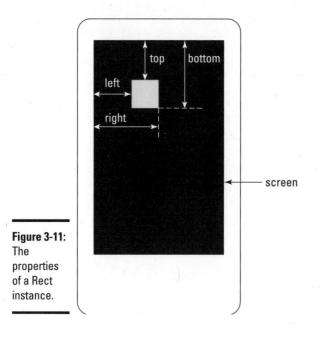

Figure 3-11:
The
properties
of a Rect
instance.

✦ Android fires `MotionEvent.ACTION_UP` when the user lifts the first finger off the screen.

✦ Android fires `MotionEvent.ACTION_POINTER_UP` when the user lifts the second finger off the screen.

✦ Android fires `MotionEvent.ACTION_MOVE` when the user drags one or more fingers along the screen's surface.

Android has constants, such as `ACTION_POINTER_2_UP` and `ACTION_POINTER_3_DOWN`, but these names are deprecated. To distinguish among three or more fingers, look for `MotionEvent.ACTION_POINTER_INDEX_MASK` in Android's SDK documentation.

The `onTouch` method in Listing 3-5 records the pixel coordinates where the user's fingers land on the screen:

✦ The `getX` method returns the number of pixels from the screen's left edge.

✦ The `getY` method returns the number of pixels from the top of the screen.

✦ In the calls to `getX` and `getY`, the `0` parameter represents the first finger that the user places on the screen.

✦ The `1` parameter represents the second finger that the user places on the screen.

Aside from this quick bookkeeping, the onTouch method defers to the handleMove method for most of the code's calculations. (The handleMove method in Listing 3-6 — shown later in this chapter — computes the white rectangle's new size and position.)

Near the end of the onTouch method, I call view.invalidate(). This tells Android that the rendering of this view on the screen is no longer valid. Thus, Android must redraw the view. That is, Android must call the view's onDraw method.

At the end of the onTouch method, the return value true indicates that the method has handled the motion event once and for all. Any other methods that think they're going to handle the motion event can go fly a kite.

This section's app shouldn't respond to a tilt of the screen. To keep the screen in landscape mode, add android:screenOrientation="landscape" to the activity's start tag in the AndroidManifest.xml document.

The details

Moving gizmos on a screen can involve some interesting math. In fact, most graphics packages use matrix transformations to adjust items' shapes and sizes. But in this section, I compromise. Instead of using the concise mathematical tools in Android's SDK, I do some simpler (and maybe more intuitive) measurements. Listing 3-6 has the code.

Listing 3-6: Dragging and Zooming

```
float newX[] = new float[2], newY[] = new float[2];
int xChange[] = new int[2], yChange[] = new int[2];
int diffX, diffY;
int newLeft = rectangle.left, newTop = rectangle.top,
    newRight = rectangle.right,
    newBottom = rectangle.bottom;

void handleMove(MotionEvent event) {
  newX[0] = Math.round(event.getX(0));
  newY[0] = Math.round(event.getY(0));
  xChange[0] = Math.round(newX[0] - oldX[0]);
  yChange[0] = Math.round(newY[0] - oldY[0]);
  oldX[0] = newX[0];
  oldY[0] = newY[0];

  switch (numberOfFingers) {
  case 1:
```

Book IV Chapter 3

An Android Potpourri

(continued)

Listing 3-6 *(continued)*

```
      newLeft = rectangle.left + xChange[0];
      newTop = rectangle.top + yChange[0];
      newRight = rectangle.right + xChange[0];
      newBottom = rectangle.bottom + yChange[0];
      if (newLeft < 0 || newRight > metrics.widthPixels) {
        newLeft = rectangle.left;
        newRight = rectangle.right;
      }
      if (newTop < 0 || newBottom > metrics.heightPixels) {
        newTop = rectangle.top;
        newBottom = rectangle.bottom;
      }
      rectangle =
          new Rect(newLeft, newTop, newRight, newBottom);

      break;

    case 2:
      newX[1] = Math.round(event.getX(1));
      newY[1] = Math.round(event.getY(1));

      diffX =
          Math.abs(Math.round(newX[1] - newX[0]))
              - Math.abs(Math.round(oldX[1] - oldX[0]));
      diffY =
          Math.abs(Math.round(newY[1] - newY[0]))
              - Math.abs(Math.round(oldY[1] - oldY[0]));

      oldX[1] = newX[1];
      oldY[1] = newY[1];

      newLeft = rectangle.left - diffX / 2;
      newTop = rectangle.top - diffY / 2;
      newRight = rectangle.right + diffX / 2;
      newBottom = rectangle.bottom + diffY / 2;
      rectangle =
          new Rect(newLeft, newTop, newRight, newBottom);
      break;
  }
}
```

The code in Listing 3-6 compares the most recent motion event's coordinates with the previous event's coordinates. With this information, the code computes the distances and directions of the user's finger movements. The code uses these values to calculate the change in the rectangle's position, size, and shape. With this information (and with the rectangle's current left, top, right, and bottom properties), the code computes new values for the rectangle's four properties.

Finally, if you do nothing to constrain the rectangle's motion, it could happen that you slide the rectangle away from the screen's visible area. To keep this from happening, I add a few `if` statements to the one-finger code. In those `if` statements, the `metrics` variable tells me the screen's width and height in pixels. (The `metrics` variable gets its values in the `onCreate` method in Listing 3-5.)

Notice the use of `float` values in Listing 3-6. Android's `MotionEvent` methods work with all kinds of devices, and some devices report touch-event locations as fractions of a pixel. After all, the touch-sensing hardware on a screen's surface is different from the light-producing hardware in the screen's guts. If the touch-sensing hardware has higher resolution than the light-producing hardware, the device can report movement in fractions of a pixel.

On the Importance of Waiting Patiently

This section deals with an important multitasking issue. Suppose your app has a feature that can take a long time to complete. For example, you create an app that displays an image on the screen. The image normally lives on a website, so your app reaches out with a URL.

While the user waits for a response from the website, your app must not appear to be frozen. The user doesn't want an interface that's unresponsive until the image appears on the screen.

Almost any part of your app's code can open an HTTP connection and request an image from the web. But if you're not careful, the request takes place in your app's main thread (the so-called *UI thread*). Like any other thread, the main thread is a one-lane road. While your HTTP request waits at a stoplight, none of your app's other features can move forward. Parts of the display don't get updated, buttons are unresponsive, and all the while the user dreams up nasty things to write on the Android Market's app ratings page.

You may be familiar with the use of Java threads. A piece of code can spawn a new thread. With two threads of execution (the main thread and the newly spawned thread), your code can do two things at once. One thread waits for a web page while the other thread handles button clicks and other user-related events. The new thread is like a side road. While a big truck clogs up this side road, cars continue to flow along the main highway.

But spawning new Java threads doesn't entirely solve the problem. Android's threading rules dictate that no thread other than the main thread can update an application's user interface. So, for example, your secondary thread can wait to get an image from the web. But after the image has been downloaded, the secondary thread can't easily display the image.

**Book IV
Chapter 3**

**An Android
Potpourri**

To fix this problem once and for all, Android has an abstract `AsyncTask` class. An `AsyncTask` does your app's time-consuming work in a separate thread and returns useful results to your app's main thread. In addition, an `AsyncTask` has methods that structure the code in a sensible, fill-in-the-blanks way.

Of course, the kinds of work that you do with an `AsyncTask` come in many forms and flavors. That's why the `AsyncTask` class has generic type parameters.

In spite of the naming, Android's `AsyncTask` class has little in common with a stack of activities that form a task. True, I sometimes use the word *task* for either a stack of activities or an `AsyncTask` instance. But the two kinds of tasks are quite different. For a refresher course on activity stacks, see Book III, Chapters 1 and 2.

Creating an AsyncTask

The `AsyncTask` in Listing 3-7 fetches an image from the web. In the meantime, the code updates a progress bar that appears on the device's screen.

Listing 3-7: Getting an Image from a Website

```
class MyAsyncTask extends
    AsyncTask<String, Integer, Bitmap> {

  int progress;

  @Override
  protected void onPreExecute() {
    progress = 0;
    button.setClickable(false);
  }

  @Override
  protected Bitmap doInBackground(String... urlArray) {
    try {
      URL url = new URL(urlArray[0]);
      HttpURLConnection connection =
          (HttpURLConnection) url.openConnection();
      connection.setDoInput(true);
      connection.connect();

      progress += 50;
      publishProgress(progress);

      InputStream input = connection.getInputStream();
      Bitmap bitmap = BitmapFactory.decodeStream(input);

      progress += 50;
      publishProgress(progress);
```

```
      return bitmap;
    } catch (IOException e) {
      e.printStackTrace();
      return null;
    }
  }

  @Override
  protected void onProgressUpdate(Integer... progressArray) {
    progressBar.setProgress(progressArray[0]);
  }

  @Override
  protected void onPostExecute(Bitmap result) {
    imageView.setImageBitmap(result);
    button.setClickable(true);
  }
}
```

The code in Listing 3-7 is an inner class; it should be nestled inside an app's main activity (or inside some other class in your app).

When you extend `AsyncTask`, you must supply three generic parameters (`<String, Integer, Bitmap>`) and four methods:

✦ **The first generic parameter (`String` in Listing 3-7) describes the type of input to the task's `doInBackground` method.**

Think of this as the type of input that the task needs in order to do its work. In Listing 3-7, the `doInBackground` method's parameter is a variable-length array of strings. The method body uses only one string (the value stored in the `urlArray`'s initial element). The code uses this string the way you'd use any web address — to fetch a web page (or in this example, an image).

✦ **The second generic parameter (`Integer` in Listing 3-7) describes the type of input to the task's `onProgressUpdate` method.**

Think of this as the type of information that describes the state of the progress bar. In Listing 3-7, the `onProgressUpdate` method's parameter is a variable-length array of `Integer` values. The method body uses only one integer (the value stored in the `progressArray`'s initial element). The code calls the progress bar's `setProgress` method to make the progress bar display the current status.

✦ **The third generic parameter (`Bitmap` in Listing 3-7) describes the result type of the task's `doInBackground` method, which is also the type of input to the task's `onPostExecute` method.**

Think of this as the type of information that's created by a run of the task. In Listing 3-7, the `onPostExecute` method feeds a bitmap (the bitmap obtained from a website) to the activity's `imageView` object.

TIP

When you create an `AsyncTask`, any or all of the three generic parameters can be `Void`. (Java's `Void` class stores the primitive `void` type — the type that refers to nothing.) When a parameter is `Void`, the `AsyncTask` doesn't use the corresponding information. For example, an `AsyncTask` with no progress bar has a middle parameter that's `Void`.

Multithreaded code, with its threads and its callbacks, can be very complicated. The `AsyncTask` class is nice because it provides preinstalled *plumbing code*. This plumbing code relieves the developer of much of the multithreaded programming burden.

Using a progress bar

I heard a story a long time ago. I don't know where I heard it. So if you're the story's originator, please contact me via e-mail, and I'll give you credit in the next edition. (And whatever you do, please don't sue me for using the story.)

Anyway, the story takes place in a tall office building with too few elevators. People would wait impatiently to go from the lobby to one of the higher floors. The building's owner got estimates for the cost of adding more elevators, and the price was staggering.

So to solve the problem, the owner installed wall-to-wall mirrors beside each of the elevators. As a result, people didn't get faster service. But everyone stopped to check their appearance in the mirrors. So from then on, no one complained about the elevators' being too slow.

Clearly, this story has an important moral. The moral is, you don't necessarily have to speed up a process. But you must keep the user busy while the process chugs along.

That's what progress bars are for. Figure 3-12 displays the progress bar in this section's example.

I define this example's progress bar with the following code:

```
<ProgressBar android:id="@+id/progressBar1"
    style="?android:attr/progressBarStyleHorizontal"
    android:max="100"

    android:layout_width="fill_parent"
    android:layout_height="wrap_content"/>
```

Android's built-in `android.R.attr.progressBarStyleHorizontal` resource describes the progress bar in Figure 3-12. The `android:max="100"` attribute tells your app to display a completed progress bar when you call `progressBar.setProgress(100)`, and to display a partially completed progress bar for values between `0` and `100`.

Figure 3-12:
A horizontal
progress
bar.

For this section's example, I might have done better using `style="?android:`
`attr/progressBarStyleLarge"`, which displays a spinning circle with no
progress percentage. But I chose the horizontal style to illustrate the usage
of progress updates. In Listing 3-7, I start with progress value 0 in the task's
`onPreExecute` method. Then, at certain points in the task's `doInBackground`
method, I call `publishProgress`. A call to `publishProgress` automatically
triggers a call to the `onProgressUpdate` method. And in Listing 3-7, my
`onProgressUpdate` method refreshes the progress bar's display.

In Listing 3-7, I select two points in the `doInBackground` method to change the
progress value and update the progress bar's display. I do this to illustrate the
usage of a horizontal progress bar. But in truth, the progress bar in Listing 3-7
might easily annoy the user. A bar with only three values (0, 50, 100) doesn't
give the user much useful information. And besides, the timing of the work in
Listing 3-7's `doInBackground` method probably isn't a 50/50 split. When you
create a real app, think carefully about updates to the progress bar. Try as hard
as you can to make them reflect the task's expected timing. And if the timing is
unpredictable, use `progressBarStyleSmall`, `progressBarStyleLarge`, or
one of the other percentage-free types in the `android.R.attr` class.

Using an AsyncTask

Listing 3-8 contains the code to use the task in Listing 3-7. To form a complete code example, paste the task from Listing 3-7 into the `MyActivity`
class of Listing 3-8. (That is, make `MyAsyncTask` be an inner class of the
`MyActivity` class.)

Listing 3-8: The Main Activity Uses an AsyncTask

```
package com.allmycode.samples;

import java.io.IOException;
import java.io.InputStream;
import java.net.HttpURLConnection;
import java.net.URL;
```

**Book IV
Chapter 3**

**An Android
Potpourri**

(continued)

Listing 3-8 *(continued)*

```java
import android.app.Activity;
import android.graphics.Bitmap;
import android.graphics.BitmapFactory;
import android.os.AsyncTask;
import android.os.Bundle;
import android.view.View;
import android.view.View.OnClickListener;
import android.widget.Button;
import android.widget.ImageView;
import android.widget.ProgressBar;

public class MyActivity extends Activity implements
    OnClickListener {

  Button button;
  ImageView imageView;
  ProgressBar progressBar;

  @Override
  public void onCreate(Bundle savedInstanceState) {
    super.onCreate(savedInstanceState);
    setContentView(R.layout.main);

    button = ((Button) findViewById(R.id.button1));
    button.setOnClickListener(this);

    imageView = (ImageView) findViewById(R.id.imageView1);
    progressBar =
        (ProgressBar) findViewById(R.id.progressBar1);
    progressBar.setProgress(0);
  }

  public void onClick(View view) {
    new MyAsyncTask().execute
      ("http://allmycode.com/JavaForDummies/"
                  + "JavaForDummies5thEdition.jpg");
  }

  // The MyAsyncTask class is in Listing 3-7.

}
```

When the user clicks a button, the code in Listing 3-8 executes a new `MyAsyncTask` instance. The result (a shameless plug for one of my Java books) is shown in Figure 3-13.

Figure 3-13:
The
completion
of the task.

This section's example gets a bitmap from the web. So to run this section's code, add `<uses-permission android:name="android.permission.INTERNET"></uses-permission>` to the application's `AndroidManifest.xml` document.

Chapter 4: Apps for Tablets

In This Chapter

✔ **Adjusting for screen size and screen orientation**

✔ **Managing multipanel activities**

Don't think about an elephant.

Okay, now that you're thinking about an elephant, think about an elephant's legs. The diameter of an elephant's leg is typically about 40 centimeters (more than four tenths of a yard).

And think about spiders of the *Pholcidae* family (the "daddy longlegs") with their hair-like legs. And think about Gulliver with his Brobdingnagian friends. Each Brobdingnagian was about 72 feet tall, but a Brobdingnagian adult had the same physical proportions as Gulliver.

Gulliver's Travels is a work of fiction. An animal whose height is 12 times a human's height can't have bone sizes in human proportions. In other words, if you increase an object's size, you have to widen the object's supports. If you don't, the object will collapse.

This unintuitive truth about heights and widths comes from some geometric facts. An object's bulk increases as the cube of the object's height. But the ability to support that bulk increases only as the square of the object's height. That's because weight support depends on the cross-sectional area of the supporting legs, and a cross-sectional area is a square measurement, not a cubic measurement.

Anyway, the sizes of things make important qualitative differences. Take an activity designed for a touchscreen phone. Zoom that activity to a larger size without making any other changes. Then display the enlarged version on a ten-inch tablet screen. What you get on the tablet looks really bad. A tiny, crisp-looking icon turns into a big, blurry blob. An e-book page adapts to display longer line lengths. But with lines that are 40 words long, the human eye suffers from terrible fatigue.

The same issue arises with Android activities. An activity contains enough information to fill a small phone screen. When the user needs more information, your app displays a different activity. The new activity replaces the old activity, resulting in a complete refresh of the screen.

If you slap this activity behavior onto a larger tablet screen, the user feels cheated. You've replaced everything on the screen even though there's room for both the old and new information. The transition from one activity to the next is jarring, and both the old and new activities look barren.

No doubt about it . . . Android needs a new look for tablet devices. And to implement this look, Android's Honeycomb release had fragments.

What Fragments Can Do For You

A *fragment* is halfway between a view and an activity. Like a view, a fragment can't survive on its own. A view lives within an activity's context. You don't display a view except to set it as an activity's content.

Yes, a fragment is something like a view. But like an activity (and unlike a view), a fragment has a lifecycle. Table 4-1 lists the fragment lifecycle methods.

Table 4-1	Fragment Lifecycle Methods
Method Name	*When Android Calls This Method*
onAttach	Called when the fragment becomes part of a particular activity
onCreate	Called when the fragment is created (similar to an activity's onCreate method)
onCreateView	Called when Android creates the fragment's visible interface (comparable to an activity's setContentView method)
onActivity Created	Called when Android finishes executing the associated activity's onCreate method
onStart	Called when the fragment becomes visible to the user (typically, when Android executes the associated activity's onStart method)
onResume	Called when the fragment begins interacting with the user (typically, when Android executes the associated activity's onResume method)

Method Name	When Android Calls This Method
onPause	Called when the fragment no longer interacts with the user (similar to an activity's onPause method)
onStop	Called when the fragment is no longer visible to the user (similar to an activity's onStop method)
onDestroyView	Called when Android destroys the fragment's visible interface
onDestroy	Called when Android clobbers the fragment (similar to an activity's onDestroy method)
onDetach	Called when the fragment ceases to be part of a particular activity

A fragment has a lifecycle. Your first response to this news might be "Oh, no! More on*SuchAndSuch* methods to manage!" But the reality is, components' lifecycle methods are your friends. Lifecycle methods coordinate the comings and goings of individual components. Sure, it means you're going to have to manage your own app's interface. But without lifecycle methods, you'd have to micromanage your own app's interaction with other apps *and* with the Android operating system.

Programming with fragments

The user interface in this section's example has three panels — a list of items, a detail pane describing whichever item is selected in the list, and a details-in-more-depth pane. On a small smartphone screen, each panel would be a separate activity. But a tablet screen in landscape mode has room for more than one panel.

Figure 4-1 shows this section's app with two of the three panels. The panel on the left displays a list of traditional Android SDK components. The panel on the right displays a description of whatever component is chosen in the list on the left. (The description is actually the first few sentences of the component's SDK documentation.) This details-on-the-right pattern is part of many user interfaces.

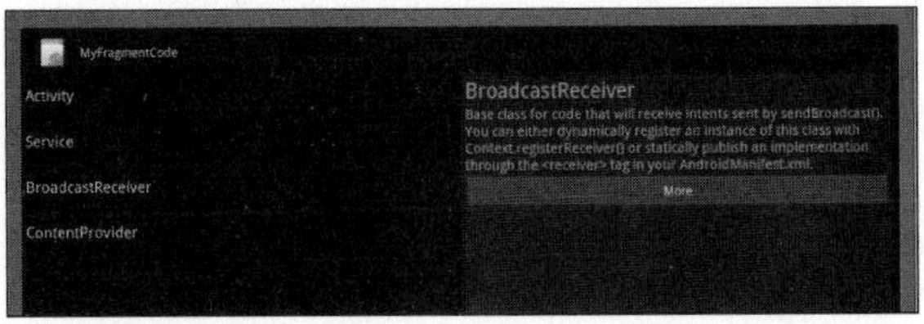

Figure 4-1:
Two
fragments
attached to
one activity.

To create the display in Figure 4-1, you build one activity. The activity has two fragments — a fragment on the left and another on the right. The left pane displays the same fragment throughout the run of the app, so you can declare that fragment in the `AndroidManifest.xml` document. The right pane displays one fragment at a time, but the fragment changes during the app's run. So you declare a frame layout in the right pane. Listing 4-1 has the code.

Listing 4-1: The main.xml Document

```
<?xml version="1.0" encoding="utf-8"?>
<LinearLayout xmlns:android=
      "http://schemas.android.com/apk/res/android"
    android:orientation="horizontal"
    android:layout_width="match_parent"
    android:layout_height="match_parent">

    <fragment class=
         "com.allmycode.frag.ComponentNamesFragment"
        android:id="@+id/component_names"
        android:layout_height="match_parent"
        android:layout_width="0px"
        android:layout_weight="1" />

    <FrameLayout android:id="@+id/docs"
        android:layout_height="match_parent"
        android:layout_width="0px"
        android:layout_weight="1"
        android:background=
          "?android:attr/detailsElementBackground" />

</LinearLayout>
```

The app's main activity code is impressively uninteresting. (See Listing 4-2.)

Listing 4-2: The Main Activity

```
package com.allmycode.frag;

import android.app.Activity;
import android.os.Bundle;

public class AllPurposeActivity extends Activity {

  @Override
  protected void onCreate(Bundle savedInstanceState) {
    super.onCreate(savedInstanceState);
```

```
    setContentView(R.layout.main);
  }
}
```

Listing 4-3 contains the `ComponentNamesFragment` class. By virtue of the layout in Listing 4-1, Android plants a `ComponentNamesFragment` on the left side of the device's screen (refer to Figure 4-1).

Listing 4-3:   A Fragment Containing a List of Items

```
package com.allmycode.frag;

import android.app.FragmentManager;
import android.app.FragmentTransaction;
import android.app.ListFragment;
import android.os.Bundle;
import android.view.View;
import android.widget.ArrayAdapter;
import android.widget.ListView;

public class ComponentNamesFragment extends ListFragment {

  final static String[] COMPONENTS = { "Activity",
      "Service", "BroadcastReceiver", "ContentProvider" };

  @Override
  public void onActivityCreated
                              (Bundle savedInstanceState) {
    super.onActivityCreated(savedInstanceState);
    setListAdapter(new ArrayAdapter<String>(
        getActivity(),
        android.R.layout.simple_list_item_activated_1,
        COMPONENTS));
  }

  @Override
  public void onListItemClick(ListView l, View v,
      int index, long id) {

    getListView().setItemChecked(index, true);
    DocsFragment docsFragment =
        DocsFragment.newInstance(index);
    FragmentManager fragmentManager =
        getFragmentManager();
    FragmentTransaction fragmentTransaction =
        fragmentManager.beginTransaction();
    fragmentTransaction.replace(R.id.docs, docsFragment);
    int backStackEntryCount =
        fragmentManager.getBackStackEntryCount();
```

(continued)

**Book IV
Chapter 4**

Apps for Tablets

Listing 4-3 *(continued)*

```
    for (int i = 0; i < backStackEntryCount; i++) {
      fragmentManager.popBackStackImmediate();
    }
    fragmentTransaction.addToBackStack(null);

    fragmentTransaction.commit();
  }
}
```

A `ListFragment` is a fragment that displays a list. Early on in the fragment's lifecycle, the code in Listing 4-3 sets a list adapter (more specifically, an `ArrayAdapter`) for the fragment. So how early is "early on?"

As in the examples from Chapter 2 (of this minibook), the `ArrayAdapter` constructor's first parameter is a context. But wait! Unlike an activity, a fragment isn't a context. So you can't use the keyword `this` for the constructor's first parameter.

Fortunately, a fragment has a `getActivity` method. A call to `get Activity` grabs the activity to which the fragment is attached. So for the `ArrayAdapter` constructor's first parameter, you can call `getActivity`. Of course, you can't call `getActivity` until the fragment is attached to an existing activity. That's why, in Listing 4-3, I override the fragment's `on ActivityCreated` method. Android calls `onActivityCreated` *after* attaching the fragment and calling the activity's `onCreate` method. So everything works as planned.

The `android.app.Activity` class's great-grandparent class is `android. content.Context`. But the `android.app.Fragment` class's parent class is plain old `java.lang.Object`. So in an activity's code, the keyword `this` refers to a context. But in a fragment's code, the keyword `this` doesn't refer to a context.

A `ListFragment` is like a `ListActivity` — except that it's a fragment, not an activity. Many of the `ListActivity` class's concepts apply as well to the `ListFragment` class. To read about Android's `ListActivity` class, see Chapter 2 in this minibook.

Like a `ListActivity`, a `ListFragment` has an `onListItemClick` method. In Listing 4-3, I respond to a click by working with a `DocsFragment`, a `FragmentTransaction`, and a `FragmentManager`:

✦ The `DocsFragment` instance in Listing 4-3 represents the right side of Figure 4-1.

✦ A fragment transaction is a bunch of things you do with fragments. For example, setting up to replace one fragment with another (as in Listing 4-3) is a transaction.

✦ A fragment manager does what its name suggests. It manages fragments' arrivals and departures.

The fragment

You don't get to see the `DocsFragment`'s code until Listing 4-4. So for now, the actual fragment created by calling `DocsFragment.newInstance` is a black box. (I shouldn't build up the suspense this way. I just don't want you to get sidetracked.)

What Listing 4-3 tells you about the new `DocsFragment` instance is that the instance knows about the current *index* — the position of the list item selected by the user. (The list is on the left side of Figure 4-1.) The `DocsFragment` class's code should use this `index` value (`0`, `1`, `2`, or `3`) to decide which component's documentation to display.

The fragment transaction

The term *transaction* comes from the world of databases. A transaction is a bunch of operations. These operations live inside an all-or-nothing bubble. That is, either all the operations in the transaction take place, or none of the operations in the transaction takes place.

In Listing 4-3, you turn a bunch of statements into a transaction. In particular, you sandwich a bunch of statements between calls to `begin Transaction` and `commit`. One of these statements, `fragment Transaction.replace(R.id.docs, docsFragment)`, prepares to replace whatever's currently in the `docs` frame layout (in Listing 4-1) with a new fragment. The replacement occurs when Android executes the `fragmentTransaction.commit` method call.

The fragment manager

An instance of the `android.app.FragmentManager` class takes care of your app's fragments. For example, in Listing 4-3 the manager's `begin Transaction` method starts a fragment transaction. The manager also helps you fiddle with your activity's stack.

Book III, Chapter 1 describes the way activities pile up on top of one another with successive `startActivity` calls. When the user presses Back, Android pops an activity off the stack. The most recently added activity is the first to be popped. It's as if Android, the boss, has an agreement with members of the Activities Union. Android fires activities in reverse order of seniority.

With the introduction of fragments in Android 3.0, an activity can have its own private stack. You can display fragment A and then call `fragment Transaction.replace` and `fragmentTransaction.addToBackStack`. The combination of method calls makes fragment B overwrite fragment A. When the user presses Back, fragment B goes away, and fragment A returns to its place on the activity's screen. Android doesn't destroy an entire activity until the activity has no fragments that it can jettison.

With the `for` loop in Listing 4-3, the fragment manager does some quick housekeeping of the activity's fragment stack. To read more about this housekeeping, cast your eyes to the next section.

Fragments, more fragments, and even more fragments

The right pane in Figure 4-1 has a More button. When the user presses this More button, the app displays a more verbose description of the selected component. To find out how this happens, stare thoughtfully (but joyfully) at the code in Listing 4-4.

Listing 4-4:   Code to Create the Fragment on the Right Side of Figure 4-1

```
package com.allmycode.frag;

import android.app.Fragment;
import android.app.FragmentTransaction;
import android.os.Bundle;
import android.view.LayoutInflater;
import android.view.View;
import android.view.View.OnClickListener;
import android.view.ViewGroup;
import android.widget.Button;
import android.widget.LinearLayout;
import android.widget.TextView;

public class DocsFragment extends Fragment {

    int index;

    public static DocsFragment newInstance(int index) {
        DocsFragment docsFragment = new DocsFragment();
```

```
  docsFragment.index = index;
  return docsFragment;
}

@Override
public View onCreateView(LayoutInflater inflater,
    ViewGroup container, Bundle savedInstanceState) {

  LinearLayout layout = new LinearLayout(getActivity());
  layout.setOrientation(LinearLayout.VERTICAL);
  TextView textView1 = new TextView(getActivity());
  textView1.setTextSize(30);
  textView1
      .setText(ComponentNamesFragment.COMPONENTS[index]);
  layout.addView(textView1);
  TextView textView2 = new TextView(getActivity());
  textView2.setTextSize(20);
  textView2.setText(DOCS[index]);
  layout.addView(textView2);

  Button button = new Button(getActivity());
  button.setText("More");
  button
      .setOnClickListener(new MyButtonListener(index));
  layout.addView(button);

  return layout;
}

public class MyButtonListener implements
    OnClickListener {
  int index;

  public MyButtonListener(int index) {
    this.index = index;
  }

  @Override
  public void onClick(View view) {
    DocsFragmentVerbose docsFragmentVerbose =
        DocsFragmentVerbose.newInstance(index);
    FragmentTransaction fragmentTransaction =
        getFragmentManager().beginTransaction();
    fragmentTransaction.replace(R.id.docs,
        docsFragmentVerbose);
    fragmentTransaction.setTransition
        (FragmentTransaction.TRANSIT_FRAGMENT_OPEN);
    fragmentTransaction.addToBackStack(null);
    fragmentTransaction.commit();
```

(continued)

Book IV
Chapter 4

Apps for Tablets

Listing 4-4 *(continued)*

```
        }
    }

    final static String[] DOCS =
        {"An activity is a single, focused thing that the"
        + " user can do. Almost all activities interact"
        + " with the user, so the Activity class takes"
        + " care of creating a window for you in which you"
        + " can place your UI with setContentView(View).",
          "A Service is an application component"
        + " representing either an application's desire"
        + " to perform a longer-running operation while"
        + " not interacting with the user or to supply"
        + " functionality for other applications to use.",
          "Base class for code that will receive intents"
        + " sent by sendBroadcast(). You can either"
        + " dynamically register an instance of this class"
        + " with Context.registerReceiver() or statically"
        + " publish an implementation through the"
        + " <receiver> tag in your AndroidManifest.xml.",
          "Content providers are one of the primary"
        + " building blocks of Android applications,"
        + " providing content to applications. They"
        + " encapsulate data and provide it to applications"
        + " through the single ContentResolver interface."
        + " A content provider is only required if you need"
        + " to share data between multiple applications."
        };
    }
```

Table 4-1 lists `onCreateView` as one of `Fragment` class's lifecycle methods. In Listing 4-4, the `onCreateView` method uses Java code to compose a layout — the layout on the right side in Figure 4-1. The listing's `onCreate View` method returns a linear layout, which is a view group, which is a view. And that view becomes the fragment's visible presence on the tablet screen.

In Listing 4-4, I define a fragment's layout using Java code instead of a res/ layout XML document. Book III, Chapter 2 goes into more detail on the usage of Java code to define views and layouts.

Building the fragment stack

In Listing 4-4, the button's `OnClickListener` replaces the right side of Figure 4-1 with a brand-new fragment — an instance of my `DocsFragment Verbose` class. And clever guy that I am, I programmed the `DocsFragment Verbose` class to display a page from the official Android documentation website. Listing 4-5 contains the code.

Listing 4-5:   A Fragment Containing a Web View

```
package com.allmycode.frag;

import android.app.Fragment;
import android.os.Bundle;
import android.view.LayoutInflater;
import android.view.View;
import android.view.ViewGroup;
import android.webkit.WebView;

public class DocsFragmentVerbose extends Fragment {

  int index;

  public static DocsFragmentVerbose
      newInstance(int index) {
    DocsFragmentVerbose docsFragmentVerbose =
        new DocsFragmentVerbose();
    docsFragmentVerbose.index = index;
    return docsFragmentVerbose;
  }

  @Override
  public View onCreateView(LayoutInflater inflater,
      ViewGroup container, Bundle savedInstanceState) {

    WebView webView = new WebView(getActivity());

    webView.loadUrl(
        "http://developer.android.com/reference/android/"
          + ((index < 2) ? "app/" : "content/")
          + ComponentNamesFragment.COMPONENTS[index]
          + ".html");

    return webView;
  }
}
```

At this point, I can describe the whole storyboard for this section's grand example:

✦ **The user sees a list — namely, the list of component names in the left fragment in Figure 4-1.**

✦ **The user selects an item in the list.**

In response, the app displays a brief description of the selected item. In Figure 4-1, the description is the first few sentences of Android's `BroadcastReceiver` documentation.

To display the description, the code in Listing 4-3 calls `replace(R.id.docs, docsFragment)`. That is, the code places a fragment into the `R.id.docs` view.

✦ **The newly displayed fragment contains a brief description and a button. (Refer to Figure 4-1.) If the user clicks the button, the app covers this fragment with an even newer fragment.**

In Figure 4-2, the new fragment displays the `BroadcastReceiver`'s online documentation page.

Figure 4-2:
A fragment contains a web view.

To load a page from the Internet, your app's `AndroidManifest.xml` document must have a `<uses-permission android:name="android.permission.INTERNET" />` element.

Trimming the fragment stack

When I created the first draft of the code in Listing 4-3, I didn't include anything about `getBackStackEntryCount` or `popBackStackImmediate`. "Whew! I'm done!" I said to myself. But then I tested the code. What I discovered in testing was that a user's attention shifts abruptly with the selection of a new list item.

Imagine selecting `BroadcastReceiver` and then clicking the More button. After a look at the `BroadcastReceiver`'s documentation page (in Figure 4-2), you turn your attention leftward to the list of components. As soon as you select a different component, you tend to forget all about broadcast receivers. So if you click the Back button, you probably don't want to rummage back through your old selections. In other words, selecting an item in the list of components represents a fresh start. When you select an item in the list of components, the app should clear whatever fragment stack you created previously.

The `for` loop in Listing 4-3 does the desired stack cleanup. The code calls the fragment manager's `getBackStackEntryCount` method to find out how many fragments you have on the stack. Then the `for` loop uses the entry count to decide how many fragments to pop off the stack. When the loop finishes its work, the stack of fragments is empty, so you can safely call the current transaction's `addToBackStack` method. The strategy works very nicely.

Getting the Best of Both Worlds

The previous sections in this chapter describe an app that uses fragments. The app works very nicely but has one tiny limitation. You must not let the user turn the tablet sideways. If the tablet device is in portrait mode, the app looks silly. (Yes, I'm being sarcastic if I call this problem a "tiny limitation.")

Figure 4-3 shows the app on a display that's taller than it is wide. You have lots of wasted space on the left side, and you have no room for the page heading (BroadcastReceiver) on the right side.

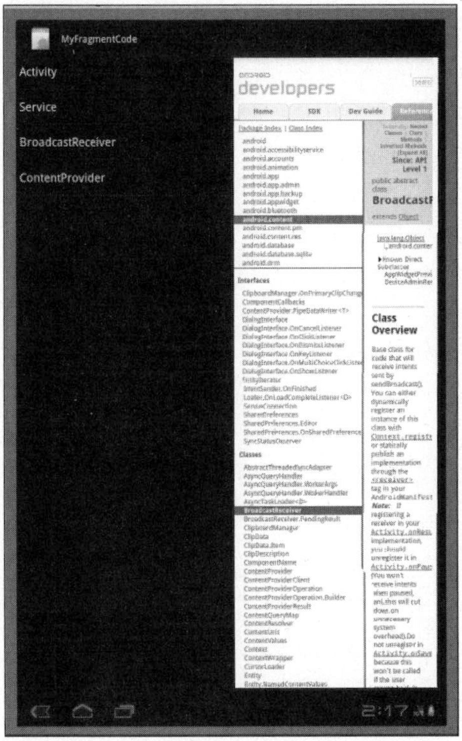

Figure 4-3: Screen orientation matters a lot!

Book IV Chapter 4

Apps for Tablets

I'm the first to admit that this book's other examples vary from plain-looking to ugly. But with other examples, the fault is with my lack of artistic flair. In this chapter's example, the fault is in the code. ("The fault, dear Brutus, is not in our arts, But in our code . . .")

To remedy the visual faux pas in Figure 4-3, you create an additional activity. The new `DocsActivityVerbose` activity has only one view — namely, a view to display the web page fragment from Listing 4-5. Unlike the narrow fragment in Figure 4-3, the new activity consumes the entire screen. (See

Figure 4-4.) You tweak the rest of the app's code to display either the `DocsFragmentVerbose` or the `DocsActivityVerbose` depending on the screen's orientation.

To adapt this chapter's app for both portrait and landscape mode, follow these steps:

1. **Start with the project that's described in Listings 4-1 to 4-5.**

You can download the code from this book's website (`www.allmy code.com/android`).

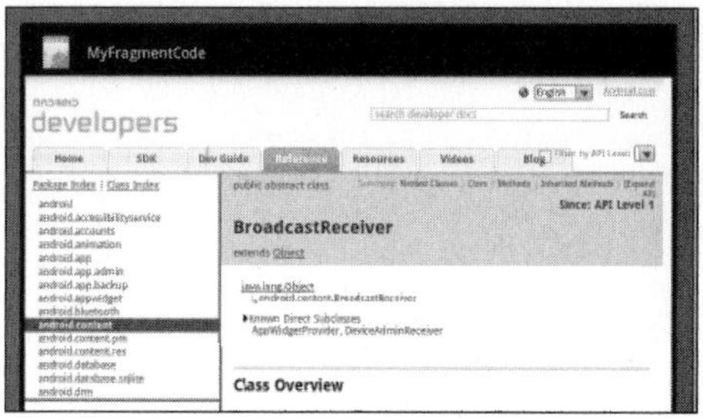

Figure 4-4:
The web
page
fragment
takes up
the entire
screen.

2. **Add a new Java class to your project.**

In Listing 4-6, I call the class `DocsActivityVerbose`.

Listing 4-6: An Activity That's a Wrapper for a Fragment

```
package com.allmycode.frag;

import android.app.Activity;
import android.app.FragmentTransaction;
import android.os.Bundle;

public class DocsActivityVerbose extends Activity {

  @Override
  public void onCreate(Bundle bundle) {
    super.onCreate(bundle);
    setContentView(R.layout.docs_verbose);

    int index = getIntent().getIntExtra("index", 0);

    DocsFragmentVerbose docsFragmentVerbose =
        DocsFragmentVerbose.newInstance(index);
    FragmentTransaction fragmentTransaction =
        getFragmentManager().beginTransaction();
    fragmentTransaction.replace(R.id.docs_verbose_frame,
```

```
        docsFragmentVerbose);
    fragmentTransaction.setTransition
        (FragmentTransaction.TRANSIT_FRAGMENT_OPEN);
    fragmentTransaction.commit();
    }
}
```

The new `DocsActivityVerbose` class performs the same fragment transaction that's performed by the `MyButtonListener` in Listing 4-4.

Notice that the code in Listing 4-6 doesn't call the `addToBackStack` method. If you called `addToBackStack` in Listing 4-6, Android would push the web page fragment on top of an initially empty fragment. Then, when the user pressed the Back button, Android would pop the web page fragment off the stack. The user would see an empty fragment that consumes the entire screen.

3. Before you forget, add an `<activity>` element to the project's `AndroidManifest.xml` document.

The new `<activity>` element looks like this:

```
<activity android:name=
    "com.allmycode.frag.DocsActivityVerbose" />
```

Like many activity classes, the new `DocsActivityVerbose` class uses its own layout resource. And sure enough, the `onCreate` method in Listing 4-6 refers to an `R.layout.docs_verbose` resource. So in the next several steps, you tweak the app's layouts and create the `docs_verbose.xml` document.

4. Right-click (Control-click on a Mac) the project's `res/layout` folder in Eclipse's Package Explorer view and then choose Copy.

5. Right-click (or Control-click on a Mac) the project's `res` folder in the Package Explorer view and then choose Paste.

Eclipse doesn't want you to create a second folder with the name `layout`. So Eclipse prompts you with a Name Conflict dialog box.

6. In the Name Conflict dialog box, enter the name layout-land **and click OK.**

When your device is in landscape mode, Android looks for a `res` folder named `layout-land`. And when your device is in portrait mode, Android looks for a `res` folder named `layout-port`. In either case, if the desired folder doesn't exist, Android falls back on the old-fashioned `res/layout` folder. (This section's example has a `layout-land` folder but no `layout-port` folder.)

Now, with folders named `res/layout` and `res/layout-land`, your app's resources can be different for the two screen orientations.

7. **Add a `docs_verbose.xml` document to the project's `res/layout` folder.**

   The code is in Listing 4-7.

Listing 4-7:   A Layout for the New DocsActivityVerbose Class

```xml
<?xml version="1.0" encoding="utf-8"?>
<LinearLayout xmlns:android=
        "http://schemas.android.com/apk/res/android"
    android:layout_width="match_parent"
    android:layout_height="match_parent">
    <FrameLayout android:id="@+id/docs_verbose_frame"
        android:layout_height="match_parent"
        android:layout_width="match_parent"
        android:layout_weight="1" />
</LinearLayout>
```

The `R.layout.docs_verbose` resource helps you when the device is in portrait mode. So the new `docs_verbose.xml` document belongs in the `res/layout` folder, not in the `res/layout-land` folder.

Having created the new `DocsActivityVerbose` class and its required layout resource, you're ready to integrate these files into the rest of the app's code. To do this, consider two situations:

- *When the user presses the More button,* you either replace the existing fragment or start your new `DocsActivityVerbose`, depending on the screen's orientation.

- *When the user turns the device sideways,* you check whether the new orientation will cause the awkward crunch, as shown in Figure 4-3. If so, back away from displaying the web page fragment.

The next few steps finish the job.

8. **Modify the `DocsFragment` code's `onClick` method (see Listing 4-8).**

Listing 4-8:   Deciding What to Do When the User Clicks a Button

```java
@Override
public void onClick(View view) {
  if (getResources().getConfiguration().orientation
          == Configuration.ORIENTATION_LANDSCAPE) {

    DocsFragmentVerbose docsFragmentVerbose =
        DocsFragmentVerbose.newInstance(index);
    FragmentTransaction fragmentTransaction =
        getFragmentManager().beginTransaction();
    fragmentTransaction.replace(R.id.docs,
        docsFragmentVerbose);
    fragmentTransaction.setTransition
```

```
    (FragmentTransaction.TRANSIT_FRAGMENT_OPEN);
  fragmentTransaction.addToBackStack(null);
  fragmentTransaction.commit();
} else {
  Intent intent = new Intent();
  intent.setClass(getActivity(),
      DocsActivityVerbose.class);
  intent.putExtra("index", index);
  startActivity(intent);
}
}
```

The original `DocsFragment` class in Listing 4-4 doesn't check the screen's orientation. But the code in Listing 4-8 responds in different ways, depending on the orientation. If the orientation is landscape, the code in Listing 4-8 mimics the code in Listing 4-4. But if the orientation is portrait, Listing 4-8 starts an instance of the new `DocsActivityVerbose` class.

9. **Add the method in Listing 4-9 to the `AllPurposeActivity` class's code.**

Listing 4-9: Intercepting a Change in the Screen's Orientation

```
@Override
public void
    onConfigurationChanged(Configuration config) {

  super.onConfigurationChanged(config);

  if (config.orientation ==
      Configuration.ORIENTATION_PORTRAIT) {
    FragmentManager fragmentManager =
        getFragmentManager();
    if (fragmentManager.getBackStackEntryCount() > 1) {
      fragmentManager.popBackStackImmediate();
    }
  }
}
```

The original `AllPurposeActivity` class is in Listing 4-2. Here in Listing 4-9, the newly added `onConfigurationChanged` method checks for danger. And by "danger," I mean being in portrait mode and displaying the web page fragment.

To be precise, the code in Listing 4-9 asks how many fragments are currently on the activity's stack of fragments. If the count is more than one, the most recently created fragment is the dreaded web page fragment. So to eliminate the danger, the code pops the web page fragment off the stack.

**Book IV
Chapter 4**

Apps for Tablets

10. **In the `AndroidManifest.xml` document, add the following attribute to the `AllPurposeActivity`'s start tag:**

```
android:configChanges="orientation"
```

This attribute tells Android not to destroy and re-create `AllPurpose Activity` whenever the user turns the device sideways. Instead, Android calls the activity's `onConfigurationChanged` method. That's good because without this attribute, Step 9 is a waste of time.

Android calls an activity's `onConfigurationChanged` method only if you add the `android:configChanges="orientation"` attribute in the `AndroidManifest.xml` document.

With the changes that you make in this section's steps, the user can turn the device sideways, upside-down, or whatever. When the user wants to see a web page, the app displays the page in a fragment or in an entire activity, whichever is best.

Book V

The Job Isn't Done Until . . .

The 5th Wave   By Rich Tennant

"Hold on, Barbara. I'm pretty sure the Android Market has an application for this."

Contents at a Glance

Chapter 1: Publishing Your App to the Android Market

In This Chapter

✔ Prepping your code

✔ Building an Android package file

✔ Opening an account in the Android Market

✔ Picking a price for your app

✔ Illustrating your app with a screen shot

✔ Uploading and publishing your application

✔ Monitoring downloads

The Honeymooners aired from 1955 to 1956 on the CBS television network in the United States. Comedian Jackie Gleason played Ralph Kramden, a bus driver living in a small Brooklyn, New York, apartment with his wife, Alice. (In earlier sketches, actress Pert Kelton had played the role of Alice. But Kelton was blacklisted by McCarthy's House Committee on Un-American Activities, so actress Audrey Meadows assumed the role of Alice.)

One of Ralph Kramden's fatal flaws was his affinity for get-rich-quick schemes. In a hilarious *Honeymooners* episode, Ralph and his buddy Ed Norton (played by Art Carney) did a live television infomercial for their Handy Housewife Helper gadgets. (Visit www.youtube.com/watch?v=yB5a6y3okeo to check it out.) Ralph's sudden stage fright made him stumble and shake instead of effectively showing off his product.

While I'm on the subject of getting rich quickly, I can segue seamlessly to the Android Market. The Android Market is the official application distribution mechanism behind Android. Publishing your application to the market enables your application to be downloaded, installed, and run by millions of users across the world. Users can also rate and leave comments about your application, which helps you identify possible usage trends as well as problematic areas that users might be encountering.

The Android Market also provides a set of valuable statistics that you can use to track the success of your application, as I show you in the last section of this chapter.

In this chapter, I show you how to publish your application to the Android Market. I also show you how to provide a couple of screen shots, a promo screen shot, and a short description of your application. To get your app into the Android Market, you have to package it in a distributable format first.

Preparing Your Code

You had a great idea, you developed the next hit application and/or game for the Android platform, and now you're ready to get the application into the hands of end users. The first thing you need to do is test your application. When you've finished testing, test some more.

After thoroughly testing your app, ask yourself what sequences of buttons you avoided clicking when you did your "thorough" testing. Then muster the courage to click the buttons and use the widgets in that strange sequence. And while you're at it, tilt the device sideways, turn the device upside down, hold the device above your head, and try using the app. If your device is a phone, interrupt the app with an incoming call.

Are you finished testing? Not yet. Have your friends test the app on their devices. Whatever you do, don't give them any instructions other than the instructions you intend to publish. Ask them about their experiences running your app.

You can "publish" your app on the Android Market so that only your designated friends can install the app. For more information, skip ahead to the "More testing" section.

Can I overemphasize the need for testing? I don't think so. When you test your app, be your app's worst enemy. Try as hard as you can to break your app. Be overly critical. Be relentless. If your app has a bug and you don't find it, your users will.

Un-testing the app

When you test an app, you find features that don't quite work. You check the logs, and you probably add code to help you diagnose problems. As you prepare to publish your app, remove any unnecessary diagnostic code, remove extra logging statements, and remove any other code whose purpose is to benefit the developer rather than the user.

In developing your app, you might have created some test data. (Is there a duck named "Donald" in your app's contact list?) If you've created test data, delete the data from your app.

Check your project's `AndroidManifest.xml` file. If the `<application>` element has an `android:debuggable="true"` attribute, remove that attribute. (The attribute's default value is `false`.)

Choosing Android versions

To distribute an application, you create an *Android Package* (APK) file. An APK file contains everything a user's device needs to know in order to run your app. You can think of an APK file as a compressed copy of the stuff displayed for a particular project in Eclipse's Package Explorer view.

Each APK file's name ends with the `.apk` extension. When you get Eclipse to run your application, Eclipse creates an APK file and installs the APK file on an emulator or a device. If your app has an activity with `"android. intent.action.MAIN"` and `"android.intent.category.LAUNCHER"`, Eclipse goes one step further and actually launches your app.

Before you jump in and create the distributable APK file, make sure that your application is available to as many users as possible. Do this by tweaking the `android:minSdkVersion` in the `AndroidManifest.xml` file:

```
<uses-sdk android:minSdkVersion="4" />
```

The `minSdkVersion` property identifies which versions of the Android platform can install this application. The Android platform, for the most part, is backward-compatible. Most of the features in API version 4 are also in API versions 8 and 9. Yes, small changes and sometimes new large components are released in each new version, but for the most part, everything else in the platform remains backward-compatible. Therefore, stating that this application needs a minimum of API version 4 (Donut) signifies that any Android operating system version 4 or greater can run the application.

Using the `minSdkVersion` information, the Android Market can determine which applications to show each user of each device. If you were to release the application right now with `minSdkVersion` set to the value of 4, and you opened the Android Market on an Android device running version 3 (Cupcake), you wouldn't find your application. Why? The Android Market filters it out for you. You, the developer, told the Android Market, "Hey! This app can run only on devices that are of API level 4 or greater!" If you were to open the Android Market on a device running API level 4 or above, you could find and install your application.

WARNING!

If you don't provide a `minSdkVersion` value in the `uses-sdk` element of the application's manifest, the Android Market defaults the `minSdkVersion` to 0, which means that this application is compatible with all Android versions. If your application happens to use a component not available in older versions of the platform (such as the Bluetooth technology in Android 2.0), and a user installs your application, he receives a run-time error informing the user that the application could not continue because an exception occurred.

For information about minimum SDK versions and target SDK versions, see Book I, Chapter 3.

Selecting an icon and a label

When you create a new Android project, Eclipse puts some default attributes in your `<application>` element's start tag:

```
<application android:icon="@drawable/icon"
             android:label="@string/app_name">
```

Before publishing your app, replace these defaults with your own values. Create nice-looking icons starting with Android's Icon Templates Pack (available for download at `http://developer.android.com/shareables/icon_templates-v2.3.zip`). Also check Android's Icon Design Guidelines at `http://developer.android.com/guide/practices/ui_guidelines/icon_design.html`. Choose a label (an app name) that grabs a customer's attention.

Set your app's own version code and version name

When you create a new Android project, Eclipse puts some default attributes in your `<manifest>` element's start tag:

```
<manifest android:versionCode="1"
          android:versionName="1.0" ... (more attributes)>
```

The version code must be an integer, and your app's code numbers must increase over time. For example, if your first published version has version code 42, your second published version must have a version code higher than 42.

Users never see the version code. Instead, users see your app's version name. You can use any string for your app's version name. Many developers use the `major-release.minor-release.point` system. For example, a typical version name might be `1.2.2`. But there are no restrictions. Android has all the dessert names, and Apple has all the jungle-cat names, so I add something like

```
android:versionName="sea squirt"
```

to my `<manifest>` start tag. (Look it up!)

Creating the APK File

When you create an app that runs on an emulator or a device, Eclipse packages your app in an APK file — one file specially formatted to contain all your app's code and all your app's data. Here's what you need to do for the packaging process to go smoothly:

1. **Open Eclipse, if it is not already open.**

2. **Right-click (Windows) or Control-click (Mac) your project and then choose Android Tools⇨Export Signed Application Package from the resulting contextual menu.**

Doing so displays the Export Android Application/Project Checks dialog box, as shown in Figure 1-1, with the current project name filled in for you.

3. **Click the Next button.**

The Export Android Application/Keystore Selection dialog box opens, as shown in Figure 1-2.

For more information about keystores, skip to the "Digitally signing your application" section.

4. **You haven't created a keystore yet, so select the Create New Keystore option.**

5. **Choose the location of your keystore.**

In Figure 1-2, notice that I don't put the new keystore in my project's directory. As I publish more apps, I'll probably use this keystore to sign other projects' APK files.

6. **Choose and enter a password that you'll remember; reenter it in the Confirm field.**

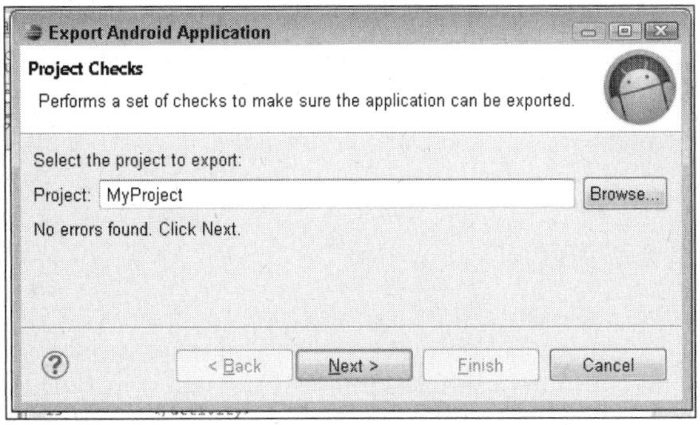

Figure 1-1:
The Export
Android
Application/
Project
Checks
dialog box.

Export Android Application

Project Checks

Performs a set of checks to make sure the application can be exported.

Select the project to export:

Project: MyProject   [Browse...]

No errors found. Click Next.

(?)   [< Back]   [Next >]   [Finish]   [Cancel]

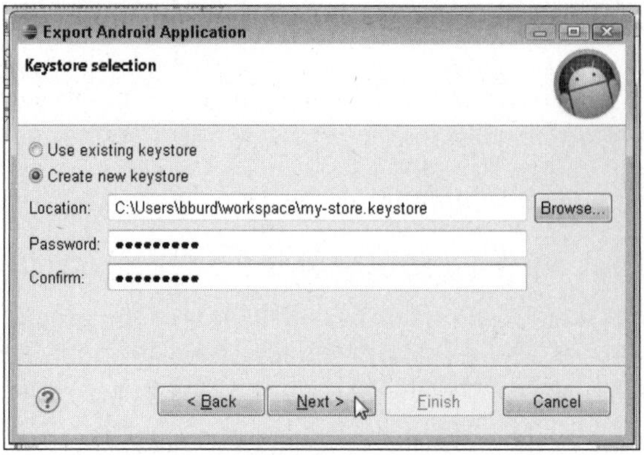

Figure 1-2:
The Export
Android
Application/
Keystore
Selection
dialog box.

Export Android Application

Keystore selection

○ Use existing keystore
◉ Create new keystore

Location: C:\Users\bburd\workspace\my-store.keystore Browse...

Password: •••••••••

Confirm: •••••••••

< Back   Next >   Finish   Cancel

7. **Click the Next button.**

   The Export Android Application/Key Creation dialog box opens.

8. **Fill out the following fields:**

   - *Alias:* This is the alias that you will use to identify the key.

   - *Password and Confirm:* This is the password that will be used for the key.

   - *Validity (Years):* This indicates how long this key will be valid for. Your key must expire after October 22, 2033. (I can't imagine how the creators of Android came up with this date! I'm wondering what kind of party I should throw when October 22, 2033, finally rolls around. Anyway, I normally insert a value of 30 years into this field to be safe.)

9. **Complete the bottom half of the dialog box (called the *Certificate Issuer* section), filling in at least one of these fields:**

   - *First and Last Name*

   - *Organizational Unit*

   - *Organization*

   - *City or Locality*

   - *State or Province*

   - *Country Code (XX)*

The items *First and Last Name, Organizational Unit,* and so on are part of the *X.500 Distinguished Name* standard. The probability of two people having the same name and working in the same unit of the same organization in the same locality is close to zero.

When you finish, your dialog box resembles Figure 1-3.

Figure 1-3:
The Export
Android
Application/
Key
Creation
dialog box.

10. **Click the Next button.**

    The final screen you encounter is the Export Android Application/
    Destination and Key/Certificate Checks dialog box, as shown in Figure 1-4.

11. **Enter a name and location for a file with an .apk extension.**

    As you develop a project, Eclipse puts APK files in the project's `bin`
    subdirectory. So that's where I put the APK file in Figure 1-4.

12. **Click the Finish button.**

    This creates the APK file in your chosen location. If you open this location,
    you see the APK file and a few other goodies. (See Figure 1-5.)

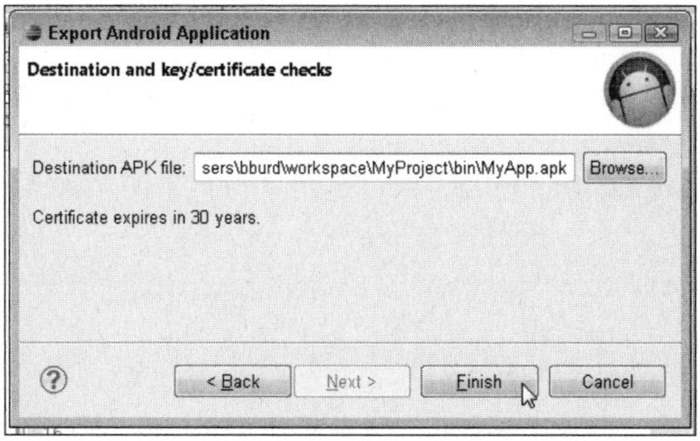

Figure 1-4:
Choosing a
name and
destination
for your APK
file.

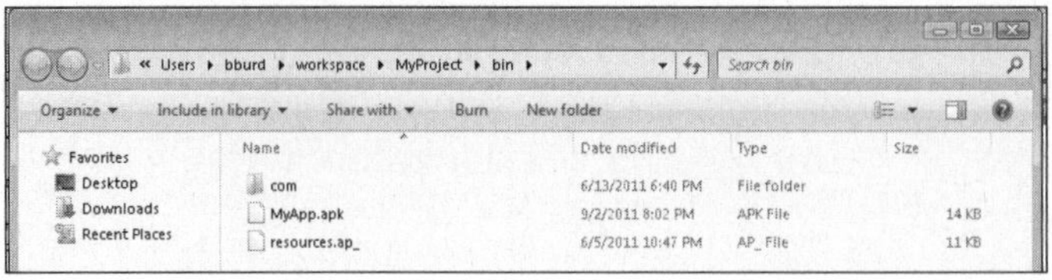

Figure 1-5:
Verifying the
destination
of the APK
file.

Congratulations! You've created a distributable APK file and a reusable keystore for future updates.

Digitally signing your application

Android requires that all installed applications be digitally signed:

✦ No ifs, ands or buts: All Android applications must be signed. The system will not install an application that is not signed.

When you test an app on an emulator or on your own device, one of Android's development tools quietly signs your app with a simple key from a `debug.keystore` file.

For bedtime reading about the `debug.keystore` file and other aspects of digital signing, see the nearby "Understanding digital signatures" sidebar.

✦ You can use self-signed certificates to sign your applications; a certificate authority is not needed.

To read all about certificate authorities, see the nearby sidebar.

✦ When you are ready to release your application to the market, you must sign it with a private key. You cannot publish the application with the debug key that signs the APK file when debugging the application during development.

✦ The certificate has an expiration date, and that expiration date is verified only at install time. If the certificate expires after the application has been installed, the application continues to operate normally.

✦ Eclipse's Android tools can do much of the work in signing your app. For finer control, you can use standard Java tools such as keytool or jarsigner to sign your APK files.

For more information on do-it-yourself signing, see Book VI, Chapter 3.

Understanding digital signatures

When you digitally sign something, you add a sequence of bits that only you can add. You use sophisticated software to create the sequence and to embed the sequence in your APK file. The software to create this sequence uses techniques from number theory. (Sometime between 1777 and 1855, Carl Friedrich Gauss called number theory "the queen of mathematics," and he wasn't kidding!)

Digital signing actually involves two sequences of bits:

✔ **A private key:** A sequence that you don't share with others.

✔ **A public key:** A sequence that you do share with others.

The private key never leaves your office, but you can display the public key on a neon sign in Times Square. If you tell someone your private key, you'd have to . . . (well, you know). But you can hire a pilot to write your public key with white smoke in the sky over the Golden Gate Bridge.

To sign an app, you run software that adds a certificate to your app. A *certificate* is a bunch of information, which includes your private key, your public key, some information to identify you, and some other information. Like your signature on a contract, a certificate's private key is difficult to fake. But with the certificate's public key, a program on the user's device verifies that your app is authentic.

A user gets keys from your app's certificate. But as a developer, you store keys apart from any certificate. You keep public and private keys in a place where your software can retrieve them — a *keystore* file. When you digitally sign an app, software grabs keys from your keystore file, uses the keys to create a certificate, and melds the certificate into your APK file. If you visit your development computer's home directory, and drill down to an .android directory (starting with a dot), you probably find the debug.keystore file. This debug.keystore file contains the keys for signing draft versions of your apps. (For help finding your home directory, see Book I, Chapter 3.)

A keystore file contains sensitive information, so every keystore file is password-pro-

tected. Android's debug.keystore file is password-protected. But unlike most keystore files, the debug.keystore file's password is freely available. The password is android. With Java's keytool program, anyone can sign any app using keys from the debug.keystore file. That's okay because the debug.keystore file's keys don't work for apps that you publish on the Android Market (or anywhere else, for that matter). So before publishing your app, run software to add your own keys to your app.

After downloading your app, a user's software applies a public key to verify that your app is signed properly. And what does that prove? Well, if a hacker tampers with your app somewhere between publication and the user's downloading, the test for proper signing detects the tampering. "Sorry," says Android, "I refuse to install this app."

But what about a malicious hacker who creates a damaging app and uses Android's freely available tools to sign it? To the world in general, the app looks fine. Signing doesn't verify that an app's developer has good intentions.

The weak link in the chain is the fact that Android apps are *self-signed.* When you add a digital signature to your app, no one else signs with you.

For scenarios that require more security (scenarios not normally associated with mobile devices), a developer can get help from a certificate authority. A *certificate authority* is an organization that issues special digital signatures — signatures that the world recognizes as very trustworthy. To get such a signature, you convince a certificate authority that you're a good person, and you pay some money to the certificate authority. Some certificate authorities issue signatures for free. These free signatures are okay, but they aren't as trusted as the paid signatures, and they don't have the same clout as the paid signatures.

You can create modular applications that can communicate with one another if the applications were signed with the same certificate. This allows the applications to run within the same process, and if requested, the system can treat them as a single application. With this methodology, you can create your application in modules, and users can update each module as they see fit. A great example of this would be to create a game and then release *update packs* to upgrade the game. Users can decide to purchase the updates that they want.

The certificate process is outlined in detail in the Android documentation. The documentation describes how to generate certificates with various tools and techniques. You can find more information about APK signing at `http://d.android.com/guide/publishing/app-signing.html`.

Creating a keystore

A *keystore* in Android (as well as in Java) is a container in which your personal certificates reside. You can create a keystore file with a couple of tools in Android:

✦ **Eclipse's Export Wizard:** This tool is installed with the Android Development Tools (ADT) and allows you to export a self-signed APK file that can digitally sign the application, as well as create the certificate and keystore (if needed) through a wizard-like process.

You use the Export Wizard in Steps 4–9 of the "Creating the APK File" section.

✦ **Java's keytool application:** The keytool application allows you to create a self-signed keystore via the command line. This tool is located in the Android SDK `tools` directory and provides many options via the command line.

The sections that follow describe the use of Eclipse's Export Wizard. (For an example of the use of Java's keytool application, see Book VI, Chapter 3.)

Safeguarding your keystore

The keystore file contains your private certificate that Android uses to identify your application in the Android Market. Back up your keystore in a safe location because if you happen to lose your keystore, you cannot sign the application with the same private key. Therefore, you cannot upgrade your application because the Android Market platform recognizes that the application is not signed by the same key and restricts you from upgrading it; the Market sees the file as a new Android application. This also happens if you change the package name of the app; Android does not recognize it as a valid update because the package and/or certificate are the same.

Don't wait! Obfuscate!

Nestled quietly inside your project's directory is a `proguard.cfg` file. This `proguard.cfg` file contains configuration information for a program that obfuscates your code. When you *obfuscate* something, you make it difficult to read. You scramble stuff and generally do the opposite of what you're supposed to do when you write clear, maintainable code.

Why do this? An obfuscated program can be executed without modification by an appropriate device. The device doesn't need a password and doesn't have to decrypt anything in order to run the code. In fact, an obfuscated program contains nothing unusual as far the Dalvik Virtual Machine is concerned. But for a person trying to reverse-engineer your code, the obfuscation is a nightmare. That's because the human mind doesn't process code mechanically. Instead, humans get the big picture; humans have to understand things in order to work with them; humans feel stress when they work with things that are terse, circuitous, and highly compressed.

So with obfuscated code, evil people can't easily figure out how your code works. They have trouble stealing your tricks and (more important) they can't easily add viruses to your published code.

Before publishing on the Android Market, you must obfuscate your app's code. Fortunately, the steps in this chapter's "Creating the APK File" section do the obfuscation for you. Eclipse's wizards apply ProGuard tools to your code, turning your code into a dizzying mess for anyone trying to tinker with it.

ProGuard is an open-source project; its website lives at `http://proguard.source forge.net`.

Creating an Android Market Account

Now that you have your APK file created, you can release the application on the Android Market. To do so, you need to create an Android Market account. To create such an account, you need a Google account. Any Google-based account, such as a Gmail account, is fine. If you don't have a Google account, you can get a free account by navigating to `www.google.com/accounts`.

This is the last exit before you enter a toll road. For an Android Market account, you pay a one-time $25 developer fee with a credit card.

To create the Android Market account, follow these steps:

1. **Open your web browser and navigate to** `http://market.android.com/publish`.

2. **On the right side of the screen, sign in with your Google account, as shown in Figure 1-6.**

Figure 1-6:
The http://
market.
android.
com/publish
page.

3. **Fill out the following fields:**

   - *Developer Name:* The name that appears as the developer of the applications you release. This could be your company name or your personal name. You can change this later, after you've created your account.

   - *Email Address:* This is the e-mail address users can send e-mails to. They normally send questions and or comments about your application if they are interested in it.

   - *Web Site URL:* The URL of your website. If you don't have a website, you can get a free Blogger account that provides a free blog to suffice as a website. You can get a free Blogger account from www.blogger.com.

   - *Phone Number:* A valid phone number at which to contact you in case problems arise with your published content.

   When you finish, your form resembles Figure 1-7.

4. **Click the Continue link.**

   On the next page, you're informed that you need to pay the $25 developer fee, as shown in Figure 1-8.

5. **Click the Continue link to pay the developer fee with Google Checkout.**

Figure 1-7:
Developer
listing
details.

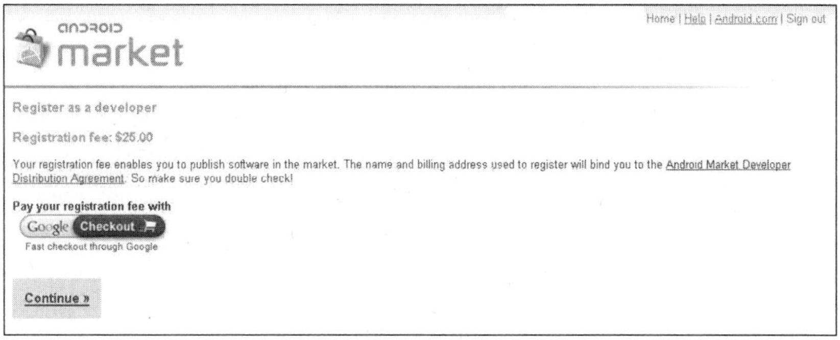

Figure 1-8:
Developer
registration
fee.

6. On the secure checkout page (see Figure 1-9), fill in your credit card
   details and billing information; then click the Agree and Continue button.

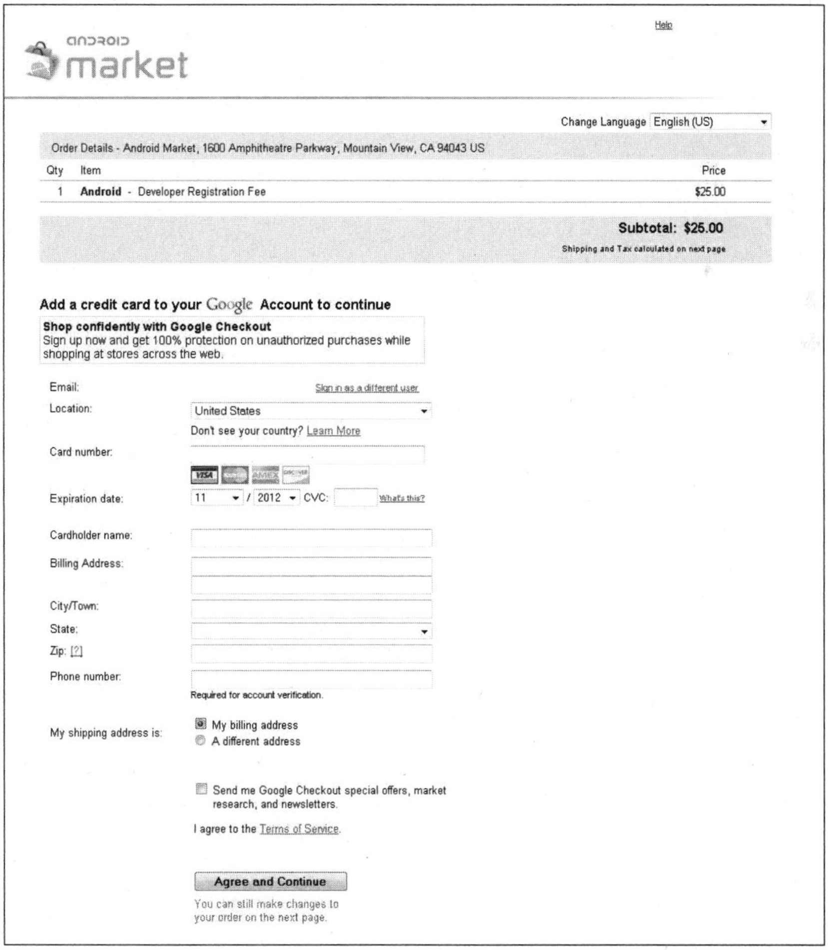

Figure 1-9:
Personal
and billing
information.

If you already have a credit card on file with Google, you may see a page listing that credit card as a payment option rather than what you see in Figure 1-9. If so, select that credit card and continue.

7. **On the resulting confirmation page (see Figure 1-10), type your password, and click the Sign In and Continue button.**

8. **On the order confirmation page (see Figure 1-11), click the Place Your Order Now button.**

   Depending on how fast your Internet connection is and how fast your order is placed, you may or may not see a loading screen.

   When the process is complete, you see a message confirming that you're an Android developer (see Figure 1-12).

Figure 1-10:
The sign-in confirmation page for registering as a developer.

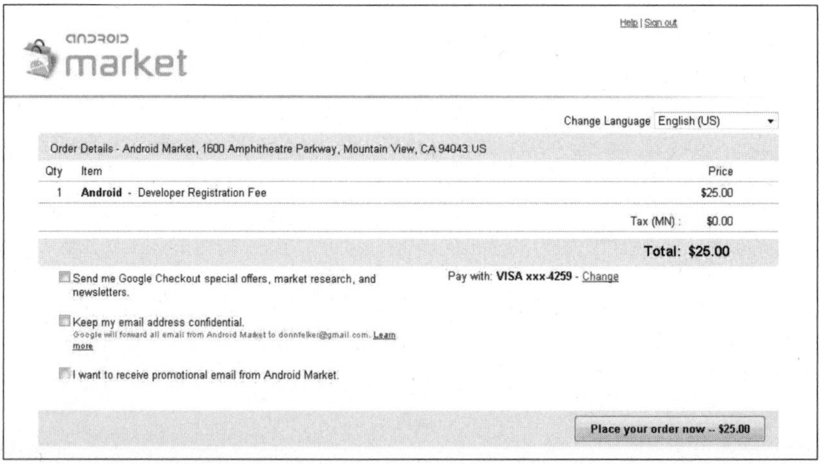

Figure 1-11:
Order confirmation.

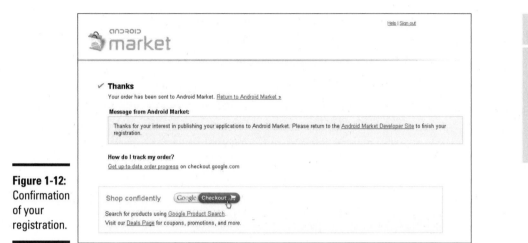

Figure 1-12:
Confirmation
of your
registration.

9. **Click the Android Market Developer Site link in the middle of the message.**

The Android Market Developer Distribution Agreement page appears. (See Figure 1-13.)

10. **(Optional) To have a paid application on the Android Market, you must set up a Google Checkout merchant account. To start setting up an account, look for the Setup Merchant Account link on the Android Market Developer Distribution Agreement page. When you set up an account, you provide**

Figure 1-13:
The
agreement
terms.

- Personal and business information
- Tax identity information (personal or corporation)
- Expected monthly revenue ($1 billion, right?)

I provide more details in the next section of this chapter.

11. **Read the terms and then click the I Agree, Continue link in the bottom left of the screen.**

You arrive at the Android Developer home page (see Figure 1-14). You've created your own Android Market account, and you can start uploading your apps.

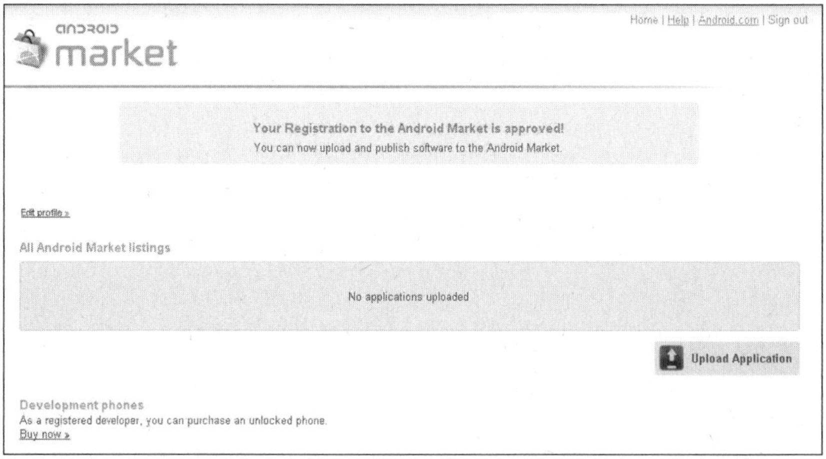

Figure 1-14: The Android developer home page.

Pricing Your Application

You have your APK file, and you're a registered Android developer. Now you're ready to get your app into users' hands, finally. But you need to ask yourself one last important question — is my app a free app or a paid app?

This decision should be made before you release your app because it has psychological consequences with potential customers/users and monetary ones for you. If your application is a paid application, you have to decide what your price point is. Look at similar applications in the Market. Most apps seem to sell from the $0.99 value range up to the $9.99 range. I rarely see an app for more than the $10 threshold. Keeping your pricing competitive with your product is a game of economics that you have to play to determine what works for your application.

The paid-versus-free discussion is an evergreen debate, with both sides stating that either can be profitable. I've done both, and I've found that both make decent income. (Yes, "free" apps can make money — check out "The free model" section a bit later in this chapter if you don't believe me.) Neither model is a sure thing — you have to figure out what works best for your application given your situation.

The paid model

If you go with a paid model, you start getting money in your pocket within 24 hours of the first sale (barring holidays and weekends, in which case, you'd receive funds the following business day). But from my experience, your application won't receive many active installs because it's a paid application. You're your own marketing team for your app, and if no one knows about your app, how is she going to know to buy it? This is a similar problem for free apps, but users can install them for free, and the mental weight of the app remaining on their device is little to none. With paid apps, this works a little differently.

All Android Market users get a free 24-hour trial period of your paid application upon initial purchase. This means a user can purchase the app and install it, Google Checkout will authorize the user's credit card on file, and the charge remains in an authorization state until 24 hours from the original purchase time. You can monitor this in your Google Checkout panel.

During those 24 hours, the user can use the fully functional application. If the user uninstalls the application within 24 hours, Google issues a full refund. If the user doesn't uninstall the app within 24 hours, the credit card authorization turns into a charge, and you receive the funds the following day.

Becoming a merchant

When you sell an app on the Android Market, Google takes a 30 percent commission. Considering Google's enormous visibility, having you get 70 percent of the revenue is a pretty good deal.

To send your app, you must first create a *merchant* account — as opposed to the Android Market account you created in the last section. To create a merchant account:

1. **Follow the steps in this chapter's "Creating an Android Market Account" section.**

2. **With your Android Market account created, point your browser to** `https://market.android.com/publish/Home`.

3. **When you arrive at your Android Market home page, click the Setup Merchant Account link.**

   Clicking this link brings you to a page with a big form to fill out. (See Figure 1-15.)

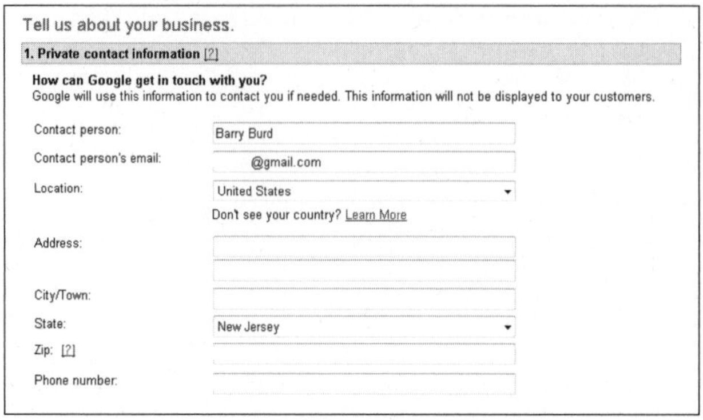

Tell us about your business.

1. Private contact information [?]

How can Google get in touch with you?
Google will use this information to contact you if needed. This information will not be displayed to your customers.

Contact person: Barry Burd

Contact person's email: @gmail.com

Location: United States

Don't see your country? Learn More

Address:

City/Town:

State: New Jersey

Zip: [?]

Phone number:

Figure 1-15:
Enter your private contact information.

4. **Tell Google your innermost secrets.**

   . . . but don't display them in Figure 1-15 of *Android Application Development All-in-One For Dummies*.

5. **On the next section of the form, fill in your publicly available contact information.**

   See Figure 1-16.

6. **In the Financial Information section of the form, show them the money.**

   See Figure 1-17.

7. **Agree to the Terms of Service (if you so choose), and click the Complete Sign Up button.**

   After doing all this, you're cleared to sell apps on Google's Android Market.

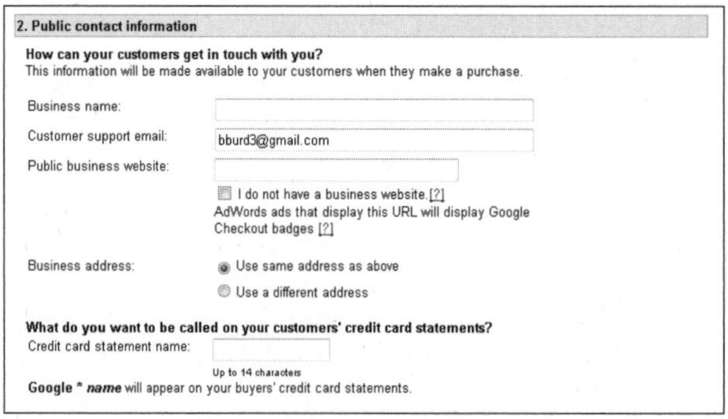

2. Public contact information

How can your customers get in touch with you?
This information will be made available to your customers when they make a purchase.

Business name:

Customer support email: bburd3@gmail.com

Public business website:

☐ I do not have a business website. [?]
AdWords ads that display this URL will display Google Checkout badges [?]

Business address: ⦿ Use same address as above
○ Use a different address

What do you want to be called on your customers' credit card statements?
Credit card statement name:

Up to 14 characters

Google * *name* will appear on your buyers' credit card statements.

Figure 1-16:
Enter your public contact information.

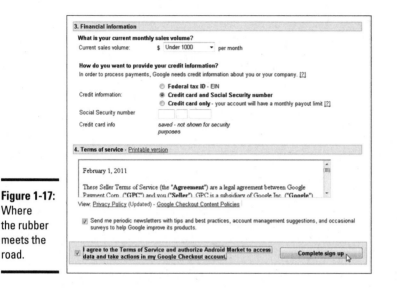

Figure 1-17:
Where
the rubber
meets the
road.

Licensing your app

To charge money for your app, you must add a license to it. Do this with
Android's Licensing Verification Library (LVL). You can download the LVL
using Android's SDK and AVD Manager. In Figure 1-18, the LVL goes by the
name *Google Market Licensing package, revision 1*.

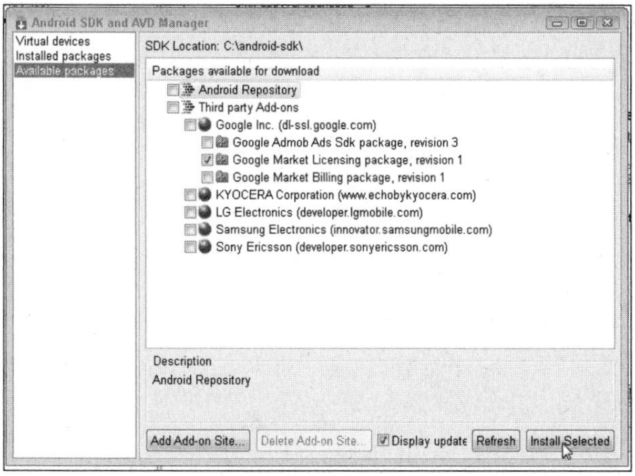

Figure 1-18:
Getting the
Licensing
Verification
Library.

To conjure up the SDK and AVD Manager, choose Window⇨Android SDK and AVD Manager from Eclipse's main menu. Or, in your development computer's command window, navigate to the Android SDK's `tools` directory and type **./android or android.bat**.

With the LVL on your development computer, you incorporate the library's code into your own project's code. As part of this process, you select a licensing policy. You have three choices:

✦ **Strict policy:** Whenever the user tries to launch your app, the device asks the Android Market server for its approval. If the user tries to launch your app when the device has no connectivity, the user is out of luck. Life's tough.

✦ **Server-managed policy:** The user's device stores a copy of the user's license. The device uses the copy when network connectivity is unavailable. The license is obfuscated (so it's tamper-resistant), and the license keeps track of trial periods, expiration dates, and other stuff. This is the default policy, and it's the policy that Google highly recommends.

✦ **Custom policy:** Create your own policy with Java code in your app. As a developer, this choice would make me nervous. But for very sensitive situations, this choice might be the best.

For all the details about the LVL, visit `http://developer.android.com/guide/publishing/licensing.html`.

More testing

When testing your app with friends in your apartment building, you don't always get reliable results. So your acquaintances living on other continents should test your app, too. In fact, test so much that you'd have trouble mailing your APK file to all your testers.

That's why the Android's LVL allows you to publish an app with invitation-only access. Figure 1-19 shows the screen in which you list your test users' Google accounts. The Test Response drop-down box lets you choose the Android Market's response to a request.

For example, in Figure 1-19, I chose LICENSED in the drop-down box. When one of my test users (`user1@gmail.com`, for example) tries to launch my app, the Market responds, "Yes, you're licensed." But notice the extent to which you can test your licensing code. If you choose NOT_LICENSED in the drop-down box, does the Market's server correctly deny the test user access to your app? And what happens if the Market responds LICENSED_OLD_KEY? Can the user launch the app? Do you want the user to be able to launch the app? All these choices help you test the robustness of your app's licensing code.

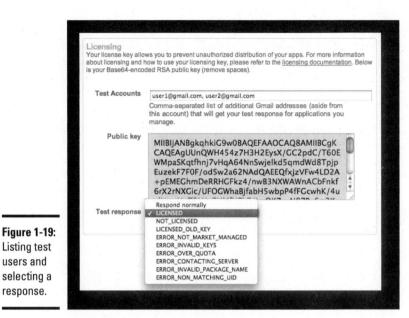

Figure 1-19:
Listing test
users and
selecting a
response.

The free model

If you choose to go the free route, users can install the application free of
charge. From my experience, 50–80 percent of the users who install your free
app will keep the application on the device, while the others uninstall it. The
elephant in the room at this point is, how do you make money with free apps?

As the age-old saying goes, nothing in life is free. The same goes for making
money on free apps. Fortunately, you have some choices:

✦ **Advertising**

Various mobile advertising agencies can provide you with a third-party
library to display ads on your mobile application. The top mobile advertising companies are Google AdSense, AdMob (which was recently
acquired by Google), and Quattro Wireless (recently acquired by Apple).

Obtaining a free account from one of these companies is fairly straightforward. They offer great SDKs and walk you through how to get ads
running on your native Android application. Most of these companies
pay on a net-60-day cycle, so it will be a few months before you receive
your first check.

✦ **In-app billing**

As a bona fide Android Market developer, you can sell goods and services directly through your application. You can sell subscriptions, kitchen utensils, and advice for the lovelorn. Users make purchases by filling in fields and clicking buttons within your application. As with the paid model, Google takes a 30 percent commission.

To set up in-app billing, you have to make significant additions to your app's code. You create a service, a broadcast receiver, an AIDL file, and some other stuff. For all the gory details, visit `http://developer.android.com/guide/market/billing/billing_integrate.html`.

Getting Screen Shots for Your Application

Screen shots are a very important part of the Android Market ecosystem because they allow users to preview your application before installing it. Allowing users to view a couple of running shots of your application can be the determining factor in whether a user installs your application. Imagine if you created a game and wanted users to play it. If you spent weeks (or months, for that matter) creating detailed graphics, you'd want the potential users/buyers of the game to see them so that they can see how great your app looks.

To grab real-time shots of your application, you need an emulator or physical Android device. To grab the screen shots, perform the following:

1. **Open the emulator and then navigate to the screen you want to capture.**

2. **In Eclipse, open the DDMS perspective.**

3. **Choose the emulator in the Devices panel, as shown in Figure 1-20.**

4. **Click the Screen Shot button to capture a screen shot.**

The Device Screen Capture dialog box appears. At first, you see the word *Capturing* instead of a screen shot. After a few seconds, the screen shot appears.

5. **In the Device Screen Capture dialog box, click the Save button.**

Your operating system prompts you for a filename, a destination folder, and all that good stuff.

6. **Finish saving the screen shot by navigating to a Save Location folder as prompted, typing a filename, and clicking Save (or whatever else you normally do when you save a file on your system).**

7. **To dismiss the Device Screen Capture dialog box, click the box's Done button.**

You can make changes on the emulator or device and refresh the screen shot dialog box using the aptly named Refresh button, as shown in Figure 1-20. After this screen shot is taken, you can publish it to the Android Market.

Click to capture screen shot.

Refresh button

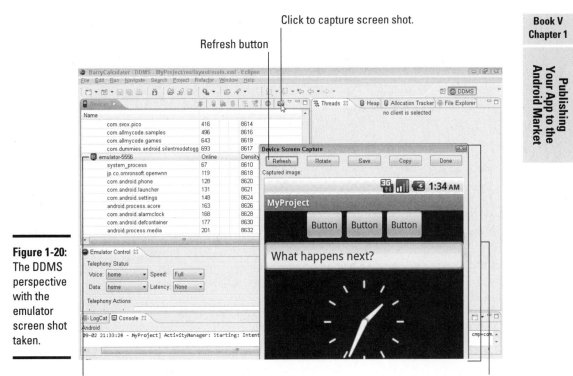

Figure 1-20:
The DDMS
perspective
with the
emulator
screen shot
taken.

Choose the emulator.

Screen shot

Uploading Your Application to the Android Market

You've finally reached the apex of the Android application development — the point when you publish the application. Publishing an application is easy; just follow these steps:

1. **On the Android developer home page (refer to Figure 1-14), click the Upload Application button.**

The Upload an Application page opens, as shown in Figure 1-21.

2. **For the Upload an .apk File field, browse to the `bin` directory of the project containing your app; in that `bin` directory, select the APK file that you concocted in the "Creating an APK File" section; then click Upload.**

If you navigate to a project's `bin` directory, and you don't see an APK file in the directory, your operating system might be hiding things such as the letters `apk` at the ends of filenames. For a solution to this problem, see the sidebar titled "Those pesky filename extensions" in Book I, Chapter 2.

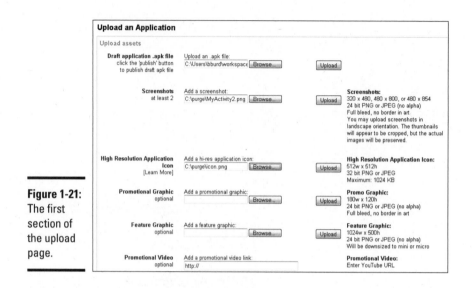

Figure 1-21:
The first
section of
the upload
page.

The Android Market uses the Java package name as the identifier inside of the market. No two applications can have the same package name. So if your first published app is in the `com.example.earnMeAMillion` package, put your second app in a `com.example.secondTimeIsACharm` package.

Your package name should help to identify you or your company. If you have a domain name, start the package name with the domain name's parts reversed. For example, I'm the proud owner of the domain name `allmy code.com`, so I publish an app with the package name `com.allmycode.clicks`. (If *you* publish an app with package name `com.allmycode.clicks`, you'll hear from my lawyer!)

3. **In the Add a Screenshot field, add two screen shots of your application.**

   The sizes of these screen shots need to be 320 pixels wide x 480 pixels high or 480 pixels wide x 854 pixels high. These screen shots allow users to preview your application in a running state without installing your application. If you're wondering whether providing screen shots is worth the hassle, consider this simple fact: Apps with screen shots have higher install rates than apps without screen shots. Screen shots are not *required* to publish the app, but not having them will negatively impact your app's install rate.

4. **Add a high-resolution application icon.**

   A high-resolution icon is 512 pixels wide and 512 pixels high. With newer Android devices having bigger and better screens, high-resolution icons are becoming an absolute necessity.

5. **(Optional) Add a promotional graphic, a feature graphic, and a promotional video.**

   Google might use these to showcase your app.

6. Scroll down the page to the Listing Details section (see Figure 1-22), and fill in the title of your application.

This text is indexed for the Android Market search.

In my experience, a great title can jump start an app's popularity.

7. Set the description for your application (refer to Figure 1-22).

This is the description that the user sees when she inspects your application to determine whether she wants to install it. All this text is indexed for the Android Market search.

8. Set the promo text of your application.

Promo text is used when your application is featured or promoted on the market. The process of getting your application featured is fairly muddy at this point and, from what I can tell, is based upon the popularity of your application. If your application gets chosen to be featured in the promo area of the market (usually the top part of the screen of each category in the Android Market), the promo text is what appears as the promotional component for it.

9. Set the application type.

The choices are Applications and Games.

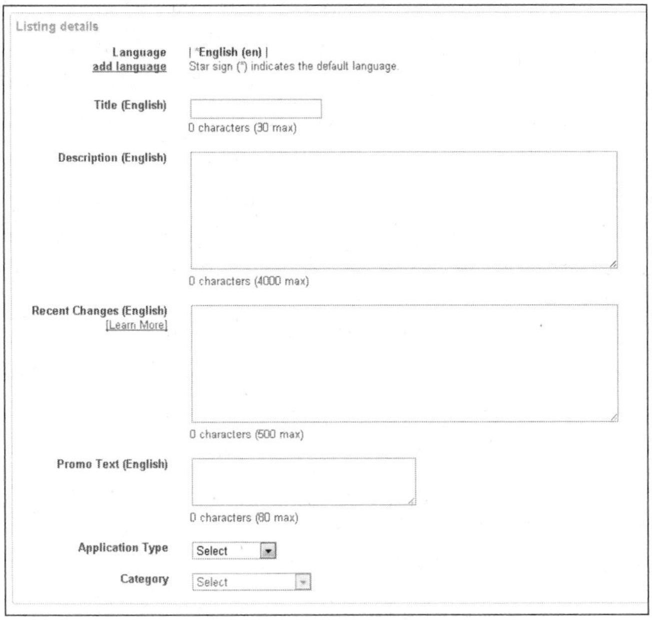

Figure 1-22:
The upload page's Listing Details section.

10. **Set the category for the app.**

The choices for type Applications include Business, Comics, Communication, Education, and many others. The choices for type Games include Arcade & Action, Brain & Puzzle, Cards & Casino, and a host of others.

11. **Scroll down the page to the Publishing Options section (see Figure 1-23), and select your Copy Protection option.**

I always choose Off. When you choose On, the file footprint on the device is usually doubled. If your app is 2MB, and you turn on copy protection, your new file footprint when installed on the device is around 4MB. I keep my files at the lowest possible setting. The reason for this is simple — if a user runs out of space on his phone, he is most likely to uninstall the largest applications in order to free up more space.

Older devices, prior to Android 2.2, could not install applications to the SD card. Therefore, internal space was limited, and when users ran out of space, they would tend to uninstall the heavyweight apps first to free the most space. If your app is very heavyweight, it will probably be removed to save space. Keeping the file small and leaving copy protection set to Off keeps you out of the crosshairs in this issue.

12. **Select the list of locations that the application needs to be visible in.**

For example, if your application is an Italian application, deselect All Locations and select Italy as the destination location. This ensures that only devices in the Italy region can see this in the Market. If you leave All Locations enabled, you guessed it — all locations can see your app in the Market.

Figure 1-23:
The upload page's Publishing Options section.

Publishing options

Copy Protection	◉ Off (Application can be copied from the device)
	○ On (Helps prevent copying of this application from the device Increases the amount of memory on the phone required to install the application.)
	The copy protection feature will be deprecated soon, please use licensing service instead
Content Rating [Learn More]	○ High Maturity
	○ Medium Maturity
	○ Low Maturity
	○ Everyone
Pricing	◉ Free ○ Paid
	Setting the price to Free is permanent; you cannot change to a price later [Learn More]

Set a price for each country/region

Default price	USD [ ]
[Auto Fill]	Automatically populate the fields with a one-time conversion to local currencies from the default price with the current exchange rate

☑ All Countries

☑ Argentina ☑ Latvia
☑ Australia ☑ Lithuania
☑ Austria ☑ Luxembourg
☑ Belgium ☑ Malta

13. **Scroll down the page to the Contact Information section (see Figure 1-24), and fill out the Web Site and Email fields (and Phone, if you want).**

    I never fill out the Phone field because, well, users will call you! Yes, they will call at midnight asking you questions, giving feedback, and so on. I prefer to communicate with customers via e-mail. If you're writing an app for a different company yet publishing it under your developer account, you can change the Web Site, Email, and Phone fields so that the users do not contact you. Users use these fields to contact you for various reasons. The most common correspondence that I receive is app feature requests and bug reports.

14. **Verify that your application meets the Android content guidelines and that you complied with applicable laws by selecting the pertinent check boxes.**

15. **Choose one of the following options:**

    - *Publish:* Saves and publishes the app to the Market in real time.

    - *Save:* Saves the changes made but does not publish the app.

    - *Delete:* Deletes all the work up until now. Don't do this.

    You can find these buttons either at the very top or the very bottom of the current page. (Look in both places. These buttons are moving targets.)

    For this exercise, click the Save button. This saves your application and returns you to the Android Developer home page, where an icon states that the app is in a saved state. (See Figure 1-25.) You can use this as a staging area until you're ready to release your app.

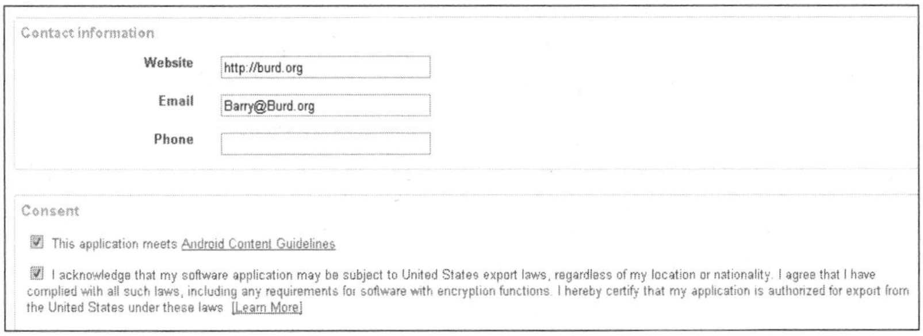

Figure 1-24:
The upload page's Contact Information and Consent sections.

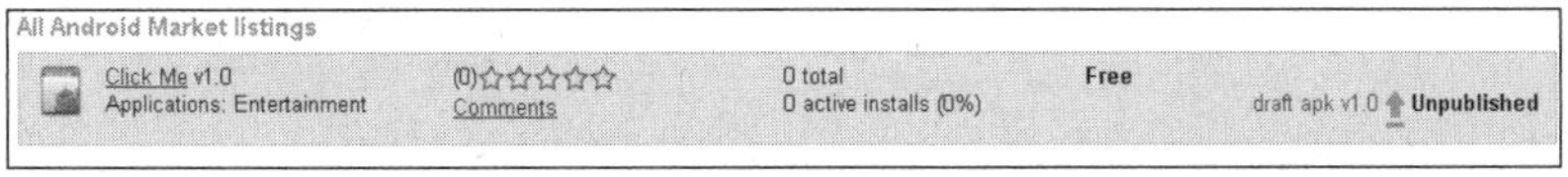

```
Contact information

         Website    http://burd.org
           Email    Barry@Burd.org
           Phone

Consent

  ☑ This application meets Android Content Guidelines

  ☑ I acknowledge that my software application may be subject to United States export laws, regardless of my location or nationality. I agree that I have
    complied with all such laws, including any requirements for software with encryption functions. I hereby certify that my application is authorized for export from
    the United States under these laws. [Learn More]
```

Figure 1-25:
The saved app on your Android Developer home page.

```
All Android Market listings

  Click Me v1.0              (0)☆☆☆☆☆      0 total                  Free
  Applications: Entertainment  Comments      0 active installs (0%)          draft apk v1.0 ⬆ Unpublished
```

16. **When you're ready to release the app, select the title of the app on the Android Developer home page.**

The Upload an Application page opens. (Refer to Figure 1-21.) On this page, some of your app information is already filled in.

17. **Scroll to the bottom of the page, and click the Publish button.**

This publishes your application to the Android Market.

You probably noticed one bonus of how Android handles application uploads: no app-approval process! Amazon's Appstore for Android has an approval process. And Apple's App Store has a rigorous screening process with a $99 yearly fee.

But with Android Market, you can create an app right now and publish it, and then users can install it right away. This means that you can perform a quick release cycle and get new features out the door as quickly as you can get them done, which is very cool.

By the way, if you search for this section's app on the Android Market, you won't find it. I published the app and then removed it from the Market. To remove the app, I chose the app title from the Android Developer home page, scrolled to the bottom, and clicked the Unpublish button. Goodbye, app!

Watching the Installs Soar

You've finally published your first application. Time to watch the millions start rolling in, right? Well, kind of. You might be an independent developer who's releasing the next best first-person shooter game, or you might be a corporate developer who's pushing out your company's Android application. Regardless, you need to be aware of the end-user experience on various devices. You have various ways of identifying how your application is doing:

✦ **Five-star rating system:** The higher average rating you have, the better.

✦ **Comments:** Read them! People take the time to leave them, so provide them the courtesy of reading them. You'd be surprised at the great ideas that people provide to you for free. Most of the time, I've found if I implement the most commonly requested feature, users get excited about it, and come back and update their comments with a much more positive boost in ratings.

✦ **Error reports:** Users who were gracious enough to submit error reports want to let you know that the app experienced a run-time exception for an unknown reason. Open these reports, look at the error, review the stack trace, and try to fix the error. An app that gets a lot of force-close errors receives a lot of really bad reviews, really quickly. Stack traces are available only for devices that run Android 2.2 and above.

✦ **Installs versus active installs:** Although this isn't the best metric for identifying user satisfaction, it is an unscientific way to determine whether users who install your app tend to keep it on their phones. If users keep your app, they probably like it!

✦ **Direct e-mails:** Users will return to the Android Market to find your e-mail address and/or website address. They will e-mail you to ask questions about features and send comments to you about their user experience. They may also send you ideas about how to improve your app, or they may ask you to create another app that does something they cannot find on the Market. People love to be part of something. I've found if I personally reply within 24 hours (less than 4 hours is really what I aim for), users become really happy with the response time. Although this is difficult to sustain if your app has a million active users, it does make users very happy to know that they can get hold of you if they run into an issue with your app that they love so much.

Keeping in touch with your user base is a large task in itself, but doing so can reap rewards of dedicated, happy customers who will recommend your application to their friends and family.

Chapter 2: Publishing Your App to the Amazon Appstore

In This Chapter

✔ Getting your app in Amazon Appstore

✔ Publishing your app

T his chapter parallels Chapter 1 in this minibook, in which I describe the process of publishing an app on Google's Android Market. Amazon's procedure is similar in some ways, and a bit different in others. (So what did you expect?)

In this chapter, I summarize the steps for publishing on Amazon Appstore for Android. I don't cover the steps in great detail for three reasons:

✦ The steps for publishing with Amazon resemble the steps for publishing with Google. You might not mind my copying and pasting text from Chapter 1 of this minibook, but to me, it wouldn't seem right.

✦ I'd go crazy if I had to reword ideas from Chapter 1 of this minibook to make them sound fresh and new in this chapter.

✦ (This one is a secret. It's just between you and me. Okay?) The editors at Wiley will go ballistic (and rightfully so) if I delay this book's publication by writing too much more material.

So time to get started! Here's Chapter 1 from this minibook written from an Amazon Appstore developer's point of view:

The Honeymooners aired from 1955 to 1956 on the CBS television network in the United States . . .

Becoming an Amazon Appstore Developer

Developing for the Amazon store costs a bit more than developing for Google's Android Market. To submit apps to the Amazon Appstore, you have to pay $99 each year. Of course, if you have a great idea for an app and you're serious about marketing the app, the $99 price of admission is well worth it.

So grab your credit card, and follow these steps:

1. **Visit** `https://developer.amazon.com/welcome.html`.

   A friendly looking page invites you to click the Get Started button.

2. **Go ahead; click the button.**

   Doing so takes you to a login page. (See Figure 2-1.)

3. **Log in with your e-mail address and password, and then click the Sign In Using Our Secure Server button.**

   A page for submitting contact information — your name, address, phone, and so on — appears.

   It goes without saying that if you do not have an Amazon password — as unlikely as that may be — you need to get one by registering with Amazon before you can submit an app to the Amazon Appstore.

4. **Fill in your contact information and then click Save.**

   Next comes the page with the Developer License Agreement.

5. **Accept the agreement if you're so inclined.**

   Like Google's Android Market, the Amazon Appstore takes a 30 percent commission for each sale of your app.

   Unlike Google's Android Market, Amazon's developer registration form asks whether you intend to charge for your apps. (Your answer isn't binding because the form for uploading an individual app has its own free-versus-paid entry.)

6. **At the end of the registration form, click Save.**

   You're ready to start uploading apps.

Figure 2-1:
Logging in
with your
regular
Amazon
password.

> **Sign In**
>
> What is your e-mail address?
>
> **My e-mail address is:** noneOfYourBusiness@Burd.org
>
> Do you have an Amazon.com password?
>
> ○ **I am a new customer.**
>   (you'll create a password later)
> ◉ **I am a returning customer, and my password is:**
>   •••••••••••
>
> [Sign in using our secure server]
>
> Forgot your password?
>
> Has your e-mail address changed since your last order?

Where to publish?

By the time you read this book, there may be other prominent Android app stores. Even now, as I write these words in 2011, there are several sites that look like alternative app stores. Some of them simply advertise and rate apps, and then link to Google's Android Market for real downloads. As a developer, your greatest concern is making your app visible on such sites.

Some hardware vendors have their own exclusive app stores. For example, owners of Samsung products can visit Samsung Apps (`http://samsungapps.com`). Owners of older Archos products don't have access to the Google Android Market, but they can download apps from the AppsLib (`http://appslib.com`).

Some time-honored websites started out by housing apps for PDAs — *personal digital assistants*, such as the Palm and the iPAQ. With the move to smartphones and tablets, these sites now distribute Android apps. Sites of this ilk include Handango, PocketGear.com, GetJar.com, and others.

In addition, most telephone carriers allow users to install apps from any website. (The mobile device's web browser visits an ordinary web page; a link on the web page points directly to an APK file.) But these days John Q. Consumer tends not to trust apps that don't come from well-known app stores, so this kind of self-publishing doesn't hold a lot of promise.

Uploading an App

Uploading an app starts with a URL. To begin uploading an app:

1. **Log in at** `https://developer.amazon.com/application/info.html`.

   After signing in, you see a form like the one in Figure 2-2.

2. **Fill in the fields on the form — including the Supported Languages field — and then click Save.**

   In the form in Figure 2-2, the Application SKU field is for your own product number, whatever that might be. If you sell enough different apps or other items to require your own product numbers, more power to you! (You can afford to pay retail for this book, so I hope you did!)

   Next up is the Merchandizing part of the form. (See Figure 2-3.)

3. **Enter all the information about the category, the price, the dates, and other stuff; then click Save.**

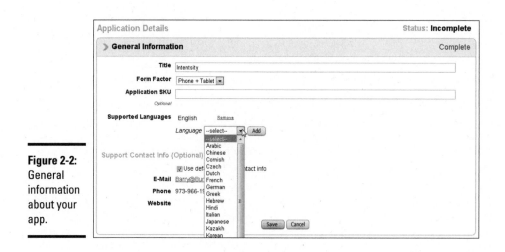

Figure 2-2:
General
information
about your
app.

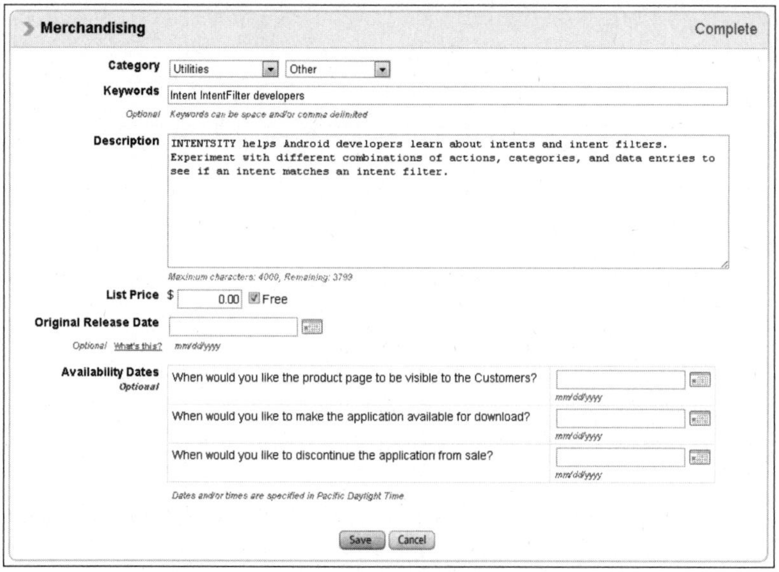

Figure 2-3:
Merchan-
dizing info
about
your app.

Figure 2-3 illustrates some important merchandizing tips from Amazon's developer pages. In my first draft of Figure 2-3, the description field contained only one sentence: `This app helps Android developers learn about intents and intent filters.` What a mistake!

Fortunately, the people who wrote Amazon's Help pages looked into their crystal ball and knew in advance that I'd write a one-sentence description starting with `This app`. The Help pages advise explicitly against using the words `This app` and against single-sentence descriptions. It's as if the Help pages say, "Barry, we know that you're going to be lazy about merchandising, so here's some important advice . . ."

Amazon's Help pages also advise against making false claims. As Shakespeare once wrote, " . . . false advertising of your app cannot be hid long; . . . at the length, truth will out."

Depending on your cultural orientation, the next form (see Figure 2-4) is either an embarrassment or a badge of honor.

4. **Make your selections in the form's drop-down boxes and then click Save.**

   The page that appears next asks for icons and screen shots. (See Figure 2-5.)

5. **Upload icons, screen shots, and other multimedia; then click Save.**

   I'm not the artistic type. So for me, the screen in Figure 2-5 is the most challenging. But after conquering the art world, I'm finally ready to upload my app. The Upload Binary page appears (see Figure 2-6).

6. **You can apply (or not apply) Amazon's *digital rights management* (*DRM*) to your app, as shown in Figure 2-6.**

   Like the DRM for Amazon Kindle books, the Appstore's DRM electronically grants permission to run each app on a device-by-device basis. And like any other scheme for managing users' privileges, the Appstore's DRM inspires vast waves of controversy in blogs and online forums.

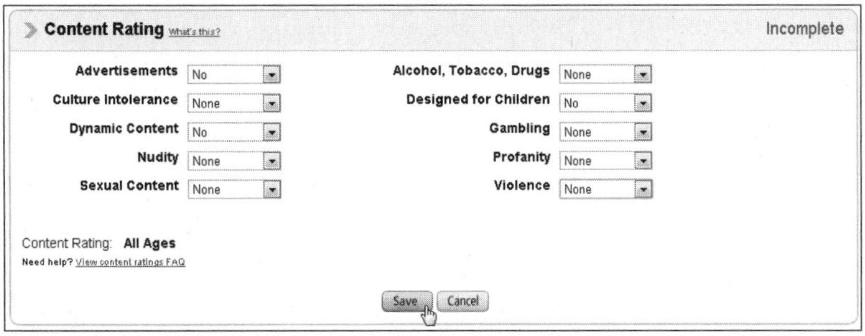

Figure 2-4:
Describing
your app's
content.

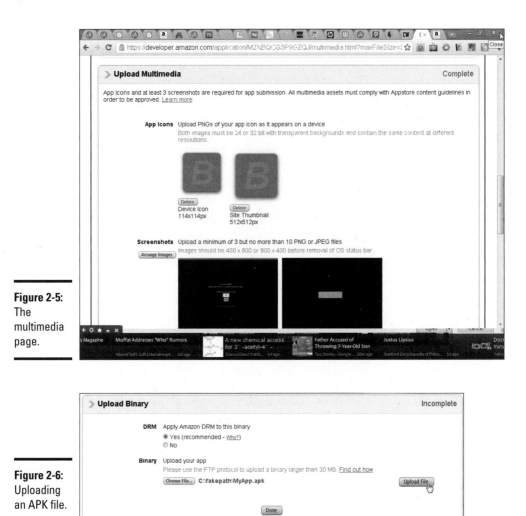

Figure 2-5:
The
multimedia
page.

Figure 2-6:
Uploading
an APK file.

Amazon doesn't publish a lot of information about the workings of its DRM scheme. But if you click the Why? link in Figure 2-6, you see the following tip: "Without the DRM, your application can be used without restrictions by any user." So when you publish a paid app, DRM is the way to go.

Chapter 1 in this minibook describes the steps in adding a digital certificate to a Google Market app. Amazon's certificate procedure isn't as nuanced. By default, Amazon applies its own certificate to each app published on the Amazon Appstore. The certificate is unique to your account. But otherwise, it's a boilerplate certificate.

If your legal situation or your technical requirements impose special demands on the kind of certificate that accompanies your app, stop checking boxes and fall back on ordinary e-mail. Submit a question with the app store's Contact Us form, and begin a dialogue with the store's administrators.

7. **Click the Choose File button to select your app's APK file and then click the Upload File button.**

8. **Click the Done button to move to the next page.**

The questions on the next page are more important than they look. (See Figure 2-7.)

9. **After some careful thought and a few rewrites, fill in the big text areas in Figure 2-7.**

Unlike Google's Android Market, apps submitted to the Amazon Appstore go through an approval process before they can be published. To qualify for publication, an app must meet Amazon's technical specifications. (Visit `https://developer.amazon.com/help/faq.html` for more info.)

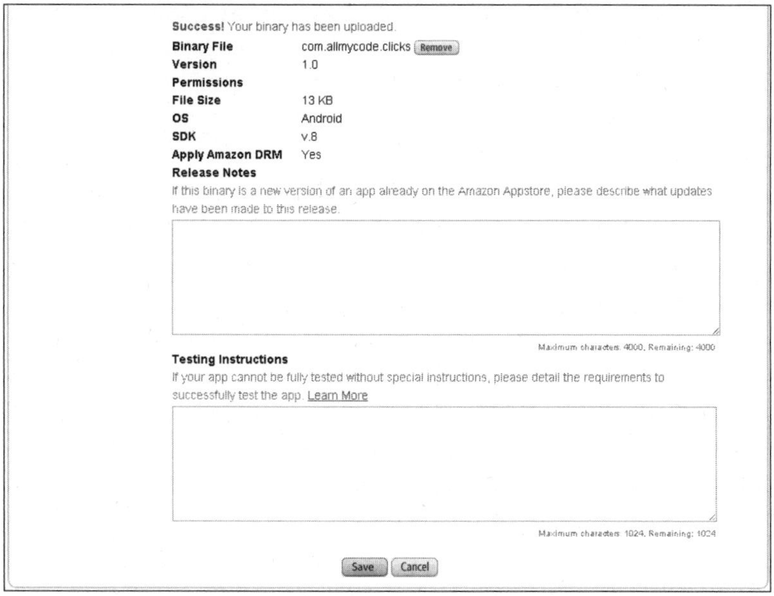

Success! Your binary has been uploaded.

Binary File	com.allmycode.clicks [Remove]
Version	1.0
Permissions	
File Size	13 KB
OS	Android
SDK	v.8
Apply Amazon DRM	Yes
Release Notes	

If this binary is a new version of an app already on the Amazon Appstore, please describe what updates have been made to this release.

Maximum characters: 4000, Remaining: 4000

Testing Instructions

If your app cannot be fully tested without special instructions, please detail the requirements to successfully test the app. Learn More

Maximum characters: 1024, Remaining: 1024

[Save] [Cancel]

Figure 2-7: Helping the folks at Amazon to test your app.

In addition, an app must meet Amazon's nontechnical specifications. These include things like the clarity of images, your right to use the images, the presence or absence in in-app advertising, the app's appropriateness for various audiences, and other things. (Again, visit `https://developer.amazon.com/help/faq.html`.)

Imagine, for a moment, that you work for Amazon. You normally enjoy testing apps that developers submit, but today you're a little grumpy. All the apps that you evaluate are beginning to look alike. And besides, the office's coffee machine isn't working!

Along comes an app that a developer has submitted. The app looks good, but it's merchandised as an update. As a tester, you want to focus on the app's new features and pay a little less attention to the previous version's features. (Yes, you want to make sure that new features don't break any of the old features, but that kind of testing requires a certain mindset.)

The problem is, the developer hasn't written enough in the Release Notes part of Figure 2-7. Without pulling up an older version of this app, you can't distinguish the new version's features from the old version's features. Maybe the new version looks the same as the old version, and the new features lurk under the hood. At best, you have to dig up an older version and compare it with the newly submitted app. At worst, you have to do some reverse engineering to figure out what has changed from one version to another.

But remember . . . The office coffee machine isn't working today. That settles it. This app is rejected.

The same thinking applies to the Testing Instructions part in Figure 2-7. As the app's developer, you're intensely aware of the app's requirements and of all your presuppositions in creating the app. But the person who tests your app knows none of this. If the lack of a simple testing prerequisite turns your app from a lifesaving utility into a useless waste of kilobytes, you must describe the prerequisite clearly in the Testing Instructions field.

Extra advertising, good marketing, and useful features make the difference between 1,000,000 downloads and 1,000 downloads. But presenting roadblocks or inconveniences in the approval process makes the difference between downloads and no downloads.

10. **When you've added all the necessary information, click Save at the bottom of the page.**

From that point on, the ball is in Amazon's court. You can check the status of your app's approval by visiting the Developer Portal and checking the portal's Dashboard. (Visit `https://developer.amazon.com/home.html`.) Amazon sends you an e-mail if any questions arise during the testing process. You also receive an e-mail when your app is approved.

Book VI

Alternative Android Development Techniques

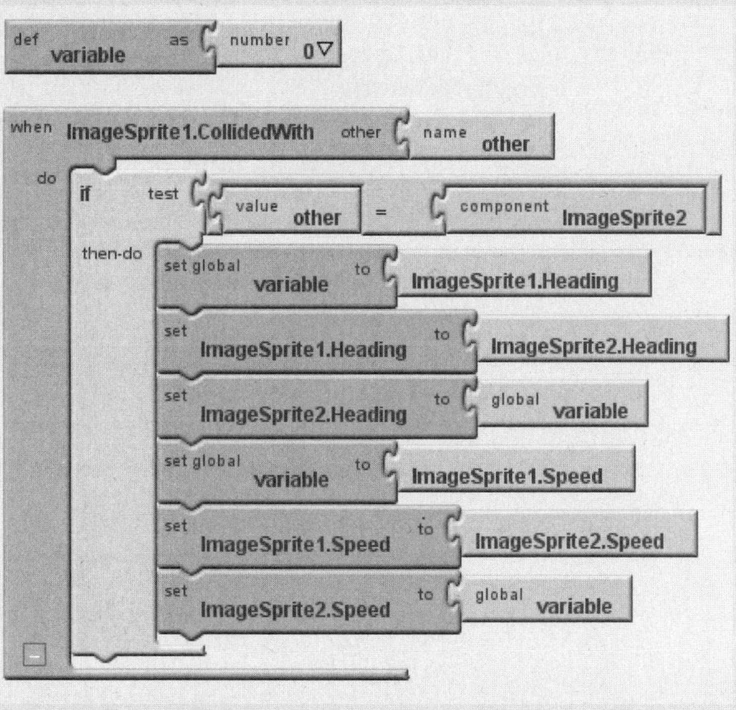

Contents at a Glance

Chapter 1: Creating Code Quickly with App Inventor

In This Chapter

✔ Designing a user interface

✔ Building program logic using visual tools

✔ Creating an Android app without typing any code

L ife is a long sequence of tradeoffs. You enjoy a big gooey dessert, but the dessert isn't healthy. You love playing in a band, but most band members don't earn a decent living. You're blessed with the ability to sleep 10 or 12 hours a day, but with all that lost time, you get behind writing *Android Application Development All-in-One For Dummies.*

And so it goes. Application development also involves tradeoffs. To use the full richness of Android's feature set, you write Java code using Eclipse and the Android API. But if you can forgo some of Android's fancier features, you can save time and effort using Google's App Inventor.

App Inventor is the GUI dessert that I describe in the first paragraph. App Inventor makes Android development easy, using a drag-and-drop paradigm for both the visual interface and for an application's logic. With App Inventor, you can't fine-tune your work the way you can with Java code. You can't make your application do some of the trickier things that Android programs do. But App Inventor hides many of the messy technical details involved in developing mobile code. For a quick, easy way to develop basic Android applications, give App Inventor a try. (In fact, for a quick, easy way to develop *not-so-basic* applications, App Inventor is worth a look.)

Getting Started with App Inventor

To begin your App Inventor experience, do the following:

1. **Visit** `http://java.com`**.**

During your visit, you can check to make sure that your computer has the Java Runtime Environment (JRE). To use App Inventor, you don't need the full Java Development Kit (JDK). But you do need the Java Runtime Environment (JRE).

If you've already followed the steps in Book I, Chapter 2, your computer has the JRE. Or if you know, for one reason or another, that your computer has the JRE, you can skip this step and go immediately to Step 4.

To develop Android apps with Eclipse, you need the Java Development Kit. In particular, you need Java SE (the development kit's Standard Edition). For more information about the Java Development Kit and the Java Runtime Environment, see Book I, Chapter 2.

2. **At the Java website, follow the steps to check whether Java is installed on your computer.**

   The website's terminology differs from the official terminology. The website offers to check whether you have "Java" on your computer. To be precise, the website checks whether your computer has the Java Runtime Environment (JRE) and whether the JRE is enabled in your web browser.

   Most computers come with the JRE preinstalled. So if you run the site's "Does my computer have Java?" test, and if the Java web page responds with a `Java is not working` message, check to make sure that Java is enabled in your web browser.

3. **Follow the instructions at** `http://java.com` **to install Java on your computer.**

   Do this if your computer doesn't have Java, or if you don't want to fiddle with your web browser's settings, or if you may already have Java but you don't care if you install Java again.

   With the JRE installed on your computer, you can proceed to Step 4.

4. **Visit** `www.appinventorbeta.com`.

   By the time you read this book, the URL for App Inventor may have changed. If so, try poking around at `www.media.mit.edu` for a pointer to App Inventor. (The MIT Media Lab took over stewardship of App Inventor from Google in August 2011.)

5. **Sign in with your Google account (or create an account if you don't already have one).**

6. **Find the link to download and install App Inventor's Setup software on your computer.**

   Download links appear in several places on the App Inventor site.

7. **Download and install App Inventor's Setup software.**

   In Windows, the Setup software installs itself in the `c:\Program Files\AppInventor` directory (or on 64-bit systems, in the `C:\Program Files (x86)\AppInventor` directory). On a Mac, the Setup software sits comfortably in the `/Applications/Appinventor` folder. In Linux, the Setup software normally nestles inside the `/usr/google/appinventor` directory.

What manner of beast is the App Inventor?

App Inventor is really three things — a *Designer*, a *Blocks Editor*, and some Setup software:

✔ With the **Designer,** you specify the appearance of your Android application's user interface.

✔ With the **Blocks Editor,** you develop your Android application's behavior. ("Here's what happens in this text box when the user clicks that button.")

Both the Designer and Blocks Editor programs live on the web. Each time you use App Inventor, you download the code for these programs from Google's servers to your computer's hard drive. While you run these programs, the programs communicate frequently with Google's servers.

✔ The **Setup software** lives locally on your computer's hard drive. This code includes some Android Software Development Kit (SDK) tools and an Android device emulator.

The Designer runs in a web browser, and the Blocks Editor runs in a Java Web Start window. A Java Web Start window is like a Java applet running outside a web browser. A run of the Blocks Editor looks very much like any ordinary program running on your desktop. But unlike most other programs, you download the Blocks Editor's code each time you use App Inventor.

When you download App Inventor's Setup software, you download and install a small portion of the Android SDK with an emulator and a few other gizmos. But the parts of App Inventor that you see most often (the Designer and the Blocks Editor) live on Google's servers, not on your computer's hard drive.

(P.S.: By the time you read this book, someone will have explained to me why the folks at Google split up App Inventor into a browser-based part and a Java Web Start part. When I find out, I'll probably be embarrassed for not having known sooner.)

WARNING!

Everything changes. Or, as the French say, "The more things change, the more things in Barry's books become out of date." I'm guessing that Google's App Inventor will change quickly while this book is in print, so don't take this chapter's instructions as gospel. Google's software people designed App Inventor from the ground up to be friendly and intuitive. So if my instructions don't match precisely what you see on your computer screen, poke around a bit. If you really get stuck, send me an e-mail. (My address is in this book's introduction.)

Creating a Project

Follow these steps to create and test a bare-bones App Inventor project:

1. **Visit** www.appinventorbeta.com.

A visit to this site brings you to one of several possible web pages. Which page you see depends on the amount of App Inventor stuff that you've already done. If you've already downloaded and installed App Inventor, the site takes you to either App Inventor's Projects page or to App Inventor's Designer page.

The Projects page lists the projects that you've created. (See Figure 1-1.)

The Designer page is the main interface to App Inventor's Designer program. On the Designer page, you lay out your Android application's screen, drag components onto the application's screen, and set the components' properties. (See Figure 1-2.)

You can navigate between the Projects page and the Designer page. When you're on the Projects page, clicking the main toolbar's New button (to create a new project) brings you to the Designer page. Alternatively, you can select the name of one of your existing projects.

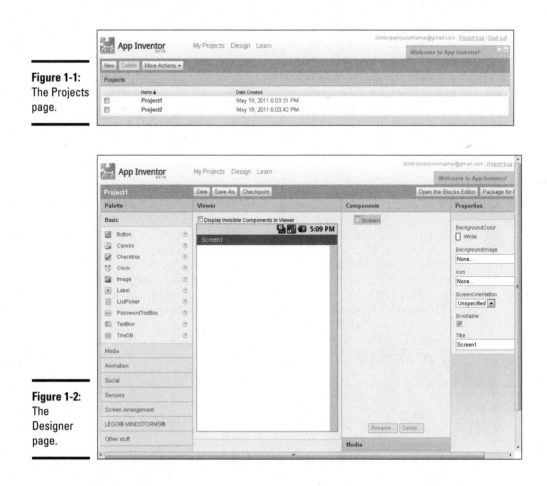

Figure 1-1:
The Projects page.

Figure 1-2:
The Designer page.

When you're on the Designer page, select the My Projects link to return to the Projects page.

Remember: Neither Ralph Lauren nor Christian Dior has anything to do with the App Inventor's Designer page.

2. **If you're not already on the Projects page, click the My Projects link to go to the Projects page.**

   In Figure 1-2, the My Projects link is at the top of the page on the right side.

3. **On the Projects page, click the New button.**

   The New App Inventor for Android Project dialog box opens.

4. **Type a project name, and click OK.**

   The Designer page opens. (See Figure 1-2.)

   At this point, App Inventor creates a skeletal Android project. You can do a quick reality check by running this project.

5. **On the Designer page, click the Open the Blocks Editor button in the upper-right corner (see Figure 1-2).**

   After you click the Open the Blocks Editor button, your computer downloads and launches the Blocks Editor program from Google's servers.

   The Blocks Editor screen contains lots of interesting thingamajigs, but for this section's minimal app, you can ignore everything except two of the buttons near the top of the screen. (See Figure 1-3.)

6. **Click the New Emulator button. (See the top of the screen in Figure 1-3.)**

   Clicking New Emulator starts the run of an Android virtual device.

7. **Wait for the emulator's startup screen to appear.**

   Android's emulator takes a long time to start running. (On my 2GHz Intel Core™ 2 Duo, the emulator's startup takes minutes, not seconds.) Sometimes, during startup, the emulator stalls, and you have to close the emulator and try launching it again. But after the emulator is fully started, it's usually quite reliable.

8. **In the emulator's screen, do whatever you normally do to unlock a phone or a tablet.**

   With your mouse, slide something from one place on the screen to another. That's usually how it's done.

9. **In the Blocks Editor, click the Connect to Device button. (Again, see the top of the screen in Figure 1-3.)**

   A list of running devices appears in a drop-down list. (See Figure 1-4.)

Book VI
Chapter 1

Creating Code
Quickly with
App Inventor

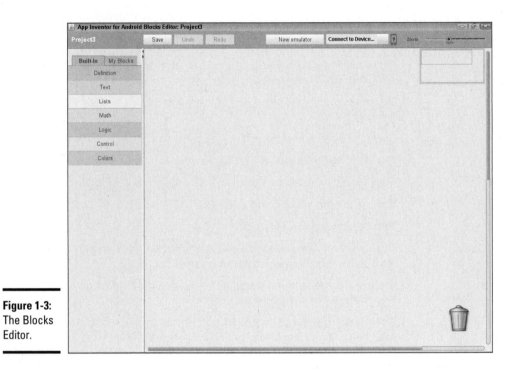

Figure 1-3:
The Blocks
Editor.

Figure 1-4:
The list of
running
devices
(emulators,
phones, and
tablets).

10. Choose a device from the drop-down list.

In Figure 1-4, the only running devices are emulators.

11. Wait for your Android application to appear on the emulator screen.

Launching an Android emulator requires the patience of a saint.

App Inventor's skeletal application is bland as any application can be. The only items on the emulator's screen are the status bar and the title bar. (See Figure 1-5.)

What's so special about the number 5554?

When you launch an Android device emulator, the new emulator's name is something like emulator-5554 or emulator-5556. The name stems from the fact that each run of an Android emulator uses two *port numbers* (two channels for communicating with the development computer). As you may already know, your web browser normally uses port number 80 to request a web page. Your e-mail program probably uses port 110, port 143, port 585, port 993, or port 995 to retrieve e-mail.

When you launch an emulator on your development computer, you can specify several port numbers for several of the emulator's networking needs. But in most of this book's examples, you start an emulator without explicitly specifying port numbers. When you don't specify port numbers, your emulator relies on default values. If you ever specify a port number other than the default, you do so because you don't want the emulator's communications to conflict with some other program's use of a particular port number. Who knows? Maybe your favorite computer game talks to the web over port 5228, the port number Android uses to obtain apps from the Android Market.

Now imagine that you have no emulators running on your development computer, and you start an emulator without specifying any port numbers. Then the new emulator uses two default port numbers — 5554 and 5555.

✔ The emulator uses port 5554 to relay its console messages (the text that appears in Eclipse's Console view).

✔ The emulator uses port 5555 to talk to the Android Debug Bridge (adb). For example, when you type **adb install myApp.apk** in your development computer's command window,

the Android Debug Bridge installs myApp.apk onto your running emulator using port 5555 to handle the communications.

If you type the command **adb devices** in your development computer's command window, you see a list of running emulators. (The list also includes any actual devices that are plugged into your computer via USB or some other fancy connection.) The list probably includes emulator-5554 because 5554 is the default console port number, and an emulator's name comes from the emulator's console port number (not from emulator's adb port number which in this example is 5555).

Time to raise the ante. Imagine that with emulator-5554 running, you go back to your development computer and start a second emulator (again, without explicitly specifying any port numbers). Then Android launches a new emulator with console port 5556 and adb port 5557. The adb port number is always one more than the console port number. To install myApp.apk on the second of the two running emulators, you'd type **adb -s emulator-5556 install myApp.apk** in your development computer's command window. If you close the first emulator, the second emulator's port numbers don't change. So after closing the first of the two emulators, when you type **adb devices**, the list of devices includes emulator-5556 and no longer includes emulator-5554.

The allowable console port numbers for Android emulators are the even numbers from 5554 to 5584 inclusive. So you can simultaneously run emulators named emulator-5554, emulator-5556, emulator-5558, and so on up to emulator-5584. I've never tried to run more than 16 emulators at once, but I'm sure that if I tried, nothing good would come of it.

Figure 1-5:
An emulator
runs your
empty App
Inventor
project.

Sure, this section's Android app is dull as dirt. But don't slam your laptop's lid shut in frustration! Keep everything running while you step through the next section's instructions.

Using the Designer

The Designer consists of five main panels, plus a few additional menus and buttons. Naturally, each of the main panels has a specific purpose. (For a gander at each of the panels, refer to Figure 1-2.) The five main panels are as follows:

✦ The *Designer palette* **contains items for you to drag into your Android application's screen.** The items in the Designer palette are called *components*. Some of the components are visible thingies (Android views and such), but other components (such as a LocationSensor) are functional rather than visible.

✦ The *Designer viewer* **is a preview of your target device's screen.** You drag components from the Designer palette to the Designer viewer.

✦ The *Components tree* **has a branch for each component that you've dropped into the Designer viewer.** Selections in the Designer viewer and the Components tree stay in sync with one another. That is, when you select a component in the Designer viewer, App Inventor automatically selects the corresponding branch of the Components tree. And when you select a branch of the Components tree, App Inventor automatically selects the corresponding component in the Designer viewer.

The bottom of the Components tree's panel has buttons for renaming and deleting components in the tree.

If you're working on a serious project (instead of goofing around with instructions in this book), rename each component that you drag into the Designer viewer. If you don't do any renaming, App Inventor assigns default names to your components — names such as Button1, Button2, and so on. Later on, when you work with these randomly named components in the Blocks Editor, you'll have trouble remembering each component's role.

✦ **The *Media panel* displays any images or other media that you've added to your project.** In Figure 1-2, the Media panel is sitting quietly below the Components tree.

✦ **The *Properties* sheet lists the properties of whatever component you select in the Designer viewer or the Components tree.** You can set a component's properties using the Properties sheet's text fields, dropdowns, and other gizmos.

**Book VI
Chapter 1**

**Creating Code
Quickly with
App Inventor**

Adding a component to your project

With the Designer, the Blocks Editor, and the emulator from the previous section still running, try the following trick:

1. **The Designer palette's components are divided into categories, so locate the Basic category.**

Refer to Figure 1-2. The Basic category is in the upper-left section of the figure.

2. **In the Basic category, locate my favorite component — the Button.**

3. **Drag the Button component from the Designer palette to the Designer viewer.**

The result is shown in Figure 1-6.

Now the real fun begins!

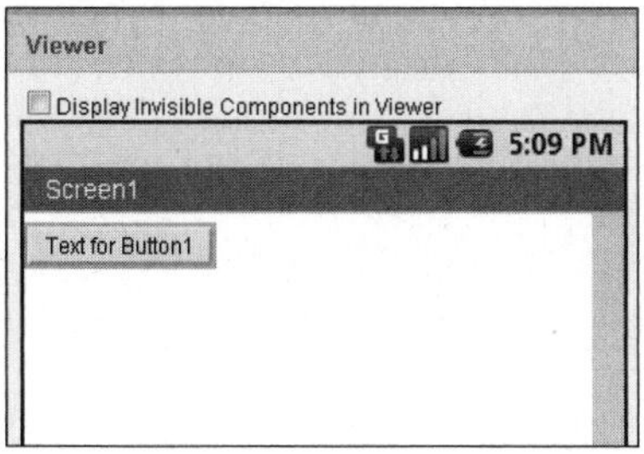

Figure 1-6:
A new
Button
component
in the
Designer
viewer.

> Viewer
> ☐ Display Invisible Components in Viewer
> 　　　　　　　　　　　🄶 📶 🔋 5:09 PM
> Screen1
> ┌─────────────┐
> │ Text for Button1 │
> └─────────────┘

4. **Look back at the emulator that you launched in Step 6 of "Creating a Project," earlier in this chapter.**

   Lo and behold! The emulator displays your modified Android app — an app with a button (See Figure 1-7.)

   In Step 9 of "Creating a Project," you forge a connection between App Inventor and an emulator. Later, when you add a button to the Designer viewer, the emulator's screen changes automatically. You don't reload your modified project onto the emulator. The App Inventor reloads for you. Hey! When you connect App Inventor to a device, you *really* connect App Inventor to the device!

5. **Create a checkpoint!**

   The Designer doesn't have an Undo feature. Instead, you create *checkpoints*. When you create a checkpoint, you create a new project containing all the changes you made since the last Save, Save As, or Checkpoint operation. After you create a checkpoint, the Designer continues to display whatever project it displayed before you created the checkpoint.

   The Checkpoint button appears above the Designer viewer in the Designer page. (See Figure 1-2.) Click this button to open the Checkpoint dialog box.

6. **In the Checkpoint dialog box, type a name for your checkpoint and then click OK.**

   The buttons above the Designer viewer have the labels Save, Save As, and Checkpoint:

   • When you click *Save,* you commit the changes you made since the previous Save or Save As operation. The Designer continues to display whatever project you save.

   • When you click *Save As,* you create a new project containing all the changes you made since the previous Save or Save As operation. After the Save As operation, the Designer displays the new project.

   • When you click *Checkpoint,* you create a new project containing all the changes you made since the last Save, Save As, or Checkpoint operation. After you create a checkpoint, the Designer continues to display whatever project it displayed before you created the checkpoint.

     To undo changes that you made to your project, return to the Projects page (by clicking My Projects on the Designer page). From the list on the Projects page, select a project that you created previously. (You created projects using the Designer's Save, Save As, and Checkpoint buttons.)

   With App Inventor (as with any other tool that you use), save your work often.

Figure 1-7:
The emulator
stays in
sync with
changes in
the Designer.

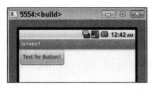

Setting component properties

Using Designer's Properties sheet, you can examine or change all kinds
of things about each component that you've placed in the Designer
viewer. Try this:

1. **Follow the previous instructions in this chapter.**

I understand. Asking you to follow all the previous instructions in this
chapter is a lot to ask. But believe me, it's worth the effort.

As a result of following those instructions, you have a Button on the
Designer viewer. ("Big deal!" you say. Well, you're on your way to
bigger and better things.)

2. **With Screen1 selected in the Components tree, find the Screen-
Orientation drop-down in the Properties sheet, and change the
selection from Unspecified or Portrait to Landscape.**

As a result, the Designer viewer's screen orientation changes to
Landscape. Congratulations! You've just turned your phone sideways.

3. **With Screen1 still selected, find the BackgroundImage field in the
Properties sheet, and select it to reveal a small BackgroundImage
dialog box.**

See Figure 1-8.

Figure 1-8:
The Back-
ground-
Image
dialog box.

4. **In the BackgroundImage dialog box, click Add.**

   The Upload File dialog box appears. (See Figure 1-9.)

5. **In the Upload File dialog box, click Choose File.**

   As a result, your operating system's Open dialog box appears.

6. **Using your operating system's Open dialog box, look for an image file on your computer's hard drive.**

7. **After choosing an image file, click OK a few times (or whatever you need to click) to back out of the Open dialog box and the Upload File dialog box.**

   As a result, the BackgroundImage field contains the name of your image file, and the Designer viewer's screen displays your image in the background. Figure 1-10 shows the Designer viewer's screen with a background image displaying the Stockton Street Tunnel in San Francisco. I took the photo with my Android phone after attending Google I/O 2011.

Because of the stuff you did in Steps 3–7, your image file appears as an option in the Designer's small Media panel. The Media panel is located below the Components tree.

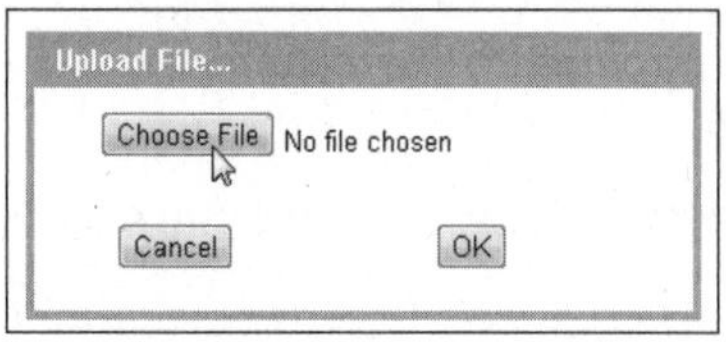

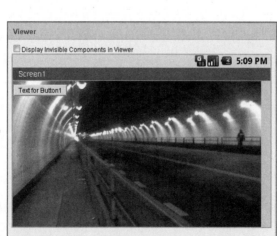

Figure 1-9:
The Upload
File dialog
box.

Figure 1-10:
There's an
image to
the Android
application's
background.

8. **In the Designer viewer (or in the Components tree), select the button that you created previously.**

   In Figure 1-10, the text on the button's face is *Text for Button1*. Select the corresponding button in your own project.

9. **In the Properties sheet, find the Text field, change the words in that field, and then press Enter.**

   In the Designer viewer, the text on the face of the button changes. (See Figure 1-11.)

Figure 1-11:
You've changed the text on the face of the button.

Arranging screen elements

The App Inventor doesn't provide all the layout facilities of Android's SDK. For example, the Designer palette has no Relative layout. And in general, the Designer's options aren't as feature-rich as the SDK's layouts. But with the Designer palette's Screen Arrangement components, you can go a long way in customizing the look of your Android app.

It's natural to wonder if you can enjoy the best of both worlds. You can create an Android app in minutes with the App Inventor. Then can you import your app into Eclipse and tweak the code with the Android SDK's high-precision tools? The answer (as of the day I write this sentence) is no. Google doesn't provide a way to translate App Inventor code into ordinary Android SDK code. I've tried one or two third-party translation tools, but none of these tools is reliable. (And for all I know, these tools might not be legal.)

I want to keep this chapter's ongoing example from becoming cluttered. So the next set of instructions starts without the changes from the "Setting component properties" section.

If you followed Steps 5 and 6 in the "Adding a component to your project" section, you can return to your checkpoint. In doing so, you return to the project as it was before changing orientation, adding a background image, and setting the button's text. But if you didn't create a checkpoint (or if you didn't do anything beyond starting a new project), don't worry. The steps in this section don't build on the steps from previous sections. (Besides, the apps that you create in this chapter are practice apps. You can experiment all you want and not hurt anything.)

For details about using checkpoints, see the "Adding a component to your project" section, earlier in this chapter.

To arrange components on the Designer viewer screen, do the following:

1. **In the Designer palette's Screen Arrangement list, find the VerticalArrangement.**

See Figure 1-12.

2. **Drag a VerticalArrangement from the palette to the Designer viewer's screen.**

An empty rectangle appears in the Designer viewer screen. (See Figure 1-13.)

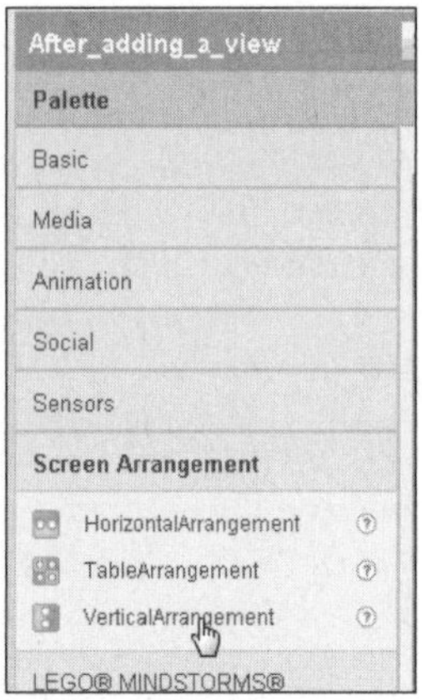

Figure 1-12:
The
Designer
palette's
Vertical-
Arrangement
component.

Figure 1-13:
The screen
contains
an empty
Vertical-
Arrangement.

3. **If you have a button on your Designer viewer's screen, drag that button into the VerticalArrangement square; if you don't already have a button, drag a new button from the Designer palette into the VerticalArrangement square.**

   The VerticalArrangement square shrinks (and maybe moves) to fully enclose the button.

4. **Drag a second button from the Designer palette into the VerticalArrangement square.**

   The VerticalArrangement square grows to accommodate the additional button. The buttons inside the arrangement appear one above the other because this arrangement is a VerticalArrangement. (See Figure 1-14.)

   Look at the quick-and-dirty layout in Figure 1-14. An Android app looks so crude if its buttons are tucked in the upper-left corner! Unlike Android's SDK, the App Inventor doesn't let you change a view's gravity. So to center the components in your application's screen, you need a hack. I describe this hack in the next several steps.

5. **In the Designer viewer or the Component tree, select the VerticalArrangement.**

6. **In the Properties sheet, select the Width field.**

   A small Width dialog box appears. (See Figure 1-15.)

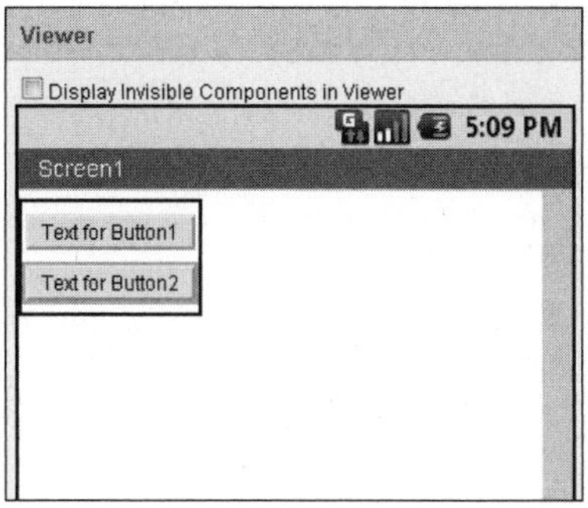

Book VI
Chapter 1

Creating Code Quickly with App Inventor

Figure 1-14: Two components inside a Vertical-Arrangement.

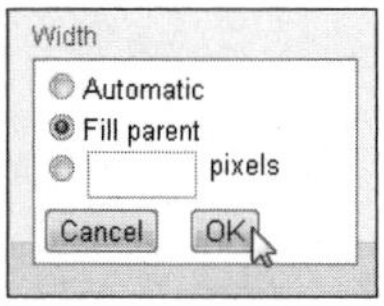

Figure 1-15: The Width dialog box.

7. **In the Width dialog box, select the Fill Parent option.**

   Again, see Figure 1-15.

8. **In the Width dialog box, click OK.**

   As a result, the VerticalArrangement stretches across the entire Designer viewer screen. (See Figure 1-16.)

   So far, so good. But here comes the embarrassing part of the layout hack.

9. **Drag two HorizontalArrangement components from the Designer palette into the VerticalArrangement.**

10. **Drag the buttons on the Designer viewer screen into the HorizontalArrangement components.**

    That is, drag one button into one HorizontalArrangement, and drag the other button into the other HorizontalArrangement. (See Figure 1-17.)

11. **Drag four new labels from the palette into the HorizontalArrangement components, and surround each button with two of the labels. (See Figure 1-18.)**

12. **Set each label's Width property to the Fill Parent option.**

    For details on setting a component's Width property, see Steps 5–8.

13. **Set both HorizontalArrangement components' properties to (yes) the Fill Parent option.**

    At this point, everything stretches across the entire Designer viewer screen. The only sore spot is the text in each of the labels.

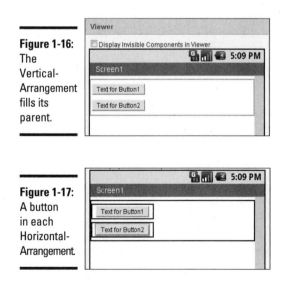

Figure 1-16: The Vertical- Arrangement fills its parent.

Figure 1-17: A button in each Horizontal- Arrangement.

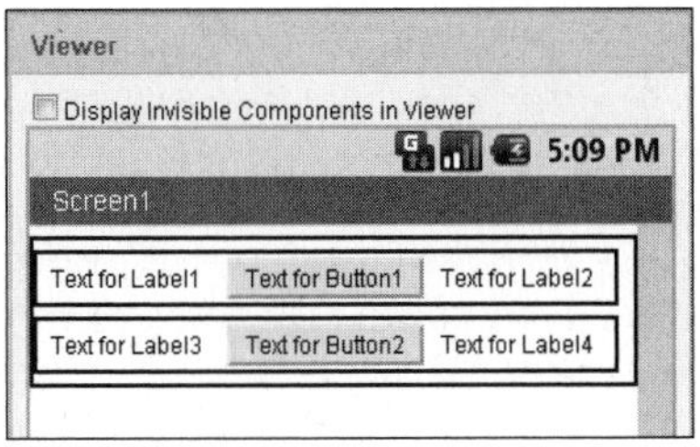

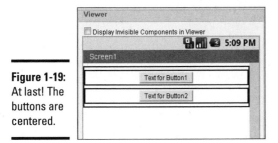

Figure 1-18:
Each
button is
surrounded
by labels.

14. **Delete the text in each of the labels, leaving behind just your button text.**

For help setting a component's text, see the "Setting component properties" section.

App Inventor doesn't treat strings the way Java treats strings. In App Inventor, the notation " " doesn't stand for the empty string. Instead, " " stands for the two-character string containing two double quotation marks. To put an empty string in one of App Inventor's label components, go to the Properties sheet and delete all characters in the component's Text field.

In the Designer viewer, the final result appears in Figure 1-19. The (beautiful) display that you see in an emulator is pictured in Figure 1-20.

**Book VI
Chapter 1**

**Creating Code
Quickly with
App Inventor**

Figure 1-19:
At last! The
buttons are
centered.

Figure 1-20:
Nice!

Using the Blocks Editor

Google's App Inventor has two major parts — a Designer and a Blocks Editor. The Blocks Editor has two big panels. These panels don't seem to have names to speak of. So for the sake of clarity, I hereby christen these panels the *Blocks palette* and the *Blocks viewer*. (In some tutorials, I've seen the Blocks viewer called the *editor,* but that terminology confuses me.)

The Blocks Editor has a palette and a viewer, and the Designer has a palette and a viewer (along with other panels). For the Designer's panels, I use the names *Designer palette* and *Designer viewer;* for the Blocks Editor's panels, I use the names *Blocks palette* and *Blocks viewer.* My terminology isn't standard. But as far as I'm concerned, the standard terminology isn't very helpful. In fact, in the official App Inventor documentation, many parts of the interface are unnamed.

You can see the Blocks palette and the Blocks viewer in Figure 1-3.

✦ **The *Blocks palette* on the left side contains building blocks for actions — the actions to be performed by your Android application.**

The Blocks palette has two tabs — Built-In and My Blocks:

- Most items on the *My Blocks tab* represent the components that you've added to the Designer's viewer — buttons, labels, screen arrangements, and other such things.

- The items on the *Built-In tab* are fundamental elements of programming logic. This includes text strings, mathematical operators, comparison operators, loops, if-then constructs, and other stuff.

✦ **The *Blocks viewer* is a preview of your application's actions.** The Blocks viewer, initially empty, consumes most of the Blocks Editor's area. As you might already have guessed, you drag items from the Blocks palette to the Blocks viewer.

The programming model for App Inventor's Blocks Editor is the Scratch development environment. Visit `http://scratch.mit.edu` for details.

Adding event handlers

In previous sections, I describe the kinds of things that most visual editors can do. In fact, Eclipse's Graphical Layout has the same kinds of drag-and-drop facilities as App Inventor's Designer, and the Graphical Layout has an added advantage. With Eclipse's Graphical Layout, you have access to most of the Android SDK features.

So what makes the App Inventor different? Why use the App Inventor instead of Eclipse and the Android SDK? With the App Inventor's Blocks Editor, you can create Android application logic by dragging and dropping things and by fitting things together. Absolutely no coding required!

Okay, what's an advantage in one setting is a disadvantage in another. Along with the Blocks Editor's "no coding required" feature comes the "no coding allowed" limitation. Anyway, App Inventor isn't a magic bullet. To create elaborate Android applications, you still need an IDE, such as Eclipse, and the full Android SDK.

In this section, you experiment with some Blocks Editor techniques:

1. **On the App Inventor's Projects page, create a new project.**

For details, see the section "Creating a Project," earlier in the chapter.

2. **Drag a button from the Designer palette and drop it onto the Designer viewer.**

For details, see the section "Adding a component to your project" — again, earlier in the chapter.

3. **Drag a label from the Designer palette and drop it onto the Designer viewer.**

Now your Application has a button (named Button1) and a label (named Label1).

4. **Open the Blocks Editor.**

For details, see the "Creating a Project" section. (You know where it is.)

5. **In the Blocks palette, click the My Blocks tab. (See Figure 1-21.)**

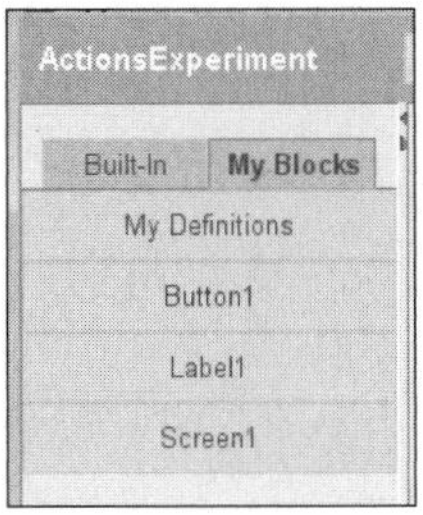

Figure 1-21:
The My
Blocks
tab in the
Blocks
palette.

6. In the My Blocks tab, click Button1. (See Figure 1-22.)

Here's where some of my earlier advice shows its real value. Previously in this chapter, I advise you to rename each component that you drag into the Designer viewer. Oddly enough, if you don't follow my advice, life is easier for me. In Step 6, you click Button1, and sure enough, your application has something with the default name *Button1.* But in practice, a Blocks palette with names such as *Button1, Label1, Button2,* and *Button3* is very confusing. Which of your buttons is *Button2?* Is it the Send Mail button or the Receive Mail button? Instead of living with the default *Button2* name, change the name to *SendMail,* or *PlaySong,* or whatever name reminds you of the button's purpose.

Anyway, in this set of steps, you've selected Button1. As a result, the expanded Blocks palette contains a bunch of puzzle pieces. Each puzzle piece (each block) has something to do with Button1. (See Figure 1-22.) Now what?

7. Click the Button1.Click block.

(If you read the fine print, the block's label is actually When Button1. Click Do.)

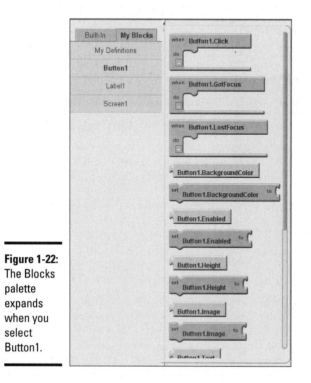

Figure 1-22:
The Blocks palette expands when you select Button1.

When you click the Button1.Click block, the other blocks on the expanded palette disappear. The Button1.Click block stands on its own in the Blocks viewer. (See Figure 1-23.)

Everybody does it. At one time or another, you'll reach into the expanded palette and click the wrong block. No problem. Simply drag the unwanted block to the trash can in the Blocks viewer's lower-right corner. (Refer to Figure 1-3.)

The Button1.Click block is an example of an *event handler:*

- An *event* is something that your application might respond to, such as a button click, the pressing of a key, a change in GPS location, or the arrival of a text message.

- An *event handler* (such as the Button1.Click block) is the part of your app that responds to the occurrence of an event.

- When an event occurs, your device automatically invokes the instructions contained in the event handler.

In this example, an event occurs when the user clicks Button1. In the Block1.Click event handler, you'll add instructions to put text in the application's other component (the Label1 component). (In fact, you'll spend the remainder of this step list doing precisely that.)

8. **In the Blocks palette, click Label1.**

Now the expanded Blocks palette contains a bunch of Label1 puzzle pieces. Notice that some of the pieces (the blocks) come in pairs. The expanded palette has a Label1.Text block and a Set Label1.Text To block.

- The *Label1.Text block* is a *getter.*

- The *Set Label1.Text To* block is a *setter.*

A getter gives you access to an existing value. A setter changes an existing value (or sets the value for the first time). Taken together, a getter and a setter allow you to examine and change the value of a component's property.

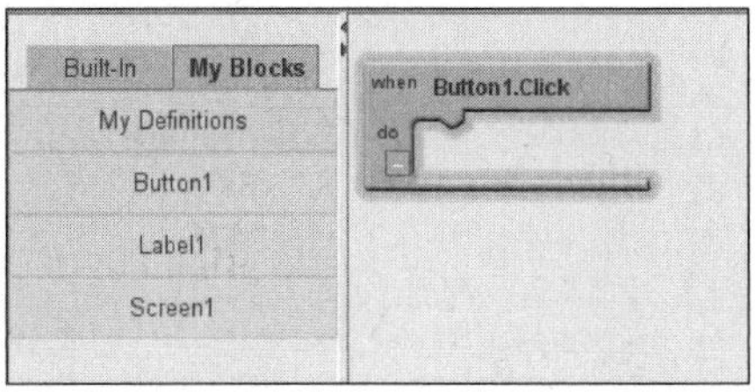

Book VI Chapter 1

Creating Code Quickly with App Inventor

Figure 1-23:
The Button1. Click block in the Blocks viewer.

Built-In	**My Blocks**
My Definitions	
Button1	
Label1	
Screen1	

when Button1.Click
do

9. **Click the Label1.Text setter block.**

The Label1.Text setter sits along with the Button1.Click event handler in the Blocks viewer.

It's time for some jigsaw-puzzle fun! Like two drifting tectonic plates, the two pieces in the Blocks viewer look as if they belong together. The Label1.Text setter can fit snugly inside the Button1.Click event handler.

10. **Drag-and-drop the Label1.Text setter block into the gap of the Button1. Click event handler block (see Figure 1-24).**

To be painfully precise, the name for one of these gaps is actually a *socket*.

If you drop the label block in the right place, your computer speaker plays a snap sound, and the combination of blocks changes in appearance just a bit. These responses indicate that you've successfully associated one block with the other. In terms of programming logic, you've said, "When the user clicks Button1, set Label1's text to . . .", and you haven't yet specified Label1's new text.

Near the top of the Button1.Click block, App Inventor displays an exclamation point inside a little box. If you hover over the box, a popup bubble says, `Warning: This clump contains an empty socket and won't be sent to the phone.` That *empty socket* is the gap in the To part of the Label1.Text setter block. The effortless emulator update that I describe in the "Adding a component to your project" section, earlier in this chapter, can't take place.

11. **Click the Built-In tab of the Blocks palette.**

12. **In the Built-In tab, click the Text item.**

A bunch of text-related blocks appears in the expanded Blocks palette. (See Figure 1-25.)

13. **In the expanded Blocks palette, click the Text item.**

As a puzzle piece, this item has only one part that connects to another piece. That part is a little knob that fits nicely into the Label1.Text setter block's empty socket.

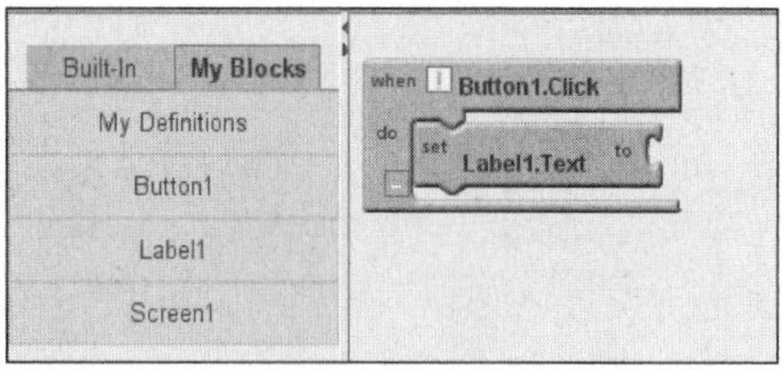

Figure 1-24:
The label
block
snaps into
the button
block.

Built-In	My Blocks
My Definitions	
Button1	
Label1	
Screen1	

when ⓘ Button1.Click
do   set Label1.Text to

14. **Drag and drop the Text block into the gap of the Label1.Text setter block (see Figure 1-26).**

You're instructing your app to set the Label1's text to something-or-other. The only remaining work is to specify what that something-or-other is.

15. **Click the bold *Text* word in the newly dropped Text piece.**

The word changes appearance, like the branch whose file you're renaming on an Explorer or Finder tree.

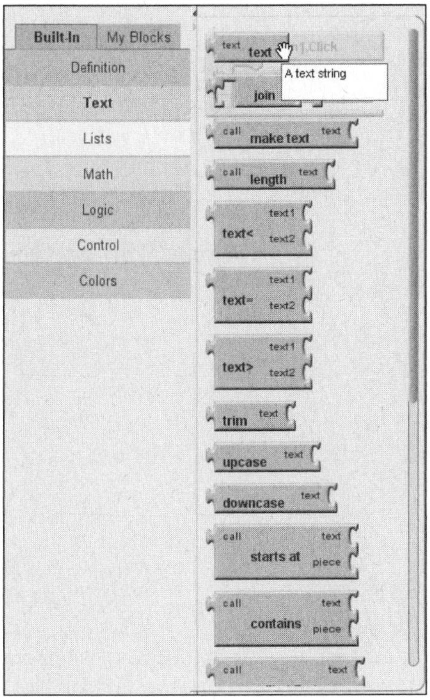

Figure 1-25:
The
expanded
Blocks
palette
displays
blocks
related to
text.

Figure 1-26:
A clump of
blocks with
no empty
socket.

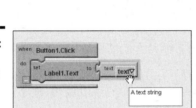

16. **Type a few characters in place of the word** *Text* **and then press Enter (see Figure 1-27).**

17. **If necessary, start an emulator and connect App Inventor to the emulator.**

For details, see the earlier section "Creating a Project."

Wait for the emulator to receive the newest changes to your Android application. And then . . .

18. **Click the button on the emulator's screen.**

The emulator responds by changing the label's text. (See Figure 1-28.)

Figure 1-27:
The block grows to hold a longer string of characters.

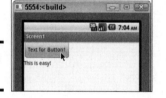

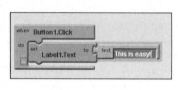

Figure 1-28:
Voilà!

Event handlers with parameters

The preceding section's event handler is very stubborn. Whenever you click the button, you get the same message: *This is easy!* If you click again, you see the same message again. This persistent behavior is a result of the work shown in Figure 1-27. In that figure, you type **This is easy!** on a block.

This section's event handler isn't nearly so stubborn. In this section, you do something like the stuff shown in Figure 1-27. But instead of typing **This is easy!** or some other specific text, you add a parameter to the Label1.Text setter block. A *parameter* is a placeholder for any text that the user types. Here's how it works:

1. **On the App Inventor's Projects page, create a new project.**

For details see the "Creating a Project" section in this chapter.

2. **Drag a button from the Designer palette and drop it onto the Designer viewer.**

3. **Drag a label from the Designer palette and drop it onto the Designer viewer.**

Now your Application has a button (named Button1) and a label (named Label1).

4. **Drag a Notifier component from the Other Stuff category of the Designer palette and then drop the Notifier onto the Designer viewer.**

A Notifier is initially invisible. (It's invisible until something interesting happens — something worth notifying the user about.) So you don't see your new Notifier in the Designer viewer's screen. But in the Components tree, you see a branch labeled Notifier1. And if you're lucky, you might peek below the Designer viewer's screen and find an icon representing Notifier1.

5. **Open the Blocks Editor.**

6. **Create the group shown in Figure 1-29.**

For help grouping blocks, see the preceding section.

The blocks in Figure 1-29 instruct your app to display a text dialog box. A text dialog box gets text from the user. (See Figure 1-30.)

In the next few steps, you create a second group of blocks.

7. **In the Blocks palette's My Blocks tab, click the Notifier1 item.**

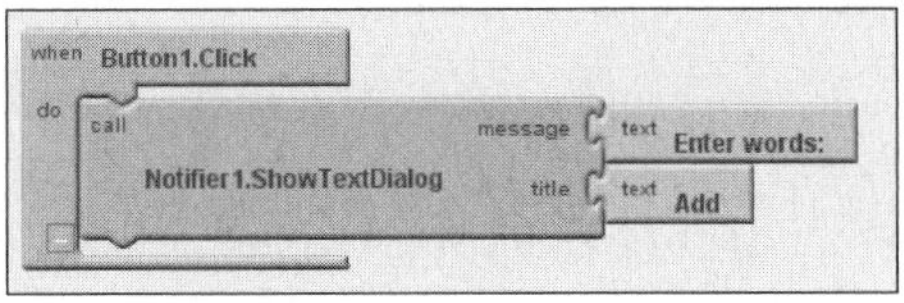

Book VI
Chapter 1

Creating Code
Quickly with
App Inventor

Figure 1-29:
When the
user clicks
the button,
the notifier
displays a
dialog box.

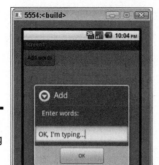

Figure 1-30:
A text dialog
box.

8. **In the expanded Blocks palette, select the Notifier1.AfterTextInput event handler block.**

When you make the selection, App Inventor adds two pieces to your Blocks viewer. (Yes, it adds *two* pieces.) Along with the event handler block, App Inventor adds a block displaying Name and Response. (See Figure 1-31.)

The extra Name Response block is a *parameter,* or placeholder. A user enters **OK, I'm typing** into the field in Figure 1-30. Then, when the user clicks OK, the user's text (*OK, I'm typing,* or whatever else the user entered) has a name. That text's name is Response.

Because the user's input text has a name, you can use that name in the rest of the handler block. You use the name to help describe an action — the action to be taken in response to the `AfterTextInput` event.

Why does the text *OK, I'm typing* need a name? The user's input text needs a name because you can't assume that the user always enters **OK, I'm typing** in the field of Figure 1-30. Somehow, you have to instruct the app to do something with whatever the user types. In Figure 1-31, the name for whatever the user types is Response.

Whatever text the user enters in Figure 1-30 goes by Response. That's fine, but how do you use Response? Here's how:

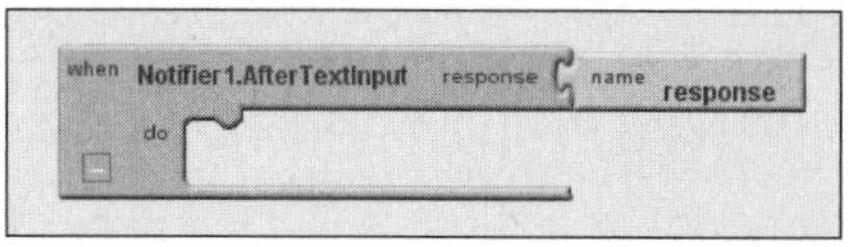

Figure 1-31:
Two blocks
for the price
of one.

9. **In the My Blocks tab, click the My Definitions category.**

A Value Response block appears (as if by magic) in the extended Blocks palette.

10. **Click the Value Response block, but for now, don't attach the block to anything else in the Blocks viewer.**

You make use of the parameter Response by plugging this Value Response block into a socket. But first, I want to show you another trick or two.

11. **Add blocks to the Notifier1.AfterTextInput event handler block to form the incomplete group shown in Figure 1-32.**

The Join block in Figure 1-32 comes from the Text category in the Blocks palette's Built-In tab. When you *join* two pieces of text, you turn the two pieces into one combined piece. (That is, you *concatenate* the two pieces.)

In this example, you plan to join three pieces of text. So in the next step, you join stuff to an existing Join block.

12. **Add another block to the Notifier1.AfterTextInput handler to form the incomplete group shown in Figure 1-33.**

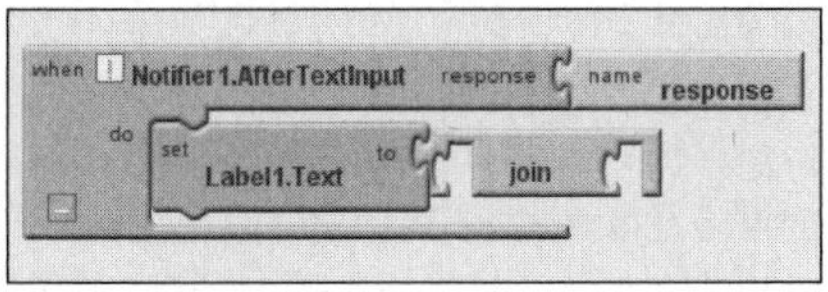

Book VI
Chapter 1

Figure 1-32:
An incomplete (but interesting) group of blocks.

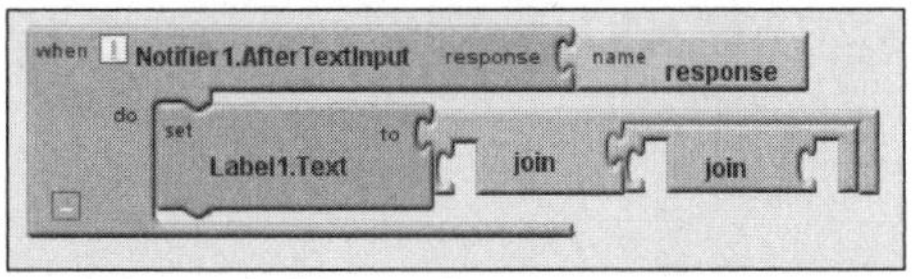

Figure 1-33:
A Join block within a Join block.

13. **Fill the empty sockets in the Notifier1.AfterTextInput block as follows:**

- *Into the leftmost socket — the remaining empty socket of your first Join block — put the Label1.Text getter block.*

- *Into the middle socket — the first empty socket on your second Join block — put a Text block containing a backslash (\ ) followed by a lowercase letter n.*

  In many modern programming languages, \n stands for an instruction to "go to the next line."

- *Into the rightmost socket — the remaining empty socket on your second Join block — put the Value Response block that you selected in Step 10.*

The resulting group of blocks is shown in Figure 1-34.

When the user finishes typing text, the combination of blocks in Figure 1-34 instructs your app to do the following:

a. Get whatever text is already on Label1.

b. Join a line break onto that text.

c. Join the user's response onto that bundle of text.

d. Put the whole bunch of joined text back into Label1.

Now you have two groups of blocks — a group to handle button clicks (in Figure 1-29) and a group to handle text input (in Figure 1-34). You can connect to an emulator and try the app. Some screen shots from a run of the app appear in Figure 1-35.

This chapter covers the general concepts behind App Inventor. Chapter 2 of this minibook describes specific App Inventor projects.

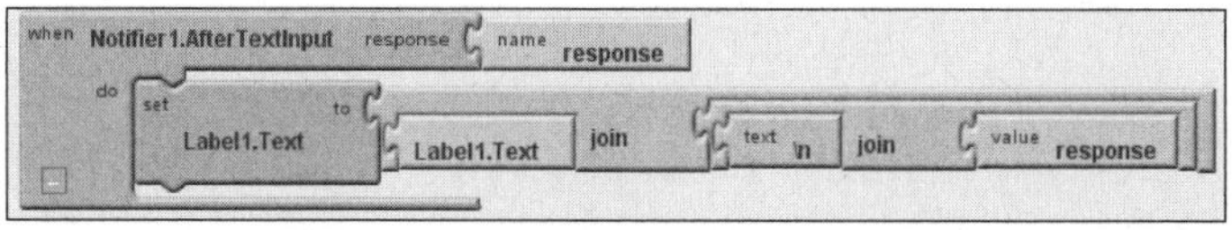

Figure 1-34:
At last! A complete event handler!

Figure 1-35:
Each
encounter
with the text
dialog box
adds a line
of text to the
label.

Chapter 2: More App Inventor Magic

In This Chapter

✔ **Taking pictures and sending messages**

✔ **Measuring a device's tilt**

✔ **Making things move on the screen**

✔ **Storing and accessing data**

✔ **Starting another app**

Chapter 1 of this minibook introduces you to the wonderful world of Google's App Inventor. "Nice to meet you," you say to App Inventor. As in any new relationship, the first getting-to-know-you encounter ends and then the let's-learn-more-about-each-other phase begins. So in this chapter, you relax with App Inventor over an espresso at lunch and find out more about creating Android applications.

Snap a Photo

App Inventor can access a device's camera. To check it out, try this:

1. **Create a new App Inventor project.**

   For details, see Chapter 1 of this minibook.

2. **Onto the Designer viewer, drop a button.**

3. **(Optional) Put the words *Start the Camera* on the face of the button.**

4. **In the Designer palette's Media category, find the Camera component.**

5. **Drag a camera from the Designer palette to the Designer viewer.**

   A camera component isn't visible, so you don't see your new camera component in the Designer viewer's screen. But in the Components tree, you see a branch labeled Camera1. And if you're lucky, you might peek below the Designer viewer's screen and find an icon representing Camera1.

Do as I say, not as I do. To make these instructions easy to follow, don't rename Camera1 to anything else (such as MyEightyMegapixelDream). But in real-life development, your components (and other things) should have consistent, informative names instead of the default names (such as Camera1) that App Inventor assigns.

6. **Open the Blocks Editor.**

   For details, see Chapter 1 of this minibook.

7. **In the Blocks viewer, align blocks, as shown in Figure 2-1.**

   For details, blah-blah-blah, Chapter 1 of this minibook, yada-yada.

8. **Fire up an emulator or connect a phone to your development computer; then test your Android application.**

   For a look at the app in action, see Figures 2-2 and 2-3.

   To get this app running, you might have to restart the Blocks Editor and the emulator. Sure, restarting takes time. But it's worth the wait.

If you're curious, Figure 2-3 is a picture of a picture of a picture. My phone takes a snapshot of my computer screen, which displays a copy of the screen on my phone, which takes a snapshot of my computer screen, and so on. I've always been curious about this kind of thing.

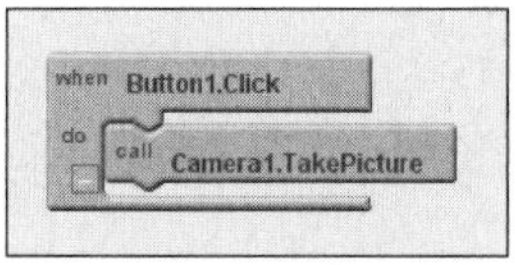

Figure 2-1:
When the user clicks the button, have the camera take a picture.

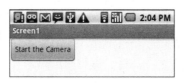

Figure 2-2:
The screen arrangement created in Steps 2 and 3.

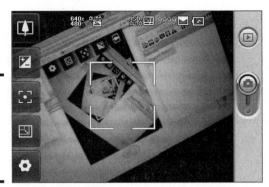

Figure 2-3:
The result
of clicking
the button
shown in
Figure 2-2.

Send a Text Message

The acronym *SMS* stands for *Short Messaging Service* — the technology that
enables text messaging from one mobile device to another. This section's
example uses App Inventor to send such a message:

1. **Create a new App Inventor project.**

2. **Onto the Designer viewer, drop two TextBox components and a
Button component.**

One text box is for a telephone number; the other text box is for a brief
message body. Clicking the button starts the message transmission.

3. **(Optional) Add a hint to each text box.**

A *hint* appears faintly inside a text box, but only when the user leaves
the text box empty. (See Figure 2-4.) To place a hint in a TextBox component, select that component in the Designer viewer or the Components
tree. Then type the stuff you want to appear ghost-like in the text box
(again, see Figure 2-4) into the Properties sheet's Hint field.

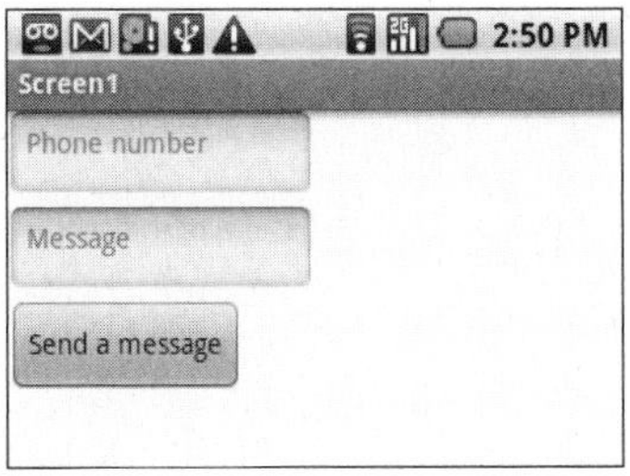

Figure 2-4:
The screen
arrangement
created in
Steps 2 to 4.

4. **(Optional) Put the words *Send a message* on the face of the button (see Figure 2-4).**

5. **On the Properties sheet, put a check mark in the NumbersOnly check box belonging to the phone number text box.**

   When the user selects a text box, NumbersOnly tells the keyboard to pop up in numeric mode. Also, NumbersOnly prevents the user from entering letters and other goofy characters into a text box.

6. **In the Designer palette's Social category, find the Texting component, and drag it from the Designer palette to the Designer viewer.**

   You don't see your new Texting component in the Designer viewer's screen. But in the Components tree, you see a branch labeled Texting1.

7. **Open the Blocks Editor.**

8. **In the Blocks viewer, add and align blocks, as shown in Figure 2-5.**

   In Figure 2-5, the second setter block is for Texting1.Message. What I call a *brief message body* in Step 2 is simply called *Message* in this setter block. So this block takes whatever is in the second text box and sends it as the body of a text message.

   You can squeeze several blocks, one after another, into a handler block's socket. In Figure 2-5, I put two setter blocks followed by a Call Texting1.SendMessage block into the Button1.Click socket. That's fine. When the user clicks Button1, the device executes the handling blocks' instructions in sequence. First, the device sets a PhoneNumber. Next, the device sets a Message (a message body, that is). Finally, the device executes, Texting1.SendMessage.

9. **Test your app on a real phone.**

   Type a telephone number and a brief message body. When you press the Send a Message button, your phone sends the text message. (If you test the app on an emulator, nothing happens when you press the Send a Message button. That's disappointing, but at least nothing bad happens!)

   For help connecting a phone or tablet device to your development computer, see Book I, Chapter 3.

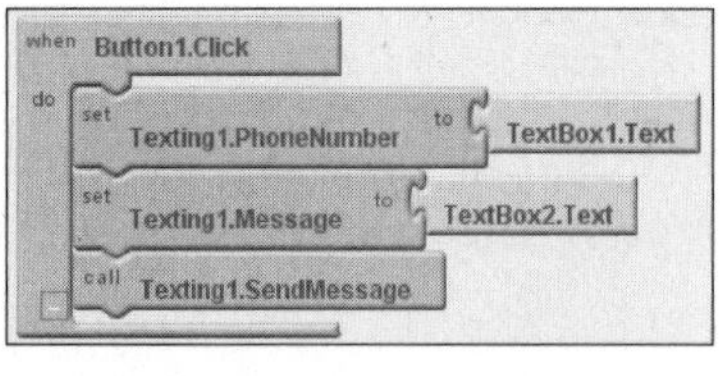

Figure 2-5:
When the user clicks the button, send a text message.

when	Button1.Click
do	set Texting1.PhoneNumber to TextBox1.Text
	set Texting1.Message to TextBox2.Text
	call Texting1.SendMessage

Travel to the Orient

A device's *orientation sensor* keeps track of the direction the device faces. A phone whose screen faces the sky and whose top faces north has zero *yaw,* zero *pitch,* and zero *roll.* If you turn the phone clockwise (keeping it flat on the ground), the yaw increases. (See Figure 2-6.) A quarter turn represents 90 degrees. So, for example, a phone whose top faces east has yaw 90. A phone whose top faces west has yaw 270.

To use orientation settings in an App Inventor project, try the following:

1. **Create a new App Inventor project.**

2. **Drop three Label components onto the Designer viewer.**

One label is for your device's yaw, another label is for the pitch, and the third label is for roll.

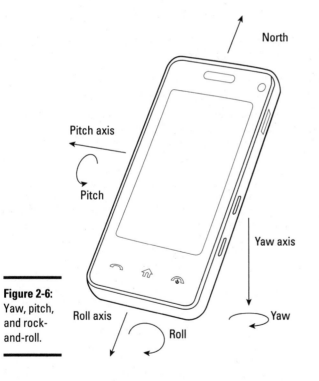

Figure 2-6:
Yaw, pitch,
and rock-
and-roll.

Angles and directions

Android's orientation and object movement functions use geometric angles to describe direction. If you've taken a geometry course, and if you haven't suppressed the memory, you may remember the following facts:

- A 0-degree angle points to the right. (Think of an analog clock whose only hand points to 3.) See the figure below.

- A 90-degree angle points upward. (Think of an analog clock whose only hand points to 12.)

- As the hand turns counterclockwise, the number of degrees increases.

- A 180-degree angle points to the left (to 9 o'clock).

- A 360-degree angle has gone counter-clockwise all the way around in a circle. Like a 0-degree angle, a 360-degree angle points to the right.

These facts (and a few others) are illustrated in the figure below.

To relate this stuff to a phone's orientation, you set a vantage point. For example, if you perform a certain (admittedly silly) experiment, your phone's yaw changes exactly the way the degrees change in the figure below. Here's the experiment:

First, put your phone on a glass table, with the phone's screen facing the ceiling and the phone's top facing north. The phone's yaw, pitch, and roll are all zero. Then, creep underneath the table and look up through the glass at the back of your phone. Position your head so that the tip of your head faces east. Now the phone's yaw changes exactly as the angles in the figure below.

To finish the experiment, get up and explain to everyone why you were lying on your back under a table.

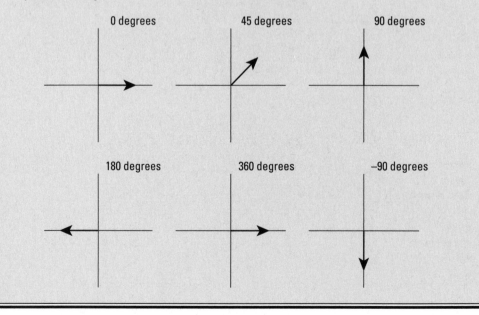

0 degrees	45 degrees	90 degrees
180 degrees	360 degrees	−90 degrees

3. **Drop an OrientationSensor component onto the Designer viewer.**

   You can find the OrientationSensor in the Designer palette's Sensors category. (What a surprise!) An OrientationSensor component isn't visible, so you don't see your new sensor in the Designer viewer's screen.

4. **Drop a Clock component onto the (very same) Designer viewer.**

   You can find the Clock component in the Designer palette's Basic category.

   The component name *Clock* is slightly misleading. The name suggests a display showing the time. But an App Inventor Clock component isn't visible. A Clock component keeps track of milliseconds and sends events to your device's operating system. (A typical event notification is something like this: "Hey, operating system! One half a second has passed since the last time I notified you.")

5. **Select your Clock component in the Components tree.**

6. **In the Properties sheet, set the TimerInterval property to 500.**

   The number 500 stands for 500 milliseconds, which is half of a second.

7. **Open the Blocks Editor.**

8. **In the Blocks viewer, align the blocks until they look like what you see in Figure 2-7.**

9. **Attach your phone to your computer, and let 'er rip!**

   For help connecting a phone or tablet device to your development computer, see Book I, Chapter 3.

   A typical run of this section's example looks like the display in Figure 2-8. (Well, it stays that way for half a second, anyway.)

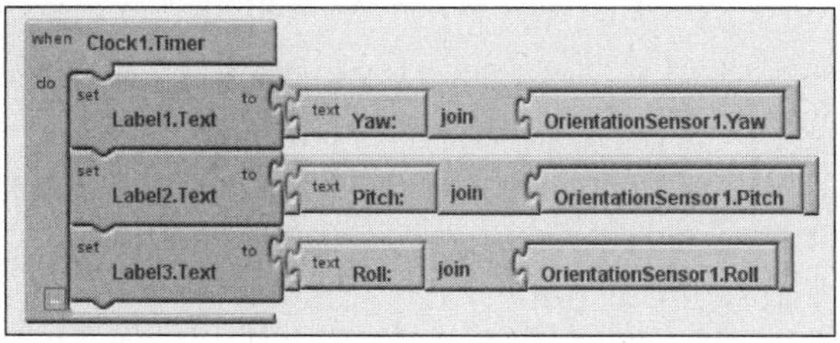

**Book VI
Chapter 2**

**More App
Inventor Magic**

Figure 2-7:
Every half
second,
refresh the
yaw, pitch,
and roll
values on
the labels.

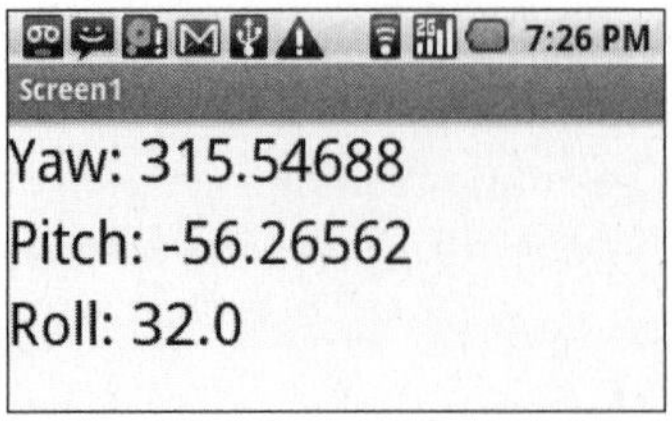

Figure 2-8:
Your app displays the device's orientation.

⚏💬🔋Ⓜ⚕⚠ 🔋📶🔋 7:26 PM
Screen1
Yaw: 315.54688
Pitch: -56.26562
Roll: 32.0

Animate!

What's more fun than making things move on a screen? (Well, I can think of a few things, but this book is about Android app development.) Anyway, App Inventor has some cool features for helping you animate objects. Follow these instructions for a simple (but helpful) example:

1. **Create a new App Inventor project.**

2. **Drop a Canvas component onto the Designer viewer's screen.**

You can find the Canvas component in the Designer palette's Basic category.

App Inventor doesn't let you drop an Animation component onto the bare Designer viewer screen. Instead, you must place a canvas on the screen and then drop an Animation component onto the canvas.

3. **Select the canvas (in the Designer viewer or in the Components tree), and then, in the Properties sheet, set the canvas's width to Fill Parent.**

4. **In the Designer palette's Animation category, find the ImageSprite component.**

An ImageSprite component is nice because it can display an image, and you can quickly program the sprite's movements on a canvas.

In computer animation, a *sprite* is a small animated image that's added to a larger scene.

5. **Drag two ImageSprite components to the canvas (the canvas that you created in Step 2).**

Try to position the two sprites so that they're both the same distance from the top of the canvas. If you have trouble getting this right, you can adjust the sprites' Y values in the Properties sheet.

6. **Use the Properties sheet to put a picture on each of the sprites.**

Each sprite has a Picture property. For the two sprites, use two different pictures. That way, when you crank up the emulator, you can tell the two sprites apart.

For help putting a picture on a sprite (or on anything else, for that matter) see Chapter 1 of this minibook.

Now you have two side-by-side sprites.

7. **Select the leftmost sprite (in the Designer viewer or in the Components tree); then, in the Properties sheet, set the sprite's properties as follows:**

   - *Enabled: Checked*

     Animation is enabled for this object. That is, the object moves.

   - *Heading:* 0

     The object starts moving in direction 0. To find out what "direction 0" is, see the sidebar "Angles and directions" in this chapter.

   - *Interval:* 100

     The object moves once every 100 milliseconds. (In other words, the object moves every tenth of a second.)

   - *Speed:* 5

     Each time the object moves, it moves in its heading direction by five pixels.

   - *Visible:* Checked

     The object appears on the device's screen.

   You can leave this sprite's other properties at their default values.

Any values that you set with the Properties sheet are the components' initial values. During the run of an app, the behavior that you configure in the Blocks Editor can change these initial values.

8. **Select the rightmost sprite (in the Designer viewer or in the Components tree); then, in the Properties sheet, set the sprite's properties as follows:**

   - *Enabled:* Checked

   - *Heading:* 180

     The object starts moving in direction 180 (the opposite of the other sprite's starting direction).

   - *Interval:* 100

   - *Speed:* 10

     Each time the object moves, it moves in its heading direction by ten pixels — twice as fast as the other sprite.

- *Visible:* Checked

- *Y:* Same as the other sprite's Y value (see Step 5)

You can leave this sprite's other properties at their default values.

Depending on your screen resolution, the sizes of your images, and the phase of the moon, your animation might look crummy when you view the animation in an emulator. If so, try adjusting some of the numbers in Steps 7 and 8.

9. **That's it! Open the Blocks Editor, connect to an emulator, and watch your app in action.**

Figure 2-9 does the best it can to show you the movement of sprites on an emulator's screen. The Calico starts on the left and moves rightward. The Burmese starts on the right and moves leftward. The two kitty cats cross past one another near the middle of the screen. When a cat reaches the screen's edge, it stops.

To make things move, you always have a second option. You can create a clock with a timer and change a sprite's position whenever the timer fires. (See Figure 2-10.) If you try this approach, don't forget to put your sprite inside a Canvas component. (Refer to Steps 2 and 3.) Outside a Canvas component, you have no explicit control over an object's X position or its Y position. For information about clocks and timers, see the "Travel to the Orient" section, earlier in the chapter.

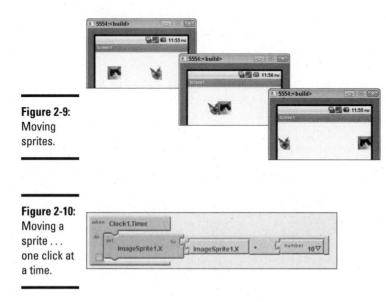

Figure 2-9:
Moving
sprites.

Figure 2-10:
Moving a
sprite . . .
one click at
a time.

Make sprites bounce off the edges of the screen

You can expand on the preceding section's example to make the sprites bounce off the screen's edges. Here's how:

1. If you haven't already done all the preceding stuff for this example — in the "Animate!" section — do it.

When placing your sprites, make sure that neither one touches the top or the bottom of the enclosing canvas.

As the sprites move from side to side, the sprites should bounce off the screen's left and right edges. To do all this, you need an *EdgeReached event handler*. Fortunately, you make yourself an EdgeReached event handler in the next few steps.

Now what happens if a sprite scrapes along the bottom of the canvas while sliding sideways? Then each of the sprite's tiny sideways movements fires an unwanted EdgeReached event. (The EdgeReached handler fires when a sprite bumps against an edge. But the handler also fires when a sprite scrapes against an edge, such as the top or the bottom of the canvas.) So the bottom line is, in this example, don't let either sprite touch the canvas's bottom line.

If your images are as tall as the enclosing canvas, you can do any of the following:

- Put a smaller image on each sprite.

- Start with large images, but shrink each image using an image-editing program before putting the images on the sprites.

- Enlarge the canvas by setting its Height property to a certain number of pixels.

- Enlarge the canvas by setting its Height property to Fill Parent.

- Use some other clever trick (an idea that strikes you in a flash of inspiration).

2. In the Blocks palette's My Blocks tab, find (and select) ImageSprite1.

The Blocks palette expands to reveal several blocks. One of these new blocks is the ImageSprite1.EdgeReached event handler.

3. Select the ImageSprite1.EdgeReached event handler block.

When you select the EdgeReached handler block, App Inventor adds two pieces to your Blocks viewer. Along with the ImageSprite1.EdgeReached block, App Inventor adds a second block displaying the words Name and Edge. (See Figure 2-11.) The second block is a parameter. The parameter represents whichever edge the sprite has reached.

To be precise, the Edge parameter's value is a number, and the number stands for one of the edges of your device's screen.

For the scoop about parameters, see Chapter 1 of this minibook.

4. **Drag an ImageSprite1.Bounce block and (from the My Definitions category) a Value Edge block into the Blocks viewer, as shown in Figure 2-11.**

Now your Blocks viewer contains an instruction you could summarize thusly:

When ImageSprite1 reaches an edge of the screen, whichever edge the sprite reached has a temporary name. That edge's temporary name is Edge. So do the following: Have ImageSprite1 bounce off of Edge.

Yesss!

5. **Repeat Steps 2–4 with ImageSprite2. (See Figure 2-12.)**

When you add a new block to the Blocks viewer, App Inventor automatically creates new (previously unused) default names for any parameters in the block. So the default name of the ImageSprite2 event handler block's parameter is Edge1. When you tell the ImageSprite2 handler which edge to bounce away from, you use the Value Edge1 block from the Blocks palette's My Definitions category.

App Inventor's parameter names are a bit different from the parameters in Java and other programming languages. You can't use the same parameter name in both the ImageSprite1.EdgeReached and ImageSprite2. EdgeReached event handlers. So App Inventor makes up different default names, Edge and Edge1, for this example's two event hander parameters.

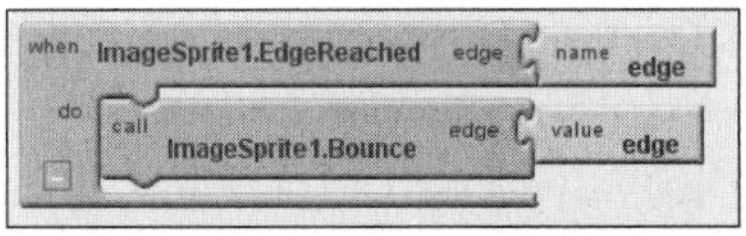

Figure 2-11:
Handling the event in which a sprite reaches the screen's edge.

Figure 2-12:
The event handler for the second sprite.

You can change a parameter's name. For example, imagine that you want to change a parameter from its default name Edge to the informative name WallReached. To make the change, click your mouse on the word Edge in the parameter block and type the word **WallReached** in place of the word Edge. And don't forget to look for any blocks in which you referred to your old Edge parameter. Change from Edge to WallReached on those blocks, too.

You're done setting up the bouncing experiment.

6. **In the Blocks Editor, connect to a device or an emulator, and watch those sprites bounce!**

Make sprites bounce away from each other

If you test the preceding section's example, you see two sprites passing each other like strangers in the night. But in a game app, you probably don't want good guys and bad guys passing each other without some kind of fracas taking place. So in this section, you handle the collision of two sprites:

1. **If you haven't already done the stuff in the preceding section, do it.**

As a result, you have two sprites moving from side to side, bouncing off the screen's edges as they travel.

2. **To the stuff already in the Blocks viewer, add the group shown in Figure 2-13.**

For details about creating groups in the Blocks viewer, see Chapter 1 of this minibook.

The big group of blocks in Figure 2-13 illustrates a few techniques that don't appear in previous sections:

- *You can create a variable.*

   A *variable* is a place to store a number, a string, or whatever. In App Inventor lingo, a variable is like a parameter, except that a parameter belongs to a particular event handler, and a variable can live on its own.

   In Figure 2-13, a variable's definition hovers independently above the other blocks. I created this variable by dragging a block from the Built-In tab's Definition category. To give the variable an initial value, I fetched a number block from the Built-In tab's Math category. Each variable has a name, and App Inventor automatically creates the default names Variable, Variable1, Variable2, and so on. In Figure 2-13, I don't mess with the default name, which is Variable.

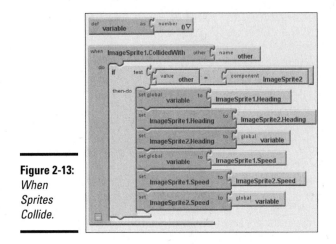

Figure 2-13:
When
Sprites
Collide.

- *You can test a condition and execute code if that condition is true.*

  In Figure 2-13, I use an If block from the Control category of the Built-In tab. The If block has two parts — a condition-testing part and a what-to-do-when-the-condition-is-true part.

- *You can use a block to refer to an entire component.*

  In Figure 2-13, the top of the If block tests to determine whether the Other thing that ImageSprite1 collided with is ImageSprite2. You can fetch the ImageSprite2 block from the ImageSprite2 category in the My Blocks tab. (The block that you want has the label Component ImageSprite2.)

  The condition in Figure 2-13 also contains a block with a little equal sign on it. You grab this block from the Logic category in the Built-In tab.

- *You can set a variable's value and get a variable's value.*

  In Figure 2-13, I use my variable to temporarily store information about ImageSprite1 while I swap the values of ImageSprite1's and ImageSprite2's motion properties. When the dust settles, ImageSprite1 has what used to be ImageSprite2's heading and speed, and ImageSprite2 has what used to be ImageSprite1's heading and speed.

  The justification for swapping the sprites' heading and speed values is the Conservation of Linear Momentum law for two objects of equal mass. Several years ago, I taught introductory college physics for a year. (Was I qualified to teach introductory college physics? Well, it's a long story.)

After creating the blocks shown in Figure 2-13, you're ready to test your app.

Only one of your app's sprites has a group of blocks like the group shown in Figure 2-13. If you have an ImageSprite1.CollidedWith event handler, you don't have an ImageSprite2.CollidedWith handler. If you mistakenly add a similar ImageSprite2.CollidedWith handler to your app, whenever the two sprites collide, your device calls both handlers, and the swapping of motion properties happens twice during one collision. That's not what you want to happen.

3. **Test your app.**

   The sprites should move back and forth, bouncing off the edges of the screen and bouncing off each other when they meet near the middle of the screen.

Using a Database

Up to this point, my App Inventor examples tend to be visual. You send a photo, animate an object, or something like that. Well, this section's example is different. This section covers the austere world of databases.

App Inventor's collection of components includes an elementary database. This section shows you how to use that database:

1. **Create a new App Inventor project.**

2. **Add two TextBox components to the project's Designer viewer.**

3. **(Optional) In the Properties sheets for each TextBox component, delete all characters from the Text fields; while you're being finicky, arrange the TextBox components nicely across the screen.**

4. **Add a ListPicker component to the Designer viewer.**

   You can find the ListPicker component in the Designer palette's Basic category.

   At the end of this section, when you see the finished app, you may argue that ListPicker isn't the best component for the work that this app does. Maybe a check box would be more user-friendly. But (darn it) I want to illustrate the use of the ListPicker somewhere in this chapter.

5. **Select ListPicker1 in the Designer viewer or the Components tree.**

   As a result, the Properties sheet has a field labeled ElementsFromString.

6. Go to the newly created ElementsFromString field on the Properties sheet, and type store, retrieve.

It should come as no surprise that ListPicker1 has something to do with a list of things. The text `store, retrieve` tells App Inventor that ListPicker1's list contains two items — the first being **store** and the second being **retrieve.**

7. (Optional) Change the text on the face of ListPicker1.

This step is optional, but seriously, the default text (Text for ListPicker1) is too ugly. Surely you can do better. In Figure 2-14, I put *store* or *retrieve* on the picker's face.

The ListPicker component in Figure 2-14 looks like a button. This is surprising because on a big, fat desktop computer screen, a "picker" wouldn't look like a button. Instead, a *picker* would be a thingie that expands to display lots of alternatives. (Imagine a drop-down list displaying the months of the year or the countries of the world.)

But on a mobile device's small screen, the best way to display alternatives is to overlay a separate panel. So when a user presses this example's ListPicker component, the device's entire screen changes to display the choices in Figure 2-15.

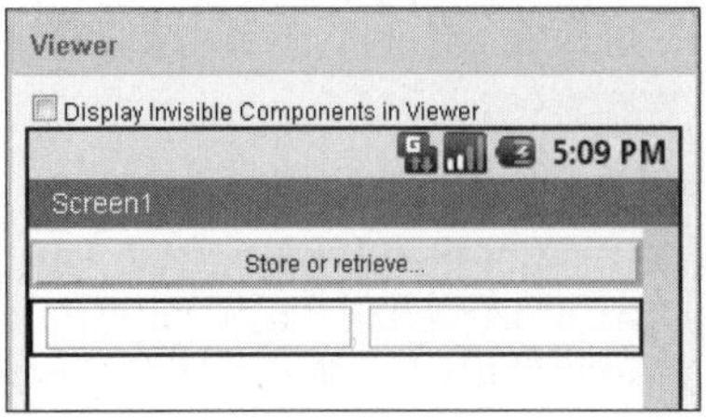

Figure 2-14:
The arrangement of visible components in this section's app.

Viewer
☐ Display Invisible Components in Viewer
🔋📶🔋 5:09 PM
Screen1
Store or retrieve...

Figure 2-15:
A list of alternatives appears on the device's screen.

In official Android terminology, the separate panel pictured in Figure 2-15 is a separate *activity*. My claim that this new activity takes over the entire screen may be outdated by the time you read this book. App Inventor will probably be able to create apps for larger tablet screens. In that case, the ListPicker's alternatives will appear in a *fragment* alongside the app's text boxes. For a word or two about activities, see the "Starting Another Android App" section, later in this chapter. For more chatter about fragments, see Chapter 4 of minibook IV.

8. **Drop a TinyDB component onto the Designer viewer.**

You can find a TinyDB component in the Basic category of the Designer palette.

You don't see TinyDB1 on the Designer viewer's screen, but TinyDB1 is now part of your app.

**Book VI
Chapter 2**

**More App
Inventor Magic**

The name *TinyDB* stands for *Tiny Database.* The name is a bit misleading because a TinyDB component has very few of the characteristics belonging to a real database. In fact, a TinyDB component's only similarity to a real database is this: Both a database and a TinyDB component control *persistent storage,* which is the saving (and retrieving) of values from one run of an app to the next. Without a TinyDB component, none of the data that you create during one run is available to any subsequent runs.

9. **Open the Blocks Editor.**

10. **In the Blocks viewer, create the group of blocks shown in Figure 2-16.**

For details about creating groups in the Blocks viewer, see Chapter 1 of this minibook.

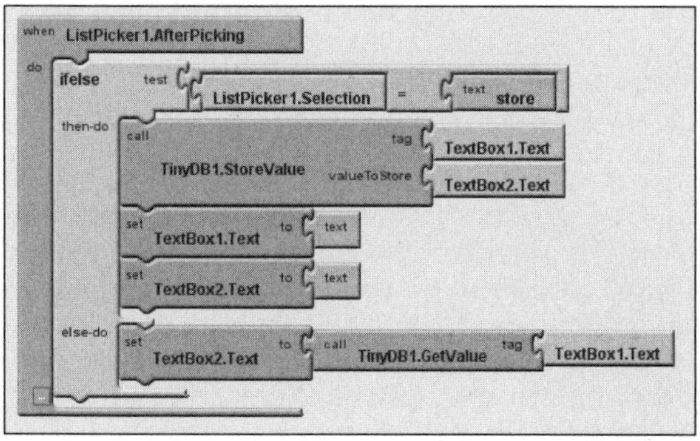

Figure 2-16:
Blocks
for simple
control of
an App
Inventor
database.

The group comes about when you do the kind of clicking, dragging, and dropping described previously in this chapter. But the group in Figure 2-16 involves a few new tricks.

- *The outermost block in Figure 2-16 is an event handler.*

  When the user clicks ListPicker1, Android displays a list containing the choices *store* and *retrieve*. Then, when the user clicks an item in the list, Android calls the ListPicker1.AfterPicking event handler.

- *The choice made by the user (in this example, either* store *or* retrieve*) becomes the value of ListPicker1.Selection.*

  In Figure 2-16, I compare ListPicker1.Selection with the word *store*. (That is, I test whether the value of ListPicker1.Selection is the word *store*.) Unless something goes horribly wrong, the only other alternative for the value of ListPicker1.Selection is the word *retrieve*.

- *The TinyDB1 component has items.*

  Each *item* has two parts — a Tag and a Value. Think of TinyDB1 as a table with two columns. (See Table 2-1.)

Table 2-1	The Number of Bunnies That Each Person Has
Name	*Number of Bunnies*
Barry	10
Harriet	14
Sam	12
Jennie	27

The first item's tag in the table is Barry; the first item's value is 10. The second item's tag is Harriet; the second item's value is 14. And so on.

If you're familiar with real databases, you might understand how tiny App Inventor's TinyDB component really is. A TinyDB component has only one table, and that table has only two columns. If you put two TinyDB components into an app, both components work with the same table. (So there's no reason to put more than one TinyDB component into an app after all.) Apps don't share their TinyDB tables with other apps. But fortunately, TinyDB data is persistent. That is, the items stored in the table during one run can be retrieved by the same app during a later run.

- *The Control category of the Built-In tab contains an Ifelse block.*

   This book's editors tell me that the word *Ifelse* is ugly. But being a computer geek, I like the word *Ifelse*. Anyway, the *Ifelse* block in Figure 2-16 says, "If the user selected *store* in ListPicker1, do one sequence of actions; otherwise, do another action." More specifically, that *Ifelse* block says the following:

```
If the user selected store, then
    store the text boxes' values as a new item
        in the database,(with TextBox1's text being
        the item's tag, and TextBox2's text being
        the item's value), and then
    clear both text boxes (by putting no characters
        in each box).
Otherwise (else)
    search TinyDB1 for an item whose tag matches
        whatever is currently in TextBox1, and
        if you find such an item, then
        put that item's value into TextBox2.
```

Book VI
Chapter 2

More App
Inventor Magic

The user might try to search for *Fred* even though TinyDB1 has no item tagged *Fred*. If TinyDB1 doesn't have an item whose tag matches whatever is in TextBox1, the call to `TinyDB1.GetValue` yields nothing. So in that case, Android clears away any characters in TextBox2. That's good, but for an app with a bit more finesse, you can perform a test like the one shown in Figure 2-17. In that test, you look for an item whose tag matches whatever is in TextBox1. If you find nothing, put (Not Found) in TextBox2.

11. Run this section's app.

   Figures 2-18 to 2-20 illustrate steps in a run of this section's app. To save some trees, these figures don't show steps like the one in Figure 2-15 (steps in which the user chooses between *store* and *retrieve*).

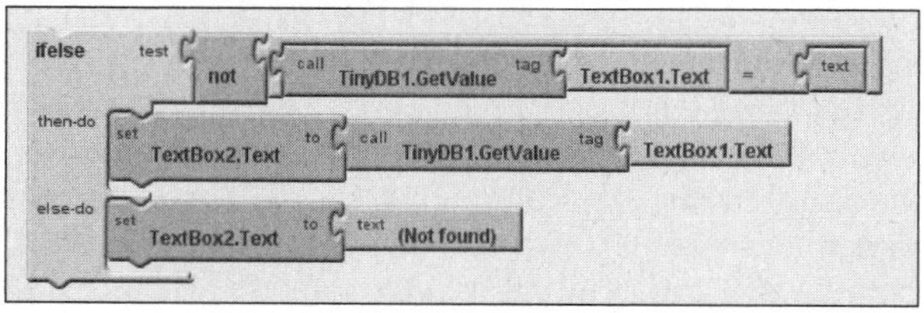

Figure 2-17:
Failing to
find, but
failing with
a flourish.

ifelse	test	not	call TinyDB1.GetValue	tag	TextBox1.Text	=	text
then-do	set	TextBox2.Text	to	call TinyDB1.GetValue	tag	TextBox1.Text
else-do	set	TextBox2.Text	to	text (Not found)

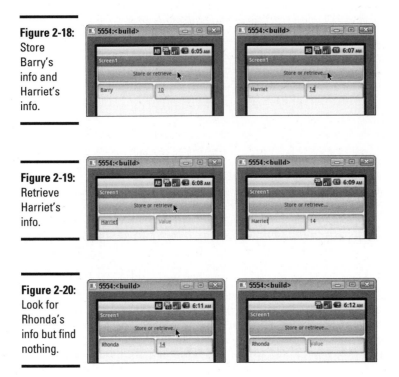

Figure 2-18: Store Barry's info and Harriet's info.

Figure 2-19: Retrieve Harriet's info.

Figure 2-20: Look for Rhonda's info but find nothing.

Starting Another Android App

One of the nice features of Android development is the ability to reuse code from existing applications. For example, if you want your app to view a web page, you don't have to create your own web browser. All you do is make a request to another app's activity.

Activities and intents

An *activity* is one "screenful" of components. Think of an activity as a form — perhaps a form for entering information to make a purchase on a website. Unlike most online forms, Android activities don't necessarily have text boxes — places for the user to type credit card numbers and such. But Android activities have a lot in common with online forms. When you put together an app's components in the Designer viewer, you're creating an Android activity.

Each activity has its own look — the initial layout of the form's components. After an activity first appears on the device screen, the layout of the activity's components might change because of certain users' actions or because of the data being displayed, the animation being used, or for other reasons.

An Android app can have several of its own activities — several different screens to display on the device's screen. In addition, an Android app can request the start of some other app's activities. For example, my game application can make a request to a web app — namely, that the web app run a page browser activity.

To start another app's activity, you typically don't use the app's name or the activity's name. For example, the official name of Android's built-in web browser is android.webkit.webView. But to display a web page, your app doesn't say, "Start running android.webkit.webView." Instead, your app creates an intent.

An *intent* is an ability — the ability to display information, for example, or the ability to edit documents, or the ability to answer phone calls. To display a web page, your app says, "Start an activity that has the `android.intent.action.` `VIEW` ability." Android's built-in `android.intent.action.VIEW` is the ability to display information, such as web pages and possibly other things.

Android's use of intents is a very good thing. Without intents, your app would have to include an instruction that says, "Start running the built-in web browser — you know, the browser named android.webkit.webView." But that instruction wouldn't be fair to org.mozilla.firefox — another web browser that you've installed on your device. So instead of naming a particular web browser, your app says, "Start running an activity whose abilities include displaying information (more formally known as the `android.` `intent.action.VIEW` ability). I leave it to the Android operating system to choose among the able activities."

For example, assume that the user has installed Firefox in addition to Android's built-in web browser. When an app issues a request to start an `android.intent.action.VIEW` activity, the device looks for apps and activities that can display information — activities with the `android.` `intent.action.VIEW` ability. If the user has already set Firefox to be the default web viewing activity, the device starts the Firefox web browser. But if the user hasn't specified a default web browser, Android displays a list asking which web browser the user wants to open. That's how intents work.

Starting an activity with App Inventor

This section's example fires up a web browser with a predetermined URL. In the example, you don't refer directly to a particular browser. Instead, you refer indirectly to a browser by requesting an activity that can fulfill an `android.intent.action.VIEW` intent. Here's how it works:

1. **Create a new App Inventor project.**

2. **Add two Button components to the project's Designer viewer.**

Book VI Chapter 2

More App Inventor Magic

3. **(Optional) Using the component's Properties sheet, put some informative text on the face of each button.**

   In Figure 2-21, I put Barry's Android Page and Barry's Java Page (a shameless plug).

4. **Add an ActivityStarter component to the Designer viewer.**

   You can find the ActivityStarter component in the Other Stuff category of the Designer palette.

   The new component, ActivityStarter1, is invisible. So you don't see ActivityStarter1 on the Designer viewer's screen.

5. **Select ActivityStarter1 in the Components tree.**

   As a result, the Properties sheet has an Action field.

6. **Go to the newly created Action field on the Properties sheet, and type android.intent.action.VIEW.**

   The text `android.intent.action.VIEW` describes an *intent* — the ability to display information. For the gory details, see the preceding section.

7. **Open the Blocks Editor.**

8. **In the Blocks viewer, create the stuff shown in Figure 2-22.**

Figure 2-21:
The look of the Designer viewer for this section's example.

Figure 2-22:
The Blocks viewer for this section's example.

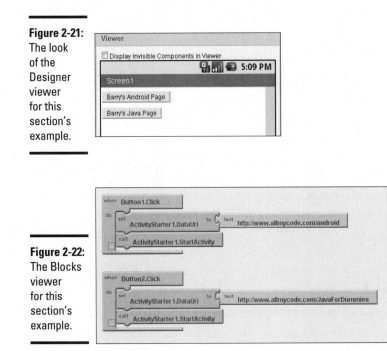

For details about creating groups in the Blocks viewer, see Chapter 1 of this minibook.

Yes, you can use URLs of your own choosing. But to keep this example simple, use URLs that begin with `http://`.

The ActivityStarter1 component has several properties. In Step 6, you set the component's Action property. And in Figure 2-22, you make the component's request more specific by assigning a URL to ActivityStarter1. Which URL you assign depends on which button the user clicks.

In Figure 2-22, notice the letters *Uri* in the property name DataUri. The letters *URI* (usually all capitalized) stand for *Universal Resource Identifier.* A URI is like a URL, except that a URI is more versatile. For a painfully correct description of URIs, visit `www.w3.org/Addressing/URL/uri-spec.html`.

Book VI
Chapter 2

9. **Run the app.**

When the app starts running, you see the buttons in Figure 2-23. Then, when you click a button, you see one of two web pages (such as the pages in Figure 2-24).

More App
Inventor Magic

Figure 2-23:
Pick a page.

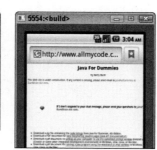

Figure 2-24:
A web page for each button.

Chapter 3: How to "Rough It" without Eclipse

In This Chapter

✔ Using the command window

✔ Thinking like an ant

✔ Gearing up for text-based development

✔ Developing with Ant and operating system commands

It's time to celebrate! You're near the end of *Android Application Development All-in-One For Dummies*. Sure, you may have skipped directly to this chapter, but that doesn't matter. This chapter contains no spoilers. This isn't where you learn that the butler murdered the heiress and that Larry Page is innocent.

Anyway, you'll be an expert Android developer in no time at all, so please rejoice in your future success by throwing a big party.

To prepare for the party, I'll bake a cake. I'm lazy, so I'll use a ready-to-bake cake mix. Let me see . . . add water to the mix, and then add butter and eggs . . . Hey, wait a minute! I just looked at the list of ingredients. What's MSG? And what about propylene glycol? That's used in antifreeze, isn't it?

I'll change plans and make the cake from scratch. Sure, it's a little harder. But that way, I get exactly what I want.

Application development works the same way. You can use ready-made tools, or you can get more control by doing things from scratch. Eclipse reduces many routine tasks to simple pointing and clicking. I highly recommend Eclipse for almost all your day-to-day Android development. But once in a while, Eclipse hides details that you'd rather see clearly. When that situation arises, you're better off using your operating system's command window.

Preliminaries

Our story begins with an operating system. The system might be Windows, Macintosh OS X, Linux, or some other system. You use this operating system to develop Android applications.

The operating system provides facilities for getting work done. Among these facilities are

✦ The ability to log onto the computer

✦ The ability to store data and code

✦ The ability to launch programs (that is, to execute code)

Along with these vague "abilities," the operating system provides one or more interfaces. In this context, an *interface* is a way of communicating with the computer — a way of saying, "Computer, run my e-mail program right now (or run the program whenever you stop displaying your annoying 'busy' icon)."

One of the oldest and most basic interfaces is a command language. A *command language* is a set of instructions that you type on your computer keyboard, along with rules for varying and combining those instructions. Each operating system has several command languages:

✦ Windows has its *Command Prompt* (called *MS-DOS* by those who blur the difference between the command language and the old text-based operating system). Windows also has fancier languages named *Windows Script Host, PowerShell,* and some others.

✦ Linux and Mac OS X have the *Bourne shell* (abbreviated *sh*), the *Bourne-again shell* (abbreviated *bash*), the *Korn shell (ksh),* the *C shell (csh),* and other command languages with amusing names.

In this book, most of my examples use the Windows Command Prompt or Linux/Macintosh bash.

Your friend, the command window

Normally you don't simply turn on your computer and start typing commands. Instead, your computer starts a nice-looking *windowing environment* (its *graphical user interface,* also known as its *GUI*), and you start pointing and clicking with your mouse. Before the computer will respond to commands, you must launch a command window, an application whose purpose is to accept your commands.

Here's how you launch your operating system's command window:

✦ **In Windows,** choose Start⇨All Programs⇨Accessories⇨Command Prompt.

✦ **In a Mac OS X Finder window,** choose Applications⇨Utilities⇨Terminal.

✦ **In Linux,** do whatever works for your distribution and your windowing environment. You poke around among the desktop's menus for something named Terminal.

After launching a command window, you're ready to start typing commands. Figures 3-1 and 3-2 display command windows on Windows and Macintosh computers.

Figure 3-1:
The command window on a computer running Microsoft Windows.

Figure 3-2:
The command window on a Mac.

When you use Eclipse to create an application, Eclipse quietly translates your mouse clicks into commands and executes the commands on your behalf. For example, in Eclipse, choose File⇨New⇨Project⇨Android Project and then fill in the fields of the New Android Project dialog box. When you click Finish, Eclipse effectively executes a command of the following kind:

```
android create project -t 10 -p MyProject
                       -a MyActivity -k com.allmycode.samples
```

Under the hood, Android application development is a bunch of commands.

Scripting

In show biz, a script is a bunch of utterances prepared in advance for actors to say. In computing, a *script* is a sequence of commands, prepared in advance for the computer to execute.

Each operating system provides ways for you to collect commands into a file and then to execute the commands in that file. Typically, you open a plain text editor, type the commands, save the file, and then type the file's name in a command window.

✦ **In Windows,** you can use Notepad and save the file with the `.bat` extension.

✦ **On a Mac,** you can use TextEdit and choose Format⇨Make Plain Text.

✦ **In Linux,** you can use gedit or KEDIT and save the file with the `.sh` extension.

The trouble with this scenario is portability. A script written for a Mac has little chance of working correctly in Linux, and a script written for Windows has almost no chance of working on a Mac.

Meet Apache Ant

To solve the preceding section's portability problem, folks at The Apache Software Foundation came up with the Ant project. *Ant* is a tool for saving and re-running sequences of commands. Ant simplifies what would otherwise be an enormous job of typing one command after another in order to create, code, and deploy an Android application.

The creators of Android have written Ant scripts to streamline the work of creating applications. And best of all, Ant isn't specific to one operating system or another. You can use Ant scripts on Windows, Mac, and Linux without making any significant changes.

Like Eclipse, Apache Ant hides details from the developer. With Android's pre-cooked Ant scripts, you don't have to type all the commands you'd normally type in the command window. The people who create Android have written portable commands and embedded them in Ant scripts. But Ant hides fewer details than Eclipse, so you're still roughing it a bit when you use Ant. And besides, you can have it both ways. You can use Ant to perform some tasks and use your operating system's command language to perform others.

An Ant's-eye view

At its heart, Ant is just another computer program. In fact, Ant is a Java program. When you run the Ant program, Ant interprets whatever instructions are coded in whatever Ant script you specify. For example, in an Ant script, the element

```
<mkdir dir="${out.classes.absolute.dir}" />
```

tells Ant to make a new directory regardless of the underlying operating system. In the element's `dir` attribute, the placeholder `${out.classes.absolute.dir}` stands for a directory name. The exact characters in the name are determined on the fly during a run of the Ant script. Because Ant scripts have placeholders (and other features), an Ant script is flexible and highly programmable.

For some background information about XML documents, see Book II, Chapter 5.

Listing 3-1 contains a small Ant script. If you don't specify otherwise, the Ant program looks for its script in a `build.xml` file.

Listing 3-1:   An Ant Script (A build.xml File)

```xml
<?xml version="1.0" encoding="UTF-8"?>
<project>
  <target name="compile">
    <mkdir dir="classes" />
    <javac srcdir="src" destdir="classes" />
  </target>

  <target name="run" depends="compile">
    <java classpath="classes" classname="Hello" />
  </target>

  <target name="clean">
    <delete dir="classes" />
  </target>
</project>
```

As an Android developer, you seldom (if ever) write Ant scripts. But it helps to be able to decipher the highlights of other developers' scripts.

A basic Ant script has a *project* element, *target* elements within the project element, and *task* elements within the target elements:

✦ **The project element is the Ant script's root element.**

✦ **Within the project element, each target element describes a starting point for execution.**

   In Listing 3-1, the `compile` target creates a `classes` directory to contain bytecode files, compiles source code files, and puts the resulting bytecode files in the newly created `classes` directories. The `run` target executes the compiled bytecode files. The `clean` target deletes the bytecode files and their directories in preparation for another compilation.

✦ **Within a target, each `task` element describes a step to be performed.**

Within the `compile` target in Listing 3-1, one task creates a `classes` directory and another task invokes `javac` (the Java compiler).

You launch Ant by starting the Ant Java program and adding the name of a target. For example, to execute the task inside the `compile` target in Listing 3-1, you type something like

```
ant compile
```

in your operating system's command window. For more detailed instructions, see the section "Android Development with Ant," later in this chapter.

One other tidbit in Listing 3-1 is worth a moment of your attention. An Ant target's execution can depend on the execution of other targets. In Listing 3-1, the `run` target's `depends` attribute indicates that running is futile without previously having compiled. So if you invoke Ant with a command like

```
ant run
```

Ant executes the `compile` target and then executes the `run` target. (If no source files need compiling, the `compile` target simply tips its virtual hat and bids you good day.)

Installing Apache Ant

To download and install Ant, do the following:

1. **Visit** `http://ant.apache.org`, **and find the Binary Distributions download page.**

2. **Pick one of the links on the Binary Distributions download page.**

   The `.zip` archive link should work for most systems, but if you're a die-hard Linux user, you may want the `.tar.gz` archive or the `.tar.bz2` archive instead.

   Android's Ant scripts require Apache Ant version 1.8.0 or later. If you find Ant 1.7, or some earlier version, ignore that version and visit `http://ant.apache.org` for the latest and greatest Ant.

   When your computer has finished downloading the archive, move on to Step 3.

3. **Do whatever you normally do to extract archive's contents.**

   Generally, I create an `ant` folder and extract the archive's contents to that `ant` folder. Of course, you may not name your new folder `ant`, or your `ant` folder may be a subdirectory of your `Applications` folder. In this chapter, I use the name ANT_HOME for whatever folder contains your Ant stuff (the files that you extract from the archive).

One way or another, your ANT_HOME directory should have a `bin` subdirectory. Inside the `bin` directory, you can find files for different operating systems. For example, a file named `ant.bat` can tell a Windows computer to run Ant. Another file, named `ant` (without the `.bat` part) can tell a Mac to run Ant. One way or another, you fall back on a command that's specific to your operating system in order to launch Ant.

The rest of this chapter describes the Android development cycle without Eclipse.

Getting Ready for Text-Based Development

Everything has to start somewhere. In this section, you start developing an Android app. You use operating system commands and Ant instead of fancier Eclipse tools.

The entire process, from start to finish, isn't very complicated. But the picky details (which operating system you have, where your Android SDK files are stored, how your computer is pre-configured, and so on) can drive you crazy. So before you take arms against a sea of semicolons, slashes, tildes, and other symbols, you should see the big picture. With that in mind, I present this overview of Android development using command line tools:

1. Create an Android project.

Do this by typing a command. The command starts with `android create project`. In this context, `android` is the name of a program, and `create project` is one of the `android` program's options.

2. Edit the project's code.

With your favorite plain text editor (Notepad, TextEdit, or whatever), hunt and peck until you've created the perfect Java code and the ideal XML documents.

3. Run a program that creates an Ant script.

Again, type a command to invoke the `android` program. But this time, add the `update project` option.

4. Run the Ant script.

Type **ant** along with an option or two. The Ant script compiles and packages your code, and installs your code on an emulator or an attached device.

With this outline in mind, I invite you to delve a bit more deeply. The rest of this chapter is details, details, details.

Preparing your system

Several of my wife's relatives are named Chris. So with identical first names and family names, it's difficult to talk about Chris's work or Chris's favorite dessert. Instead, I have to identify people by location. I say "Chris from California" or "Chris from Boston." If I mistakenly say "Chris from Bavaria," I'm in a bit of trouble because my wife has no relatives in Bavaria.

The same thing happens when you type **android** in your development computer's command window. Your computer may have several files named android, each in a different directory. And many directories have nothing to do with Android and have no android file. So typing **android** in a command window might be like yelling for Chris in the streets of Bavaria.

To help sort all this out, your operating system keeps track of a PATH.

Your *PATH* is a list of directories containing programs that you execute frequently. When you type a program's name on a line in a command window, your operating system looks for files with that name in each of the PATH list's directories. With your PATH set correctly, you can launch a program by typing the program's name. You don't have to type the (possibly long) name of whatever directory houses the program.

In my household, our unspoken PATH includes California. So instead of saying "Chris in California," I can simply say "Chris." To refer to a different relative I have to say "Chris in Boston" or "Chris in Schenectady."

In this section's steps, adjust your PATH:

1. **Launch a command window.**

For details, see the section "Your friend, the command window," earlier in this chapter.

2. **In the command window, type** cd / **and then press Enter (that's the letters** cd, **followed by a space, a slash, and Enter).**

This command brings you to your computer's root directory. The root directory is a neutral place from which you can safely follow the instructions in Step 3.

3. **Discover which software tools are in your development computer's PATH.**

For this chapter's examples, your PATH should contain Java tools, Android tools, and Ant tools.

- *To find out whether your PATH includes Java development tools, type **javac -version** in a command window.*

If the computer responds with something like

```
javac 1.7.0
```

your PATH includes Java development tools. If, instead, your computer responds with something like

```
'javac' is not recognized as a command
```

or with something like

```
javac: command not found
```

your PATH doesn't include Java development tools. Either way, make note of the result.

- *To find out whether your PATH includes Android development tools, type* **android** *in a command window.*

  If your computer responds by opening an Android SDK and AVD Manager window, your PATH includes the Android development tools. You can close the Android SDK and AVD Manager window and move on with your tests.

  If your computer responds with a no such command message, your PATH doesn't include the Android development tools.

- *To find out whether your PATH includes Ant tools, type* **ant -version** *in a command window.*

  If your computer responds with something like

  ```
  Apache Ant(TM) version 1.8.2
  ```

  your PATH includes Ant tools. If, instead, your computer responds with a no such command message, your PATH doesn't include Ant tools.

4. **Find the home directories for any software tools that aren't in your PATH.**

   For each software tool that gives you a no such command message in Step 3, search your hard drive for the directory containing the tool.

   - *Your JAVA_HOME directory has a name such as jdk1.7.0 (or with some variation on that name).*

     Your JAVA_HOME directory contains a subdirectory named bin, and the bin subdirectory contains a javac.exe file, or simply javac. (This javac file is the Java compiler. For more info, see Chapter 2 of minibook II.)

     When you find a directory that qualifies as a JAVA_HOME directory, make note of that directory's name. For example, on my Windows computer, that directory's full name is C:\Program Files (x86)\java\jdk1.6.0_25.

In a few cases, your hard drive might have two or more directories containing Java tools. This business seldom causes trouble. If you find more than one JDK directory on your hard drive, simply choose one of the directories to be your `JAVA_HOME` directory. The same holds for directories containing Android tools, and for directories containing Ant tools.

- *Your `ANDROID_HOME` directory has `android` in its name.*

  This home directory has subdirectories: `tools` and `platform-tools`. The `tools` and `platform-tools` folders contain programs to help you develop Android apps. For details, see Book I, Chapter 2.

- *You create the `ANT_HOME` directory in this chapter's "Installing Apache Ant" section.*

  The `ANT_HOME` directory contains a `bin` subdirectory. The `bin` subdirectory has several files: `ant`, `antRun`, and so on. Each of these files plays a role (on one operating system or another) in launching Apache Ant.

5. **For any software tools that aren't in your PATH, add subdirectories of the corresponding home directories to your PATH.**

   When you type **javac**, you want your computer to execute the `javac` program in the `bin` subdirectory of your `JAVA_HOME` directory. In other words, you want the `JAVA_HOME` directory's `bin` subdirectory in your PATH. The `ANDROID_HOME` directory has two subdirectories containing programs — the `tools` directory and the `platform-tools` directory. So you want both of those subdirectories in your PATH.

   Your work for this step depends on your development computer's operating system.

   - *Windows*

     On my Windows computer, my `JAVA_HOME` directory is `C:\Program Files (x86)\java\jdk1.6.0_25`, my `ANDROID_HOME` directory is `C:\Program Files (x86)\Android\android-sdk`, and my `ANT_HOME` directory is `C:\ant`. So to add software directories to my PATH, I type the commands in Listing 3-2.

Listing 3-2: Modifying Your PATH on a Windows Computer

```
set JAVA_HOME=C:\Program Files (x86)\java\jdk1.6.0_25
set ANDROID_HOME=^
C:\Program Files (x86)\Android\android-sdk
set ANT_HOME=C:\ant
set PATH=%PATH%;%JAVA_HOME%\bin;%ANDROID_HOME%\tools;^
%ANDROID_HOME%\platform-tools;%ANT_HOME%\bin
```

Listing 3-2 contains four commands. Each command begins with `set`. But Listing 3-2 has six lines because two of the commands in the listing are very long. Neither of these long commands fits between the book's margins.

With each long command, I type part of the command on one line; then I end that line with the Windows line-continuation character (^); then I continue the command on the next line. When you type your commands, you can break a command into two or more lines with the ^ character. Alternatively, you can type each long command as if you're typing past the edge of the window. A long command wraps automatically onto the next line whenever you reach the edge of the window.

After typing the stuff in Listing 3-2, you can check your work by typing **echo %PATH%** and then pressing Enter. When you do, you see a long list of directories ending with the names or your `JAVA_HOME`, `ANDROID_HOME`, and `ANT_HOME` directories. A semicolon separates each directory in the list from the next directory in the list.

When you type the stuff from Listing 3-2 in a particular command window, the `set` commands have no effect on the PATH in any other command windows. For example, imagine that you have two command windows open — Window 1 and Window 2. Type the commands in Listing 3-2 in Window 1. Then the PATH in Window 1 includes your `JAVA_HOME`, `ANDROID_HOME`, and `ANT_HOME` directories, but the PATH in Window 2 might not include those directories. After doing all that, open a third window — Window 3. This third window's PATH might not include the `HOME` directories. The moral of this story is, if you switch to a different command window, type the stuff in Listing 3-2 in the new command window.

- *Macintosh*

  The stuff in Step 3 tells me that my Mac's PATH already includes Java tools and Ant tools. And in Step 4, I find that my Mac's `ANDROID_HOME` directory is `/Applications/android-sdk`. So to add software directories to my PATH, I type the commands in Listing 3-3.

Listing 3-3: Modifying Your PATH on a Macintosh

```
export ANDROID_HOME=/Applications/android-sdk/
export PATH=${PATH}:\
${ANDROID_HOME}/tools:${ANDROID_HOME}/platform-tools
```

Listing 3-3 contains two commands. Each command begins with `export`. But Listing 3-3 has three lines because one of the commands in the listing is very long. Neither of these long commands fits between the book's margins.

With each long command, I type part of the command on one line; then I end that line with the Unix line-continuation character (\); then I continue the command on the next line. When you type your commands, you can break a command into two or more lines with the \ character. Alternatively, you can type each long command as if you're typing past the edge of the window. A long command wraps automatically onto the next line whenever you reach the edge of the window.

After typing the stuff in Listing 3-3, you can check your work by typing **echo ${PATH}** and then pressing Enter. When you do, you see a long list of directories ending with the names of any directories that you add in your version of Listing 3-3. A colon separates each directory in the list from the next directory in the list.

When you type the stuff from Listing 3-3 in a particular command window, the `set` commands have no effect on the PATH in any other command windows.

Creating a project

With your PATH set correctly, you can proceed to create a new Android project:

1. **Set your PATH.**

For more detailed instructions than you ever wanted, see the preceding section. Use the same command window as you march through the rest of this section's steps.

2. **Create a directory to store this chapter's Android projects, and change your directory to be that new directory.**

On a Windows computer, I type the following two commands:

```
md %HOMEPATH%\MyAndroidProjects
cd %HOMEPATH%\MyAndroidProjects
```

On a Mac, I type these two commands:

```
mkdir ~/MyAndroidProjects
cd ~/MyAndroidProjects
```

The notion of changing your directory isn't difficult to understand, but that same notion is difficult to describe rigorously. When you use a command window, you're always positioned in one directory or another. For example, when you first open a command window, you may be positioned at *C:\Users\yourname* or */Users/yourname*. You can change the place where you're positioned by typing the `cd` command, along with the name of the directory where you want to land.

At any point in time, the directory in which you're positioned is your *working directory*. In this step, you make a new directory (with the `md` or `mkdir` command). Then, with the `cd` command, you change directories (so that the newly created directory is your working directory).

On a typical computer, each user has her own directory (a place to store settings, documents, data, and other stuff). On a Windows computer, `%HOMEPATH%` stands for your user directory. (Normally, `%HOMEPATH%` stands for `C:\Documents and Settings\`*your-user-name* or `C:\Users\ `*your-user-name*.) On a Mac, the tilde symbol (~) stands for your user directory. (Normally, ~ stands for `/Users/`*your-user-name*.)

As you jump from one directory to another (using the `cd` command), you can check to make sure that you've landed where you want to land. On a Windows computer, the two-letter `cd` command (with nothing after the letters `cd`) tells the computer to display your working directory's name. On a Mac, the corresponding command is `pwd`.

**Book VI
Chapter 3**

How to "Rough It" without Eclipse

3. At last, create an Android project!

If you run Windows, type the command in Listing 3-4. If you use a Mac, type the same command with backslashes (\) instead of hooks (^) at the ends of the first four lines.

Listing 3-4: Creating an Android Project, Windows Style

```
android create project --target "android-8" ^
                       --name MyProject ^
                       --path MyProject ^
                       --activity MyActivity ^
                       --package com.allmycode.samples
```

In Listing 3-4, the hook (^) is the Windows line-continuation character. Similarly, the backslash (\) is the Macintosh line-continuation character. To read more about line-continuation characters (and why my fanatical book authoring habits compel me to use them), see the section "Preparing your system," earlier in this chapter.

The `android` tool (which comes with your download of Android's SDK) has many uses. One use of this tool is to create a brand-new Android project. In Listing 3-4, you follow the tool name `android` with the action name `create project`. (No mystery about the action name!)

Following `create project`, you have some options.

- *In the* `--target` *option,* `"android-8"` *represents Froyo, also known as Android 2.2.*

  To see a list of acceptable target names, type **android list targets** in the command window. Then replace `"android-8"` with whatever target name works for you.

When I type `android list targets`, the computer displays a list that includes lines like `id: 7` or `"android-8"`. Accordingly, I can use the number `7` in place of `"android-8"` in each of my commands. But be careful. The string `"android-8"` refers to Froyo on all computers. But the number `7` means "the seventh target installed on *this* computer." On another development computer, the seventh installed target might not be Froyo.

- *In the `--name` option, I use the boring, old `MyProject` name.*

  As with each of these options, try not to duplicate the hum-drum stuff that I do in Listing 3-4. Instead, use a project name that meets your needs.

- *The `--path` option gives the computer a name for a new directory (the directory that contains your new Android project).*

  I'm lazy, so I reuse the name `MyProject`. The new `MyProject` directory becomes a subdirectory of your working directory. (In Step 2, I named my working directory `MyAndroidProjects`.)

- *The `--activity` option tells your computer to create a bare-bones Android activity.*

  Again, in Listing 3-4, laziness compels me to create `MyActivity.java`. And no, I never choose the word *password* for any of my passwords.

- *The `--package` option supplies a package name for the project's Java code.*

  I'm selfish about sharing my package name. So please use your own package name.

Having created an Android project, you're almost ready to package your application. But of course, you're not completely ready. Here are a few more steps:

4. **Edit your project's Java code and your project's XML files.**

   No big deal, right? Yes, this step is a big deal, but this chapter isn't about writing Java code and tweaking XML files.

   If you're avoiding Eclipse, I recommend the TextPad editor on a Windows computer. (For a look at the TextPad editor, visit `http://textpad.com`.) On a Mac, I recommend TextEdit, but before saving a JAVA file or an XML file for the first time, choose Format⇨Make Plain Text.

5. **In the command window, type the following command:**

   ```
   android update project --path MyProject
   ```

   The `android` tool's `update project` action customizes your project's `build.xml` file (your project's Ant script).

Your computer interprets the --path name MyProject as being relative to your working directory. The command in this step works only if your working directory is the same as the working directory in Step 3.

6. Start an emulator.

It's never too soon to start an Android emulator. (You never know how long the emulator will take to start itself up.)

To launch an emulator, you have several alternatives:

• *You can run the* android *script.*

   Typing **android** with no other words on the command line causes Android to launch its SDK and AVD Manager. (See Book I, Chapter 2.) From the SDK and AVD Manager, you can start the emulator of your choice.

• *You can run the* emulator *program.*

   For example, imagine that you've already created an AVD named Froyo1. You can type emulator -avd Froyo1 to start an emulator based on your Froyo1 AVD.

• *You can run Eclipse and start an emulator the way you normally do with an Eclipse project.*

One way or another, get an emulator running.

Android Development with Ant

Having done the stuff in this chapter's "Creating a project" section, you're ready to compile and test your Android app. You can do all the heavy lifting in one step. But for finer control, you may prefer a multi-step approach:

1. Follow the preceding section's instructions . . .

   . . . which means also following the instructions from two sections back, which in turn means following instructions from the beginning of time, and so on.

2. In the command window, go to the directory containing your Android project.

   Here's a quick recap: In the preceding section, I go to my own user directory, %HOMEPATH% in Windows, and called ~ (the tilde symbol) on a Mac. From there I travel to a subdirectory which I call MyAndroidProjects. Then, in Listing 3-4, I create a MyProject directory (a subdirectory of MyAndroidProjects). In this MyProject directory, I whip up all the ingredients of an Android project (the src files, the res files, and all that other good stuff).

So if you do exactly as I do in the preceding section, you have an Android project in a `MyProject` directory. You want your working directory to be that `MyProject` directory.

On a Windows computer, type the following command:

```
cd %HOMEPATH%\MyAndroidProjects\MyProject
```

On a Mac, type this command:

```
cd ~/MyAndroidProjects/MyProject
```

3. **(Optional) Run an Ant script by typing**

   ```
   ant compile
   ```

   In Step 5 of the preceding section, you create an Ant script for your project. As luck would have it, that Ant script contains a `compile` target. When you invoke Ant with that `compile` target, your computer generates your project's `R.java` file and compiles all the Java source files associated with your project.

   This `ant compile` step is optional. If you skip this step, the run of Ant in Step 4 will invoke the `compile` target on your behalf.

4. **(Optional) Run an Ant script by typing**

   ```
   ant debug
   ```

   The Ant script from Step 5 of the preceding section contains a `debug` target. When you invoke Ant with that `debug` target, your computer performs all the tasks in the script's `compile` target and packages your project into an APK file.

   This `ant debug` step is optional. If you skip this step, the run of Ant in Step 5 will invoke the `compile` and `debug` targets on your behalf.

5. **Run an Ant script by typing**

   ```
   ant install
   ```

   The Ant script from Step 5 of the preceding section contains an `install` target. When you invoke Ant with that `install` target, your computer performs all the tasks in the script's `compile` and `debug` targets and loads the APK file onto an emulator (or to an Android device connected to your development computer).

6. **Test your app.**

   In some cases, your app starts immediately on the emulator or the device. In other cases, you have to click the app's icon to make the app run. One way or another, pat yourself on the back. You've created an Android app without help from Eclipse or from any other IDE.

You can examine Ant's action in detail. For example, to find out what Ant does when it runs the `compile` target, type **ant -verbose -logfile myLog.txt compile**. Then view the `myLog.txt` file.

To read about Ant-based Android development straight from the horse's mouth, visit `http://developer.android.com/guide/developing/building/index.html#detailed-build`.

Android Development with Operating System Commands

Many years ago I took a car repair course. I wanted to save money on maintenance, but I didn't have a natural talent for mechanical matters. During one class session, I got stuck under a car while I was testing the transmission fluid level. The teacher threatened to push the car out to the parking lot (with me underneath the car) if I wasn't out from under the vehicle by the end of the day's class.

Anyway, I wasn't good at repairing things, so I gave up pretty quickly. But a year later, I was cruising along I-94 on my way to the Milwaukee airport. I had just enough time to catch my flight. But between the 35th Street and 26th Street exits, my car turned itself off. As I coasted to the highway's shoulder, I wondered if I could catch a later flight.

When my panic eased off a bit, I got out of the car and lifted the hood. My eyes gravitated immediately toward a wire that was disconnected from its thingamabob. A few other parts were dangling in suspicious ways, but from my experience in the car repair course, I knew that this particular wire had to be reconnected to its thingamabob. I connected the wire, started up my car, and got to the airport in time to catch my flight.

So that's my story. Understanding the inner workings of things may seem esoteric at first. But in the long run, very little knowledge goes to waste. You're always better off knowing more than you absolutely need to know.

The story about car repair gives me an excuse for writing this section. Hardly anyone develops Android apps without Eclipse and without Ant scripts. But seeing the underlying process (which part of the application comes from which step on the development computer) helps you understand how Android apps tick.

So in this section, I present a batch of Windows commands (that is, a Windows BAT file) to create, compile, and install an Android app. I've made a reasonable effort to make the batch file portable so that the file runs correctly on any up-to-date Windows computer. But I make no promises. If the commands in Listing 3-5 don't work on your computer, don't beat your head against the wall trying to make the commands work. Connect the car's wire back onto the thingamabob, but don't get stuck checking transmission fluid under the car.

So much for the apologies . . . Listing 3-5 contains the commands.

Listing 3-5: Creating an Android App with Your Bare Hands

```
set JAVA_HOME=C:\Program Files (x86)\java\jdk1.6.0_25

set JRE_HOME=C:\Program Files (x86)\java\jre6

set ANDROID_HOME=^
C:\Program Files (x86)\Android\android-sdk

set ANT_HOME=C:\ant

set PATH=%PATH%;%JAVA_HOME%\bin;%ANDROID_HOME%\tools;^
%ANDROID_HOME%\platform-tools;%ANT_HOME%\bin

rem Uncomment the next command if you
rem want to start an emulator
rem
rem start "Starting the emulator..." emulator ^
rem -scale 0.75 -avd Froyo1

cd "%HOMEPATH%\MyAndroidProjects"

call android create project ^
  --target "android-8" ^
  --name MyNextProject ^
  --path MyNextProject ^
  --activity MyActivity ^
  --package com.allmycode.samples

set MY_PROJECTS=%HOMEPATH%\MyAndroidProjects

set THISPROJ=%MY_PROJECTS%\MyNextProject

cd "%THISPROJ%"

mkdir gen

mkdir bin\classes

aapt package -f -m -M AndroidManifest.xml -S res ^
  -I "%ANDROID_HOME%\platforms\android-8\android.jar" ^
  -J gen

set CLASSPATH="%THISPROJ%\bin\classes";^
"%THISPROJ%";^
C:\ant\lib\ant-launcher.jar;^
C:\ant\lib\ant-antlr.jar;^
```

```
C:\ant\lib\ant-apache-bcel.jar;^
C:\ant\lib\ant-apache-bsf.jar;^
C:\ant\lib\ant-apache-log4j.jar;^
C:\ant\lib\ant-apache-oro.jar;^
C:\ant\lib\ant-apache-regexp.jar;^
C:\ant\lib\ant-apache-resolver.jar;^
C:\ant\lib\ant-apache-xalan2.jar;^
C:\ant\lib\ant-commons-logging.jar;^
C:\ant\lib\ant-commons-net.jar;^
C:\ant\lib\ant-jai.jar;^
C:\ant\lib\ant-javamail.jar;^
C:\ant\lib\ant-jdepend.jar;^
C:\ant\lib\ant-jmf.jar;^
C:\ant\lib\ant-jsch.jar;^
C:\ant\lib\ant-junit.jar;^
C:\ant\lib\ant-junit4.jar;^
C:\ant\lib\ant-netrexx.jar;^
C:\ant\lib\ant-swing.jar;^
C:\ant\lib\ant-testutil.jar;^
C:\ant\lib\ant.jar;^
"%JAVA_HOME%\lib\tools.jar"

set CLASSPATH=%CLASSPATH%;"%JRE_HOME%\lib\ext\QTJava.zip"

set SOURCEPATH="%THISPROJ%\src";"%THISPROJ%\gen"

set BOOTCLASSPATH=^
"%ANDROID_HOME%\platforms\android-8\android.jar"

javac -d "%THISPROJ%\bin\classes" ^
  -classpath %CLASSPATH% ^
  -sourcepath %SOURCEPATH% ^
  -target 1.5 ^
  -bootclasspath %BOOTCLASSPATH% ^
  -encoding UTF-8 ^
  -g ^
  -source 1.5 ^
  "%THISPROJ%\src\com\allmycode\samples\*.java"

call dx --dex --output=%THISPROJ%\bin\classes.dex ^
  %THISPROJ%\bin\classes

aapt package -f --debug-mode ^
  -M "%THISPROJ%\AndroidManifest.xml" ^
  -S "%THISPROJ%\res" ^
  -I "%ANDROID_HOME%\platforms\android-8\android.jar" ^
  -F "%THISPROJ%\bin\MyActivity-debug-unaligned.ap_"

call apkbuilder ^
  %THISPROJ%\bin\MyActivity-debug-unaligned.apk ^
```

(continued)

**Book VI
Chapter 3**

How to "Rough It"
without Eclipse

Listing 3-5 *(continued)*

```
-v ^
-u ^
-z "%THISPROJ%\bin\MyActivity-debug-unaligned.ap_" ^
-f "%THISPROJ%\bin\classes.dex"

keytool -genkey -v ^
  -keystore "%MY_PROJECTS%\my-keystore.keystore" ^
  -alias my-alias -keyalg RSA -validity 10000

"%JAVA_HOME%\bin\jarsigner" -verbose ^
  -certs ^
  -keystore „%MY_PROJECTS%\my-keystore.keystore" ^
  „%THISPROJ%\bin\MyActivity-debug-unaligned.apk" my-alias

„%JAVA_HOME%\bin\jarsigner" -verify ^
  -keystore „%MY_PROJECTS%\my-keystore.keystore" ^
  „%THISPROJ%\bin\MyActivity-debug-unaligned.apk"

zipalign -f 4 ^
  "%THISPROJ%\bin\MyActivity-debug-unaligned.apk" ^
  "%THISPROJ%\bin\MyActivity-debug.apk"

rem Uncomment the next command if you get an
rem INSTALL_PARSE_FAILED_INCONSISTENT_CERTIFICATES error
rem
rem adb uninstall com.allmycode.samples

adb install -r "%THISPROJ%\bin\MyActivity-debug.apk"
```

Google's official documentation is vague on the subject of command-line Android development, and unofficial web postings aren't much better. To figure out how to create Listing 3-5, I ran Android's Ant scripts with `verbose` output and logged the output to a text file. The output of `ant -verbose -logfile myLog.txt install` displays a detailed list of the commands that Ant executes, along with the options used in each command.

Here's what happens in Listing 3-5:

1. The first several commands set some variables.

 Commands that come later in Listing 3-5 refer back to these variables.

2. In Windows, `rem` denotes a comment.

 The computer doesn't execute commented text. If you remove some `rem`s near the beginning of Listing 3-5, the computer executes the command to launch an Android emulator.

3. The command `android create project` builds the skeletal outline of an Android project.

Using `android-8` (also known as Froyo), the `android` program creates a `MyNextProject` directory. In that directory, `android` creates a project and a `MyActivity.java` file. In addition, the program creates `main.xml`, `strings.xml`, `AndroidManifest.xml`, and other good stuff.

4. In Listing 3-5, the first invocation of the `aapt` program generates `R.java`.

   `aapt` stands for *Android Asset Packaging Tool.*

5. The `javac` command compiles your project's Java source files.

   After executing `javac`, you have several newly created Java bytecode (`.class`) files.

6. The `dx` command goes one step further in translating your code.

   The `dx` command turns your `.class` files (and other project stuff) into a `.dex` file — a *Dalvik executable* file.

   For the scoop about Dalvik executables, see Book II, Chapter 2.

7. In Listing 3-5, the second invocation of the `aapt` program packages your project's resources into a single file.

   The single file's name is *something-or-other*`.ap_`. The underscore in the `ap_` extension reminds you that this file isn't ready for prime time. This `.ap_` file contains the stuff in your project's `res` folder but not the executable `.dex` files.

8. The `apkbuilder` creates a real live Android app package (an APK file).

   In Listing 3-5, `apkbuilder` creates a file named `MyActivity-debug-unaligned.apk`. The file `MyActivity-debug-unaligned.apk` is an Android app package — an APK file with executables and all. But you can't run this APK file on a phone or an emulator. Your package still needs some tweaking.

9. The `keytool` program with the `-genkey` option creates a cryptographic signature; the `jarsigner` program adds the cryptographic signature to your Android project file.

   In order to run (on a device or an emulator), an Android project file must be *signed*. You must add proof that the file comes from you and not from a malicious hacker. But a project file isn't like a contract or a work of art. You can't autograph a project file with a felt-tip pen.

   Instead, you "sign" a file by adding your own sequence of bits — a sequence that belongs only to you. One algorithm that helps to create such bit sequences is *RSA encryption.* (That's *Rivest, Shamir, and Adleman* encryption, if you want to know.)

**Book VI
Chapter 3**

How to "Rough It" without Eclipse

Before you sign a file, you need a *key* — a big number that you apply to the bits in your file. For example, imagine encrypting a secret message by changing *A*s to *C*s, changing *B*s to *D*s, changing *C*s to *E*s, and so on. The word *Android* becomes *Cpftqkf*. Then the "big" number that you apply to your file's letters is 2. If, instead of applying 2, you applied the number 3, you would change *A*s to *D*s, *B*s to *E*s, and so on.

Anyway, the run of `keytool` in Listing 3-5 creates a key with 617 digits. Then a run of `jarsigner` applies the key to your Android app file.

When `keytool` runs, your computer prompts you for some identifying information. Each piece of information is part of the *X.500 Distinguished Name* standard. For example, here's a snippet from a run of `keytool` on my development computer:

```
Enter keystore password: (I make up a password.)
Re-enter new password: (I repeat the password.)
What is your first and last name?
  [Unknown]:  Barry Burd
What is the name of your organizational unit?
  [Unknown]:  Global Headquarters
What is the name of your organization?
  [Unknown]:  Burd Brain Consulting
What is the name of your City or Locality?
  [Unknown]:  Madison
What is the name of your State or Province?
  [Unknown]:  NJ
What is the two-letter country code for this unit?
  [Unknown]:  US
Is CN=Barry Burd, OU=Global Headquarters,
 O=Burd Brain Consulting, L=Madison, ST=NJ,
 C=US correct?
  [no]:  yes
```

10. The `zipalign` program aligns bytes in Android app file (see the nearby sidebar).

You always align after you sign. Aligning can't mess up a previous signing. But if you do it in reverse order, signing can mess up a previous aligning.

11. A run of `adb` with the `install` option copies your Android application onto an emulator or a connected device.

If `adb` has a choice of running emulators or connected devices, you can specify a particular emulator or device. For example, to install onto `emulator-5556` instead of `emulator-5554`, add the `-s emulator-5556` option to the `adb` command.

Byte off more than you can view

The Android operating system (along with all other Unix-like systems) has a mmap program. The letters mm in mmap stand for *memory-mapped* input and output. The mmap program grabs data from a file and makes the data available to applications. The mmap program is a real workhorse, providing quick and efficient data access for many apps at once.

The nimbleness of mmap doesn't come entirely for free. For mmap to do its work, certain values must be stored so they start at four-byte boundaries. To understand four-byte boundaries, think about a chunk of data in your application's APK file. A *byte* is eight bits of data (each bit being a 0 or a 1). So four bytes is

32 bits. Now imagine two values (Value A and Value B) stored one after the other in your APK file. (See the figure here.) Value A consumes three bytes, and Value B consumes four bytes.

Without four-byte alignment, the computer might store the first byte of Value B immediately after the last byte of Value A. If so, Value B starts on the last byte of a four-byte group. But mmap works only when each value starts at the beginning of a four-byte group. So Android's zipalign program moves data as shown in the lower half of the figure below. Instead of using every available byte, zipalign wastes a byte in order to make Value B easy to locate.

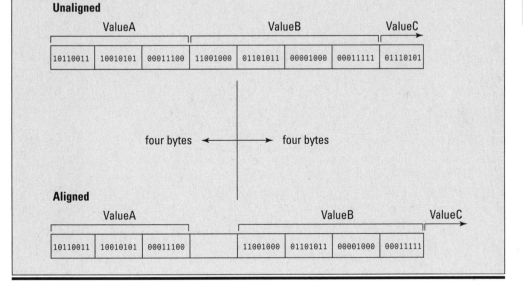

Chapter 4: Going Native

In This Chapter

✔ **Connecting C code to Java code**

✔ **Creating an Android app with native code**

Sometimes, you have to get your hands dirty. You have to pop the hood and figure out why smoke comes out of your car. You have to bake a cake for that special friend who's allergic to the ingredients in store-bought cakes. Or, in order to build the perfect mobile app, you must bypass Android's comfortable Java coating and dig deep to find your true inner geek. You must create part of an app in the primitive, nuts-and-bolts, down-and-dirty language called C.

Book II, Chapter 2 explains how Java puts a virtual machine between your processor's hardware and a running application. Java programs don't turn directly into sets of instructions that your processor can then run. Instead, your processor runs a set of instructions, or a virtual machine. (Your Android device runs the Dalvik Virtual Machine; your laptop computer runs the Java Virtual Machine.) The virtual machine interprets a Java program's instructions and carries out these instructions on your processor's behalf.

Anyway, this added layer of software (between the Java instructions and your processor's circuits) has both benefits and drawbacks. Isolation from the hardware enhances portability and security. But the added software layer might slow down a program's execution. The layer also prevents Java from micromanaging the processor.

Imagine solving your allergic friend's problem by ordering a cake directly from a local bakery. "My friend has a wheat allergy. Can you make the cake without using any wheat products?" At a classy establishment, the baker knows how to avoid wheat gluten. But your friend is also allergic to *carrageenan polysorbate 80,* an emulsifier found in many commercial food products. "Please don't use any carrageenan polysorbate 80," you say. And the person behind the bakery counter says, "We'll try our best. We can't check for every chemical in every ingredient that we use."

So you leave the bakery without completing the order. For the sake of your friend's health, you need complete control over the baking process. Delegating some of the work to a baker in the back room (or to a virtual machine executing instructions on behalf of your device's processor) just isn't good enough.

Another potent reason for using non-Java code is to avoid rewriting code that you already have — code written in another programming language. Imagine having a thousand-line C program that reliably computes a decent daily investment strategy. (No, I don't have such a program, in case you're wondering.) The program does lots of fancy calculations, but the program has no user-friendly interface. The code has no windows, no buttons, and nothing nice for the user to click. You want to package this program inside an Android application. The app presents choices to the user, computes today's investment strategy with its complicated formulas, and then displays details of the strategy (in a friendly, colorful way) on the user's screen.

You can try rewriting the C program in Java. But translating between two closely related languages (such as C and Java) is a virtual rat's nest. The translation is often messy and unreliable. A better plan is to write the user interface as an Android Java app and let your Java app defer to your existing C program only for the intricate investing strategy calculations. All you need is a way to exchange information between a Java program and a C program.

The Native Development Kit

The creators of Android realized that developers would want to use non-Java code. So Android has a framework that mediates between Java and other languages. As you might have guessed from this section's title, that framework is *NDK — Native Development Kit*. With Android's NDK, you can write code that executes directly on a mobile device's processor without relying on a virtual machine to carry out the instructions.

Getting the NDK

The NDK doesn't come as part of Android's standard software development kit — its *SDK*. In fact, you don't get the NDK by checking for available packages in the Android SDK and AVD Manager. The NDK is a separate archive file, available for download at `http://developer.android.com`. (If I'm lucky, the particular URL will still be `http://developer.android.com/sdk/ndk` when you read this chapter.) On Windows, the NDK archive is usually a `.zip` file. For Mac or Linux, the NDK archive is usually a `.tar.bz2` file.

After downloading the NDK archive, double-click this archive file to display the file's contents. Then drag the file's contents (not the file itself — the stuff *inside* the archive file) to a handy place on your development computer's hard drive. (On my Windows computer, I see only one item, a folder named `android-ndk` inside the downloaded archive. I drag this folder to the root of my C: drive. As a result, I have a folder named `c:\android-ndk`.)

Make note of the folder containing your unzipped NDK materials (or your "un-bz2ed" and "untared" NDK materials). I refer to this folder in later sections. I call it your NDK_HOME directory.

Getting a C compiler

In this chapter's big example, a C program performs a portion of an application's work. So to run this chapter's big example, you need a C compiler. If you run Mac OS X or Windows, you may or may not have a C compiler. If you run Linux on your development computer, you can gloat because you already have everything set up correctly. (Actually, don't gloat. Simply skip this "Getting a C compiler" section.)

Getting a C compiler for Windows

Windows users can get a C compiler by following these steps:

1. **Visit** http://cygwin.com.

2. **At the Cygwin website, look for the Cygwin installation file.**

   The file that I found is tastefully named setup.exe. But remember, your filename mileage may vary.

3. **Download the Cygwin installation file and then double-click the installation file to begin running it.**

   The names setup.exe and "installation file" are slightly deceiving. When you run this file, the computer starts a program that offers to download more code from the web.

4. **Click Next to page through the installation's initial dialog boxes.**

   After clicking Next to go from one dialog box to another, you reach the Select Packages dialog box. (See Figure 4-1.)

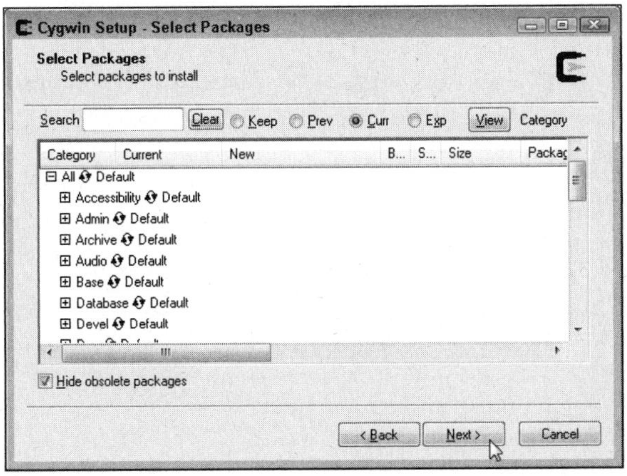

Figure 4-1:
Cygwin's
setup
program
offers
you some
packages.

In Figure 4-1, the word *Default* next to each category (next to Accessibility, Admin, and so on) indicates that you intend to download the minimal amount of Cygwin software in each of these categories. Cygwin's documentation recommends running the installation file twice. The first time you run this installation, you accept all the defaults shown in Figure 4-1.

5. **With the defaults on the Select Packages dialog box, click Next.**

The installation of Cygwin (with a minimum set of components) proceeds on your computer.

To do Android NDK development, you need a bit more than Cygwin's minimum toolset.

6. **Run the Cygwin installation file a second time.**

7. **Again, click Next to page through the initial dialog boxes.**

When at last you see the Select Packages dialog box, you see a list of categories, each displaying the word *Default*.

8. **Expand the Devel branch of the list (see Figure 4-2).**

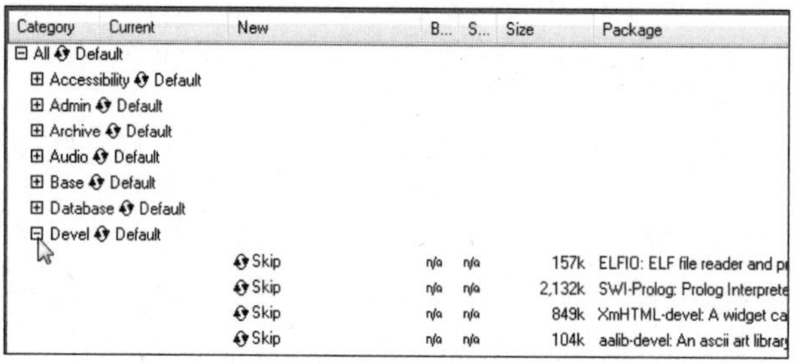

Figure 4-2:
Expanding
the Devel
category's
branch.

Why label this branch Development when a simple Devel tells the whole story?

9. **Within the Devel branch, look for a `make` item (see Figure 4-3).**

Somewhere on that `make` item's row, you see the word *Skip*.

10. **Repeatedly click the place where you see Skip until you see a version number instead of Skip.**

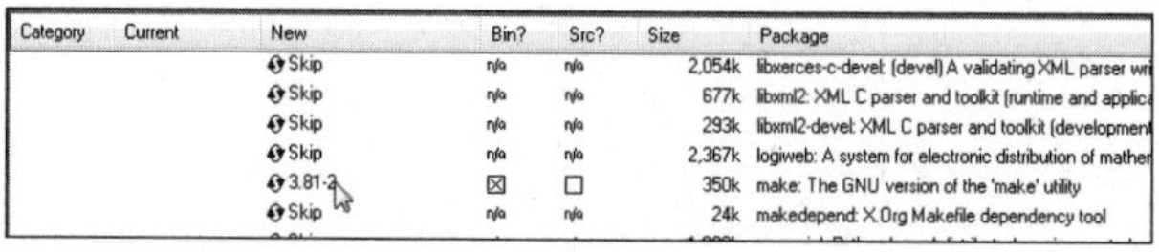

Figure 4-3:
Installing
the make
utility.

In Figure 4-3, I click the same place until I see 3.81-2 instead of Skip. As you click that place, you may see Source instead of Skip, or you may see other version numbers. If you have a choice of different version numbers, choose the highest. (That's the safest thing to do.)

11. In the lower-right corner of the Select Packages dialog box, click Next.

When the installation is finished, you have all the Cygwin tools that you need.

Getting a C compiler for Macintosh

Mac users must install Xcode in order to compile C programs. In addition, Mac users must install the Unix development support that comes optionally with Xcode.

Check to see whether you already have what you need:

1. Open a Terminal window.

You find the Terminal app in the Utilities subfolder of your Mac's Applications folder.

2. In the Terminal windows, type the words which make **and then press Return.**

The computer should respond with something like

```
/usr/bin/make
```

If you see this response (or a line closely resembling this response), you already have make installed on your Mac. (Or maybe you have Mac installed on your make! I don't know.) If instead, the computer responds with nothing but another prompt, you have to install the make tool on your Mac.

Here's how you install the make tool on your computer:

1. Locate your Macintosh OS X installation materials.

I use the generic word *materials* because Apple is moving quickly toward downloads instead of DVDs. Anyway, if you have OS X on a DVD, search high and low for the DVD. If you paid for an OS X download, do whatever you do to access the Mac OS X operating system installation download.

2. Visit your installation materials in a Finder window.

3. In the window's search field, type Xcode.

A bunch of items appears in the Finder window's main panel.

4. Look for an item named Xcode.mpkg (or something very close to that name) and double-click the item.

Welcome to the Xcode Installer, says your Macintosh.

5. **Click Continue and agree to everything until you see a list of options to install (see Figure 4-4).**

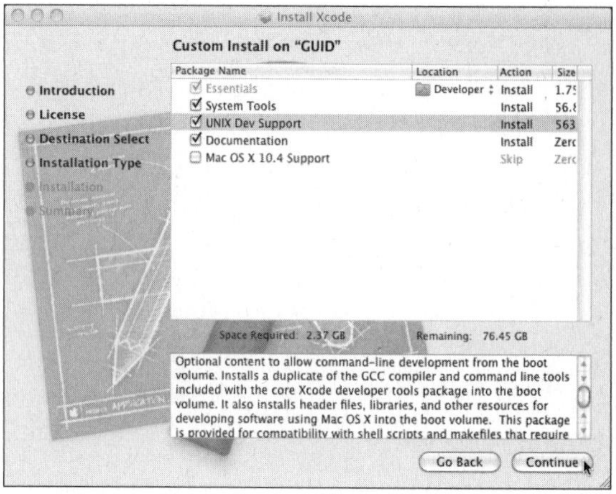

Custom Install on "GUID"

Package Name	Location	Action	Size
☑ Essentials	Developer :	Install	1.7!
☑ System Tools		Install	56.!
☑ UNIX Dev Support		Install	563
☑ Documentation		Install	Zerc
☐ Mac OS X 10.4 Support		Skip	Zerc

Space Required 2.37 GB   Remaining: 76.45 GB

Optional content to allow command-line development from the boot volume. Installs a duplicate of the GCC compiler and command line tools included with the core Xcode developer tools package into the boot volume. It also installs header files, libraries, and other resources for developing software using Mac OS X into the boot volume. This package is provided for compatibility with shell scripts and makefiles that require

Go Back   Continue

Figure 4-4:
Xcode
installation
options.

6. **Make sure that the UNIX Dev Support option is selected.**

    Again, see Figure 4-4. The UNIX Dev Support option contains the make utility that you need in order to create Android NDK code. This make utility is not installed by default. (Well, anyway, it wasn't installed the first time I installed Xcode.)

7. **Click Continue to proceed with the installation.**

    When the installation is completed, you have the C tools that you need.

Eclipse has some very nice plug-ins to help you work with C/C++ code and with Android's NDK. For this chapter's example, I don't describe these tools. (I don't want you to trudge through two hours of downloading to prepare for half an hour of application developing.) But if you plan to make extensive use of Android's NDK, check out Eclipse's CDT (the C/C++ Development Tooling project). Also visit the Sequoyah project's web pages (www. eclipse.org/sequoyah). *Sequoyah* is a set of tools to help you debug your Android NDK code.

Creating an Application

An NDK-enabled application is almost exactly like an ordinary Android application, except it's different! (That's a joke, by the way.) To create a simple NDK-enabled application, do the following:

1. **Use Eclipse to create a new Android project (see Figure 4-5).**

   You can choose any project name you want, but if you want to follow along with the steps in my example, name the project `MyNDKProject`. Also, select the Android 2.2 target with application name `My NDK App` and activity name `MyActivity`. For the package name, select `com.allmycode.examples.ndk`.

   Books I and II have all the information you'd need to create an "ordinary" simple Android application.

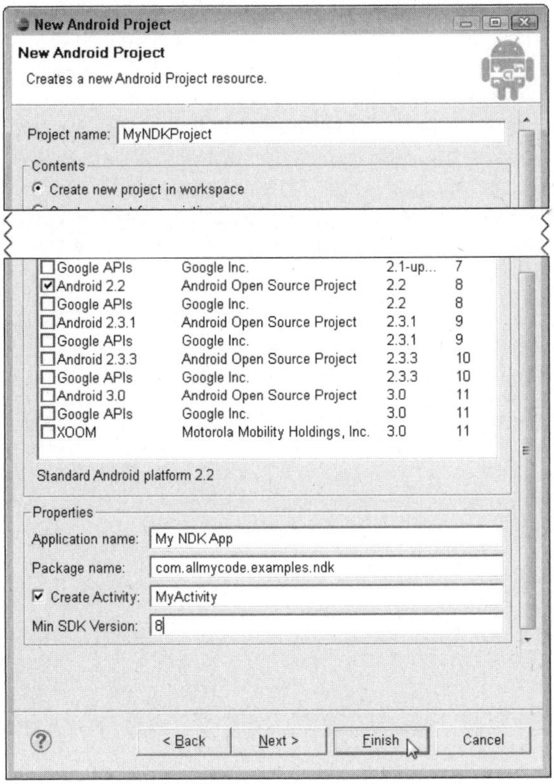

> **New Android Project**
>
> **New Android Project**
> Creates a new Android Project resource.
>
> Project name: | MyNDKProject
>
> Contents
> ⦿ Create new project in workspace
>
> | | | | |
> |---|---|---|---|
> | ☐ Google APIs | Google Inc. | 2.1-up... | 7 |
> | ☑ Android 2.2 | Android Open Source Project | 2.2 | 8 |
> | ☐ Google APIs | Google Inc. | 2.2 | 8 |
> | ☐ Android 2.3.1 | Android Open Source Project | 2.3.1 | 9 |
> | ☐ Google APIs | Google Inc. | 2.3.1 | 9 |
> | ☐ Android 2.3.3 | Android Open Source Project | 2.3.3 | 10 |
> | ☐ Google APIs | Google Inc. | 2.3.3 | 10 |
> | ☐ Android 3.0 | Android Open Source Project | 3.0 | 11 |
> | ☐ Google APIs | Google Inc. | 3.0 | 11 |
> | ☐ XOOM | Motorola Mobility Holdings, Inc. | 3.0 | 11 |
>
> Standard Android platform 2.2
>
> Properties
> Application name: | My NDK App
> Package name: | com.allmycode.examples.ndk
> ☑ Create Activity: | MyActivity
> Min SDK Version: | 8|
>
> ⑦   < Back   Next >   Finish   Cancel

Figure 4-5:
Creating your new project.

2. **With the Graphical Layout editor, add an EditText view to `main.xml` (the main layout).**

   For details about adding an EditText view and for details about some of the next several steps, see Book II, Chapter 1 and Book III, Chapter 2.

3. **Using the Graphical Layout editor, add a button to `main.xml` (the main layout).**

4. **Assign a name to the button's Click Event listener.**

If you're following along at home, I give the button's Click Event listener the name onButtonClick. That is, I use the Properties view to set the button's onClick property to onButtonClick.

5. **Add Event Listener code to your app's activity.**

I don't know about your activity, but my activity contains the following Event Listener code:

```
public void onButtonClick(View v) {

    Editable name = ((EditText) findViewById(R.id.editText1)).getText();
    Toast.makeText(getApplication(), getString() + name,
                                   Toast.LENGTH_LONG).show();
}
```

Most of this Event Listener code is fairly harmless. But please remember that the names in the code must correspond to names in your project. For example, the method name (in my example, onButtonClick) must be the same as the name you assigned as the button's onClick listener in Step 4. Also, the ID editText1 must be same as the ID of the view that you created in Step 2.

The only unusual thing about the Event Listener code is the call to a method named getString. You don't declare getString the way you declare most Java methods.

6. **To your activity class (named MyActivity in Step 1) add the following code:**

```
public native String getString();

static {
    System.loadLibrary("my-jni-app");
}
```

With or without Android, the Java technology suite comes with a *JNI* — the *Java Native Interface* — framework. The purpose of JNI is to help Java programs communicate with code written in other programming languages. This step's code is the way JNI tells your program to expect the getString method's body to be written in a language other than Java.

The first line

```
public native String getString();
```

tells Java to look for the body of getString somewhere else (outside the Java class in which the line appears). The rest of the code

```
static {
    System.loadLibrary("my-jni-app");
}
```

tells your program to look for method bodies in a place called my-jni-app. And wha'ddaya know? This section's example includes some C-language code in a file named my-jni-app.c.

Listing 4-1 pulls together all the code in your MyActivity.java file.

Listing 4-1: Your Project's Main Activity

```
package com.allmycode.examples.ndk;

import android.app.Activity;
import android.os.Bundle;
import android.text.Editable;
import android.view.View;
import android.widget.EditText;
import android.widget.Toast;

public class MyActivity extends Activity {
    /** Called when the activity is first created. */
    @Override
    public void onCreate(Bundle savedInstanceState) {
        super.onCreate(savedInstanceState);
        setContentView(R.layout.main);
    }

    public native String getString();

    static {
        System.loadLibrary("my-jni-app");
    }

    public void onButtonClick(View v) {

        Editable name =
          ((EditText) findViewById(R.id.editText1)).getText();
        Toast.makeText(getApplication(), getString() + name,
          Toast.LENGTH_LONG).show();
    }
}
```

7. **In Eclipse's Package Explorer tree, right-click the MyNDKProject branch and choose New⇨Folder. (On a Mac, use Control-click in place of right-click.)**

Eclipse displays a New Folder dialog box.

8. **In the New Folder dialog box's Folder Name field, type** jni **and then click Finish.**

The Package Explorer's tree has a new branch labeled jni. At this point, it helps to check the location of the jni folder. In Figure 4-6, the jni folder is an immediate subdirectory of MyNDKProject (the main project folder). The `jni` folder is on a level parallel with `res`, `assets`, `Android 2.2`, and so on. This location is important because a folder in the wrong location means that Java can't find your code. (Besides, it's really easy to mess up a new folder's location in Eclipse's Package Explorer.)

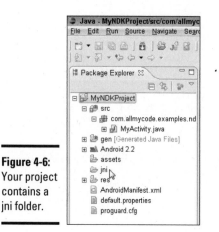

Figure 4-6:
Your project contains a jni folder.

In Figure 4-6, notice that the `MyActivity.java` branch displays an ugly red blotch (an X inside a red rectangle). This blotch reminds you that you haven't yet created the `getString` method's body.

9. **In Eclipse's Package Explorer, right-click the new `jni` folder's branch and then choose New➪File.**

Eclipse opens its New File dialog box.

10. **In the New File dialog's File Name field, type** Android.mk **and then click Finish.**

An `.mk` file is like a C-language `make` file, except it's shorter. For more information, see the "Android.mk files" sidebar.

11. **Repeat Steps 9 and 10 to create yet another file in the `jni` folder.**

12. **In the New File dialog box's File Name field, type** my-jni-app.c **and then click Finish.**

This new file is destined to contain code written in C. You can give the file any name you want, as long as that name matches the name in the `loadLibrary` call in Step 6. Also, in this example, you're creating C code, so the filename should end with the `.c` extension.

13. **Using Eclipse's editor, type the following code into the `Android.mk` file:**

```
LOCAL_PATH := $(call my-dir)
include $(CLEAR_VARS)
LOCAL_MODULE := my-jni-app
LOCAL_SRC_FILES := my-jni-app.c
include $(BUILD_SHARED_LIBRARY)
```

This code tells the computer how to put the parts of your project together into an Android application. For more details, see the "Android. mk files" sidebar.

Android.mk files

An `Android.mk` file tells your computer where your project's files are located. The computer uses this information to *build* your project (that is, to combine your files into a full-fledged Android application). I copied the `Android.mk` file in Step 13 from Android's documentation pages (with only minor changes of my own). This `Android.mk` file provides five pieces of information:

✔ **The starting point for relative filenames inside this `Android.mk` file:** In this case, the starting point (the `LOCAL_PATH`) is the directory containing the `Android.mk` file (the `$(call my-dir)` directory).

✔ **That all instructions stored in the `$(CLEAR_VARS)` file must be included as part of the project:** These instructions initialize things like `LOCAL_MODULE`, `LOCAL_SRC_FILES`, `LOCAL_C_INCLUDES`, `LOCAL_CFLAGS`, and others. (By *initialize*, I mean "set as undefined.") Two of these variables become defined by subsequent lines in the `Android.mk` file.

✔ **The `LOCAL_MODULE` name:** In this case, the `LOCAL_MODULE` name is `my-jni-app`. This means that the library file containing the compiled C code is stored in a file whose name has `my-jni-app` in the middle.

Android always puts `lib` before the middle and puts `.so` after the middle. So the full name of the library file is `libmy-jni-app.so`. (This `lib` and `.so` business comes from naming conventions in Unix and Linux.) Sure enough, when you finish this chapter's instructions, you have a file named `libmy-jni-app.so` in your Eclipse project.

✔ **The location for your stored C source code (that is, `LOCAL_SRC_FILES`):** Here, the C source code is stored in a file named `my-jni-app.c`. (You create a new, empty `my-jni-app.c` file in Step 12. You put a C program in that file in Step 14.)

✔ **That all instructions stored in the `$(BUILD_SHARED_LIBRARY)` file must be included as part of the project:** This file contains instructions to scoop up all the available information and then build an Android project from the Java code, the C code, the binary files, and all the other useful things in your project directories.

For more information, including a list of available variables and commands, see the file named `ANDROID-MK.html` in your `NDK_HOME` folder's `docs` subfolder.

14. **Using Eclipse's editor, type the code from Listing 4-2 into the** `my-jni-app.c` **file.**

Listing 4-2: Your C Program

```
#include <string.h>
#include <jni.h>

jstring
Java_com_allmycode_examples_ndk_MyActivity_getString
  (JNIEnv* env, jobject obj)
{
    return (*env)->NewStringUTF(env, "Hello, ");
}
```

If you're not a seasoned C programmer, you may be wondering what the code in `my-jni-app.c` means. Well, you're in luck. There's a sidebar for that! (The sidebar's name is "C programming in 600 words or less.")

For the next several steps, you jump from Eclipse to your development computer's command line windows.

C programming in 600 words or less

You won't become a C programmer by reading this chapter, but you might want to know something about the C code in Listing 4-2.

First of all, C code doesn't normally run on a virtual machine. You compile your C program into a *native executable* file — a low-level binary file that runs only on an Intel x86 processor, an ARM processor, or some other kind of processor. This absence of a virtual machine makes C much more dependent on exotic binary file types. When you finish this chapter's steps, you have the `.c` file in Step 14, but you also have an `.o` object file, an `.o.d` file, and some `.so` library files,

I'll be criticized by the purists for trying to translate Listing 4-2 into Java. Even so, you can use my fake Java code to understand the C program:

```
/*
 * Disclaimer:
 * This is a rough translation
   of the
 * C program in Listing 4-2.
   This code
 * illustrates the meaning of
   the
 * my-jni-app.c program. But
   this Java
 * code cannot replace the
   my-jni-app.c
 * program in Listing 4-2.
 */
package com.allmycode.
   examples.ndk;

import java.lang.String;
import java.lang.Runtime;

public class MyActivity {

    public String getString()
```

```
    {
        return "Hello, ";
    }
}
```

The actual `my-jni-app.c` program in Listing 4-2 defines a single method — the method `Java_com_allmycode_examples_ndk_MyActivity_getString`. The long method name follows JNI rules to implement the `getString` method in Listing 4-1. The `MyActivity` class in Listing 4-1 declares a native method whose fully qualified name is `com.allmycode.examples.ndk.MyActivity.getString`. To form the C-language JNI name in Listing 4-2, you replace the dots with underscores and preface the whole business with `Java_`.

The C programming language doesn't sweep pointers under the rug. In C, you use asterisks and arrows to refer explicitly to pointers, and you can use pointers to pass objects to functions. For example, the name `JNIEnv` refers to a class whose objects have about 200 fields. Each `JNIEnv` field is a pointer to a function. When you call the method in Listing 4-2, you pass a pointer to a `JNIEnv` object. (That is, you pass something of type `JNIEnv*`.)

The parameter `env` stores that pointer to a `JNIEnv` object. (See the nearby figure.)

In a C program, when you type ***env**, you're dereferencing the pointer stored in `env`. In other words, `*env` stands for whatever object `env` points to. So in Listing 4-2, `(*env)` stands for a `JNIEnv` object.

In C, an expression like `x->y` is shorthand for "the thing pointed to by the `y` field of the `x` object." In Listing 4-2, the text `(*env)->NewStringUTF` stands for the function that's pointed to by the `NewStringUTF` field of `*env`. In other words, `(*env)->NewStringUTF` stands for the current JNI environment's version of the `NewStringUTF` function.

The `return` statement in Listing 4-2 creates a new `java.lang.String` object (which is called a `jstring` object in a JNI C program). The new `String` object becomes part of the Java calling environment, and the Java calling environment gets the return value `"Hello, "`.

And if this isn't complicated enough, the whole thing works a bit differently when you shun plain old C and write your native code in C++ instead. Whew!

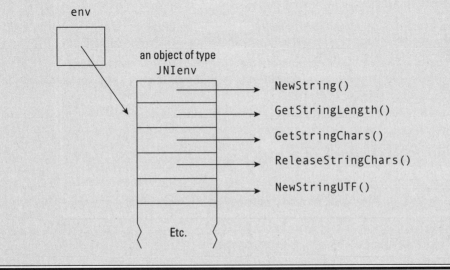

15. Open a command window on your computer.

- *Windows:* Choose Start➪All Programs➪Accessories➪Command Prompt.

- *Macintosh:* Double-click the Terminal app, which is in the `Utilities` subfolder of your Mac's `Applications` folder.

- *Linux:* Well . . . er . . . it depends on your Linux distribution. If you're a Linux user, you're probably laughing right now because you know how to launch a Terminal window (or the Shell) and you use it all the time.

16. In the command window, use the Change Directory command (cd) to navigate to the directory containing your Android project.

If you're not sure where your Android project lives, return to Eclipse and choose File➪Switch Workspace➪Other. Eclipse's Select a Workspace dialog box pops up, showing you the name of your current workspace. On a Windows computer, you see something like `c:\Users\`*your-user-name*`\workspace`. Copy the text from the leftmost slash onward. In the command window, type

```
cd \Users\your-user-name\workspace\MyNDKProject
```

and then press Enter. (I'm assuming that you followed my lead in Step 1 by naming your project MyNDKProject. If not, substitute your own project's name here.)

17. Recall the location of the Android SDK on your development computer.

In Book I, Chapter 2, I call this location your `ANDROID_HOME` directory. On my computer, the `ANDROID_HOME` directory is `c:\android-sdk-windows`, but on your computer, the directory may be different.

Don't navigate away from your Android project's directory. Or if you do navigate away in order to find the `ANDROID_HOME` directory, navigate back to the Android project's directory before proceeding to the next step.

18. In the command window, type the following command and then press Enter:

- *Windows users:*

```
ANDROID_HOME\tools\android update project --path .
```

- *Mac and Linux users:*

```
ANDROID_HOME/tools/android update project --path .
```

The only difference between the Windows command and everyone else's command is that Windows uses backslashes.

So, for example, on my computer, I type the following:

```
c:\android-sdk-windows\tools\android
update project --path .
```

I begged the people at John Wiley & Sons, Inc., to publish a book whose pages are two feet wide, but they didn't do it! When you type this step's command, you don't intentionally start a new line anywhere in the middle of the command. The command that I type on my computer looks like it's two lines long here, but that's only because this book's page is too narrow. Normally you just keep typing along one line. (And if your computer's command window takes its own initiative to wrap your typing to a new line, you're okay.)

This is a well-kept secret: The Windows command line accepts forward slashes (as well as backslashes) as file separators. The command for Mac and Linux works on Windows, too!

This step's `android update project` command creates a `build. xml` file. This `build.xml` file contains a set of instructions telling Java how to bundle your application. This project needs a `build.xml` file because of the special NDK stuff in the project.

If all goes well, your command window responds to your command with text like

```
Updated local.properties
Updated file MyNDKProject\build.xml
Updated file MyNDKProject\proguard.cfg
```

The next part of the process involves running a Unix/Linux shell script. To do this on a Windows computer, use Cygwin.

19. **(Windows only) Launch Cygwin.**

The Cygwin command window opens. It looks a lot like the ordinary Windows command box. But Cygwin understands Unix/Linux commands.

20. **(Windows only) Type the following command into the Cygwin command window and then press Enter:**

```
cd /cygdrive/c
```

In the Cygwin world, this command gets you to the root of your Windows C: drive. If your project is on some other drive (say, your X: drive), type the command `cd /cygdrive/x` instead.

21. **(Windows only) In the Cygwin window, use the familiar Change Directory command (`cd`) to navigate to the directory containing your Android project.**

In other words, repeat the stuff you did in Step 16, but when you type the directory's full path name, use forward slashes and omit the leftmost slash. On my computer, I type

```
cd Users/bburd/workspace/MyNDKProject/
```

In general, you type something like

```
cd Users/your-user-name/workspace/MyNDKProject/
```

22. **Type the following command and then press Enter:**

    ```
    NDK_HOME/ndk-build
    ```

    On my Windows computer, I unzipped the NDK materials to a `C:\ android-ndk-r5b` folder. So in this step, I type

    ```
    /cygdrive/c/android-ndk-r5b/ndk-build
    ```

    The extra `/cydrive/c` stuff is to make Cygwin happy.

    On my Macintosh, I was lazy enough to leave the archived NDK in my Downloads folder. So I type

    ```
    /Users/my-user-name/Downloads/android-ndk-r5b/ndk-build
    ```

By default, the `ndk-build` command operates on whatever folder you're sitting in when you issue the command. So before issuing this step's command, navigate to your Android project's directory. Windows users: Follow Steps 19 through 21. Mac and Linux users: You're already positioned at the project's directory by virtue of Step 16. Don't drift away while the Windows users take time to get their ducks in a row.

After issuing the `ndk-build` command, your computer responds with a message like this:

```
Compile thumb  : my-jni-app <= my-jni-app.c
SharedLibrary  : libmy-jni-app.so
Install        : libmy-jni-app.so =>
                 libs/armeabi/libmy-jni-app.so
```

Congratulations! The message indicates that your C code has been translated into a usable library for ARM processors.

23. **In Eclipse's Package Explorer, right-click the `MyNDKProject` branch, and in the resulting contextual menu, choose Refresh.**

    As usual, Macintosh users should Control-click instead of right-click.

    Here's what's going on: In Steps 15 through 22, you march away from your Eclipse window and work in one or more command windows. In doing so, you create some new files inside your `MyNDKProject` directory. That's all well and good as far as you're concerned, but in Step 1, you use Eclipse to create the `MyNDKProject` directory. So you've modified an Eclipse project without using Eclipse to make the modification.

You have to tell Eclipse to wake up, look around, and figure out what changed while Eclipse wasn't watching. In other words, Eclipse must update its notion of what files are in its `MyNDKProject` directory. To do this, you right-click and choose Refresh.

With all the stuff you have to do to create an NDK app, you can easily forget to refresh your Eclipse project. (I forget all the time.) Make yourself a mental note reminding yourself about this refresh step.

After refreshing your project, Eclipse's Package Explorer displays three folders that you don't normally see in an Android project: `jni`, `libs`, and `obj`. (See Figure 4-7.)

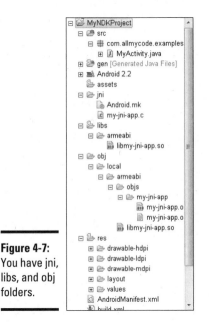

Figure 4-7:
You have jni, libs, and obj folders.

24. Run your Android project.

After some delay (and much anticipation), you see a screen like the one in Figure 4-8.

25. Type your name in the EditText view and then click the button.

A toast notification appears on your emulator's screen. In Figure 4-9, the name Barry comes from the activity's EditText view. (It's no big deal.) But initial text in the notification comes from a C-language program — namely, the program in Listing 4-2.

Figure 4-8:
Your app
starts
running.

Figure 4-9:
You've
made toast!

Sure! Fetching a `"Hello"` string from a C program isn't the most useful app you've ever seen. But the ability to call C code to help with an Android app's work has lots of potential.

The most common hurdle for new NDK programmers involves correctly connecting a method call with its method. In Listing 4-1, for example, your Java program calls `getString()`, but with all the naming conventions and linking tricks, the system may not see the connection to the C-language method `Java_com_allmycode_examples_ndk_MyActivity_getString` in Listing 4-2. Your application crashes, and Eclipse's LogCat view displays an `UnsatisfiedLinkError`.

If this happens to you, retrace your steps. The connection between a Java method and its corresponding C/C++ method can be very brittle. Check the spelling of names, check the messages you receive when you invoke ndk-build, and check your folder structure. If you're patient and persistent, you can get the stars and planets to align beautifully.

ARM alphabet soup

A run of the ndk-build command creates a folder named armeabi. What's that all about?

The acronym *ARM* comes originally from the term *Advanced RISC Machines*, which in turn comes from *Advanced Reduced Instruction Set Computing Machines*. (I love these multilevel acronyms!) The company named ARM, Ltd., designs and licenses its ARM processors for use in mobile devices around the world. (ARM, Ltd., doesn't build processors. Instead, the company does all the thinking and sells ideas to processor manufacturers.)

The acronym *ABI* stands for *Application Binary Interface*. An ABI is like an API, except that an ABI describes the way one piece of software communicates with another on a binary level. For example, in an API you'd say, "To create a string that represents an object, call the object's toString method." In an ABI, you might say, "A signed double word consists of 8 bytes and has byte-alignment 8 [whatever that means]."

The ARM EABI is ARM's *Embedded Application Binary Interface. Embedded* refers to the tendency of ARM processors to appear in specialized devices — devices other than general-purpose computers. For example, the main processor inside your laptop isn't an embedded processor. Your laptop's main processor does general-purpose computing — word processing one minute and playing music the next. In contrast, an embedded processor sits quietly inside a device and processes bits according to the device's specialized needs. Your car is loaded with embedded processors.

You may argue that the processor inside your mobile device isn't a special-purpose processor. Thus, the *E* in *ARM EABI* doesn't apply to mobile development. Well, argue all you want. This terminology's usage can wobble in many directions, and regardless of what you think is inside your phone, many phones use ARM processors, and the ndk-build command creates code according to ARM EABI specifications.

Index

J

K

Q

R